D1112101

COGNITIVE NEUROPSYCHOLOGY IN CLINICAL PRACTICE

COGNITIVE NEUROPSYCHOLOGY IN CLINICAL PRACTICE

Edited by

David Ira Margolin
Departments of Neurology and Psychiatry
University of California, San Francisco
Fresno-Central San Joaquin Valley Medical Education Program
and the Cognitive Neuroscience Laboratory at the
Fresno Veterans Administration Medical Center
Fresno, California

New York Oxford
OXFORD UNIVERSITY PRESS
1992

Oxford University Press

Oxford New York Toronto
Delhi Bombay Calcutta Madras Karachi
Petaling Jaya Singapore Hong Kong Tokyo
Nairobi Dar es Salaam Cape Town
Melbourne Auckland

and associated companies in
Berlin Ibadan

Published by Oxford University Press, Inc.,
200 Madison Avenue, New York, New York 10016

Oxford is a registered trademark of Oxford University Press

Library of Congress Cataloging-in-Publication Data
Cognitive neuropsychology in clinical practice / edited by David Ira Margolin.
p. cm. Includes bibliographical references and index.
ISBN 0-19-506422-4
1. Cognition disorders. 2. Clinical neuropsychology.
I. Margolin, David Ira.
[DNLM: 1. Attention. 2. Cognition. 3. Cognition Disorders—psychology. 4. Language Disorders—psychology.
5. Neuropsychology. WL 103 C6765]
RC553.C64C65 1992 616.8—dc20
DNLM/DLC 91-24105 CIP

9 8 7 6 5 4 3 2 1

Printed in the United States of America
on acid-free paper

With love, to Slim and Ruth

Contents

Preface

This book reveals why the 1990s, the "Decade of the Brain," is an extremely exciting and fruitful time for clinicians who study disorders of behavior and intelligence. The recent past has witnessed breathtaking advances in neuroimaging technology which have set the stage for major breakthroughs in understanding brain-behavior relationships. At the same time, there has been revolutionary growth in the scientific study of human intelligence. That growth is embodied in two new disciplines, cognitive psychology and cognitive neuropsychology—the former dealing with normal intelligence and the latter with disorders of intelligence.

Reviewing the list of contributors provides a valuable insight into the dynamics of cognitive neuropsychology. Like the intended readership, the contributors of this book come from diverse backgrounds, including cognitive psychology, clinical neuropsychology, neurology, psychiatry, speech pathology, and rehabilitation. The unifying factor is that they all approach the study of behavior from a cognitive neuropsychological perspective. Guided by information-processing models of cognitive function, they dissect apart complex disorders of behavior revealing the impaired information-processing components that account for each disorder.

The goal of this book is to introduce cognitive neuropsychology to a broad audience. Sufficient introductory material is provided to orient readers who are interested in disorders of higher cortical function, but have no background in psychology. On the other hand, each topic is explored in sufficient depth to serve as a reference resource for cognitive psychologists and cognitive neuropsychologists. Perhaps clinical neuropsychologists have the most to gain from this volume. They will be familiar with the clinical disorders, but will see them examined with new instruments forged by experimental psychology and information-processing models of cognitive function. These cognitive neuropsychological assessment techniques and materials are described in sufficient detail to allow clinicians to incorporate them into their clinical repertoire. Most of the authors have developed original test materials which they will make available upon request.

My work was supported by the Department of Veterans Affairs Research and Development Service. Portions of the book were reviewed by Arnold E. Andersen, M.D.; Adam Drewnowski, Ph.D.; Terrence S. Early, M.D.; Robert

Hierholzer, M.D.; Debra Sue Pate, Ph.D.; and Roberta Goodman-Schulman, Ph.D. Michael Posner, Ph.D., and Fran Friedrich, Ph.D., provided very helpful guidance in the selection of contributors. Sheryl Carter's excellent secretarial support was invaluable. Cynthia Meyer and her medical library staff at the University of California, San Francisco, Fresno-Central San Joaquin Valley Medical Education Program, were extremely helpful. J. J. Margolin's input and support were greatly appreciated. Thanks to Aaron, Jenny, and Brandon for their interest and enthusiasm. Finally, it was a pleasure working with Joan Bossert and Louise Page at Oxford University Press.

Contributors

Marlene Behrmann, Ph.D.
Rotman Research Institute of Baycrest Centre
North York, Ontario
Canada M6A 2E1

Penni Blaskey, Ph.D.
The Learning Center of the Eye Institute
Pennsylvania College of Optometry
Philadelphia, Pennsylvania 19141

Sally Byng, Ph.D.
National Hospitals
College of Speech Science
London, England

Alfonso Caramazza, M.D.
Cognitive Science Center
The John Hopkins University
Baltimore, Maryland 21218

H. Branch Coslett, M.D.
Philadelphia, Pennsylvania 19130

Mark A. Demitrack, M.D.
University of Michigan Medical Center
Director of Clincal Research
Michigan Eating Disorders Program
Ann Arbor, Michigan 48109

Andrew W. Ellis, Ph.D.
Department of Psychology
University of York
Heslington
York, Y01 5DD England

Edward P. Feher, Ph.D.
Memory Assessment Clinics
Bethesda, Maryland 20814

Sue Franklin, Ph.D.
Department of Psychology
University of York
Heslington
York, Y01 5DD England

Roberta Goodman-Schulman, Ph.D.
Speech-Language Pathologist
Reisterstown, Maryland 21136

Eric Granholm II, M.A.
Univeristy of California at Los Angeles
Department of Psychology
Los Angeles, California 90024

Walter Harley, Ph.D.
Microsoft Corporation
Redmond, Washington 98052

Argye E. Hillis, Ph.D.
Director, Neurological Rehabilitation
Health South Rehabilitation Corporation
Baltimore, Maryland 21234

William J. Jagust, M.D.
Department of Neurology
University of California, Davis
Lawrence Berkeley Laboratory
Berkeley, California 94704

Tedd Judd, Ph.D.
Department of Mental Health
Pacific Medical Center
Seattle, Washington 98144

Janice Kay, Ph.D.
Department of Psychology
University of Exeter
Exeter, England EX4 4QG

Paul Macaruso, Ph.D.
Neurolinguistics Laboratory at Massachusetts General Hospital
Boston, Massachusetts 02108

David Ira Margolin, M.D., Ph.D.
The Cognitive Neuroscience Laboratory at the Fresno Veterans Administration Medical Center
Fresno, California 93703

Randi C. Martin, Ph.D.
Department of Psychology
Rice University
Houston, Texas 77251

Michael McCloskey
Cognitive Science Center
The John Hopkins University
Baltimore, Maryland 21218

Beth A. Ober, Ph.D.
Division of Human Development
Department of Applied Behavioral Sciences
University of California, Davis
Davis, California 95616

Howard Poizner, Ph.D.
Rutgers Center for Molecular and Behavioral Neurosciences
University Heights
Newark, New Jersey 07102

Bruce R. Reed, Ph.D.
U.C. Davis/Northern California Alzheimer's Disease Center
Alta Bates Herrick Hospital
Berkeley, California 94704

Lynn C. Robertson, Ph.D.
Cognitive Neuropsychology Lab
Neurology Department
University of California, Davis
Davis, California 95616

David P. Roeltgen, M.D.
Hahnemann Medical School
Philadelphia, Pennsylvania 19102

Eleanor M. Saffran, Ph.D.
Temple University School of Medicine
Philadelphia, Pennsylvania 19104

Jennifer R. Shelton
Department of Psychology
Rice University
Houston, Texas 77251

John F. Soechting, Ph.D.
Department of Physiology
University of Minnesota
Minneapolis, Minnesota 55455

Carolyn Szostak, Ph.D.
Cognitive Neuroscience Center
National Institute of Health
Bethesda, Maryland 20205

Herbert Weingartner, Ph.D.
Cognition Section
Gerontology Research Center
National Institute of Aging
Baltimore, Maryland 21224

Laura S. Yaffee
Department of Psychology
Rice University
Houston, Texas 77251

COGNITIVE NEUROPSYCHOLOGY IN CLINICAL PRACTICE

Introduction

DAVID IRA MARGOLIN

According to Gardner (1985, p. 28) cognitive science was officially recognized in 1956. Although the birth records of cognitive psychology and cognitive neuropsychology are less precise, there is no doubt that they have both experienced rapid growth spurts in the recent past. This book documents the tentative first steps of a third generation of cognitive science—clinical cognitive neuropsychology.

Part I reviews the foundations of clinical cognitive neuropsychology. The first chapter traces its lineage, introducing the theoretical frameworks, experimental paradigms, and vocabulary which have been adopted and adapted from a rich pool of parent disciplines. The contributors to this volume come from a varied assortment of backgrounds which is reflective of the discipline itself. Predictably, a fascinatingly heterogeneous group of assessment techniques have emerged. The contributors were told to describe their assessment materials and procedures in sufficient detail to allow readers naive to this field to incorporate these techniques into their clinical repertoire. Whenever possible, authors have followed this editorial mandate, and in keeping with the spirit of their endeavor, most have agreed to make selected testing materials available to others.

Chapter 2 focuses on the process of making the diagnosis of dementia of the Alzheimer's type for purposes of clinical care and clinical research. This provides the opportunity to document the impact which cognitive neuropsychology has had on the conceptualization and development of screening cognitive/mental status examinations.

Part II consists of three chapters which discuss very different patient populations: schizophrenics, stroke patients, and anorectics. The common thread is that disorders of attention play a prominent role in the various behavioral disturbances seen in these patients. Chapter 3 on schizophrenia is presented first, because of Granholm's broad historical review of attention and resource/capacity limitations. In addition to providing a synopsis of reaction time (RT) experimentation in schizophrenia, Granholm discusses two treatment strategies which arise from the information processing approach.

Robertson in Chapter 4 turns to a topic more familiar to most cognitive psychologists and cognitive neuropsychologists—disorders of attention resulting from stroke. She skillfully ties together three important paradigms: covert orienting, visual search, and local/global processing.

In Chapter 5, Demitrack, Szostak, and Weingartner take the information processing approach into relatively uncharted territory—disorders of food intake and body image. They offer an exciting framework for characterizing patients in terms of a performance profile. This profile charts the effects of cognitive (e.g., attention and memory) and noncognitive (e.g., arousal and affect) variables on each patient's performance. In addition, their chapter is unique for its discussion of the relationships between changes in neurotransmitters and cognitive performance. Furthermore, many clinicians will appreciate the authors' method for quickly surveying attention and memory.

Part III covers short-term and long-term memory disorders. In Chapter 6, Shelton, Martin, and Yaffee include an authoritative review of theories and models of short-term memory followed by a very practical step-by-step approach to assessing patients. They take full advantage of this opportunity to juxtapose theoretical and empirical arguments and make a convincing case for the existence of separate phonological and semantic short-term memory systems. Their final section on remediation provides a glimpse of the potential of theory-based approaches to memory rehabilitation, presenting an exciting challenge to cognitive therapists.

In Chapter 7, Feher and Martin do an admirable job of summarizing the complicated literature on long-term memory disorders. Their critique of standard assessment tests of memory from the perspective of current theories of memory should be particularly informative for practicing neuropsychologists. A detailed coherent framework for testing long-term memory is provided, including recommendations on how to test implicit memory.

Part IV of the book consists of five chapters dealing with various facets of language. Starting with the coin of the realm, spoken language, Ellis, Kay, and Franklin (Chapter 8) explain how to assess patients with anomia. Their emphasis is on distinguishing semantic from phonological processing deficits. Implications of their view of anomia in planning and executing speech therapy are discussed in detail.

Reading disorders have played a major role in the rise to prominence of cognitive neuropsychology. Hillis and Caramazza (Chapter 9) do this topic justice by explaining the theoretical basis for an information processing model of reading, demonstrating the use of the *Johns Hopkins University Dyslexia Battery*, which is based upon that model, and presenting a sober discussion of the potential for developing therapeutic strategies based upon this model.

In Chapter 10, Margolin and Goodman-Schulman follow a very similar format with respect to spelling disorders. A model of spelling presented in 1984 is updated based upon subsequent clinical evidence. An assessment tool, the *Johns Hopkins University Dysgraphia Battery*, is described and demonstrated. The influence of current parallel distributing processing or neural network models on previous models, which were more serial and static in nature, is discussed.

Roeltgen and Blaskey (Chapter 11) provide exposure to the relatively understudied field of developmental cognitive neuropsychology. Developmental reading and spelling disorders are analyzed and compared to the analogous acquired disorders discussed in the preceding three chapters. In addition to the questions faced by those studying acquired disorders, developmental neuropsychologists must contemplate how these skills are learned to begin with. Roeltgen and Blaskey discuss the two theories—modular (or independent) development and sequential acquisition. These theories are put to the test against patient data on the *Battery for Linguistic Analysis of Writing and Reading* developed by Roeltgen.

Behrmann and Byng, in Chapter 12, look at rehabilitation of language disorders, putting a very nice cap on this part. Their chapter reinforces the information-processing models of reading and spelling presented in the preceding chapters and illustrates, by literature review and case reports, how rehabilitation plans can be structured on the basis of these models.

Leading off the fifth part, "Other Domain-Specific Disorders," is Coslett and Saffran's chapter on visual processing disorders. Their synthesis of the clinical and the theoretical, the neurologic and the psychologic, is the quintessence of clinical cognitive neuropsychology. The complexity of this chapter indicates that the maturation of clinical cognitive neuropsychology will be a long and difficult process; at the same time, the potential payoff and excitement of this endeavor is vividly portrayed.

In Chapter 14, Macaruso, Harley, and McCloskey discuss assessment of acquired dyscalculia. Their job is complicated by the infrequent occurrence of selective disorders of number processing and the relatively small relevant literature. Nevertheless, they present a coherent and compelling information processing model of number processing, an assessment scheme, and case reports which demonstrate the utility of their model and testing procedures.

Poizner and Soechting's groundbreaking work on the microquantification of apraxia (Chapter 15) relies more heavily on high-technology equipment than the other chapters. This is a double-edged sword. Their advanced technology permits a high level of chronometric and spatial sophistication which may lead to advances in our understanding of the cognitive components of motor control. On the other hand, the technical demands of these procedures are a stumbling block to their widespread clinical application. Balancing technological sophistication against clinical practicality is likely to become increasingly challenging for clinical cognitive neuropsychologists as time goes on.

Judd approaches a relatively virgin topic in the field—music and other arts (Chapter 16). The development of cognitive models in the arts is lagging behind models of language, memory, or visuospatial function; so while Judd reviews the relevant literature, he does not attempt to create a broad model of music performance. The strength of this chapter lies in its well thought-out discussions of clinical assessment and rehabilitation planning.

Ober, Reed, and Jagust, in Chapter 17, bring the volume to a satisfying close. Familiar topics, including disorders of attention, language, memory, visuospatial analysis, and mental imagery, are approached from a fresh perspective—that of the neuroimager. A remarkably cogent overview of neuroimaging techniques provides a sturdy frame of reference for reviewing studies which relate structural and functional brain changes with cognitive changes in each of the aforementioned domains.

PART I

FOUNDATIONS

1

Clinical Cognitive Neuropsychology: An Emerging Speciality

DAVID IRA MARGOLIN

The field of cognitive science encompasses all of the different approaches to studying intelligent systems (Simon & Kaplan, 1989). Gardner (1985) and others (Posner, 1978; Posner & Shulman, 1979; Posner, Pea, & Volpe, 1982; Miller & Gazzaniga, 1984) have done an excellent job of chronicling the birth and early development of this still rapidly evolving science. Cognitive psychology and cognitive neuropsychology are two branches of cognitive science which study the same intelligent system—the human brain. They differ in that cognitive psychologists study normal brain function, while cognitive neuropsychologists study individuals with brain dysfunction. Excellent resources exist which provide overviews of cognitive psychology (Posner, 1978; Lachman, Lachman, & Butterfield, 1979; Eysenck & Keane, 1990) and cognitive neuropsychology (Ellis & Young, 1988; Shallice, 1988; Posner, 1989a). Much of the discussion in this chapter pertains to both cognitive psychologists and cognitive neuropsychologists. In order to avoid repeated use of those two labels, I will use the term *cognicians* when the discussion applies to practitioners of both disciplines.

Since cognitive neuropsychology involves the study of patients, it may seem redundant to introduce the term clinical cognitive neuropsychology, as I have done in this chapter's heading. In reality, an interest in cognitive neuropsychology is not always accompanied by an interest in practical clinical issues, such as determining the anatomical location and etiology of the lesion or treating patients. Shallice (1989, Chapter 9) has even coined the term *ultra-cognitive* neuropsychologist to describe those who study cognitive consequences of brain lesions, but have no interest in, or belief in the value of, defining the neural basis of cognition. Similarly, current cognitive neuropsychology publications differ substantially in the degree to which they emphasize theoretical as opposed to practical issues.

As evident from the title, this book concentrates on the clinical applications of cognitive neuropsychology. This chapter lays the groundwork for the subsequent discussions of specific clinical disorders by reviewing some of the more well-established concepts, vocabulary, experimental paradigms, and assessment techniques in cognitive neuropsychology, as well as touching upon current controversial issues and newer topics of investigation.

INTELLIGENCE IS MULTIFACETED

For most of this century, the dominant view in psychology was that human intelligence is a unidimensional monolithic attribute or capacity (Gardner, 1983). That view has been officially pronounced dead (Lezak, 1988), although its wraith may linger for some time. It has been replaced by the concept of intelligence as a multifaceted multidimensional array of capacities. Howard Gardner's 1983 book, *Frames of Mind*, has been very influential in explaining the principle of multiple intelligences to nonclinicians. He defined six "relatively autonomous" types or "frames" of intelligence: Linguistic, musical, logical-mathematical, spatial, bodily-kinesthetic, and personal. He later subdivided personal intelligence into intrapersonal and interpersonal intelligence (Gardner, 1987). Cognicians are far from reaching a consensus as to the number or names of the facets of intelligence, but I daresay that most would agree that Gardner's categories represent broad divisions of intelligence which can be divided further. Gardner's suggests that we conceptualize his six frames as "elements in a chemical system, basic constituents which can enter into compounds of various sorts and into equations" (1983, p. 279). Using this metaphor, cognicians can be described as searching for the subatomic particles that make up these elements and investigating how these irreducible "building blocks" of intelligence interact with one another to produce intelligent behaviors.

In preparation for this ambitious search, cognitive psychologists have borrowed from the accumulated knowledge of a diverse group of ancestral disciplines including philosophy, anthropology, neurology, psychiatry, basic neuroscience, linguistics, computer science, information theory, human engineering, communication engineering, and of course, several divisions of psychology—neobehaviorism, neuropsychology, and verbal learning (Posner, 1978; Lachman et al., 1979; Gardner, 1985).

The legacy of information theory is reflected prominently in the terminology of cognitive psychologists. They view human intelligence as reflecting the integrated action of multiple discrete *information processing modules* (or components or units). Each module can be conceptualized as a basic unit of intelligence which cannot be fractionated further using current technology (the subatomic particles of intelligence). A module can be conceptualized as having two dimensions: the type of information stored there (the code or format), and what is done to that information (the procedures or operations) (Caramazza, 1984).

Cognitive neuropsychologists who study brain-damaged individuals to learn more about how the normal brain processes information are implicitly or explicitly making three assumptions: (1) information-processing modules can function independently (the modularity principle; Morton, 1981); (2) brain damage can impair modules differentially (the fractionation assumption; Caramazza, 1984); (3) observing the behavioral consequences of damage to that module or set of modules reveals how it (or they) function in the normal brain (the transparency condition; Caramazza, 1984).

It is important to realize that cognicians have no monopoly on the adjective *cognitive*. Much in psychology which is termed cognitive has little in common with the work discussed in this book. Most of the widespread "cognitive" psychotherapies and "cognitive" neurorehabilitation programs, for example, bear only a superficial similarity to cognitive neuropsychology in that they all make reference to human thinking. As a rule, these other "cognitive" approaches do not share cognitive neuropsychology's theoretical and methodological grounding in cognitive psychology.

Conceptualizing intelligence as a network of modules is a refinement of, not a radical departure from, nineteenth century "localizationist" views of higher cortical functions. Carl Wernicke's 1874 theory, for example, held that language is dependent upon circumscribed groups of "simple psychic elements" (Wernicke, 1874/1968; see Margolin, 1991, for a detailed comparison of Wernicke's theory of language with contemporary information-processing theories). Modern cognicians are fond of illustrating the functional relationships between information-processing modules in the form of flow charts, similar to those used by computer programmers. Those flow charts are also known as box-and-arrow models. The boxes contain stores of information and procedures for manipulating (activating, retrieving, and transforming) that information. The arrows show the path and direction of information flow among the boxes (von Eckardt, 1978; Lachman et al., 1979, pp. 124–127; Shallice, 1979, 1981; Coltheart, 1987; Ellis, 1987). These box-and-arrow models are featured prominently in this volume.

THE CHRONOMETRIC APPROACH AND REACTION TIME (RT) METHODOLOGY

Reaction times (RT) provide an intuitively appealing indirect measure of brain function and efficiency. The use of RT methodology in psychology dates back to at least 1868 when Donders (1868/1969) theorized that the amount of time required to perform a given behavioral task was the sum of the time required to perform all of the constituent stages involved in that task. As a corollary, the RT difference between a more complex task and a simpler task reflects the amount of time needed to perform the cognitive operations involved in the more difficult task but not in the simpler task.

More recently, this "subtraction method" has been endorsed and expanded (Sternberg, 1969; Gottsdanker & Shragg, 1985) and is now commonly employed by cognitive psychologists and cognitive neuropsychologists. The most straightforward application of the subtraction method involves comparison of two uncomplicated tasks, the simple reaction time (SRT) task and the choice reaction time (CRT) task. In the SRT, subjects make a simple motor response to a specified stimulus (e.g., pressing a response key every time the number 1 appears on the computer screen). The RT measures how long it takes the subject to perceive the stimulus and execute the motor response. The conceptual and design simplicity of this task belie its power. For example, Foster et al. (1983) found that the SRT was the best overall correlate (negative) of cerebral glucose metabolism in a group of dementia of the Alzheimer's type (DAT) subjects.

In a CRT task, there are two different stimuli, each uniquely linked to one of two different responses (e.g., pressing key number 1 when number 1 appears and pressing key number 2 when the number 2 appears). The SRT and CRT tasks require the same peripheral steps (i.e., perception and motor response) but the CRT requires the addition of more central processing including a decision-making step (selecting the appropriate response). Subtracting the SRT from the CRT thus provides an indirect measure of decision-making time (see Margolin, Chapter 2, for a discussion of RT data in studies of aging and dementia).

The chronometric approach to neuropsychology is not confined to the use of reaction times as a dependent variable. Timing parameters such as stimulus presentation duration and interstimulus interval frequently serve as independent variables. In such experiments, either accuracy or RT are used as the dependent variable. The timing parameters can be manipulated so as to identify the optimal information-processing time for a given task (Posner, 1978, pp. 8–9).

HOW MANY SUBJECTS?

When providing clinical care (e.g., diagnostic assessment or treatment), cognitive neuropsychologists usually analyze the data from one patient at a time. In clinical research, however, pooled data from multiple patients are often analyzed together. Some cognitive neuropsychologists object vehemently to that practice. Caramazza (1986) and Caramazza and McCloskey (1988), for example, argue that even the most carefully constructed group of patients will be too heterogenous to permit valid or intelligible analyses, because important individual effects will be averaged out. This point is well taken, but most cognitive neuropsychologists still believe that, when patients are carefully selected, group studies are a valid and informative methodology (Caplan, 1988; Shallice, 1989).

This type of careful selection requires that each subject be studied in sufficient detail to ensure that all of the individuals in the group are matched along the relevant variables. As Marshall and Newcombe (1984, p. 70) put it, "There are no useful groups in neuropsychology; there are only groupings of individuals. And in order to be grouped in a rational, theoretically revealing fashion, the member must first be investigated in highly detailed single-case studies." In cognitive neuropsychological studies, patients within a group should be matched both for the behavioral abnormality (e.g., anomia [Chapter 8] or inattention [Chapters 3 to 5]) and the putative causative information-processing deficits (such as loss of semantic or lexical phonological information in anomia, or disruptions of disengage, move, or engage operations in inattention). The term *group case study* (Caramazza & Martin, 1983) has been proposed for this methodology, which distinguishes it from group studies where patients are grouped together based on a common syndrome diagnosis (e.g., Broca's aphasia). In such group studies, patients are lumped together on the basis of behavioral similarities which may only be superficial rather than reflecting common underlying information processing deficits. In studying anomia, for example, the group case study approach would separate patients with anomia due to phonological processing deficits from patients with anomia due to semantic processing deficits, which the prototypical group study would not.

With respect to single case studies, most cognicians are familiar with case reports where the behavioral phenomena are so compelling that no statistical analyses are necessary. This approach is common in the clinical neurology literature. More subtle effects can be detected thanks to statistics that are designed for single subjects. These statistical techniques are not new, but there has recently been a reawakening of interest in them (Guyatt et al., 1986; Wilson, 1987; Guyatt et al., 1990; Behrmann & Byng, see Chapter 12).

AUTOMATIC VERSUS EFFORTFUL

Viewed as a dichotomy, automatic tasks are those which can be performed without cognitive effort and thus do not interfere with other tasks, and non-automatic or effortful tasks are those which require cognitive effort (Posner, 1978, p. 91; Posner & Rafal, 1987). Alternatively, the amount of cognitive effort required to perform a task may be distributed along a continuum. In either model, effort is closely related to attention and consciousness. These concepts are fully developed in Part II of the book, *The Pervasive Influence of Attention.*

NEURAL NETWORKS

The 1980s witnessed a quantum change in the field—the influence of neural network models of cognitive function (a.k.a. connectionist or parallel distributed processing models; see Anderson, Silverstein, Ritz, & Jones, 1977; Anderson & Hinton, 1981; McClelland & Rumelhart, 1981; McClelland & Rumelhart, 1986; Rumelhart & McClelland, 1986; Anderson & Rosenfield, 1988; McClelland, 1988; Caudill, 1989; Mesulam, 1990; Schwartz, 1990). Unlike the box-and-arrow models which can be understood and even created without consideration of underlying neural structure or function, neural network models are based on an analogy to the human brain. The highly interdisciplinary origin of this class of models is underscored by the fact that they have been developed in conjunction with computer programs which simulate the activity of neurons. In these models/programs, neurons are portrayed as simple information-processing elements or nodes.

Each element receives graded excitatory or inhibiting input from the other nodes to which it is connected. The ultimate output of the network is defined by the weighted sum of all the input taken in parallel. Translating these concepts into operating computer programs has thus necessitated a radical departure from conventional programming methods where data and instructions are stored in specific memory locations and are retrieved in a sequential fashion as instructed by the program.

Neural network models are not inherently incompatible with the concepts represented in box-and-arrow models (Allport, 1985; Bechtel, 1988). The concepts of directionality of information flow (i.e., input vs. output), qualitatively distinct types of information (e.g., semantic vs. phonological), and connections between the different types are all preserved in the network models. These distinctions are represented in the form of different layers of nodes and their interconnections. The network models are highly interactive, postulating simultaneous bidirectional information flow across multiple levels. In contrast, box-and-arrow models usually show information flowing in one direction one step at a time.

One obvious advantage of the network models over the box-and-arrow models is that in addition to providing a conceptual framework for understanding cognitive processes, the network models provide a computational tool for testing and refining the models. The modeler/programmer must specify the functional details of the network, including the pattern and strength of activation in sufficient detail to run the program, and the output must simulate normal behaviors. Perturbations can also be introduced into the system in an attempt to stimulate the effects of neurological lesions. Existing work along those lines includes very simple simulations of acquired disorders of associative memory (Wood, 1978, 1982), naming (Gordon, 1982), and reading comprehension (Hinton & Sejnowski, 1986).

Reference to neural network models is made in only two chapters (10 and 13) of this volume, indicating that this line of investigation is just beginning to influence cognitive neuropsychologists. Ultimately, however, its impact is likely to be profound. Once the effects of neurological lesions can be accurately simulated, the opportunity will exist to develop cognitive rehabilitation techniques to reverse or compensate for the effects of the "lesion." In this approach the models will have to conform to the types and patterns of errors produced by patients. At the same time, examination of the programmed perturbations needed to produce a successful lesion simulation will provide insight into the pathophysiology of the actual cognitive deficit.

STATE-OF-THE-ART: A GLIMPSE INTO THE FUTURE?

One of the exciting promises of cognitive neuropsychology is the potential for identifying neural substrates of cognitive operations and procedures. The best example of work which interfaces neural and cognitive techniques comes from Posner and his colleagues. Posner (1989b) has proposed a general framework for conceptualizing the relationship between cognitive events and biological effectors/substrates at various levels of analysis. Posner's five levels of analysis include the elementary operations required (e.g., moving and engaging attention), the neural structures which are involved (e.g., occipital lobe, parietal lobe, midbrain), the type of neural activity involved (component analysis, in his terms; e.g., facilitation vs. inhibition), and the types of cells involved (e.g., rods and cones, cortical neurons). In groundbreaking work, Petersen, Fox, Posner, Mintum, and Raichle (1988) demonstrated how the PET scan can be applied toward localizing particular information-processing modules to specific brain regions; this study is described in more detail by Ober, Reed, and Jagust in Chapter 17, which looks at neuroimaging and cognition. Recent advances in the technical aspects of neuroscience (e.g., neuroimaging and computer technology) have been astounding. Advances in describing and understanding acquired cognitive abnormalities and identifying the underlying information processing deficits have been less dramatic. One goal of clinical cognitive neuropsychology is to narrow this technology-behavior gap. This is a prerequisite for the development of more veridical information-processing models of cognition.

REFERENCES

Allport, D. A. (1985). Distributed memory, modular subsystems and dysphasia. In S. Newman & R. Epstein (Eds.), *Current perspectives in dysphasia* (pp. 32–60). Edinburgh: Churchill Livingstone.

Anderson, J. A., & Hinton, G. E. (1981). Models of information processing in the brain. In G. E. Hinton & J. A. Anderson (Eds.), *Parallel models of associative memory* (pp. 9–48). Hillsdale, NJ: Erlbaum.

Anderson, J. A., & Rosenfield, E. (Eds.). (1988). *Neurocomputing: Foundations of research*. Cambridge, MA: MIT.

Anderson, J. A., Silverstein, J. W., Ritz, S. A., & Jones, R. S. (1977). Distinctive features, categorical perception, and probability learning: Some applications of a neural model. *Psychological Review*, *85*:413–451.

Bechtel, W. (1988). Connectionism and rules and representations systems: Are they compatible? *Philosophical Psychology*, *1*:5–16.

Caplan, D. (1988). On the role of group studies in neuropsychological and patho-psychological-research. *Cognitive Neuropsychology*, *5*:535–548.

Caramazza, A. (1984). The logic of neuropsychological research and the problem of patient classification in aphasia. *Brain and Language*, *21*:9–20.

Caramazza, A. (1986). On drawing inferences about the structure of normal cognitive systems from the analysis of patterns of impaired performance: The case for single-patient studies. *Brain and Cognition*, *5*:41–66.

Caramazza, A., & Martin, R. C. (1983). Theoretical and methodological issues in the study of aphasia. In J. B. Hellige, (Ed.), *Cerebral hemisphere asymmetry: Method, theory, and application* (pp. 18–45). New York: Praeger Scientific.

Cramazza, A., & McCloskey, M. (1988). The case for single-patient studies. *Cognitive Neuropsychology*, *5*:517–528.

Caudill, M. (1989). *Neural networks primer*. San Francisco: Miller Freeman.

Coltheart, M. (1987). Functional architecture of the language-processing system. In M. Coltheart, G. Sartoni & R. Job (Eds.), *The cognitive neuropsychology of language* (pp. 1–26). London: Erlbaum.

Donders, F. C. (1969). On the speed of mental processes. In W. G. Koster (Ed. and Trans.), *Attention and performance II (Acta Psychologica, 30)* (pp. 412–431). Amsterdam: North Holland. (original work published 1868.)

Ellis, A. W. (1987). Intimations of modularity, or, the modularity of mind. Doing cognitive neuropsychology without syndromes. In M. Coltheart, G. Sartori & R. Job (Eds.), *The cognitive neuropsychology of language* (pp. 397–408). London: Lawrence Erlbaum.

Ellis, A. W., & Young, A. W. (1988). *Human cognitive neuropsychology*. Hillsdale, NJ: Erlbaum.

Eysenck, M. W., & Keane, M. T. (1990). *Cognitive psychology: A student's handbook.* Hillsdale, NJ: Erlbaum.

Foster, N. L., & Chase, T. N., Fedio, P., Patronas, N. J., Brooks, R. A., & Di Chiro,

G. (1983). Alzheimer's disease: Focal cortical changes shown by positron emission tomography. *Neurology*, *33*:961–965.

Gardner, H. (1983). *Frames of mind: The theory of multiple intelligences.* New York: Basic Books.

Gardner, H. (1987). The assessment of intelligences: A neuropsychological perspective. In M. Meier, A. Benton, & L. Diller (Eds.), *Neuropsychological rehabilitation* (pp. 59–70). New York: Guilford.

Gardner, H. (1985). *The mind's new science: A history of the cognitive revolution.* New York: Basic Books.

Gordon, B. (1982). Confrontation naming: Computational model and disconnection simulation. In M. A. Arbib, D. Caplan, & J. C. Marshall (Eds.), *Neural models of language processes* (pp. 511–530). New York: Academic Press.

Gottsdanker, R., & Shragg, G. P. (1985). Verification of Donder's subtraction method. *Journal of Experimental Psychology: Human Perception and Performance*, *11*:765–776.

Guyatt, G. H., Keller, J. L., Jaeschke, R., Rosenbloom, D., Adachi, J. D., & Newhouse, M. T. (1990). The n-of-1 randomized control trial: Clinical usefulness. *Annals of Internal Medicine*, *112*:293–299.

Guyatt, G., Sackett, D., Taylor, D. W., Chong, J., Robert, R., & Pugsley, S. (1986). Determining optimal therapy—randomized trials in individual patients. *New England Journal of Medicine*, *314*:889–892.

Hinton, G. E., & Sejnowski, T. J. (1986). Learning and relearning in Boltzmann machines. In D. E. Rumelhart & J. L. McClelland (Eds.), *Parallel distributing processing: Vol. 1 Foundations* (pp. 282–317). Cambridge: MA: MIT.

Lachman, R., Lachman, J. L., & Butterfield, E. C. (1979). *Cognitive psychology and information processing: An introduction*. Hillsdale, NJ: Erlbaum.

Lezak, M. (1988). IQ: R.I.P. *Journal of Clinical and Experimental Neuropsychology*, *10*:351–361.

Margolin, D. I. (In press). Cognitive neuropsychology: Resolving enigmas about Wernicke's aphasia and other higher cortical disorders. *Archives of Neurology*, 48:751–765.

Marshall, J. C., & Newcombe, F. (1984). Putative problems and pure progresss in neuropsychological single-case studies. *Journal of Clinical Neuropsychology*, *6*:65–70.

McClelland, J. C. (1988). Connectionist models and psychological evidence. *Journal of Memory and Language*, *27*:107–123.

McClelland, J. C., & Rumelhart, D. E. (1981). An interactive model of context effects in letter perception: Part 1. An account of basic findings. *Psychological Review*, *88*:375–407.

McClelland, J. C., & Rumelhart, D. E. (1986). *Explorations in the microstructure of cognition, Volume 2: Psychological and biological models.* Cambridge, MA: MIT.

Mesulam, M. M. (1990). Large-scale neurocognitive networks and distributed processing for attention, language, and memory. *Annals of Neurology*, *28*:597–613.

Miller, G. W., & Gazzaniga, M. S. (1984). The cognitive sciences. In M. S. Gazzaniga (Ed.), *Handbook of cognitive neuroscience* (pp. 3–11). New York: Plenum Press.

Morton, J. (1981). The status of information processing models of language. *Philosophical Transactions of the Royal Society of London*, *295B*:387–396.

Petersen, S. E., Fox, P. T., Posner, M. I., Mintum, M., & Raichle, M. E. (1988). Positron emission tomographic studies of the cortical anatomy of single-word processing. *Nature*, *331*:585–589.

Posner, M. I. (1978). *Chronometric explorations of mind.* Hillsdale, NJ: Erlbaum.

Posner, M. I. (Ed.). (1989a). *Foundations of cognitive science*. Cambridge, MA: Bradford/MIT Press.

Posner, M. I. (1989b). Structures and functions of selective attention. In T. Boll & B. K. Bryant (Eds.), *Clinical neuropsychology and brain function: Research, measurements and practice* (pp. 173–202). Washington, DC: American Psychological Association.

Posner, M. I., Pea, R., & Volpe, B. (1982). Cognitive neuroscience: Developments toward of science of synthesis. In J. Mehler, M., Garrett, and E. Walker (Eds.), *Perceptives on mental representation: Experimental and theoretical studies of cognitive processes and capabilities* (pp. 251–276). Hillsdale, NJ: Erlbaum.

Posner, M. I., & Rafal, R. D. (1987). Cognitive theories of attention and the rehabilitation of attentional deficits. In M. Meier, A. Benton, & L. Diller (Eds.). *Neuropsychological rehabilitation* (pp. 182–201). New York: Guilford.

Posner, M. I., & Shulman, G. I. (1979). Cognitive science. In E. Hearst (Ed.), *The first century of experimental psychology* (pp. 371–406). Hillsdale, NJ: Erlbaum.

Rumelhart, D. E., & McClelland, J. L. (1986). *Parallel distributed processing: Exploration in the microstructure of cognition: Vol. 1 Foundations*. Cambridge, MA: MIT.

Schwartz, E. L. (Ed.). (1990). *Computational neuroscience*. Cambridge, MA: Bradford/MIT Press.

Shallice, T. (1979). Case study approach in neuropsychological research. *Journal of Clinical Neuropsychology*, *1*:183–211.

Shallice, T. (1981). Neurological impairment of cognitive processes. *British Medical Bulletin*, *37*:187–192.

Shallice, T. (1989). *From neuropsychology to mental structure*. Cambridge, UK: Cambridge University Press.

Shallice, T. (1988). Specialization within the semantic system. *Cognitive Neuropsychology*, *5*:133–142.

Simon, H. A., & Kaplan, C. A. (1989). Foundations of cognitive science. In M. I. Posner (Ed.), *Foundations of cognitive science* (pp. 1–48). Cambridge, MA: Bradford/MIT Press.

Sternberg, S. (1969). The discovery of processing stages: Extensions of Donder's method. *Acta Psychologica*, *30*:276–315.

von Eckardt, B. (1978). Inferring functional localization from neurological evidence. In E. Walker (Ed.), *Explorations in the biology of language* (pp. 27–66). Montgomery, VA: Bradford Books.

Wernicke, C. (1968). The symptom complex of aphasia (Trans.). *Boston Studies in the Philosophy of Science*, *4*:34–97. (Original work published 1874).

Wilson, B. (1987). Single-case experimental design in neuropsychological rehabilitation. *Journal of Clinical and Experimental Neuropsychology*, *9*:527–544.

Wood, C. C. (1978). Variations of a theme on Lashley: Lesion experiments of the neural model of Anderson, Silverstein, Ritz, & Jones. *Psychological Review*, *85*:582–591.

Wood, C. C. (1982). Implications of simulated lesion experiments for the interpretation of lesions in real nervous systems. In M. A. Arbib, D. Caplan, & J. C. Marshall (Eds.), *Neural models of language processes* (pp. 485–509). New York: Academic Press.

2

Probing the Multiple Facets of Human Intelligence: The Cognitive Neuropsychologist as Clinician

DAVID IRA MARGOLIN

Most of the chapters in this book, like most of the publications in this field, concentrate on disorders within a single cognitive domain (e.g., dyscalculia, dysphasia, dyslexia, dyspraxia); they demonstrate how cognitive neuropsychologists, guided by the relevant information-processing models, utilize fine-tuned psychometric tests in order to define as precisely as possible the cognitive deficit(s) underlying a given patient's disorder.

This approach has had a profound impact upon the practice of neuropsychology, but since the cognitive neuropsychology approach has specialized in detailed analyses of circumscribed problems, it has had much less of an impact upon how clinicians initially diagnose and classify patients. Through a discussion of the clinical syndrome of dementia of the Alzheimer's type (DAT), this chapter reveals the subtle but increasingly important influence of cognitive neuropsychology on the initial diagnostic workup of patients—including the use of wide-ranging, screening, or survey assessments of intellect (i.e., mental status tests).

DEMENTIA OF THE ALZHEIMER'S TYPE: DIAGNOSTIC CRITERIA

Clinical research is only as valid as the diagnoses given to the patient participants. At least for the moment, there is a consensus regarding the proper diagnostic criteria for DAT (McKhann et al., 1984; American Psychiatric Association [APA], 1987, pp. 103–107, 119–121). The diagnosis of DAT can be conceptualized as a two-step process, the first step is to determine that the patient has a dementia rather than some qualitatively different type of behavioral disturbance. The second step involves differentiating between Alzheimer's disease and the myriad other causes of dementia. The label dementia is appropriate when a patient has experienced a multifaceted intellectual decline (involving at least two qualitatively different types of intelligence) which is severe enough to "interfere significantly with work or usual social activities or relationships with others" (APA, 1987, p. 103). In addition, the intellectual deterioration takes place in the setting of a normal level of consciousness (normal sensorium) and normal (at least grossly) attention. These latter two features distinguish dementia from the other major category of multifaceted behavior change, delirium (in psychiatric terms) or encephalopathy (in neurological terms) (APA, 1987, pp. 100–103).

The second step, determining the etiology of the dementia, consists in large part of documenting the time course of the intellectual deterioration. DAT has an insidious onset and is gradually progressive, while multi-infarct dementia is characterized by abrupt episodes of deterioration (stepwise course) (APA, 1987, pp. 121–123). Despite their simplicity, careful application of these criteria along with a not-too-onerous series of laboratory tests (Katzman, 1986) is associated with an impressive 80% to 100% diagnostic accuracy for Alzheimer's disease (Sulkava, Haltia, Paetau, Wikstrom, & Palo, 1983; Huff, et al., 1987; Martin, et al., 1987; Wade, et al., 1987; Tierney, et al., 1988; Boller, Lopez, & Moossy, 1989; Forette, et al., 1989). This represents a substantial improvement over the 50% (or less) accuracy afforded by earlier less well-specified criteria (Kay, 1977; Garcia, Reding, & Blass, 1981; Katzman, 1986).

Despite this relatively high degree of accuracy, the workup described so far is insufficient to diagnose Alzheimer's disease definitively. Currently, the diagnosis of *definite* Alzheimer's disease requires documentation of specific microscopic changes—senile plaques and neurofibrillary tangles—in addition to the history of gradual cognitive decline. It is crucial to note that neither of these pathological changes are pathognomonic for Alzheimer's disease. They both occur in limited numbers in normal brains, their prevalence increasing with age (Matsuyama, 1983; Ulrich, 1985; Crystal et al., 1988). Conventional wisdom holds that the plaques and tangles occur in normal brains in smaller quantities than in Alzheimer's brains, but there are no universally accepted quantitative standards for distinguishing between normality and pathology based upon neuropathological changes alone (Ulrich, 1985; Crystal et al., 1988; Tierney et al., 1988). Furthermore, Alzheimer's changes, particularly neurofibrillary tangles, occur in large numbers in chronic neurological disease of diverse etiologies (Wisniewski, Jervis, Moretz, & Wisniewski, 1979).

Given the requirement of histological verification for the diagnosis of definite Alzheimer's disease, the great majority of clinical research in this area has thus relied upon patients with *probable* or *possible* (McKhann et al., 1984) Alzheimer's disease. Many investigators use terms such as dementia of the Alzheimer's type (DAT) or Alzheimer's-type dementia to reflect this diagnostic uncertainty. An aggressive worldwide search is under way to uncover some type of biological marker (e.g., neuropsychological, neurochemical, or genetic abnormality) or behavioral marker which is specific for, or at least highly correlated with, DAT (Katzman, 1986). The goal is to approach 100% diagnostic accuracy even in the absence of a brain biopsy. At present, however, the most powerful diagnostic tools are a detailed medical history and careful general physical, neurological, psychiatric, and cognitive status examinations.

FIRST THINGS FIRST: THE HISTORY

The quest for an accurate diagnosis is common ground for clinicians and clinical researchers. While the emphasis of this book is on the unique contributions of cognitive neuropsychology to the neurosciences, the cognitive neuropsychologist's initial workup of a patient should not differ from conventional medical or psychological approaches. Regardless of the examiner's discipline or precise orientation, obtaining an accurate and sufficiently detailed history should be the first priority.

It is standard teaching in clinical neurology that the clinician should be able to diagnose many (if not most) diseases solely on the basis of a well-taken history. This is equally applicable to neuropsychology. As the well-known neurologist Adolph Sahs has been quoted as saying, "If you have 30 minutes to see a patient, spend 29 on the history, one on the examination, and none on the EEG and skull x-ray" (Joynt, 1987, p. 562). Clearly, the results of psychological testing, no matter how exhaustive or well designed the tests, cannot be interpreted in a vacuum. Gross deficits are unlikely to be misinterpreted, but there is no neuropsychological equivalent of Babinski's sign (an abnormal reflex which is a reliable indicator of pathology of the nervous system).

Given the nature of the disease, it is imperative to obtain a history from at least one collateral source who knows the patient well. The history taking is not complete until the interviewer has (1) painted a clear picture of the individual's premorbid behavior, (2) determined the time course and pattern of the behavior change, and (3) documented the current level of cognitive functioning. Table 2-1 lists some of the important historical points which should be covered in making these determinations. Descriptions of the subject's premorbid abilities should be supplemented by documentation if possible (e.g., school grades, writing samples, samples of art or craftwork). Standardized questionnaires provide an important adjunct to the history; they are helpful in differentiating DAT from such other causes of dementia as alcoholism (Selzer, 1971), multiple cerebral infarcts (Hachinski et al., 1975; Rosen, Terry, Fuld, Katzman, & Peck, 1980), and depression (Yesavage, et al., 1983; Alexopoulos, Abrams, Young, & Shamoian, 1988; Reynolds, et al., 1988; Rovner, Broadhead, Spencer, Carson, & Folstein, 1989).

AXES I LOVE TO GRIND

Nomenclature

As mentioned earlier, patients with suspected but non-biopsy-proven Alzheimer's disease should be referred to by a diagnostic label which accurately reflects the appropriate degree of clinical uncertainty, such as: possible or probable Alzheimer's disease, dementia of the Alzheimer's type, or Alzheimer's-type dementia. In my opinion, the adjective senile (e.g., senile dementia or senile dementia of the Alzheimer's type) has no place in dementia terminology. The word *senile* means to age, so that the term senile dementia conveys the false (according to most investigators) impression that aging per se (i.e., normal aging) is an independent etiology of dementia. Even when the term is used solely to convey chronological information (i.e., that the patient is over the age of 65), it is problematic since it has not been established that Alzheimer's disease oc-

Table 2-1 History Checklist

I. Establishing a premorbid profile

1. Education
2. Hobbies
3. Reading material
4. Letter writing
5. Following current events
6. Investments
7. Checkbook
8. Income tax
9. Travel
10. Social contacts

II. Onset and time course of behavior change

1. Describe earliest changes in behavior (forgetfulness, word finding, using objects, navigating, judgment)
2. Approximate onset
3. Pattern of progression (steady vs. episodic/stepwise)
4. Rate of decline (rapid vs. slow)
5. Any periods of recovery?
6. Who has noticed changes outside of the family?

III. Current function

1. Describe typical day (time awakes, meals, physical activity, activity outside the home)
2. Does he/she drive? (Any changes in driving skills noted? Accidents or near accidents? Getting lost?)
3. Change in sleeping or eating pattern?
4. Evidence of depression? (sad, blue, crying, hopeless)

curring before the age of 65 is clinically or biologically distinct from Alzheimer's disease occurring after the age of 65 (Crook, Ward, & Austin, 1979). Even if age-related differences in Alzheimer's disease do exist, the age 65 is an arbitrary cutoff.

Intellectual Decline in Alzheimer's: Continuum or Dichotomy?

It is common to encounter references to the stages of Alzheimer's disease (e.g., Cummings & Benson, 1983; Reisberg, 1983; Strub & Black, 1988). While these staging schemas can provide a convenient clinical shorthand for conveying information about the severity of dementia, the danger is that they imply that DAT progresses in discrete stages and in an orderly, predictable fashion. That implication is fundamentally at odds with the diagnostic criterion that DAT follows an insidious gradually progressive course (APA, 1987, p. 121; McKhann et al., 1984, p. 940). Moreover, it is becoming increasingly clear that there is considerable interpatient heterogeneity in the pattern and time course of intellectual decline in this disease (Friedland, 1988; Martin et al., 1986; Martin, 1987).

SURVEY TECHNIQUES: NOT MISSING THE FOREST FOR THE TREES

Contemporary mental status or cognitive status tests are legion and range from a minimalist approach (e.g., Katzman, 1981) to exhaustive (and exhausting) standardized batteries. Most clinicians seek an instrument which strikes a good balance between brevity on the one hand and breadth and depth on the other hand, and which can be administered within 10 to 20 minutes without elaborate props. Some of the more widely used instruments include: the Mini-Mental State Examination (Folstein, Folstein, & McHugh, 1975; Teng & Chui, 1987; Bleecker, Bolla-Wilson, Kawas, & Agnew, 1988), the Cognitive Capacity Screening Examination (Jacobs, Bernhard, Delgado, & Strain, 1977); the Short Portable Mental Status Questionnaire (Pfeiffer, 1975); and the Mattis (1976) Dementia Scale. Descriptions of these widely used tests are readily available (e.g., Lezak, 1983; Schmitt, Ranseen, & DeKosky, 1989) and will not be repeated here. As one might expect, these brief tests have high false-negative rates (i.e., do not detect subtle degrees of pathology) particularly in patients with predominantly nonverbal deficits (Nelson, Fogel, & Faust, 1986).

A brief mental status test developed in Britain, The Information-Memory-Concentration Test (IMC; Blessed, Tomlinson, & Roth, 1968), and a version slightly modified for use in the United States (mIMC; Katzman et al., 1983) have become widely used, at least in part, because some attempt has been made to validate these measures against neuropathological data. Blessed et al. (1968) found that there was a statistically significant negative correlation between IMC scores and mean plaque counts (averaged across multiple cortical areas) in a group of 60 elderly individuals. It is crucial to note, however, that this was a very heterogeneous group of subjects, which included patients with neurodegenerative diseases, delirium, "functional psychoses," and the physically ill without overt cognitive impairment. Twenty-six patients were labeled as having "senile dementia," but only two of them were judged to have probable Alzheimer's disease. The correlation between the IMC scores and plaque counts was not significant in this "senile dementia" group. Katzman et al. (1983) found a significant correlation between mIMC test scores and plaque counts in 38 autopsied patients, but the same caveat applies. Their sample included nondemented subjects, patients with multiple infarcts, and DAT patients. Recently, Salmon et al. (1990) have reported a significant inverse correlation between mIMC scores and several biological markers of Alzheimer's disease in the frontal lobes of 13 Alzheimer's patients. Those markers included neurofibrillary tangles, synapse density, and choline acetyltransferase activity (plaque counts did not correlate significantly with mIMC scores; Dr. Salmon, personal communication, January 28, 1991).

Over the last 10 years, the mIMC has gained wide acceptance in both clinical and research settings. Early data indicated that eight errors or less could be considered within normal limits for the geriatric population (Fuld, 1978; Katzman et al., 1983), but subsequent reports have proven that criterion too lenient. Katzman et al. (1989) studied 434 individuals between the ages of 75 and 85 who were functional in their community, ambulatory, and "presumably nondemented." Subjects who made zero to two errors on the IMC had less than 0.6%

per year chance of developing DAT, while those with five to eight errors had a rate of over 12% per year. Those data of course beg the question as to whether the poorer scoring individuals were truly normal at the time of initial testing.

Longitudinal studies extending up to six years indicate that the IMC is a useful measure for charting the rate of intellectual decline in DAT subjects. The findings that the rate of change in the IMC scores is independent of age (across the age range of 52–96 years) or place of residence (community vs. nursing home) (Katzman et al., 1988) attest to the robustness of this test.

Since 1985 we have been using a relatively newly developed instrument, the Neurobehavioral Cognitive Status Examination (NCSE; Kiernan, Mueller, Langstrom, & Van Dyke, 1987; Schwamm, Van Dyke, Kiernan, Merrin, & Mueller, 1987; Kiernan, 1989; Meek, Clark, & Solana, 1989). This test consists of eleven measures of behavior. Two of them—level of consciousness and attention—can be described as measuring more pervasive (domain general, horizontal) mental activity which has a general influence on many, if not all, other tasks. The other nine measures probe more discrete (domain specific, vertical) cognitive processes, including orientation, memory (verbal learning), construction, calculation, similarities, judgment, and three subtests of language (comprehension, repetition, and naming). For eight of the measures a screening item difficult enough to result in a 20% failure rate for normal subjects is administered. Only if this screening item is failed is a series of items of graded difficulty administered. For example, the screen for the attention task is repeating six digits; if the subject fails the screen then 3-, 4-, 5-, and 6-digit numbers are given in that order. This test can thus typically be administered to normals in about 15 to 20 minutes; mildly demented subjects take somewhat longer.

Despite its brevity, this test is more sensitive to cognitive dysfunction than is the Mini-Mental State Exam or the Cognitive Capacity Screening Examination (Schwamm et al., 1987). The NCSE is commercially available and comes with all necessary props except for several readily available common objects (e.g., keys, pen, paper) which are used in the auditory comprehension subtest. The four-page scoring booklet is mostly self-explanatory, but a scoring manual is provided. Attractive features of the booklet include a graphic display of the patient's scores with the range of normal scores shaded in. For scores below the range of normal, the severity of the deficit is quantified along an ordinal scale (mild, moderate, or severe). It is thus immediately apparent whether the deficit is unifaceted or multifaceted, and what the pattern of the deficits is. Space is provided for documenting important clinical information (e.g., handedness, medications, education, occupation).

The NCSE: Cognitive Profiles

Figure 2-1 shows the composite NCSE profile of 13 of our subjects who fit the diagnostic criteria for probable DAT (McKhann et al., 1984), compared with 13 older normals matched as closely as possible for age and education (descriptions of individual patients are presented in Table 2-2). The average age for the DAT group was 71.3 years compared with 69.8 for the older normals [$F(1,24) = .19$; P = N.S.], and the education levels were 12.2 years versus 14.6 years,

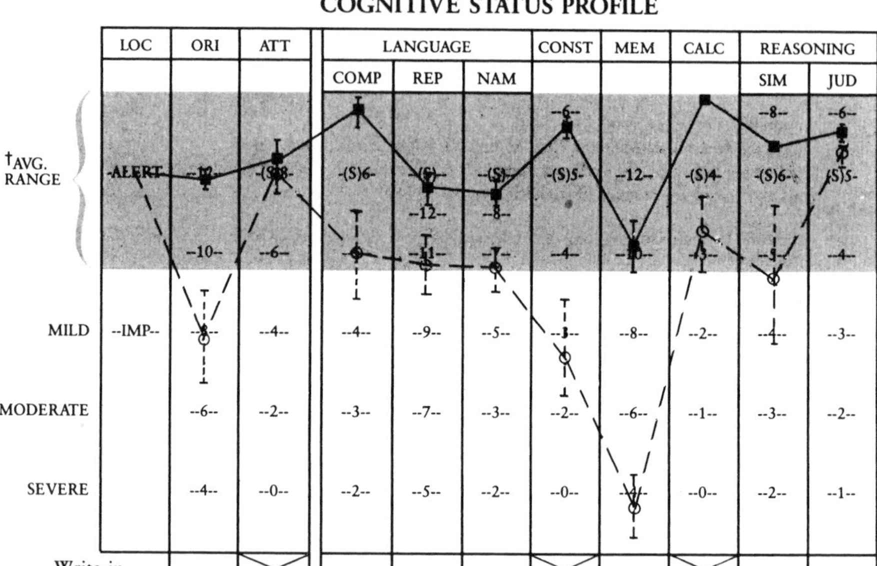

Figure 2-1 The continuous line indicates the composite NCSE profile of 13 older normals. The broken line is the composite of 13 DAT subjects. (Reprinted with permission from the Northern California Neurobehavioral Group, Inc., 1986.)

respectively [$F(1,24) = 3.77$; P = N.S.]. By definition, both groups had a normal level of consciousness. The DAT group was significantly (Table 2-3) impaired on eight of the remaining ten subtests; attention and judgment were the exceptions. The most severe deficits, by far, were in the orientation and memory subtests. This observation underscores a point which is well known to clinicians who have worked with amnestic patients: orientation is primarily a test of new

Table 2-2 Clinical Profiles of DAT Patients

Patient	Severity of Dementia	Age	Gender	Education (years)	Duration of Dementia (years)	IMC Score
DW	Very mild	53	M	10	1–2	12
WH	Very mild	64	M	18	3	8
IK	Very mild	66	M	6	1–2	6
CD	Very mild	73	M	12	2	8
LP	Very mild	74	M	12	2–3	6
JL	Very mild	76	F	12	2	5
DP	Mild	57	M	18	6	22
MB	Mild	69	F	12	1–2	10
RA	Mild	71	M	12	2–5	4
MV	Mild	79	F	10	7	16
FC	Mild	81	M	18	5	18
JC	Mild	81	M	10	4–5	19
LH	Moderate	82	M	8	1–2	22

Table 2-3 NCSE Subtest Scores for DAT versus Older Normals

Subtest	$F[1,24]$
Orientation	17.0*
Attention	0.3
Comprehension	10.1*
Repetition	6.0*
Naming	10.2*
Construction	18.6*
Memory	65.7*
Calculation	15.5*
Similarities	8.6*
Judgment	0.9

*$p < .05$.

learning. On the NCSE, for example, there are seven questions: name, age, current location, city, date, day of week, and time of day. Except for the subject's name, answering the other questions requires that the subject remember recently encountered verbal or visual information. It is not surprising, therefore, that this subtest is affected in DAT.

The memory subtest is a test of verbal learning, a form of episodic memory. Four unrelated words are presented auditorily for immediate repetition and for later recall. If spontaneous recall is unsuccessful, a semantic category cue is given, followed by a 3-choice recognition trial if needed. This subtest thus offers considerably more detailed information about verbal learning than other bedside exams. The disproportionately severe deficit on the memory subtest of the NCSE is consistent with the well-documented verbal learning deficits in DAT (see Morris & Kopelman, 1986, for review). Such deficits tend to be the earliest impairment and remain the most salient feature throughout the course of the disease.

The moderate impairment in constructional praxis is congruent with the well-documented fact that the Performance IQ is more impaired than the Verbal IQ in groups of DAT subjects (Martin et al., 1986; Bayles & Kaszniak, 1987, pp. 236–239). The three language subtests—comprehension, repetition, and naming—were relatively equally affected: they were all impaired to a mild degree. These data are consistent with a considerable literature which indicates that language deficits are a common, if not universal, consequence of DAT (Appell, Kertesz, & Fisman, 1982; Bayles & Kaszniak, 1987, pp. 114–132; Margolin, 1988; Margolin, Pate, Friedrich, & Elia, 1990).

The performance of the DAT subjects on the attention task did not differ significantly from normal. The NCSE utilizes digit span as the measure of attention, so that scores on this subtest reflect both immediate memory function and the allocation and sustaining of attention. Other investigators have also found digit span to fall within normal limits in DAT (Weingartner et al., 1981; Weingartner, Grafman, Boutelle, Kaye, & Martin, 1983; Vitaliano, Breen, Albert, Russo, & Prinz, 1984; Martin, Brouwers, Cox, & Fedio, 1985), but some have found it to be mildly to substantially impaired (Nebes, Martin, & Horn, 1984; Eslinger, Damasio, Benton, & Van Allen, 1985; Jorm, 1986). Presumably

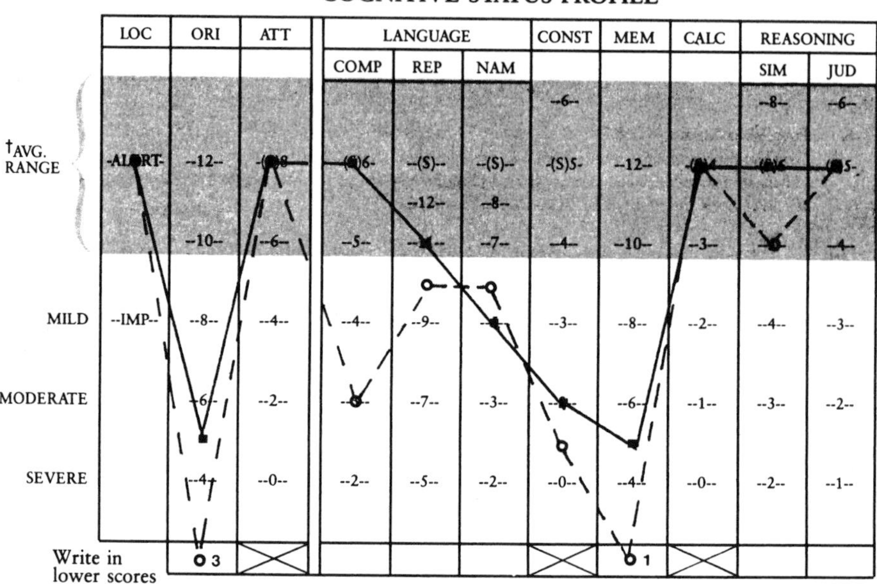

Figure 2-2 NCSE profiles of DAT patient M.V. from 5/86 (continuous line) and 3/89 (broken line). (Reprinted with permission from the Northern California Neurobehavioral Group, Inc., 1986.)

differences in the severity of the dementia account for some of the discrepancy in these data, but it will take time to sort out the role of other confounding variables. For clinical purposes, the salient point is that, up until very late in the course of the disease, DAT subjects usually appear to be alert and attentive. The finding that judgment is relatively spared is noteworthy but not easily explained. It would be interesting to see if scores on that subtest correlated with quality of judgment in natural settings (i.e., is knowing the right thing to do predictive of actually doing the right thing?).

Overall, our data are very much in line with those of Kiernan, who reports that mild-moderate DAT patients "are usually alert and attentive and demonstrate relatively preserved language functions. They frequently show evidence of mild disorientation and have difficulty with constructional and memory tasks. Their performance on calculation and verbal reasoning tasks is highly variable and often remains largely unimpaired in early stages of the disease" (Kiernan, 1989, p. 258).

The NCSE is an excellent vehicle for documenting the pattern and temporal course of cognitive decline in individual DAT patients. Figure 2.2 shows the results of two administrations of the NCSE to one of our DAT subjects, M.V. The two administrations were given approximately three years apart. This right-handed woman presented in September of 1985 at age 79 with a chief complaint of forgetfulness. She had recently moved from another city to live with her daughter, but described herself as "just visiting." She was still active socially, including participating in a woman's club and visiting with friends. This history was confirmed by her daughter who dated the onset of her mother's memory problem to around 1978 with subsequent gradual deterioration. Examples for the memory problem included misplacing objects and forgetting her grandson's name.

As can be seen from Figure 2-2, the most severe deficits in the May 1986 administration of the NCSE were in the tasks that put the heaviest load on recent verbal memory and new learning. In addition, there were mild language and constructional problems. Her knowledge of current events was severely limited, providing further documentation of the recent verbal memory deficit. The rest of the neurological examination showed only some mild left-sided weakness. A CT scan performed in June 1984 showed mild atrophy, and an MRI performed in June 1988 showed moderate atrophy. The rest of the dementia workup was within normal limits. M.V. was tested at approximately six-month intervals over the next 2½ years. Her daughter reported a progressive memory disturbance characterized by repetitive questioning, with a relatively preserved personality. During the most recent testing round (March 1989), it was reported that the patient had become fatigued, anorectic, and hypersomnolent. Nevertheless, she continued to attend adult day care 40 hours per week. The neurological examination had changed to reveal some pathology of emotion (Poeck, 1969); she laughed and cried without apparent cause or change in reported mood. The NCSE from March 1989 documented the reported decline in orientation and memory. Furthermore, the multifaceted nature of the impairment had become much more apparent, with speech comprehension and repetition deficits emerging. As is typical for the DAT patients as a group, attention and judgment were relatively immune to the disease.

Data-Driven Mini-Batteries

Several investigators have taken a qualitatively different approach to screening for DAT, the use of multivariate statistical techniques. Multivariate analyses can be used, for example, to identify the minimal number of cognitive tasks which differentiate DAT from normality. This application can be conceptualized as a search for a convenient behavioral marker of DAT, analogous to the search for a pathognomonic biological marker (Katzman, 1986). In 1984, Storandt, Botwinick, Danziger, Berg, and Hughes demonstrated that a battery of four psychological tests—consisting of the logical memory and mental control subjects of the WMS, Form A of the Trailmaking Test, and word fluency for the letters S and P—was 98% accurate in differentiating mild dementia patients from normal age-matched controls. These four measures were selected from a much larger group of tests based on the results of stepwise discriminate function analyses. The authors indicated that the following formula could be used for classifying subjects as normal or demented based upon the results (raw scores) of these four tests [$Y = (-0.455) \times$ logical memory and $(-0.066) \times$ trailmaking $+ (-0.036) \times$ verbal fluence score $+ (0.130) \times$ mental control $+ 3.588$), $Y > 0$ = demented, $Y < 0$ = normal. Widespread acceptance of this formula may have been undermined by the fact that the formula was alluded to in the narrative of the article rather than explicitly provided in equation form, which might be problematic given that it was published in a very clinically oriented neurology journal.

Subsequent investigations have verified that this type of battery is useful in distinguishing between patients with mild (or more severe) dementia and normal subjects, but is not clinically useful in discriminating between very early dementia and normality, or differentiating among dementias of different etiologies (Eslinger et al., 1985; Tierney, Snow, Reid, Zorzitto, & Fisher, 1987; Storandt & Hill, 1989). Other measures, however, some of them selected on a theoretically motivated basis, have been reported to differentiate between DAT and dementias of other etiology, including depression (Weingartner et al., 1982), Huntington's disease (Moss, Albert, Butters, & Payne, 1986), multiple cerebral infarcts (Perez et al., 1975), and Parkinson's disease (Freedman & Oscar-Berman, 1986; Mayeux, Stern, Sano, Cote, & Williams, 1987; Stern, Mayeux, Sano, Hanser, & Bush, 1987).

This work is encouraging, but there are formidable barriers to be overcome before a behavioral marker for DAT is defined. As discussed earlier, there is good evidence that the currently accepted neuropathological gold standards for determining the etiology of dementia are actually made of less precious metals. For instance, there has been a considerable degree of overlap in the autopsy findings in patients diagnosed with Parkinson's disease and patients diagnosed with DAT (Hakim & Mathieson, 1979; Whitehouse, Hedreen, White, & Price, 1983; Gasper & Gray, 1984; Rogers, Brogan, & Mirra, 1985; Leverenz & Sumi, 1986; Ditter & Mirra, 1987; Boller et al., 1989) and between patients diagnosed with DAT and patients diagnosed with multi-infarct dementia (Rosen et al., 1980; Molsa, Paljarvi, Rinne, Rinne, & Erkki, 1985; Wade et al., 1987).

There is also a certain catch-22 inherent in this work. The usual strategy is to match two or more dementia groups for overall degree of dementia and then to use more fine-grained measures of behavior to look for subtle differences in the pattern or degree of cognitive deficits which differentiate among the groups. Frequently, however, the procedures used to rate the level or severity of dementia have involved some of the same measurements of cognitive function which are used to discriminate one etiologically distinct dementia group from another. We feel that the Clinical Dementia Rating Scale (discussed in the following section) does the best job of avoiding this methodological pitfall.

Dementia Severity

Current authoritative diagnostic criteria are remarkably vague when it comes to discussions of dementia severity. The APA (1987) criteria, for example, requires that the intellectual disturbance be severe enough that it "significantly interferes with work or usual social activities or relationships with others" (p. 107). The NINCDS-ADRDA work group criteria (McKhann et al., 1984) are even less well specified: "dementia is the decline of memory and other cognitive functions in comparison with the patient's previous level of function (p. 940). Some of the reasons for this lack of specificity have already been discussed. For instance, the clinical presentation of DAT is very variable and the tools for measuring the behavior change are diverse. Perhaps the most important impediment to clearly defining the diagnostic criteria for dementia is our ignorance regarding the cognitive changes which are caused by the normal aging process. The most coherent effort to operationally define those changes has come from a National Institute of Mental Health Work Group (Crook et al., 1986). The Work Group coined the term age-associated memory impairment (AAMI) to describe memory problems due to normal aging and proposed diagnostic criteria to be used for research studies.

This work was a very valuable starting point, and the criteria need to be more precisely defined (a recent paper by Blackford & LaRue, 1989, offers some suggestions along these lines). One of the key inclusionary criteria, for example, is "complaints of memory loss reflected in such everyday problems as difficulty remembering names of individuals following introduction, misplacing objects, difficulty remembering multiple items to be purchased or multiple tasks to be performed, problems remembering telephone numbers or zip codes, and difficulty recalling information quickly or following distraction" (p. 270). This criterion is clearly on the right track, but it is broad enough that the interrater reliability is likely to be low. Reliability would probably be better if the criteria were more precisely and operationally defined. For example, more detailed criteria could specify the required severity and frequency of memory complaints and whether such complaints are spontaneously provided or elicited by the examiner. Until the cognitive parameters of normal aging are defined more clearly, the diagnostic gray zone between normal aging and early dementia will represent a major stumbling block in designing a valid rating system for dementia.

Of the numerous dementia rating scales available (see Overall, 1989, for a review), the Clinical Dementia Rating Scale (CDR) is my personal favorite. Developed at Washington University, and in use there since 1977, the CDR ratings of dementia are based on assessment of the patient's memory, orientation, judgment and problem solving, participation in the community, continued engagement with hobbies and activities at home, and personal care (Hughes, Berg, Danziger, Coben, & Martin, 1982; Berg et al., 1982; Berg 1984). Information obtained from collateral sources is an important component of this assessment. A CDR score of zero indicates no cognitive impairment; scores of 0.5, 1, 2, and 3 correspond to questionable, mild, moderate, and severe dementia, respectively. The subject receives one of these five ratings for each of the six categories. Brief verbal descriptions are provided to assist in the rating. For example, the CDR 0.5 for the memory category is "mild consistent forgetfulness; partial recollection of events; 'benign' forgetfulness. The CDR 2.0 is "severe memory loss; only highly learned material retained; new material rapidly lost." Recently this group has advocated use of the "sum of boxes" (adding the numerical scores from each category resulting in a range of 0 to 18) as a more differentiated measure of cognitive function than a single overall CDR score (Berg et al., 1988; Rubin, Morris, Grant, & Vendegna, 1989). The CDR instructions are appealing in that they freely acknowledge the role of clinical judgment in the rating process. Raters are instructed to "consider the subject's function only in relation to cognitive ability and to the subject's past performance, not to that of the general population" (Hughes et al., 1982, p. 567).

The usefulness of the CDR is greatly enhanced by the rich body of clinical data which has been harvested by the Washington University group. Burke et al. (1988) found the CDR to have high interrater reliability and Morris, McKeel, Fulling, Torack, and Berg (1988) demonstrated the construct validity of the CDR in an autopsy study. All 26 of their DAT patients (17 had mild, 5 had moderate, and 4 had severe dementia by the CDR) had Alzheimer's disease confirmed by autopsy. Two subjects who were rated as normal (CDR = 0) did not have Alzheimer's changes at autopsy.

Predictably, the CDR has been very useful in the longitudinal study of dementia. The fate of 42 of their DAT subjects has been charted over a period of almost 7 years. At the start of the study, all 42 subjects were rated as having mild dementia. Over the course of one year 21 patients progressed from mild to moderate or to severe dementia, and 20 remained mild (one was lost to follow up, Berg et al., 1984). Eighteen of the 42 completed four rounds of testing over four years; five remained mild over the four years (Botwinick, Storandt, & Berg, 1986). Only four of the original 42 were still alive 6.8 years into the study. Two were still rated as having mild dementia, the other two had progressed to moderate dementia (Botwinick, Storandt, Berg, & Boland, 1988).

The CDR of 0.5—the "questionable" score—is turning out to be a category of tremendous importance. Recall that, in this category, function is either normal or of minimal severity (i.e., mild, doubtful, or slight impairment). It is crucial to know the ultimate outcome of those assigned to this category, since both researchers and clinicians are keenly interested in studying the earliest stages of this disease. Rubin et al. (1989) studied 16 subjects with an initial CDR of 0.5 over a period of 7 years. Over that period of time, 11 of the 16 either had Alzheimer's disease verified by autopsy or had advanced to a more severe stage of dementia. Ten of Morris et al.'s (1991) patients who were initially assigned a CDR of 0.5 eventually came to autopsy. They all met neuropathological criteria for Alzheimer's disease. Similarly, 86% (6 out of 7) of our subjects who were rated 0.5 at the initial testing session progressed to more severe stages of dementia within 26 months. These data suggest that a CDR of 0.5 usually does represent a very early stage of Alzheimer's disease rather than the cognitive consequences of normal aging. Consequently, in our lab we now refer to patients with CDR ratings of 0.5 as having very mild dementia rather than questionable dementia. No matter how well defined the criteria, some individuals will fall through the cracks. We use the term *equivocal* dementia for individuals whom we suspect are not normal even though their CDR is zero.

Another key finding of the Rubin et al. study was that the very mild (0.5) dementia group cannot be clearly distinguished from either normal elderly or mild (1.0) dementia patients on the basis of cross-sectional neuropsychological testing alone. It is the pattern of test results over time which provides the most useful information as to the presence or absence of dementia (Storandt & Hill, 1989). Given the crucial role of longitudinal decline in making the diagnosis of early DAT, Rubin et al. suggest that consideration should be given to obtaining premorbid neuropsychological testing as a public health policy analogous to mammography screening for cancer.

Morris and Fulling's (1988) report provides another perspective on the difficulty of distinguishing between normality and pathology in very old subjects. They describe a man who was enrolled in their longitudinal study on aging and dementia as a normal control at age 82 who died from pneumonia at age 85. An extensive battery of neuropsychological tests was administered at entry, at 13 months, and 30 months after entry. His performance was quite stable over the first 13 months, except for deterioration on the Trailmaking test-part A, and he was rated as normal (CDR = 0) for the first two sessions. At the 30-month evaluation, there was deterioration in the Boston Naming Test and the digit-symbol substitution subtest of the WAIS, but one examiner still rated him as normal. Two other clinicians rated him as questionably demented (CDR = 0.5), based mainly on his wife's observation of subtle cognitive impairment over the preceding six months. He died four months after the last assessment; autopsy showed prominent neuropathological changes indicative of Alzheimer's disease. This report dramatically highlights the limits of our ability to accurately distinguish between the earliest stages of DAT and the cognitive changes which are sometimes associated with apparently normal aging. As Morris and Fulling (1988) say, "Existing brief cognitive scales may be inadequate for detecting early dementia in the general population." The salient point here is that no test or group of tests can serve as a substitute for careful history taking, longitudinal assessment, and good clinical judgment. Henderson (1989, p. 82) puts this nicely when he recommends the "lead standard" for diagnosing DAT—"longitudinal assessment by experts of all the data."

Chronometric Measures of Behavior

Many of the standard instruments in neuropsychology include performance time as a parameter in computing the patient's score, but cognitive psychology has brought the chronometric analysis behavior to a new level of precision and conceptual sophistication (Sternberg, 1969a; Posner, 1978; Welford, 1988). A principal component of the chronometric approach is the use of reaction time (RT) measurements as a dependent variable. That practice is motivated by the fact that the brain requires a finite amount of time to process information. Presumably, changes in cognitive capacity and efficiency may be reflected in changes in the speed or pattern of RT before overt failures in performance occur. If RT tasks were indeed more sensitive than pass/fail or percent correct tasks, then RT tasks could be very useful in the detection of early dementia and in improving the ability to differentiate between cognitive changes due to normal aging and the earliest manifestations of Alzheimer's disease or some other dementing illness.

Estimates of decision-making time have been derived in this fashion for both older normals and patients with dementia of various etiologies. Older normals and DAT subjects have been found to be slower than younger normals on reaction time tasks, but there are crucial quantitative and qualitative differences between older normals and DAT subjects (Nebes & Madden, 1988). In most studies, for example, decision-making time has been found to be significantly longer in DAT groups than in the older controls (Ferris, Crook, Sathananthan & Gershan, 1976; Pirozzolo, Christensen, Ogle, Hansch, & Thompson, 1981;

Table 2-4 Cognitive Neuroscience Laboratory Protocol

Questionnaires and Rating Scales	Paper-and-Pencil Tests	Reaction Time (RT) Tests
Clinical Dementia Rating (CDR) (Hughes et al., 1982)	Information-Memory-Concentration Test—modified (mIMC) (Katzman et al., 1983)	Simple RT vs. Choice RT (Margolin et al., 1987)
Ischemia Score—modified (Rosen et al., 1980)	Neurobehavioral Cognitive Status Exam (NCSE) (Kiernan et al., 1987)	Phasic Alerting (Margolin et al., 1987)
Geriatric Depression Scale (Yesavage et al., 1983)	WAIS-R Short Form (Adams et al., 1985)	Sternberg Memory Scan (Sternberg, 1969b)
Michigan Alcohol Screening Test (Selzer, 1971)	Weschler Memory Scale—revised (Wechsler, 1987)	Covert Orienting (Posner, 1989)
Memory Functioning Questionnaire (MFQ) (Gilewski & Zelinski, 1988)	Remote Memory Battery (Albert et al., 1981)	Letter Matching (Posner & Snyder, 1975)
Cornell Depression Scale (Alexopoulos et al., 1988)	Estimation Test—modified (Shallice & Evans, 1978)	Lexical Priming (Margolin, 1988)
	Cookie Theft Picture Description (Goodglass & Kaplan, 1983)	
	Semantic Category Fluency (Mattis, 1976)	
	Controlled Oral Word Fluency (Benton & Hamsher, 1983)	
	Boston Naming Test (Kaplan et al., 1983)	
	Visual Form Discrimination (Benton & Hamsher, 1983)	
	Colored Progressive Matrices (Raven et al., 1977)	

Vrtunski, Patterson, Mack & Hill, 1983; Mahurin & Pirozzolo, 1986; Margolin, Friedrich, Elia, & Keller, 1987; Gordon & Carson, 1990).

The study by Vrtunski et al. (1983) nicely demonstrates how making a simple modification in an experimental paradigm can lead to a substantial increase in information gleaned. In addition to recording RTs in a CRT task, they measured the amount of force subjects exerted on the response key (via pressure transducers). DAT subjects were not only slower than older normals—they were indecisive. When producing a response, the normals had a rapid crisp deviation from a steady baseline with a rapid return to baseline. DAT subjects showed much more variability and fragmentation both in pressing the key and releasing it.

Despite its simplicity, the SRT paradigm can be quite a powerful measure of behavior. Foster et al. (1983), for example, found that the SRT measure had a strong negative correlation with cortical glucose metabolism measured by PET scan in Alzheimer's patients. Similarly, Nebes and Madden (1988) used a meta-analysis incorporating a wide range of RT tasks to document qualitative differences between the cognitive changes associated with normal aging and those associated with DAT.

We rely heavily on RT tasks of behavior in our work on aging and dementia. Table 2-4 summarizes the testing protocol that we use in our clinical research which includes a "Cognitive Battery" of RT tasks (see Poon, 1983; Wens, Baro, & d'Ydewalle, 1989, for descriptions of closely related approaches). We have found significant group differences between normal and DAT subjects in cross-sectional analyses of paper-and-pencil tasks (Margolin et al., 1990) and reaction time tasks (Margolin & Friedrich, 1985; Margolin, Friedrich, Elia, & Keller, 1987; Margolin, 1988). Cluster and discriminate function analyses of our longitudinal (up to 5 years) data are being performed to determine which behavioral measures constitute the most effective discriminating variables for predicting group membership (e.g., normal vs. DAT; DAT vs. other etiologically distinct dementia groups). The likelihood of finding such behavioral markers for the various dementing illnesses will increase along with advances in defining and measuring the constituent information processing modules of human intelligence. The increased diagnostic accuracy afforded by these markers will obviously enhance the practice of cognitive neuropsychology in both clinical care and clinical research settings.

REFERENCES

Adams, R. L., Smigielski, J., & Jenkins, R. L. (1985). Development of a Satz Mogel short form of the WAIS-R. *Journal of Consulting and Clinical Psychology, 52*, 908.

Albert, M. S., Butters, N., & Brant, J. (1981). Patterns of remote memory in amnesic and demented patients. *Archives of Neurology, 38*, 495–500.

Alexopoulos, G. S., Abrams, R. C., Young, R. C., & Shamoian, C. A. (1988). Cornell scale for depression in dementia. *Biological Psychiatry, 23*, 271–284.

American Psychiatric Association. (1987). *Diagnostic and statistical manual of mental disorders* (3rd ed., rev.). Washington, DC: Author.

Appell, J., Kertesz, A., & Fisman, M. (1982). A study of language functioning in Alzheimer's patients. *Brain and Language*, *17*, 73–91.

Bayles, K. A., & Kaszniak, A. W. (1987). *Communication and cognition in normal aging and dementia*. Boston: College-Hill Press.

Benton, A. L., & Hamsher, K. (1983). Multilingual aphasia examination: *Manual of instructions*. Iowa City: AJA Association.

Berg, L. (1984). Clinical dementia rating. *British Journal of Psychiatry*, *145*, 339.

Berg, L., Danziger, W. L., Storandt, M., Coben, L. A., Gado, M., Hughes, C. P., Knesevich, J. W., & Botwinick, J. (1984). Predictive features in mild senile dementia of the Alzheimer type. *Neurology*, *34*, 563–569.

Berg, L., Hughes, C. P., Coben, L. A., Danziger, W. L., Martin, R. L., & Knesevich, J. (1982). Mild senile dementia of Alzheimer's type: Research diagnostic criteria recruitment and description of a study population. *Journal of Neurology, Neurosurgery and Psychiatry*, *45*, 962–968.

Berg, L., Miller, J. P., Storandt, M., Duchek, J., Morris, J. C., Rubin, E. H., Burke, W. J., & Coben, L. A. (1988). Mild senile dementia of the Alzheimer type: 2. Longitudinal Assessment. *Annals of Neurology*, *23*, 477–484.

Blackford, R. C., & LaRue, A. (1989). Criteria for diagnosing age-associated memory impairment: Proposed improvements from the field. *Developmental Neuropsychology*, *5*, 295–306.

Bleecker, M. L., Bolla-Wilson, K., Kawas, C., & Agnew, J. (1988). Age specific norms for the Mini-Mental State Exam. *Neurology*, *38*, 1565–1568.

Blessed, G., Tomlinson, B. E., & Roth, M. (1968). The association between quantitative measures of dementia and of senile change in the cerebral grey matter of elderly subjects. *British Journal of Psychiatry*, *114*, 797–811.

Boller, F., Lopez, O. L., & Moossy, J. (1989). Diagnosis of dementia: Clinicopathologic correlations. *Neurology*, *39*, 76–79.

Botwinick, J., Storandt, M., Berg, L. (1986). A longitudinal, behavioral study of senile dementia of the Alzheimer's type. *Archives of Neurology*, *43*, 1124–1127.

Botwinick, J., Storandt, M., Berg, L., & Boland, S. (1988). Senile dementia of the Alzheimer type: Subject attrition and testability in research. *Archives of Neurology*, *45*, 493–496.

Burke, W. J., Miller, J. P., Rubin, E. H., Morris, J. C., Coben, L. A., Duchek, J., Wittels, I. G., & Berg, L. (1988). Reliability of the Washington University Clinical Dementia Rating. *Archives of Neurology*, *45*, 31–32.

Crook, R. H., Ward, B. E., & Austin, J. H. (1979). Studies of aging of the brain IV. Familial Alzheimer's disease: Relation to transmissible dementia, aneuploidy, and microtubular defect. *Neurology*, *29*, 1402–1412.

Crook, T., Bartus, R. T., Ferris, S. H., Whitehouse, P., Cohen, G. D., & Gershon, S. (1986). Age-associated memory impairment: Proposed diagnostic criteria and measures of clinical change. Report of a National Institute of Mental Health Work Group. *Developmental Neuropsychology*, *2*, 261–276.

Crystal, H., Dickson, D., Fuld, P., Masur, D., Scott, R., Mehler, M., Masdeau, J., Kawas, C., Aronson, M., & Wolfson, L. (1988). Clinico-pathologic studies in dementia: Nondemented subjects with pathologically confirmed Alzheimer's disease. *Neurology*, *38*, 1682–1687.

Cummings, J. L., & Benson, D. F. (1983). *Dementia: A clinical approach*. Boston: Butterworths.

Ditter, S. M., & Mirra, S. S. (1987). Neuropathologic and clinical features of Parkinson's disease in Alzheimer's disease patients. *Neurology*, *37*, 754–760.

Eslinger, P., Damasio, A. R., Benton, A. L., & Van Allen, M. (1985). Neuropsychological detection of abnormal mental decline in older persons. *Journal of the American Medical Association*, *253*, 670–674.

Ferris, S., Crook, T., Sathananthan, G., & Gershon, S. (1976). Reaction time as a diagnostic measure in senility. *American Geriatrics Society*, *24*, 529–533.

Folstein, M. F., Folstein, S. E., & McHugh, P. R. (1975). Mini-mental state: A practical method for grading the cognitive state of patients for the clinician. *Journal of Psychiatric Research*, *12*, 189–198.

Forette, F., Henry, J. F., Orgogozo, J. M., Dartigues, J. F., Pere, J. J., Hugonot, L., Israel, L., Loria, Y., Goulley, F., Lallemand, A., & Boller, F. (1989). Reliability of clinical criteria for the diagnosis of dementia. *Archives of Neurology*, *46*, 646.

Foster, N. L., Chase, T. N., Fedio, P., Patronas, N. J., Brooks, R. A., & DiChito, G. (1983). Alzheimer's disease: Focal cortical changes shown by positron emission tomography. *Neurology*, *33*, 961–965.

Freedman, M., & Oscar-Berman, M. (1986). Selective delayed response deficits in Parkinson's and Alzheimer's disease. *Archives of Neurology*, *43*, 886–890.

Friedland, R. P. (1988). Alzheimer's disease: Clinical and biological heterogeneity. *Annals of Internal Medicine*, *109*, 298–311.

Fuld, P. (1978). Psychological testing in the differential diagnosis of the dementias. In R. Katzman and R. D. Terry (Eds.), *Aging, Vol. 7. Alzheimer's disease: Senile dementias and related disorders* (pp. 184–192). New York, Raven Press.

Garcia, C. A., Reding, M. J., & Blass, J. P. (1981). Overdiagnosis of dementia. *Journal of the American Geriatric Society*, *29*, 407–410.

Gaspar, P., & Gray, F. (1984). Dementia in idiopathic Parkinson's disease: A neuropathological study of 32 cases. *Acta Neuropathologica* (Berl), *64*, 43–52.

Gilewski, M. J., & Zelinski, E. M. (1988). Memory functioning questionnaire (MFQ). *Psychopharmacology Bulletin*, *24*, 665–670.

Goodglass, H., & Kaplan, E. (1983). *The assessment of aphasia and related disorders*, (2nd ed.). Philadelphia: Lea & Febiger.

Gordon, B., & Carson, K. (1990). This basis for choice reaction time slowing in Alzheimer's disease. *Brain and Cognition*, *13*, 148–166.

Hachinski, V. C., Iliff, L. D., & Zilhka, E., DuBoulay, G. H., McAllister, V. L., Marshall, J., Ross Russell, R. W., & Symon, L. (1975). Cerebral blood flow in dementia. *Archives of Neurology*, *32*, 632–637.

Hakim, A. M., & Mathieson, G. (1979). Dementia in Parkinson's disease: A neuropathologic study. *Neurology*, *29*, 1209–1214.

Henderson, A. S. (1989). Methodological issues in standard assessment. In T. Hovaguimian, S. Henderson, Z. Khachaturian, & J. Orley (Eds.), *Classification and diagnosis of Alzheimer's disease: An international perspective* (pp. 78–86). Toronto: Hogrefet Huber.

Huff, F. J., Becker, J. T., Belle, S. H., Nebes, R. D., Holland, A. L., & Boller, F. (1987). Cognitive deficits and clinical diagnosis of Alzheimer's disease. *Neurology*, *37*, 1119–1124.

Hughes, C. P., Berg, L., Danziger, W. L., Coben, L. A., & Martin, R. L. (1982). A new clinical scale for the staging of dementia. *British Journal of Psychiatry*, *140*, 566–572.

Jacobs, J. W., Bernhard, M. R., Delgado, A., & Strain, J. J. (1977). Screening for organic mental syndromes in the medically ill. *Annals of Internal Medicine*, *86*, 40–46.

Jorm, S. J. (1986). Controlled and automatic information processing in senile dementia: A review. *Psychological Medicine*, *16*, 77–88.

Joynt, R. J. (1987). Adolph L. Sahs, M.D. (1906–1986). *Archives of Neurology*, *44*, 562.

Kaplan, E., Goodglass, H., & Weintraub, S. (1983). *Boston naming test*. Philadelphia: Lea & Febiger.

Katzman, R. (1981). Early detection of senile dementia. *Hospital Practice*, June, 61–76.

Katzman, R. (1986). Alzheimer's Disease. *New England Journal of Medicine*, *314*, 964–973.

Katzman, R., Brown, T., Fuld, P., Peck, A., Schechter, R., & Schimmel, H. (1983). Validation of a short orientation-memory-concentration test of cognitive impairment. *American Journal of Psychiatry*, *14*, 734–739.

Katzman, R., Aronson, M., Fuld, P., Kawas, C., Brown, T., Morgenstern, H., Frishman, W., Gidez, L., Eder, H., & Ooi, W. L. (1989). Development of dementing illnesses in an 80-year-old volunteer cohort. *Annals of Neurology*, *25*, 317–324.

Katzman, R., Brown, T., Thal, L. J., Fuld, P. A., Aronson, M., Butters, N., Klauber, M. R., Wiederholt, W., Pay, M., Renbing, X., Ooi, W. L., Hofstetter, R., & Terry, R. (1988). Comparison of rate of annual change of mental status score in four independent studies of patients with Alzheimer's disease. *Annals of Neurology*, *24*, 384–389.

Kay, D. W. K. (1977). The epidemiology and identification of brain deficit in the elderly (pp. 11–26). In C. Eisdorfer & R. O. Friedel (Eds.), *Cognitive and emotional disturbance in the elderly*. Chicago: Year Book Medical Publishers, Inc.

Kiernan, R. I. (1989). Cognitive status testing: History, present status and future directions. In J. Mueller (Ed.), *Neurology and Psychiatry: A meeting of minds*. (pp. 248–265). Basel, Karger.

Kiernan, R. J., Mueller, J., Langston, J. W., & Van Dyke, C. (1987). The neurobehavioral cognitive status examination: A brief but differentiated approach to cognitive assessment. *Annals of Internal Medicine*, *107*, 481–485.

Levernenz, J., & Sumi, S. M. (1986). Parkinson's disease in patients with Alzheimer's disease. *Archives of Neurology*, *43*, 662–664.

Lezak, M. (1983). *Neuropsychological assessment* (2nd ed.). New York: Oxford University Press.

Mahurin, R. K., & Pirozzolo, I. J. (1986). Chronometric analysis: Clinical applications in aging and dementia. *Developmental Neuropsychology*, *2*, 345–362.

Margolin, D. I. (1988). Lexical priming by pictures and words in aging, stroke and dementia (Doctoral dissertation, University of Oregon). *Dissertation Abstracts International*, *49B*, 1416. University Microfilms No. 88-08,692).

Margolin, D. I., & Friedrich, F. J. (October, 1985). *Picture priming in anomia*. Presented at the meeting of the Academy of Aphasia. Pittsburgh, PA.

Margolin, D. I., Friedrich, F. J., Elia, E., & Keller, W. J. (February, 1987). Arousal and decision making in aging and dementia. Presented at the meeting of the International Neuropsychological Society, New Orleans, LA. *Journal of Clinical and Experimental Neuropsychology*, *9*(1), 78, 1987.

Margolin, D. I., Pate, D. S., Friedrich, F. J., & Elia, E. (1990). Dysnomia in dementia and in stroke patients: Different underlying cognitive deficits. *Journal of Clinical and Experimental Neuropsychology*, *12*, 597–612.

Martin, A. (1987). Representations of semantic and spatial knowledge in Alzheimer's patients: Implications for models of preserved learning in anomia. *Journal of Clinical and Experimental Neuropsychology*, *9*, 191–224.

Martin, A., Brouwers, C., Cox, C., & Fedio, P. (1985). On the nature of the verbal memory deficit in Alzheimer's disease. *Brain and Language*, *25*, 323–341.

Martin, A., Brouwers, C., Lalonde, F., Cox, C., Teleska, P., Fedio, P., Foster, N. C., & Chase, T. N. (1986). Towards a behavioral typology of Alzheimer's patients. *Journal of Clinical and Experimental Neuropsychology*, *8*, 594–610.

Martin, E. M., Wilson, R. S., Penn, R. D., Fox, J. H., Clasen, R. A., & Savoy, S. M. (1987). Cortical biopsy result in Alzheimer's disease: Correlations with cognitive deficits. *Neurology*, *37*, 1201–1204.

Matsuyama, H. (1983). Incidence of neurofibrillary change, senile plaques, and granulovacular degeneration in aged individuals. In B. Reisberg (Ed.), *Alzheimer's disease: The Standard Reference* (Chapter 20). New York, The Free Press.

Mattis, S. (1976). Mental status examination for organic mental syndrome in the elderly patient. In L. Bellack & T. Katasu (Eds.), *Geriatric psychiatry: A handbook for psychiatrists and primary care physicians* (pp. 77–121). New York: Grune & Stratton.

Mayeux, R., Stern, Y., Sano, M., Cote, L., & Williams, J. B. W. (1987). Clinical and biochemical correlates of bradyphrenia in Parkinson's disease. *Neurology*, *7*, 1130–1134.

McKhann, G., Drachman, D., Folstein, M., Katzman, R., Price, D., & Stadlan, E. M. (1984). Clinical diagnosis of Alzheimer's disease: Report of the NINCDS-ADRDA Work Group under the auspices of Department of Health and Human Services Task Force on Alzheimer's Disease. *Neurology*, *34*, 939–944.

Meek, P. S., Clark, H. W., & Solana, V. L. (1989). Neurocognitive impairment: Unrecognized component of dual diagnosis in substance abuse treatment. *Journal of Psychoactive Drugs*, *21*, 153–160.

Molsa, P. K., Paljarvi, L., Rinne, J. O., Rinne, U. K., & Erkki, S. (1985). Validity of clinical diagnosis in dementia: A prospective clinicopathological study. *Journal of Neurology, Neurosurgery, and Psychiatry*, *48*, 1085–1090.

Morris, J. C., & Fulling, K. (1988). Early Alzheimer's disease: Diagnostic considerations. *Archives of Neurology*, *45*, 345–349.

Morris, J. C., McKeel, D. W., Fulling, K., Torack, R. M., & Berg, L. (1988). Validation of a clinical diagnostic criteria for Alzheimer's disease. *Annals of Neurology*, *24*, 17–22.

Morris, J. C., McKeel, D. W., Storandt, M., Rubin, E. H., Price, J. L., Grant, E. A., Ball, M. J., & Berg, L. (1991). Very mild Alzheimer's disease: Informant-based clinical, psychometric, and pathologic distinction from normal aging. *Neurology*, *41*, 469–478.

Morris, R. G., & Kopelman, M. D. (1986). The memory deficits in Alzheimer's type dementia: A review. *Quarterly Journal of Experimental Psychology*, *38A*, 575–602.

Moss, M. B., Albert, M. S., Butters, N., & Payne, M. (1986). Differential patterns of memory loss among patients with Alzheimer's disease, Huntington's disease, and alcoholic Korsakoff's syndrome. *Archives of Neurology*, *43*, 239–246.

Nebes, R. D., & Madden, D. J. (1988). Different patterns of slowing produced by Alzheimer's disease and normal aging. *Psychology and Aging*, *3*, 102–104.

Nebes, R. D., Martin, D. C., & Horn, L. C. (1984). Sparing of semantic memory in Alzheimer's disease. *Journal of Abnormal Psychology*, *93*(3), 321–330.

Nelson, A., Fogel, B. S., & Faust, D. (1986). Bedside cognitive screening instruments: A critical assessment. *Journal of Nervous and Mental Disease*, *174*, 73–83.

Overall, J. E. (1989). A guide to the main instruments. In T. Hovaguimian, S. Henderson, Z. Khachatuian, & J. Orley (Eds.). *Classification and diagnosis of Alzheimer's disease: An International Perspective* (pp. 65–77). Toronto: Hogrefe and Huber.

Perez, F. I., Rivera, V. M., Meyer, J. S., Gay, J. R. A., Taylor, R. L., & Mathew, N. T. (1975). Analysis of intellectual and cognitive performance in patients with multi-infarct dementia, vertebrobasilar insufficiency with dementia, and Alzheimer's disease. *Journal of Neurology, Neurosurgery, and Psychiatry*, *38*, 533–540.

Pfeiffer, E. (1975). A short portable mental status questionnaire for the assessment of organic brain defects in elderly patients. *Journal of the American Geriatrics Society*, *23*, 433–441.

Pirozzolo, F. J., Christensen, K. J., Ogle, K. M., Hansch, E. C., & Thompson, W. G. (1981). Simple and choice reaction time in dementia: Clinical implications. *Neurobiology of Aging*, *2*, 113–117.

Poeck, K. (1969). Pathophysiology of emotional disorders associated with brain damage. In P. J. Vinken, & G. W. Bruyn (Eds.), *Handbook of clinical neurology: Vol. 3* (Chapter 20). Amsterdam: North Holland Publishing Co.

Poon, L. W. (1983). Application of information-processing technology in psychological assessment. In T. H. Crook, S. T. Ferris & R. Bartus (Eds.), *Assessment in geriatric psychopharmacology* (Chapter 18). USA: Mark Powley.

Posner, M. I. (1978). *Chronometric explorations of mind.* Hillsdale, NJ: Lawrence Erlbaum.

Posner, M. I. (1989). Structures and functions of selective attention. In T. Boll & B. K. Bryant (Eds.), *Clinical neuropsychology and brain function: Research, measurements and practice*. Washington, DC: American Psychological Association.

Posner, M. I., & Snyder, C. R. R. (1975). Facilitation and inhibition in the processing of signals. In P. M. A. Rabbitt and S. Dornic (Eds.), *Attention and Performance V.* (Chapter 41). New York: Academic Press.

Raven, J. C., Court, J. H., & Raven, J. C. (1977). *Manual for Raven's progressive matrices and vocabulary scales.* London: H. K. Lewis.

Reisberg, B. (Ed.). (1983). *Alzheimer's disease: The standard reference.* New York: The Free Press.

Reynolds, C. F., Hoch, C. C., Kupfer, D. J., Buysse, D. J., Houck, P. R., Stack, J. A., & Campbell, D. W. (1988). Bedside differentiation of depressive pseudodementia form dementia. *American Journal of Psychiatry*, *145*, 1099–1103.

Rogers, J. D., Brogan, D., & Mirra, S. S. (1985). The nucleus basalis of Meynert in neurological disease: A quantitative morphological study. *Annals of Neurology*, *17*, 163–170.

Rosen, W. G., Terry, R. D., Fuld, P. A., Katzman, R., & Peck, A. (1980). Pathological verification of ischemia score in differentiation of dementia. *Annals of Neurology*, *7*, 486–488.

Rovner, B. W., Broadhead, J., Spencer, M., Carson, K., & Folstein, M. F. (1989). Depression and Alzheimer's disease. *American Journal of Psychiatry*, *146*, 350–353.

Rubin, E. H., Morris, J. C., Grant, E. A., & Vendegna, T. (1989). Very mild dementia of the Alzheimer type I: Clinical Assessment. *Archives of Neurology*, *46*, 379–382.

Salmon, D., Masliah, E., DeTeresa, R., Hansen, L., Butters, N., Katzman, R., & Terry, R. (1990). Neuropsychological-neuropathological correlates in Alzheimer's disease. *Society for neuroscience abstracts*, *16*, 148.

Schmitt, F. A., Ranseen, J. D., & Dekosky, S. T. (1989). Cognitive mental status examinations. *Clinics in Geriatric Medicine*, *5*, 545–564.

Schwamm, L. H., Van Dyke, C., Kiernan, R. J., Merrin, E. L., & Mueller, J. (1987). The neurobehavioral cognitive status examination: Comparison with the cognitive capacity screening examination and the mini-mental state examination in a neurosurgical population. *Annals of Internal Medicine*, *107*, 486–491.

Selzer, M. L. (1971). The Michigan Alcoholism Screening Test. The Quest for a New Diagnostic Instrument. *American Journal of Psychiatry*, *127*(12), 89–94.

Shallice, T., & Evans, M. E. (1978). The involvement of the frontal lobes in cognitive estimation. *Cortex*, *14*, 294–303.

Stern, Y., Mayeux, M. D., Sano, M., Hanser, W. A., & Bush, T. (1987). Predictors of disease course in patients with probable Alzheimer's disease. *Neurology*, *37*, 1649–1653.

Sternberg, S. (1969a). The discovery of processing stages: Extensions of Donder's method. *Acta Psychologica*, *30*, 276–315.

Sternberg, S. (1969b). Memory-scanning: Mental processes revealed by reaction-time experiments. *American Scientist*, *57*, 421–457.

Storandt, M., Botwinick, J., Danziger, W., Berg, L., & Hughes, C. (1984). Psychometric differentiation of mild senile dementia of the Alzheimer type. *Archives of Neurology*, *41*, 497–499.

Storandt, M., & Hill, R. D. (1989). Very mild senile dementia of the Alzheimer type: II. Psychometric test performance. *Archives of Neurology*, *46*, 383–386.

Strub, R. L., & Black, F. W. (1988). *Neurobehavioral disorders: A clinical approach*. Philadelphia: F. A. Davis.

Sulkava, R., Haltia, M., Paetau, A., Wikstrom, J., & Palo, J. (1983). Accuracy of clinical diagnosis in primary degenerative dementia: Correlation with neuropathological findings. *Journal of Neurology, Neurosurgery and Psychiatry*, *46*, 9–13.

Teng, E. L., & Chui, H. C. (1987). The modified mini-mental state (3MS) examination. *Journal of Clinical Psychiatry*, *48*, 314–318.

Tierney, M. C., Snow, W. G., Reid, D. W., Zorzitto, M. L., & Fisher, R. H. (1987). Psychometric differentiation of dementia: Replication and extension of the findings of Storandt and coworkers. *Archives of Neurology*, *44*, 720–722.

Tierney, M. C., Fisher, R. H., Lewis, A. J., Zorzitto, M. L., Snow, W. G., Reid, D. W., & Nieuwstraten, P. (1988). The NINCDS-ADRDA Work Group criteria for the clinical diagnosis of probable Alzheimer's disease: A clinical pathological study of 57 cases. *Neurology*, *38*, 359–364.

Ulrich, J. (1985). Alzheimer's changes in nondemented patients younger than sixty-five: Possible early stages of Alzheimer's disease and senile dementia of Alzheimer type. *Annals of Neurology*, *17*, 273–277.

Vitaliano, P. P., Breen, A. R., Albert, M. S., Russo, J., & Prinz, P. N. (1984). Memory, attention, and functional status in community-residing Alzheimer type dementia patients and optimally healthy aged individuals. *Journal of Gerontology*, *39*, 58–64.

Vrtunski, P. B., Patterson, M. B., Mack, J. L., & Hill, G. O. (1983). Microbehavioral analysis of the choice reaction time response in senile dementia. *Brain*, *106*, 929–947.

Wade, J. P. H., Mirsen, T. R., Hachinski, V. C., Fisman, M., Lau, C., & Merskey, H. (1987). The clinical diagnosis of Alzheimer's disease. *Archives of Neurology*, *44*, 24–29.

Wechsler, D. (1987). *Wechsler adult intelligence scale-revised: Manual*. San Antonio: The Psychological Corporation.

Weingartner, H., Grafman, J., Boutelle, W., Kaye, W., & Martin, P. R. (1983). Forms of memory failure. *Science*, *221*, 380–382.

Weingartner, H., Kaye, W., Smallberg, S., Cohen, R., Ebert, M. H., Gillin, J. C., & Gold, P. (1982). Determinants of memory failures in dementia. In S. Corkin (Ed.), *Aging, Vol. 19, Alzheimer's disease: A report of progress* (pp. 171–176). New York: Raven Press.

Weingartner, H., Kaye, W., Smallberg, S., Ebert, M. H., Gillin, J. C., & Sitaram, N. (1981). Memory failures in progressive idiopathic dementia. *Journal of Abnormal Psychology*, *90*(3), 187–196.

Welford, A. T. (1988). Reaction time, speed of performance, and age. *Annals of the New York Academy of Sciences*, *515*, 1–17.

Wens, L., Baro, F., & d'Ydewalle, G. (1989). The information processing approach in clinical memory assessment. In T. Hovaguimian, S. Henderson, Z. Khachaturian & J. Orley (Eds.), *Classification and diagnosis of Alzheimer's disease: An international perspective* (pp. 103–112). Toronto: Hogrefe & Huber.

Whitehouse, P. J., Hedreen, J. C., White, C. L., & Price, D. L. (1983). Basal forebrain neurons in the dementia of Parkinson disease. *Annals of Neurology*, *13*, 243–348.

Wisniewski, K., Jervis, G. A., Moretz, R. C., & Wisniewski, H. M. (1979). Alzheimer neurofibrillary tangles in diseases other than senile and presenile dementia. *Annals of Neurology*, *5*, 288–294.

Yesavage, J. S., Brink, T. L., Lum, O., Huang, V., Adey, M., & Leirer, V. O. (1983). Development and validation of a geriatric depression screening scale: A preliminary report. *Journal of Psychiatric Research*, *17*, 37–49.

PART II

THE PERVASIVE INFLUENCE OF ATTENTION

3

Processing Resource Limitations in Schizophrenia: Implications for Predicting Medication Response and Planning Attentional Training

ERIC GRANHOLM II

> I can't concentrate on television because I can't watch the screen and listen to what is being said at the same time . . . I seem to be always taking in too much at the one time and then I can't handle it and can't make sense of it (Patient 25). My mind's away. I have lost control. There are too many things coming into my head at once and I can't sort them out (Patient 21). My mind is going too quick for me. It is all bamboozled. All the things are going too quick for me. Everything's too fast and too big for me (Patient 6).

These firsthand descriptions of how schizophrenic patients experience their cognitive deficits (McGhie & Chapman, 1961) illustrate that patients with schizophrenia are easily overwhelmed by the processing demands of simple daily activities. This suggests that schizophrenics are overloaded by a variety of cognitive tasks that normal individuals find much less difficult. Investigators studying the cognitive neuropsychological deficits of schizophrenics have confirmed a wide variety of processing deficiencies, ranging from poor icon formation to poor abstract thinking across a variety of cognitive tasks (Broga & Neufeld, 1981; Goldstein, 1986; Nuechterlein & Dawson, 1984).

The present chapter describes ways in which the practicing neuropsychologist might understand the variety of cognitive impairments observed in schizophrenia and participate in the care of schizophrenic patients. Processing resource theory (Kahneman, 1973; Norman & Bobrow, 1975) will be reviewed briefly in the following section and is then utilized to describe and understand the cognitive deficits commonly observed in schizophrenia. Based on a resource limitations model of cognitive impairments in schizophrenia, some preliminary guidelines for predicting medication response and planning attentional training programs will be presented.

EVOLUTION OF PROCESSING RESOURCE THEORY

When processing stimuli in the environment, one is generally concerned with analyzing inputs and eventually acting upon them. Since the processes by which these goals are accomplished occur at a finite rate (i.e., our information processing system can analyze, decide about, and transform a limited number of items per unit of time), certain channels or subsets of stimuli impinging upon the system must be selectively attended to for processing to avoid information overload. Thus, the concepts of selective attention and resource or capacity limits are closely related, and deficient performance due to capacity overload is commonly referred to as a "selective attention deficit" (Schneider & Shiffrin, 1977).

Stage Theories

Stage theories of selective attention attempt to identify a specific stage or bottleneck at which capacity limits are reached and subsets of information are given selective attention in the information processing sequence. One classical theory (Broadbent, 1958), views human attention as being mediated by a single limited-capacity channel. Sensory input is thought to converge onto a switch that selects an input channel (e.g., ear receiving input), while filtering or holding other inputs in a short-term store until a response can be initiated. Thus, second or unselected signals can be lost, since they are not permitted to enter the channel until processing is completed on the first input.

Treisman (1964) later expanded on this model to include classification filters that select either an input source or dimensions of messages coming from a source. The output of these filters provides "functional channels" that can be selected for processing. Broadbent (1971) also expanded on his original model to include three progressively more complex mechanisms to govern information flow through the limited-capacity channel: (1) *Filtering*, which refers to the selection of stimuli according to physical features (e.g., ear of presentation or sex of voice in a dichotic listening task); (2) *categorizing*, which refers to selecting stimuli according to class membership; and (3) *pigeonholing*, which refers to a biasing process, whereby the perceptual threshold is lowered for stimuli that possess specific characteristics. Other stage theorists (e.g., Welford, 1967) located the limited-capacity channel or bottleneck later in the processing sequence, at response-initiation and decision-making stages. Nonetheless, the emphasis of these limited-capacity channel theories is on the notion that selective attention occurs at a specific stage of information processing.

Researchers (e.g., Moray, 1967), however, began to find that limited-capacity channel models had difficulty accounting for new findings. For example, when subjects were given extensive practice in choice reaction time studies, performance decrements normally observed at higher processing loads (e.g., increased number of choices) were eliminated (Moray, 1967). The failure to find performance deficiencies after practice, despite increased demands for rapid processing at higher loads, suggested a channel of nearly unlimited capacity. In addition, varying difficulty of response to a second stimulus in a sequence was found to affect responses to both the first and the second stimulus (Gophor & Donchin, 1986). If, as proposed by stage theorists, a second stimulus is not examined until after the first is completed, how can its difficulty affect processing of the first? Kahneman (1973) also showed that processing of a second stimulus does not always wait until analysis of and response to a first is completed. Data generated by a classical debate over whether selection occurred early versus late in processing revealed that neither model could account for the vast research stimulated by the debate (e.g., see Gophor & Donchin, 1986).

Such findings suggested that the information processing system is active and dynamic, and attempts to fully characterize it with data-driven, peripheral models neglected dynamic characteristics, such as operating modes (e.g., parallel vs. serial). While peripheral structures, such as early precategorical selection processes likely exist, one must address the multiplicity of mechanisms and processes which appear to be operating simultaneously at various times during task performance.

Resource Theory

Moray (1967) conceptualized the human operator, not at as a limited-capacity channel, but as a limited-capacity *central processor*. The crucial difference here is that the capacity limits of the system do not lie in the physical limitations of a structure or transmission line; rather, "the functions performed on the message themselves take up the capacity of the transmission system" (Moray, 1967, p. 87). Thus, for example, the apparent unlimited ability of the central processor to operate at higher processing loads after extensive practice in choice reaction time studies can be conceptualized as the result of perceptual learning or discovery of more efficient strategies for transforming inputs, which leads to more efficient processing and consequent saving of the central processor's resources.

Moray's (1967) proposal is closely related to Knowles' (1963) conceptualization of the human processor as possessing a "pool of resources," which is broadly conceptualized as a limited commodity that enables performance of cognitive tasks. This view, like Moray's (1967), stresses that resources can be flexibly allocated in graded quantity between separate operations. With this flexibility, there was no need to propose a locus of a specific bottleneck, since deficits would be observed on a wide variety of tasks at several stages of processing whenever the resource demands of the task exceed the overall amount of processing resources available to the system.

Kahneman (1973) later expanded resource theory and stressed the intensive, energetical aspects of attention. He proposed that an information input specific to a structure and a nonspecific, enabling input labeled *capacity*, which is analogous to a fuel, are both necessary for completion of mental activity. The nonspecific commodity of capacity (or resources) is drawn from a limited pool that can be flexibly allocated in accordance with enduring dispositions (e.g., allocate to all novel stimuli) or momentary intentions (e.g., allocate to the right ear).

The notion of a single pool of nonspecific processing resources has been called into question, and some theorists have proposed the existence of multiple independent resources pools (Navon & Gophor, 1979; Wickens, 1984). However, the notion of multiple resource pools and the number and types of pools that might exist is one of the more debated issues in resource theory (e.g., see Hirst & Kalmar, 1987; Navon, 1984). This chapter will focus more on the overall amount of resources available from the pool(s) drawn upon by a specific task. In addition, since there is currently little consensus about exactly what constitutes a resource, resources are broadly conceptualized here as the limited pool(s) of fuel(s), processes, skills, and structures that are available at a given moment for performance of cognitive tasks (Hirst & Kalmar, 1987). Similar to arousal and activation, resources are not directly observable entities. They represent a hypothetical commodity to be utilized and consumed for the purpose of information processing. The use of this concept simply provides a means for describing the human brain as a resource-dependent system, in that there are clear limits on its ability to perform.

Automatic and Controlled Processing

In discussing competition for resources and capacity limitations, it is also crucial to consider the mode of information processing employed on a task. Not all types of processing are subject to the constraints of a limited-resource system. Several investigators (Schneider, Dumais, & Shiffrin, 1984; Posner & Snyder, 1975; Hasher & Zacks, 1979) draw a distinction between a resource-demanding, controlled mode of processing and a relatively resource-free, automatic mode of processing. Controlled processing is a relatively slow, generally serial processing mode which is resource-limited. By contrast, automatic processing is a relatively fast, generally parallel processing mode which requires few or no resources. Processes which are widely believed to be controlled processes include rehearsal, serial search, and mental arithmetic. Automatic processes include simple recognition, verbatim repetition, and encoding of spatial and frequency information about stimuli.

The distinction between controlled and automatic processing becomes blurred, however, when one considers that different types of controlled processes are assumed to require different amounts of resources. For example, in verbal memory encoding, semantic elaboration may require more resources than phonemic or graphemic strategies of encoding (Glenberg & Adams, 1978), and simple recognition is assumed to require less resources than recall operations (Hasher & Zacks, 1979). It is thus unclear whether automatic and controlled processes represent two ends of a continuum or are discrete processes.

Work by Schneider and colleagues (1984) has provided important insight into this question. Their studies indicate that automatic processes can be broken down (e.g., Schneider et al., 1984) into *informational* processes, which are responsible for the parallel encoding of input stimuli to various code levels in short-term store (e.g., visual features and category codes), and *actional* processes, such as operations that direct attention and controlled processes to specific inputs without utilizing resources in the act (i.e., automatic attention responses) or that produce overt responses (e.g., push a button). Actional processes develop through practice with consistent stimuli that always give rise to a relevant, nonconflicting response. For example, on a visual letter detection task where a target stimulus (e.g., T) does not appear on any trial as a distractor letter that should be ignored, the target always receives a positive response (e.g., always push a button for T). In this example, the target stimulus T is "consistently-mapped" onto the button-push response, so sufficient practice should lead to the development of automatic attention responses for the target stimulus. One of the most beneficial features of consistent-mapped practice is that the processing of information can become resource-free through the development of automatic operations; thus, increasing the human processor's capacity to process information.

For a process to reach the resource-free stage in its development, it may require thousands of trials of practice (Schneider et al., 1984). However, it is important to stress that automatic processing develops gradually, in stages, through interactions with controlled processing (Schneider et al., 1984). Depending primarily on the amount of practice, controlled processing may be facilitated through the partial use of underdeveloped automatic operations (moderate practice) or processes may be more completely responsible for performance (extensive practice). Schneider & Fisk (1983) point out that, the benefits of automatic processing can be observed in as few as 10 to 50 trials in normal subjects, and that, as a rule of thumb, they observe the benefits of automaticity within 200 trials when conditions are engineered to facilitate automatization.

COGNITIVE FUNCTIONING IN SCHIZOPHRENIA

Resource-Limitations Hypothesis

The evolution of theories attempting to explain cognitive impairments in schizophrenia has followed a similar path to that of the cognitive psychology of selective attention described above. Many studies have attempted to identify a specific dysfunctional stage of processing to account for the nearly global cognitive impairments that characterize schizophrenia (for a review, see Broga & Neufeld, 1981). For example, researchers have proposed deficiencies involving information extraction deficits in very early precategorical stages (e.g., Saccuzzo & Braff, 1986) or response organization deficits in late processing stages (e.g., Broen & Storms, 1967). Early processing deficits would result in some degradation of input stimuli, thereby adversely affecting subsequent stages of information processing. Deficits in response organization and execution would similarly produce impairments on a variety of tasks, regardless of the efficiency of processing at earlier stages.

Just as the resource theories refuted the notion of a bottleneck at a specific early or late stage in the information processing sequence, more recent theories of schizophrenic impairments (Gjerde, 1983; Knight & Russell, 1978; Nuechterlein & Dawson, 1984) have refuted the hypothesis that there is a single defective processing stage underlying the schizophrenic patient's nearly global cognitive dysfunctions. These newer theories propose that since it is currently not possible to implicate any specific mechanism(s) as the cause of observed limitations on schizophrenic patients' performance, it may prove more useful to pool performance limitations and consider them to reflect an abnormal reduction in the *availability* of a hypothetical resource pool (Nuechterlein & Dawson, 1984).

Several literature reviews (Knight & Russell, 1978; Gjerde, 1983; Nuechterlein & Dawson, 1984) have suggested that deficits are often observed in patients with schizophrenia on tasks that are judged to make higher demands for processing resources, but that schizophrenics perform at or near normal levels when demands for resources appear lower. Findings that schizophrenics appear more adversely affected by higher resource demands than controls suggest that patients reach the limits of their available resources at lower processing loads than do controls. This is consistent with the hypothesis that a reduction, relative to controls, in the amount of processing resources available for essential cognitive operations is responsible for the schizophrenic patient's variety of cognitive deficits with higher processing loads (Nuechterlein & Dawson, 1984).

Normal amounts of processing resources may not be available to schizophrenic patients for several reasons (Nuechterlein & Dawson, 1984): (1) The actual pool of resources may be smaller or more limited in schizophrenics; (2) Resources may not be mobilized and allocated efficiently in accordance with task demands, despite intact resource pools; (3) Excessive resources may be wasted on processing of task-irrelevant stimuli, leaving fewer resources available (remaining) for task-relevant operations; and/or (4) Automatic processes might be disrupted, which would require that resource-demanding controlled processing be utilized to carry out processing normally accomplished through resource-free automatic operations (for a more detailed discussion, see Nuechterlein & Dawson, 1984). The notion that schizophrenics experience processing overload due to deficient resource availability is commonly reflected in patients' descriptions of their cognitive deficits, such as those presented at the beginning of this chapter.

Problems Measuring Resource Limitations

Several difficulties arise in the examination of the resource-limitations hypothesis. Studies often cited as providing evidence in support of the resource-limitations hypothesis (which are briefly reviewed below) have not directly measured either the subjects' resource availability or the resource demands of the tasks employed. The relative resource demands of a task are estimated on the basis of the task's processing load; with more resources presumably required on tasks with higher processing loads. However, relative processing load is usually intuitively estimated on the basis of the intensity (i.e., number of repetitions of an operation carried out per time unit) or complexity (i.e., number of operations or cognitive mechanisms required) of a task's structure. Increasing the number of items on verbal list recall task, for example, increases the intensity of the task, since the subject is under greater time pressure to increase rehearsal rate to compensate for stimulus decay. A visual detection task where subjects must detect a specific target only when it follows another specific target increases the complexity of the task over a single target task by introducing a memory component. Increasing task intensity and/or complexity, as well as increasing reliance on controlled rather than automatic processing, usually results in a decline in quality of performance and is assumed to increase the task's processing load and thus its resource demands (Kahneman, 1973).

Estimating processing load in this intuitive way is problematic for several reasons. First, this procedure can confuse task processing load with task difficulty, which refers to a psychometric difference between tasks in quality of performance. One cannot assume that differences between tasks in quality of performance reflect differences between tasks in processing load. This assumption neglects the interaction between the task and the subject. Subjects increase resource allocation when task processing load increases, so quality of performance will not necessarily decline with increased load, and subjects will likely maintain stable performance levels until resource limits are reached (Gophor & Donchin, 1986). Thus, using psychometric differences in the quality of performance (difficulty) between tasks is not an adequate procedure for estimating processing load and resource demands.

Norman and Bobrow (1975) pointed out another problem with making assumptions about processing load and resource limits on the basis of psychometric changes in quality of performance. They proposed the term *resource-limited* to describe tasks and operations which are facilitated (i.e., show improved performance) by increased resource allocation until resource limits are reached. In contrast, a task is *data-limited*, when increased resource allocation does not facilitate performance; that is, regardless of the amount of spare resources the subject might allocate to the task, performance remains limited by the quality (e.g., perceptibility) of the stimulus data. The assumption that subjects will only show performance decrements when resource limits are reached is not valid unless one can be certain that task performance is not, or has not become, data-limited. Thus, the major problem with using intuitive judgements and changes in quality of performance to estimate processing load and resource limitations is that a task may be made more difficult (i.e., performance decrements might be observed) for a variety of reasons; not all of which are related to resource limitations.

Evidence for Resource Limitations

Several studies commonly cited as evidence for resource limitations in schizophrenia are summarized in Table 3-1 and will be selectively reviewed in this section. The purpose of this review is not to provide an exhaustive summary of the relationship between resource limitations model and the extensive research on cognitive functioning in schizophrenia (see Nuechterlein & Dawson, 1984; Knight & Russell, 1978). Rather, a brief review will be provided in order to illustrate how the resource-limitations hypothesis might be utilized to explain the information processing impairments observed in schizophrenia.

The resource-limitations hypothesis predicts that patients with schizophrenia will reach the limits of their available resources with lower demands for resources (i.e., at lower processing loads) than will controls with normal resource utilization. That is, on controlled processing tasks, schizophrenic patients should evidence a higher error rate or increased reaction time relative to controls, under conditions of higher processing load. Little or no deficit should be observed on

Table 3-1 Cognitive Neuropsychological Measures Consistent with the Resource-Limitations Hypothesis

Tasks and Conditions	Processing Load[a]	Performance[b]	References
Sensory Storage and Read Out			
Backward Masking Task			
Longer interstimulus intervals	Lower	+	Saccuzzo & Braff, 1986
Briefer interstimulus intervals	Higher	–	Saccuzzo et al., 1974
Partial-Report Span of Apprehension Task			
1- to 4-letter arrays	Lower	+	Asarnow et al., 1991
8- to 12-letter arrays	Higher	–	
Sustained Focused Attention			
Continuous Performance Test			
Single clear target	Lower	+/–	Asarnow & MacCrimmon, 1978
With distraction	Higher	–	Nuechterlein & Dawson, 1984
Sequential target	Higher	–	Orzack & Kornetsky, 1966
Degraded target	Higher	–	Wohlberg & Kornetsky, 1973
Selective and Divided Attention			
Dichotic Listening Task			
Slow presentation rate	Lower	+	Korboot & Diamani, 1976
Rapid presentation rate	Higher	–	Payne et al., 1970
Organized stimuli	Lower	+	Pogue-Geile & Oltmanns, 1980
Random stimuli	Higher	–	Wielgus & Harvey, 1988
Simple shadowing set	Lower	+	Wishner & Wahl, 1974
Complex shadowing set	Higher	–	
Short-Term Recall and Recognition Memory			
Recognition Memory Tasks	Lower	+	Bauman, 1971
Recall Memory Tasks	Higher	–	Gjerde, 1983
Active organization not required	Lower	+	Koh, 1978
Active organization required	Higher	–	Larsen & Fromholt, 1976
Incidental recall/induced organization	Lower	+	Neale & Oltmanns, 1980
			Russell et al., 1975

[a]Relative intuitive judgments made within category (see text).

[b]+ = normal performance; – = deficient performance relative to normal controls.

tasks with lower processing load and tasks carried out through primarily automatic operations which are less likely to exceed schizophrenic patients' available resources. As summarized in Table 1 and discussed below, schizophrenic patients' performance is impaired almost exclusively when processing loads and resource demands are intuitively judged to be higher, but not when load and demands appear lower. This consistent pattern across several cognitive domains is consistent with the notion that patients with schizophrenia exhaust their resource supplies at processing loads which are lower than the loads required to deplete a normal individual's supplies. While the results of these studies are consistent with the resource-limitations hypothesis, all of the studies require intuitive judgments about processing load and resource limits on the basis of task intensity and complexity and differences in quality of performance. Thus, they are open to the criticisms discussed above and do not conclusively support the resource-limitations hypothesis.

Sensory Storage and Read Out

In Saccuzzo, Hirt, and Spencer's (1974) backward masking task, subjects were required to report which of two possible target letters were presented in a briefly exposed display that was followed by a briefly exposed noninformational, patterned mask stimulus (e.g., two partially overlapping W's). The mask is assumed to limit the available amount of processing time for the previously presented target-letter display. Nonpsychotic psychiatric patients and normal controls showed decreased detection accuracy relative to their no-mask condition accuracy with 50 or 100 msec interstimulus intervals (between the display and mask), but reached their no-mask condition level of performance when the interstimulus interval was 150 msec or greater. In contrast, schizophrenic patients required longer interstimulus intervals (i.e., 300 msec or more) to achieve their no-mask level of detection accuracy and showed decreased accuracy relative to their no-mask performance with 50, 100, and 150 msec interstimulus intervals. These findings suggest that the schizophrenic patients required more time than controls to process the stimuli.

This backward masking deficit has been observed in remitted schizophrenics free of significant thought disorder, in nonpsychotic, schizophrenia-spectrum (e.g., schizotypal personality disorder) subjects, and in college subjects with a schizotypic 2-7-8 code type on the MMPI (Saccuzzo & Braff, 1986). Although depressed patients do not show the backward masking deficit, patients with actively symptomatic schizoaffective or bipolar disorder do show evidence of this deficit (Saccuzzo & Braff, 1986).

From a resource theory framework, when increased demands for resources are made by increasing the intensity of processing (i.e., increased time pressure for transfer from iconic store or for posticonic processing with the briefer interstimulus intervals), schizophrenic patients' performance suffered. This interpretation is consistent with deficits involving either smaller pools of resources or a failure to rapidly mobilize and utilize intact resources. Patients may also fail to reject the mask as irrelevant and thus may wastefully allocate resources to processing of masks, leaving fewer resources for task-relevant processing.

Another task extensively studied in cognitive neuropsychological investigations in schizophrenia is the forced-choice partial-report span of apprehension (SOA) task. This task is designed to assess the number of items that can be apprehended or attended to at one time by tachistoscopically presenting varying numbers of letters in a visual matrix and asking subjects to report which of two predesignated target letters are presented in the display. In our recent review of SOA studies in schizophrenia (Asarnow, Granholm, & Sherman, 1991), we noted that, in all seven studies in which actively psychotic schizophrenic patients were compared to normal controls, the patients detected significantly fewer target stimuli than controls in higher processing load conditions (8- to 12-letter arrays). In contrast, when the processing load was low (1- to 4-letter arrays), schizophrenics and controls did not differ in detection rates.

In addition to being sensitive to schizophrenic psychosis, impairments at higher processing loads on the SOA have been observed in schizophrenic patients in a remitted, nonpsychotic state; foster children whose biological mothers were schizophrenic; nonpsychotic biological mothers of schizophrenic patients; and individuals with schizotypic or psychosis-prone characteristics (Asarnow et al., 1991). Schizophrenics also detect fewer targets on the SOA at higher workloads than partially remitted manic patients and psychiatric controls (Asarnow et al., 1991). A few studies utilizing a narrow display visual angle have failed to replicate some of these findings, and these failures suggest that increases in the visual angle of displays (which increases search demands) are at least partially related to SOA impairments (see Asarnow et al., 1991, for a more detailed discussion). Findings of deficient SOA detection at higher processing loads (increased intensity) are consistent with the notion that schizophrenics have a general problem recruiting sufficient processing resources to carry out the discrete computational functions required to rapidly scan the iconic image for the target stimuli within the time limitations of iconic persistence.

Sustained Focused Attention

On one well-studied measure of sustained (from 8 to 30 min), focussed attention, the continuous performance test (CPT), subjects are typically required to press a response key every time a critical target stimulus (e.g., an X or a 7) appears in a random sequence of individually presented letter or digit distractors, which are shown at 40- to 100-msec exposure durations. Chronic schizophrenics obtain significantly lower target hit rates than normal control subjects on this version of the CPT (Orzack & Kornetsky, 1966) and this impairment is observed in acute and remitted phases of the illness (Asarnow & MacCrimmon, 1978). However, deficits are not always observed on the CPT in patients in remitted stages, unless distraction or other factors which increase burden on controlled processing resources are present. For example, the deficits of patients in remitted stages are more clearly evidenced when subjects are required to actively ignore distracting stimuli (digits presented aurally; Asarnow & MacCrimmon, 1978), and when a sequential target version of the CPT is used which incorporates a memory component (increased complexity) by requiring that subjects respond only when a 5 occurs on one trial *and* a 9 occurs on the next trial (Wohlberg & Kornetsky, 1973). Processing has been further burdened in CPT studies by debilitating automatic encoding operations and increasing demands for controlled stimulus comparison operations by degrading (blurring) stimuli (Nuechterlein & Dawson, 1984). When demands for processing resources were increased through these manipulations, remitted patients (and children at high risk for developing schizophrenia) evidenced CPT deficits relative to controls, but in the absence of these manipulations deficits in these individuals were less frequently observed (for a review, see Nuechterlein & Dawson, 1984).

Selective and Divided Attention

Studies utilizing dichotic listening tasks have shown that schizophrenic patients are excessively susceptible to the effects of distraction on information processing tasks. In this paradigm, subjects are asked to listen to a message and repeat (shadow) it *out loud*, while ignoring an irrelevant message played simultaneously either in a different ear or a different voice. The stimulus messages employed in these paradigms have ranged from random digits, letters or word strings to related sentences, and logical prose passages. When shadowing random word lists, schizophrenic patients commonly make more shadowing omission errors than controls when irrelevant word lists are introduced (Payne, Hochberg, & Hawks, 1970; Wishner & Wahl, 1974). These impairments are, however, reduced when shadowing semantically and syntactically structured textual information (Wielgus & Harvey, 1988; Pogue-Geile & Oltmanns, 1980). Since automatic processes are employed more in organizing, deciphering, and coding textual material than in processing random messages, textual material likely required less resource-demanding controlled processing for organization and monitoring than random stimuli (Pogue-Geile & Oltmanns, 1980). Thus, consistent with the resource-limitations hypothesis, the reduced processing burden of monitoring textual rather than random material alleviated the schizophrenic patients' shadowing difficulties.

Korboot and Diamani (1976) did not find shadowing deficits in paranoid or chronic schizophrenics, when the stimulus presentation rate was approximately 30 items per minute, and these investigators point out that the stimulus input rate and pressure to respond (increased intensity) in their study may not have been high enough to sufficiently burden processing. Support for this notion comes from the finding of deficient shadowing due to interference effects with faster (50 items per minute), but not slower (25 items per minute), presentation rates (Wishner & Wahl, 1974). Thus, higher demands for resources, in the form of increased pressure to respond (increased intensity), lead to overload in the monitoring and processing of the more rapidly presented information.

Short-Term Recognition Memory

Several studies have found normal recognition memory in schizophrenic patients (for a review see Koh, 1978), and a common finding is that recall, but not recognition, is deficient in schizophrenics (Gjerde, 1983; Koh, 1978). From a resource-theory framework, the elaborative encoding and retrieval processes required for recall are more resource demanding than for recognition, and Hasher and Zacks (1979) include simple recognition in their list of relatively automatic, resource-free functions. Thus, intact recognition and impaired recall performance in schizophrenics is consistent with the notion that these patients have insufficient resources available for the more resource-demanding recall tasks.

However, intact recognition is not universally found in schizophrenia. Several studies provide evidence that schizophrenic patients' recognition performance is deficient when elaborative controlled processing at encoding could be used to improve performance. For example, schizophrenics display deficient recognition performance for high-association, but not low-association, word pairs (Russell, Bannatyne, & Smith, 1975), and they failed to improve their recognition performance when the potential for organization of trigrams (i.e., alphabetic ordering by the first letter) was provided and pointed out to subjects (Bauman, 1971). Thus, unlike controls, schizophrenics failed to take advantage of opportunities for elaboration of high-association word pairs and high organization trigram lists. By contrast, stimuli with low potential for semantic elaboration gave controls less of an opportunity to utilize their spare resources and display their superior controlled mnemonic abilities. These findings suggest that schizophrenic patients' recognition memory is not normal when more complex organizational processes are crucial for normal recognition memory.

Short-Term Recall Memory

Investigations of recall performance in schizophrenia have also led to the conclusion that schizophrenic patients' recall performance is consistently below that of controls, because they fail to carry out controlled organizational and elaborative mnemonic processes necessary for adequate memory functioning (Koh, 1978; Neale & Oltmanns, 1980). Unlike controls, patients with schizophrenia do not make normal use of categorical clustering of word lists, do not benefit from affective clustering of word lists based on "pleasantness," do not show normal levels of idiosyncratic, subjective organization of random word lists, and do not show normal release from proactive interference (for a review see Koh, 1978). However, manipulations that facilitate mnemonic organization, such as sorting words into categories until a predetermined organizational consistency is achieved (Larsen & Fromholt, 1976) or inducing semantic encoding through a levels-of-processing incidental recall paradigm (Koh & Peterson, 1978), produce normal recall in schizophrenics. This pattern of failed spontaneous use of mnemonic strategies, despite normal ability to utilize such strategies when elicited experimentally, suggests deficient mobilization and utilization of these resources, rather than structural defects in short- or long-term memory (Koh, 1978).

Several studies have investigated serial position effects in the recall of schizophrenics. In the absence of distracting stimuli, schizophrenic patients show a normal serial position effect in word or digit list recall (Oltmanns, 1978), which is characterized by superior recall for the first (primacy effect) and last (recency effect) few items presented in a list. However, unlike controls, patients show a decreased primacy effect in the presence of distraction (opposite sex voice reading distractor words between target words), but show normal recency effects (Oltmanns, 1978). The primacy effect is assumed (e.g., Bjork, 1975) to be due to the transfer of initial items to long-term store through active elaborative rehearsal (i.e., semantic associations formed), while the recency effect is assumed to be the result of more passive rote maintenance rehearsal (e.g., articulatory loop). Thus, from a resource theory framework, the additional resources required to actively ignore the distracting stimuli may have left the patients with too few resources to carry out the more resource-demanding elaborative rehearsal processes necessary to transfer initial items to long-term store.

Critique and Future Directions

While the pattern of findings reviewed above is consistent with a resource-limitations hypothesis, it is impossible to utilize intuitive judgments of processing load level based on task intensity and complexity to conclude that impairments observed in schizophrenic patients are the result of resource limitations. Alternative hypotheses involving data limitations, rather than resource limitations, can explain the impairments observed on many of the tasks reviewed in this section. For example, on the backward masking task, the mask, through integration with the target, may result in degradation of the target, suggesting that the backward masking deficit might reflect an early perceptual sensitivity problem with processing the relevant target attributes embedded in the integrated target-mask stimulus composite (Saccuzzo & Braff, 1986). This problem might be described within Broadbent's (1971) framework as a failure in pigeonholing, i.e., a failure to lower the perceptual threshold for letter-like features. On the degraded-target version of the CPT, impairments could be due to a similar form of perceptual sensitivity deficit.

In addition, following Posner's model of covert orienting in visual attention (Posner & Presti, 1987), the SOA deficit might be explained by an impairment in one of the specific computational systems (disengage, move, engage) involved in visual search. Both normal controls and schizophrenics show a consistent pattern of target location effects on the SOA task (Asarnow et al., 1991). For example, detection from the top half of arrays is generally better than detection from the bottom half, which suggests at least one move of the attentional spotlight from one to another area of the display is carried out on the SOA. An impairment in any one discrete visual search operation (engage, move, disengage) would have an additive negative effect on detection from larger arrays, since more disengage, move, and engage operations are required with more display items. Posner and colleagues (1988) have recently reported some evidence for a disengage deficit in schizophrenics, but this impairment was only observed for targets appearing in the right visual field. A problem with disengage, move or engage functions would leave schizophrenic patients with less ability to scan the arrays and extract relevant information. This would be a data limitation, not a resource limitation. These alternatives to a resource-limitations explanation illustrate the difficulties with employing intuitive judgments of processing load in the single-task paradigm. Regardless of the amount of reserve resources subjects might possess, performance might decline due to limitations in subjects' ability to perceive, extract, and process relevant task data.

In addition to problems with differentiating resource-limitations from data-limitations, it is circular to reason that schizophrenics have excessive resource limitations because they perform worse on tasks that are difficult for them than on tasks that are easy. The circularity arises from assuming that condition A has higher resource demands than condition B because subjects perform worse in condition A than B, and then reasoning that worse performance in condition A than B also indicates that subjects have excessive resource limitations. This strategy utilizes performance quality as both the independent variable and the dependent variable within the same paradigm.

As noted above, it is necessary to determine the specific factor that makes a task *difficult*; that is, that results in a decline in performance. Is a task difficult because it exceeds resource limits or because data limits are reached? More direct measures of processing load and resource limitations are needed, and relying on any single measure of load is unlikely to be reliable. Three types of measures have been employed: (1) subjective, (2) psychophysiological, and (3) secondary task procedures. Subjective report has not been widely accepted, because it has proved unreliable and invalid (Gophor & Donchin, 1986).

Psychophysiological measures, especially changes in pupil diameter (Beatty, 1982), have proved much more reliable and have been employed extensively by Kahneman (1973). Beatty (1982) suggested that the task-evoked changes in pupillary dilation response may index the overall processing load of a task in a way analogous to how an amperage meter indexes the total amount of electricity used by the many electronic appliances in a house. In a review of pupillometric studies, Beatty (1982) reported meaningful parallels between intuitive estimations of processing load and task-evoked pupillary response in normal individuals. For example, a task requiring memory for digits resulted in progressively greater pupillary response as the number of digits increased from 1 to 7, and increasing the number of multiplicands in mental arithmetic problems increases pupillary response. Pupillary measures have been used in schizophrenics, who show smaller than normal dilation responses to relevant and informative stimuli (Steinhauer & Zubin, 1982), possibly suggesting abnormally low resource allocation to relevant stimuli. The notion that psychophysiological measures might index resource allocation has also been proposed by Dawson (1989) who found that, in normals, magnitude of electrodermal orienting responses correlated with amount of reaction time slowing on a secondary task (reflecting amount of resource allocation to primary task performance) in a dual-task paradigm. The use of psychophysiological measures can be useful in validating intuitive estimates of processing load and resource allocation and would be best applied within the same study where assumptions about these variables are made across subject groups.

The secondary task procedure, which was specifically designed to test resource limits, has been the most widely utilized and accepted measure of resource limitations (Gophor & Donchin, 1986; Norman & Bobrow, 1975). In the dual-task paradigm, subjects are asked to favor performance of a primary task but to simultaneously perform a secondary task. Findings of decrements in overall performance on both tasks during dual-task relative to single-task performance and decrements in secondary task performance as a function of increasing processing load on the primary task are taken to reflect resource limitations (Gophor & Donchin, 1986). If one can perform each of the two tasks separately, but is unable to perform them together in the dual-task condition, what makes per-

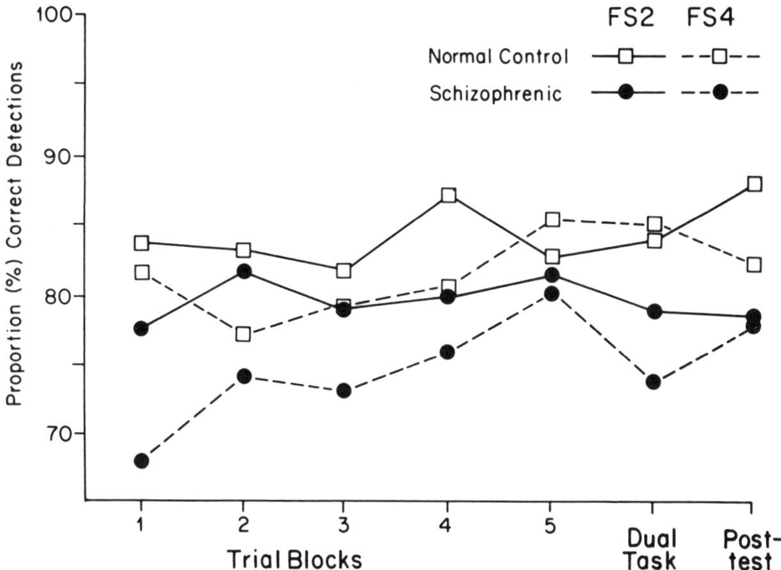

Figure 3-1 Mean percentage of correct target detections by schizophrenic patients and normal controls on a multiple-frame search task for frame sizes 2 and 4 (FS2, FS4) in five blocks of practice and during (Dual Task) and after (Posttest) simultaneous performance of an auditory shadowing task. (Reproduced with permission from E. Granholm et al., *Journal of Abnormal Psychology*, Vol. 100, 22–30; Copyright © 1991 by the American Psychological Association, Inc.)

formance more difficult? The notion of a data limitation or stage deficit cannot account for successful single-task performance. The dual-task paradigm allows one to more directly conclude that task performance is made too difficult because insufficient resources are available for adequate dual-task performance.

In a recent experiment carried out in our laboratory (Granholm, Asarnow, & Marder, 1991), we employed a dual-task paradigm in an attempted to circumvent the difficulties of previous single-task studies and more directly examine whether schizophrenic patients suffer limitations in controlled processing resources. A hybrid memory and visual search task, the multiple-frame search task (MFST) was employed, on which a series of twelve 2 × 2 letter arrays (frames) were presented on each trial, with each letter frame immediately followed by patterned masks in each of the four letter positions (Schneider & Shiffrin, 1977). Subjects were asked to search the series of frames for either a T or F target, under two processing load conditions: two or four letters per frame. Since the targets never appeared as distractors on any trial (consistent-mapping), sufficient practice on this task should result in the development of automatic detection responses for the targets, which is inferred when detection rates become independent of processing load (Schneider & Shiffrin, 1977).

As shown in Figure 3-1, at the beginning blocks of practice (64 trials per block), chronic schizophrenic patients and normal controls differed significantly, especially at the higher processing load. In contrast, at the end of 320 trials of practice (block 5), the two groups did not differ significantly. The patients may have developed automatic detection responses, as evidenced by the elimination of load effects on target detection accuracy in the patient group; however, it is not possible to determine if patients reached a *normal* level of automatization. Since no load effect was found in controls at block one, use of the elimination of load effects with practice as an index of automatization was compromised for controls, and therefore could not be used as a dependent measure for group comparisons of level of automatization achieved.

Because the elimination of load effects was unexpectedly compromised as a measure of automatization in controls, an additional index of automatization was explored in a secondary analysis. The presence of a target-location effect (i.e., better detection from the top vs. bottom half of arrays), which has been used as evidence for serial search (e.g., Snodgrass & Townsend, 1980), was found for both patient and control groups at the beginning of practice, but was significantly reduced by practice to a similar degree in both groups. This finding of decreased use of controlled serial search (decreased target-location effects) suggests similar development of automatic detection responses with practice in the two groups. Thus, initial differences between groups may reflect the patients' deficient utilization of controlled processing, which was alleviated by development of automatic detection responses after practice. These findings are consistent with theories postulating greater difficulties with resource-dependent controlled processing but normal automatic processing in patients with schizophrenia (Neale & Oltmanns, 1980; Callaway & Naghdi, 1982).

To further probe the extent to which detection was automated on the MFST, following the fifth block of MFST practice, subjects were required to simultaneously perform on the MFST and an auditory shadowing task (dual-task condition), where they repeated random letters presented at the rate of one every two seconds. In the dual-task condition, the MFST accuracy of the patients deteriorated, but nonsignificantly, relative to their single-task (block 5) level of performance, while the controls' MFST accuracy remained much more stable (see Figure 3-1). Thus, although neither group's MFST performance was *significantly* affected by the additional demands of the dual-task condition, the patients' performance was somewhat more adversely affected, suggesting that they may not have automated detection to the same degree as normals.

In the dual-task condition, the patients also showed impaired shadowing accuracy, relative to controls and relative to their own single-task shadowing performance. This finding indicates that, unlike controls, patients were left with insufficient resources to maintain shadowing (secondary) task performance during simultaneous (primary) MFST performance. A stage or data-limitation deficit cannot account for the findings that the patients' single-task shadowing accuracy and practiced MFST detection accuracy did not differ significantly from that of controls. Performance decrements were only observed during the increased processing load of the dual-task condition, where the patients' resource availability was exceeded.

IMPLICATIONS FOR TREATMENT

The resource-limitations hypothesis provides a foundation for exploring the use of cognitive neuropsychological tasks in assessment for treatment planning in schizophrenia. The following discussion focuses on the potential use of cognitive neuropsychological testing for guiding medication management. Subsequently, speculations on the potential benefits of attentional training programs designed to reduce the likelihood of resource overload will be presented.

Predicting Medication Response

Several studies (see Spohn & Strauss, 1989) suggest that antipsychotics improve schizophrenic patients' performance on cognitive tasks. For example, in a seminal study, Spohn and colleagues (1977) withdrew medications from 63 chronic schizophrenic patients for a six-week washout period and subsequently gave either chlorpromazine or placebo. They found that patients on antipsychotics, but not patients on placebo, made increasingly more correct detections on single-target CPT and full-report SOA tasks across the course of treatment (up to 8 weeks). Several cognitive functions appear to be enhanced by antipsychotic treatment, including improved sustained attention, increased channel capacity (e.g., visual span of apprehension), enhanced registration, and decreased distractibility (Spohn & Strauss, 1989).

Since researchers have been unable to clearly identify the specific cognitive mechanism(s) that are altered by antipsychotic treatment (Spohn & Strauss, 1989), it may prove useful to bypass specific mechanistic hypotheses and conceptualize improvements in information processing as a general improvement in resource utilization following antipsychotic treatment. Of course, the dual-task paradigm can be utilized to test the notion that, as opposed to alleviating a specific dysfunction at a particular stage of processing, antipsychotics increase general resource availability and use. Evidence in support of this hypothesis would be provided by finding no differences between single-task performance of a moderate-processing-load task in the absence, relative to presence, of antipsychotic treatment, while finding decrements in performance on the task in a dual-task condition in the absence, relative to presence of antipsychotic treatment. Finding no effect of antipsychotics on single-task performance would suggest that the subjects' ability to carry out the specific cognitive operations required by the task are unchanged by antipsychotics. Finding that antipsychotics improve performance of the task in the dual-task condition would suggest that these drugs increase the subjects' resource availability.

It is important to point out that not all antipsychotic medications improve processing on all neuropsychological tasks, and, indeed, some medications may impair specific functions (Heaton & Crowley, 1981). Negative effects primarily appear to be due to anticholinergic effects, which result from either anticholinergic medications given to treat the extrapyramidal side effects of antipsychotics or from the antipsychotic medication itself, which can have significant anticholinergic effects (Heaton & Crowley, 1981; Spohn & Strauss, 1989). The greater anticholinergic effects of aliphatics and piperdines, relative to piperazines, are associated with greater impairments in normal individuals on attention and motor tasks, although greater neuroleptic anticholinergic effects have *not* been associated with greater impairments in attention and motor functioning in schizophrenic patients (Heaton & Crowley, 1981). Similarly, the adverse effect of anticholinergic activity on memory tasks is now well known in normal subjects but has not been investigated in schizophrenic patients (Frith, 1984). In contrast, medications with less anticholinergic activity (e.g., piperazines) have few negative cognitive effects and generally improve the cognitive and psychomotor performance of both schizophrenics and controls (Heaton & Crowley, 1981).

Although antipsychotic medications appear to reduce many cognitive impairments in schizophrenic patients, this effect appears to characterize only a subgroup of schizophrenic patients. Several studies have shown that only approximately 40–60% of schizophrenics evidence processing deficits on the CPT and SOA (Asarnow & MacCrimmon, 1981; Orzack & Kornetsky, 1966). Based on such individual differences on SOA task performance, Asarnow and Marder and colleagues (Asarnow, Marder, Mintz, Van Putten, & Zimmerman, 1988; Marder, Asarnow, & Van Putten, 1984) have recently reported several findings related to predicting short- and long-term medication response in the treatment of schizophrenia. Marder and colleagues (1984) found that SOA performance generally improves over a three-week period with low-dose antipsychotic treatment. However, there was considerable variability in the effects of antipsychotics on SOA performance. Approximately one-third of the schizophrenics in the sample actually detected fewer targets on the SOA after antipsychotic treatment than when not on medication at baseline. Individual differences in SOA performance predicted symptom response to antipsychotic: The schizophrenic patients who showed the best baseline SOA performance or the greatest initial improvement (over 7 days) on the SOA also showed the greatest *reduction* in thought disorder (over 14 days) in response to antipsychotic treatment.

Parallel findings of symptom remission and improvements in information processing following antipsychotic treatment has lead to the suggestion (Cornblatt, Lezenweger, Dworkin, & Erlenmyer-Kimling, 1985; Nuechterlein, Edell, Norris, & Dawson, 1986; Spohn et al., 1977) that schizophrenic patients' information processing impairments may be a central mediating mechanism of schizophrenic symptoms, and that medications reduce vulnerability to develop schizophrenic symptoms through their enhancement of information-processing abilities (Orzack, Kornetsky & Freeman, 1967; Spohn et al., 1977). While this hypothesis is intriguing, most studies that support the above parallels do not conclusively rule out the possibility that the direction of causation is reversed; that is, that normalization of symptomatology allows greater focus on cognitive tasks which results in better performance (Spohn & Strauss, 1989).

Some findings, however, suggest that processing impairments on some tasks are not the result of interference from symptomatology. For example, Nuechterlein and colleagues (1986) showed that SOA and CPT impairments measured after discharge from the hospital (i.e., after significant symptom remission) correlated backwards in time with in-patient symptom severity. In addition, the SOA, CPT and backward masking impairments all appear to be a stable trait of patients, which is consistently observable through psychotic and remitted (i.e., reduced-symptom) states. However, the causal relationships between symptomatology, information processing and medication regimen cannot be conclusively determined on the basis of even the best-designed medication studies, since medication manipulations generally lead to concurrent changes in symptoma-

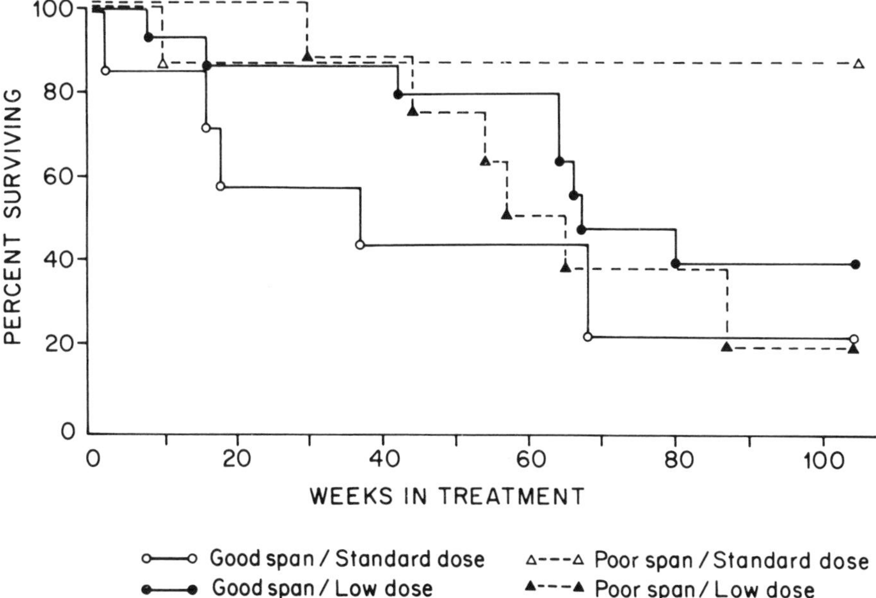

Figure 3-2 Proportion of patients free of symptom exacerbations ("surviving") in schizophrenic outpatients with good and poor SOA performance maintained on low (5 mg) and standard (25 mg) doses of fluphenazine decanoate. (Reproduced with permission from R. F. Asarnow et al., *Archives of General Psychiatry*, Vol. 45, 822–826; copyright © 1988 by the American Medical Association.)

tology and information processing (see Spohn & Strauss, 1989, for a more detailed discussion).

Despite this problem, correlations between changes in information-processing and psychiatric symptoms may be useful in identifying a clinically meaningful subgroup of patients who are likely to respond best to antipsychotic medications. The importance of identifying whether individual schizophrenic patients belong to this subgroup of patients is illustrated by a recent study by Asarnow and colleagues (1988) which provides dramatic evidence of how individual differences in performance on the SOA might predict which patients are best maintained with a standard versus lower dose of antipsychotic medication over the *long term*. After a four-week wash-out period, chronic schizophrenic outpatients were assigned to 5 or 25 mg of fluphenazine decanoate every two weeks and were assessed for symptom exacerbation (worsening on Brief Psychiatric Rating Scale cluster scores) and SOA performance at baseline and repeatedly throughout a two-year period. Patients were assigned to subgroups according to low (5 mg) or standard dosage (25 mg) of antipsychotic medication and according to whether they showed intact resource utilization (good SOA performance) or resource deficits (poor SOA performance), using an impairment cut score of less than 30 (out of 40) correct detections on the SOA ten-letter array (high processing load) condition. Figure 3-2 compares the survival rates (i.e., proportion of subjects remaining free of psychotic exacerbations over time) for the four patient groups.

Clearly, a standard dose of antipsychotic medication has dramatically different effects on schizophrenic patients with resource deficits (poor SOA) versus those with normal resource utilization (good SOA): An 86% survival rate was found for patients in the poor-span, standard-dose group, but only a 21% survival rate was found for patients in the good-span, standard-dose group. It is possible that a standard dose of antipsychotic may have some unknown toxic effect on schizophrenic patients who have normal resource utilization (good SOA). In contrast, a standard dose given to patients with excessively limited resource availability (poor SOA) has a protective effect of forestalling relapse, particularly during the second year of treatment, when most patients in the poor-span, low-dose group (22% two-year survival rate) begin to exacerbate and relapse.

If these findings are replicated and extended, the practicing clinical neuropsychologist might eventually employ tasks developed in cognitive psychology, like the SOA, in assessment for making medication recommendations. Decisions about medication dosage are currently made on a fairly trial-and-error basis, since there are no useful tools for predicting dose-related outcomes for an individual patient. In light of the risk of tardive dyskinesia, akathisia, and other negative effects of higher dosages, it would clearly be beneficial for the practicing clinician to be able to make recommendations about optimal antipsychotic dosage based on individual differences on cognitive neuropsychological tasks. Patients who evidence greater resource limitations on information processing tasks may have better outcomes at a standard dose, while patients with relatively normal resource utilization may fair better with low-dose treatment approaches.

Additional research is needed to validate such an approach and to identify the task and patient characteristics for which this approach might be most effective. For example, the use of the cut-score of 30 correct detections (out of 40 trials) on the ten-letter array SOA task (Asarnow & MacCrimmon, 1981) to define good and poor performance on individual patients is most appropriate for patients similar to those employed in Asarnow et al. (1988), who were chronic, stabilized patients who had been receiving antipsychotic medication for at least two months. The 30-correct cutoff, and the low-dose approach itself, is likely not appropriate for acute patients. Subtle changes in the parameters of the task (e.g., display visual angle) may also drastically change the appropriate cutoff score (Asarnow et al., 1991). The Marder et al. (1986) and Asarnow et al. (1988) studies employed small sample sizes with all male, relatively chronic schizophrenic patients who were able to be maintained on a standard dose of neuroleptic, which calls into question the generalizability of these results. More standardized and convenient computer-administered versions of this task are currently being developed (Asarnow, personal communication), and replication of these findings with the computer format is warranted. More accurate and confident prediction of which patients are most likely to benefit from long-term, standard-dose antipsychotic treatment might be gained by identifying those patients who perform below normal limits at higher processing loads across several of the tasks listed in Table 3-1. Additional research is needed to examine these issues.

Planning Attentional Training

Numerous studies suggest that the cognitive deficits observed in patients with schizophrenia can be remediated by nonpharmacologic means (Adams, Brantley, Malatesta, & Turkat, 1981; Benedict & Harris, 1989; Magaro, Johnson, & Boring, 1986). As noted above, several studies (Koh, 1978; Koh & Peterson, 1978; Larsen & Fromholt, 1978) reported that the passive, inefficient mnemonic strategies employed by schizophrenics can be remediated when elaborate encoding is induced by the experimenter, or adequate training of the required strategy is provided.

Recent studies have shown that reinforcement is an important component of cognitive training in schizophrenic patients. In their attempts to train patients to do the Wisconsin Card Sorting Task (WCST), Goldberg and colleagues (1987) failed to find maintenance of improvement on the WCST in chronic schizophrenics who were given instruction concerning strategies for improving performance. In contrast, Green and colleagues (1990) found that a subgroup of chronic schizophrenics were able to achieve and maintain improved performance on the WCST, when given both instruction and monetary reinforcement for correct responses. Reinforcement may increase the patient's motivation to participate in training and improve reflection on and internalization of the meaning of new strategies for carrying out component operations (see also Meichenbaum & Cameron, 1973). If the finding that only a subgroup of schizophrenics can benefit from cognitive remediation with reinforcement is replicated, future studies should identify which individual patients are likely to benefit from rehabilitation programs, especially since these programs are costly and scarce.

Other studies report that schizophrenic patients' performance improves when they are provided with an opportunity to practice on reaction time and other speeded information processing tasks; and on digit span, memory, and problem-solving tasks (Magaro et al., 1986; Benedict & Harris, 1989; Adams et al., 1981). It is not clear why patients improve after practice on all of these tasks, although many of the procedures employed involve extensive practice and consistent mapping of stimuli and responses which are critical conditions to allow the development of automatic processes. This suggests that some improvement on these tasks may be due to greater reliance on resource-free automatic, rather than resource-dependent controlled processing.

Many of these practice tasks are widely available as computerized modules in cognitive training programs (Magaro et al., 1986; Ben-Yishay, Piasetsky, & Rattok, 1987), which have been employed with head injury patients. However, the validity of these approaches is still somewhat controversial since many of the beneficial effects on cognition observed in head-injured patients have not been thoroughly evaluated against the effects of spontaneous recovery (e.g., see Ponsford & Kinsella, 1989). Similarly, evaluation of cognitive training programs in schizophrenia must address the possibility that variables, such as remission of acute positive symptoms and enhancement of information processing abilities with antipsychotic treatment, are responsible for observed benefits. In addition, the impact of cognitive training on the real-life functioning and symptoms of patients must be examined to justify the use of training the procedures. These factors have not been thoroughly addressed in past research (Magaro et al., 1986) and must be explored in future research prior to widespread use of training programs.

In sum, several findings indicate that the cognitive deficits of patients with schizophrenia can be remediated through provision of instructional strategies, reinforcement and practice. These findings suggest that schizophrenic patients may possess but fail to effectively use the resources necessary to carry out many cognitive tasks. Instructing patients to employ strategies designed to more adequately capitalize on the resources that they do possess may facilitate more efficient processing and better coping with information overload.

Meichenbaum and Cameron (1973) employed a self-instructional training procedure which incorporated modeling, instructions, examples, discussion, and rehearsal to provide schizophrenics with strategies for capitalizing on their processing resources. In Meichenbaum's study, patients were trained to covertly guide themselves through cognitive tasks by using instructional sets and imagery, by monitoring and evaluating responses, and by making coping and reinforcing self-statements. This training led to decreased "sick talk" in an interview, improved performance on digit recall with distraction and proverb interpretation tasks, and the training generalized to an inkblot task, on which patients evidenced reduced thought disorder. These findings suggest that cognitive-behavioral techniques may be helpful in teaching schizophrenic patients new strategies for capitalizing on the resources that they do possess.

In addition, since automatic processing abilities may remain relatively intact in schizophrenics (Callaway & Naghdi, 1982; Neale & Oltmanns, 1980; Granholm et al., 1991, described above), it may be possible to functionally increase the amount of resources *available* to schizophrenic patients by training them to automate cognitive operations when possible. Substitution of resource-free automatic processes for resource-demanding controlled processes or reautomatization of deficient operations when possible would free resources for concurrent controlled processing. There is some evidence that automatic attention responses trained in the laboratory are not specific to the trained targets and may transfer to facilitate processing of other exemplars within the same class of stimuli as the trained targets. For example, Schneider and Fisk (1984) trained normal subjects to detect consistently mapped words from specific categories (e.g., colors) on a MFST, and after extensive practice subjects were presented novel words from the trained categories. Comparisons between the original stimuli used in training and the novel words on a reaction time measure showed that reaction time for the novel words was at least 92% that of the trained words. These findings demonstrate significant positive transfer between trained and novel stimuli. This is particularly important in considering transfer between laboratory training and real-world situations. However, it is possible that consistently mapped practice with well-defined categories (e.g., colors) will yield greater automatization and greater transfer than practice with more complex, real-world categories (e.g., facial expressions of emotions).

Nonetheless, it is tempting to speculate that it may be possible to similarly train schizophrenic patients to attend to important classes of environmental stimuli by employing extensive consistent-mapped practice. For example, in order to respond appropriately during an ordinary social encounter, one must attend to and recognize a great many subtle cues in the faces, voices, postures, and gestures of others which occur numerous times per second. We must rapidly encode and categorize this information in order to respond appropriately and avoid overload. Andorfer (1984) suggested that a failure to process affective patterns in social situations might account for several common clinical manifestations of schizophrenia, and he proposed retraining of schizophrenics to recognize facial configurations of various emotions. A consistent-mapping procedure employed in such retraining would facilitate the automatization of the categorization of facial cues, much in the same way exemplars of one color can be trained to be automatically differentiated from exemplars of others. A range of cues associated with a specific emotion could be trained to elicit a categorization response (e.g., happy, sad) for only those cues, through extensive consistent-mapped practice. The automatization of affective pattern recognition would free resources for more efficient controlled tracking of social interactions.

It will likely be most beneficial to combine attentional training therapies with current medication, communication, and social skills therapies. Brenner (1989) employs such a multimodal treatment approach, which progresses through a gradual shift from emphasis on cognitive processes toward social skills, and he notes that ability to process information adequately is a necessary, but not sufficient, condition for generalization of social behavior change. Spaulding and colleagues (1989) also propose a multimodal treatment approach which includes cognitive-behavioral techniques, medication, social skills training, and attentional and cognitive retraining interventions. Although the attentional training procedures proposed in this section logically follow from research on cognitive functioning in schizophrenia and from a resource-limitations model of schizophrenia, they have not been subjected to rigorous experimental evaluation individually or as a cohesive treatment program and are highly speculative.

SUMMARY

As a cognitive neuropsychologist working forward from a resource-limitations model of information processing impairments in schizophrenia, I have proposed potential avenues for neuropsychologists to increase their research activities and their ability to assist in the treatment of patients with schizophrenia. Research examining the validity of the resource-limitations explanation of cognitive impairments in schizophrenia should employ a dual-task design and incorporate psychophysiological measures to validate assumptions about task processing load and resource limitations. In consultation with psychiatrists, neuropsychologists might design, study, and eventually employ procedures for making recommendations regarding optimal medication dose on the basis of patients' performance on cognitive tasks sensitive to resource deficiencies. In rehabilitation settings, neuropsychologists might design, study, and eventually implement attentional training programs directed at alleviating resource limitations and reducing processing overload. The notions of processing resources and the resource-limitations hypothesis may prove to be theoretically useful constructs for explaining observed information-processing impairments and guiding treatment planning in schizophrenia.

ACKNOWLEDGMENTS

I would like to thank Drs. Robert F. Asarnow, Michael J. Goldstein, and Keith H. Nuechterlein as well as the authors of other chapters in this volume who commented on this work. Preparation of this chapter was supported by NIMH research grants MH14584 and MH30911.

REFERENCES

Adams, H., Brantley, P., Malatesta, V., & Turkat, I. (1981). Modification of cognitive processes: A case study of schizophrenia. *Journal of Consulting and Clinical Psychology*, *49*, 460–464.

Andorfer, J. C. (1984). Affective pattern recognition and schizophrenia. *Journal of Clinical Psychology*, *40*, 403–409.

Asarnow, R. F., Granholm, E., & Sherman, T. (1991). Span of apprehension in schizophrenia. In S. Steinhauer, J. H. Gruzelier & J. Zubin (Eds.), *Handbook of Schizophrenia, Vol. 5, Neuropsychology, psychophysiology, and information processing*. pp. 335–370. Amsterdam: Elsevier.

Asarnow, R. F., MacCrimmon, D. J. (1978). Residual performance deficit in clinically remitted schizophrenics: A marker of schizophrenia? *Journal of Abnormal Psychology*, *87*, 597–608.

Asarnow, R. F., & MacCrimmon, D. J. (1981). Span of apprehension deficits during the postpsychotic stages of schizophrenia: A replication and extension. *Archives of General Psychiatry*, *38*, 1006–1011.

Asarnow, R. F., Marder, S. R., Mintz, J., Van Putten, T., & Zimmerman, K. E. (1988). The differential effect of low and conventional doses of fluphenazine decanoate on schizophrenic outpatients with good or poor information processing abilities. *Archives of General Psychiatry*, *45*, 822–826.

Bauman, E. (1971). Schizophrenic short-term memory: The role of organization at input. *Journal of Consulting and Clinical Psychology*, *36*, 4–19.

Beatty, J. (1982). Task-evoked pupillary responses, processing load and the structure of processing resources. *Psychological Bulletin*, *91*, 276–292.

Benedict, R. H. B., & Harris, A. E. (1989). Remediation of attention deficits in chronic schizophrenic patients: A preliminary study. *British Journal of Clinical Psychology*, *28*, 187–188.

Ben-Yishay, Y., Piasetsky, E. B., & Rattok, J. (1987). A systematic method for ameliorating disorders in basic attention. In M. Meier, A. Benton & L. Diller (Eds.), *Neuropsychological Rehabilitation*. (pp. 165–181). New York: Guilford Press.

Bjork, R. A. (1975). Short-term storage: The ordered output of a central processor. In Restle, Shiffrin, Custellan, Lindeman & Pison (Eds.), *Cognitive Theory, Vol. 1* (pp. 151–171). Hillsdale, NJ: Lawrence Erlbaum Associates.

Brenner, H. D. (1989). The treatment of basic psychological dysfunctions from a systemic point of view. *British Journal of Psychiatry*, *155*, 74–83.

Broadbent, D. E. (1958). *Perception and Communication*. London: Pergamon Press, Ltd.

Broadbent, D. E. (1971). *Decision and Stress*. London: Academic Press, Inc.
Broen, W. E., Jr., & Storms, L. N. (1967). A theory of response interference in schizophrenia. In B. A. Maher (Ed.), *Progress in Experimental Personality Research, Vol. 4*. New York: Academic Press.
Broga, M. I., & Neufeld, R. W. J. (1981). Evaluation of information sequential aspects of schizophrenic performance: I. Framework and current findings. *The Journal of Nervous and Mental Disease*, *169*, 558–568.
Callaway, E., & Naghdi, S. (1982). An information processing model for schizophrenia. *Archives of General Psychiatry*, *39*, 339–347.
Cornblatt, B. A., Lenzenweger, M. F., Dworkin, R. H., & Erlenmeyer-Kimling, L. (1985). Positive and negative schizophrenic symptoms, attention, and information processing. *Schizophrenia Bulletin*, *11*, 397–407.
Dawson, M. E. (1980, October). Psychophysiology at the interface of clinical science, cognitive science, and neuroscience. Presidential address at 29th annual meeting of the Society for Psychophysiological Research, New Orleans, LA.
Frith, C. D. (1984). Schizophrenia, memory and anticholinergic drugs. *Journal of Abnormal Psychology*, *93*, 339–341.
Gjerde, P. F. (1983). Attentional capacity dysfunction and arousal in schizophrenia. *Psychological Bulletin*, *93*, 57–72.
Glenberg, A., & Adams, F. (1978). Type I rehearsal and recognition. *Journal of Verbal Learning and Behavior*, *17*, 455–463.
Goldberg, T. E., Weinberger, D. R., Berman, K. F., Pliskin, N. H., & Podd, M. (1987). Further evidence for dementia of the prefrontal type in schizophrenia. *Archives of General Psychiatry*, *44*, 1008–1014.
Goldstein, G. (1986). The neuropsychology of schizophrenia. In I. Grant & K. Adams (Eds.), *Neuropsychological Assessment of Neuropsychiatric Disorders* (pp. 221–243). New York: Oxford University Press.
Gopher, D. & Donchin, E. (1986). Workload—examination of the concept. In K. R. Boff, L. Kaufman & J. P. Thomas (Eds), *Handbook of Perception and Human Performance, Vol. 2, Cognitive Processes and Performance* (pp. 41-1 to 41-49) New York: Wiley and Sons.
Granholm, E., Asarnow, R. F., & Marder, S. R. (1991). Controlled information processing resources and the development of automatic detection responses in schizophrenia. *Journal of Abnormal Psychology*, *100*, 22–30.
Green, M. F., Ganzell, S., Satz, P., & Vaclav, J. F. (1990). Teaching the Wisconsin Card Sort to schizophrenic patients. *Archives of General Psychiatry*, *47*, 91–92 (Letter).
Hasher, L., & Zacks, R. T. (1979). Automatic and effortful processes in memory. *Journal of Experimental Psychology: General*, *108*, 356–388.
Heaton, R. K., & Crowley, T. J. (1981). Effects of psychiatric disorders and their somatic treatments on neuropsychological test results. In S. B. Filskov and T. J. Boll (Eds.), *Handbook of Clinical Neuropsychology* (pp. 481–525). New York: Wiley-Interscience.
Hirst, W., & Kalmar, D. (1987). Characterizing attentional resources. *Journal of Experimental Psychology: General*, *116*, 68–81.
Kahneman, D. (1973). *Attention and effort*. Englewood Cliffs, NJ: Prentice-Hall.
Knight, R. G., & Russell, P. N. (1978). Global capacity reduction in schizophrenia. *British Journal of Social and Clinical Psychology*, *17*, 275–280.
Knowles, W. B. (1963). Operator loading tasks. *Human Factors*, *5*, 151–161.
Koh, S. D. (1978). Remembering of verbal materials by schizophrenic young adults. In

S. Schwartz (Ed.), *Language and cognition and schizophrenia* (pp. 55–99). Hillsdale, NJ: Lawrence Erlbaum.

Koh, S. D., & Peterson, R. A. (1978). Encoding orientation and the remembering of schizophrenic young adults. *Journal of Abnormal Psychology, 87*, 303–313.

Korboot, P. J., & Diamani, N. (1976). Auditory processing speed and signal detection in schizophrenia. *Journal of Abnormal Psychology, 85*, 287–295.

Larsen, S. F., and Fromholt, P. (1976). Mnemonic organization and free recall in schizophrenia. *Journal of Abnormal Psychology, 85*, 61–65.

Magaro, P. A., Johnson, M. H., & Boring, R. (1986). Information processing approaches to the treatment of schizophrenia. In R. E. Ingram (Ed.), *Information Processing Approaches to Clinical Psychology* (pp. 283–304). New York: Academic Press.

Marder, S. R., Asarnow, R. F., & Van Putten, T. (1984). Information processing and neuroleptic response in acute and stabilized schizophrenic patients. *Psychiatry Research, 13*, 41–49.

McGhie, A., & Chapman, J. (1961). Disorders of attention and perception in early schizophrenia. *British Journal of Medical Psychology, 34*, 103–116.

Meichenbaum, D., & Cameron, R. (1973). Training schizophrenics to talk to themselves: A means of developing attentional controls. *Behavior Therapy, 4*, 515–534.

Moray, N. (1967). Where is capacity limited? A survey and a model. *Acta Psychologica, 27*, 84–92.

Navon, D. (1984). Resources—A theoretical soup stone? *Psychological Review, 91*, 216–234.

Navon, D., & Gopher, D. (1979). On the economy of the human information processor. *Psychological Review, 86*, 214–255.

Neale, J. M., & Oltmanns, T. F. (1980). *Schizophrenia* (Chapter 3) (pp. 102–161). New York: John Wiley and Sons.

Norman, D. A., & Bobrow, D. G. (1975). On data-limited and resource-limited processes. *Cognitive Psychology, 7*, 44–64.

Nuechterlein, K. H., & Dawson, M. E. (1984). Information processing and attentional functioning in the course of schizophrenic disorder. *Schizophrenia Bulletin, 10*, 160–203.

Nuechterlein, K. H., Edell, W. S., Norris, M., & Dawson, M. E. (1986). Attentional vulnerability indicators, thought disorder, and negative symptoms. *Schizophrenia Bulletin, 12*, 408–426.

Oltmanns, T. (1978). Selective attention in schizophrenic and manic psychoses: The effect of distraction in processing. *Journal of Abnormal Psychology, 87*, 212–225.

Orzack, M. H., & Kornetsky, C. (1966). Attention dysfunction in chronic schizophrenia. *Archives of General Psychiatry, 14*, 323–326.

Orzack, M. H., Kornetsky, C., & Freeman, H. (1967). The effects of daily administration of carphenazine on attention in the schizophrenic patient. *Psychopharmacologia, 11*, 31–38.

Payne, R. W., Hockberg, A. C., & Hawks, D. V. (1970). Dichotic stimulation as a method of assessing the disorder of attention in overinclusive schizophrenic patients. *Journal of Abnormal Psychology, 76*, 185–193.

Pogue-Geile, M. F., & Oltmanns, T. F. (1980). Sentence perception and distractibility in schizophrenic, manic and depressed patients. *Journal of Abnormal Psychology, 89*, 115–124.

Ponsford, J. L., & Kinsella, G. (1989). Evaluation of a remedial programme for attentional deficits following closed-head injury. *Journal of Clinical and Experimental Neuropsychology, 10*, 693–708.

Posner, M. I., Early, T. S., Reiman, E., Pardo, P. J., & Dhawan, M. (1988). Asymmetries in hemispheric control of attention in schizophrenia. *Archives of General Psychiatry*, *45*, 814–821.

Posner, M. I., & Presti, D. (1987). Selective attention and cognitive control. *Trends in Neuroscience*, *10*, 12–17.

Posner, M. I., & Snyder, C. R. P. (1975). Attention and cognitive control. In R. L. Solso (Ed.), *Information Processing and Cognition: The Loyola Symposium* (pp. 55–85). Hillsdale, NJ: Lawrence Erlbaum Associates.

Russell, P. N., Bannatyne, P. A., & Smith, J. F. (1975). Associative strength as a mode of organization in recall and recognition: A comparison of schizophrenics and normals. *Journal of Abnormal Psychology*, *84*, 122–128.

Saccuzzo, D. P., & Braff, D. L. (1986). Information-processing abnormalities in schizophrenic and psychotic patients: Trait and state dependent components. *Schizophrenia Bulletin*, *12*, 447–459.

Saccuzzo, D. P., Hirt, M., & Spencer, T. J. (1974). Backward masking as a measure of attention in schizophrenia. *Journal of Abnormal Psychology*, *83*, 512–522.

Schneider, W., Dumais, S. T., & Shiffrin, R. M. (1984). Automatic and controlled processing and attention. In R. Parasuraman, J. Beatty & J. Davies (Eds.), *Varieties of Attention* (pp. 1–27). New York: Academic Press.

Schneider, W., & Fisk, A. D. (1983). Attention theory and mechanisms for skilled performance. In R. A. Magill (Ed.), *Memory and Control of Action* (pp. 119–143). New York: North Holland Publishing Co.

Schneider, W., & Fisk, A. D. (1984). Automatic category search and its transfer. *Journal of Experimental Psychology: Learning, Memory and Cognition*, *10*, 1–15.

Schneider, W., & Shiffrin, R. M. (1977). Controlled and automatic human information processing: I. Detection, search and attention. *Psychological Review*, *84*, 1–66.

Snodgrass, J. G., & Townsend, J. T. (1980). Comparing parallel and serial models: Theory and implementation. *Journal of Experimental Psychology: Human Perception and Performance*, *6*, 330–354.

Spaulding, W., Garbin, C. P., & Crinean, W. J. (1989). The logical prerequisites for cognitive therapy of schizophrenia. *British Journal of Psychiatry*, *155*, 68–73.

Spohn, H. E., Lacoursiere, R. B., Thompson, K., & Coyne, L. (1977). Phenothiazine effects on psychological and psychophysiological dysfunction. *Archives of General Psychiatry*, *34*, 633–644.

Spohn, H. E., & Strauss, M. E. (1989). Relation of neuroleptic and anticholinergic medication to cognitive functions in schizophrenia. *Journal of Abnormal Psychology*, *98*, 367–380.

Steinhauer, S., & Zubin, J. (1982). Vulnerability to schizophrenia: Information processing in the pupil and event-related potential. In E. Vsdin & I. Handin (Eds.), *Biological Markers in Psychiatry and Neurology*. New York: Pergamon Press.

Treisman, A. M. (1964). Monitoring and storage of irrelevant messages in selective attention. *Journal of Verbal Learning and Verbal Behavior*, *3*, 449–459.

Welford, A. T. (1967). A single channel operation in the brain. *Acta Psychologica*, *27*, 5–22.

Wickens, C. D. (1984). Processing resources in attention. In R. Parasuraman, J. Beatty & J. Davies (Eds.), *Varieties of Attention* (pp. 63–102). New York: Academic Press.

Wielgus, M. S., & Harvey, P. D. (1988). Dichotic listening and recall in schizophrenia and mania. *Schizophrenia Bulletin*, *14*, 689–700.

Wishner, J., & Wahl, O. (1974). Dichotic listening in schizophrenia. *Journal of Consulting and Clinical Psychology*, *42*, 538–546.

Wohlberg, G. W., & Kornetsky, C. (1973). Sustained attention in remitted schizophrenics. *Archives of General Psychiatry*, *28*, 533–537.

4

Perceptual Organization and Attentional Search in Cognitive Deficits

LYNN C. ROBERTSON

The study of attention and higher order perception in neuropsychology has lagged behind investigations of many other cognitive disorders such as aphasia and dementia. One contributing factor may be that intact language and memory are required for successful social interaction. This property makes it relatively easy for patients or family members and close friends to detect even small changes in these capacities. Conversely, perception is a much more private affair, and if a deficit is reported at all, it will often be in the form of "needing my eyes checked." Thus, in order to isolate cognitive dysfunction in patients with suspected perceptual dysfunction, it seems critical to use procedures that can reveal deficits at preconscious or unconscious stages of processing. Cognitive psychology has been very successful in this regard. Methods such as reaction time, signal detection, multidimensional scaling, priming, and the use of time-limited displays were all advanced to examine the underlying cognitive processes and internal representations that were often unknown or unavailable to the subject. The recent application of these methods and their resulting information processing models to neuropsychological investigations has advanced our understanding of many attentional and perceptual deficits in ways that were not possible with traditional methods.

In the area of attentional disturbance, this advance is especially evident in the study of unilateral visual neglect, and this will be the topic of the first section. The results have settled some arguments and have raised others. While the use of the term *hemi-inattention* to refer to neglect was once considered a matter of faith, neglect is now conceived by many neuropsychologists as an attentional disorder. It will become clear as the discussion continues that the type of attention involved in neglect is quite specific. It is not a lack of vigilance or concentration as seen in frontal patients, nor is it a general lack of awareness or arousal often seen with diffuse brain disease or in patients with brain stem involvement. Rather, attentional deficits in unilateral visual neglect seem to be due to hypersensitivity to information on the ipsilateral or intact side of space. Attention becomes focussed on information on the ipsilateral side at the expense of information on the contralateral side. The ability to selectively focus (or engage) attention on the ipsilateral side remains intact, while the ability to defocus (or disengage) attention from the intact side is altered.

Posner and his colleagues performed the seminal studies to demonstrate these effects and did so after prolonged investigation of spatial attention in normals. Their work is an excellent example of the development of theory within cognitive neuroscience that has had a direct impact on neuropathological classification, and it will be discussed at length in the first section of this chapter. The theory was developed from findings in normals followed by converging evidence supporting the theory from studies with patient populations. The cognitive level of the theory has remained basically unchanged by neuropsychological data, and indeed has received substantial support by demonstrating that proposed component operations can be independently affected by damage to different areas of the human brain.

In the second part of the chapter, I will discuss a rather different topic—higher order perceptual deficits in the analysis of global and local levels of visual form. These investigations have implications for theories of normal and abnormal perceptual organization and are also critical for theories of functional hemispheric asymmetry in higher order visual analysis. By focusing on one type of perceptual problem, I hope to show how neuropsychological data can play a somewhat different role. In the area of neglect, a theory developed within traditional cognitive psychology has received support from neuropsychological data. In the study of global/local analysis, a theory developed within cognitive psychology has been substantially changed by neuropsychological data. In this case component operations were uncovered that were unsuspected by testing normals alone. Although the distinction between theory application and theory development within neuropsychology should be kept in mind, it is the case that whichever way one proceeds, increased understanding of patients' cognitive deficits and their underlying neural pathology will surely follow.

Finally, the topic selections do not mean that other investigations of attentional and perceptual dysfunction in basic science have had little reciprocal influence—quite the contrary. The interplay between cognitive theories and neuropsychology has been broad and is becoming more frequent. For instance, Marr's (1982) theory of vision relied heavily on Warrington and Taylor's (1978) findings that certain patients could identify common views of objects as well as normals but had difficulty in identifying uncommon views. The study of prosopagnosia and hemisphere laterality has influenced models of face perception to a large degree (Ellis, 1986; Newcombe, 1979; Sergent, 1986; Young, 1986). Work in "blindsight" (Weiskrantz, 1986) has forced closer examination of the relationship between awareness and normal perception, and Humphreys and Riddoch and their colleagues (Humphreys & Riddoch, 1984; Humphreys & Riddoch, 1987; Humphreys, Riddoch, & Quinlan, 1985; Riddoch & Humphreys, 1987) have repeatedly demonstrated the value of neuropsychological data in several domains of perception. I will not review these lines of investigation, but rather focus on specific problems in order to explore the neuropsychological and cognitive psychological implications in depth.

VISUAL NEGLECT AND SPATIAL ATTENTION

Interest in visual neglect has had a long history with theorists falling into two main groups: those who attribute this type of neglect to lower order visual-sensory defects (Battersby et al., 1956; Bender, 1952; Denny-Brown, & Banker; 1954) and those who argue for higher order cognitive processes (McFie, Piercy, & Zangwill, 1950). Lower order deficits have always been problematic for cognitive theories of visual neglect, because this type of neglect is most often seen with large lesions that often affect visual primary cortex or optic fibers. This of course results in substantial visual loss in the visual field contralateral to the lesion. To complicate matters even further, clinical signs of neglect generally dissipate rapidly (between 8 and 40 weeks post injury depending on what survey one reads). Even if lesions do not include visual areas on CT or MRI scans, there are likely to be metabolic abnormalities in distant sites that may affect vision, and this is especially so in acute states. Until recently, the major argument against the role of lower order visual deficits in visual neglect was that patients could be found who did not show any signs of neglect but who had as severe, if not more severe, visual deficits than those patients who did have clinical signs. For instance, patients with a dense homonymous hemianopia search the contralateral side of space while patients with neglect do not (Heilman, Watson, & Valenstein, 1985). However, to argue against lower order processes on this basis is to assume that the visual deficit contributing to neglect is a field cut and not some other visual problem that might arise as a function of occipital damage and may not have been tested (e.g., lowered contrast sensitivity).

Despite this problem, recent studies have helped to quell the voices of the sensory deficit advocates (and in fact should quiet them entirely) by demonstrating that neglect occurs even on internally generated images where no sensory stimulus is presented. Bisiach et al (1981) asked subjects with visual neglect to *imagine* themselves facing a well known landmark in a plaza in Milan from one end of the plaza and to report the buildings surrounding it. The same patients were then asked to imagine themselves at the opposite end of the plaza and do the same. In both cases, patients with visual neglect reported fewer items on the contralesional side of their internally generated images.

Other neuropsychological evidence questioning sensory interpretations has shown that visual extinction can occur even when stimuli are presented wholly within the intact visual field (Ladavas, 1987). Finally, a 90° rotation of a patient with visual neglect can result in both viewer-centered neglect (e.g., the left side relative to the orientation of the head) and environment-centered neglect (e.g., the left side of the room; Calvanio, Petrone, & Levine, 1987; Farah et al., in press). Rotating the patient dissociates an environmental and viewer-centered frame of reference, and these studies demonstrate that neglect is relative to both frames. These findings showed that neglect could occur even within the intact visual field and be reduced within the neglected field under appropriate conditions.

Findings such as these have generated new alternative theories of neglect based on higher order cognitive processes. Theorists can be roughly divided into two camps: those who advocate deficits in spatial representation (Bisiach &

Berti, 1985) and those who argue for deficits in spatial attention (Eglin, Robertson, & Knight, 1989; Heilman, 1979; Heilman, Watson, & Valenstein, 1985; Mesulam, 1985; Posner, Walker, Friedrich, & Rafal, 1984). The issue is basically whether or not attention is directed away from the neglected field because there is nothing meaningful in that field to attend to (due to an altered representation of space), or that attention cannot be directed into the neglected side because it gets stuck on the intact side. Although these models are very different theoretically, the message for the clinician is that neglect depends on higher order cognitive operations that either interact with spatial attention or are directly attentional in nature.

At least two information processing theories derived from studies in cognitive psychology have been useful in understanding the role of spatial attention in visual neglect. One was proposed by Posner (1980) and includes a covert attentional scanner that has been said to operate somewhat analogous to a beam of light. Another is based on feature intergration theory first proposed by Treisman and Gelade (1980). Although these two theories have emphasized different aspects of attention, both are concerned with what factors direct attentional search through the visual field and both have been used to identify the underlying cognitive deficits in visual neglect.

Posner's Covert Scanner

The impact of Posner's theory on the study of neglect is well known. In a series of experiments with normals and neurologically impaired patients, Posner and his colleagues (Posner, 1980; Posner, Inhoff, Friedrich, & Cohen, 1987; Posner, Cohen, & Rafal, 1982; Rafal, Posner, Friedman, Inhoff, & Bernstein, 1988; Rafal & Posner, 1987) have shown that the movement of attention through space can occur without accompanying eye movements. They have further shown that this covert movement of attention through the visual field can be broken down into component processes: move, engage, and disengage. The idea is that spatial attention has components similar to those needed for eye movements, and similar to an eye movement, attention must be moved to a given location, stopped at that location, and then disengaged from the location to go elsewhere.

A typical paradigm used to test attentional scanning is as follows: Three boxes appear on the screen in front of subjects, and subjects are told to keep their eyes fixated on the central box. A trial begins with one of the two peripheral boxes brightened for a few milleseconds. This box is the cue that tells the subject a target will likely appear at the location of the cue, as opposed to the opposite location where the box did not brighten. A target then appears at variable intervals from cue onset. The target is most likely to occur at the cued location, but on a small number of trials it appears at the opposite, uncued location. In either case the subject is to respond to its appearance by pressing a button measuring reaction time. The absolute reaction time is relatively unimportant in these experiments. Rather, the meaningful measures are the mean difference in reaction time between different cue-target intervals and the difference in reaction time between trials in which the target appears in the cued location (valid trials) and those in which it appears on the opposite side in the non-cued location (invalid trials). (A stylized pattern of results typically found in normals

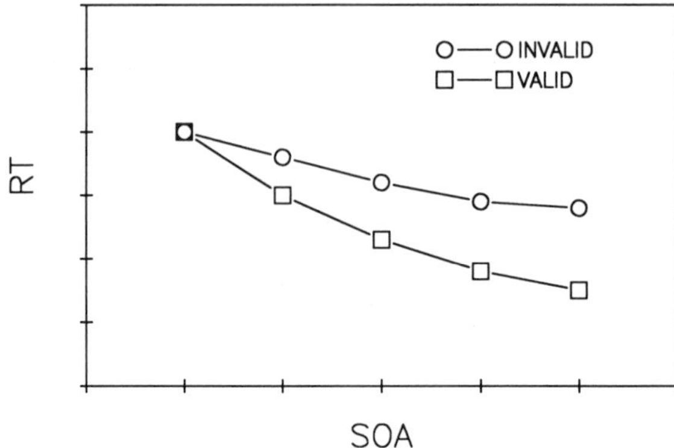

Figure 4-1 Characterized results of Posner et al.'s findings. Validly and invalidly cued functions are plotted over increasing stimulus onset asynchrony (SOA).

is shown in Figure 4-1.) If the cue signals the attentional mechanism to move to the cued location in anticipation of an upcoming target, response time should decrease as the cue-target interval (stimulus onset asynchrony or SOA) increases, and it does because it takes time to move to the expected location. If the target occurs in the invalid location, reaction time should be longer than when it occurs in the valid location, because attention would be at the wrong location when the target appeared. This also occurs. Furthermore, the difference between valid and invalid trials should be absent or negligible at short SOAs but increase as the interval increases, because the longer the SOA the more likely it is that the subject's attention has been moved and engaged. This effect also occurs.

Patients with parietal damage (not necessarily exhibiting signs of neglect) show a different pattern of results that suggests difficulty in disengaging from a cued location in the ipsilateral field (intact side) in order to respond to a target in the contralateral field (neglected side; Posner et al., 1984). The function that represents the movement of attention (valid trials) is relatively normal in these patients whether the target appears in the intact or neglected field. Reaction time decreases over SOA for valid trials. Conversely, reaction time is substantially slowed for targets appearing in the neglected field on invalid trails (i.e., the cue is in the intact field with the target in the neglected field). This delay does not occur when the cue is in the neglected field and the target in the intact field. Attention appears to get stuck on the intact side, and the patients have difficulty disengaging attention from this side to move to a target presented in the neglected field.

These patients were able to respond to the target when it was presented on the contralateral side to the lesion on valid trials. However, they were slower than normals to respond to a target on the contralateral side when the cue designated the intact side. This difference in speed rather than accuracy is important. If a traditional measure of neglect had been used—one based on number of omissions or percent correct—a deficit may not have been detected, and, in fact, 5 of the 15 patients had no clinical signs of neglect; 2 were classified as having "minimal" neglect which was actually intermittent signs of extinction; and only one was classified as having "moderate" neglect, which was defined as consistently missing information on the neglected side. Thus, deficits in responding to contralateral targets were found in some relatively high functioning chronic patients even when they did not show obvious signs of clinical neglect. Morrow and Ratcliff (1988) more recently showed that this effect occurs with larger magnitudes in patients with obvious clinical signs of neglect. Together with Posner et al., these findings are consistent with the idea that neglect is best conceived as a continuum from extinction to severe neglect. More will be said about this idea later.

Other studies have further supported the independence of component processes in visual attention on similar tasks. For instance, pulvinar damage produces a deficit in engaging attention (Rafal & Posner, 1987). Conversely, studies with patients with midbrain lesions have shown a deficit in movement but none in engage and disengage operations (Rafal et al., 1988). Damage to these areas seldom produces neglect in humans. However, the data demonstrate that the different processing components of spatial attention can be independently affected by lesions in different areas of the visual system.

Treisman's Feature Integration Theory

Which stimuli require attention and which do not? If we knew when attention was needed and were able to manipulate attentional demands systematically, we would be a step closer in identifying the types of stimuli and tasks that could prove useful in diagnosing and understanding neglect. Again, neuropsychology has benefited from procedures and theories developed in cognitive psychology. Feature integration theory states that features such color or orientation are processed in parallel without attentional demands, while a stimulus that contains more than one feature (called a conjunction) requires attention in order to conjoin the features into a perceived object (Treisman, 1988; Treisman & Gelade, 1980). This theory predicts that as overall attentional demands increase, conjunctions will be harder to find, but that the detection of features will be unaffected by such demands, and evidence to this effect has been repeatedly found in normals.

Although feature integration theory is well known among experimental psychologists and cognitive neuroscientists, the practicing clinician may be unaware of it, and I will outline it briefly before continuing. The theory as initially proposed by Treisman states that primitive features such as color or orientation are processed in parallel by something she calls "feature detectors." Features require no attentional resources and are automatically encoded. However, in order to perceive the conjunction of features such as a red dot with a line through it as an integrated form, attention directed to the location of the form is required. The theory receives support from several studies showing that identifying features such as a red dot is as rapid when there is only a single red dot on the page as when there are a number of other non-red dots (see Figure 4-2A). Reaction time to detect the red dot is independent of the number of distractors. Conversely, when a red dot with a line bisecting it is to be detected (see Figure 4-3B, 4-3C, and 4-3D), objects have to be serially scanned in order to find the

A

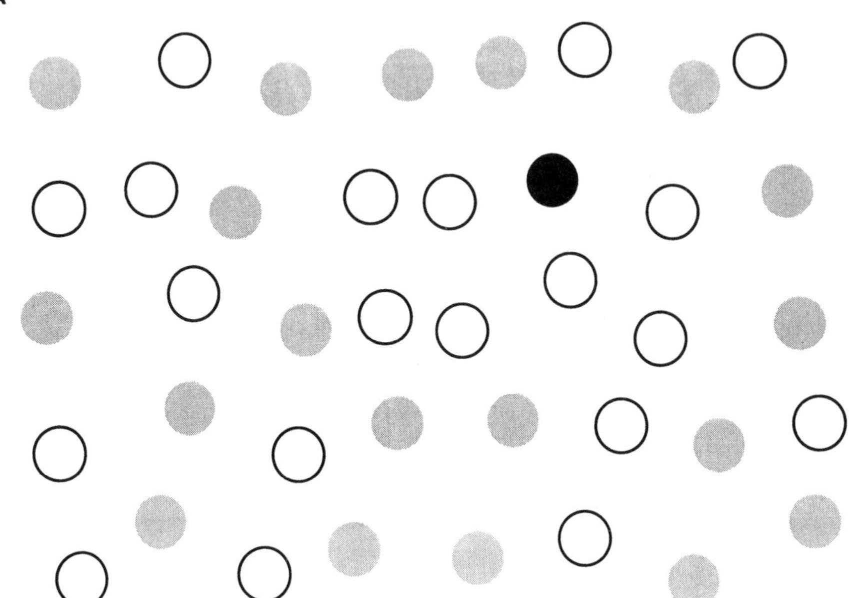

Figure 4-2 Stimulus characterization of stimulus patterns used in the Eglin et al. (1989) study of search performance in patients with neglect. (The original stimuli were in color with red represented by the black dots, blue by the open dots and yellow by the grey dots.) (A) Feature search stimulus—target is on the right with 19 same-side distractors and 20 opposite-side distractors. (B) Conjunction search stimulus—target is on the left with 0 same-side distractors and 20 opposite-side distractors. (C) Conjunction search stimulus—target is on the left with 19 same-side distractors and 0 opposite-side distractors. (D) Conjunction search stimulus—target is on the left with 19 same-side distractors and 20 opposite-side distractors.

conjunction of red and line. In this case reaction time increases linearly with increasing number of distractors in the display.[1]

Eglin, Robertson, and Knight (1989) and Riddoch and Humphreys (1987) exploited this fact by examining search for features and conjunctions in patients with visual neglect. Again, if the major source of neglect were attentional, neglect should be observed when patients searched for a conjunction and not when they searched for a feature. The prediction was that patients with neglect, at least those who were testable, would be able to respond equally rapidly to a feature like a red dot among other dots (Figure 4-2A), whether the red dot was presented on the neglected or intact side of space. On the other hand, locating a conjunction should create great difficulty when appearing on the side contralateral to the lesion because spatial attention is required to detect such a target. Although clinically, patients who are tested at bedside often look as if they could not attend to anything on the neglected side no matter what task was used, features are typically not tested. Such questions as "is there something red?" are not asked when the only thing red is on the neglected side. The fact that many patients with neglect also have visual field deficits makes the response to such

B

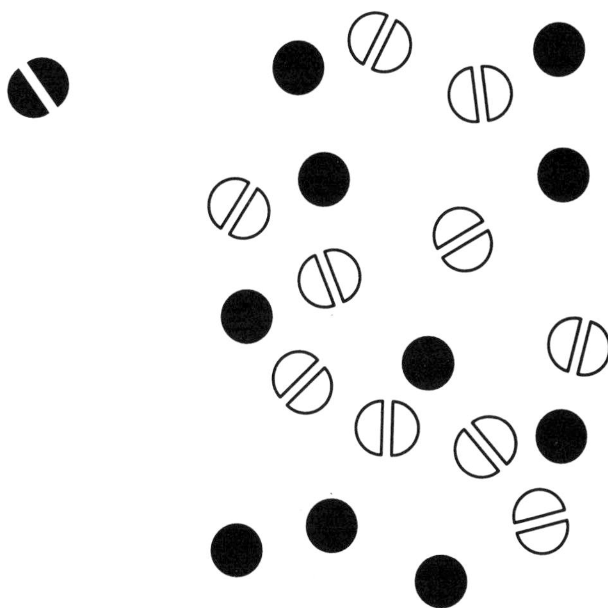

Figure 4-2 *(Continued)*

a question even more difficult to interpret especially in the acute stage. In fact, on the basis of a study by Riddoch and Humphreys (1987), we (Eglin, Robertson, & Knight, 1989) suspected that patients with neglect would be able to respond to features equally well on the neglected and intact side but would not be able to respond to conjunctions on the neglected side when distractors were on the intact side. As it turned out we were wrong. Informal bedside testing of the first patient with right middle cerebral artery infarct showed that he had difficulty locating conjunction targets on the neglected side, but he eventually found them on all but a handful of trials (less than 4%). This occurred despite the fact that he had a severe case of neglect with all the classical signs. In the Albert's line cancellation task, he would not cancel more than the first two columns of lines on the right side even when encouraged to do so; denied hemiparesis of his left leg; did not orient into left space; and could not copy the left side of simple figures. Yet given time, both the feature and conjunction targets were salient enough to be found on the contralateral side even by a person with such severe neglect. This was in contrast to Riddoch and Humphrey's (1987) findings where high error rates occurred on the neglected side. This is likely due to the fact that they used a presence/absence task and we used a location task. This means that on half the trials in their study no target was present and the subject was asked to say yes or no. Our data demonstrate that as long as a patient knows a target is somewhere in the array on each trial, search will continue until the target is found, and the patient will eventually attend to the neglected side on his own accord. We went on to test six more patients with severe neglect (they

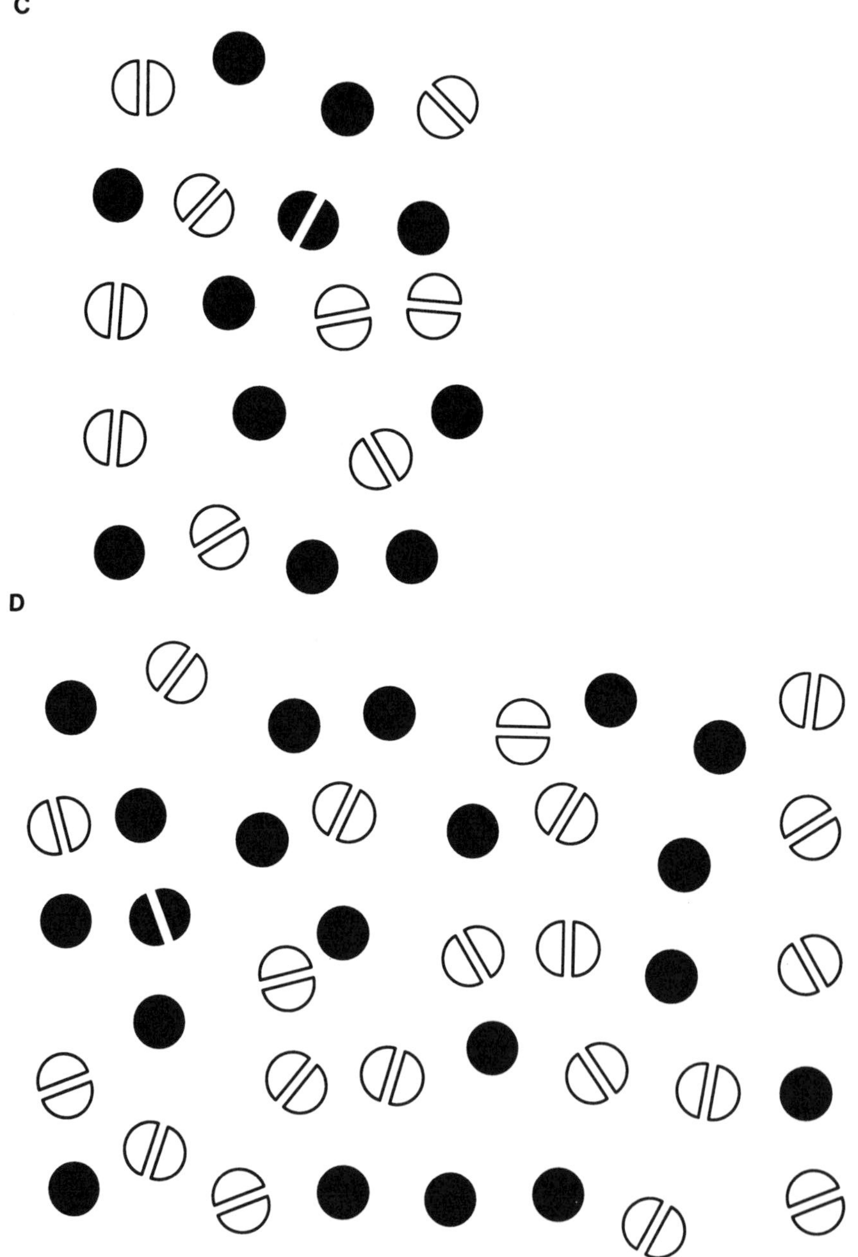

Figure 4-2 *(Continued)*

could not cancel lines across the midline of the page in Albert's line cancellation task even when urged to do so), and we found the same effects.

In testing these patients we used a Treisman feature and conjunction search task varying the number of distractors in the display, but added an additional factor of left or right side target crossed with the number of left and right side

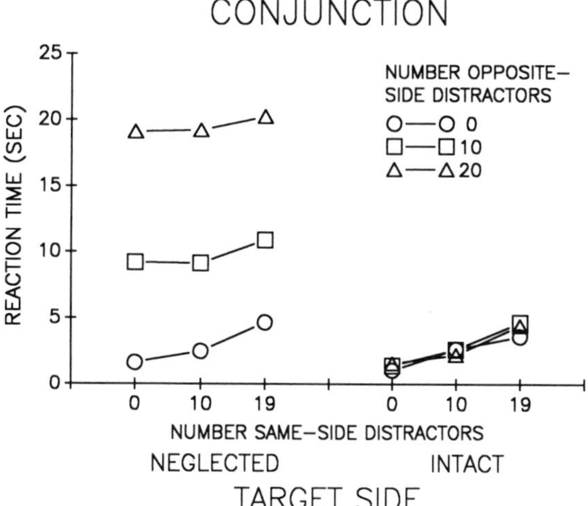

Figure 4-3 Reaction time for conjunction search as a function of number of same-side and opposite-side distractors.

distractors. Thus, the number of targets and distractors varied independently on each side of the array so we could examine the influence of distractors on the intact and neglected sides. Several important findings emerged and they can be seen in Figure 4-3. I will first discuss the conjunction search data.

First, search rates on the neglected and intact sides were the same when no distractors appeared on the opposite side (the O-opposite side distractor condition in Figure 4-3). In other words, when nothing was on the intact side, patients searched the neglected side as easily as they did the intact side and began the search as rapidly. Second, in all cases the functions on the intact and neglected sides increased linearly and equally with increasing number of distractors *on the same side as the target* (i.e., there was serial search whether on the intact or neglected side). Once attention was directed to the neglected field, search occurred in the same way as in the intact field. Third, distractors on the neglected side had no effect at all on responding to targets on the intact side (the three opposite-side distractor functions over-lap for the intact side in Figure 4-3). Unlike normals who are influenced by the number of dots across the entire visual display, in patients, only distractors on the intact side affect search on the intact side. Despite the fact that neglected side targets were responded to when no distractors were on the intact side to draw attention, the distractors on the neglected side were completely ignored when attention was drawn to the intact side. In contrast, the number of distractors on the intact side affected the time to begin searching for a target on the neglected side. This difficulty increased disproportionately as the attentional demands (i.e., the number of distractors) on the intact side increased. These findings are consistent with a disengage problem, but the problem is one of disengaging from the intact side of space. It is as if the patients searched the intact side several times before moving to the neglected side, and the time to search the intact side increased with the number of distractors on that side.

Like Posner et al.'s (1984) patients, subjects were able to move their attention into the neglected side as fast as they could move it into the intact side *as long as no distractors appeared on the intact side.* This finding also demonstrates that visual field or eye movement deficits could not account for the results. Subjects were able to move into the neglected field when no distractors were on the intact side. Futhermore, once attention was moved into the neglected side, search continued through that side at the same rate as on the intact side (i.e., attention acted normally once it was moved to the neglected side).

As with Posner et al.'s subjects who were relatively unimpaired clinically, our subjects with obvious and severe visual neglect had no difficulty in responding to targets on the neglected side when nothing appeared on the intact side to draw attention to it. When stimulation was present on the intact side attention was drawn to it, and the subjects had difficulty disengaging attention to move it into the neglected side. More importantly, as the attentional demands of patterns on the intact side increased, the time to move to the neglected side increased as well.

Unlike Riddoch and Humphreys' (1987) study where no neglect was found for feature search, performance in the feature task in our study was similar to that in the conjunction task. Whereas Riddoch and Humphrey found evidence for intact parallel preattentive search, we did not. Again, the reason is likely to be that they used a presence/absence task, while we used a location task. In a presence/absence task, subjects only have to say whether or not a feature was there and not *where* it was. By introducing a location task, we forced the patients to locate targets. In fact, feature integration theory proposes that conjunction search occurs serially because conjunctions must be located among a group of distractors. Features are searched in parallel and need not be located to know of their presence. By changing to a task in which locating the objects was required, we overcame the high error rates in conjunction search that Riddoch and Humphreys found, but at the same time added an extra demand for locating the object for feature search.

What relevance do these findings have for clinical practice? First, they demonstrate very clearly that the degree of neglect observed will be a function of the attentional demands on the intact side of space. They also demonstrate that the nature and number of patterns used can have profound effects on whether or not clinical neglect will be observed. For instance, the number of lines and their spacing on a line cancellation task could be crucial. If only a few lines appeared on the intact side, no signs of neglect might be found, while manipulating the physical characteristics of the lines on the intact side (e.g., density, length, orientation) may reveal substantial neglect.

Posner et al.'s findings are also important for this argument. Recall that only one of their patients had moderate signs of neglect. Whether patients were classified as having neglect or not, they showed disengage problems under timed conditions. Neglect, at least in part, appears to lie on a continuum of an attentional disengagement deficit. Even small changes can make a large difference in how attention demanding a stimulus might be. Obviously, some standardization is required. It would seem impossible to equate the attentional demands of, say, a flower a patient is asked to draw with clock numbers or with a line cancellation task. Also the number of lines, their density, and even the length of lines to be cancelled should have an effect on how far a patient will traverse across the page into the neglected side before stopping. An interesting and elegantly simple example of this was recently reported by Mark, Kooistra, and Heilman (1988) by having patients erase lines rather than cancel them, a very easy task to use at bedside. Conversely, just because a patient cancels all lines on a page, draws both sides of a flower equally well, places the numbers on a clock appropriately, and has no observable signs of neglect does not mean there is no neglect present. These same patients placed in Posner et al.'s or Eglin et al.'s task may show a slowing into contralateral space that would not be detected on standard tests.

Perhaps it would help to keep in mind that neglect and extinction refer to behavioral phenomena and have no special significance as a classification other than what we give them. A disengage deficit that varies in degree of severity is not a replacement for these categories but is one of the likely component operations that contributes to the phenomena. If we find that this disengagement deficit is most correlated with parietal damage but does not occur with other areas of damage that produce clinical neglect, then we are a step further toward being able to predict specific behavioral signs of neglect on the basis of lesion site and also closer to an understanding of the neural basis of neglect. Obviously there is more to neglect than simple disengagement of attention. Anosognosia, allesthesia and the patients' seeming unawareness of the neglected side must all be explained. However, the data I have discussed in this section go a long way in understanding at least one fundamental operation that contributes to visual neglect. It is left to future studies to determine the degree to which disengage operations interact with others to result in the collection of deficits observed in patients suffering from hemispatial visual neglect.

VISUAL ORGANIZATION OF GLOBAL AND LOCAL LEVELS

It may seem a long jump from neglect to the perception of global and local levels, but in fact there has been a history in neuropsychology associating right parietal lobe function with neglect and with disruption of the global analysis of form. Although we are not clear about the relationship between deficits in responding to global parts of objects and neglect, or even if there is one, in clinical populations it is the case that similar lesions can cause either type of problem and sometimes both. As will be seen in this section, whatever the relationship, it is not a simple one, and I will not be able to answer the question fully, but there are some intriguing commonalities that will become evident as the discussion progresses. However, the first order of business for the present purposes is to examine how cognitive models and methods have helped in understanding processes that contribute to the perceptual disruption of global and local levels of form.

Objects are perceived as parts embedded within other objects (i.e., local objects are perceived as parts of global objects). However, a drawer does not lose its "drawerness" by being embedded within a desk, nor is it necessary for a desk to include drawers to be a desk. What mechanism does the visual system

```
EEEE
E
EEEE
   E
EEEE
```

Figure 4-4 Example of hierarchically constructed stimulus. The letter "S" is at the global level and the letter "E" at the local.

use to accomplish this integration yet segregation of objects within objects? In order to address this question, I will first discuss evidence from cognitive psychology. This will then be extended to the study of brain injured patients and a discussion of how this work has clarified the component operations and the anatomical correlates involved. Unlike in neglect, a theory developed in normals has not received convergent evidence from research with patients. Rather the work with patients has suggested a different theory of normal cognition.

Level Advantage and Theoretical Concerns

It was originally thought that perceptual wholes were built up from their constituent parts, but the gestalt psychologists demonstrated quite clearly that this need not be the case (see Robertson, 1986, for an overview). The perceived whole could be *different* from the sum of its parts. In an era of information processing, the question has been rephrased as what is processed first, the whole or its parts. Do wholes emerge from their parts with parts being perceived first, or are parts parsed from their wholes with wholes being perceived first?

It was Krech in 1938 who first suggested that objects were perceived in a "hierarchical order of levels of perceptual organization" with higher levels of the hierarchy being perceived before lower levels (Krech and Calvin, 1953; Krechevsky, 1938). This hypothesis was based on the fact that learning to discriminate visual stimuli proceeded from the more general to the more specific. In 1977, Navon echoed this hypothesis within an information processing framework. He proposed a model that he termed "global precedence." According to this model, the visual system proceeded from global information (higher levels of the hierarchy) to local information (lower levels of the hierarchy). The model was based on two findings, a global advantage in reaction time and global interference. Responses for identifying global forms were overall faster than for local forms in a pattern with global and local levels such as shown in Figure 4-4. In addition to this global advantage, the identity of the global form increased reaction time to respond to the local form when it was inconsistent (i.e., a global S would interfere with identification of a local E), but inconsistent local forms did not slow reaction time in identifying global forms. This asymmetrical slowing reflected global interference and supported the model of global procedure, since information could not be ignored in responding to local information, but the reverse was true. Hypothetically, both global advantage and global interference were due to the same underlying operations of global precedence.

Several subsequent studies demonstrated that these effects could be changed by changes in the sensory quality of the input (retinal location, the relative size of the two levels, visual angle, etc.) or by changes in task demands (e.g., divided vs. focused attention conditions, spatial uncertainty, instructions, etc.), and the theory fell into disfavor as a result (Hoffman, 1980; Kimchi & Palmer, 1982; Kinchla & Wolfe, 1979; Kinchla, Solis-Macias, & Hoffman, 1983; Lamb & Robertson, 1988; Miller, 1981; Pomerantz, 1983; Robertson & Palmer, 1983). However, Navon never claimed that other perceptual and cognitive operations were irrelevant in global advantage and global interference. He made it very clear that global precedence occurred "all else being equal" (1981). Operationally, this meant that there was equal performance for isolated large and small letters, but global advantage and global interference when the same sized letters were arranged hierarchically. In Navon's view, global precedence was a principle of the visual perceptual system, but its observation could only be guaranteed if differential stimulus quality between global and local levels and task parameters were controlled or ruled out as possible causes for the effects. Despite this claim, various researchers have continued to either trivialize Navon's findings as an artifact of visual sensory processes or to explain them as an effect of a higher order cognitive mechanism such as control over attentional distribution to global or local levels. As a backdrop to this debate, the issue of whether perception begins with local or global levels remained unanswered with some evidence supporting local to global processing and other evidence supporting global to local processing as proposed by Navon. As will be seen in the following paragraphs, the data from neuropsychological evidence has shown that the visual system does both and could possibly do them both at the same time.

The neuropsychological data have also shown that the pattern of performance is a combination of both automatic perceptual processes and controlled attentional processes. As a result of these data a more complex model of hierarchical organization than Navon's has emerged (Robertson & Lamb, 1991). This model includes several cognitive mechanisms that can be independently affected by neural damage yet are interconnected in the normal brain. These mechanisms interact to produce the final output in normals that results in a global or local level advantage or level interference. These mechanisms include one that is biased toward global information (i.e., produces faster response times to global than local levels of Figure 4-4) and is disrupted by right superior temporal and adjacent caudel parietal lobe lesions (RSTG); another that is biased toward local levels and is disrupted by analogous left posterior lesions (LSTG); a third that controls attentional allocation to global and local levels and is disrupted by more rostal inferior parietal lesions (IPL); and a fourth that interconnects global and local levels and appears to rely on cross communication between left and right posterior regions.

This componential model emerged as a result of many studies performed in brain-injured patients and from studies with normals reported in the cognitive literature. In the beginning we did not suspect that we would find such rich pasture for theoretical development as we did. Our original purpose in testing neurological patients was to test Navon's model in patients to determine whether processing global and local levels could be disrupted independently. Was there one mechanisn that processed one level first and then the other; or were there two mechanisms—one dedicated to global analysis and one to local? Toward this end, we began rather crudely. At first, we were not terribly concerned with the underlying neural structures involved in such organization, but rather in the use of regional damage to test for independence between cognitive processes, and indeed we found such evidence. Patients with right hemisphere damage did not recall or recognize, and were less influenced by global level information than local. Patients with left hemisphere damage did not recall or recognize and were less influenced by local information than global (Delis, Robertson, & Efron, 1986; Robertson & Delis, 1986). This occurred whether the stimuli were linguistic or nonlinguistic in nature.

Several subsequent studies in chronic patients, using slightly different methods but all measuring reaction time, supported these results. The global or local reaction time advantage observed depended on the hemisphere involved. Right hemisphere damage resulted in a local advantage, and left hemisphere damage resulted in a global advantage relative to controls (Lamb, Robertson, & Knight, 1989; Lamb, Robertson, & Knight, 1990; Robertson, Lamb, & Knight, 1988; Robertson & Lamb, 1991). These findings were also consistent with studies using half field presentation in normals (Martin, 1979; Sergent, 1982). It is important that all patients were able to respond to both levels, but the order of response was different. This suggests that the hemispheres are not dichotomous in their level of response (global or local) but dichotomous in the relative time of availability of global or local information measured against some baseline condition. If normals produce a baseline global reaction time advantage in a given task, an RSTG (right superior temporal gyrus with adjacent parietal involvement) group will show a reduced global advantage and a left STG group an increased global advantage. If normals show no baseline advantage, right hemisphere patients will show a local advantage and left hemisphere a global advantage.

Unlike the initial experiments, the studies with reaction time used relatively high functioning patients with smaller lesions who were at least six months post injury to reduce effects of edema on adjacent regions. By utilizing such groups, we have repeatedly shown that damage to right or left STG produces the asymmetry; whereas damage limited to inferior parietal regions does not. More recently we have also found normal performance in patients with dorsolateral prefrontal lesions (Robertson, Lamb, & Knight, 1990). It therefore appears that processes supported by the RSTG in normals are biased toward analyzing global information, and others supported by the LSTG are biased toward analyzing local information.

The findings suggest a somewhat different notion of hemisphere asymmetry in global/local analysis than previously held. First, the asymmetry seems to be produced by isolated lesions in inferior posterior regions, specifically STG regions. Second, the asymmetry is not all or none. It is simply a bias toward one level or the other that makes information at one level available before information at the other. Third, there are two mechanisms, one that makes global information available before local and one that does the reverse. All else being equal, there are both global and local advantage in the perceptual system.

HEMISPHERE LATERALITY AND GLOBAL/LOCAL LEVELS

Perhaps the findings that left and right hemisphere damage differentially effect levels of a stimulus pattern are not particularly surprising. Neuropsychologists have suggested for some time that the perception of parts and their wholes are analyzed by separate mechanisms. Right posterior damage often results in test scores that reflect difficulty in responding to a visual pattern as a whole, while left hemisphere damage often results in difficulty responding to the parts. Such observations led to various theories of functional hemisphere asymmetry suggesting that the right hemisphere was specialized for processing wholes, gestalts, or configurations, while the left hemisphere was specialized for processing parts or details. Although these theories were little more than a description of the observations, the differences between right and left hemisphere damaged patients in responding to parts and their wholes were reliable and robust (see Bradshaw & Nettleton, 1981; De Renzi, 1982, for overviews). Until recently cognitive psychologists essentially ignored such data, and for the most part neuropsychologists ignored findings in the cognitive literature.

The more recent findings make important clarifications about the type of part-whole relationships that are disrupted. In a hierarchical stimulus the so-called parts are simply lower level wholes nested within higher level wholes. There are wholes at both the global and local levels. It is therefore not quite correct to conceive of the breakdown observed in right or left hemisphere injured patients as due to a deficit in processing parts or details on the one hand and wholes or gestalts on the other (cf. Robertson & Delis, 1986). In the pattern in Figure 4-4, a local letter is as much a whole in its own right as the global letter. They are both whole forms with their own parts (e.g., horizontal and vertical lines, angles, etc.). One benefit of using a form of this type is that the wholes at the two levels are interchangeable. The E's in Figure 4-4 can be changed to S's, yet the global level will remain the same, and the global level can be changed to an E without affecting the identity of the local level. This property makes these figures more useful as experimental stimuli than clinical instruments such as the Rey-Osterreith, block design, or normal scenes.

Investigations in neuropsychology have been detoured by the idea that functional asymmetry is related to parts and wholes in some general sense which has given rise to such all-encompassing theories as analytic versus holistic processing (Bradshaw & Nettleton, 1981), or detail versus configural processing (Kaplan, 1976) in accounting for performance asymmetries. Differences between right and left hemisphere damaged patients do not reflect an all or none response. It simply takes longer to respond to local than global information in chronic patients if left STG damage occurs and longer to respond to global than local information if right STG damage occurs. Whatever is lateralized in responding to global and local levels of complex visual scenes, it is difficult for it to be explained by simplified theories that postulate hemispheric bifurcation of processing parts and wholes. The real question, of course, is what cognitive mechanisms and/or stimulus parameters are responsible for the performance differences between left and right STG groups. Our first attempt to answer this question is the subject of the next section.

Attention and the Inferior Parietal Lobe

We began by asking what role attention might play in the observed performance asymmetries between right and left injured patients and found a fascinating set of results. These results showed that the distribution of attention between global and local levels was disrupted by IPL lesions, while patients with STG lesions who exhibited the asymmetry were perfectly capable of controlling the distribution of attention to the two levels even though they had an overall bias toward one level or the other (Robertson, Lamb, & Knight, 1988). (There was also an overall reaction time advantage in the IPL group that was either due to a speed-accuracy trade-off or to something more interesting like disruption of inhibition. Since we cannot discriminate between these accounts, I will not pursue it further.)

As in almost every other area of neuropsychological research (aphasia, dementia, apraxia, etc.), the concept of a unitary mechanism has become untenable. In clinical lore, patients with frontal lesions have "attentional deficits." However, the deficits seem to be a vigilance problem (i.e., a deficit in sustaining attention; Stuss & Benson, 1987). Another type of attention called "selective attention" refers to the ability to attend to relevant aspects in a stimulus, ignoring irrelevant aspects. Perhaps the best example is the cocktail party effect in which one can attend to the conversation of one person while ignoring virtually all conversation from other persons. Although there has been a great deal of investigation in cognitive psychology on how this selectivity might occur (e.g., is the information filtered early or late), the important point for now is that there is some device that is able to select specific aspects of the sensory array on which to attend while ignoring others. Kahneman (1973) presented several findings suggesting that attention to selected aspects was "capacity limited." That is, attention allocated to one aspect of an array could consume all resources available, while attention divided between two or more aspects divided the resources and performance changed accordingly.

Capacity limitation of attentional resources predicted that the more attentional resources given to one aspect of the stimulus, the less would be available for others. Thus, performance would become better for an item as more resources were allocated to it and worse as resources were allocated to other aspects. There would be cost/benefit trade-offs in performance. Kahneman further proposed that there was effort involved in allocating resources. Certain processing did not require effort and therefore did not require attentional resources. These were automatic processes (see also Shiffrin and Schneider, 1977; Schneider & Shiffrin, 1977). For instance, certain information like a person's own name will be heard from an unattended source even when concerted concentration is focused on something else, and highly practiced tasks such as driving a car can be accomplished while carrying on a conversation, although this cannot be accomplished very well when one is learning to drive (testimonies by teenagers to the contrary). Spelke, Hirst, and Neisser (1976) showed that, with extended practice, subjects can even read and comprehend a text while writing dictated words without any decrement in performance. Decrements in performance were observed in initial testing sessions consistent with attention being divided between the two tasks at the beginning of testing and producing cost/benefit trade-offs. As learning progressed, fewer and fewer resources were necessary to a point where attention was not needed at all. The tasks had become effortless and automatic. In sum, there are processes that are resource independent and processes that are resource dependent.

Capacity limitations and controlled and automatic processes are relevant for how global and local performance can be changed and what portions of the cortex support these different functions. Recall that capacity limitations predict that when attention is allocated to one aspect of a display, response to that aspect will benefit and response to other aspects will suffer (i.e., trade-offs in performance will occur). This also happens in responding to global and local levels in normals. Kinchla et al. (1983) varied the probability that a target would appear at either the global or local level of a hierarchical pattern hypothesizing that subjects would change their allocation of attention between the two levels in accordance with the probability schedules. His evidence supported this hypothesis. When local targets were more likely, responses were easier for local targets and harder for global targets compared to a 50/50 neutral condition. When global targets were more likely, responses were easier for global targets and harder for local targets.

We replicated these effects in older normal subjects. Kinchla et al. used college-age students; whereas our subjects were older adults with a mean age of about 55. We also replicated the effects in patient groups with frontal lesions and a group with left temporal-parietal lesions (STG) but not with more superior left parietal (IPL) lesions (Robertson, Lamb, & Knight, 1988). (In this study right hemisphere damaged subjects could not be broken down into STG and IPL groups.) The relevant data are replotted from the original article in Figure 4-5 which included LSTG, LIPL and RTP (large right temporal-parietal) groups with right hemisphere lesions overlapping STG and IPL regions. Notice that LSTG patients were faster at responding to global targets in the 50/50 baseline condition, while RTP patients showed the reversed pattern as expected. In contrast, the LIPL group, like the normal controls, showed no significant bias toward one level or the other. The findings were quite different in the conditions where target probabilities were different for the two levels. The LIPL patients showed reduced trade-offs over baseline conditions indicative of a deficit in reallocating attention under the different probability schedules. In fact, there were no significant differences between probability schedules for this group. The LSTG patients showed a normal cost/benefit tradeoff relative to their baseline condition. Although their reaction times were predictably biased toward local targets overall, the tradeoff was evident and robust as it was in normals. In other words, LIPL patients showed no evidence of controlling attention normally to the two levels over probability schedules, while LSTG patients did.

Controlled attentional processes and the automatic perceptual encoding of global and local levels can be disrupted independently. Because LSTG patients did reallocate attention normally even with a large change in level advantage, attentional processes cannot be the basis for the local advantage. It follows that the hemisphere asymmetry in responding to global and local level information

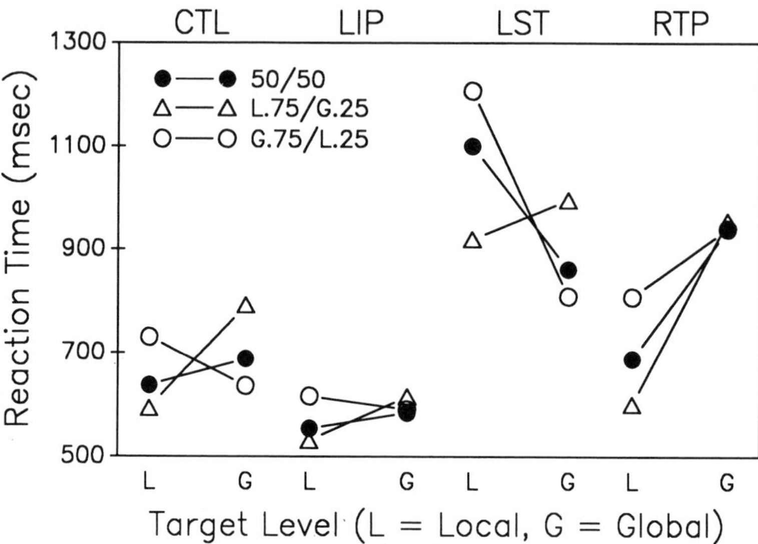

Figure 4-5 Reaction time as a function of target level for the global bias, local bias, and no bias conditions.

that we have consistently observed between RSTG and LSTG is not due to deficits in controlled attentional processes.

To this point, we have isolated three cognitive operations involved in responding to hierarchical patterns: one that is biased toward local information, one biased toward global information, and one that controls attentional distribution between global and local levels. There is also a fourth operation that we think functions to integrate the two levels, and this will be the topic of the next section.

Interaction Between Levels, Hemisphere Transfer, and Simultanagnosia

The fact that we naturally want to call a local element a *part* of the global form signifies the degree to which we perceive the two levels of structure as interconnected, despite the fact that there are whole forms at the two levels. We never lose that fact perceptually. Nothing I have described so far has addressed the issue of how the two levels could be linked together to form an integrated pattern. Understanding this integration seems especially relevant for the study of certain types of visual agnosia. Simultanagnosia, for instance, refers to a deficit in integrating parts to form a whole (Kinsbourne & Warrington, 1963), a deficit also described in Humphreys et al's. (1985) case of a person who had what they termed "integrative visual agnosia" (Humphreys & Riddoch, 1987).

In order to understand this problem fully for the integration of global and local levels, it will first be necessary to return to Navon's original findings. Recall that global precedence theory was based on two effects, an overall global advantage (collapsed over consistency) and global interference in responding to the local level, but not vice versa (an interaction between level and consistency). Navon argued that interference occurred because global information was processed before local (i.e., global advantage and global interference were derived from the same underlying process, namely global precedence). However, this has not received consistent support. Subsequent studies in normals have shown that the level advantage and level interference can vary independently, supporting independence between global advantage and global interference (Navon & Norman, 1983; Lamb & Robertson, 1989b). Global interference can even be found when there is a large local reaction time advantage (Lamb & Robertson, 1989a). Facilitation is also evident between levels under certain conditions (Miller, 1981; Robertson & Palmer, 1983). We have argued that the facilitation and interference between levels reflects an integration process separate from a level identification process (Lamb, Robertson, & Knight, 1989; Robertson & Lamb, 1991). To support this argument, we have repeatedly shown that groups with IPL lesions produce normal interactions between global and local levels, while STG lesions eliminate the interaction completely. Note that interaction is eliminated in the same patient groups who produce an asymmetric overall advantage to global or local levels. However, there is a very important difference between the effect of STG lesions on advantage and interference. A lesion in LSTG causes an overall global advantage and a lesion in RSTG causes an overall local advantage, but the effect of a lesion *on either side* is to eliminate the interaction between the two levels.

This does not mean that integration never occurs in these patients. The elimination of the interaction in our studies was found with time-limited displays (100 msec), and subjects were clearly able to perform activities of daily living that would require some form of perceptual integration. None were suffering from clinical signs of neglect or simultanagnosia or obvious integrative visual agnosia in Humphreys and Riddoch's terms. However, when pushed, our subjects had trouble with the structural organization of the pattern in a way that suggests a problem in placing local elements in an overall pattern as in simultanagnosia and Humphrey and Riddoch's case of "integrative agnosia" (a case referred to as John). The investigators concluded that John had difficulty binding parts into a whole and found, as we did, a lack of interaction in this patient using stimuli like those we have been using.

One question that inevitably arises is how we could be testing the same deficit as in John, since he had bilateral inferior occipital temporal infarcts—lesions generally considered necessary to produce visual agnosia. How can we reconcile our findings in LSTG and RSTG patients with results from these other investigators? One way is to consider the deficit as a disconnection syndrome between asymmetrically represented input channels. Lesions that disrupt the cross talk between inferior posterior areas can result in a reduction or elimination of interaction between the two levels. Bilateral inferior temporal-occipital infarcts should produce the most severe deficits in this respect, and indeed they do. John had difficulty integrating parts of visual stimuli even when a pattern was presented to him without time limits.

In summary, the cognitive and neuropsychological data collected to date have pointed to a more complex theory of hierarchical organization of global/local levels of a visual pattern than either neuropsychologists or cognitive psychologists suspected. I have summarized our findings on the right side of Table

Table 4-1

Region Damaged	Performance Decrement
Left STG	Slower local than global identification (relative to controls) No global/local interaction Normal tradeoffs associated with attention
Right STG	Slower global than local identification (relative to controls) No global/local interaction Tradeoffs unknown but probably normal
Left IPL	Normal global/local identification Normal global/local interaction Reduced or absent tradeoffs
Right IPL	Normal global/local identification Normal global/local interaction Probable reduced tradeoffs

4-1. Frontal patients are not represented, as we found them to be normal (Robertson et al., 1990).

Finally, a schematic outline of the regions and interconnections which seem to support various functional components of global/local analysis are presented in Figure 4-6. I fully admit that this figure presents little more than a correlation of the lesion sites to the functional component believed to be associated with the particular deficit in performance. It is well known that a lesion in one region affects several other sites via efferent and afferent connections. Given the limitations of lesion studies, the schematic in Figure 4-6 should be considered a

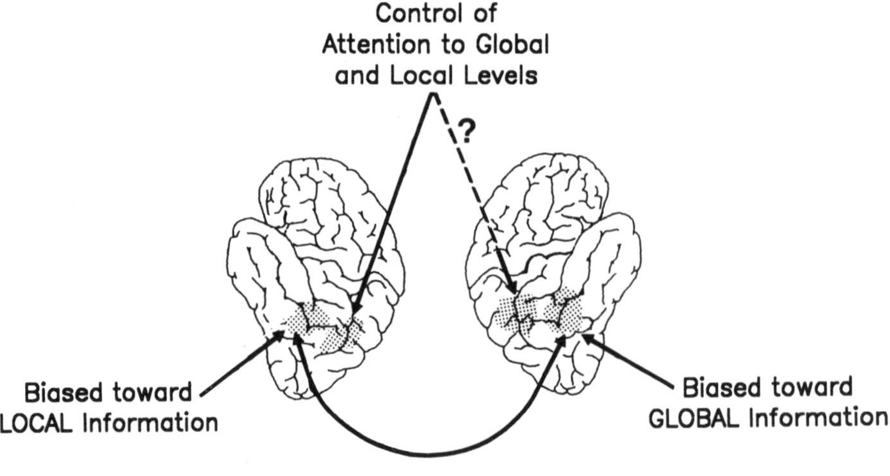

Figure 4-6 Schematic drawing of proposed component operations in analyzing hierarchical patterns and regions of neural damage that are sufficient to disrupt each operation.

working model in need of verification by investigations of lesions in strongly connected regions and/or by physiological measures. We obviously have much further to go than we have come, but clearly the combination of cognitive theory and neuropsychological investigations into perception of hierarchically arranged visual stimuli has taken us further in our understanding of the component processes and their underlying neural mechanisms than either area of investigation has been able to do alone.

CONCLUSION

In this chapter, I have tried to show how the application of perceptual and attentional theories derived from cognitive psychology can improve our understanding of specific types of deficits. In discussing deficits of attention and perceptual organization, I presented findings from brain injured patients with focal cortical lesions to demonstrate how cognitive theory can influence and be influenced by neuropsychological investigations. The examples I discussed in the section on neglect demonstrate how a deficit that has resisted understanding is becoming harnessed by applying cognitive methodology and theories to the problem. The examples from studies of global and local perceptual dysfunction demonstrate how theories of normal cognition can be changed by neuropsychological findings.

The message for testing patients is similar in both cases. Posner et al. (1984) were able to demonstrate deficits in attentional shifts to contralateral space in patients who had few or no clinical signs of neglect at the time of testing. By using brief displays and measuring reaction time, they were able to find a performance deficit with behavioral properties similar to neglect that were evident way beyond the acute stage. Similarly, cognitive tasks that measured response to global and local levels of a pattern were able to detect deficits in patients who showed few signs of impairment in everyday life nor any sign of neglect, simultanagnosia or visual agnosia upon examination. In either case, the story is not complete, nor will it be in the near future. Nevertheless, the influence of cognitive psychology has changed the nature of neuropsychological investigation of these and other deficits and will clearly continue to do so.

ACKNOWLEDGMENTS

I wish to thank David Margolin and Robert Rafal for their comments and careful reading of previous versions of this paper. I also wish to thank Linda Kerth and John Lackey for figure preparation and Marvin Lamb and Mirjam Eglin for their intellectual inspiration. Preparation of this manuscript was supported by VA Medical Research funds and by ADAMHA grant award #AA06637.

NOTE

1. Although some recent investigators have questioned the underlying basis of these effects (e.g., Duncan & Humphreys, 1989; Wolfe, Cave, & Franzel, 1989), it remains a

fact that features such as color do not typically produce a significant linearly increasing slope as distractor numbers increase, while the conjunction of features generally do.

REFERENCES

Battersby, W. S., Bender, M. B., Pollack, M., & Kahn, R. (1956). Unilateral spatial agnosia (inattention) in patients with cerebral lesions. *Brain*, *79*, 68–93.

Bender, M. B. (1952). *Disorders in perception*. Springfield, IL: C. C. Thomas

Bisiach, E., & Berti, A. (1985). Dyschiria: An attempt at its systemic explanation. In M. Jeannerod (Ed.), *Neurophysiological and neuropsychological aspects of spatial neglect*. N. Holland: Elsevier Science Publishers.

Bisiach, E., Capitani, E., Luzzatti, C., & Perani, D. (1981). Brain and conscious representation of outside reality. *Neuropsychologia*, *19*, 543–551.

Bradshaw., J. L., & Nettleton, N. C. (1981). The nature of hemispheric specialization in man. *The Behavior and Brain Sciences*, *4*, 51–91.

Calvanio, R., Petrone, P. N., & Levine, D. N. (1987). Left visual spatial neglect is both environment-centered and body-centered. *Neurology*, *37*, 1179–1183.

Delis, D. C., Robertson, L. C., & Efron, R. (1986). Hemispheric specialization of memory for visual hierarchical stimuli. *Neuropsychologia*, *24*, 205–204.

Denny-Brown, D., & Banker, B. (1954). Amorphosynthesis from left parietal lesions. *Archives of Neurological Psychiatry*, *71*, 302–313.

DeRenzi, E. (1982). *Disorders of space exploration and cognition*. New York: Wiley

Duncan, J., & Humphreys, G. W. (1989). Visual speech and stimulus similarity. *Psychological Review*, *96*, 433–458.

Eglin, M., Robertson, L. C., & Knight, R. T. (1989). Visual search performance in the neglect syndrome. *Journal of Cognitive Neuroscience*, *4*, 372–381.

Ellis, H. D. (1986). Introduction: processes underlying face recognition. In R. Bruyer (Ed.), *The neuropsychology of face perception and facial expression*. (pp 1–17). Hillsdale, NJ: Lawrence Erlbaum Associates.

Farah, M. J., Brunn, J. L., Wong, A. B., Wallace, M. A., & Carpenter, P. A. (1990). Frames of reference for allocating attention to space: Evidence from the neglect syndrome. *Neuropsychologia 28*, 335–347.

Heilman, K. M. (1979). Neglect and related disorders. In K. M. Heilman & E. Valenstein (Eds.), *Clinical neuropsychology* (1st ed) (pp 268–307). New York: Oxford University Press.

Heilman, K. M., Watson, R. T., & Valenstein, E. (1985). Neglect and related disorders. In K. M. Heilman & E. Valenstein (Eds.), *Clinical neuropsychology* (2nd ed.) (pp. 243–293). New York: Oxford University Press.

Hoffman, J. R. (1980). Interaction between global and local levels of a form. *Journal of Experimental Psychology: Human Perception & Performance 6*, 222, 234.

Humphreys, G. W., Riddoch, M. J., & Quinlan, P. T. (1985). Interactive processes in perceptual organization: Evidence from visual agnosia. In M. I. Posner & O. S. M. Marin (Eds.). *Attention & Performance XI* (pp. 301–318). Hillsdale, NJ: Lawrence Erlbaum.

Humphreys, G. W., & Riddoch, M. J. (1987). *To see but not to see: A case study of visual agnosia*. London: Lawrence Earlbaum Associates.

Humphreys, G. W., & Riddoch, M. J. (1984). Routes to object constancy. *Quarterly Journal of Experimental Psychology*, *36A*, 385–415.

Kahneman, D. (1973). *Attention and effort*. Englewood Cliffs, NJ: Prentice-Hall.

Kaplan, E. (1976). *The role of the uncompromised hemisphere in focal organic disease*.

Paper presented at the American Psychology Association meeting, Washington, DC.

Kimchi, R., & Palmer, S. (1982). Form and texture in hierarchically constructed patterns. *Journal of Experimental Psychology: Human Perception & Performance 8*, 521–535.

Kinchla, R. A., Solis-Macias, V., & Hoffman, J. (1983). Attending to different levels of structure in a visual image. *Perception & Psychophysics*, *33*, 1–10.

Kinchla, R. A., & Wolfe, J. M. (1979). The order of visual processing: "top-down," "bottom-up," or "middle-out." *Perception & Psychophysics 25*, 225–231.

Kinsborne, M., & Warrington, E. K. (1963). The localizing significance of limited simultaneous visual form perception. *Brain*, *86*, 697–702.

Krech, D., & Calvin, A. (1953). Levels of perceptual organization and cognition. *The Journal of Abnormal and Social Psychology*, *48*, 394–400.

Krechevsky, I. (Later changed to Krech, D.) (1938). An experimental investigation of the principle of proximity in the visual perception of the rat. *Journal of Experimental Psychology*, *22*, 497–523.

Ladavas, E. (1987). Is the hemispatial deficit produced by right parietal lobe damage associated with retinal or gravitational coordinates. *Brain*, *110*, 167–180.

Lamb, M. R., & Robertson, L. C. (1988). The processing of hierarchical stimuli: Effects of retinal locus, locational uncertainty and stimulus identity. *Perception & Psychophysics 44*, 172–181.

Lamb, M. R., & Robertson, L. C. (1989a). The effect of visual angle on global and local reaction times depends on the set of visual angles presented. *Perception & Psychophysics 47*, 489–496.

Lamb, M. R., & Robertson, L. C. (1989b). Do response time advantage and interference reflect the order of processing of global and local level information? *Perception & Psychophysics*, *46*, 254–258.

Lamb, M. R., Robertson, L. C., & Knight, R. T. (1989). Effects of right and left temporal parietal lesions on the processing of global and local patterns in a selective attention task. *Neuropsychologia*, *27*, 471–483.

Lamb, M. R., Robertson, L. C., & Knight, R. T. (1990). Component mechanisms underlying the processing of hierarchically organized patterns: Inferences from patients with unilateral cortical lesions. *Journal of Experimental Psychology: Learning, Memory & Cognition*, *16*, 471–483.

Mark, V. W., Kooistra, C. A., & Heilman, K. M. (1988). Hemispatial neglect affected by non-neglected stimuli. *Neurology*, *38*, 1207–1211.

Marr, D. (1982). *Vision*. San Francisco: W. H. Freeman.

Martin, M. (1979). Hemisphere specialization for local and global processing. *Neuropsychologia*, *17*, 33–40.

McFie, J., Piercy, M. R., & Zangwill, O. L. (1950). Visual spatial agnosia associated with lesions of the right hemisphere. *Brain*, *73*, 167–190.

Mesulam, M-M. (1985). Attention, confusional states, and neglect. In M-M. Mesulam (Ed.), *Principles of behavioral neurology* (pp. 125–168). Philadelphia: F. A. Davis.

Miller, J. (1981). Global precedence in attention and decision. *Journal of Experimental Psychology: Human Perception and Performance*, *7*, 1161–1185.

Morrow, L., & Ratcliff, G. (1989). The disengagement of covert attention and the neglect syndrome. *Psychobiology*, *16*, 261–269.

Navon, D. (1977). Forest before trees: The precedence of global features in visual perception. *Cognitive Psychology*, *9*, 353–383.

Navon, D. (1981). Do attention and decision follow perception? Comment on Miller.

Journal of Experimental Psychology: Human Perception and Performance, *7*, 1175–1182.

Navon, D., & Norman, J. (1983). Does global precedence really depend on visual angle? *Journal of Experimental Psychology: Human Perception and Performance*, *9*, 955–965.

Newcombe, F. (1979). The processing of visual information in prosopagnosia and acquired dyslexia: Functional versus physiological interpretations. In O. J. Osborne, M. M. Grunsberg & J. R. Eisler (Eds.), *Research in psychology and medicine*. London: Academic Press.

Pomerantz, J. R. (1983). Global and local precedence: Selective attention in form and motion perception. *Journal of Experimental Psychology: General*, *112*, 516–540.

Posner, M. I. (1980). Orienting of attention. *Quarterly Journal of Experimental Psychology*, *32*, 3–25.

Posner, M. I., Cohen, A., & Rafal, R. D. (1982). Neural systems control of spatial orienting. *Philosophical Transcripts of the Royal Society of London*, *B298*, 187–198.

Posner, M. I., Inhoff, A. W., Freidrich, F. J., & Cohon, A. (1987). Isolating attentional systems: A cognitive-anatomical analysis. *Psychobiology*, *15*, 107–121.

Posner, M. I., Walker, J. A., Friedrich, F. J., & Rafal, R. D. (1984). Effects of parietal injury on covert orienting of attention. *Journal of Neuroscience*, *4*, 1863–1874.

Rafal, R. D., & Posner, M. I. (1987). Deficits in human visual spatial attention following thalamic lesions. *Proceedings of the National Academy of Science*, *84*, 7349–7353.

Rafal, R. D., Posner, M. I., Friedman, J. H., Inhoff, A. W., & Bernstein, E. (1988). Orienting of visual attention on progressive supranuclear palsy. *Brain*, *111*, 267–280.

Riddoch, M. J., & Humphrey, G. W. (1987). Perceptual and action systems in unilateral visual neglect. In M. Jeannerod (Ed.), *Neurophysiological and neuropsychological aspects of spatial neglect*. North-Holland: Elsevier Science.

Robertson, L. C. (1986). From gestalt to neo-gestalt. In T. J. Knapp & L. C. Robertson (Eds.), *Approaches to cognition: Contrasts and controversies* (pp. 159–188). Hillsdale, NJ: Lawrence Erlbaum Associates.

Robertson, L. C., & Delis, D. C. (1986). "Part-whole" processing in unilateral brain damaged patients: Dysfunction of hierarchical organization. *Neuropsychologia*, *24*, 363–370.

Robertson, L. C., & Lamb, M. R. (1991). Neuropsychological contributions to theories of part/whole organization. *Cognitive Psychology 23*, 299–330.

Robertson, L. C., Lamb, M. R., & Knight, R. T. (1988). Effects of lesions of temporal-parietal junction on perceptual and attentional processing in humans. *Journal of Neurosciences*, *8*, 3757–3769.

Robertson, L. C., Lamb, M. R., & Knight, R. T. (1990). *Posterior/anterior contributions in responding to global and local levels of visual stimuli*. Paper presented at the International Neuropsychology Society meeting, Orlando, FL.

Robertson, L. C., & Palmer, S. E. (1983). Holistic processes in the perception and transformation of disoriented figures. *Journal of Experimental Psychology: Human Perception and Performance*, *9*, 203–214.

Schneider, W., & Shiffrin, R. M. (1977). Controlled and automatic human information processing. I. Detection, search and attention. *Psychological Review*, *84*, 1–66.

Sergent, J. (1982). The cerebral balance of power: Confrontation or cooperation? *Journal of Experimental Psychology: Human Perception and Performance*, *8*, 253–272.

Sergent, J. (1986). Methodological constraints on neuropsychological studies of face perception in normals. In R. Bruyer (Ed.), *The neuropsychology of face perception and facial expression* (pp. 91–124). Hillsdale, NJ: Lawrence Erlbaum Associates.

Shiffrin, R. M., & Schneider, W. (1977). Controlled and automatic human information processing II. Perceptual learning, automatic attending and general theory. *Psychological Review*, *84*, 127–190.

Spelke, E., Hirst, W., & Neisser, U. (1976). Skills of divided attention. *Cognition*, *4*, 215–230.

Stuss, D. T., & Benson, D. F. (1987). The frontal lobes and control of cognition and memory. In E. Perecman (Ed.), *The frontal lobes revisited*. New York: The IRBN Press.

Treisman, A. (1988). Features and objects: The fourteenth Bartlett memorial lecture. *Quarterly Journal of Experimental Psychology*, *40A*, 201–247.

Treisman, A. M., & Gelade, G. (1980). A feature integration theory of attention. *Cognitive Psychology*, *12*, 97–136.

Warrington, E. K., & Taylor, A. M. (1978). Two categorical stages of object recognition. *Perception*, *7*, 695–705.

Weiskrantz, L. (1986). *Blindsight: A case study and implications*. New York: Oxford University Press.

Wolfe, J. M., Cave, K. R., & Franzel, S. L. (1989). Guided search: An alternative to the feature integration model of visual search. *Journal of Experimental Psychology: Human Perception & Performance 15*, 419–433.

Young, A. W. (1986). Subject characteristics in lateral differences for face processing by normals. In R. Bruyer (Ed.), *The neuropsychology of face perception and facial expression* (pp. 167–299). Hillsdale, NJ: Lawrence Erlbaum Associates.

5

Cognitive Dysfunctions in Eating Disorders: A Clinical Psychobiological Perspective

MARK A. DEMITRACK, CAROLYN SZOSTAK, and HERBERT WEINGARTNER

The purpose of this chapter is to provide a systematic program for understanding the cognitive abnormalities in patients with eating disorders. We will do this by formulating an analytic framework which can be useful in the psychobiological study of many different forms of cognitive impairments. The usefulness of this framework for understanding cognitive failures in such diverse neuropsychiatric disorders as dementia, depression, and amnestic syndromes will be demonstrated by presenting a brief discussion of syndrome-specific changes reproduced using drug challenges in normal individuals. We will then selectively review the clinical manifestations of cognitive dysfunction in patients with eating disorders. This information will be used to formulate testable hypotheses about the psychobiology of cognition in patients with eating disorders. Finally, we will provide an integrative discussion relating data on the cognitive changes seen in these patients with what is known about the underlying neurobiology of eating disorders in order to suggest a rational program of future research.

COGNITION: SOME DEFINITIONS

Cognition, in its broadest sense, refers to a diverse arena of higher mental functions, including learning and memory. Cognitive processes, however, also include all of the mental operations that are involved in sensory integration, including attention (both conscious attention and attentive processes outside of conscious awareness), the encoding and decoding memory processes that operate on incoming information, as well as the acquisition, retention, and retrieval of previously experienced data. Also included are components of sensorimotor function that may modify perception, the state of arousal of the subject, and the experience of feeling states as these are elicited and associated with both internal and external sources of information. We therefore use the term cognition synonomously with the conscious and nonconscious expressions of higher cortical functions. We propose here a clinically useful framework for organizing these attributes that groups together those functions which are intrinsic to the processing, storage, retention, and retrieval of information versus those which are extrinsic to the information processing but nevertheless act to modulate the efficiency of these intrinsic cognitive processes (Tariot & Weingartner, 1986; Squire & Davis, 1981). Components of the intrinsic and extrinsic cognitive operations which are of relevance to the present chapter are discussed in detail below.

Intrinsic Cognitive Processes

Episodic vs. Semantic (Knowledge) Memory

Recent learning and memory can be conceptualized along two contrasting dimensions of episodic and semantic memory. Episodic memory represents the acquisition, consolidation, and retrieval of events consisting of information about a particular event based on the temporal and spatial organization of the data (Tulving, 1982). As such, episodic memory is context and sequence bound. It records a specific, biographical piece of memory with information about what occurred, with whom, when, and what was the precise sequencing of events. Standard clinical bedside testing often assesses this aspect of recent memory. Disruptions in the organization of episodic memory may arise from a multitude of pathologic processes and therefore are not often in and of themselves of specific diagnostic significance.

On the other hand, certain memories are not context or sequence bound but instead provide information about how things relate to one another, the procedures and skills that are involved in the execution of certain events and many aspects of one's sense of self that allow an individual to display specific, enduring personality attributes. This aspect of memory, to which we refer as semantic or knowledge memory, is, along with episodic memory, generally considered to represent a portion of long-term memory (Weingartner et al., 1983). As such, semantic, knowledge, memories provide schemata which enables us to systematically organize our internal knowledge base of the world and the expectations we can be prepared to make of that world. Indeed, it appears that disruptions in knowledge memory are fundamental deficits in senile dementia of the Alzheimer's type (Weingartner et al., 1983). A prominent role for cholinergic pathways in the functioning of these types of memories can be gleaned from pharmacologic challenges in normal individuals (Drachman & Leavitt, 1974; Wolkowitz et al., 1985; Sunderland et al., 1987) and is circumstantially supported by the profound alterations in cholinergic neurotransmission which are evident in the neuropathology of Alzheimer's disease (Whitehouse et al., 1982; Davies & Maloney, 1976). These points will be elaborated in subsequent sections of this chapter.

Effortful vs. Automatic Processes

The degree to which a mental task requires the conscious effort and attentional capacity of the individual may be used to distinguish two important qualitative aspects of learning and memory processes (Hasher & Zacks, 1979, 1984; Hirst & Volpe, 1984; Weingartner, Burns, Diebel, & LeWitt, 1984; Weingartner, Chen, Sunderland, Tariot, & Thompson, 1987; Kahneman, 1973). These distinctions concern the extent to which particular cognitive tasks require a significant degree of attentional capacity to the exclusion of other operations or whether these tasks may occur in parallel with other mental processes often outside of the conscious awareness of the individual. Cognitive tasks which are employed with regularity in conscious and intentional decision-making and problem-solving involve the sustained effort of the subject for their appropriate completion. These operations have been referred to collectively as effortful cognitive processes. In general, the cognitive capacity available to perform such tasks is finite in amount. While attending to the acquisition and processing of information for a particular primary task, an individual will have a proportionate reduction of cognitive capacity for the performance of any subsidiary tasks. In contrast, certain cognitive processes proceed seemingly without the need for conscious attention or intentional activity. We refer to such processes here as automatic operations. They require little of the overall cognitive capacity of the subject and can therefore occur in parallel with other conscious or nonconscious mental activities.

Specific patterns of failure of either effortful or automatic cognitive processing are seen in a variety of neuropsychiatric syndromes. For example, cognitive operations requiring sustained attention are disrupted while automatic memory processes are spared in patients with depressive illness (Cohen, Weingartner, Smallberg & Murphy, 1982; Silberman, Weingartner, & Post, 1983; Weingartner et al., 1984). On the other hand, in progressive dementias such as Alzheimer's dementia, the functioning of both effortful and automatic cognitive processing can be disrupted (Weingartner et al., 1981c). As will be discussed further in the sections to follow, information obtained from drug challenge studies implicates a relatively important role for certain classical neurotransmitters in mediating the expression of these mental processes.

Explicit vs. Implicit Memory

A related conceptual scheme to the effortful/automatic distinction involves a typology of memory based on the psychological experience (awareness) of the individual during the process of memory recall (Graf & Schacter, 1985; Schacter, 1987). Certain events are said to be explicitly remembered when the individual experiences a conscious and intentional recollection of certain memories in order to complete a particular cognitive task. This process may bridge the domains of both episodic and semantic memories and in this manner conceptualizes a slightly different memory store. Alternatively, events may be demonstrated to have been recalled without the conscious or intentional recollection of the individual being tested. Such a process may be manifest by the facilitation of task performance over repeated trials, without awareness of the previous testing trials. The precise neurobiologic substrates for these processes are far from clear and may well depend on the functional integrity of multiple interconnecting systems. For example, arousal, the attentional demands of the task, and the capacity for planning and judgment characteristic of certain neocortical domains may influence implicit memory.

Cognitive Operations: A Developmental Perspective

The acquisition of cognitive processes follows a hierarchical, developmental progression. It is generally thought that stages of cognitive development proceed such that attributes of earlier stages are embedded in and serve as necessary conditions for the emergence of more complex processing strategies. For example, Piaget (1952[1936]) described the progression in children through sensorimotor, preoperational, concrete operational, and formal operational stages, with each stage building upon the constructs appearing in previous ones. Recent studies suggest that a developmental progression can also be seen in the acquisition of the learning and memory strategies outlined above. Semantic memory, for example, appears at an ontogenically earlier stage in infants than episodic memory. The latter appears no earlier than eight to nine months of age (Schacter & Moscovitch, 1984). One of the last developmental cognitive achievements and one of the least well understood is the capacity for metacognition, or the judgment of and knowledge about the processing and performance of one's own cognitive experiences (Flavell, 1979). It has been noted that this capacity is incompletely developed in young children. In other words, they are unable to accurately judge what variables will affect the outcome of particular cognitive strategies and the awareness or feeling that they know a certain thing (Flavell et al., 1970).

Assessment of cognitive failures along a developmental dimension may have considerable theoretical and clinical interest in the evaluation of cognitive dysfunctions in the eating disorders. It is known that a biological consequence of the starvation associated with these illnesses is an apparent hormonal regression to a prepubertal state. For example, the circadian secretory pattern of luteinizing hormone (Boyar et al., 1974) and the production of adrenal androgens (Zumoff et al., 1983) reverts to an ontogenically prepubertal level in underweight anorexics, returning to normal with remission of the starved state. Coincident with this biological regression often is an apparent psychological regression which serves to ward off the integration of painful issues associated with normal maturation (Crisp, 1965). Whether the confluence of these psychobiological factors reinforces the persistence or biases towards the use of ontogenically primitive cognitive processes in the starved patient is an intriguing possibility, but has yet to be formally investigated.

Extrinsic Processes

In addition to the intrinsic cognitive operations already discussed, overall cognitive performance can be modulated by a number of activities that are not directly part of the primary cognitive processes, yet still have a rather proximate influence on these intrinsic cognitive operations. These activities, here referred to as extrinsic or noncognitive operations, may have important effects on the efficiency of the cognitive output of the individual.

Arousal

Arousal is a multidetermined construct, for which no truly satisfactory definition exists in the literature. For the purposes of this chapter, we consider arousal to be a unitary concept which generally reflects the degree of activation of the sympathetic nervous system. Changes in the level of arousal will alter an individual's ability to attend to incoming stimuli. Such disturbances have been shown to adversely affect procedural learning as well as the ability to access and utilize previously stored information (Eysenck, 1977; Clark, Milberg, & Ross, 1983).

Increasing levels of arousal may be associated with a number of clinically observed behavioral states, for example, anxiety. Eysenck has emphasized the role of anxiety and its associated physiologic arousal on the operation of effort-demanding cognitive operations and the allocation of processing resources (Eysenck, 1979). The primary effect of increased anxiety is the initiation of task-irrelevant activities, such as an obsessive overconcern with the quality of one's performance, which eventually impairs overall task performance (Eysenck, 1979). The higher the level of anxiety of the individual, the higher the intensity of task-irrelevant activities and, hence, the more effort is expended to compensate for the distracting effects of processing these task-irrelevant events. Such increased effort may be effective up to a certain point in maintaining the overall quality of task performance; however, as the burden of task-irrelevant processing mounts, the available working memory is reduced, resulting in impairment of task performance. A response to the anxiety-induced increase in task-irrelevant processing is a narrowing of attentional focus as the effort-driven cognitive operations are overloaded (Easterbrook, 1959; Eysenck, 1979).

These empirically derived principles which relate anxiety and arousal to task performance were first described by Yerkes and Dodson (1908). The basic assumptions of these observations are, first, that an inverted U-shaped relationship exists between anxiety or arousal and overall task performance and, second, that the optimal level of arousal for a particular task is negatively correlated with increasing task diffculty. These relationships are graphically displayed in Figure 5-1. Since heightened levels of arousal and psychomotor activation are common accompaniments of the starved state in eating disorders, arousal is an important consideration in the interpretation of any alteration in cognitive performance in patients with eating disorders.

Reinforcement

The degree to which an individual may be directed to preferentially attend to certain stimuli and not others will alter significantly the acquisition of information related to the reinforced event (Coles et al., 1986). Eating disordered behavior involves a significant distortion or bias toward selective attention to the rewarding and aversive properties of food intake and weight gain. It would therefore be important to consider the relative reinforcing capacity of the stimulus being provided in the assessment of cognitive dysfunction in these illnesses.

Emotional/affective state

Changes in mood state may profoundly alter the individual's responsiveness to certain stimulus information (Bower, 1981; Weingartner, Miller, & Murphy, 1977; Weingartner, Murphy & Stillman, 1978). In addition, mood state may influence the accessibility of information in a mood congruent fashion. For example, when subjects are asked to freely recall personal experiences, those who are tested in a sad or unhappy mood retrieve more sad memories than pleasant ones (Teasdale & Fogarty, 1979). The converse is true for subjects tested in a happy mood. Mood-congruent access and retrieval of information is

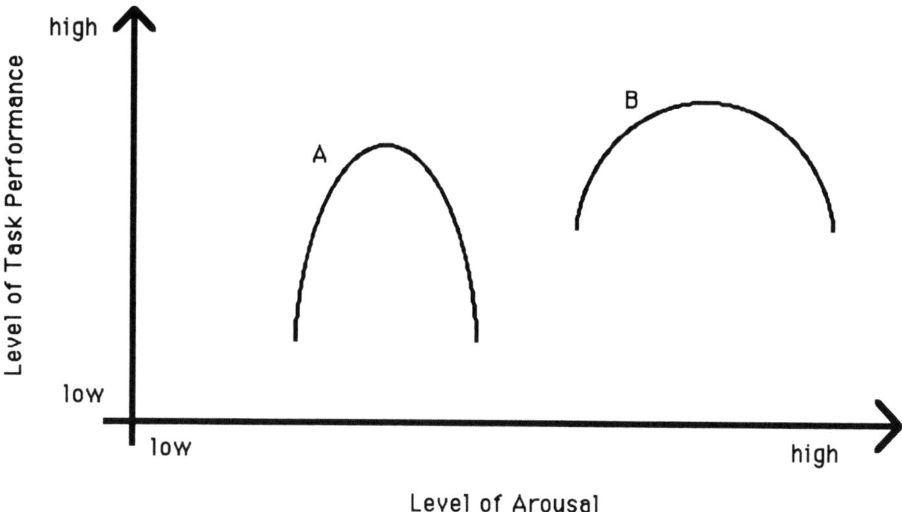

Figure 5-1 Relationship between quality of task performance and level of arousal with respect to task difficulty.

also evident in patients with major depression (Teasdale, 1983; Weingartner et al., 1978).

In regard to patients with eating disorders, it is noteworthy that some degree of affective distress, often characterized as rapid, unstable fluctuations in mood, is evident in nearly all eating disordered patients, particularly in severe states of starvation (Johnson & Larson, 1982; Norman & Herzog, 1983).

Dissociative Capacity

Alterations in mood state can also have significant effects on acquisition and retrieval of information. Experimentally, it has been shown that retrieval of previously acquired information is facilitated if the state—which can be defined pharmacologically, environmentally, and emotionally—of the subject is consistent across acquisition and retrieval conditions (Smith, 1979; Eich, 1980; Bower, 1981). Dissociations of state can result in a failure of the normal integration of thoughts, feelings, memories, and actions into a unified sense of consciousness.

While most experiments have assessed the dissociative effects of state on episodic memory, it has also been found that aspects of knowledge memory, implicit learning and metacognition can be modulated by a person's state (Fogarty & Helmsley, 1983; Natale & Hantas, 1982; Teasdale, Taylor, & Fogarty, 1980; Weingartner et al., 1977, 1978). One interpretation of state-dependent retrieval is that the state of the subject serves as a discriminative stimulus. Thus, mood states may be associated with state-specific hierarchies of responses and stored information that are part of knowledge memory. These hierarchies may,

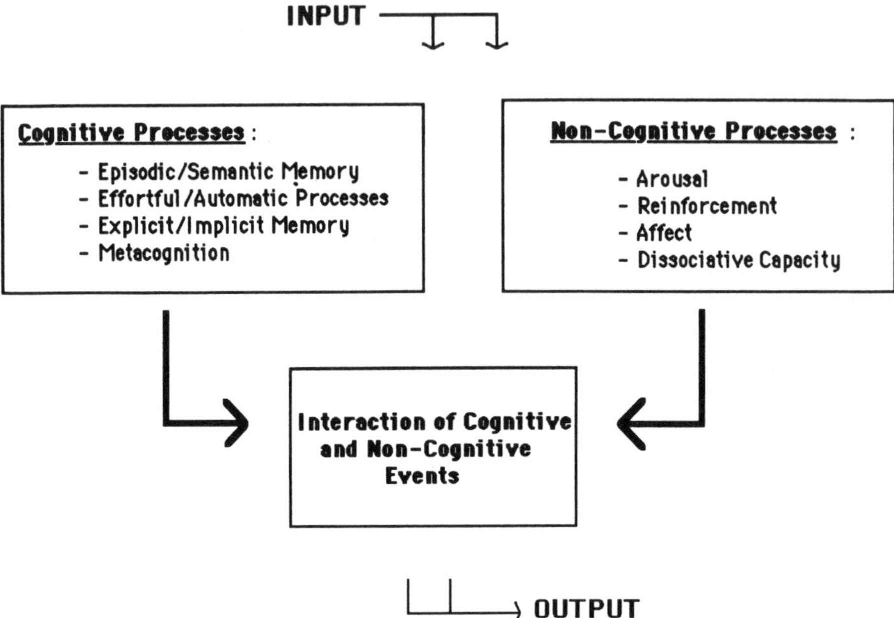

Figure 5-2 Domains of cognitive and non-cognitive processes.

in turn, determine how recent or episodic events are processed or encoded. The specific nature of the retrieval process may also be determined by one's state.

These issues are of considerable theoretical and clinical interest given the high frequency of dissociative experiences reported by eating disordered patients (Demitrack, Putnam, Brewerton, Brandt, & Gold, 1990b) and, hence, the presence of unstable fluctuations in conscious state. These dissociations of state may, in part, be prompted by certain behavioral traits which characterize these patients such as severe food restriction, repeated periods of bingeing and purging and repeated bouts of self-harm. Such events may serve as profound physiologic stressors which, in turn, may alter the patients' conscious state or may serve as contextual cues for the induction of dissociative states and in so doing perpetuate or enhance the propensity for the patient to dissociate. The degree and frequency to which alterations in conscious state will have significant effects on both the allocation of attention and the context-dependent storage and retrieval of certain stimuli has yet to be fully elucidated. A schematic representation of these intrinsic, cognitive operations and extrinsic, noncognitive events and their potential interrelationships are presented in Figure 5-2.

NEUROBIOLOGIC CORRELATES OF COGNITIVE FUNCTIONS: INFORMATION FROM PHARMACOLOGIC CHALLENGE STUDIES

A central theme of this chapter concerns the multiplicity of higher cortical functions, collectively referred to as cognition, which may be organized in a paradigm of functional domains which have demonstrable psychobiological correlates. A number of strategies have been employed to assist in elucidating the biologic correlates of the various intrinsic and extrinsic processes outlined above. One approach has been the use of pharmacologic challenges in normal individuals. While such methodologies have been very revealing, they are also associated with some shortcomings. First, for example, it is unlikely that these diverse processes can be parsimoniously explained by unitary defects in single neurochemical systems. Second, the pharmacologic agents employed are not completely selective for one neurochemical pathway, but usually involve alterations in a number of systems at once, blurring conclusions about the specificity for a particular cognitive or noncognitive process. In spite of these caveats, the available data have provided meaningful insights which highlight the usefulness of a component analysis of higher mental activities along the functional domains suggested in the preceding framework. In the following section, we will provide a selective review of studies examining neurotransmitter and neuropeptide systems of particular interest to the clinical syndromes discussed here.

Acetylcholine

There is a clear role for cholinergic neurotransmission in the phenomenology of memory (Deutsch, 1971). Scopolamine, a central muscarinic cholinergic antagonist, has been used extensively in normal individuals to investigate the nature of cholinergic effects on memory (Drachman & Leavitt, 1974). In general, the administration of scopolamine interferes with the acquisition and storage of new information (Safer & Allen, 1971; Ghoneim & Mewaldt, 1975, 1977). It has also been reported that scopolamine disrupts the retrieval of information previously stored in knowledge memory (Drachman & Leavitt, 1974; Wolkowitz et al., 1985). Further evidence that these deficits are related to changes in cholinergic activity is provided by the finding that these deficits can be reversed, at least in part, by the administration of physostigmine, a cholinesterase inhibitor.

Another source of evidence supporting the involvement of cholinergic neural systems in cognition are the results obtained from clinical studies. As described in the next section, Alzheimer's disease is characterized clinically by progressive memory impairments. A central role for acetylcholine in the neuropathology of this illness is suggested by the substantial loss of cholinergic cell bodies within the nucleus basalis of Meynert (Whitehouse et al., 1982) and the decrease in presynaptic choline acetyltransferase, an enzyme involved in the synthesis of acetylcholine (Davies & Maloney, 1976) that occurs in patients with this disease. The severity of cholinergic cell damage has also been found to correlate with the degree of memory impairment in these patients (Perry et al., 1978). Parenthetically, it has been reported that short-term treatment with agents that enhance cholinergic activity, such as tetrohydroaminoacridine and physostigmine, produces some improvement in cognitive performance in Alzheimer patients (Summers, Majouski, March, Tachiki, & Kling, 1986; Mohs et al., 1985).

Finally, it should be noted that the effects of scopolamine on memory in young subjects mimics the changes seen with normal aging (Drachman & Leavitt,

1974), and the effects of scopolamine in older normals mimics the changes seen in Alzheimer's disease (Sunderland et al., 1987).

Monoamine Neurotransmitters

The extent to which cognition processing is subserved by the monoaminergic neurotransmitter systems has been assessed primarily through the use of stimulants such as amphetamine, which putatively could affect cognition processes by directly releasing the neurotransmitters, dopamine and norepinephrine, and/or by blocking catecholamine reuptake. Although studies in experimental animals have yielded reproducible effects on learning and memory variables (McGaugh, 1973; Alpern & Jackson, 1978), the results of human studies have been less conclusive. In general, it appears that performance on tasks requiring sustained effort and attention are enhanced to a greater extent by increased activity of monoamine systems than performance involving automatically processed information (Weiss & Laties, 1962; Hamilton, Bush, Smith, & Peck, 1982; Newman, Weingartner, Smallberg, & Caine, 1984). These effects are also more apparent in subjects who are fatigued prior to testing (Weiss & Laties, 1962). As such, although cognitive performance is modulated by changes in monoaminergic activity, it is unclear whether these systems have specific effects on intrinsic cognitive processes or if the observed impairments are secondary to effects on extrinsic parameters such as arousal and reinforcement.

Neuropeptides (Vasopressin and Oxytocin)

Over the past several years there has been an enormous interest in the role of neuropeptides and cognition. Two of the more interesting and extensively studied neuropeptides, with respect to the present chapter, are the neurohypophyseal hormones, vasopressin and oxytocin. In 1965, deWeid demonstrated that removal of the posterior and intermediate lobes of the pituitary in the rat facilitated extinction of a conditioned avoidance response without influencing the acquisition of the avoidance response. Further studies, in a variety of animal species, have led to the hypothesis that these effects are mediated by alterations in the availability of vasopressin and oxytocin. Since then, researchers have employed a variety of paradigms, permitting assessment of the roles of vasopressin and oxytocin in both memorial and motivational processes (Lande, Flexner, & Flexner, 1972; Walter, Hoffman, Flexner, & Flexner, 1975; Rigter & VanRiezen, 1974). In general, it has been suggested that vasopressin enhances the consolidation and retrieval of conditioned behavior, while oxytocin works in an antithetical fashion (de Weid, 1980).

Vasopressin's role in cognitive functions has also been assessed in a variety of clinical populations, including head injury patients, alcoholics, and patients with dementia (Oliveros et al., 1978; Jenkins, Mather, Coughlin, & Jenkins, 1982; Tinklenberg, Pfefferbaum, & Berger, 1981, 1982; Weingartner et al., 1981a,b). The results from these studies suggest a facilitatory role for vasopressin in effortful memory. In contrast, oxytocin appears to exert a disruptive effect on the recall of recently stored information (Fehm-Wolfsdorf, Born, Voight, &

Fehm, 1984; Kennett, Devlin, & Ferrier, 1982; Ferrier, Kennett, & Devlin, 1980). It remains unclear, however, whether the observed effects reflect a direct influence of these peptides on cognition or whether they are, in fact, secondary to alterations in arousal or attention. To this end, it has been speculated that the cognitive effects of neurohypophyseal hormones may be mediated principally via peripheral mechanisms which may be part of the organism's integrated arousal response (Le Moal, Bluthe, Dantzer, Bloom, & Koob, 1987). As such, the enhancement of selective attention and facilitation of effortful cognitive functions produced by vasopressin could reflect increased arousal. It is interesting to note that the effects of vasopressin resemble those induced by central and peripheral catecholamines and other stimulants (McGaugh, 1983a,b). Consistent with these ideas are findings which suggest that vasopressin acts to increase catecholamine activity in the brain (Tanaka, DeKloet, deWied, & Versteeg, 1977) and that the behavioral effects of vasopressin may be dependent upon an intact catecholaminergic system (Kovacs et al., 1979, 1980).

Gamma-amino butyric acid (GABA)

The role of GABA in cognition has been inferentially determined largely from studies using benzodiazepines. The best documented cognitive effect of benzodiazepines is the induction of anterograde amnesia (Wolkowitz et al., 1987; see Lister, 1985, for review). Phenomenologically, these agents disrupt the encoding and consolidation of newly learned information without affecting access to previously acquired knowledge. It is interesting to note that the pattern of cognitive deficits induced by the benzodiazepines is similar to the clinical syndrome of anterograde amnesia observed in Korsakoff's disease (see next section).

The amnestic effects of the benzodiazepines can be reversed by the administration of the benzodiazepine antagonist RO 15-1788 (O'Boyle et al., 1983). In contrast, the deficits are not altered when cholinergic agents are administered (Ghoneim & Mewaldt, 1977). This suggests that the effect of benzodiazepines on memory is mediated, at least indirectly, by GABA and not by cholinergic mechanisms. Taken together, these findings support the idea that episodic and knowledge memory are psychobiologically distinct processes. However, as discussed previously, interpretation of these observations is complicated by our lack of understanding regarding the degree to which the effects of benzodiazepines reflect effects of extrinsic, noncognitive events such as sedation or alteration of affective state. It is also important to recall the caveats mentioned at the beginning of this section and to use caution accordingly in interpreting the data as indicating that impaired access to knowledge memory is attributable to a unitary defect in cholinergic neurotransmission. For example, benzodiazepines can produce similar cognitive effects in normal individuals, albeit at extremely high dosages (Block, DeVoe, Stanley, Stanley, & Pomara, 1985). Moreover, the disruption in memory produced by scopolamine in experimental animals can be reversed by nootropic agents and drugs which block the reuptake of serotonin (Flood & Cherkin, 1985; Verloes et al., 1988). In sum, the retrieval of information from knowledge memory may occur via dysregulation in a variety of neurochemical systems.

CLINICAL EXAMPLES: UNIQUE TYPES OF COGNITIVE CHANGES

In this section we will describe three clinical syndromes that are associated with cognitive deficits. By considering the cognitive profiles associated with these syndromes, we hope to demonstrate the conceptual usefulness of the cognitive domains outlined in the beginning of the chapter.

Dementia of the Alzheimer Type

The nature of the cognitive deficits associated with dementia of the Alzheimer's type is dependent upon the severity of illness. Early in the disease, deficits in attention, coding, processing, and the retrieval of information may be evident (Weingartner et al., 1982). In addition to the deficits in these intrinsic cognitive processes, patients with Alzheimer's disease often develop alterations in mood (Miller, 1980). These mood changes, in combination with deficits in learning and memory, may make a differential diagnosis of the cognitive dysfunction of depression from the dementia of Alzheimer's disease problematic (see below). As the disease progresses, there is a gradual deterioration resulting in major neuropsychiatric impairment (e.g., disorientation for time, place, and person, apraxias, and aphasias). Hypothetically, alterations in extrinsic, noncognitive processes may also progress to involve impairments in the sensorimotor integration of incoming information either through motor apraxias or alterations in visual or auditory processing and gross disintegration of the individual's personality and interpersonal functioning.

Some patients with moderately impaired Alzheimer's disease demonstrate an impairment of memory regardless of the attentional demands of the task (Weingartner et al., 1981c). That is, there is an inability to process information, whether it involves a fixed capacity (effort demanding) or unlimited capacity (automatic processing). It has been suggested that these deficits reflect a specific impairment in the accessing and use of previously stored knowledge (Weingartner et al., 1983). This, in turn, would result in an inability to develop new learning strategies and, furthermore, disrupt the retrieval of biographical information. While alterations in effort-demanding processes may be seen in other syndromes, such as depression (Reus, Silberman, Post, & Weingartner, 1979; Cohen et al., 1982), the presence of impaired access to knowledge memory appears to represent a core distinguishing feature in the cognitive expression of Alzheimer's dementia. These data and the findings from the studies of anticholinergic effects in normal individuals cited above, provide compelling evidence to suggest that the deficits in access to knowledge memory in these patients are closely coupled to the profound derangements in cholinergic neurotransmission.

Anterograde Amnesias: Korsakoff's Disease

This syndrome represents one of the most extensively studied amnestic disorders (Butters & Cermak, 1980; Victor, Adams, & Collins, 1971; Milner, 1970). The primary intrinsic cognitive process deficit in Korsakoff's patients can be described generally as a failure in recent memory, reflected by an inability to form episodic, context-dependent memories (Weingartner et al., 1983). Further characterization of the deficits has revealed that these patients have a preserved capacity to learn and that they can, in fact, demonstrate procedural learning of complex tasks involving perceptual-motor function (Corkin, 1968) as well as pattern-analysis (Cohen & Squire, 1980). It is noteworthy that this learning proceeds outside of awareness of the individual. That is, they can neither recall the learning context nor whether the particular acquired skills were ever learned. In other words, these patients manifest dysfunctions in explicit learning while implicit memory operations remain intact. In contrast to the cognitive deficits associated with Alzheimer's dementia, access to previously acquired knowledge appears to be preserved in Korsakoff's amnesia (Weingartner et al., 1983). Whether there are alterations in the incorporation of effortful or automatically processed events in unclear. As a specific subset of patients with anterograde amnesias, patients with Korsakoff's disease also have important abnormalities in domains of extrinsic, noncognitive processes. Clinically, they may appear apathetic and without motivation, suggesting significant disturbances in neurobiologic systems both subserving mechanisms of reward and reinforcement and mediating alterations in intrinsic cognitive operations (Cummings, 1983; Reuler, Girard, & Cooney, 1985).

Neuropathologic studies have implicated the hippocampus, mammillary bodies, fornix and medial dorsal nucleus of the thalamus as major loci of dysfunction in the expression of anterograde amnesias (Milner, 1970; Mishkin, 1978; Victor et al., 1971; Warrington & Weiskrantz, 1982). In the case of Korsakoff's disease, thiamine deficiency associated with chronic alcohol use plays a central role in the development of the syndrome. Other agents or structural alterations which lead to derangement in the functioning of these brain regions can lead to impairments in the anterograde processing of information.

Affective Illness

Patients with depression almost always report some degree of poor concentration or difficulty in remembering information they previously knew. As noted above, these complaints along with the evidence provided by bedside cognitive testing can make it quite difficult to distinguish elderly, depressed patients without Alzheimer's disease from patients with early stages of Alzheimer's-type dementia (Caine, 1981). However, a closer examination of the cognitive profile of the depressed patient reveals differences from that observed in some patients with early stages of Alzheimer's dementia.

In depression, there is a selective decrement in the ability to perform tasks which require sustained attention, concentration or effort (Cohen et al., 1982; Reus et al., 1979). The motivational strategies, which may normally ensure adequate processing of such information, are also impaired (Akiskal & McKinney, 1975). On the other hand, a depressed patient performs no differently from normal individuals on measures of automatic memory processes (Silberman et al, 1983). For example, depressed patients will do poorly when learning an extensive list of information which requires elaborating a scheme by which to organize and process the specific items on the list. However, they will remember incidental information related to the testing context, such as the location of the room or color of the furniture. In contrast to patients with dementia, depressed patients also show preserved access to previously stored knowledge (Hilbert, Niederehe, & Kahn, 1976; Glass, Uhlenhuth, Hartel, Matzus, & Fishman, 1981). Thus, in depression, the specific cognitive deficit appears to involve the effortful processing of information.

Conceptual formulations of the alterations in thinking style of these patients highlight their pervasive negative attribution to certain environmental events (Akiskal & McKinney, 1975). There is a heightened awareness of the failures rather than the successes of their personal accomplishments and a tendency to focus on negative or pessimistic occurrences as supportive evidence for their negative view of themselves and the world. The extent to which the presence of extrinsic or noncognitive factors, such as the intensity of depression or the level of arousal, may play a role in the expression of the cognitive impairments is incompletely understood. It has been speculated that neurobiologic systems subserving self-stimulation and reward may be prominently involved in the anhedonia or loss of motivation and interest evident in these patients (Akiskal & McKinney, 1975) and, as well, the tendency to focus on negative life experience as sole environmental reinforcers.

COGNITIVE DYSFUNCTION IN EATING DISORDERS: CLINICAL MANIFESTATIONS AND A COMPONENT ANALYSIS OF COGNITION

Anorexia nervosa is an idiopathic illness characterized by a failure to maintain one's body weight above a minimum expected amount coupled with an obsessive pursuit of thinness and an intense fear of weight gain. In women, there is also a loss of normal menstrual function (American Psychiatric Association, 1987, pp. 65–69). Patients with bulimia nervosa engage in repeated, uncontrollable episodes of binge eating (rapid consumption of a large quantity of food in a short period of time). This is associated with a variety of maneuvers such as vomiting, laxative abuse, use of diet pills, or excessive exercising which are designed to rid the body of the unwanted effects of food intake (American Psychiatric Association, 1987, pp. 65–69).

In general, it has been frequently mentioned that these patients appear to have an impaired ability to monitor internal physiologic and feeling states, described as a defect in interoceptive awareness (Bruch, 1962). When confronted with the cognitive and affective demands of normal interpersonal functioning, the absence of adequate interoceptive awareness often leads to overwhelming anxiety and a loss of an integrated sense of self. Contributing to this impaired sense of self-integration and breakdown of basic interpersonal skills are a number of peculiarities of cognitive style and abnormalities of extrinsic cognitive processes.

These patients are often described as being unable to experience the simultaneous existence of qualitatively opposite attributes. This inability is referred to as dichotomous thinking (Garfinkel & Garner, 1982). Also, as an apparent consequence of the preoccupation with food intake, the tremendously reinforcing qualities of weight loss and the fear of loss of control in their own lives, these patients may selectively attend to and abstract information from ongoing events which serves to support a distorted memory of reality. Alteration in mood, especially depression, is a common accompaniment of these illnesses (Johnson & Larson, 1982; Norman & Herzog, 1983), particularly in emaciated patients or in patients incapacitated by multiple bingeing and purging episodes throughout the day. The starvation state itself also produces an increase in arousal and psychomotor activity (Keys, 1950). Anxiety may then persist well into weight recovery or after cessation of bingeing and purging. Finally, as noted above, these patients demonstrate a significant degree of dissociative experience (Demitrack et al., 1990b), a finding which may be a result of or exacerbated by the behaviors characteristic of the illness itself.

It may be speculated that simply as a result of the emaciation and metabolic derangements associated with the disordered eating behavior that patients may be expected to manifest cognitive failure on an organic basis alone. Indeed, computed tomographic studies have shown cerebral ventricular enlargement and sulcal widening in underweight anorexics which appear to be reversible, resolving when the same patients were examined after weight restoration (Heinz, Martinez, & Haenggeli, 1977; Krieg et al., 1988). These findings did not correlate with the length of illness but did bear a positive relationship to the magnitude of weight loss. Positron emission tomography using the ^{18}F-2-fluoro-2-deoxyglucose method revealed disturbances in regional cerebral glucose metabolism in the underweight state which normalized when compared to studies in the same patients after weight recovery. Specifically, there was evidence of hypermetabolism in caudate nucleus and temporal cortex bilaterally (Herholz et al., 1987).

Studies of neuropsychological function add some interesting dimensions to the structural and functional neuropathologic findings cited above. Using a battery of neuropsychological assessments, Hamsher, Halmi, and Benton (1981) examined a group of 20 patients with anorexia nervosa while underweight and at the end of weight recovery. These same patients were then contacted one year after discharge to evaluate long-term outcome and weight stability. Notably, at low weight there was evidence of attentional difficulties, as demonstrated by impairment of mental arithmetic tasks and retarded reaction times on a forced-choice task. There were also significant deficits in short-term visual memory and in long-term information retrieval. Eighty-five percent of patients with none or only one cognitive deficit at weight recovery demonstrated a favorable outcome one year after discharge compared with 71% of patients with two or more cognitive deficits who manifested a poor outcome at one year. Interestingly, these investigators also reported a relationship between the cognitive impairment and levels of affective distress and arousal. Specifically, their data suggest that an increase in arousal, as reflected by elevated measures of anxiety, is correlated with greater cognitive impairment in low weight anorectics.

In contrast to these results, Witt, Ryan, and Hsu (1985) examined a group of underweight anorexics using a variety of tests designed to assess attention, memory, associative learning, and psychomotor state. While their test group did not differ from normal controls on measures of attention, immediate or delayed visual memory or psychomotor state, a significant impairment was noted on a symbol-digit paired associate learning task. Interestingly, the degree of impairment did not correlate with level of weight loss but did bear a significant inverse relationship to duration of illness.

While these studies highlight the clinical presence of a broad spectrum of cognitive dysfunction in these patients, the approach has largely been task-oriented rather than directed at identifying the specific domains of cognition that are disrupted in anorexia and bulimia nervosa. By evaluating the efficiency of task performance alone, there is a tendency to obscure the overall picture of the cognitive dysfunctions and, as a result, inferences regarding biological correlates of these disturbances becomes quite difficult.

In a preliminary study from our group, Strupp, Weingartner, Kaye, and Gwirtsman (1986) used a series of paradigms to assess cognitive dysfunction in patients with anorexia nervosa according to the component functions of automatic and effortful processing as outlined in the framework described earlier. Seventeen patients with anorexia nervosa were included in the study. This was a heterogeneous group comprised of 11 patients who were nutritionally stabilized but still at low weight, along with 6 patients studied after restoration of normal body weight for a mean duration of 34 months. Measures of effortful processing included: (1) a prompted recall task, (2) a picture-word paired associate learning task, (3) a continuous recognition task, and (4) a recall task of randomly organized or categorically related lists. Automatic processing was assessed by two methods: (1) recall of item presentation as a picture or a word in task 2, and (2) the frequency monitoring/assessment of items presented in task 3. As a group, patients performed no differently from controls on measures of effortful processing but demonstrated a significant impairment on the two measures of automatic processing. It is interesting to note that when comparing low-weight with weight-recovered patients, the six recovered patients exhibited greater impairment than low-weight patients on the frequency monitoring measure of automatic processing. This latter finding suggests that the alterations in automatic processing may not be weight dependent in a unitary sense but emerge from the confluence of physiological changes (e.g., increased psychomotor activation) and cognitive events (e.g., increased reinforcement) associated with the changes in eating behavior and weight. The potential implications of these points will be elaborated upon in the sections to follow.

Automatic and Effortful Processing: The Possible Role for Altered Reinforcement and Increased Dissociative Capacity

At first glance, it may seem inconsistent that patients with anorexia nervosa should manifest such a notable difference in the pattern of cognitive failure compared to that seen in patients with depressive illness. Indeed, there appears to be a familial clustering of eating disorders and affective illness suggesting a common biological substrate (Winokur, March, & Mendels, 1980; Kassett, Maxwell, Gershon, Brandt, & Jimerson, 1989). Also, patients with anorexia nervosa and bulimia nervosa often present with a concurrent diagnosis of major affective disorder (Johnson & Larson, 1982; Norman & Herzog, 1983). A brief discussion of these findings may shed some light on the usefulness of a component analysis of the pattern of cognitive failure in patients with eating disorders and may inform our subsequent discussion of studies of plasma and cerebrospinal fluid neurochemicals in these patients.

As described previously, effortful and automatic cognitive operations are sensitive to alterations in levels of anxiety and arousal (Eysenck, 1979). Since evidence exists to suggest that patients with depression as well as patients with eating disorders manifest an increase in levels of arousal and anxiety, examination of this dimension alone would not allow a prediction of the observed changes in effortful and automatic processing in these two patient groups. We hypothesize that there are two additional parameters of interest which may help in understanding the differing cognitive findings seen here. The first parameter concerns the degree to which an individual is responsive to certain reinforcing cues from the environment. Responsiveness to reinforcement is related to the aspired ideals of the individual relative to their past performance (i.e., the degree of goal discrepancy, as discussed by Eysenck, 1979). A low degree of goal discrepancy would be expected to increase responsivity to reinforcing cues; while a high degree of goal discrepancy would reduce such responsiveness to reinforcement (i.e., a state of "learned helplessness"; Eysenck, 1979). In contrast to the anhedonia and negative self-evaluation characteristic of patients with depression, the eating-disordered individual has often successfully accomplished their goal of weight reduction (low goal discrepancy) and also receives a tremendous internal sense of reinforcement from this behavior (increased reinforcement). Furthermore, with respect to the Yerkes-Dodson Law (1908), an increase in responsiveness to reinforcement will yield a reduction in perceived task difficulty and therefore a higher level of arousal for optimal task performance. Conversely, the higher the goal discrepancy for a particular task, the higher the perceived task difficulty, and the less tolerant the individual will be, even for minor levels of anxiety and arousal (Figure 5-3). Such alterations in responsiveness to reinforcement may underlie the relative preservation of effortful processing in patients with eating disorders described above.

The second parameter of interest here involves the degree to which the individual may be able to disrupt information processing specifically with respect to performance for subsidiary tasks or automatically processed information. We noted previously that patients with eating disorders, unlike individuals with depression, demonstrate significant capacity for dissociative experience (Demitrack et al., 1990b). We hypothesize that this increase in dissociative capacity may lead to a disruption in information processing, resulting in impairments in the perception and processing of stimuli which are not currently the focus of attention (i.e., incidental or extraneous information).

In other words, the confluence of both an alteration in responsiveness to reinforcement and the occurrence of dissociative states in the eating disordered patient leads to a relative preservation of effort-demanding processes on the one hand, and a disruption of automatically processed information on the other.

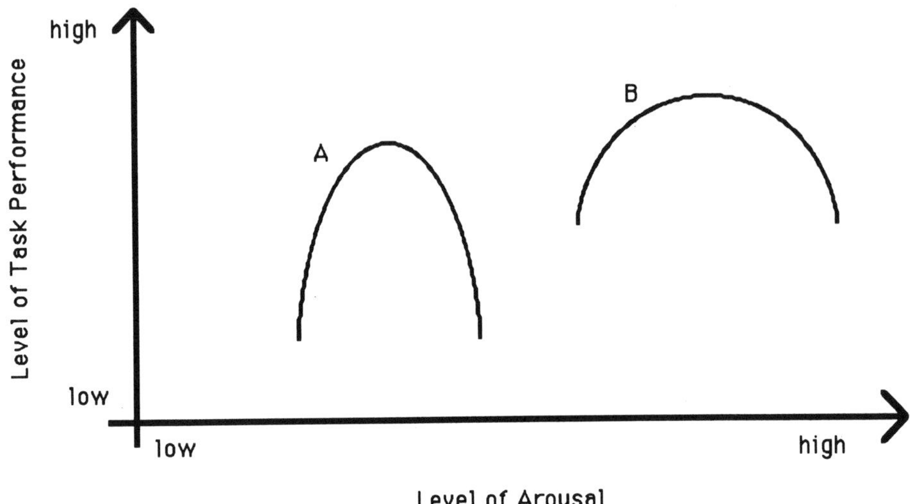

Figure 5-3 Relationship between quality of task performance and level of arousal with respect to degree of individual goal discrepancy.

This approach of contrasting the component domains of cognitive function in terms of both intrinsic cognitive operations and extrinsic operations which modulate these intrinsic processes may be graphically displayed as profiles of spared and impaired cognitive function. Examples of differential profiles present in depression and anorexia nervosa are presented in Figures 5-4 and 5-5. This framework allows for a concise description of syndrome-specific alterations in

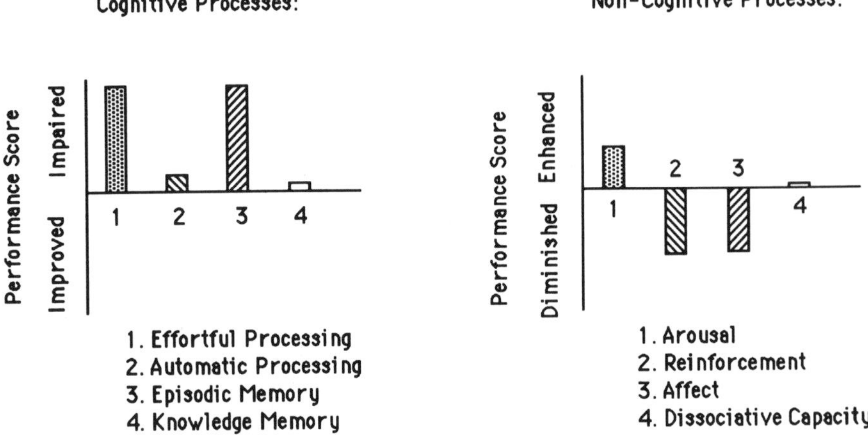

Figure 5-4 Profile of hypothetical impairments in cognitive and noncognitive processes in a depressed patient.

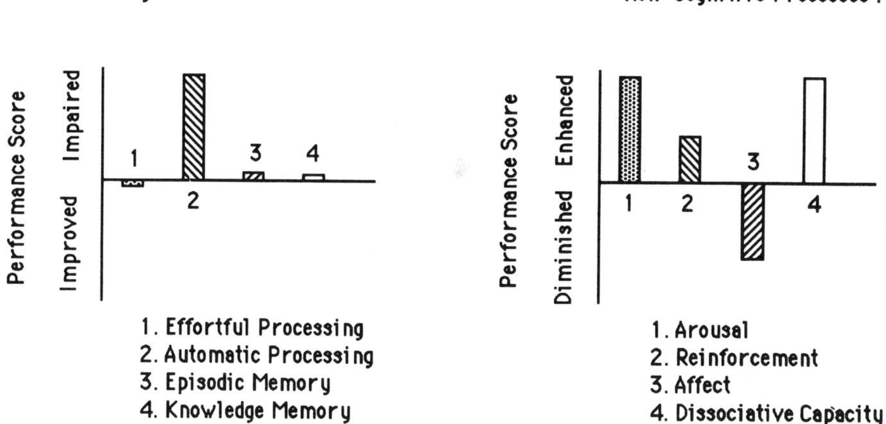

Figure 5-5 Profile of hypothetical impairments in cognitive and noncognitive processes in a patient with anorexia nervosa.

the domains of interest and may assist in the formulation of underlying neurobiologic mechanisms of altered cognition.

COGNITIVE DYSFUNCTION IN EATING DISORDERS: POTENTIAL NEUROBIOLOGIC CORRELATES

In previous sections we described the potential role for abnormalities in specific neurotransmitter and neuromodulator systems as mediators in the expression of certain types of cognitive failure. While not meant to imply a simplistic one-to-one congruence of neurotransmitter dysregulation with cognitive deficit, the data obtained from drug challenge studies in normal individuals suggest that prominent abnormalities in one or another biological substrate may be shown to bias toward the occurrence of predictable patterns of cognitive failure. In this section we will highlight some of what is known about the neurobiologic basis of eating disorders. We will do this with particular reference to neurochemical systems which may be speculated to play a central role in the clinically manifest patterns of cognitive failure seen in these patients.

The regulation of feeding involves a complex, centrally mediated integration of multiple metabolic signals which coordinate the acquisition and utilization of food. The importance of certain hypothalamic nuclei serving as nodal points in the central integration of incoming feeding signals and the coordinated output of neuroendocrine and autonomic responses is well accepted at this point. The lateral and ventromedial hypothalamus serve as principle components of the central neuroanatomy of feeding. Lesions of the lateral hypothalamus result in reductions in food intake (Teitelbaum & Epstein, 1962) while destruction of the ventromedial hypothalamus produces syndromes of hyperphagia and obesity (Hetherington & Ranson, 1940; Brobeck, Tepperman, Blong, 1943). Initial models of the central regulation of nutrient balance posited a simple *dual center* control hypothesis based on these hypothalamic regions alone. It is clear though, that while the lateral and ventromedial hypothalamus are placed prominantly in the hierarchy of neuroanatomical structures involved in feeding, the feeding response itself is a complex event incorporating such other disparate brain regions as the cerebral cortex; subcortical regions such as the globus pallidus; limbic brain regions including the septum, hippocampus, and amygdala; and other hypothalamic regions such as the arcuate and paraventricular nuclei.

There has been extensive research establishing a clear role for the monoamine neurotransmitters in the regulation of this central feeding system. For example, it is well known that central injections of norepinephrine in the lateral and medial hypothalamus are potent stimuli increasing feeding (Grossman, 1962). Alternatively, destruction of the dopaminergic fiber tracts of the nigrostriatal pathway leads to a hypophagic syndrome similar to that seen in animals with lesions of the lateral hypothalamus (Ungerstedt, 1970; Fibiger, Zis, & McGur, 1973). Interest has also been generated in determining the role of serotonin in mediating satiety. This appears to occur largely through actions at the ventromedial hypothalamus (Latham & Blundell, 1979). Finally, the effects of GABA are less clear but may involve a more indirect modulation of primary feeding effects of norepinephrine or dopamine. While the precise interplay of these systems is far from clear, their importance in homeostasis of the feeding system via effects at a hypothalamic level is firmly established.

A number of neuropeptides have been shown to be associated with reduction in feeding, including cholecystokinin (CCK; Smith & Gibbs, 1984) and bombesin (Morley, Levine, Gosnell, & Billington, 1984a), peptides which are found distributed in both gastrointestinal tract as well as the brain. The satiating effects of CCK appear to be mediated by peripheral stimulation of the vagus nerve and activation of specific brainstem nuclei (Crawley & Kiss, 1984). This latter pathway may also produce the central activation of another neuropeptide of interest, oxytocin (Verbalis, McCann, McHale, & Stricker, 1986; Renaud, Tang, McCann, Stricker, & Verbalis, 1987). The interrelationship of these systems is not yet completely understood. Release of the hypothalamic neuropeptide corticotropin-releasing hormone (CRH), which coordinates activation of the pituitary-adrenal axis during stress, also results in profound reduction in food intake and activation of the sympathetic nervous system (Levine, Rogers, Kneip, Grace, & Morley, 1983; Brown, Fisher, Spiess, Rivier, Rivier, & Vale, 1982). These effects appear to be mediated by action of CRH at the paraventricular nucleus (Krahn, Gosnell, Morley, & Levine, 1988). In addition to these appetite-supressing neuropeptides, a number of neuropeptides have been shown to have potent orexigenic effects. These include the opioid peptides, beta-endorphin (Tseng & Cheng, 1980; Leibowitz & Hor, 1982) and dynorphin (Morley & Levine, 1983; Essatara et al., 1984), as well as neuropeptide Y (Clark, Kalra, Crowley, & Kalra, 1984; Stanley & Leibowitz, 1984).

Ongoing studies, to be outlined below, from investigators in our group are consistent with the expectation that alterations in feeding, as seen in the clinical syndromes of anorexia and bulimia nervosa, would be associated with disturbances in specific neuropeptides and monoamine neurotransmitters. We have employed methodologic approaches involving measurement of cerebrospinal fluid (CSF) levels of these substances in conjunction with examination of peripheral responses to specific neuroendocrine challenge paradigms. Cerebrospinal fluid measures are of particular relevance to the present discussion in that the CSF may function as a physiologically meaningful communication pathway in the brain (Post et al., 1983). This would potentially allow the central release of neurochemicals to orchestrate activation of multiple disparate brain regions and hence more complex behavioral events.

Underweight patients with anorexia nervosa were noted in initial studies to have reduced CSF levels of the dopamine metabolite, homovanillic acid (HVA), and the serotonin metabolite 5-hydroxyindole acetic acid (5-HIAA), which appeared to normalize with weight recovery (Kaye, Ebert, Raleigh, & Lake, 1984). More recent studies have suggested persistent changes in central serotonin function. In anorexic patients who have remained at a stable recovered weight for an average of 30 months, CSF 5-HIAA levels are elevated in comparison to normal females (Kaye, Gwirtsman, & Ebert, 1989). Studies of norepinephrine and its metabolites further support the hypothesis of altered monoamine neurotransmission in eating disordered patients. Acutely ill patients with anorexia nervosa demonstrate normal levels of CSF norepinephrine; however, these levels were decreased compared to controls in a group of anorexic patients who maintained a stable recovered weight for an average of 20 months (Kaye et al., 1984). In addition, long-term weight recovered anorexics demonstrate reductions in plasma levels of the norepinephrine metabolite 3-methoxy-4-hydroxyphenylglycol (MHPG) and in lying and standing levels of norepinephrine (Kaye, Jimerson, Lake, & Ebert, 1985).

Parenthetically, this latter finding of relatively normal noradrenergic function during the underweight state of anorexia nervosa, with marked reductions in peripheral and central measures of norepinephrine metabolism after long term weight recovery, contrasts with findings in melancholic depression. These studies suggest an activation of central noradrenergic systems as reflected by normal or increased levels of CSF norepinephrine (Post et al., 1984; Christensen, Vestergaard, Sorenson, & Rafaelson, 1980), elevated plasma norepinephrine (Wyatt, Portnoy, Kupfer, Snyder, & Engelman, 1971; Lake et al., 1982; Roy, Pickar, Linnoila, & Potter, 1985) and increased CSF and urinary MHPG (Koslow et al., 1983). In a related vein, resolution of the depressed state in response to antidepressant treatment is associated with decreases in CSF and urinary MHPG (Linnoila, Karoum, Calil, Kopin, & Potter, 1982).

A prominent neuroendocrine disturbance in both depression and anorexia nervosa is the marked hypercortisolism seen during the active phases of each illness. Studies from our group using a paradigm of intravenous challenge with CRH have provided circumstantial evidence to suggest that in both of these illnesses, the hypercortisolism arises from a defect at or above the level of the hypothalamus (Gold et al., 1986a,b). We and others have further shown that in both underweight anorexics and in depressed patients, CSF levels of the hypothtlamic neuropeptide corticotropin-releasing hormone (CRH) are elevated in comparison with normals (Hotta et al., 1986; Kaye et al., 1987). These data strongly implicate hypersecretion of CRH as a common pathophysiologic defect in the hypercortisolism of these illnesses.

In contrast, examination of a related pair of hypothalamic neuropeptides, vasopressin and oxytocin, reveals striking differences in CSF milieu of eating disordered and depressed patients. Both vasopressin and oxytocin have well established physiologic roles when released from neuronal terminals in the posterior pituitary. Vasopressin is classically known as the antidiuretic hormone (Robertson, 1977). In response to increasing plasma osmolality, vasopressin is released into the systemic circulation and acts at the kidney to prevent the diuresis of free water and hence reduce the osmolality of the intravascular compartment. The principal roles for oxytocin are to promote uterine contraction during parturition and milk letdown during the post-partum period (Forsling, 1986). Interestingly, central administration of both vasopressin and oxytocin have been shown to have antithetical effects on a variety of learning and memory paradigms in animals. As described elsewhere in this chapter, vasopressin appears to enhance consolidation and delay extinction of aversively conditioned behaviors; while oxytocin leads to disruption of the consolidation and retrieval of such behaviors. We have previously speculated that changes which would serve to exaggerate the secretion of vasopressin with or without concomitant reduction in the secretion of oxytocin may be one of a number of biological substrates which would bias the individual toward a narrowing of cognitive focus and a perseverative awareness of particular thoughts (Gold et al., 1983). Though as yet not formally examined, such a hypothesis finds a potentially attractive application in understanding the nature of the eating disordered patients exaggerated preoccupation with the aversive consequences of food intake and weight gain.

We have previously shown that underweight anorexics demonstrate erratic release of vasopressin into the plasma in response to osmotic stimulation. This abnormality is almost always associated with hypersecretion of vasopressin into the CSF (Gold et al., 1983). More recently we have shown similar findings in normal weight bulimic patients studied after cessation of bingeing and purging for one month (Demitrack et al., 1989). In addition, CSF levels of oxytocin are reduced in anorexics studied while underweight but return to normal after short-term weight recovery (Demitrack et al., 1990a). Normal weight patients with bulimia nervosa do not show this reduction in centrally directed oxytocin. In contrast to these findings in patients with eating disorders, depressed patients have been shown by our group and others to have reductions in centrally directed levels of vasopressin (Gold, Goodwin, Post, & Robertson, 1981; Gjerris, Hammer, Vendsborg, Christensen, & Rafaelson, 1985). In addition, CSF levels of oxytocin in patients with depression appear to be no different than normal (Gold et al., 1980).

The causes and consequences of these multiple monoamine and neuropeptide abnormalities in the CSF of patients with eating disorders and depression are far from clear. However, the presence of patterns of change which are dissimilar between specific disease syndromes and the awareness of specific behavioral effects of these neurochemicals suggests that simultaneous assessment of behavioral and biological events may have merit. For example, the finding of normal and reduced noradrenergic tone in conjunction with exaggerated vasopressin release in anorexia nervosa with the converse relationship in patients with depression may have relevance in understanding the relationship among the noncognitive parameters of attention, arousal, and mood with the individual performance on measures of automatic and effortful cognitive operations. The approach outlined here would suggest that the cognitive assessment proceed by contrasting the component domains of function in terms of both intrinsic cognitive operations and extrinsic operations which modulate these intrinsic processes and then graphically displaying the profiles of spared and impaired function (Figures 5-4, 5-5). As such, this framework would provide a coherent quantification of cognitive dysfunction which may then be compared and contrasted in an iterative fashion with simultaneously obtained biological parameters. Hence, the approach we propose here may serve as a rational starting point for examining the interaction between biological and cognitive events.

ACKNOWLEDGMENT

We would like to acknowledge the Upjohn Corporation for their generous support of this work.

REFERENCES

Akiskal, H. S., & McKinney, W. T. (1975). Overview of recent research in depression. *Archives of General Psychiatry*, *32*, 285–305.

Alpern, H. P., & Jackson, S. J. (1978). Short-term memory: A neuropharmacologically distinct process. *Behavioral Biology*, *22*, 133–146.

American Psychiatric Association. (1987). *Diagnostic and statistical manual of mental disorders* (pp. 65–69). (3rd ed., rev.).

Block, R. I., DeVoe, M., Stanley, B., Stanley, M., & Pomara, N. (1985). Memory performance in individuals with primary degenerative dementia: Its similarity to diazepam-induced impairments. *Experimental Aging Research*, *11*, 151–155.

Bower, G. H. (1981). Mood and memory. *American Psychologist*, *36*(2), 129–148.

Boyar, R. M., Katz, J. L., Weiner, H., Kapen, S., Finkelstein, J. W., Weitzman, E. D., & Hellman, L. (1974). Anorexia nervosa: Immaturity of the 24-hour LH secretory pattern. *New England Journal of Medicine*, *291*, 861–865.

Brobeck, J. R., Tepperman, J., & Long, C. N. H. (1943). Experimental hypothalamic hyperphagia in albino rat. *Yale Journal of Biological Medicine*, *15*, 831–853.

Brown, M. R., Fisher, L. A., Spiess, J., Rivier, C., Rivier, J., & Vale, W. (1982). Corticotropin-releasing factor: Actions on the sympathetic nervous system and metabolism. *Endocrinology*, *111*, 928–931.

Bruch, H. (1962). Perceptual and conceptual disturbances in anorexia nervosa. *Psychosomatic Medicine*, *24*, 187–194.

Butters, N., & Cermak, L. S. (1980). *Alcoholic Korsakoff's syndrome*. Orlando: Academic Press.

Caine, E. D. (1981). Pseudodementia: Current concepts and future directions. *Archives of General Psychiatry*, *38*, 1359–1364.

Christensen, N. J., Vestergaard, P., Sorensen, T., & Rafaelson, O. J. (1980). Cerebrospinal fluid adrenaline and noradrenaline in depressed patients. *Acta Psychiatrica Scandinavica*, *61*, 178–182.

Clark, J. J., Kalra, P. S., Crowley, W. R., & Kalra, S. P. (1984). Neuropeptide Y and human pancreatic polypeptide stimulate feeding behavior in rats. *Endocrinology*, *115*, 427–429.

Clark, M. S., Milberg, S., & Ross, J. (1983). Arousal cues arousal-related material in memory: Implications for understanding mood on memory. *Journal of Verbal Learning Verbal Behaviors*, *22*, 633–649.

Cohen, N. J., & Squire, L. R. (1980). Preserved learning and retention of pattern-analyzing skill in amnesia: Dissociation of knowing how and knowing that. *Science*, *210*, 207–210.

Cohen, R. M., Weingartner, H., Smallberg, S., & Murphy, D. L. (1982). Effort and cognition in depression. *Archives of General Psychiatry*, *39*, 593–597.

Coles, M. G. H., Donchin, E., & Porges, S. W. (1986). *Psychophysiology: Systems, processes and applications*. New York: Guilford Press.

Corkin, S. (1968). Acquisition of motor skill after bilateral medial temporal lobe excision. *Neuropsychologica*, *6*, 255–266.

Crawley, J. N., & Kiss, J. Z. (1984). Tracing the sensory pathway from gut to brain regions mediating the actions of cholecystokinin on feeding and exploration (p. 533). *Society of Neuroscience Abstracts*, *10*.

Crisp, A. H. (1965). Clinical and therapeutic aspects of anorexia nervosa: A study of 30 cases. *Journal of Psychosomatic Research*, *9*, 67–68.

Cummings, J. L., & Benson, D. F. (1983). Dementia: A clinical approach (p. 43). Boston: Butterworth Publishers.

Davies, P., & Maloney, A. J. (1976). Selective loss of central cholinergic neurons in Alzheimer's disease. *Lancet*, *ii*, 1403–1405.

Demitrack, M. A., Lesem, M. D., Kalogeras, K., Brandt, H. A., Granger, L., & Gold, P. W. (1989, December). Plasma and cerebrospinal fluid abnormalities of arginine vasopressin secretion in patients with bulimia nervosa. American College of Neuropsychopharmacology annual meeting, Maui, Hawaii.

Demitrack, M. A., Lesem, M. D., Listwak, S. J., Brandt, H. A., Jimerson, D. C., & Gold, P. W. (1990a). Cerebrospinal fluid oxytocin in anorexia nervosa and bulimia nervosa: Clinical and pathophysiologic considerations. *American Journal of Psychiatry*, *147*(7), 882–886.

Demitrack, M. A., Putnam, F. W., Brewerton, T. D., Brandt, H. A., & Gold, P. W. (1990b). Relation of Clinical Variables to Dissociative Phenomena in Eating Disorders. *American Journal of Psychiatry*, *147*(9), 1184–1188.

de Weid, D. (1980). Behavioral actions of neurohypophyseal peptides. *Proceedings of the Royal Society of London* [Biol], *210*, 183–195.

de Weid, D. (1965). The influence of the posterior and intermediate lobe of the pituitary and pituitary peptides on the maintenance of a conditioned avoidance response in rats. *International Journal of Neuropharmacology*, *4*, 157–167.

Deutsch, J. A. (1971). The cholinergic synapse and the site of memory. *Science*, *174*, 783–794.

Drachman, D. A., & Leavitt, J. (1974). Human memory and the cholinergic system. *Archives of Neurology*, *30*, 113–121.

Easterbrook, J. A. (1959). The effect of emotion on cue utilization and the organization of behavior. *Psychological Reviews*, *66*, 183–201.

Eich, J. E. (1980). Cue-dependent nature of state-dependent retrieval. *Memory and Cognition*, *8*, 157–173.

Essatara, M'B., Morley, J. E., Levine, A. S., Elson, M. K., Shafer, R. B., & McClain, C. J. (1984). The role of the endogenous opiates in zinc deficiency anorexia. *Physiology and Behavior*, *32*, 475–478.

Eysenck, M. W. (1979). Anxiety, learning and memory: A reconceptualization. *Journal of Research in Personality*, *13*, 363–385.

Eysenck, M. W. (1977). *Human memory*. New York: Pergamon Press, Inc.

Fehm-Wolfsdorf, G., Born, J., Voight, K-H., & Fehm, H-L. (1984). Human memory and neurohypophyseal hormones: Opposite effects of vasopressin and oxytocin. *Psychoneuroendocrinology*, *9*(3), 285–292.

Ferrier, B. M., Kennett, D. J., & Devlin, M. C. (1980). Influence of oxytocin on human memory processes. *Life Science*, *27*, 2311–2317.

Fibiger, H. C., Zis, A. P., & McGur, E. G. (1973). Feeding and drinking deficits after 6-hydroxydopamine administration in the rat: Similarities to the lateral hypothalamic syndrome. *Brain Research*, *55*, 135–148.

Flavell, J. H. (1979). Metacognition and cognitive monitoring: A new area of cognitive-developmental inquiry. *American Psychologist*, *34*(10), 906–911.

Flavell, J. H., Friedrichs, A. G., & Hoyt, J. D. (1970). Developmental changes in memorization processes. *Cognitive Psychology*, *1*, 324–340.

Flood, J. F., & Cherkin, A. (1985). Fluoxetine enhances memory processes in mice. *Psychopharmacology*, *93*, 36–43.

Fogarty, S. L., & Helmsley, D. R. (1983). Depression and the accessibility of memories. *British Journal of Psychiatry*, *142*, 232–237.

Forsling, M. L. (1986). Regulation of oxytocin release. In: D. Pfaff & D. Ganten (Eds.), *Current topics in neuroendocrinology* (Vol. 6). Berlin and Heidelberg: Springer-Verlag.

Garfinkel, P. E., & Garner, D. M. (1982). Anorexia nervosa: A multidimensional perspective (p. 272). New York: Brunner/Mazel.

Ghoneim, M. M., & Mewaldt, S. P. (1975). Effects of diazepam and scopolamine on storage, retrival, and organisational processes in memory. *Psychopharmacologia*, *44*, 257–262.

Ghoneim, M. M., & Mewaldt, S. P. (1977). Studies on human memory: The interactions of diazepam, scopolamine, and physostigmine. *Psychopharmacology*, *52*, 1–6.

Gjerris, A., Hammer, M., Vendsborg, P., Christensen, N. J., & Rafaelson, O. J. (1985). Cerebrospinal fluid vasopressin—Changes in depression. *British Journal of Psychiatry*, *147*, 696–701.

Glass, R. M., Uhlenhuth, E. H., Hartel, F. W., Matzus, W., & Fischman, M. W. (1981). Cognitive dysfunction and imipramine in outpatient depressives. *Archives of General Psychiatry*, *38*, 1048–1051.

Gold, P. W., Goodwin, F. K., Ballenger, J. C., Weingartner, H., Robertson, G. L., & Post, R. M. (1980). Central vasopressin function in affective illness. In: D. deWeid, P. A. vanKeep (Eds.), *Hormones and the brain*. London: MTP Press.

Gold, P. W., Goodwin, F. K., Post, R. M., & Robertson, G. L. (1981). Vasopressin function in depression and mania. *Psychopharmacology Bulletin*, *17*, 7–9.

Gold, P. W., Gwirtsman, H. E., Avgerinos, P. C., Nieman, L. K., Gallucci, W. T., Kaye, W., Jimerson, D., Ebert, M., Rittmaster, R., Loriaux, D. L., & Chrousos, G. P. (1986b). Abnormal hypothalamic-pituitary-adrenal function in anorexia nervosa: Pathophysiologic mechanisms in underweight and weight-corrected patients. *New England Journal of Medicine*, *314*(21), 1335–1342.

Gold, P. W., Kaye, W. H., Robertson, G. L., & Ebert, M. H. (1983). Abnormalities in plasma and cerebrospinal fluid vasopressin in patients with anorexia nervosa. *New England Journal of Medicine*, *308*, 1117–1123.

Gold, P. W., Loriaux, D. L., Roy, A., Kling, M. A., Calabrese, J. R., Kellner, C. H., Nieman, L. K., Post, R. M., Pickar, D., Gallucci, W., Avgerinos, P., Paul, S., Oldfield, E. H., Cutler, G. B., & Chrousos, G. P. (1986a). Responses to corticotropin-releasing hormone in the hypercortisolism of depression and Cushing's disease: Pathophysiologic and diagnostic implications. *New England Journal of Medicine*, *314*(21), 1329–1335.

Graf, P., & Schacter, D. L. (1985) Implicit and explicit memory for new associations in normal and amnestic subjects. *Journal of Experimental Psychology*, [Learn. Mem. Cogn.] *11*, 501–518.

Grossman, S. P. (1962) Direct adrenergic and cholinergic stimulation of hypothalamic mechanisms. *American Journal of Physiology*, *202*, 872–882.

Hamilton, M. J., Bush, M., Smith, P., & Peck, A. W. (1982). The effect of buspirone, a new antidepressant drug, and diazepam, and their interaction in man. *British Journal of Clinical Pharmacology*, *14*, 791–797.

Hamsher, K. deS., Halmi, K. A., & Benton, A. L. (1981). Prediction of outcome in anorexia nervosa from neuropsychological status. *Psychiatry Research*, *4*, 79–88

Hasher, L., & Zacks, R. T. (1979). Automatic and effortful processes in memory. *Journal of Experimental Psychology*, [Gen.] *108*, 356–388.

Hasher, L., & Zacks, R. T. (1984). Automatic processing of fundamental information: The case of frequency of occurrence. *American Psychologist*, *39*, 1372–1388.

Heinz, E. R., Martinez, J., & Haenggeli, A. (1977). Reversibility of cerebral atrophy in anorexia nervosa and Cushing's syndrome. *Journal of Computer-Assisted Tomography*, *1*(4), 415–418.

Herholz, K., Krieg, J-C., Emrich, H. M., Pawlik, G., Beil, C., Pirke, K-M., Phal, J. J., Wagner, R., Weinhard, K., Ploog, D., & Heiss, W-D. (1987). Regional cerebral glucose metabolism in anorexia nervosa measured by positron emission tomography. *Biological Psychiatry*, *22*, 43–51.

Hetherington, A. W., & Ranson, S. N. (1940). Hypothalamic lesions and adiposity in rat. *Anatomical Record*, *78*, 149–172.

Hilbert, N. H., Niederehe, G., Kahn, R. L. (1976). Accuracy and speed of memory in depressed and organic aged. *Educational Gerontology*, *1*, 131–146.

Hirst, W., & Volpe, B. T. (1984). Automatic and effortful encoding in amnesia. In Gazzaniga, M. S. (Ed.). *Handbook of cognitive neuroscience*. (pp. 369–386). New York: Plenum Press.

Hotta, M., Shibasaki, T., Masuda, A., Imaki, T., Demura, H., Ling, N., & Shizume, K. (1986). The responses of plasma adrenocorticotropin and cortisol to corticotropin-releasing hormone (CRH) and cerebrospinal fluid immunoreactive CRH in anorexia nervosa patients. *Journal of Clinical Endocrinology Metabolism*, *62*(2), 319–324.

Jenkins, J. S., Mather, H. M., Coughlin, A. K., & Jenkins, D. O. (1982). Desmopressin and desglycinamide vasopressin in post-traumatic amnesia. *Lancet i*, 39.

Johnson, C., & Larson, R. (1982). Bulimia: An analysis of moods and behavior. *Psychosomatic Medicine*, *44*, 341–351.

Kahnemann, D. (1973). *Attention and effort*. Englewood Cliffs, NJ: Prentice Hall.

Kassett, J., Maxwell, E. M., Gershon, E. S., Brandt, H. A., & Jimerson, D. C. (1989, May). A family study of psychiatric disorder associated with bulimia nervosa (Abstract No. 207). American Psychiatric Association annual meeting, San Francisco.

Kaye, W. H., Ebert, M. H., Raleigh, M., & Lake, C. R. (1984). Abnormalities in CNS monoamine metabolism in anorexia nervosa. *Archives of General Psychiatry*, *41*, 350–355.

Kaye, W. H., Gwirtsman, H. E., & Ebert, M. H. (1989, May). Serotonin: A trait disturbance in anorexia nervosa? American Psychiatric Association Annual Meeting, (Abstract No. 391). San Francisco.

Kaye, W. H., Gwirtsman, H. E., George, D. T., Ebert, M. H., Jimerson, D. C., Tomai, T. P., Chrousos, G. P., & Gold, P. W. (1987). Elevated cerebrospinal fluid levels of immunoreactive corticotropin-releasing hormone in anorexia nervosa: relation to state of nutrition, adrenal function, and intensity of depression. *Journal of Clinical Endocrinology and Metabolism*, *64*(2), 203–208.

Kaye, W. H., Jimerson, D. C., Lake, C. R., & Ebert, M. H. (1985). Altered norepinephrine metabolism following long-term weight recovery in patients with anorexia nervosa. *Psychiatry Research*, *14*, 333–342.

Kennett, D. J., Devlin, M. C., & Ferrier, N. M. (1982). Influence of oxytocin on human memory processes: Validation by a control study. *Life Sciences*, *31*, 273–275.

Keys, A., Brozek, J., Henschel, A., Mickelson, O., & Taylor, H. L. (1950). *The biology of human starvation* (Vol. 1). Minneapolis: University of Minnesota Press.

Koslow, J. H., Maas, J. W., Bowden, C. L., Davis, J. M., Hanin, I., & Javaid, J. (1983). CSF and urinary biogenic amines and metabolites in depression and mania: A controlled, univariate analysis. *Archives of General Psychiatry*, *40*, 999–1010.

Kovacs, G. L., Bohus, B., & Versteeg, D. H. G. (1979). The effects of vasopressin on memory processes: The role of noradrenergic neurotransmission. *Neuroscience*, *4*, 1529–1537.

Kovacs, G. L., Vecsei, L., Medve, L., & Telegdy, G. (1980). Effects of endogenous vasopressin content of the brain on memory processes: The role of catecholaminergic mechanisms. *Experimental Brain Research*, *38*, 357–361.

Krahn, D. D., Gosnell, B. A., Morley, J. E., & Levine, A. S. Behavioral effects of corticotropin-releasing factor: Localization and characterization of central effects. *Brain Research*, *443*, 63–69, 1988.

Krieg, J-C., Pirke, K-M., Lauer, C., & Backmund, H. (1988). Endocrine, metabolic, and cranial computed tomographic findings in anorexia nervosa. *Biology and Psychiatry*, *23*, 377–387.

Lake, C. R., Pickar, D., Ziegler, M. G., Lipper, S., Slater, S., & Murphy, D. L. (1982). High plasma norepinephrine levels in patients with major affective disorder. *American Journal of Psychiatry*, *139*, 1315–1318.

Lande, S., Flexner, J. B., & Flexner, L. B. (1972). Effect of corticotropin and desglycinamide-9-lysine vasopressin on suppression of memory by puromycin. *Proceedings of the National Academy of Science USA*, *69*(3), 558–560.

Latham, C. J., & Blundell, J. E. (1979). Evidence for the effect of tryptophan on the pattern of food consumption in free feeding and food deprived rats. *Life Sciences*, *24*, 1971–1978.

Leibowitz, S. F., & Hor, L. (1982). Endorphinergic and alpha-noradrenergic systems in the paraventricular nucleus: Effects on eating behavior. *Peptides*, *3*, 421–428.

Le Moal, M., Bluthe, R-M., Dantzer, R., Bloom, F. E., & Koob, G. F. (1987). The role of arginine vasopressin and other neuropeptides in brain-body integration. In: S. M. Stahl, S. D. Iversen & E. C. Goodman (Eds.), *Cognitive neurochemistry*, (pp. 203–232). Oxford University Press, Oxford.

Levine, A. S., Rogers, B., Kneip, J., Grace, M., & Morley, J. E. (1983). Effect of centrally administered CRF on multiple feeding paradigms. *Neuropharmacology*, *22*, 337–339.

Linnoila, M., Karoum, F., Calil, H. M., Kopin, I. J., & Potter, W. Z. (1982). Alteration of norepinephrine metabolism with desipramine and zimelidine in depressed patients. *Archives of General Psychiatry*, *39*, 1035–1028.

Lister, R.G. (1985). The amnesic action of benzodiazepines in man. *Neuroscience and Biobehavioral Reviews*, *9*, 87–94.

McGaugh, J. L. (1973). Drug facilitation of learning and memory. *Annual Review of Psychology*, *13*, 229–241.

McGaugh, J. L. (1983a). Hormonal influences on memory. *Annual Review of Psychology*, *34*, 297–323.

McGaugh, J. L. (1983b). Preserving the presence of the past: Hormonal influences on memory storage. *American Psychologist*, *38*, 161–174.

Miller, N. E. (1980). The measurement of mood in senile brain disease: Examiner ratings and self-reports. In: J. O. Cole & J. E. Barret (Eds.), *Psychopathology in the Aged* (pp. 97–118). New York: Raven Press.

Milner, B. (1970). Memory and the medial temporal regions of the brain. In: K.H. Pribram, D. E. Broadbent (Eds.), *Biology of memory* (pp. 29–50). Orlando: Academic Press.

Mishkin, M. (1978). Memory in monkeys severely impaired by combined but not by separate removal of amygdala and hippocampus. *Nature*, *273*, 297–298.

Mohs, R. C., Davis, B. N., Johns, C. A., Mathe, A. A., Greenwald, B. S., Horvath, T. B., & Davis, K. L. (1985). Oral physostigmine treatment of patients with Alzheimer's disease. *American Journal of Psychiatry*, *142*, 28–33.

Morley, J. E., & Levine, A. S. (1983). Involvement of dynorphin and kappa opioid receptor in feeding. *Peptides*, *4*, 797–800.

Morley, J. E., Levine, A. S., Gosnell, B. A., & Billington, C. J. (1984). Neuropeptides and appetite: The contribution of neuropharmacological modeling. *Federation Proceedings*, *43*, 2903–2907.

Natale, M., & Hantas, M. (1982). Effect of temporary mood states on selective memory about the self. *Journal of Personality and Social Psychology*, *42*, 927–934.

Newman, R. P., Weingartner, H., Smallberg, S., & Caine, D. (1984). Effortful and automatic memory processes: Effects of dopamine. *Neurology*, *34*(6), 805–807.

Norman, D. K., & Herzog, D. B. (1983). Bulimia, anorexia nervosa, and anorexia nervosa with bulimia: A comparative analysis of MMPI profiles. *International Journal of Eating Disorders*, *2*, 43–52.

O'Boyle, C., Lambe, R., Darragh, A., Taffe, W., Brick, I., & Kenny, M. (1983). RO-15-1788 antagonizes the effects of diazepam in man without affecting its bioavailability. *British Journal of Anaesthesiology*, *55*, 349–355.

Oliveros, J. C., Jandali, M. K., Timsit-Berthier, M., Remy, R., Behghezal, A., Audibert, A., & Moeglan, J. H. (1978). Vasopressin amnesia. *Lancet*, *i*, 41.

Piaget, J. (1952[1936]). *The origins of intelligence in children*. New York; International Universities Press.

Perry, E. K., Tomlinson, B. E., Blessed, G., Bergmann, K., Gibson, P. H., & Perry, R. H. (1978). Correlation of cholinergic abnormalities with senile plaques and mental test scores in senile dementia. *British Medical Journal*, *2*, 1457–1459.

Post, R. M., Jimerson, D. C., Ballenger, J. C., Lake, C. R., Uhde, T. W., & Goodwin, F. K. (1984). Cerebrospinal fluid norepinephrine and its metabolites in manic depressive illness. In: R.M. Post & J.C. Ballenger (Eds.), *Neurobiology of mood disorders* (pp. 539–553). Baltimore: Williams and Wilkins.

Post, R. M., Gold, P. W., Rubinow, D. R., Bunney, W. E. Jr., Ballenger, J. C., & Goodwin, F. K. (1983). Cerebrospinal fluid as neuroregulatory pathway: Peptides in neuropsychiatric illness. In: J. H. Wood (Ed.), *Neurobiology of cerebrospinal fluid 2* (pp. 107–141) New York: Plenum Publishing.

Renaud, L. P., Tang, M., McCann, M. J., Stricker, E. M., & Verbalis, J. G. (1987). Cholecystokinin and gastric distension activate oxytocinergic cells in rat hypothalamus. *American Journal of Physiology*, *253* (Reg. Integr. Comp. Physiol. 22), R661–R665.

Reuler, J. B., Girard, D. E., & Cooney, T. G. (1985). Wernicke's encephalopathy. *New England Journal of Medicine*, *312*, 1035–1039.

Reus, V. I., Silberman, E., Post, R. M., & Weingartner, H. (1979). D-amphetamine: Effects on memory in a depressed population. *Biological Psychiatry*, *14*, 345–356.

Rigter, H., & Van Riezen, H. (1974). The effects of ACTH and vasopressin analogues on CO2-induced retrograde amnesia in rats. *Physiology and Behavior*, *13*, 381–388.

Robertson, G. L. (1977). The regulation of vasopressin function in health and disease. *Record of Progress in Hormone Research*, *33*, 333–385.

Roy, A., Pickar, D., Linnoila, M., & Potter, W. Z. (1985). Plasma norepinephrine level in affective disorders: Relationship to melancholia. *Archives of General Psychiatry*, *42*, 1181–1185.

Safer, D. J., & Allen, R. P. (1971). The central effects of scopolamine in man. *Biological Psychiatry*, *3*, 347–355, 1971.

Schacter, D. L. (1987). Implicit memory: History and current status. *Journal of Experimental Psychology* [Learn. Mem. Cogn.], *13*, 501–518.

Schacter, D. L., & Moscovitch, M. (1984). Infants, amnesics and dissociable memory systems. In: M. Moscovitch (Ed.), *Infant memory: Its relation to normal and pathological memory in humans and other animals* (pp. 173–216). New York: Plenum Press.

Silberman, E. K., Weingartner, H., & Post, R. M. (1983). Thinking disorder in depression. *Archives of General Psychiatry*, *40*, 775–780.

Smith, G. P., & Gibbs, J. (1984). Gut peptides and postprandial satiety. *Federation Proceedings*, *43*, 2889–2892.

Smith, S. M. (1979). Remembering in and out of context. *Journal of Experimental Psychology*, Human Learn. Mem. *5*(5), 460–471.

Squire, L. R., & Davis, H. P. (1981). The pharmacology of memory: A neurobiological perspective. In: R. George, R. Okun & A. K. Cho (Eds.), *Annual review of pharmacology and toxicology* (Vol. 21) (pp. 323–356).

Stanley, B. G., & Leibowitz, S. F. (1984). Neuropeptide Y: Stimulation of feeding and drinking by injection into the paraventricular nucleus. *Life Sciences*, *33*, 2635–2642.

Strupp, B. J., Weingartner, H., Kaye, W., & Gwirtsman, H. (1986). Cognitive processing in anorexia nervosa; A disturbance in automatic information processing. *Neuropsychobiology*, *15*, 89–94.

Summers, W. K., Majouski, L. V., March, Q. M., Tachiki, K., & Kling, A. (1986). Oral tetrahydroaminoacridine in long-term treatment of senile dementia of the Alzheimer type. *New England Journal of Medicine*, *315*, 1241–1245.

Sunderland, T., Tariot, P. N., Cohen, R. M, Weingartner, H., Mueller, E. A., & Murphy, D. L. (1987). Anticholinergic sensitivity in patients with dementia of the Alzheimer type and age-matched controls: A dose-response study. *Archives of General Psychiatry*, *44*, 418–426.

Tanaka, M., De Kloet, E. F., de Wied, D., & Versteeg, D. H. G. (1977). Arginine-8-vasopressin affects catecholamine metabolism in specific brain nuclei. *Life Science*, *20*, 1799–1808.

Tariot, P. N., & Weingartner, H. (1986). A psychobiologic analysis of cognitive failures. *Archives of General Psychiatry*, *43*, 1183–1188.

Teasdale, J. D. (1983). Negative thinking in depression: Cause, effect or reciprocal relationship? *Advances in Behavior Therapy*, *5*, 3–25.

Teasdale, J. D., & Fogarty, S. J. (1979). Differential effects of induced mood on retrieval of pleasant and unpleasant events from episodic memory. *Journal of Abnormal Psychology*, *88*, 248–257.

Teasdale, J. D., Taylor, R., & Fogarty, S. J. (1980). Effects of induced elation-depression on the accessibility of memories of happy and unhappy experiences. *Behavior Research and Therapy*, *18*, 339–346.

Teitelbaum, P., & Epstein, A. N. (1962). The lateral hypothalamic syndrome: Recovery of feeding and drinking after lateral hypothalamic lesions. *Psychology Review*, *69*, 74–90.

Tinklenberg, J. R., Pfefferbaum, A., & Berger, P. A. (1981). 1-desamino-D-arginine vasopressin (DDAVP) in cognitively impaired patients. *Psychopharmacology Bulletin*, *17*, 206–207.

Tinklenberg, J. R., Pigache, R., Pfefferbaum, A., Berger, P. A., & Kopell, B. S. (1982). 8-L-Arginine-9-desglycinamide-vasopressin (organon 5667) and cognitively impaired patients. *Psychopharmacology Bulletin*, *18*, 202–204.

Tseng, L., & Cheng, D. S. (1980). Acute and chronic administration of beta-endorphin and naloxone on food and water intake in rats. *Federal Proceedings*, *39*, 606.

Tulving, E. (1982). *Elements of episodic memory*. New York: Oxford.

Ungerstedt, U. (1970). Is interruption of the nigro-striatal dopamine system producing the 'lateral hypothalamic syndrome'? *Acta Psychologica Scandinavica*, *80*, 35A.

Verbalis, J. G., McCann, M. J., McHale, C. M., & Stricker, E. M. (1986). Oxytocin secretion in response to cholecystokinin and food: Differentiation of nausea from satiety. *Science, 232*, 1417–1419.

Verloes, R., Scotto, A. M., Gobert, J. & Wulfert, E. (1988). Effects of nootropic drugs in a scopolamine-induced amnesia model in mice. Psychopharmacology, *95*, 226–230.

Victor, M., Adams, R. D., & Collins, G. H. (1971). The Wernicke-Korsakoff syndrome. Boston: Blackwell Scientific Publications.

Walter, R., Hoffman, P. L., Flexner, J. B., & Flexner, L. B. (1975). Neurohypophyseal hormones, analogs and fragments: Their effect on puromycin-induced amnesia. *Proceedings of the National Academy of Science*, *USA 72*(10), 4180–4184.

Warrington, E. K., & Weiskrantz, L. (1982). Amnesia: A disconnection syndrome? *Neuropsychologia*, *20*, 233–248.

Weingartner, H., Burns, S., Diebel, R., & LeWitt, P. A. (1984). Cognitive impairments in Parkinson's disease: Distinguishing between effort-demanding and automatic cognitive processes. *Psychiatry Research*, *11*, 223–235.

Weingartner, H., Chen, R. M, Sunderland, T., Tariot, P. N., & Thompson, K. (1987). Diagnosis and assessment of cognitive dysfunctions in the elderly. In Meltzer, H. (Ed.), *Psychopharmacology: The third generation of progress* (pp. 909–919). New York: Raven Press.

Weingartner, H., Gold, P., Ballenger, J. C., Smallberg, S. A., Summers, R., Rubinow, D. R., Post, R. M., & Goodwin, F. K. (1981a). Effects of vasopressin on human memory function. *Science*, *211*, 601–603.

Weingartner, H., Grafman, J., Boutelle, W., et al. (1983). Forms of memory failure. *Science*, *221*, 380–382.

Weingartner, H., Kaye, W., Smallberg, S., Cohen, R. M., Ebert, M. H., Gillin, J. C., & Gold, P. W. (1982). Determinants of memory failures in dementia. In: S. Corkin, K. Davis, J. Growdon, E. Usdin & R. Wurtman (Eds.), *Alzheimer's disease: A review of progress* (Vol. 19) (pp. 171–176). New York: Raven Press.

Weingartner, H., Kaye, W. H., Smallberg, S. A., Ebert, M. H., Gillin, J. C., & Sitaram, N. (1981c). Memory failures in progressive idiopathic dementia. *Journal of Abnormal Psychology*, *49*, 187–196.

Weingartner, H., Kaye, W., Gold, P., Smallberg, S., Peterson, R., Gillin, J. C., & Ebert, M. (1981b). Vasopressin treatment of cognitive dysfunction in progressive dementia. *Life Sciences*, *29*, 2721–2726.

Weingartner, H., Miller, H., & Murphy, D. L. (1977). Mood-state-dependent retrieval of verbal associations. *Journal of Abnormal Psychology*, *86*(3), 276–284.

Weingartner, H., Murphy, D. L., & Stillman, R. C. (1978). Mood state dependent learning. In: F. C. Colpaert and J. C. Rosecrans (Eds.), *Stimulus properties of drugs: Ten years of progress*. Amsterdam: Elsevier/North-Holland Biomedical Press.

Weiss, B., & Laties, V. G. (1962). Enhancement of human performance by caffeine and the amphetamines. *Pharmacology Review*, *14*, 1–36.

Whitehouse, P. J., Price, D. L., Struble, R. G., Clark, A. W., Coyle, J. T., & DeLong, M. R. (1982). Alzheimer's disease and senile dementia: Loss of neurons in the basal forebrain. *Science*, *215*, 1237–1239.

Winokur, A., March, V., & Mendels, J. (1980). Primary affective disorder in relatives of patients with anorexia nervosa. *American Journal of Psychiatry*, *137*, 695–698.

Witt, E. D., Ryan, C., & Hsu, L. K. G. (1985). Learning deficits in adolescents with anorexia nervosa. *Journal of Nervous and Mental Disorders*, *173*(3), 182–184.

Wolkowitz, O. M., Tinklenberg, J. R., & Weingartner, H. (1985). A psychopharmacological perspective of cognitive functions: II. Specific pharmacological agents. *Neuropsychobiology*, *14*, 133–156.

Wolkowitz, O. M., Weingartner, H., Thompson, K., Pickar, D., Paul, S. M., & Hommer, D. W. (1987). Diazepam induced amnesia: A neuropharmacological model of an "organic amnestic syndrome." *American Journal of Psychiatry*, *144*, 25–29.

Wyatt, R. J., Portnoy, B., Kupfer, D. J., Snyder, F., & Engelman, K. (1971). Resting plasma catecholamine concentrations in patients with depression and anxiety. *Archives of General Psychiatry*, *24*, 65–70.

Yerkes, R. M., & Dodson, J. D. (1908). The relation of strength of stimulus to rapidity of habit formation. *Journal Composition of Neurology Psychology*, *18*, 459–482.

Zumoff, B., Walsh, B. T., Katz, J. L., Levin, J., Rosenfeld, R. S., Kream, J., & Weiner, H. (1983). Subnormal plasma dehydroepiandrosterone to cortisol ratio in anorexia nervosa: A second hormonal parameter of ontogenetic regression. *Journal of Clinical Endocrinology and Metabolism*, *56*(4), 668–672.

APPENDIX

An Example of a Methodological Approach That Can Be Used to Simultaneously Assess Different Forms of Memory Functions in the Same Subject in Repeated Measures Experimental Designs

Each of the domains of cognitive functioning outlined in the present chapter can be assessed using a growing number of laboratory-based procedures. The methods that are described here have been developed in our laboratory and have been validated in a series of studies in young, middle-aged, and elderly normal volunteers and in studies contrasting groups of memory-impaired patients such as those suffering from dementia, amnesia, depression, mania, anxiety, and attentional dysfunctions as well as in studies that involve many different types of drug treatments of both normal or impaired subjects (see text for references).

In studies that assess alterations in cognitive functioning in response to some drug treatment, it would be useful to obtain some quantitative index of functioning in several domains. The problem that is, however, often faced by the experimenter interested in capturing the features of cognitive effects is the limited time available for assessing cognitive functioning. Each of the methods that are ordinarily used to measure the separate components of cognitive function can often require a considerable amount of time. This of course is of limited practical usefulness in studies where the observed effects may last for no more than a few minutes. In our laboratory we have developed a number of procedures that will allow an experimenter to assess several different types of functions at the same time. One of the procedures that we have used in many of our studies allows us to assess multiple cognitive domains in about 10 minutes of testing time.

The task begins by having the subject listen to 18 words read one at a time at a 2-sec rate. The subject is instructed to remember these words. All of the words have been systematically selected from a single category, e.g., vegetables. Six of the 18 words are read once, and six of the words are repeated to the subject. The subject's first task is to respond to each word that is heard for the second time. This is a simple measure of *vigilance* and *attention*. Five minutes later, after an activity-filled delay in which some other cognitive function is assessed, the subject is asked to remember as many of the words as they can from the previously read list of vegetables, a measure of *effort-demanding memory functions*. The subject is likely to remember some once-presented items, more of the twice-presented words, and is also likely to generate some intrusions. The subject is then asked to judge the certainty that a recalled word was a stimulus in the list that was read earlier, a measure of *meta-cognition*. The subject is then asked to identify which word was read once and which word was read twice, a measure of *automatic memory functions*.

The activity-filled delay that occurs between the time the subject has first heard the list and when memory is tested is used to measure other aspects of cognitive function. For example, access to *semantic knowledge* can be assessed by having the subject generate as many items as they can from an alternate category name, e.g., parts of a house. Alternatively, access to knowledge in long-term memory, or *semantic memory*, can be assessed by having the subject solve word or picture puzzles. This can be accomplished in several ways. One procedure we use is to ask subjects to identify degraded pictures of common objects which are reconstructed in a series of controlled steps. The task of the subject is to identify what the given stimulus object is. After ten seconds, if the subject is unsuccessful, more information is given, that is, more of the stimulus is exposed. The time to solve these perceptual or word problems serves as an efficient and sensitive measure of access to *semantic memory* in the case of word problems, or *knowledge memory* in the case of perceptual puzzles. Later, the subject can be asked to remember the stimuli that they had identified earlier, a measure of *explicit memory*. However, it is also possible to again present these same word or picture puzzles that had been solved earlier along with equivalent new problems that require solution. The amount of time that is saved in trying to again identify these same stimuli compared to equally difficult new stimulus material is a measure of *implicit memory* functioning. Subjects ordinarily solve the same problem again much faster even if they have no conscious awareness of having solved that stimulus problem before. (Category lists are available from the primary author upon written request.)

PART III
MEMORY

6

Investigating a Verbal Short-Term Memory Deficit and Its Consequences for Language Processing

JENNIFER R. SHELTON, RANDI C. MARTIN, and LAURA S. YAFFEE

Although general neuropsychological assessment batteries often contain subtests that rely on short-term memory, little further investigation is typically carried out to investigate the source of poor performance on these subtests. Moreover, deficits on these subtests are often mistakenly attributed to factors other than short-term memory. For example, the WAIS (Wechsler, 1958) has a digit span subtest that assesses both forward and backward span. Poor performance on this subtest relative to other verbal scales is often attributed to anxiety or distractibility (Moldawsky & Moldawsky, 1952), though there is little evidence indicating that such factors contribute to poor performance in the majority of cases (Frank, 1964; Guertin, Ladd, Frank, Rabin, & Heister, 1966). There is some evidence that a large discrepancy between performance on forward and backward span may be indicative of a deficit in concentration; however, poor performance on both components is more likely to be a strong indicator of a verbal short-term memory deficit (Lezak, 1976). On diagnostic batteries for aphasia, a subtest consisting of sentence repetition is often included (e.g., Boston Diagnostic Aphasia Exam, Goodglass & Kaplan, 1972; Western Aphasia Battery, Kertesz, 1979). If speech perception and articulation are preserved, poor performance on this subtest is assumed to indicate some level of impairment of a repetition capacity that translates auditory input into speech output (Goodglass & Kaplan, 1972). However, it is clear that sentence repetition draws on a variety of verbal abilities including verbal short-term memory, and poor performance on this task may be indicative of a short-term memory deficit. A deficit to short-term memory could have adverse consequences for a variety of other tasks which may be important to the patient's everyday functioning. Therefore, it is important for a clinician to identify whether a patient performs poorly on these aforementioned tasks due to a short-term memory deficit. Further, it is important to discern the exact nature of the short-term memory deficit (e.g., whether the deficit derives from an inability to rehearse or an inability to retain phonological

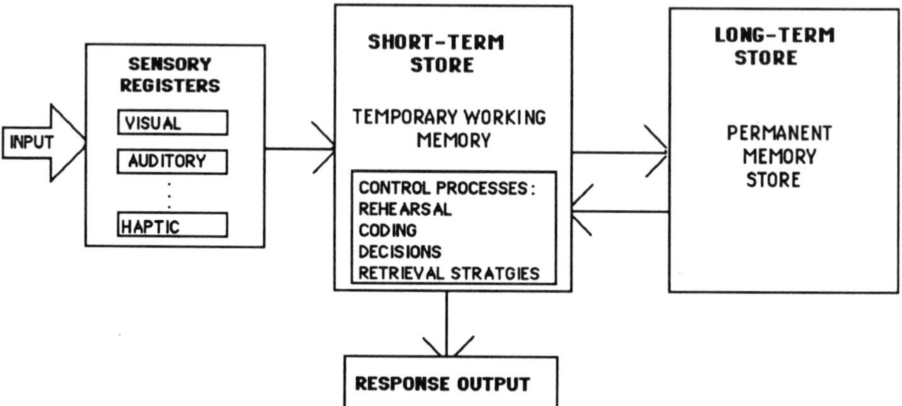

Figure 6-1 Modal model of memory. (Based on Atkinson & Shiffrin, 1968.)

information), since the consequences of the deficit will differ depending on which aspect of short-term memory has been affected.

Several different types of models of short-term memory have been proposed in the cognitive psychology literature. In the 1960s, the first models of short-term memory were developed to account for data accumulated with normal subjects on verbal recall tasks (e.g., Atkinson & Shiffrin, 1968; Waugh & Norman, 1965). Although many somewhat different models were proposed, they had many features in common, and a model containing these common features has come to be termed the "modal model" (Murdock, 1974). The modal model (see Figure 6-1) operated in a serial fashion and consisted of three memory stores: the sensory store, the short-term store and the long-term store. Information in the sensory store had only a very brief duration and had to be recoded into a more durable code to be retained in short-term memory. Short-term memory served as a general working memory space in which information was held while various types of operations (e.g., grouping or organizing information, rehearsal) were performed. Information had to be maintained in short-term memory before memory traces could be laid down in the long-term store. According to Waugh and Norman's (1965) version of the modal model, during every unit of time there was a fixed probability that information would be transferred from short-term to long-term memory. Consequently, the longer that information was retained in short-term memory the greater the probability of transfer to long-term memory. Similarly, in the Atkinson and Shiffrin model, the longer an item was retained in short-term memory, the greater the strength of the trace of the item in long-term memory and the greater the opportunity for applying various coding operations to enhance long-term retention. Rehearsal was assumed to be an important means by which information was maintained in short-term memory.

During the 1970s, a number of findings led to the downfall of the modal model (see Crowder, 1982, for a review). One problematic finding was that greater rote rehearsal did not enhance the likelihood that an item would enter long-term memory (Craik & Watkins, 1973). Also, the view that short-term

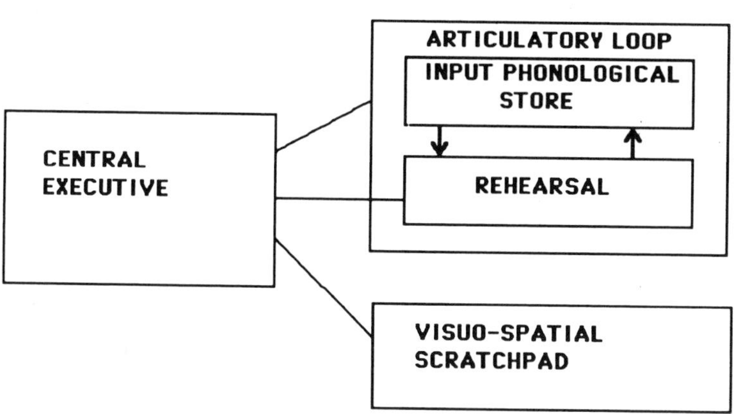

Figure 6-2 Working memory model. (Based on Baddeley, 1986, pp. 74–144.)

memory, as assessed by traditional span tasks, reflected the capacity of a general working memory space for all information processing was challenged by results from dual task experiments. If the capacity of working memory was reflected by the amount of information that could be recalled in a span task, then having subjects retain a span load of digits or words (i.e., about six items) should use up the capacity of working memory and prevent the simultaneous performance of other information processing tasks. However, several studies showed that simultaneously retaining six unrelated items had either a minimal effect or no effect on reasoning or comprehension tasks (e.g., Baddeley & Hitch, 1974; Klapp, Marshburn, & Lester, 1983). Baddeley (1986) proposed a working memory model (see Figure 6-2) that could account for many of the findings that caused difficulty for the modal model. This model outlines several components to working memory, which include a central executive and two slave systems: a visuo-spatial scratchpad and an articulatory loop. In Baddeley's recent formulation of the model (Baddeley, 1986), the central executive acts as an attention-controlling system similar to the supervisory system in Norman and Shallice's (1986) model of attention. That is, the central executive is a limited capacity system that carries out the conscious direction of activities, including the control of the slave systems. The slave systems are assumed to have dedicated capacities of their own and to carry out their functions at a more automatic level. The articulatory loop is used to maintain speech representations whereas the visuo-spatial scratchpad is used to maintain visual representations that are derived from perception or retrieved from memory. In this model, rehearsal maintains information in the articulatory loop, but does not serve as the primary means for enhancing transfer to long-term memory. Also, information can be maintained in the articulatory loop while the central executive carries out various types of processes on other sources of information.

In both the normal and neuropsychological literature, the articulatory loop component of Baddeley's working memory model has received the greatest amount of attention and will be discussed below. Although early formulations of the articulatory loop assumed that coding was solely in terms of articulatory representations (Baddeley & Hitch, 1974), the current formulation assumes two components to the articulatory loop: a phonological store which maintains speech in a nonarticulatory phonological code and a rehearsal process which depends on an articulatory code. That is, during rehearsal the phonological code is used to create an articulatory code. Internal execution of this articulatory code (i.e., rehearsal) serves to refresh the phonological code. Auditorily presented items are assumed to have automatic access to the phonological store whereas visually presented items must be converted to a phonological form via an articulatory process in order to be deposited in the phonological store. Baddeley (1986) has argued that the rehearsal loop is responsible for memory span phenomena (pp. 75–107).

There are several findings which support these claims. First, a phonological similarity effect, in which reduced span is found for lists of letters or words that sound similar, has been established for both auditory and visual presentation (e.g., Conrad, 1964; Baddeley, 1966). These findings support the view that span lists are maintained in a phonological form. A second finding is a word length effect, in which span has been found to be greater for lists comprised of short words (e.g., one-syllable words) than for lists comprised of longer words (e.g., four-syllable words). The word length appears to be dependent on the time taken to say the words rather than the number of phonemes in the words, since Baddeley, Thomson, and Buchanan (1975) showed that span was smaller for words with long vowels than words with short vowels even though the words were matched in number of phonemes. The word length effect thus supports the involvement of an articulatory rehearsal process in span. Articulatory suppression, that is having the subjects articulate irrelevant syllables or words during a span task, has been found to have different effects on auditory and visual presentation. With auditory presentation, the phonological similarity effect remains, but the word length effect is eliminated under suppression. With visual presentation, neither the phonological similarity effect nor the word length effect survives suppression. These results support the notion that visual information must be converted through an articulatory process in order to enter the phonological store whereas auditory information has direct access. With visual presentation and suppression, the items cannot be converted to phonological form, and thus both the phonological similarity effect and the word length effects are eliminated. With auditory presentation, the items enter the phonological store directly, resulting in the phonological similarity effect; however, the use of suppression prevents rehearsal and thus eliminates the word length effect.

The findings reviewed above provide strong support for the role of phonological and articulatory processes in memory span tasks. Yet several other findings are not easily accommodated by this model. For one, memory span is greater for words than nonwords (Brener, 1940) and greater for nonwords rated higher in meaningfulness than for nonwords rated low in meaningfulness (Salter, Springer, & Bolton, 1976). Also, Crowder (1978) demonstrated that memory span for phonologically uniform lists (e.g., write-right-right-write-rite-write) that are visually presented show only a small decrease in performance as compared to phonologically distinct lists that still share the same degree of visual similarity.

Both of these findings would seem to implicate a lexical contribution to memory span that is not phonological in nature. In addition, Watkins (1977) and Brooks and Watkins (1990) demonstrated that word frequency and semantic category interact with serial position effects in memory span. If phonological information alone were responsible for the results of span tasks, then one would not expect these semantic variables to affect performance on span tasks. These findings suggest a semantic component as well. It is not clear how lexical or semantic components could be incorporated into Baddeley's working memory model. Possibly these effects might be attributed to contributions from the central executive to span tasks. However, the central executive's role as an attention-controlling mechanism does not provide any obvious link with a role in maintaining lexical or semantic information.

Other problematic findings for the model come from studies demonstrating modality effects in short-term memory, that is, better recall or auditorily than visually presented word lists. It might be argued that such a result could be accommodated on the grounds that the articulatory process involved in phonological recoding for visual presentation takes up time or capacity that is not required with auditory presentation. Watkins, Watkins, and Crowder (1974) discussed several findings that refute this explanation. For example, a modality effect is obtained if one compares recall of visually presented items which are spoken aloud versus spoken subvocally (Conrad & Hull, 1968). Speaking items aloud should require at least the same, if not more, time and capacity in phonological recoding as required for internal speech, and yet recall is superior when the auditory input is added from the subject's own voice. The auditory advantage suggests that there is a specifically auditory component to memory span that is distinct from a phonological component.

Some recent models of short-term memory have taken a multiple-representations approach, that is, conceiving of verbal memory in terms of all the different types of codes (i.e., auditory, visual, phonological, articulatory, morphological, semantic, syntactic) that might be involved in language processing (Monsell, 1984; Barnard, 1985; Schneider & Detweiler, 1987). Because of all the types of codes that might be involved and the different types of processes that might be applied to them, it is difficult to characterize these models in terms of the simple box-and-arrow diagrams that have been used in many information-processing models. Nonetheless, all of these authors have made attempts at specifying their models in this fashion. As an example, consider the system-level depiction of Schneider and Detweiler's model, shown in Figure 6-3. Each of the modules on the circle (e.g., auditory, lexical) is a processing module with its own dedicated storage capacity. The different levels of each module represent different levels of processing within that domain. For example, within the speech domain, the levels might represent phonemes, syllables, and words. Each of the modules is directly connected with each of the others via the innerloop. Different modules may be active simultaneously and communicating with other modules. In this model, there is no single capacity that is drawn upon by all tasks. Interference between simultaneously performed tasks occurs only when these tasks draw on the same processing modules.

The most important assumption of these models for the present discussion

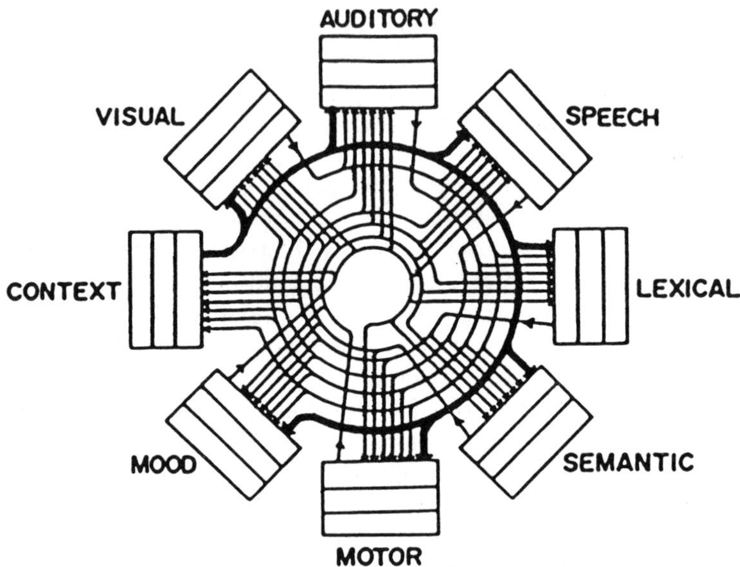

Figure 6-3 Multiple representation memory model. (Based on Schneider & Detweiler, 1987, Fig. 3, p. 64.)

is that verbal short-term memory may depend not only on the maintenance of phonological or articulatory information, but involve the maintenance of other types of information as well. For example in Schneider and Detweiler's model, auditory, speech, lexical, and semantic modules might all be activated and serve to retain different aspects of the information in the list. In a sense, these models are expanding on Baddeley's notion that there may be different buffers or storage capacities that contribute to short-term memory. However, they add buffers beyond the phonological and visual slave systems proposed in Baddeley's working memory model. The clinical implication of these multiple-capacity working memory models for neuropsychological studies is that impaired verbal short-term memory in brain-damaged patients may derive from a variety of sources, not all of which are phonological or articulatory in nature.

NEUROPSYCHOLOGICAL EVIDENCE

Some early neuropsychological evidence on short-term memory contributed to the demise of the modal model. According to the modal model, one would predict that patients with a deficit in short-term memory should show impaired long-term memory. If this deficit was interpreted as a reduction in the capacity of short-term memory, then fewer items could be simultaneously retained in short-term memory by these patients, and consequently the rate of transfer to long-term memory should be reduced. If the deficit was interpreted as more rapid decay from short-term memory, then weaker long-term memory traces would be developed. These predictions were challenged by the results of studies in which a patient with impaired short-term memory showed normal long-term memory performance (e.g., Warrington & Shallice, 1969; Shallice & Warrington, 1970).

A number of recent studies have examined short-term memory in brain-damaged patients in light of Baddeley's working memory model. Support for the phonological component of Baddeley's model has been found in several patients who show short-term memory deficits consistent with a disruption of phonological storage (e.g., Saffran & Marin, 1975; Caramazza, Basili, Koller, & Berndt, 1981; Vallar & Baddeley, 1984; Friedrich, Glenn & Marin, 1984; Martin, 1987). These patients show better recall with visual than auditory presentation, although recall with visual presentation is still below normal. This reversal of the normal modality effect is assumed to result from these patients' being able to rely on visual short-term memory for the visually presented lists, but having to rely on very reduced phonological storage for the auditorily presented lists. These patients also show no phonological or word length effects with visual presentation, and no word length effect with auditory presentation. Several factors argue against interpreting these patients' results in terms of a disruption of rehearsal. For one, their spans are smaller than what is found for normal subjects under articulatory suppression (for example, see Baddeley et al., 1975, for the results for normal subjects under suppression). Second, articulatory suppression in normal subjects does not eliminate the auditory advantage, but rather exaggerates it (Levy, 1971), presumably because suppression disrupts the ability to recode visual items to a phonological form. Finally, many of these patients are fluent speakers. This last factor argues against a rehearsal deficit to the extent that the articulatory processes involved in overt speech overlap with those involved in rehearsal. Such an assumption appears warranted due to the interfering effects on span tasks that derive from articulating irrelevant speech.

Other patients have been identified who appear to have better preserved phonological storage but show a deficit in rehearsal. These patients show similar effects as the phonological storage cases with regard to the absence of phonological similarity and word-length effects, however they show better recall with auditory than visual presentation (Martin, 1987). In addition, some of these cases have shown normal performance on a recognition memory probe task (i.e., a task in which a subject must decide if a probe item was presented in a list; Feher, 1987). This task appears to tap phonological storage but is not aided by rehearsal.

Some researchers have argued that recent neuropsychological evidence implies that the two-component articulatory loop model needs to be revised into a system with at least three components: an input phonological store, an output phonological store, and a rehearsal mechanism that transfers information between these two stores (Monsell, 1987; Howard & Franklin, 1990). A separation between input and output phonological representations has been posited on several grounds, one of which is the existence of patients who show semantic errors in single-word repetition (e.g., saying "woman" for "lady"; Shallice, 1988). The semantic errors indicate that the patient has accessed the appropriate semantic domain and thus must have perceived the phonological information correctly. Such errors would not be expected if the same phonological representation served both speech perception and production. Although such evidence supports the existence of separate input and output phonological representations, it does not demonstrate that a storage capacity specific to output representations is involved in short-term memory. Convincing evidence for an output phonological *store* would be a patient who showed poor performance on a task presumed to tap the input phonological store, but good performance on a memory task involving output phonology. A case presented by Allport (1984) provides some evidence in this regard. This patient performed poorly on a matching span task; that is, a task requiring the subject to determine if two-word sequences are the same or different. In contrast, the patient performed better on a serial recall task, at least when the inter-item interval was sufficiently long. On the basis of this patient's and other patients' performance, Allport argued that the matching span task taps the input phonological buffer, which was damaged in this patient. The patient's good performance on serial recall with a slow presentation rate was attributed to the patient using the inter-item interval to translate the input phonological form to an output phonological form which could be stored in the output buffer. When the presentation rate was increased or articulatory suppression was required, the patient's serial recall was seriously impaired. Although such findings are suggestive, it is possible that the patient was using some other type of coding (e.g., imagery) during the slow presentation rate. Clearly more evidence is needed before the separation between input and output phonological stores can be considered well established.

In contrast to the numerous studies on phonological and articulatory deficits in span, only a few studies have examined whether lexical or semantic retention deficits may be observed that impair performance on traditional short-term memory tasks. One study that has often been cited as evidence against semantic effects in short-term memory, but in favor of lexical effects, was carried out by Warrington (1975). She examined span performance for two patients who showed disruptions of semantic memory. She compared span for known words (i.e., words the patients could define to some degree) against span for unknown words (i.e., words the patients could not define) and span for unknown words versus nonwords. Both patients showed only a slight and nonsignificant superiority for the known word lists over the unknown word lists, although both showed significantly better performance on the unknown words than on the nonwords. Warrington interpreted these findings as demonstrating that memory span did not depend on semantic information but did depend on lexical information (what she termed "word-form" information, p. 654). However, Warrington's criterion for determining that a word was known to the patients was rather lax. For example, if the patient provided only a correct superordinate term when asked to define a word (e.g., saying "animal" to "crab"), the word was classified as known. Comprehension tests that probed knowledge of the words claimed to be unknown showed that the patients could often recognize the superordinate of these terms. Consequently, the degree of difference in knowledge between the words classified as known and unknown is unclear. Also, the difference between unknown words and nonwords is not purely one of lexical status since the patients evidently had some semantic information about words claimed to be unknown.

A study that reported evidence favoring a semantic component to span was carried out by Saffran and N. Martin (1990). They examined the performance of two patients who showed evidence of reduced phonological retention capacity, but who differed with respect to the effects of lexical status and imagability on span and the interaction of these factors with serial position. For example, one of the patients was very poor at recalling items in the first serial position of a list and showed a large effect of imagability on recall of these items, recalling high imagability items better than low imageability items. They argued that this patient's patient poor performance on list initial items was due to a deficit in retaining semantic information. A rich semantic code (as was available for the high imagability items) was necessary to boost performance in this position.

Recently, a patient has been identified in our lab who has a short-term memory deficit which appears to be lexical or semantic, rather than phonological, in nature (Martin, Yaffee, & Shelton, 1989). This patient (A.B.) shows normal effects of phonological and articulatory manipulations on span yet has a span of only two to three items. On memory span tests, he shows evidence of difficulty in retaining semantic information. Details of this patient's performance are presented in the section that outlines the series of tests needed to establish the nature of a short-term memory deficit and its consequences for language processing. The performance of a patient who shows a phonological retention deficit (E.A.) will also be presented in order to demonstrate the contrasting patterns that might be expected from these different deficits.

CONSEQUENCES OF SHORT-TERM MEMORY DEFICIT FOR LANGUAGE PROCESSING

Beyond establishing that a patient has a short-term memory deficit of a particular type, it is important to consider the consequences of this memory deficit for everyday functioning. Certainly one would expect patients with a short-term memory deficit to be impaired on everyday tasks that have memory requirements similar to those of typical short-term memory tasks; that is, tasks requiring the retention of random lists of items. For example, one might expect patients with reduced verbal short-term memory capacity to have difficulty with the short-term retention of telephone numbers, with the retention of a list of items that someone has asked them to buy, or with remembering sets of comparative prices that a clerk has told them. Such difficulties have been reported by patients with phonological short-term memory deficits (Vallar & Baddeley, 1984; Friedrich, Martin, & Kemper, 1985).

In addition to these situations in which the memory requirements are analogous to those in traditional short-term memory tasks, it is possible that more general language difficulties would follow from a verbal short-term memory deficit. For the past several years, there has been a great deal of interest not only in the possible nature of short-term memory deficits in brain-damaged patients, but also in the consequences of limited short-term memory capacity for sentence processing (e.g. Saffran & Marin, 1975; Butterworth, Campbell, & Howard, 1986; Friedrich et al., 1985; Martin, 1987; Vallar & Baddeley, 1984).

Most theories of sentence comprehension assume that a working memory system is used to retain the partial results of phonological, semantic, and syntactic processing until a final intepretation of the sentence is constructed. Also, theories of sentence production assume that sentence planning proceeds in several stages from the construction of central message level representations to peripheral motor planning (Garrett, 1975; Fromkin, 1971), with the implication that higher level representations must be maintained in working memory while more peripheral representations are constructed. To the extent that the verbal memory capacities that are tapped by short-term memory tasks overlap with those involved in sentence processing, one might expect patients with reduced span to show impaired sentence processing.

Most of the research on the relationship of short-term memory and sentence processing has been carried out on patients who have been shown to have phonological retention deficits. One surprising finding is that spontaneous speech production in these patients may be normal or near normal (Shallice & Butterworth, 1977; Vallar & Baddeley, 1984). Such findings suggest that the phonological store tapped by span tasks is an input capacity rather than an output capacity.[1] With regard to sentence comprehension, a great deal of research has examined the extent to which a phonological memory representation is needed for the syntactic analysis of the sentence. Some have argued that a phonological representation is needed prior to the application of syntactic analyses (Caramazza et al., 1981), perhaps to maintain order information or the representation of function words and inflections (Martin & Caramazza, 1982). Others have argued that a phonological representation is needed in order to maintain the output of syntactic analyses prior to semantic interpretation (Saffran, 1990). None of these arguments has been particularly well-supported since a number of patients have been identified with phonological short-term memory deficits who are yet capable of detecting long-distance grammatical disagreements between words in a sentence and who can understand syntactically complex sentences (Vallar & Baddeley, 1984; Butterworth et al., 1986; Howard, 1989). These findings support the results of studies of normal subjects that imply "immediacy of processing;" that is, findings indicating that the structure and interpretation of the sentence are developed as quickly as possible on a word-by-word basis (Just & Carpenter, 1987). Consequently, there is no need to retain several words in a phonological form prior to syntactic analysis, or after syntactic analysis and prior to semantic interpretation.

Even though a phonological memory representation may not be critical for the first pass analysis of a sentence, it is possible that a phonological representation is necessary as a backup representation that is used whenever the first analysis of a sentence proves incorrect and a second attempt must be made (Martin, 1990; Caplan & Waters, 1990). Although such a hypothesis appears plausible, the minimal data available on this point does not support this contention. Both Martin (1990) and Howard (1989) showed that patients with phonological short-term memory deficits showed good comprehension of garden-path sentences; that is, sentences that were specifically designed to lead to an initial misinterpretation (e.g., "The woman walked along the river near the bank where she had her savings account").

Despite the fact that a phonological short-term memory deficit alone does not appear to *cause* syntactic processing problems, it may be the case that a phonological short-term memory deficit in conjunction with a mild syntactic deficit will exacerbate the consequences of the syntactic deficit. For example, suppose that a patient had a mild syntactic deficit that consisted of slowed processing relative to normal subjects. Then, for short, syntactically simple sentences, the patient's syntactic processing might be able to keep pace with the spoken input and correctly analyze the sentence. However, if the sentence was longer or more complex, it is possible that the processing could not keep up with the sentence as it was perceived, and consequently, some of the input might have to be stored phonologically while analysis of an earlier portion was completed. Thus, for a patient with slowed syntactic processing, immediacy of processing would not hold, and the patient might be more dependent than a normal person on being able to retain information in a phonological form prior to syntactic analysis. If the patient *also* had a phonological short-term memory deficit, comprehension might be very impaired for long or complex sentences. If such a combination of deficits were present, one might expect the patient to do poorly on the comprehension of syntactically complex sentences for auditory presentation. On the other hand, if the sentences were presented visually and remained available for rereading until a response was made, the patient would not have to rely on phonological short-term memory, and thus, would be expected to show better performance (Martin, Jerger, & Breedin, 1987; Martin, 1990).

Although a phonological short-term memory deficit alone does not appear to have direct consequences for syntactic processing, patients with this type of memory deficit have consistently shown difficulty with the verbatim repetition of sentences, sometimes paraphrasing the sentences in their responses rather than repeating them exactly (Saffran & Marin, 1975; Butterworth et al., 1986; Martin, Shelton & Yaffee, 1989). The patients' preservation of the gist of the sentences in their attempts at repetition indicates that they have understood the sentences at least fairly well. However, their phonological memory deficit makes then unable to recall exactly which words were used. Consistent with this conclusion of preserved comprehension without retention of exact wording are findings indicating that some of these patients can accurately select pictures to match sentences for the same sentences that they cannot repeat (Butterworth et al., 1986; Howard, 1989; Martin, 1990).

Only a few studies have examined the relationship between lexical or semantic short-term memory deficits and sentence processing deficits. Martin and Feher (1990) showed that for several patients with varying degrees of restriction in short-term memory span, the ability to comprehend sentences with varying number of content words was highly related to span. The sentences were similar to those on the Token Test (De Renzi & Vignolo, 1962) such as "Touch the large red circle and the small green square". For sentences of varying syntactic complexity, however, there was not a relation between comprehension and memory span. Martin and Feher (1990) assumed that the patients' short-term memory deficits were due to a phonological storage deficit and interpreted the sentence comprehension results as indicating that a backup phonological representation might be needed for sentences with heavy semantic load, particularly when there was little semantic coherence among the words in the sentence. However, it is possible that these patients had a deficit in the retention of semantic information, instead of, or in addition to, a phonological short-term memory deficit, and the semantic retention deficit caused the comprehension difficulties on the semantically loaded sentences.

The only other evidence on the consequences of a semantic retention deficit for sentence processing appears to come from the patient A.B. discussed earlier (Martin, Shelton, & Yaffee, 1989). Details of his performance on sentence processing tasks is presented in the next section and compared with that of patient E.A. who shows a phonological short-term memory deficit. To anticipate the results, A.B. shows better verbatim repetition than E.A., but poorer comprehension. It appears that A.B.'s relatively well-preserved ability to retain phonological information results in repetitions which are closer to the target than are E.A.'s. However, his difficulty in retaining semantic information compromises his ability to repeat and to understand all of the content information in a sentence.

In summary, the consequences of a short-term memory deficit on sentence processing depend on the exact nature of the short-term memory deficit. A phonological short-term memory deficit impairs verbatim recall of sentences as well as word lists. It does not appear to have major effects on comprehension when the phonological short-term memory deficit exists in isolation; however, in combination with other deficits, severe comprehension deficits may be found when sentences are presented auditorily. A semantic retention deficit also affects sentence repetition, but results in a different pattern of repetition errors. Sentence comprehension is also affected by a semantic short-term memory deficit in that poor comprehension is found for sentences with high semantic load.

INVESTIGATING THE NATURE OF A SHORT-TERM MEMORY DEFICIT AND ITS CONSEQUENCES FOR LANGUAGE PROCESSING

If a clinician identifies a patient who could possibly have a short-term memory deficit, as evidenced by reduced memory span or poor sentence repetition on a standardized test battery, several tests could be carried out to determine whether this pattern is due to a short-term memory deficit, and, if so, the nature of that deficit and its effects on other tasks. It should be reiterated that patients with a verbal short-term memory deficit may not be obviously impaired in speech production. Thus, the absence of aphasic production patterns should not be used to rule out the possibility of a verbal short-term memory deficit. In the sections below, we describe two patients that appear to have contrasting short-term memory deficits, and we outline the procedures that could be used to assess short-term memory and language processing for sentences that make varying demands on short-term memory. The results from these two patients should help to clarify the different patterns of results that might be obtained which would be indicative of certain types of short-term memory impairments.

Patient Biological and Clinical Backgrounds

Patient E.A. was 48 years old when she had a CVA in 1975 that involved the left temporal and parietal lobes. She has a college degree and is right-handed, but reported that she was ambidextrous until she broke her left arm at the age of 5. E.A. has fluent speech and fits the pattern of conduction aphasia, showing good comprehension and production and very impaired sentence repetition. She makes only rare phonemic paraphasias in her speech production. In 1979, patient A.B., who is right-handed, began to experience right hemiparesis. At that time he was 59 years old and a practicing lawyer. He was operated on for a left frontal hematoma, and postoperatively he showed a dense global aphasia, which resolved over several months into a mild aphasia. A.B. is fluent in terms of his articulatory abilities. He shows word finding difficulties in spontaneous speech, but his confrontation naming is above normal. On standard clinical aphasia batteries he shows only mild comprehension deficits.

Both patients' narrative speech has been analyzed using the method developed by Saffran, Berndt, and Schwartz (1989). In this procedure, the patient is asked to tell a familiar story such as the Cinderella story, and their productions are scored on both morphological (e.g., proportion of verb inflections, proportion of nouns preceded by determiners) and structural characteristics (e.g., proportion of sentences well-formed, proportion of embedded constructions). E.A. and A.B. scored within one standard deviation of the mean for normal controls on most of the measures. However, E.A.'s speech rate (i.e., words per minute) was two standard deviations below the normal mean and A.B.'s was far below the normal mean (he spoke at about half the rate of normal subjects). Also, A.B. was below the normal range on the structural elaboration index which measures the number of words included in noun phrases and verb phrases.

Preliminary Testing

The first step in assessing a possible short-term memory deficit in a patient is to rule out any other factors that may have caused the patient to perform poorly on the span task. Language or information processing difficulties other than short-term memory deficits could produce poor performance on short-term memory tasks. For example, although it is unlikely that most patients performing poorly on memory span tasks do so because of an attention deficit, it is possible that for some patients attention deficits do cause poor performance. If the patient has difficulty attending to other tasks that require concentration but not short-term memory, than an attention problem rather than or in addition to a short-term memory problem would most likely be implicated. A subtle attention deficit as the source of a verbal memory deficit could be ruled out if the patient performed well on a non-verbal short-term memory task. (See discussion under *Nonverbal Span* for a description of some nonverbal tasks.) Of course, if a patient also performed poorly on nonverbal short-term memory tests, some other task would have to be used to rule out an attention deficit. A continous performance test could be administered in which the subject has to attend to an auditory or visual display and respond (by pressing a response button or tapping) when a pre-selected target is presented. One such task was administered by Warrington and Shalice (1969) in which the subject was given a category, such as animals, and was asked to tap each time a word belonging to the category was presented. The subject was then presented with a 40-word list, which was read at a rate of one item per second, in which 10 of the words were animals. This procedure was repeated with three other categories. If a subject performed poorly on this task, an attention problem rather than a short-term memory problem may be implicated. If such a categorization task would be too difficult for a given patient, a simpler task such as tapping every time a particular word appeared could be used.

If screening tests involving short-term memory have been administered that require a verbal response (such as in the Digit Span subtest of the WAIS), difficulties due to speech production deficits could be a possible source of poor performance. For example, patients with articulatory difficulties might perform poorly because it takes them a long time to produce each word, and by the time they have produced one or two words in a memory span list, they have forgotten the rest. One way to isolate a memory problem would be to administer a test in which the response mode was nonverbal (e.g., pointing to pictured objects or Arabic numerals).

Possible speech perception difficulties must also be addressed. In order to evaluate whether a speech perception deficit is interfering with performance on memory span tasks, a speech discrimination test may be administered. For example, one section of the Minnesota Test for the Differential Diagnosis of Aphasia (Schuell, 1965) includes a speech perception test that assesses phoneme discrimination. In this subtest the examiner says a word and the patient must choose between two pictures with phonologically similar names (e.g., for the word "peas," the distracting picture is "knees"). A similar test could easily be developed by the clinician that would involve presenting pairs of identical or phonologically similar words (e.g., "keep"–"keep", "keep"–"sleep") and asking the patient to determine whether the pairs are the same or different. Normal subjects would be expected to score nearly 100% correct on such a test.

Tests for more subtle speech perception deficits (such as discrimination tests using synthetic or natural speech syllables differing in only a single phonetic feature) are probably not necessary. Recent evidence from our lab (Martin & Breedin, 1990) indicates that patients with impairments on such difficult discrimination tasks (but good performance on tasks involving easier discriminations) can perform normally on verbal short-term memory tasks.

Patient Performance on Preliminary Tests

Neither E.A. nor A.B. demonstrates any attention difficulties. On a continuous performance task in which the subjects were instructed to tap every time a particular word was spoken, neither subject made any errors. Previous studies have shown that E.A. has a mild speech perception deficit (Friedrich et al., 1984). On a recent speech discrimination test involving natural speech syllables differing in a single phonetic feature, E.A. scored 90% correct and A.B. scored 97% correct. A group of age-matched controls obtained a mean score of 97.6% correct with a range of 95 to 100. On an easier discrimination test involving natural speech syllables (i.e., the nonmatching phonemes differed in two or more phonetic features), both E.A. and A.B. scored within normal range.

GENERAL TESTING CONSIDERATIONS FOR MEMORY SPAN TASKS

The tests presented below will focus on verbal span. Span could also be measured, for example, with environmental sounds or with pictorial stimuli. However, we are mainly concerned with deficits in span for verbal material and with the relationship of these deficits to sentence processing. Only brief consideration will be given to tests of nonverbal short-term memory.

The following considerations should be employed in testing for short-term memory deficits. First, a sufficient number of trials should be given to the patient at each set size (e.g., at least 10 lists per set size) in order to determine that the pattern is consistent. Span is then determined as the set size at which the patient misses 50% of the lists. For example, if a patient can correctly recall all the lists at set size 2 but only half of the lists at set size 3, the patient would be said to have a span of 3. If the 50% performance level falls between two set sizes, then span can be estimated by interpolating between the two set sizes to estimate the set size at which 50% performance would occur. For example, if a patient scores 80% at set size 2 and 30% at set size 3, span would be estimated to be 2+ (the observed percentage correct/the percentage correct to meet criterion) which, in this case would be 2+ (30/50) = 2.6.

Second, a pointing response rather than a verbal response should be used with all patients that have language production deficits. The pointing response is important because if spoken recall is required, a patient who has trouble articulating or who has word-finding difficulties may show a reduced span for those reasons rather than from reduced short-term memory capacity. In using a pointing response, all the possible items in the list (e.g., the digits one through nine) should be arranged randomly on a sheet of paper. For words, either the written word (for patients with preserved reading abilities), or a picture depicting the word, should be on the response sheet. Before testing begins, the patient should be asked to point to each item as it is said out loud by the tester. This is done to insure that the patient can recognize the pictures or printed words.

With the pointing procedure described above, it is possible that the patient would develop a spatial strategy to perform the task rather than relying on verbal short-term memory. That is, the patient might imagine the pictured object and its location on the page as each item is presented and use this spatial image to recall the items. To prevent the use of such a strategy, several different random configurations of the items should be developed and a response sheet with a new arrangement should be given after each set size. When a new arrangement is given, the patient should again be asked to point to each item as it said aloud by the researcher. It is essential that the patient not be allowed to look at the response sheet while a list is being given. The response sheet should be face down while each list is presented and turned over after the last item in the list is presented.

Third, it is recommended that the researcher present all the memory span lists once visually and once auditorily. The comparison of auditory versus visual presentation is important in establishing the specific nature of the short-term memory deficit. In relation to this point, the researcher should carry out the testing for the various lists (e.g., phonologically similar versus dissimilar lists) and different modalities over several testing sessions in order to avoid fatigue and frustration for patients who have short-term memory deficits. If this is not possible, testing of the various lists should have as much intervening material as possible and this material should not be related to short-term memory tests.

Fourth, the rate of presentation should be consistent across lists of different set sizes and for different modalities. A typical presentation rate is one item per second. For auditory presentation, it is probably wise to create a tape in order to better control the rate. For visual presentation, the researcher should use a computer to present list items, if possible. If this is not feasible, words should be presented on index cards and the cards should be shown to the patient at the recommended rate.

Fifth, on standardized intelligence tests, memory span is typically assessed by measuring both forward and backward span. Since it is not clear what backward span measures in addition to memory span (i.e., attention or reasoning abilities), only forward span should be used in diagnosing a short-term memory deficit.

The following memory span tasks can be used to determine if the short-term memory deficit is articulatory, phonological, or lexical-semantic in nature. It is assumed that the clinician has already established that the patient performs poorly on digit span and repetition tests found on assessment batteries and that the poor performance is not due to the variables mentioned earlier. In addition to span tasks, some other short-term memory tasks are included that can be used to provide converging evidence on the nature of the short-term deficit.

MEMORY TESTS THAT ISOLATE PHONOLOGICAL FACTORS IN SHORT-TERM MEMORY

Auditory vs. Visual Presentation

Word lists should be created that contain words which are all the same length and the same frequency of occurrence (this can be determined from norms of word frequency; e.g., Kucera & Francis, 1969). Ten to twelve words should be chosen to make up the test set. Set sizes should range from 2 to 5 and each set size should contain 10 lists. Patients should be tested on recall for both visual and auditory presentation.

One piece of evidence for a disruption to a phonological store is the absence of a modality effect or a reverse modality effect. Normal individuals should show better performance for auditory than visual presentation. Patients with phonological short-term memory deficits do not show this normal pattern of performance and typically show better performance with visual presentation. As discussed earlier, their better performance with visual presentation is attributed to their ability to rely on intact visual storage.

Table 6-1 Proportion Correct for E.A. and A.B. on Phonological Short-Term Memory Tasks[a]

	Control	E.A.	A.B.
Mode of Presentation			
Set sizes		(2–5 items)	
Auditory	n.a.	.43	.38
Visual	n.a.	.50	.25
Phonological Similarity			
Letters			
Set sizes	(3–6 items)	(2–3 items)	
Auditory			
Similar	.65	.58	.53
Dissimilar	.86	.65	.85
Visual			
Similar	.68	.88	.18
Dissimilar	.79	.68	.33
Words			
Set sizes	(5 items)	(2–3 items)	
Auditory			
Similar	.40	.30	.30
Dissimilar	.65	.70	.65
Visual			
Similar	.30	.30[b]	.18
Dissimilar	.57	.35[b]	.40
Word Length (auditory)			
Set sizes	(3–6 items)	(2–5 items)	
1 syllable	.59	.38	.43
2 syllable	.52	.41	.32
Digit Matching Span			
Set sizes	(3–6 items)	(2–6 items)	
	.96	.66	.78

n.a. = not available.

[a]Numbers represent proportion correct averaged across set sizes.

[b]Percent correct for three-item lists; E.A. was not tested on 2 item lists.

On a serial recall task using concrete word lists and a pointing response, patient E.A. showed the pattern of performance expected from a patient with a phonological deficit in short-term memory in that she showed better performance on visually presented materials than auditorily presented materials. It would be expected that a patient with a lexical-semantic deficit would show the normal modality effect and A.B. did show better performance with auditorily than visually presented lists. The results for both patients are shown in Table 6-1.

Phonological Similarity

Ten letters should be chosen that are phonologically similar (e.g., Z, P, B, etc.) to create 10 lists at each set size. These would make up the phonologically similar lists. Ten lists at each set size should also be created with letters that are phonologically dissimilar (e.g., A, R, L, etc.). Phonologically similar and dissimilar word lists could also be used. However, if testing with visual presentation is also to be used, care must be taken to insure that the phonologically similar words are not also more visually similar than are the phonologically dissimilar words. To create phonologically similar and dissimilar word lists we have used the phonologically similar set (talk, awe, bought, paw, got, cot, taught, dock) which is matched in terms of the number of letter repetitions within a set with the phonologically dissimilar set (owe, bright, cat, thought, pal, goat, tale, deck).

Normal subjects show worse performance on lists containing letters that are phonologically similar than on lists where letters are phonologically dissimilar because they are using a phonological code to retain information. Patients with a phonological short-term memory deficit would not be expected to show this effect for visually presented lists, since it would not be their advantage to convert visually presented items to a phonological form. However, several patients who have been described as having a phonological short-term memory deficit show a phonological similarity effect for auditory presentation. The interpretation has been that although these patients have very reduced phonological capacity, the capacity is not zero. Since auditorily presented verbal information appears to be automatically coded phonologically, theses patients tend to rely on their reduced phonological capacity for auditorily presented items. In order for these patients not to show a phonological similarity effect, they would have to develop a conscious strategy of converting phonological information into some non-phonological code for retention.

Performance for both patients and age-matched controls is shown in Table 6-1. For both the letters and words E.A. shows a phonological similarity effect for auditory presentation. For the visually presented letters, E.A. actually performs better on the phonologically similar lists than on the phonologically dissimilar lists. For the visually presented words, E.A. shows a slight advantage for the phonologically dissimilar lists, but this difference is far from significant. A.B. does show a significant phonological similarity effect for both auditorily and visually presented letters and words.

Word Length

Ten one-syllable words should be chosen to make up the short word length list, for example: Rome, class, switch, verse, goat, Maine, math, zinc, mumps, Greece. Ten two-syllable words should be chosen to make up the long word-length list, for example: Paris, Texas, reading, iron, subject, sofa, donkey, measles, novel, China. The words in the two lists were matched for frequency as should be the case with any additional lists that are created.

Normal subjects show worse performance with two-syllable words than one-syllable words of the same list length. Worse performance on the two-syllable words is presumably due to articulatory rehearsal since two syllable words take longer to articulate than one syllable words. Therefore, a patient with a severe articulatory rehearsal deficit would not be expected to show this effect if he could not engage in rehearsal. Also, since the role of articulatory rehearsal is presumed to be the maintenance of a phonological code, patients with a phonological short-term memory deficit would not be expected to show a word length effect. It is possible that a patient with partially impaired rehearsal might produce an exaggerated effect of word length, but this has not been reported in the literature.

E.A. does not show a word length effect with one- and two-syllable words, as would be expected from a patient with a phonological short-term memory deficit. Although A.B. does have a greatly reduced span, he does show a word length effect. The results for both patients and age-matched controls are shown in Table 6-1.

Digit Matching Span

The digits one through nine can be used to create 20 item lists for each set size (e.g. set size 2–5). Fifty percent of these lists (i.e., 10 lists) should be used to create a matching trial (e.g., 4, 7, 2, 6–4, 7, 2, 6). Nonmatching sequences are created for the other 50% of the lists by reversing the order of two consecutive digits in the original lists (e.g., 5, 3, 1, 9–5, 1, 3, 9). The position of the switched letters should be balanced across list positions. All of the sequences should then be randomized. The task is to determine if two auditorily presented sequences are the same or different.

Matching span has been argued to be a fairly pure measure of phonological memory (Allport, 1984). Since the patient does not have to reproduce the list either orally or by pointing, the need for articulatory rehearsal may be minimized. However, the test does tap memory for order information, which appears to be an important component of phonological memory. Also, since random series of digits have little meaning, memory for semantic information would be expected to make little contribution to this task. Thus, a patient with a phonological short-term memory deficit might show worse performance on this test than on other span tests that involve words.

The results for both patients and age-matched controls are shown in Table 6-1. E.A. shows a pattern consistent with the assumption that she has a phonological short-term memory deficit. Her matching span for digits, which carry little semantic information, is worse than A.B.'s. In contrast, for concrete noun lists (reported under mode of presentation) which carry much more semantic information, E.A.'s serial recall is better than A.B.'s.

Summary of Patient Performance: Phonological Short-Term Memory Tasks

E.A. shows a pattern of performance expected from a patient with a phonological deficit in short-term memory. She shows a reverse modality effect, no effect of phonological similarity for visual presentation and no effect of word length. A.B., on the other hand, shows a normal pattern of performance on all the phonological tasks although his span is greatly reduced. Thus, it would be difficult to attribute his short-term memory deficit to exactly the same source as E.A.'s. Although he probably has some restriction in his capacity for phonological retention, this restriction appears to be less severe than E.A.'s given that he shows phonological effects and that his matching span is larger than hers. E.A.'s better performance than A.B. on the concrete word lists suggests that A.B. may have difficulty retaining semantic information. Below, tests are described which can be used to assess lexical-semantic short-term memory in patients with reduced span.

SHORT-TERM MEMORY TASKS THAT ISOLATE SEMANTIC FACTORS AFFECTING SPAN

Several memory tasks can be given to test their ability to retain information in a semantic code. Performance can be assessed on a auditory recognition probe task and a memory span task that compares low-frequency words and nonwords matched on phonemes.

Recognition Probe

In the probe task, the subject is presented with a four item list and then a fifth probe item, the task being to say whether or not the probe item was one of the four list items. The lists are presented auditorily at the rate of one item per second. Probes can either match the list item or, on nonmatching trials, can be unrelated, semantically related (i.e., synonymous) or phonologically related (i.e., rhyming) to one of the list items. 48 lists should be created with half of the probes being contained in the list. On the 24 nonmatching trials, one-third of the probes should be semantically related to a list item (e.g., arm, hat, friend, bed, probe = cap), one-third phonologically related (e.g., fence, pool, car, hair, probe = school), and one-third unrelated to any list item. Each position in the four-item list should be probed equally often on both the matching trials, and on the phonologically and semantically related nonmatching trials.

If a patient with a phonological deficit is retaining list information in a lexical-semantic code, it would be expected that a patient would make more errors on a memory probe task when the probe was semantically related to the list item than when it was unrelated. However, a patient using only a phonological code to retain list information (i.e., a lexical-semantic deficit) would not be likely to make these semantic errors but would make errors on the phonologically related probes.

As shown in Table 6-2, E.A. makes the most errors on semantically related probes whereas A.B. makes no errors on these probes. The largest proportion of A.B.'s errors occur on the phonologically related probes.

Word vs. Nonword

Retention for 2 to 4 item low-frequency word lists and nonword lists can be used to assess whether list information is being held in either a phonological or lexical-semantic code. The low frequency words and the nonwords should be matched for phonological similarity. For example, the low-frequency list might consist of the words: hog, toe, pet, rot, hid, gal, web, tat, cab, lag. The nonword

Table 6-2 Proportion Correct for E.A. and A.B. on Lexical-Semantic Short-Term Memory Tasks

	Control	E.A.	A.B.
Recognition Probe			
Matching	.97	.90	.91
Unrelated			
Phonological	.95	.87	.83
Semantic	.99	.67	1.00
Word versus Nonword			
Set sizes[a]	(4–6 items)	(2–3 items)	
Word	.63	.45	.50
Nonword	.51	.10	.45

[a]Numbers represent proportion correct averaged across set sizes.

list might consist of: cag, bal, heb, wat, tor, het, pid, tal, gog, tob. Lists should be presented auditorily, although visual presentation can also be tested if desired.

Normal control subjects show better performance for the word lists than the nonword lists for auditory presentation. This indicates that they can make use of a lexical-semantic code as well as a phonological code to retain information. A patient with a lexical-semantic deficit would not be expected to show a difference in performance for the word and nonword lists. However, a patient with a phonological deficit would be expected to show better performance on the word lists if they are using a lexical-semantic code to retain list information.

Table 6-2 presents the results for both patients and age-matched controls on this test. E.A. shows better retention of words over nonwords. A.B., on the other hand, shows no significant difference in words over nonwords.

Summary of Patient Performance on Lexical-Semantic Short-Term Memory Tests

The performance for these two patients on the phonological span tasks and the lexical-semantic span tasks indicates that although both E.A. and A.B. have deficits in short-term memory, their deficits are very different in nature. Although it is unlikely that his phonological retention capacity is normal, A.B. appears to have a better ability to retain phonological information than does E.A. However, it appears that E.A. has a better ability to retain semantic information since she performs better than A.B. with concrete word lists. She also performs better with word than nonword lists while A.B. does not show this effect. Further evidence of E.A.'s retention of words in a semantic form was obtained in the probe task in which she made many errors on the semantically related trials, while A.B. made no such errors. The different pattern of performance for the two patients suggests that there may be two components involved in short-term memory, a phonological component and a lexical-semantic component. This conclusion is contrary to the model proposed by Baddeley (1986) since this model does not easily accommodate a contribution from semantic information in span tasks. However, this pattern would be consistent with a multiple stores model such as that of Schneider and Detweiler (1987).

Nonverbal Span

Finally, if nonverbal short-term memory abilities are a concern, span should be assessed on tasks that are nonverbal as well. Often patients with language deficits perform normally on nonverbal short-term memory tasks. One such task that was administered to E.A. and A.B. assessed nonverbal auditory memory. In this task, they had to tap out tone sequences by pointing to spatial locations on the table that corresponded to high or low tones. Tones were presented at the rate of two tones per second with lists ranging in length from 3 to 6 items. Normal subjects were able to produce 93% of the 4-item lists (range: 88–96), 83% of the 5-item lists (range: 75–96) and 66% of the 6-item lists (range: 54–79). The data from this task for E.A. were previously reported in Friedrich et al. (1984). E.A. was able to reproduce 96% of the 3-item lists, 83% of the 4-item lists, 67% of the 5-item lists and 37% of the 6-item lists. This performance is remarkable compared to her performance on word lists even though it is slightly below normal range. A.B. did not perform quite as well; he correctly reproduced 83% of the 3-item lists, 67% of the 4-item lists, 33% of the 5-item lists and 8% of the 6-item lists. Still, compared to his performance on verbal span tasks his performance is impressive.

To assess visuo-spatial aspects of nonverbal memory, one could assess a patient's ability to recall the order in which spatial locations are pointed to by the experimenter. A test which assesses nonverbal span in this way is the Corsi Blocks test (described in Milner, 1971, pp. 274–275). One could use this test or some version of this test to assess nonverbal span.

The dissociations between nonverbal and verbal short-term memory that have been observed for E.A. and other patients (e.g., Shallice & Warrington, 1974) constitute important evidence that buffers beyond the articulatory loop and visuo-spatial scratchpad must be postulated. Consequently, these findings also support the multiple stores position such as that postulated by Schneider and Detweiler (1987).

TESTS THAT INVESTIGATE LANGUAGE PROCESSING IN PATIENTS WITH SHORT-TERM MEMORY DEFICITS

Once the nature of the short-term memory deficit has been established, the researcher may wish to assess how this deficit affects the patients' ability to repeat and comprehend sentences. The following tasks may be employed for patients with short-term memory deficits to investigate the ways in which their reduced memory spans affect their sentence processing abilities.

Preliminary Testing

In order for the patients' performance on these tasks to be meaningfully related to their short-term memory abilities, it is necessary to insure that the patients can comprehend the words in the sentences when the words are presented in isolation. If the patients have well-preserved vocabularies—as evidenced, for example, by good performance on the PPVT (Dunn & Dunn, 1981) or on the vocabulary section of the WAIS (Wechsler, 1958)—then this issue would not be of great concern. A.B. received a standardized score of 110 on the PPVT, thus showing good single-word comprehension. Although E.A. has not been tested on the PPVT, she scored in the 97th percentile in the vocabulary section on the Gates-MacGinitie Test (Gates & MacGinitie, 1968). However, if patients do have single-word comprehension difficulties, then care must be taken to construct sentences with simple words that they can understand. In some cases, the tests below use a restricted vocabulary that is the same across sentences of different lengths, and begin with sentences with few content words. If the patients do well on the sentences with few words, one can rule out a single-word comprehension deficit as a complicating factor.

Beyond single word comprehension, it is necessary to insure that the patients have syntactic abilities that are sufficient for analyzing the types of sentence constructions employed in the tests. This could be assessed by comparing comprehension for visual presentation (with unlimited time for viewing the sentence) versus auditory presentation. Visual presentation should minimize the demands on short-term memory. If a patient does well on a given construction with visual presentation, one can assume that their syntactic abilities are sufficiently well-preserved to analyze these sentence types, at least when given unlimited time to do so. Of course, for performance with visual presentation to be meaningfully interpreted, the patient must have preserved reading abilities.

General Testing Considerations for Sentence Processing Tests

For auditory sentence comprehension tests, the sentences should be presented to the subject at a normal rate of speech. It is preferable to pre-record the sentences on a cassette tape to control for speech rate. If the task involves pictures, they should *not* be in view until the sentence has been completed, since the patient could avoid the memory demands of auditory testing by being able to eliminate picture alternatives as key words in the sentence were perceived. Sentences should not be repeated since repetition of the sentence may serve to boost memory for certain elements of the sentence that were lost from short-term memory on the first presentation.

In the present context, the purpose of visual testing is to minimize short-term memory demands in order to determine if performance is enhanced. Consequently, for visual presentation, the sentences should remain in view at all times during the trial. If pictures are used, they should be presented at the same time as the sentences.

For repetition tasks, the sentences to be repeated should be presented at a normal rate of speech, and if possible should be recorded on a cassette. Since this task investigates short-term memory, sentences should only be heard by the subject once. The patients' repetitions should be recorded and later transcribed so their exact wording is preserved.

Patient Performance on Sentence Processing

The patients E.A. and A.B., whose short-term memory data were discussed earlier, have been tested on many sentence comprehension and repetition tasks. As with their memory span data, they show contrasting patterns on the language processing tasks that fit well with the assumption that E.A. has a phonological retention deficit and A.B. a semantic retention deficit. Their data are discussed in conjunction with the description of the tests used to assess sentence processing.

TESTS OF SENTENCE COMPREHENSION

The following sections present several tests that may be administered to patients with short-term memory deficits that will help the clinician to reveal sentence comprehension deficits that may not be apparent in less structured conversational interactions. Some of these sentences use syntactically simple sentences with varying amounts of content information. One might expect that patients with a semantic retention deficit would show increasingly impaired performance as the amount of content information increased. On the other hand, it is possible that patients with pure phonological retention deficit would perform well on these tasks (Butterworth et al., 1986).

The second type of task includes sentences that vary in syntactic complexity but where the amount of semantic information is kept constant. Some patients with very restricted short-term memory spans have been shown to perform well on syntactically complex sentences (Martin, 1987). However, as discussed earlier, it is possible that a short-term memory deficit would interact with mild sentence processing deficits to produce impaired performance with auditory presentation, though performance with visual presentation might be unimpaired.

For all of the comprehension tests, performance with auditory presentation could be compared to performance with visual presentation. Good performance with visual presentation would verify that the patients could understand the content words and syntactic structures of the sentences, and that any difficulty with auditory presentation could thus not be attributed to these factors. On the other hand, if the patients showed similar patterns of impaired performance for auditory and visual presentation, it would be unlikely that their short-term memory deficit was the source of the comprehension difficulty.

Sentences with Varying Semantic Load

Sentence-Picture Matching

Administration of this task requires construction of pictures containing the appropriate referents for the content words.[2] In this task, a sentence is spoken (e.g., "The old man was carrying the tired girl"). Then a picture is presented, and the subject must decide if the picture matches the sentence. In the nonmatching pictures, a substitution should be made for an attribute described by an adjective (e.g., old), or the attribute should be attached to the wrong person or object. In order to vary the amount of content information, sentences with

Table 6-3 Sentences with Simple Syntactic Structures and Varying Numbers of Content Words and Performance for Patients E.A. and A.B.

1 Adjective before Nouns: The old man was carrying the tired girl.
2 Adjectives before Nouns: The new red truck was hauling the heavy old furniture.
2 Adjectives before Nouns + Prepositional Phrase: The new blue car with tinted windows was splashing the angry little girl.

	Percent Correct	
	E.A.	A.B.
1 Adjective before Nouns	100	83
2 Adjectives before Nouns	83	33

different numbers of adjectives and prepositional phrases can be used (see examples in Table 6-3). Eight trials for each sentence type would be a minimum for establishing the effect of increasing semantic load. For visual presentation, the sentence and picture should be presented together and remain available until the patient makes a response. Only the sentences with one and two adjectives before each of two nouns were presented auditorily to E.A. and A.B. for sentence-picture matching. The results from this task are presented in Table 6.3.

Token Test Sentences

This task is similar to the sentence-picture matching task. However, it has the advantage that the materials are commercially available, and many clinicians would already have a copy of this test. The first four sections of the Token Test (DeRenzi & Vignolo, 1962) use sentences with simple syntactic structures but with increasing numbers of content words, as shown in Table 6-4. (The fifth section introduces sentences with more complex syntactic structures, and so the results for that should be kept separate from those from the earlier parts of the tests.)

On this test, subjects respond by touching the appropriate tokens (upon the completion of the command). In order to test for the effects of short-term memory load in administering this test, the tokens should be out of view when the sentence is spoken.[3] Otherwise the patient might be able to identify the appropriate tokens as the sentence is spoken, and use some sort of spatial memory for the location of the tokens in responding. Even patients with severe

Table 6-4 Example of Sentences with Simple Syntactic Structure and Varying Numbers of Content Words (Token Test Sentences and Performance for Patients and Control Subjects

	Percent Correct		
	E.A.	A.B.	Controls
1. Touch the red square.	92	100	
2. Touch the large white circle.	75	83	
3. Touch the green square and the yellow circle.	58	58	99.6
4. Touch the small yellow circle and the large green square.	42	0	97.1

short-term memory deficits should be able to perform well on the first section if they can understand the meaning of the content words in these sentences, since there are only two informative content words in the shortest sentences (e.g., "Touch the green square"). Only patients who did well on this first section would be of interest for examining the effects of memory load. Patients who did poorly would presumably have some difficulty understanding the meaning of the size, shape, and color words.

For visual presentation, in order to minimize memory demands, the sentence should remain in view until the patient has made a response.

Twelve sentences of each of the four types shown in Table 6-4 were presented auditorily. In terms of overall level of performance, E.A. performed somewhat better than A.B., responding correctly on 32/48 commands whereas A.B. responded correctly on 29/48 commands. The results for each sentence type are presented in Table 6-4 along with data from age-matched control subjects. Twenty control subjects were tested, and the mean data is presented. Since the control subjects did so well on the two most difficult sentence types, Types 1 and 2 were not administered.

With visual presentation, E.A. scored 100% correct and A.B. scored 98% correct overall.

Attribute Questions

We have developed a comprehension test for attributes of objects that was based on a similar task used by McCarthy and Warrington (1987). In this task, the patient is asked 20 simple attribute questions such as "Which is quick, a deer or a snail?" and "Which is quiet, a concert or a library?" In our version of the task, none of the attributes or exemplars were repeated across trials. This was done to minimize interference between the responses for different trials. If a patient has difficulty with this task, the questions can be revised to include only one noun and one attribute (e.g., "Is a deer quick?" "Is a concert quiet?"), to determine if minimizing the amount of semantic information improves performance.

E.A. scored 100% correct on this task. A.B. had a very difficult time with this task, answering only 20% of the questions corectly on the first presentation. He often could produce no answer and asked that the question be repeated. With visual presentation, A.B. scored 100% correct indicating that he knew which objects had which attributes. Also, with the shorter questions (e.g. "Is a deer quick?"), he scored 100% correct.

Sentences with Complex Syntactic Structures

Relative Clause Sentences

A comprehension test of relative clause sentences with differing syntactic structures can be administered. Table 6-5 presents examples of types of sentences that could be used. All of the sentences are matched in number of content words and in the complexity of the semantic information conveyed by the sentences. Types I and II contain two active clauses whereas types III and IV contain one passive clause. In type III, the passive is in the main clause, and in type IV the

Table 6-5 Examples of Relative Clause Sentence Types

I. The boy that had red hair carried the girl.
II. The boy that carried the girl had red hair.
III. The boy that had red hair was carried by the girl.
IV. The boy that was carried by the girl had red hair.
V. The boy that the girl carried had red hair.

passive is in the embedded clause. Type V differs from the rest in that the embedded clause is an object relative construction rather than a subject relative construction. Types III, IV, and V should be more difficult than types I and II since the passive and object relative constructions are considered to be more complex syntactic structures than the active and subject relative constructions. Among these three more complex constructions, one might expect the type IV and V sentences would be the most difficult since the unusual construction is contained in the embedded clause rather than the main clause. That is, in these sentence types, subjects have to retain the syntactic representation of the main clause while processing the difficult embedded clause construction. Previous results using this task have been presented in Martin (1987).

For auditory presentation, the sentence should be spoken and then two picture alternatives presented to the subjects. Their task is to choose the picture that matches the sentence. On half of the trials, the incorrect picture should depict a reversal of the agent and the object, and on the other half, the incorrect picture should depict the attribute attached to the wrong noun. For example, when the sentence "The boy that had red hair carried the girl" is presented, the distractor picture could either depict a girl carrying a boy with red hair (reversal of agent and object) or a boy carrying a girl with red hair (attribute attached to wrong noun). In our version of this task, 12 trials of each sentence type were presented. Again, for visual presentation, the sentence should be presented with the pictures and remain in view until the picture is selected.

The results for E.A. and A.B. for auditory presentation were presented in Martin (1987) and are shown in Table 6-6 along with results for visual presentation. In contrast to the results with the semantically complex sentences, A.B. performed at a higher level than E.A., with the difference evident on the most difficult constructions, types IV and V. With visual presentation, E.A.'s performance improved substantially on the type IV sentence, though remaining near chance on the type V sentences. A.B.'s scores with visual presentation are

Table 6-6 Percent Correct on Relative Clause Sentences for Patients E.A. and A.B.

	I	II	III	IV	V
Auditory					
E.A.	92	92	92	58	42
A.B.	96	100	92	84	72
Visual					
E.A.	83	92	92	92	67
A.B.	92	96	96	88	88

similar to those with auditory presentation but with slightly better performance on the type V sentences.

E.A.'s poor performance on the type IV and V sentences with auditory presentation suggests that she has some syntactic processing difficulty, since other patients with phonological short-term memory deficits have been shown to perform well on relative clause sentences similar to those employed here (Butterworth et al., 1986). Her better performance on the type IV sentences with visual than auditory presentation suggests that her phonological memory deficit plays a role in her poor comprehension of these sentnces, since when the sentence remains available her performance improves considerably. As discussed in Martin (1990), it is possible that for E.A. syntactic processing is slowed or inefficient which causes her to have to rely on her deficient phonological memory when processing auditory sentences.

Summary of Comprehension Data

For sentences with heavy semantic load, A.B.'s performance is worse than E.A.'s, consistent with the contention that A.B. has a deficit in the short-term retention of semantic information. The discrepancy in their performance was most striking for the attribute questions. For the syntactically complex relative clause sentences, both patients performed at a high level except on the two most difficult sentence types where A.B. performed better than E.A. For these most difficult sentence types, E.A. showed better performance for visual than auditory presentation, suggesting that her phonological memory deficit contributed to her poor performance on these sentence types. A.B. performed fairly well on even the most syntactically complex sentences and showed a similar level of performance for auditory and visual presentation. Consequently, it appears that his semantic retention deficit does not impair his comprehension of syntactic information.

TESTS OF SENTENCE REPETITION

As mentioned in the introduction, aphasia batteries often include tests of sentence repetition. In these batteries, repetition is often treated as if it were a single language faculty, rather than the result of the functioning of a composite of abilities. However, it is clear that repetition can be impaired in many different ways depending on the nature of the underlying deficit. For example, repetition can be impaired because patients have articulatory or phonological deficits that distort their output, or because patients have speech perception deficits that impair recognition of the input. Even if the source of the repetition deficit is a short-term memory deficit, different patterns of repetition can be observed depending upon which specific component of short-term memory is impaired. Several previous studies have shown that patients with a phonological short-term memory deficit perform very poorly on sentence repetition, at least in terms of verbatim responses. However, they perform well in terms of retaining the gist of the sentences (e.g., Martin et al., 1989). In contrast, one might expect

Table 6-7 Percent Omission and Semantic Substitution Errors on Sentences with Simple Syntactic Structures for Patients E.A. and A.B.

	E.A.		A.B.	
	Omission	Substitution	Omission	Substitution
Determiners	4	13	4	0
Nouns	12	17	3	3
Verbs	0	43	0	8
Adjectives	35	6	30	8

patients with preserved phonological short-term retention but impaired semantic retention to better preserve the exact wording of a sentence. However, with increasing semantic load, they may be unable to retain all of the semantic information in the sentence, and consequently omit some of this information in their repetition.

Sentences with Varying Semantic Load

Sentences like those in the sentence-picture matching test described previously can be used for repetition. Their responses can be scored in terms of percent of different word types (nouns, adjectives, verbs, function words) accurately recalled, and percentage of different error types (e.g., omissions, semantically related substitutions). Also, the percentage of sentences which are accurately paraphrased could be noted.

On this task, A.B. performed much better than E.A. This result contrasts markedly with their comprehension results where E.A. performed better than A.B. In terms of number of sentences recalled verbatim, A.B. performed well on the easiest of the sentences (75% correct on sentences with one adjective before the nouns), whereas E.A. repeated none of these sentences verbatim. A.B. also recalled verbatim 25% of the sentences with two adjectives before the nouns. Again, E.A. did not reproduce any of the sentences exactly; E.A. often paraphrased the sentences. While both patients omitted a large number of adjectives, E.A. also made quite a few semantic substitutions whereas A.B. did not (see Table 6-7). These results are consistent with the idea that A.B. is able to hold a phonological representation of the sentences, while E.A. is relying on a semantic code to repeat the sentences.

Syntactically Complex Sentences

Sentences like those in the relative clause test could be used for repetition. A variety of other sentence types could be used as well, since there is no need to constrain the set to sentences which are easily depicted. Some other types of syntactically complex sentences are presented in Table 6-8 including adverbial phrases, complements, and conjoined sentences. A scoring procedure similar to that for the sentences with varying semantic load could be used.

E.A.'s repetition of syntactically complex relative clause sentences has been discussed in Friedrich, Martin, & Kemper (1985). Among the sentences used in that study were some like the Type II and V sentences used in the comprehension

Table 6-8 Examples of Syntactically Complex Sentences

Adverbial phrase: The boy did his homework before watching television.
Complements: The girl hoped the exam would be easy.
Conjoined: The teacher ate her breakfast and the children played a game.

test described earlier. Given E.A.'s poor comprehension of the Type V sentences, it should perhaps not be surprising that she performed extremely poorly on the repetition of this sentence type, repeating none verbatim and reversing the roles of agent and object on five out of eight sentences. On the sentences with the Type II construction, she repeated three out of eight verbatim, and preserved the correct role relations on six of the eight sentences, though changing the form of the sentence. Again, in terms of verbatim repetition, her comprehension exceeded her repetition performance as she scored 92% correct on the comprehension test, but repeated only 38% of the sentences exactly.

A.B. has also repeated sentences with these two types of constructions. On the Type II sentences, he repeated two of eight verbatim. On the remainder he made minor errors, substituting either "that's," "who is" or "who's" for "that is." On the Type V sentences, he repeated six of eight verbatim, made a verb omission error on one sentence, and made two noun substitutions on the remaining sentence.

E.A. and A.B. have also repeated sentences like those shown in Table 6-8. Examples of their repetitions are shown in Table 6-9. A.B. recalled 86% of the adverbial phrases perfectly; whereas E.A. was not able to reproduce any without error. A.B. repeated 67% of the complement sentences verbatim, as compared to 10% for E.A. On the conjoined sentences, A.B. repeated 13% of the sentences correctly and E.A. was not able to reproduce any verbatim. Their error patterns are shown in Table 6-10. A.B. made many errors involving omissions, substitutions, or additions of one word while E.A. paraphrased many of the sentences, retaining the gist, but not the exact wording, as evidenced by the first example sentence in Table 6-9. A.B.'s omissions were often nonobligatory items, although the items were often prenominal adjectives rather than items in a prepositional phrase.

Summary of Repetition Results

A.B.'s verbatim repetition was superior to E.A.'s for all sentence types, even for the semantically loaded sentence types that A.B. had difficulty compre-

Table 6-9 Examples of Repetition of Syntactically Complex Sentences by Patients E.A. and A.B.

Target:	After eating dinner, the man walked the dog.
E.A.:	After supper, the man took his dog for a walk.
A.B.:	(perfect repetition)
Target:	The sleepy little boy was watching a funny old movie.
E.A.	The young child was watching TV.
A.B.	The sleepy boy was watching an old movie.

Table 6-10 Percent Error Types on Syntactically Complex Sentences for Patients E.A. and A.B.

	One Word[a]	Paraphrase
E.A.		
Complements	70	10
Adverbial clause	0	86
Conjoined	0	63
A.B.		
Complements	20	0
Adverbial clause	14	0
Conjoined	87	0

[a]Omission, substitution, or addition of one word.

hending. The fact that A.B. is better at verbatim recall than E.A. may be attributed to his superior ability to retain the phonological information from sentences. Worse verbatim recall for E.A. may be attributed to her inability to retain phonological information and her consequent reliance on the semantic information in sentences. While she was able to recall the gist of many types of sentences, she was very poor at repeating sentences verbatim.

The contrast between the repetition and comprehension data for A.B. and E.A. is also consistent with their differing short-term memory deficits. E.A. is generally able to rapidly extract and retain the semantic information from sentences (except for those few sentence types with syntactic constructions she cannot understand), and consequently shows good comprehension. She often shows evidence of using this semantic interpretation of the sentence to guide her repetition, since she tends to preserve the gist of the sentences but not the exact wording. A.B., on the other hand, cannot retain all of the semantic information in sentences with many content words, and consequently, often shows worse comprehension than E.A. However, because of his better retention of phonological information, his repetitions are often closer to the target.

Outline of Testing Procedures

A summary of the tests that have been described in this chapter are outlined in Table 6-11. This lists the tasks we described and indicates in which capacity each test would be appropriate. This table can be used as a reference guide for selecting appropriate tests to use when one is interested in investigating a short-term memory deficit.

IMPLICATIONS OF THE NATURE OF A SHORT-TERM MEMORY DEFICIT FOR REMEDIATION

At present, it is not clear that therapy can be directed at improvement of the specific aspect of short-term memory that is impaired in a particular patient. There have been no studies that have isolated different aspects of short-term

Table 6-11 Summary of Clinical Assessment of Short-Term Memory Disorders

- *Variables to be eliminated through testing when isolating a short-term memory deficit*
    - Auditory perception of speech and/or nonspeech
    - Attention
- *Determining the nature of the short-term memory deficit*
    - *Phonological Test Manipulations*
        - Phonological similarity
        - Mode of Presentation
        - Word Length
        - Matching Span
    - *Lexical-Semantic Test Manipulations*
        - Recognition Probe
        - Word/Nonword
- *Implications of a Short-Term Memory Deficit on Language Processing*
    - *Sentence Comprehension*
        - *Sentences with Varying Semantic Load and Simple Syntax*
            - Sentence Picture Matching
            - Token Test
            - Attribute Questions
        - *Sentences with Complex Syntactic Structures*
            - Relative Clause Sentences
    - *Sentence Repetition*
        - *Sentences with Varying Semantic Load and Simple Syntax*
            - Sentences from Picture Matching Task
        - *Sentences with Complex Syntactic Structures*
            - Sentences from Relative Clause Task
            - Adverbial Phrases, Complements and Conjoined Sentences

memory and attempted to remediate these. However, a patient could be advised to adopt strategies to minimize the impact of his or her short-term memory deficit. Patients with any type of short-term memory deficit could be advised to write down telephone numbers or other types of random lists. If someone is speaking these lists to them, the patients could be advised to ask the speaker to say them one item at a time so that they could write them down.

More specific strategies could be adopted depending on the exact nature of a patient's deficit. For a patient with a phonological retention deficit but preserved semantic retention, the patient could be advised to adopt a conscious strategy of rapidly recoding random lists of information into more meaningful representations. Patient E.A. had adopted such a strategy on her own in attempting to recall lists of letters or words. For word lists, she would try to think of semantic relations among the words, and for lists of letters to think of words that began with each letter. Constructing visual images from the words or creating sentences containing the list items could also be used. Normal subjects often adopt such mnemonic stategies when attempting to retain information over the long term, but rely on phonological information over the short term. Phonological short-term memory deficit patients could adopt these strategies to aid retention over the short term. For patients with a semantic retention deficit, such a strategy would be likely to be ineffective.

In the realm of language processing, patients with a phonological short-term memory deficit would be likely to be less impaired than patients with a semantic short-term memory deficit, unless verbatim recall of sentences is required. Patients with a semantic retention deficit could be warned that they would be likely to have difficulty comprehending all of the information in long sentences with many content words. Family members and others who would be communicating with patients with semantic short-term memory deficits could be advised to minimize the amount of information conveyed in individual sentences, breaking down what might usually be conveyed in a single sentence into smaller sentence units.

These comments on possible remediation strategies should be considered only suggestive at this point, and certainly not definitive with regard to the range of coping strategies that patients might adopt to minimize the consequences of a short-term memory deficit. Much future research is needed to determine what types of strategies might be most effective for patients with particular deficits. However, even in the absence of such research, innovative clinicians who had used the tests described here would have substantial knowledge regarding the patient's preserved and impaired capacities that could be used to guide them in elaborating on or adding to these suggestions in devising a treatment strategy.

CONCLUSIONS

Although short-term memory has been considered an important component of information processing models of cognition since the early 1960s, little has been done in the way of developing standardized clinical tests for examining a short-term memory deficit. Digit span, the one measure of short-term memory that is often included in clinical test batteries, is often interpreted as a measure of attention rather than of short-term memory. Even when digit span is considered indicative of short-term memory capacity, there may be no additional testing to determine whether the short-term memory deficit is limited to verbal materials, and, within the verbal domain, whether retention of a specific type of verbal code has been affected.

The aim of this chapter has been to present a theoretically based account of verbal short-term memory and its relation to language processing, and to suggest tests that could be used to determine the nature of a short-term memory deficit and its effects on repetition and comprehension. It is hoped that use of these tests will provide the clinician with a better understanding of the patient's spared and impaired capacities, and consequently lead to more effective remediation strategies.

ACKNOWLEDGMENT

Preparation of this manuscript was supported in part by NIH grant no. DC00218.

NOTES

1. This finding may be explained by assuming separate input and output phonological stores and assuming that these patients have a damaged input phonological store and a

preserved output phonological store. However, if they have a preserved output phonological store that could be used in span tasks, then one might expect their span to be larger. A possible explanation that would adhere to the assumption of separate input and output phonological stores would be that these patients have a disruption of the input store and disruption of the process that translates directly between the input and output stores. See Howard & Franklin, 1990; and Monsell, 1987, for further discussion concerning the translation process.

2. Copies of this test and the other language processing tests that have been developed in our lab may be obtained from the authors: Psychology Dept., Rice University, P.O. Box 1892, Houston, TX 77251.

3. This is not the standard procedure for administration. Therefore, the norms provided for the Token Test are not appropriate.

REFERENCES

Allport, D. A. (1984). Auditory-verbal short-term memory and conduction aphasia. In H. Bouma & D. Bouwhuis (Eds.), *Attention & performance X*. Hillsdale, NJ: Erlbaum.

Atkinson, R. C., & Shiffrin, R. M. (1968). Human memory: A proposed system and its control process. In K. W. Spence and J. T. Spence (Eds.), *The psychology of learning and motivation: Advances in research and theory* (Vol. 2). New York: Academic Press.

Baddeley, A. D. (1966). Short-term memory for word sequences as a function of acoustic semantic and formal similarity. *Quarterly Journal of Experimental Psychology, 18*, 362–365.

Baddeley, A. D. (1986). *Working memory*. Oxford, England: Clarendon Press.

Baddeley, A. D., & Hitch, G. J. (1974). Working memory. In G. Bower (Ed.), *Recent advances in learning and motivation* (Vol. VIII). New York: Academic Press.

Baddeley, A. D., Thomson, N., & Buchanan, M. (1975). Word length and the structure of short-term memory. *Journal of Verbal Learning and Verbal Behavior, 15*, 575–589.

Barnard, P. (1985). Interacting cognitive subsystems: A psycholinguistic approach to short-term memory. In A. Ellis (Ed.), *Progress in the psychology of language* (Vol. 2). London: Lawrence Erlbaum.

Brener, R. (1940). An experimental investigation of memory span. *Journal of Experimental Psychology, 26*, 467–482.

Brooks, J. O., III & Watkins, M. J. (1990). Further evidence on the intricacy of memory span. *Journal of Experimental Psychology: Learning, Memory, and Cognition, 16*, 1134–1141.

Butterworth, B., Campbell, R., & Howard, D. (1986). The uses of short-term memory: A case study: *The Quarterly Journal of Experimental Psychology, 38A*, 705–737.

Caplan, D., & Waters, G. (1990). Short-term memory and language comprehension: A critical review of the neuropsychological literature. In G. Vallar & T. Shallice (Eds.), *Neuropsychological impairments of short-term memory*, Cambridge, England: Cambridge University Press.

Caramazza, A., Basili, A. G., Koller, J., & Bernedt, R. S. (1981). An investigation of repetition and language processing in a case of conduction aphasia. *Brain and Language, 14*, 235–271.

Conrad, R. (1964). Acoustic confusion in immediate memory. *British Journal of Psychology, 55*, 75–84.

Conrad, R., & Hull, A. J. (1968). Input modality and the serial position curve in short-term memory. *Psychonomic Science*, *10*, 135–136.

Craik, F. I. M., & Watkins, M. (1973). The role of rehearsal in short-term memory. *Journal of Verbal Learning and Verbal Behavior*, *12*, 599–607.

Crowder, R. G. (1978). Memory for phonologically uniform lists. *Journal of Verbal Learning and Verbal Behavior*, *17*, 73–89.

Crowder, R. G. (1982). The demise of short-term memory. *Acta Psychologica*, *50*, 291–323.

De Renzi, E., & Vignolo, L. A. (1962). The Token test: A sensitive test to detect receptive disturbances in aphasia. *Brain*, *85*, 665–678.

Dunn, L., & Dunn, L. (1981). *Manual for forms L and M of the Peabody Picture Vocabulary Test—Revised.* Circle Pines, MN: American Guidance Service.

Feher, E. (1987). *An examination of short-term memory deficits in non-fluent aphasics.* Unpublished doctoral dissertation, Rice University, Houston, TX.

Frank, G. (1964). The validity of retention of digits as a measure of attention. *Journal of General Psychology*, *71*, 329–336.

Friedrich, F., Glenn, C., & Marin, O. S. M. (1984). Interruption of phonological coding in conduction aphasia. *Brain and Language*, *22*, 253–296.

Friedrich, F., Martin, R. C., & Kemper, S. (1985). Consequences of a phonological coding deficit in sentence processing. *Cognitive Neuropsychology*, *2*, 385–412.

Fromkin, V. A. (1971). The non-anomalous nature of anomalous utterances. *Language*, *47*, 27–52.

Garrett, M. F. (1975). The analysis of sentence production. In G. H. Bower (Ed.), *The psychology of learning and motivation* (Vol. 9). New York: Academic Press.

Gates, A. I., & MacGinitie, W. H. (1968). *Gates-MacGinitie Reading Tests: Readiness skills.* New York: Teachers College Press.

Goodglass, H., & Kaplan, E. (1972). *Assessment of aphasia and related disorders.* Philadelphia: Lea & Febiger.

Guertin, W. H., Ladd, C. E., Frank, G. H., Rabin, A. I., & Hiester, D. S. (1966). Research with the Wechsler Intelligence Scales for adults: 1960–1965. *Psychological Bulletin*, *66*, 385–409.

Howard, D. (1989). Does a short-term memory deficit cause impaired sentence comprehension? Paper presented at the International Conference on Cognitive Neuropsychology, Harrogate, U.K.

Howard, D., & Franklin, S. (1990). Memory without rehearsal. In G. Vallar & T. Shallice (Eds.), *Neuropsychological Impairments of short-term memory*, Cambridge, England: Cambridge University Press.

Just, M. A., & Carpenter, P. A. (1987). *The psychology of reading and language comprehension.* Massachusetts: Allyn & Bacon.

Kertesz, A. (1979). *Aphasia and associated disorders.* New York: Grune & Stratton.

Klapp, S. T., Marshburn, E. A., & Lester, P. T. (1983). Short-term memory does not involve the "working memory" of information processing: The demise of a common assumption. *Journal of Experimental Psychology: General*, *112*, 240–264.

Kucera, H., & Francis, W. N. (1967). *Computational analysis of present-day American English.* Providence: Brown University Press.

Levy, B. A. (1971). The role of articulation in auditory and visual short-term memory. *Journal of Verbal Learning and Verbal Behavior*, *10*, 123–132.

Lezak, M. D. (1976). *Neuropsychological Assessment.* New York: Oxford University Press.

Martin, R. C. (1987). Articulatory and phonological deficits in short-term memory and their relation to syntactic processing. *Brain and Language*, *32*, 137–158.

Martin, R. C. (1990). Neuropsychological evidence on the role of short-term memory in sentence processing. In G. Vallar & T. Shallice (Eds.), *Neuropsychological impairments of short-term memory*, Cambridge, England: Cambridge University Press.

Martin, R. C., & Breedin, S. (1990). *Dissociations between speech perception and phonological short-term memory*. Unpublished manuscript.

Martin, R. C., & Caramazza, A. (1982). Short-term memory in the absence of phonological coding. *Brain and Cognition*, *1*, 50–70.

Martin, R. C., & Feher, E. (1990). The consequences of reduced memory span for the comprehension of semantic versus syntactic information. *Brain and Language*, *38*, 1–20.

Martin, R. C., Jerger, S., & Breedin, S. (1987). Syntactic processing for auditory and visual sentences in a learning disabled child: Relation to short-term memory. *Developmental Neuropsychology*, *3*, 129–152.

Martin, R. C., Shelton, J. R., & Yaffee, L. S. (1989). *Short-term memory and sentence processing*. Paper presented at the Psychonomics Society, Atlanta, GA.

Martin, R. C., Yaffee, L., & Shelton, J. (1989). *Consequences of a deficit in semantic retention for short-term memory, long-term memory and sentence processing*. Paper presented at the International Conference on Cognitive Neuropsychology, Harrogate, UK.

McCarthy, R. A., & Warrington, E. K. (1987). Understanding: A function of short-term memory? *Brain and Language*, *110*, 1565–1578.

Milner, B. (1971). Interhemispheric differences in the localization of psychological processes in man. *British Medical Bulletin*, *27*, 272–277.

Moldawsky, S., & Moldawsky, P. C. (1952). Digit span as an indicator of anxiety. *Journal of Clinical and Consulting Psychology*, *16*, 115–118.

Monsell, S. (1984). Components of working memory underlying verbal skills: A "distributed capacities" view. In H. Bouma & D. G. Bouwhuis (Eds.), *Attention and performance, X*. London: Lawrence Erlbaum Associates.

Monsell, S. (1987). On the relation between lexical input and output pathways for speech. In D. A. Allport, D. MacKay, W. Prinz & E. Scheerer (Eds.), *Language perception and production: Relationships between listening, speaking reading and writing* (pp. 273–311). London: Academic Press.

Murdock, B. B. (1974). *Human memory: Theory and data*. Potomac, MD: Erlbaum.

Norman, D., & Shallice, T. (1986). Attention to action: Willed and automatic control of behavior. In R. J. Davidson, G. E. Schwartz & D. Shapiro (Eds.), *Consciousness and self-regulation* (Vol. 4). New York: Plenum Press.

Saffran, E. M. (in press). Short-term memory impairment and language processing. In Caramazza, A. (Ed.), Advances in cognitive neuropsychology and neurolinguistics.

Saffran, E. M., Berndt, R. S., & Schwartz, M. (1989). The quantitative analysis of agrammatic production: procedure and data. *Brain and Language*, *37*, 419–439.

Saffran, E. M., Marin, O. S. M. (1975). Immediate memory for word lists and sentences in a patient with deficient auditory short-term memory. *Brain and Language*, *2*, 420–433.

Saffran, E. M., & Martin, N. (1990). Neuropsychological evidence for lexical involvement in STM. In G. Vallar & T. Shallice (Eds.), *Neuropsychological impairments of short-term memory*, Cambridge, England: Cambridge University Press.

Salter, D., Springer, G., & Bolton, L. (1976). Semantic coding versus the stimulus suffix effect. *British Journal of Psychology*, *67*, 339–351.

Schneider, W., & Detweiler, M. (1987). A connectionist/control architecture for working memory. In G. Bower (Ed.), *The psychology of learning and motivation: Advances in research and theory* (Vol. 21) (pp. 54–119). New York: Academic Press.

Schuell, H. (1965). *Differential diagnosis of aphasia with the Minnesota test*. Minneapolis: University of Minnesota Press.

Shallice, T. (1988). *From neuropsychology to mental structure*. Cambridge: Cambridge University Press.

Shallice, T., & Butterworth, B. (1977). Short-term memory impairment and spontaneous speech. *Neuropsychologia*, *15*, 729–735.

Shallice, T., & Warrington, E. K. (1970). Independent functioning of the verbal memory stores: A neuropsychological study. *Quarterly Journal of Experimental Psychology*, *22*, 261–273.

Shallice, T., & Warrington, E. K. (1974). The dissociation between short-term retention of meaningful sounds and verbal material. *Neuropsychologia*, *12*, 553–555.

Vallar, G., & Baddeley, A. D. (1984). Phonological short-term store, phonological processing and sentence comprehension: A neuropsychological case study. *Cognitive Neuropsychology*, *1*, 121–141.

Warrington, E. K. (1975). The selective impairment of sementic memory. *Quarterly Journal of Experimental Psychology*, *27*, 635–657.

Warrington, E. K., & Shallice, T. (1969). The selective impairment of auditory verbal short-term memory. *Brain*, *92*, 885–896.

Watkins, M. J. (1977). The intricacy of memory span. *Memory & Cognition*, *5*, 529–534.

Watkins, M. J., Watkins, O. C., & Crowder, R. G. (1974). The modality effect in free and serial recall as a function of phonological similarity. *Journal of Verbal Learning and Verbal Behavior*, *13*, 430–447.

Waugh, N. C., & Norman, D. A. (1965). Primary memory. *Psychological Review*, *72*, 89–104.

Wechsler, D. (1958). *The measurement and appraisal of adult intelligence* (4th ed.). Baltimore: Williams & Wilkins.

7

Cognitive Assessment of Long-Term Memory Disorders

EDWARD P. FEHER and RANDI C. MARTIN

In recent decades cognitive psychology has displaced behaviorism as the predominant approach in human experimental psychology. This paradigm shift has most affected the realms of theory and research, but has also had major impact on clinical practice. Perhaps most affected among practitioners have been clinical neuropsychologists, in their attempts to specify the changes in intellectual skills that occur as a result of brain disease or injury. American clinical neuropsychology grew up around the Halstead-Reitan battery of tests, an approach that was geared to the detection of brain disease but which was atheoretical in terms of describing cognitive functioning. Such an approach is no longer tenable in view of the increasing sophistication of human information-processing models. Clinical neuropsychologists are now expected to go beyond the mere detection of cognitive impairment. Detailed descriptions of the patient's cognitive deficits are now expected, together with recommendations regarding rehabilitative and compensatory strategies to ameliorate or to circumvent the deficits. The practitioner in clinical neuropsychology must therefore be well versed in current information-processing models and must be knowledgeable in the use of assessment procedures that apply these models to clinical practice. This chapter will provide an overview of clinical memory assessment from these two perspectives. Specifically, current theoretical conceptions of long-term memory (LTM) will be briefly reviewed (for a discussion of short-term memory, see Chapter 6). Clinical assessment of LTM disorders will then be discussed, including a critique of commonly used tests. The neuroanatomy of memory disorders will also be briefly reviewed. A profile of cognitive abilities can be derived without reference to brain anatomy, but a knowledge of brain-behavior relationships is often important in establishing prognosis and in cases of differential diagnosis.

THEORETICAL CONCEPTIONS OF LTM

Types of LTM

LTM is viewed by memory theorists as a more or less permanent record of one's experiences and knowledge. Early memory models stated that, while short-term memory is based on a phonological code, information in LTM is organized on the basis of meaning, i.e. a given piece of information is stored with closely related pieces of information (Kintsch & Buschke, 1969). For example, the term Wimbledon would be associated with such bits of information as "tennis tournament," "played on grass," "takes place in Great Britain," and so on (Collins & Loftus, 1975). In recent years, theoretical conceptions of short-term memory and LTM have become more complex, going beyond the phonology versus meaning dichotomy stressed by early models. Thus, while phonological coding is still considered the major code for verbal short-term memory, more attention is being given to multiple processing capacities (e.g., "working memory;" Baddeley, 1986). With regard to LTM, the trend toward greater complexity has been even more pronounced, with numerous subtypes of LTM being proposed.

One of the most influential attempts to fractionate LTM into components is that of Tulving (1972). He proposed the existence of two complementary LTM systems, episodic memory and semantic memory. Episodic memory is autobiographical in nature, consisting of memories of life events or episodes set in a spatiotemporal context (a specific time and place). Memory for a meeting with an old friend would be an example of an episodic memory. Semantic memory, on the other hand, consists of knowledge of the world (e.g., facts, concepts, vocabulary), independent of the context in which the knowledge was initially learned. "$E = mc^2$," "Columbus discovered America in 1492," and "High cholesterol predisposes to heart attacks" are pieces of information typical of the kind stored in semantic memory.

Tulving's theory grew out of cognitive psychology and the study of normal memory, but there have been attempts to apply his system to the syndrome of amnesia. Kinsbourne and Wood (1975) were early proponents of this view. They pointed out that amnesics do not forget the vocabulary and syntax of language, social amenities, or other much rehearsed skills (Wood, Ebert, & Kinsborne, 1982). In contrast, amnesics have great difficulty in retaining new episodic information and many have difficulty remembering specific episodes from their past. Wood, Ebert, and Kinsbourne (1982) cite the case of a 9-year-old girl who was left "densely amnesic" after herpes encephalitis, but who was able to return to school and to learn many traditional academic skills despite failure to remember the particular episodes in which learning took place. Tulving (Tulving, Schacter, McLachlan, & Moscovitch, 1988) also cites an amnesic case as supportive of the episodic-semantic dissociation. Patient KC cannot remember episodes of his past life, but he can recall much factual information that he learned in the past, suggesting that "KC's episodic memory system has ceased functioning, whereas his semantic memory system . . . has suffered less damage" (Tulving, 1989, p. 363).

Many theorists remain cautious about or flatly reject the proposal that semantic memory is preserved but episodic memory is defective in amensia. Squire (1987) argues that amnesics have difficulty with both semantic memory and episodic memory. The apparent dissociations cited by Wood and Kinsbourne and by Tulving are attributed to failure to distinguish between anterograde amnesia (AA) and retrograde amnesia (RA). AA is the inability to learn new information; RA refers to the inability to retrieve previously learned information. (It has long been known that, in addition to poor learning ability, amnesics have difficulty remembering events or information that had been stored prior to the event causing the amnesia.) Squire reasons that the intact language and intact general knowledge of memory-impaired patients are due to the fact that RA is generally time limited, occurring for a time period of a few seconds to a few years prior to the injury. Information acquired before this period is intact. He further argues that, with regard to learning new information, amnesics' impaired learning ability applies equally to episodic and semantic memory. Squire's argument receives support from a recent study by Gabrieli, Cohen, and Corkin (1988). It was shown that, for certain types of information, the severely amnesic patient HM has acquired very meager semantic knowledge since his amnesia onset in 1957. HM performed very poorly on knowledge of post-1950s words (e.g., acid rain, flower child, soul food) and on recognition of post-1950s famous names (e.g., Sylvester Stallone, Ivan Lendl). In a similar study, Gabrieli et al. (1983) attempted to teach HM the meanings of eight new words. He showed almost no new learning, even though he was given 115 trials per day for 10 days.[1]

The episodic-semantic controversy in amnesia may appear puzzling. Why not simply perform careful research to examine the nature of amnesics' learning abilities and the nature of their RA, and let the results resolve the question of whether episodic memory alone or both episodic and semantic memory are affected? Failure to resolve the issue rests on several factors. First, it is difficult to devise adequate procedures for assessing RA (see Squire & Fox, 1980, for a discussion). Second, reported cases of learning of semantic information in amnesia have not been sufficiently documented. For example, the child reported by Wood et al. (1982) appears to present a striking dissociation between disrupted episodic memory and preserved ability to learn academic subjects; however, little quantitative information is provided regarding her disrupted and spared memory abilities. Third, Tulving's theory is vague with regard to the crucial issue of the relationship between semantic memory and episodic memory. Semantic memories are, after all, acquired during the course of life episodes. When and how does a given memory become a part of semantic memory in addition to or instead of being a part of episodic memory? This issue has been insufficiently addressed, attenuating the usefulness of Tulving's model as a framework for understanding the amnesic syndrome.

Apart from Tulving's episodic-semantic dichotomy, numerous other classifications of LTM have been proposed. Whereas Tulving's system grew out of observations of normal memory and was later applied to amnesia, many other schemes were directly based on studies of amnesic patients. Specifically, many studies have demonstrated that amnesia is selective, that even severely impaired amnesics can sometimes perform within or near the normal range on certain tasks. An early demonstration by Milner and colleagues (Milner, 1966; Corkin, 1968) showed that patient HM could acquire certain motor abilities (pursuit rotor and mirror tracing), though he acquired these skills more slowly than normal subjects. A later study by Brooks and Baddeley (1976) showed that other amnesics could acquire similar motor skills at a normal rate. Learning of perceptual skills, such as reading of mirror-inverted script, may also be normal in amnesic patients (Cohen & Squire, 1980; Moscovitch, Winocur, & MacLachlan, 1986). Amnesic patients have also been shown to learn skills that are not clearly perceptual or motor in nature, though often at a rate below that of normal subjects. Amnesic patients have learned to solve jigsaw puzzles (Brooks & Baddeley, 1976), to apply a numerical rule (Wood et al., 1982), to learn a serial pattern (Nissen & Bullemer, 1987), and to acquire simple microcomputer programming skills (Glisky, Schacter, & Tulving, 1986). Their performance has also been shown to be within the normal range on a variety of classical conditioning tasks (Weiskrantz & Warrington, 1979).

Several recent findings on "priming" effects have attracted a great deal of attention because these studies demonstrated normal memory in amnesics based on a single prior exposure to a stimulus. In an early study, Warrington and Weiskrantz (1970) showed amnesic patients a set of words and subsequently gave them a yes/no recognition test and a test in which they were given the first three letters of the words and asked to complete them. As expected, the amnesic patients performed very poorly on the recognition memory task. In contrast, on the stem completion task the amnesics were as likely as normal control subjects to complete the word stems with studied words (and more likely than subjects who had not studied the words prior to the test). These findings and others by Warrington and Weiskrantz (1968, 1970, 1978) led to numerous studies on the nature of priming effects. Studies with normal and amnesic subjects demonstrated that prior exposure to a set of words speeded lexical decision for the words (Moscovitch, 1982), increased the likelihood of using the words as free association responses (Shimamura & Squire, 1984), and facilitated perception of the words when presented tachistoscopically or in degraded fashion (Jacoby & Dallas, 1981).

Some researchers have claimed that priming effects derive solely from the activation of previously acquired knowledge structures (Graf, Squire, & Mandler, 1984; Diamond & Rozin, 1984). According to this reasoning, priming effects in amnesics do not reflect normal learning of new information, but rather a normal temporary increase in the activation of old information. Some recent studies suggest, however, that priming may be demonstrated for newly acquired information. Graf and Schacter (1985) showed that, for both normal and amnesic subjects, prior exposure to words in the context of another word (e.g., window—reason) resulted in greater priming when the words were presented in the same context (e.g., window—rea____) than when presented in a different context (e.g., kindly—rea____). Such priming would have to result from the formation of new associations during the study phase. McAndrews, Glisky, and Schacter (1987) used a sentence puzzle procedure in which subjects were asked to think of a key word that made a sentence comprehensible (e.g., the word "parachute" for the sentence, "The haystack was important because the cloth ripped"). Severely impaired amnesics who could not distinguish old from new sentences on a recognition memory test could provide many of the solutions for the previously presented puzzles. These findings remain controversial, however, as Schacter and Graf (1986) later showed that the priming for new associations only held for their mildly amnesic cases, suggesting that it resulted from partially preserved explicit memory abilities. In addition, Shimamura and Squire (1989) were unable to replicate Graf and Schacter's findings.

Not surprisingly, theorists have suggested dichotomous classifications of LTM in an attempt to capture the distinction between impaired and preserved abilities in amnesia. Proposed classifications have included implicit vs. explicit memory, declarative vs. procedural memory, memory vs. habit, taxon vs. locale, vertical vs. horizontal associations, working memory vs. reference memory, plus others. (See Squire, 1987, for a list of 15 proposed dichotomous classifications of LTM.) Two representative dichotomies will be briefly described.

The declarative/procedural dichotomy has been championed by Cohen and Squire. Declarative memory, which is dysfunctional in amnesia, is "memory that is directly accessible to conscious recollection. It can be declared. It deals with the facts and data that are acquired through learning" (Squire, 1987, p. 152). Procedural memory is spared in amnesia and consists of "learned skills or modifiable cognitive operations . . . the acquired information is embedded in procedures, or it occurs as changes in how pre-existing cognitive operations are carried out" (Squire, 1987, p. 158). Procedural learning is said to occur in an incremental and automatic manner without conscious awareness. Declarative memory is often learned in a single trial and results in a stored representation that is available to conscious recollection.

One difficulty with the procedural/declarative dichotomy is that priming effects derive from a single prior exposure to the studied materials, and thus differ from other preserved memory abilities that depend on a slow, incremental learning process. Cohen (1984) argued that priming effects could be grouped with other examples of preserved memory, on the grounds that priming derives from the activation of previously acquired procedures. However, the recent demonstrations of priming for newly acquired knowledge cause difficulty for this account.

A second classification system that has gained wide currency is that of implicit versus explicit memory. According to Schacter (1987a), "Memory for a recent event can be expressed explicitly, as conscious recollection, or implicitly, as a facilitation of performance without conscious recollection" (p. 501). Explicit memory is assessed by traditional tests of free recall, cued recall, and recognition. In contrast, when implicit memory is assessed, "instead of being asked to try to remember recently presented information, subjects are simply required to perform a task . . . memory is revealed by a facilitation or change in task performance that is attributable to information acquired during a previous study episode" (p. 501), which is not explicitly remembered by the patient. Schacter draws parallels between explicit and implicit memory and older terms from the psychology literature: conscious memory vs. unconscious memory, and memory with awareness vs. memory without awareness.

Some researchers have used the terms explicit memory and implicit memory descriptively (as exemplified by the previous quotations). Other researchers have made the stronger claim that there are two different memory systems which have distinct properties. Amnesic patients are said to have a disrupted explicit memory system and a preserved implicit memory system. As with the procedural/declarative dichotomy, however, it is not clear that all the preserved aspects of memory that have been demonstrated in amnesics can be treated as part of one memory system. For example, priming effects that are observed for the repetition of single stimuli are unaffected by study tasks that emphasize superficial versus semantic processing of the stimuli (Jacoby & Dallas, 1981; Jacoby, 1983). In contrast, the priming for sentence puzzles obtained by McAndrews et al. necessarily depends on semantic processing of the sentence. Beyond these dissociations in the effects of study manipulations, different types of priming have been found to dissociate in different types of brain-damaged patients. Heindel, Salmon, Shults, Walicke, and Butters (1989) demonstrated that patients with Huntington's disease showed impaired priming on a motor task but preserved priming on a lexical task, whereas Alzheimer patients showed the reverse pattern. One would not expect to find such dissociations if there were a single implicit memory system.

One possible response to the finding of dissociations among procedural/implicit memory tasks is to posit the existence of many different non-recollective memory systems.[2] That is, it can be argued that there are *many* memory systems, differing in various ways, and that any simple dichotomy will not do justice to the complexity of memory. Squire (1987), although defending the declarative/procedural approach, concludes that "procedural learning does not appear to depend on any one structure or location. Indeed, procedural memory is not a single thing. It is a collection of different abilities, each dependent on its own specialized processing system" (p. 161). Schacter (1987a), in a similar vein, states that "whether implicit and explicit memory depend on a single underlying system or on multiple underlying systems is not yet resolved . . ." (p. 501).

LTM Processes

The discussion thus far has focussed on types of LTM. LTM can also be considered from the point of view of memory processes, an approach that dominated amnesia research in the 1970s and which is currently seeing a resurgence, though along different lines. The information processing approach assumes that human memory, similar to computer memory, consists of encoding processes, a memory store or stores, and retrieval processes. The encoding process translates the information to be stored into a code used by the central nervous system. The memory store consists of the brain areas and the brain changes which serve to hold the information for future use. The retrieval process searches the information stored in the brain and retrieves the particular item that the individual wishes to remember.

Considerable research in the 1970s was devoted to a debate over whether defective encoding processes or defective retrieval processes were responsible for the amnesic syndrome. Warrington and colleagues championed the defective retrieval position. As evidence, they demonstrated that amnesics perform much better with cued recall than with free recall, with performance attaining normal levels on certain types of tasks (Warrington & Weiskrantz, 1970; 1978). The suggestion from this finding was that encoding and storage of memories are adequate in amnesia but that unassisted retrieval of memories is impaired. A second piece of evidence cited by Warrington was the claim that amnesics show excessive intrusion errors during attempted recall (Warrington & Weiskrantz, 1973). This finding was taken as evidence of excessive interference during retrieval processes.

In contrast to the claims of retrieval theorists, Butters and Cermak argued that amnesia could best be explained as a failure to encode information sufficiently. That is, amnesics were said to fail to encode information to deep or semantic levels during learning. In one set of studies it was shown that semantic cueing was less beneficial to Korsakoff amnesics than to normal control subjects (Butters & Cermak, 1980). In other studies, the semantic relatedness of word lists was manipulated, and it was found that Korsakoff patients were less susceptible to semantic variables than control subjects (Cermak & Butters, 1973; Cermak, 1982), presumably because of the amnesics' failure to encode information adequately.

In recent years the debate between retrieval theories and encoding theories has all but died out. Warrington and colleagues explicitly renounced their allegiance to the claim that amnesia can be best viewed as a defect in retrieval mechanisms (Warrington & Weiskrantz, 1982). Butters has muted his claims regarding deficient encoding in amnesics, conceding that some of the experimental findings might apply only to Korsakoff amnesics and not to amnesics in general (Butters, Salmon, Heindel, & Granholm, 1988). This turn of events arose out of several findings. Some of the recognition memory tasks used by Warrington are now considered implicit memory tasks (e.g., recognition of fragmented words, word stem completion), and the relative preservation of performance in amnesics is now attributed to this fact rather than to facilitation of retrieval. With regard to Butters' findings of aberrant performance by Korsakoff patients on certain encoding tasks, it has been argued that this may occur, not because of amnesia per se, but because Korsakoff patients suffer damage to other brain systems (i.e., frontal lobe systems). The notion of defective encoding has also been criticized on other grounds. Rozin (1976) asked, if amnesic patients can carry on an adequate conversation (thus demonstrating adequate encoding, at some level, of incoming information), how can it be argued that their "encoding" mechanisms are defective. Finally, Meudell and Mayes (1982; Mayes & Meudell, 1984) have pointed out methodological flaws in several of the supposed supportive studies, and have persuasively argued that, at our present state of knowledge, separation of encoding, storage, and retrieval deficits in memory-impaired subjects may not be possible.[3]

Another proposed memory process should be briefly discussed. It has long been known from animal experiments that recently formed memories can be abolished by electroconvulsive shock and by other methods of temporarily disrupting brain function (Schneider & Plough, 1983; McGaugh, 1989). The effect of the disruption is time limited. Very recent memories are most susceptible to disruption, with memories becoming less susceptible over time. These observations led to the proposal that memories undergo a period of consolidation. Newly formed memories gradually become less susceptible to disruption, due to some physiological process which "strengthens" the memories. Squire (1982; 1987) has been the chief proponent of applying this model to human memory. He attributes RA to the fact that brain injury disrupts consolidation processes.

Depending on the severity of the injury, the RA may encompass a time period of a few seconds or a period of several years. With regard to AA, Squire regards this aspect of amnesia as a *storage* deficit. In the absence of certain brain regions (those damaged in amnesia), new memories cannot be established (entered into long-term store) and consolidation of the memories cannot be initiated.

Consolidation theory has been criticized by some workers in the field of human memory. Kinsbourne (1987) terms it "incoherent," pointing out the implausibility of a physical consolidation process occurring over many years, since RA in some patients has been reported to exceed 10 years (e.g., Cermak & O'Connor, 1983). Kinsbourne also argues that consolidation theory cannot account for the phenomenon of shrinking RA. (In patients with an acute brain injury, the time period of RA tends to decrease as the patient recovers. This suggests that the memories were not "lost," as would be expected if a consolidation process were disrupted, but were temporarily not retrievable.) In defense of consolidation theory, it should be pointed out that Squire's account meets the phenomenon of RA head-on, whereas other theories generally skirt the issue. (For example, why is it that only recently formed memories become temporarily unretrievable?) In any case, the only justifiable conclusion at present is that attempts to describe amnesia as a unitary deficit in a given memory process (retrieval, encoding, consolidation) have met with little success.

Recently, a processing approach has been advocated to explain the findings on implicit memory (Roediger, Weldon, & Challis, 1989b; Moscovitch et al., 1986). Roediger and colleagues (Roediger, Srinivas, & Weldon, 1989a) have concentrated on explaining the findings from normal subjects rather than on explaining the amnesia findings. As discussed earlier, a number of variables have been shown to have large effects on explicit memory tests but not on implicit memory tests. For example, deeper processing of items during the study phase has a large effect on a yes/no recognition task (an explicit task) but has no effect on perceptual identification (an implicit task; Jacoby & Dallas, 1981). Rather than interpreting such findings in terms of different stores with different properties, Roediger has interpreted these results in terms of "transfer-appropriate processing." According to this principle, processing at the time of study will benefit later performance to the extent that processing at study matches that at test. Most implicit memory tests, such as stem completion or perceptual identification, involve mainly perceptual or "data-driven" processing. Consequently, these tasks will benefit from any study manipulation that involves perceptual processing of the same stimuli, but will show less benefit from any manipulation that involves semantic or "conceptually-driven" processing. In contrast, standard explicit memory tests involve conceptual processes in retrieval. Consequently, these tasks will show more benefit the greater the conceptual processing required at study, and will show less benefit the greater the emphasis on data-driven processing at study.

According to the transfer-appropriate processing view, it should be possible to find dissociations among different implicit tasks. For example, if an implicit memory task involved conceptually-driven processes, then it should be affected by degree of conceptual processing at study, unlike data-driven implicit tasks that are unaffected by such manipulations. Such a pattern was found by Graf and Schacter (1985) in a study of priming for word pairs. Additional dissociations between the effects of different variables among implicit tasks are reported in Roediger et al. (1989a; 1989b) and Blaxton (1989). Of course, one could accommodate these findings by postulating many different implicit memory systems that obey different principles (see Tulving & Schacter, 1990, for such an account), but a more parsimonious account is provided by the transfer-appropriate processing principle.

Despite the success of the transfer-appropriate processing approach in accounting for findings in the normal literature, it is not clear how the approach extends to findings on amnesia. One possibility would be to claim that amnesics' difficulties with recall and recognition tasks can be attributed to a deficit in conceptually driven processing. However, this argument seems similar to the already discredited view that amnesics have difficulties with deeper levels of processing. As it stands, the transfer-appropriate processing approach fails to account for amnesics' intact cognitive processing abilities in the face of inability to make conscious recollections concerning the past occurrence of events.

In order to explain amnesic patients' inability to explicitly recall past experiences despite adequate processing, Schacter, McAndrews, and Moscovitch (1988) suggested that amnesia results from the disconnection of memory mechanisms from a "consciousness mechanism." The consciousness mechanism itself is not damaged in amnesia, since conscious experience apart from memory is normal in these patients. According to this view, it should be possible to demonstrate that all types of memory can be established in amnesic patients in normal fashion, if one could find the appropriate implicit task to reveal the presence of the information. To support this view, many more studies along the lines of the McAndrews et al. study would be needed, to demonstrate the presence of memory for complex new information through the use of implicit tasks.

A study by Glisky, Schacter, and Tulving (1986) appears to be the most ambitious attempt so far to assess the acquisition of complex knowledge in memory-impaired patients. The skills involved learning to use some computer commands, to write simple programs, and to save programs on disk and retrieve them. Though showing much slower learning than control subjects, all of the amnesic subjects managed to master the lessons up to a near perfect level of performance, and they showed retention over periods of a month or more. This was the case even for one densely amnesic patient (KC; Tulving, 1989) who could consciously recall none of his experiences with the computer. Despite these impressive accomplishments, the knowledge acquired by the amnesic patients differed from that acquired by the normal subjects. The amnesic patients were unable to answer questions about the commands they had learned if the wording of the questions differed in minor ways from the wording in the original instructions. Also, they were unable to integrate information from different lessons to create programs different from the ones that they had been trained on. The normal subjects could easily carry out these transfer tasks. Glisky et al. concluded that the amnesics had learned highly specific stimulus-response associations rather than developing a more general mental model of the procedures involved in programming.

The findings of Glisky et al. suggest that the memory disruption in amnesic patients is more than a disconnection from consciousness. The data suggest that the amnesics are unable to learn new material in a fashion that allows for generalization to new problems. Perhaps an inability to consciously reflect on what has been learned prevents generalization from occurring. It would be valuable to determine whether the amnesics failed to make inferences about the nature of programming during the learning process, or whether they made such inferences but failed to remember them.

NEUROANATOMY OF MEMORY

Considerable progress has been made in determining the brain regions involved in human memory. One major advance occurred in 1953 when a 27-year-old severe epileptic, now known in the memory literature as patient HM, underwent an experimental technique to control his intractable seizures. Surgery was performed, excising the medial temporal lobes, including the hippocampus, amygdala, and entorhinal cortex. The operation rendered HM severely amnesic, implicating this brain region as important to human memory (Milner, 1966). Considerable other evidence is supportive of this conclusion. Patients with herpes encephalitis, anoxia, and bilateral strokes who have suffered damage to the medial temporal lobes have been rendered amnesic (Squire & Zola-Morgan, 1988). Severity of amnesia has been shown to correlate with degree of hippocampal involvement, and lesions restricted to the hippocampus cause amnesia, implicating this structure as the most crucial temporal lobe region for memory functioning (Squire & Zola-Morgan, 1988).

Another landmark study in the neuropathology of memory was the work of Victor, Adams, and Collins (1971) with alcoholic patients. There is continuing debate about the exact location of the brain lesions that occur in alcoholism (Mair, Warrington, & Weiskrantz, 1979; von Cramon, Hebel, & Schuri, 1985; Mayes, Meudell, Mann, & Pickering, 1988), but certain facts are clear based on the large number of patients studied by Victor et al. and by other similar studies (see Victor, Adams, & Collins, 1989, for a recent review). First, a severe amnesic disorder (Korsakoff's syndrome) occurs in a small percentage of alcoholics. Second, the crucial lesions in these patients involve the mammillary bodies and/or certain areas of the thalamus. The medial dorsal nucleus has long been considered the crucial thalamic area, but recent careful studies suggest that neighboring brain regions may also be of importance (Mair et al., 1979; von Cramon et al., 1985; Mayes et al., 1988). In addition to studies of alcoholics, research with patients suffering strokes, tumors, and localized trauma has been supportive of the conclusion that the mammillary bodies and medial dorsal nucleus are parts of a memory system (Whitty & Zangwill, 1977; Weiskrantz, 1987). An issue that remains poorly understood is the relationship between the hippocampus and the mammillary bodies/medial dorsal nucleus. That is, it is unknown whether these brain areas constitute a single memory circuit or two (or more) parallel circuits (for more detailed discussions, see Weiskrantz, 1985, Squire, 1987).

Although the brain areas described above subserve memory functions, it is likely that other brain regions are also involved. Many years ago Lashley set out in search of the engram, the putative site of memory storage. He performed numerous ablation studies in rats, but was unable to localize memory to a particular area, and concluded that memory storage was dispersed throughout the brain. Lashley's conclusion can be attributed to shortcomings in his methodological approaches (Squire, 1987), but considered from another perspective, his argument has considerable validity. Although the hippocampus, mammillary bodies, and thalamus are involved in memory functions, most theorists do not consider them the actual storehouse for memories. Rather, it is believed that they serve to *establish* memories stored in other brain regions. One suggestion is that engrams are stored in cerebral cortex, near the regions in which perceptual processing of incoming stimuli occurs (Morris, Kandel, & Squire, 1988). For a given memory episode, the visual aspects of the memory would be stored near visual processing areas, the auditory components of the memory would be stored near auditory processing areas, and so on. This theoretical approach has the advantage of parsimony, since processing functions (and corresponding brain areas) would closely overlap with memory functions and corresponding brain regions. Such a memory system also combines aspects of strict localizationism and the more holistic approach espoused by (Lashley, 1963), thus reconciling a long-standing theoretical conflict regarding brain organization.

It should be noted that the neuroanatomic system outlined above applies to only certain types of memory. The memory abilities *preserved* in amnesics would of course not be dependent on the hippocampus, mammillary bodies, or medial dorsal nucleus. Suggestions have been made relating "habit memory" to the basal ganglia (Mishkin, Malamut, & Bachevalier, 1984), classical conditioning of certain motor responses to the cerebellum (Thompson, 1983), and working memory to frontal and parietal regions (Weiskrantz, 1987; Fuster, 1989). However, such proposals are either very preliminary or have been applied to animal work only and will not be reviewed here.

Frontal Lobe Lesions

Apart from classical amnesic syndromes, one other type of memory dysfunction should be discussed. There has been much debate about memory problems after frontal lobe lesions. Some experts claim that such patients "are not amnesic in the ordinary sense . . . they do not have the deficits in recall, recognition, or sense of familiarity that have come to be associated with amnesic disorders" (Squire, 1987). This observation receives support from experimental studies of patients with frontal lobe injuries (e.g., Stuss & Benson, 1986). It also agrees with clinical experience: these patients typically obtain memory test scores within or very near the normal range. Despite these findings, family members frequently report that patients with frontal injury are "forgetful." Several explanations have been offered to account for this apparent contradiction. First, there is evidence that frontal damage selectively impairs certain aspects of memory. Milner has shown that remembering the temporal order of events is dependent on the frontal lobes (Petrides & Milner, 1982; Bowers, Verfaellie, Valenstein, & Heilman, 1988). We recently saw a closed head injury patient with frontal contusions on CT scanning whose wife commented, "He can't remember whether something happened today, yesterday, or last week." There have also been numerous reports that frontal patients are more susceptible to interference than other types of memory-impaired patients (Schacter, 1987b; Parkin, Leng, Stanhope, & Smith, 1988). Other suggestions are that frontal patients underutilize memory strategies and that they suffer attentional deficits. The failure of frontal patients to adequately self-monitor their behavior might be yet another contributing factor (termed "forgetting to remember" by Hecaen and Albert, 1978). Finally, frontal cortex may be involved in certain short-term or working memory functions, especially with regard to spatial abilities (e.g., Goldman-Rakic, 1987; Baddeley & Wilson, 1988). The lessons to be learned from this debate are that memory is not a unitary phenomen, and that memory cannot be assessed in isolation. Adequate memory assessment must take into account different aspects of memory as well as memory-related skills and other cognitive abilities. These points will be stressed again later when clinical memory testing is discussed.

AMNESIA VS. AMNESIAS

Amnesia (or, more generally, memory disorders) can be grouped in terms of etiology or in terms of neuroanatomy. In terms of etiology, one can speak of Alzheimer's disease, closed head injury, anoxia, herpes encephalitis, and so on. In terms of neuroanatomy, many writers have distinguished two main groups: hippocampal amnesia and diencephalic amnesia. The former of course involves damage to the hippocampus; the latter involves damage to the mammillary bodies and/or thalamus. These classification systems have merit, but imprecision arises in some instances. Certain syndromes are not clearly understood in terms of the neuroanatomy of the memory disorder. For example, certain types of cerebrovascular accidents can produce profound memory loss (e.g., rupture of anterior communicating artery aneurysm), but remain poorly understood regarding neuropathology of the memory impairment. The basis of memory loss in so-called multifocal syndromes such as closed head injury also remains incompletely understood.

Setting aside the above caveats, it remains useful to debate the existence of amnesia versus amnesias. That is, it can be asked if amnesic syndromes are essentially the same regardless of etiology or underlying pathology, or whether significant differences exist among amnesias. Lhermitte and Signoret (1972) were early proponents of the latter approach, but Butters is perhaps the best-known and most vocal proponent (Butters, 1984; Butters, Salmon, Heindel, & Granholm, 1988). Butters' major arguments are as follows. First, amnesics of different etiology can be distinguished with regard to pattern of RA. Alcoholic Korsakoff patients have a "gradient" of retrograde memory loss, with very remote memories being relatively spared in the face of rather extensive RA. In contrast, Alzheimer patients and Huntington patients display an equivalent loss of remote memories from all periods of their lives. A third group of patients includes HM and patients receiving ECT, who have a limited RA, for a few years prior to the brain insult. Apart from differing patterns of RA, Butters contends that amnesics differ in terms of encoding versus retrieval deficits. Korsakoff patients are said to have encoding difficulty, failing to process incoming stimuli on a sufficiently deep level as to allow adequate retention. Huntington's disease patients, on the other hand, have a retrieval deficit. They perform poorly on recall testing but their performance on recognition testing approaches normal levels.

Other proposals have been made regarding differences among amnesic syndromes. Huppert and Piercy (1978) reported that forgetting rates differed among diencephalic amnesics and hippocampal amnesics. The latter patients showed a faster rate of forgetting, after amount of initial learning was roughly equated. This finding has generated many replication attempts and much controversy, to be discussed shortly. Other claims of differences among amnesic groups address issues of susceptibility to interference and number of intrusion errors. The most often stated claims are that alcoholic Korsakoff patients are more prone to interference effects than other amnesics, and that Korsakoff patients and patients with Alzheimer's disease make more intrusion errors than other amnesics (Butters et al., 1988).

In contrast to the "many amnesias" point of view, Weiskrantz (among others) has argued that the core amnesic syndrome does not differ across patients (Weiskrantz, 1985; 1987; see also Baddeley & Wilson, 1988). Weiskrantz attributes the claimed differences among amnesics to quantitative differences (i.e., some patients have more severe memory impairment than others), to differences in the purity of the syndrome (some amnesics have additional brain lesions outside of memory circuits), and to methodological problems. For example, with regard to forgetting rates, he points out that the size of the forgetting rate differences reported by Huppert and Piercy was in fact quite small. Further, the hippocampal and diencephalic groups differed somewhat in terms of initial learning. The failure to closely equate the two groups might therefore account for the obtained small differences in forgetting rates. Numerous replication attempts (e.g., Squire, 1981; Freed, Corkin, & Cohen, 1987; Huppert & Kopelman, 1989) have failed to settle the issue: evidence has accumulated both for and against forgetting rate differences among amnesics. One researcher has published results on both sides of the issue (cf. Kopelman, 1985; Huppert & Kopelman, 1989), and one patient has been cited as having both a normal forgetting rate (Freed, Corkin, & Cohen, 1987) and an abnormally rapid forgetting rate (Huppert & Piercy, 1978). At present the only justifiable conclusion is that differences among amnesic groups in terms of forgetting rate have yet to be firmly established.

With regard to the supposed differences among amnesics in RA, Weiskrantz argues that these findings are more apparent than real. He states that "both animal and clinical evidence suggest that the greater the degree of anterograde amnesia . . . the greater the retrograde amnesia" (Weiskrantz, 1985, p. 393). In British studies, Weiskrantz and colleagues have obtained a flat and extensive retrograde memory loss across past decades when severely amnesic patients were tested (Sanders & Warrington, 1971). The less extensive RA reported by American researchers for Korsakoff patients and patients receiving ECT is attributed to lesser severity of amnesia and to differences in assessment methods (Weiskrantz, 1985).

Contrary to Weiskrantz, several researchers claim that the relationship between RA and AA is small and that dramatic dissociations occur in rare patients. Goldberg et al. (1981), Roman-Campos, Poser, and Wood (1980), and Andrews, Poser, and Kessler (1982) have reported patients with extensive RA but minimal AA. These cases would seem to represent strong evidence that AA and RA need not be highly correlated and are subserved by separate brain mechanisms. One puzzle, however, is why new memories should be easily stored and retrieved in the face of inability to retrieve old memories. After all, new memories gradually become old. The fact that newly formed memories remain available to these patients suggests that their RA is due to a *loss* of premorbid memories rather than to a retrieval deficit. However, this conclusion is contrary to the phenomenon of shrinking RA, which suggests that RA is due to a retrieval deficit. These issues are of much theoretical importance, and their resolution will require better measures of RA and careful documentation of additional patients with dissociations between RA and AA.

As mentioned, the claim has been made that Korsakoff amnesics are especially prone to interference effects and that Korsakoff amnesics and Alzheimer patients generate a high number of intrusion errors on memory testing. Interference effects are categorized as proactive or retroactive. The usual procedure is to have the subject learn two word lists. Intrusions due to proactive interference occur when words on the first list occur on attempted recall of the second list. Intrusions due to retroactive interference occur when words on the second list occur on attempted recall of the first list. Patients may also show a high number of intrusions of other items not on any list. There are two problems with the claim that certain amnesic groups can be distinguished by a high rate of intrusions and interference effects. First, the research evidence is inconsistent. Several studies have documented a high rate of these effects in Alzheimer and alcoholic Korsakoff patients (Kramer et al., 1988; Fuld, Katzman, Davies, & Terry, 1982; Hart, Smith, & Swash, 1986; Miller, 1978; Butters, 1984; Butters, Wolfe, Granholm et al., 1986). However, other studies have failed to find differences between amnesic groups (Shindler, Kaplan, & Hier, 1984; Ober, Koss, Friendland, & Delis, 1985; Lowenstein et al., 1989). The second problem with these claims is that most Korsakoff and Alzheimer patients do not have a *pure* amnesia. Both groups suffer some degree of prefrontal atrophy, and it has been argued that frontal damage accounts for susceptibility to interference effects. Taken as a whole, the evidence reviewed above does not strongly support claims that amnesic syndromes deriving from different etiologies or different lesion locations can be differentiated in consistent ways. Nonetheless, there are examples of individual cases that differ strikingly from the typical amnesic syndrome (e.g., patients with severe RA and mild AA). Consequently, the particular pattern of memory disruption in an individual patient may not be useful in differential diagnosis, but would have implications for patient care and remediation.

Material-Specific Memory Disorders

Despite the controversy regarding "amnesia versus amnesias," it is well accepted that memory loss can differ depending on lateralization of brain injury. Milner and others have shown that left hippocampal injury is associated with verbal memory impairment, whereas right hippocampal injury is associated with visual or spatial memory impairment. For example, right temporal lobe patients perform poorly on memory of geometric designs (Milner, 1968), faces (Kimura, 1963), visual and tactual mazes (Kimura, 1963; Milner & Teuber, 1968), and spatial location (Smith & Milner, 1981). Conversely, left temporal lobe patients are very impaired on verbal memory tasks (Milner, 1966; von Cramon, Hebel, & Schuri, 1988). Verbal versus visuospatial memory differences have also been described with lateralized injury to the thalamus, although the evidence is less firm than for unilateral temporal lobe injury (Speedie & Heilman, 1982, 1983). It should also be admitted that clear-cut material-specific memory disorders are not a universal finding with unilateral temporal lobe damage. Certain studies fail to report such findings in certain patients (e.g., von Cramon, Hebel, & Schuri, 1988). These inconsistencies might be explained by patient characteristics (e.g., long-standing epilepsy may affect lateralization of function) or by choice of assessment measures (tests may be more or less pure as measures of verbal memory and visual memory; see the following discussion).

One unresolved issue with regard to material-specific memory disorders has to do with the use of alternative coding methods. It has been argued that much nonverbal material can be encoded via verbal descriptors, confounding the assessment of "visual memory." For example, the Wechsler Memory Scale (WMS) and Wechsler Memory Scale-Revised (WMS-R) Visual Reproduction subtests have been criticized on these grounds (Mayes, 1986; Loring & Papanicolaou, 1987; Loring, 1989). The issue remains controversial, however. Milner argues that verbal classification of visual material aids immediate reproduction from memory but is not beneficial after a delay, when "the hastily improvised verbal labels do not suffice to reinstate the original pattern, and may even be misleading" (Milner & Teuber, 1968, p. 335). More infomation is needed regarding this debate. Purposes of clinical memory assessment include isolating the severity of verbal versus visuospatial memory impairment. To achieve this goal more information is needed regarding the extent to which nonverbal stimulus material can be encoded by verbal means. It would also be of interest to compare use of verbal encoding strategies across subjects, since patients may vary in the use of alternative memory strategies.

ASSESSMENT OF MEMORY DISORDERS

The following sections provide a discussion of explicit and implicit memory tests that could be used by clinical practitioners. With regard to explicit memory tests, a number of standardized instruments are available. With regard to implicit memory testing, there are no standardized tests currently in use. Consequently, the tests we suggest are drawn from the experimental literature. After a discussion of selected explicit and implicit memory tests, we present a step-by-step procedure for choosing appropriate tests.

Assessment of Explicit Memory

Wechsler Memory Scale-Revised

The original WMS was as widely criticized as it was widely used (Prigatano, 1978). A similar fate probably awaits the WMS-R. Similar to its predecessor, it has major strengths and major weaknesses. The WMS-R consists of nine separate subtests, and total administration time is roughly one hour. We doubt that many clinicians administer the entire WMS-R, given the lengthy administration time and given weaknesses of certain subtests. For example, the Visual Paired Associates subtest involves learning a color associated with each of six line drawings, and may be susceptible to performance via verbal mediation. Certain subtests (e.g., Mental Control) do not assess memory per se. Adequate norms are not available for certain subtests. (For a more detailed critique of the WMS-R see Loring, 1989.)

With regard to an information processing perspective, the WMS-R adheres to the basics. Immediate memory (tested by Digit Span and Visual Memory Span subtests) is differentiated from LTM (assessed by several subtests). Within immediate memory and LTM, verbal memory is differentiated from visual memory (e.g., Digit Span vs. Visual Memory Span, Logical Memory vs. Visual Reproduction). Beyond these dichotomies, the WMS-R does not attempt a more detailed or sophisticated breakdown of memory deficits. This approach may be a strength rather than a weakness, since there is abundant evidence for the STM/LTM and verbal memory/visual memory dichotomies which the WMS-R does address, but less evidence for some of the other claims regarding the isolation of specific memory processes (e.g., encoding, retrieval).

An additional strength of the WMS-R is that the Logical Memory, Visual Reproduction, and Verbal Paired Associates subtests have a lengthy history of clinical usefulness. These three tasks are very similar to subtests of the original WMS, which have been demonstrated to differentiate memory-impaired subjects from normal subjects. The WMS was much criticized for not using a delay interval for the Logical Memory and Visual Reproduction subtests, and this approach has been built into the WMS-R. The WMS-R versions of Logical Memory and Visual Reproduction are also superior to the WMS with respect to the availability of adequate norms, a crucial and often neglected need for clinical assessment.

One additional criticism of the WMS-R should be mentioned. It has been pointed out that performance on the Visual Reproduction subtest is confounded in some patients by constructional apraxia, since the task requires a drawing response. There is merit to this argument, although a rough estimate of the contribution of constructional apraxia to poor performance can be obtained by having the patient copy the designs after completion of memory testing.

Buschke Selective Reminding Procedure

The Buschke Selective Reminding Procedure, which has become quite popular in recent years, espouses a more sophisticated approach than does the WMS-R. The subject attempts to learn a word list across several trials. After each trial, there is a reminder only of the words not recalled on that trial. This approach shortens testing time (on traditional word list learning the subject is told all the words on the list on each trial). More importantly, the selective reminding procedure allows generation of a variety of scores, including Sum Recall, Long-Term Retrieval, Short-Term Recall, Long-Term Storage, Consistent Long-Term Retrieval, and Random Long-Term Retrieval (see Buschke & Fuld, 1974, for details of scoring). Most important among the scores are those which are said to separate retrieval ability from ability to enter information into long-term store.

The popularity of the Buschke procedure lies in several factors: the reduced testing time, the fact that word list learning may be a more sensitive measure than story recall (von Cramon et al., 1988), and the information processing approach embodied in the separation of retrieval deficits from storage deficits. Despite these advantages, we have two major criticisms of the test. First, the Buschke test is in actuality a procedure and not a test. The selective reminding approach is constant across test users, but the word list, the number of words, and the number of trials vary widely (Hannay & Levin, 1985). For this reason there are only fragmentary norms available (e.g., Larrabee, Trahan, Curtiss, & Levin, 1988). There is also little information available concerning the number of words and number of trials that would maximize sensitivity to mild memory impairment, while also taking into account time constraints, subject frustration level (the task is difficult for many patients), and other factors.

Our second criticism has to do with the claim that the selective reminding procedure can separate "retrieval deficits" from "storage deficits." Buschke assumes that, if a patient fails to recall a word that had been recalled from long-term store previously, then the word can be assumed to still be in LTM, and the patient's recall failure must represent a "retrieval failure." This assumption is open to criticism on theoretical grounds. Furthermore, it has not been shown that the selective reminding method for assessing retrieval failure yields results similar to other methods purported to assess retrieval deficits (e.g., comparison of recall performance versus recognition performance). Further, there is little evidence that patients with damage to a certain brain region have prominent "retrieval failure" (as assessed by the selective reminding procedure), whereas patients with damage to a different brain region have relatively intact retrieval but defective ability to enter information into long-term store. Until such evidence has been gathered, the selective reminding procedure would seem to offer little beyond traditional list learning tasks.

California Verbal Learning Test

The California Verbal Learning Test (CVLT) involves learning a list of 16 words (from four semantic categories) over five trials. The subject is then given one learning and recall trial of a second list of 16 words. Free recall of the *first* list is then requested, followed immediately by cued recall by category name of the first list. After a 20-minute delay, free recall and cued recall of the first list are again requested. Finally, yes/no recognition testing is administered (the 16 words on the list are intermixed with 16 distractor words). In addition to scoring the number of words recalled and the number correct on yes/no recognition, the CVLT calls for recording extra-list items (intrusions and perseverations) on recall trials.

Unlike the Buschke procedure, the CVLT uses a standard set of words, a standard number of words, and a standard number of learning trials. Normative data are also available. Scoring of the CVLT generates numerous scores, including list A total recall, semantic cluster ratio, serial cluster ratio, percent primacy recall, percent recency recall, learning slope, list B recall, list B vs. list A trial 1 recall, short delay free recall, short delay vs. trial 5 recall, short delay cued recall, long delay free recall, long delay cued recall, recognition hits, false positives, free recall intrusions, cued recall intrusions, and perseverations. (For details of scoring and interpretation, see Delis, Freeland, Kramer, & Kaplan, 1988). Certain interpretations of CVLT scores are straightforward: for example, total recall, percent primacy recall, percent recency recall, and learning slope are interpreted as they would be for any list learning task. Other CVLT interpretations attempt a more sophisticated breakdown of memory impairment (e.g., comparing encoding and retrieval processes, measuring proactive interference, assessing the number and type of intrusion errors). Our major criticism of the CVLT parallels our criticism of the Buschke procedure. Certain of the scoring procedures can yield conclusions that are not yet well supported by research. For example, there is insufficient evidence that the purported separation of retrieval processes and encoding processes has theoretical or clinical validity. The CVLT also assesses susceptibility to interference and number of intrusions and perseverations. Clinical lore and some research studies suggest that frontal lobe patients and Alzheimer patients produce a high number of perseverations/intrusions relative to other diagnostic groups, but the overall research evidence is in fact contradictory (see earlier discussion). These findings weaken the claim of the CVLT developers that "Error analysis can contribute to the characterization of different memory disorders." In addition, issues of incremental validity need to be addressed. For example, if frontal lobe patients do show interference effects on the CVLT, does this finding add useful knowledge to clinical assessment of such patients? If interference effects are obtained only in patients with blatant "frontal symptoms," the answer may be "no."

To be fair, our criticisms of the Buschke procedure and of the CVLT should be taken as applying to naïve and unsophisticated use of these tests. If they are used with full knowledge of their limitations, they represent useful clinical tools. Our concern is that, if used without a knowledge of the research literature and of the complexities of an information processing approach to memory, they can lead to overly facile descriptions of memory disorders.

Rey-Osterreith Figure

This test assesses visual memory. As with many neuropsychological instruments, there are various permutations of the test and various scoring procedures. The most common administration procedure is to have the subject copy the Rey-Osterreith figure (a complex geometric design), to immediately reproduce it from memory, and to reproduce it from memory again after a delay. Scoring involves assigning one point for each unit correctly reproduced (e.g., cross in upper left corner).

A disadvantage of the Rey-Osterreith figure is the absence of normative data and standard administration methods (although fragmentary norms are available; see Lezak, 1983). On the other hand, the test has been used in a large number of research studies (e.g., Kimura, 1963; Milner, 1968). Not surprisingly, patients with documented brain injury perform less well than normal control subjects. Also, there is evidence that patients with right-sided injury perform more poorly on the Rey-Osterreith figure than on verbal memory tests (Milner, 1968).

For the clinician wishing to choose between the Rey-Osterreith figure and the WMS-R Visual Reproduction subtest, there are few data available. The Rey-Osterreith has been used extensively in research studies, whereas the WMS-R offers better standardization and norms. A visual memory test beyond these two instruments is much needed. Use of stimuli other than geometric designs would be useful. Ability to recognize faces, for example, is more likely to be perceived as a "real world" task, and would be useful with subjects threatened by "artificial" psychological tests. Warrington's Recognition Memory Test (Warrington, 1984) includes a facial memory subtest. The subject is shown 50 faces, one every three seconds. Fifty pairs of faces are then presented, with the subject choosing the previously presented face in each pair. This test holds much promise as a clinical instrument, but has not yet been well-validated in research studies in the United States. Computerized tests of facial memory have recently been developed by Crook and colleagues, utilizing advanced computer imaging technology (Larrabee & Crook, 1989). These tests combine a high degree of "face validity" with simulation of everyday memory tasks and will gain wider use as neuropsychologists increasingly make use of computer-based assessment.

Assessment of Implicit Memory

As reviewed earlier, much recent attention has been devoted to the study of preserved memory abilities in amnesia. Little clinical application has been made of these findings, even though it is an axiom among rehabilitation neuropsychologists to use preserved abilities to circumvent impaired abilities. One reason for the failure to use tests of implicit memory is that much of the research on implicit memory is quite recent, and insufficient time has elapsed for the findings to be adapted for clinical practice. A second reason, related to the first, is that there are no standardized tests of these abilities. A third reason is that the usefulness of these preserved abilities in the everyday life of the patient may not be obvious. However, it is now becoming evident that some simple preserved abilities (e.g., priming in word fragment completion) may be used to facilitate the acquisition of more complex types of information (e.g., learning of computer commands; see Glisky et al., 1986). Preserved implicit memory skills may enable amnesic patients to learn the use of memory aids, or may allow for the acquisition of some occupational skills. Below we discuss some implicit memory tests drawn from the experimental literature that merit exploration as clinical assessment tools. The tasks chosen are those which showed substantial retention in amnesic patients and which appear easy to administer. Because of the absence of normative data, it would be necessary to test a sample of normal subjects prior to administering the tests to patients.

Word Stem Completion

This task examines priming for word-stem completion. In the first phase, subjects are required to carry out a study task on a set of words. Typically, experimenters have asked subjects to read the words aloud or to make judgments about the words such as rating them for pleasantness. In the second phase, word stems are presented (usually the first three letters) and subjects are asked to complete the word with the first word that comes to mind. Usually half of the stems presented in the second phase are based on the words presented in the first phase. The other half consists of words not previously presented, which provides a baseline measure for the likelihood of completing the stems in the absence of prior study. The delay between the first and second phases affects the amount of priming, with larger priming effects at shorter delays.

In group studies with normal subjects, the studied and nonstudied items are counterbalanced across subjects. Thus, when results are averaged across subjects, the baseline and priming completion rates reflect performance on the same word targets. Difficulties arise in adapting this procedure to the assessment of individual patients. In testing a single case, it is not possible that a given word target can be both presented and not presented. The alternative is to divide the set of word targets randomly into studied and nonstudied items and to have a sufficiently large number of items in each set so that idiosyncratic characteristics of words in either the studied or nonstudied sets do not bias the priming effect in either direction.

Another reason for having a large number of stimuli is that the size of the priming effect in normal subjects is usually fairly small. Normal subjects typically complete 20% to 30% more of the word stems for the studied words than for the nonstudied words. If there were only 20 studied words, this would translate into an average advantage of four to six items completed for words primed by prior study. It might be difficult to detect whether a patient fell below the normal range if such a small number of words were used. Thus, it would seem advisable to use at least 40 words in the study phase, randomly chosen from a set of 80 target words, and to present all 80 stems in the stem completion phase.

In choosing the word targets, some researchers have used words whose stems have at least 10 possible completions as indicated by 10 or more different entries in a pocket dictionary (Graf et al., 1984). This criterion was used in order to reduce the likelihood of producing the high frequency target without prior study. However, some evidence suggests that the use of low-frequency target words results in larger priming effects (MacLeod, 1989). Appendix 7-1 (see end of chapter) presents two sets of 80 word stimuli. The first set consists of target words having stems with ten or more completions in a pocket dictionary (*Webster's Vest Pocket Dictionary*, 1981). The second set consists of five-letter target words which are low-frequency but familiar words. The stems for each of these words have two or more possible five-letter word completions.

It is important that the word stem completion task not be presented as an explicit memory test. Graf et al. (1984) have shown that when the stems are treated as cues for memory recall, amnesics perform much more poorly than controls. However, when instructions emphasize completing the stems with the first word that comes to mind, amnesics show the same completion rate as controls.

It may be helpful at this point to summarize how the word completion test would be administered. Assume that the 80 words from set 2 in Appendix 7.1 were to be used. The words would be randomly divided into a studied set and a nonstudied set. In the study phase, only the studied words would be presented visually. The subject would be asked to read each word aloud, or make some judgment about each word. A time limit should be set for each word (e.g., 5 sec), in order to ensure the same amount of exposure for each word across subjects. Then an intervening task would be used that took several minutes (e.g., from 3 to 15 min) that would serve to clear short-term memory. The next step would be to present the three-letter stems for the studied and nonstudied words in a randomized order and ask the subject to complete the stem with the first five-letter word that comes to mind. For set 1, the target words are of different lengths, and the length of the subject's response would not be specified. Again a time limit for each stem should be used (e.g., 10 sec), since subjects may not be able to think of any word that completes some stems. The results would be scored by counting the number of stems for the studied words that were completed with the studied word, and the number of stems for the nonstudied words that were completed with the target nonstudied word. To evaluate whether the amount of priming was normal, data from control subjects would have to be obtained for the same materials and procedures. Data from a study of 20 undergraduate Rice University students that used the words in set 2 and a 15-minute intervening task between study and test showed an average priming effect of 10 words (25%) and a standard deviation of 3.75.

Sentence Puzzle Solution

This variation of the priming task developed by McAndrews et al. (1987) assesses implicit memory for more complex information than the word stem completion task. As discussed earlier, subjects in the McAndrews et al. study were given a set of sentence puzzles in which a key word or phrase had to be generated to make the sentence meaningful. For example, for the sentence "The person was unhappy because the hole closed," the key words were "pierced ears." The puzzles were selected to have a low baseline solution rate (about 12%). In the study phase subjects were given one minute to solve the puzzles, and were provided the answer if they could not solve it. After a delay ranging from one minute to one week, subjects were given the puzzles again along with some new puzzles and asked to solve them. For the repeated puzzles the completion rate was much higher for the second presentation than for the first, even for severely amnesic patients.

Unlike the word stem completion task, where the size of priming effects appears unrelated to severity of memory loss, severely amnesic subjects showed a lower solution rate for sentence puzzles than moderately impaired amnesics, and the moderately impaired amnesics showed a lower solution rate than the normal controls. In fact, the control subjects had solution rates of 100% at short delays and very high solution rates even at the one week delay. McAndrews et al. state that they could not prevent normal subjects from relying on explicit recall. That is, it was impossible to disguise the task in such a way that normal subjects would not realize that they had seen the puzzles previously. Presumably the moderately impaired amnesics also employed some explicit memory which resulted in their higher performance than the severely impaired amnesics. However, even the severely impaired amnesics showed solution rates of 63% at one-week delay. (Recall that the baseline solution rate on the first presentation was only 12%.) Despite their relatively high solution rates, the severe amnesics were completely unable to distinguish new from old puzzles.

An assessment of the amnesic patients' implicit recall can be made by comparing solution rate when the puzzles are presented the second time to solution rate on the first presentation. An interesting comparison that could be made within an individual subject would be the ability to recognize if puzzles had been previously presented versus the ability to solve the puzzles with the key word or phrase. Such a comparison would help to sort out the contribution of explicit and implicit memory impairment.

The puzzles that were used by McAndrews et al. included the 20 puzzles from Auble, Franks, and Soraci (1979, Appendix A) that were most difficult for subjects to solve spontaneously. To use these materials to test individual amnesic subjects, the subjects should be instructed that they will be seeing sentences whose meaning is not immediately apparent, but which could be made sensible by thinking of a key word or phrase. A few practice examples should then be presented. The practice examples might be drawn from the set of easier sentences in the Auble et al. study. Then the 20 difficult puzzles could be presented in a random order with the subject being allowed a limited amount of time to solve the puzzle (60 sec in the McAndrews et al. study). At the end of the time limit, the subject would be told the key word or words. After a time delay, memory would be assessed by presenting the same sentences in a different random order.

Pilot data were collected using the 20 difficult sentences from the Auble et al. (1979) study and a 30-minute filled delay between first and second administration. Data from 20 undergraduate Rice University students showed an average solution rate of 3.75/20 (s.d. = 1.9) on the first administration and 17.6/20 (s.d. = 1.4) on the second administration. Eight normal elderly subjects (ages 55 to 70) had an average solution rate of 3.1/20 (s.d. = 2.4) on the first administration and 14.8/20 (s.d. = 2.6) on the second administration.

If a recognition test is to be incorporated (to test explicit memory), it would be necessary to include a second set of 20 sentences mixed in with the original 20 during the second administration. Subjects would then be asked whether the sentence had previously been presented.

Implicit Memory Testing: General Comments

Two procedures for adapting implicit memory tests to the clinical setting have been described. Implicit memory assessment is of course not an end in itself. The results must be clinically useful with regard to predicting behavior or with regard to facilitating rehabilitation. There are few data addressing these issues in the research literature. The clinician must therefore serve in a quasi-research role, generating his/her own data and hypotheses. To cite one example, memory-impaired patients are often taught strategies to circumvent their memory loss (e.g., mnemonics, use of visual imagery, use of memory notebooks). Ability to learn such strategies may to some extent involve implicit or procedural memory, and it would be of interest to determine the ability of various implicit memory tests to predict successful learning of memory strategies. A second, similar example would involve teaching of specific occupational skills, in which the work skills are analyzed as to their specific nature. Success in learning the job skills would be expected to vary across tasks and across subtasks (and across patients). The point of interest would be to determine the extent to which various explicit and implicit memory measures predicted success on different types of tasks.

The study of Glisky et al. (mentioned above) outlined another approach to the use of preserved implicit memory skills. The "method of vanishing cues" was utilized. Patients were taught a computer-related vocabulary via a procedure in which the subjects were cued with as many letters of the target word as needed to elicit the correct response. Letters were then gradually withdrawn until the subject could produce the response without cues. This teaching approach (which has obvious similarities to the word stem completion task) was designed to tap preserved implicit memory skills so as to permit the acquisition of new abilities. Learning was achieved, although with significant limitations (see earlier discussion). The important point is that additional, similar approaches need to be attempted with memory-impaired patients, to expand our understanding of the use of preserved implicit memory skills in the design of rehabilitation programs.

Memory Assessment: Step-by-Step Procedures

The following section will discuss assessment of memory-related abilities, followed by a review of the dimensions of memory that should be evaluated as part of the memory assessment process.

Assessment of Memory-Related Abilities

An important initial step, prior to memory assessment per se, involves evaluating the intactness of sensory-perceptual skills. Verbal LTM assessment must take into account auditory deficits, and visual LTM assessment must take into account visual impairment. Such deficits are not uncommon, especially in the elderly population which accounts for a large proportion of referrals for memory testing. Ideally, audiological and ophthalmological examination reports would be available; if not, the clinician can roughly evaluate vision and hearing using brief screening tests. A pocket eye chart can be used to assess visual acuity. Visual fields can be assessed by having the patient detect fingers. Hearing can be roughly assessed by ability to detect light finger rub. Beyond the assessment of sensory deficits, higher level perceptual skills should also be tested. Aphasic deficits can be assessed by standard aphasia batteries. Visuoperceptual impairment can be assessed by a variety of tests (e.g., facial discrimination tests, figural discrimination tests, gestalt closure tests; see Lezak, 1983). Visual assessment can also include tests of visual scanning and of visual neglect.

If deficits are detected on sensory or perceptual testing, an estimate of the contribution to memory impairment must be made. In some cases memory

Table 7-1 Conceptualization of Memory Assessment

Immediate memory vs. LTM
Verbal memory vs. visual memory
Explicit memory vs. implicit memory
Recall performance vs. recognition performance
Forgetting rate
Episodic memory vs. semantic memory
Remote memory
Interference effects; confabulation
Metamemory

testing will not be possible because of the severity of the perceptual impairment. Other patients will have no detectable sensory or perceptual impairment. Many cases will fall into a grey area, however, and there are no hard and fast rules for "subtracting" sensory-perceptual impairment from memory impairment. The usual solution is to describe the nature and the severity of the sensory-perceptual deficits in the neuropsychological report and to briefly discuss (often in vague terms) the possible impact on memory. This state of affairs could be improved if perceptual tests and memory tests were more closely linked. For example, a test of memory for faces could be followed by a facial discrimination test using the memory test stimuli. Additional test development along these lines is much needed.

A second step in LTM assessment is to determine the intactness of attentional skills. Some degree of attentional impairment is common with brain disease, and certain syndromes are characterized by marked attentional deficits (e.g., delirium, severe frontal lobe pathology). If attentional dysfunction is present, ability to enter information into LTM will be affected. To assess attention a variety of clinical tests are available. Some require sophisticated equipment (e.g., the Continuous Performance Test); others require little or no equipment and can be performed at bedside (e.g., the sustained attention task of Strub and Black, 1977). Attention can also be evaluated qualitatively, independent of standard tests, by noting arousal level, responses to extraneous stimuli, coherence of stream of speech, and so on. As with sensory-perceptual deficits, there is no formula for determining the contribution of attentional impairment to memory performance. Such assessment is left to clinical judgment and is usually described qualitatively.

LTM Assessment: Conceptualization and Choice of Tests

The information-processing approach mandates the testing of memory skills across several different dimensions, rather than as a unitary entity. The theoretical background outlined earlier dictates the dimensions to be assessed. A framework for memory assessment (and for the following discussion) is provided in Table 7-1.

An initial step in memory assessment is to separate immediate memory from LTM. This may seem obvious to some, but clinicians have not always been careful in this regard. For example, the original WMS failed to include delayed recall trials. As a result, "normal" performance could be achieved by some memory-impaired patients on the basis of intact immediate memory skills (Prigatano, 1978). Memory testing should include separate tests of short-term memory (e.g., digit span, word span) and of LTM. If tests are administered which tap both immediate memory and LTM (e.g., list learning, immediate recall of stories), procedures should be included to separate the contributions of each memory store. For list learning tasks (e.g., the Buschke procedure) this can be accomplished by analysis of serial position effects, use of a sufficient number of trials to assess learning, and use of a delayed recall trial. For tasks such as story recall (e.g., Logical Memory subtest of WMS-R) delayed recall performance should be compared with immediate recall performance (and with performance on immediate memory tests such as word span and sentence repetition).

Striking dissociations between immediate memory performance and LTM performance are seen in two types of patients. Amnesic patients have severely defective LTM in the face of intact immediate memory, whereas certain patients with focal perisylvian damage have the converse pattern (see chapter 6). Even if a pure amnesia or pure immediate memory syndrome is not present, a lesser degree of dissociation between LTM and immediate memory may be present. With regard to clinical implications, impairment in LTM has obvious significance, since inability to form new memories will interfere with many activities. The significance of impaired immediate memory is less understood (for a discussion, see Chapter 6).

LTM assessment should include measures of both verbal memory and visual memory. Verbal and visual memory tests can be selected from those described earlier, or from others that are available (see Lezak, 1983; Squire, 1987). The WMS-R and Warrington's Recognition Memory Test offer both verbal and visual subtests. Most other available tests assess either verbal memory alone or visual memory alone (e.g., the CVLT and the Rey-Osterreith, respectively). This does not preclude comparison of verbal versus visual memory, but problems may arise in the use of normative data from two different samples.

A dissociation between verbal and visual memory performance carries implications for laterality of the brain lesion (left hemisphere vs. right hemisphere). It also carries implications for the everyday tasks which will present difficulty for the patient (for example, intact memory for conversation but poor memory for unfamiliar faces). In actual fact, little research has been performed to confirm the latter expectation. That is, there has been little research relating dissociations on verbal vs. visual memory tests to dissociations in real world abilities. This situation may be rectified by recent interest in increasing the "ecologic validity" of memory tests (see Crook & Larrabee, 1988).

Traditional memory assessment has included only tests of explicit memory. However, depending on the purposes of assessment, evaluation of implicit memory may also be desirable. Assessment of implicit memory is likely to be of most interest in a rehabilitation setting. Such a setting would allow for lengthy assessment and for design of experimental memory tasks, both needed for implicit memory assessment. As these issues were discussed above, they will not be reviewed further here.

Theoretical claims have been made with regard to dissociations between recall performance and recognition performance in different etiologies of amnesia

(Butters, 1984). The evidence is not yet convincing, but it remains possible (though unproven) that individual patients might show preserved recognition with impaired recall. If so, such a pattern would be important for patients' everyday functioning, as such patients would presumably be unable to recall information when questioned, but would be able to recognize people and places upon seeing them. If the clinician wishes to compare recall and recognition performance, a few tests are available. The CVLT yields measures of both recall and recognition. Certain versions of the Buschke selective reminding procedure use a delayed recall trial followed by a delayed recognition trial. Tests without a recognition format (e.g., Logical Memory of WMS-R) can be extended to include such testing if the clinician is so inclined, but normative data are of course not available for such an approach.

As reviewed earlier, some have argued that forgetting rate varies across etiologies of amnesia, but this remains a matter of dispute. Methodological considerations also make measurement of forgetting rate difficult. Initial learning must be equated across subjects; accomplishing this can be difficult given the wide range of memory impairment in brain-injured patients. Also, the lengthy delay intervals (e.g., 24 hours, 1 week) used in experimental studies would be impractical in the clinic. Of the standardized tests available, the Paired Associates subtest of the WMS-R is one of the few to use a learning to criterion approach followed by a delayed recall trial. "Forgetting" is scored in terms of amount of information retained after a delay. However, many memory-impaired patients fail to achieve the criterion of perfect performance. Comparison across patients is therefore problematical. In sum, at present assessment of forgetting rate remains of questionable usefulness in the clinical setting.

The assessment of episodic memory versus semantic memory has also failed to achieve wide use among clinicians. The major reason was discussed earlier: dispute over whether amnesia can be characterized in terms of the episodic/semantic dichotomy. A second reason involves the extreme difficulty in assessing episodic memory for personal events. Life episodes are by definition idiosyncratic to the subject; testing such personal memories in a valid, reliable fashion is not easily accomplished. Most such testing by clinicians has been informal, e.g., asking about family events, job-related incidents, etc. Needless to say, the usefulness of information obtained in this fashion is open to question, since the responses are difficult to verify and standardization of such procedures is difficult to achieve.

It is well-known that loss of old memories occurs in memory disorders (see earlier discussion). However, assessment of remote memory encounters difficulties similar to the assessment of episodic vs. semantic memory. Tests of remote memory have required patients to identify photographs of famous individuals, to answer questions about news events, and to identify television shows that were broadcast for only one season (Squire & Fox, 1980). None of these tests has achieved wide clinical use. It is difficult to be sure that the patient knew the information premorbidly; remote memory tests need to be constantly updated as time passes; assessment of remote memory is a time-consuming procedure. For the clinician interested in remote memory assessment, such tests can be obtained from the research literature (e.g., Beatty, Salmon, Bernstein, & Butters, 1987) or by writing to their creators.

Qualitative Analysis of Memory Test Performance

Thus far the approach we have described has been to assess memory via specific tests—that is, visual versus verbal tests, explicit versus implicit tests, and so forth. In performing an information-processing analysis, certain *within-test* aspects of performance can also provide useful information. For example, interference effects can be analyzed, to test the possibility that the patient is highly susceptible to such effects. Certain memory tests have such measures built in (e.g., the CVLT). On other tests the examiner can obtain such information via qualitative analysis. For instance, the WMS-R Logical Memory subtest requires recall of two stories. A patient prone to interference effects may confuse information between the two stories, a fact that is easily noted.

Qualitative analysis of memory test performance can also be used to assess confabulation. Kopelman (1987) has provided a useful framework for the assessment of this phenomenon. He distinguishes between spontaneous and provoked confabulation. The former occurs both on testing and in conversation, tends to be grandiose and fantastic, and is seen with frontal lobe pathology. The latter occurs only when the patient's memory is probed by questioning, does not have the fantastic quality of spontaneous confabulation, and is seen in all etiologies of memory decline. The theoretical basis of confabulation remains poorly understood, and its clinical correlates have not been explored in detail. Nonetheless, brief evaluation of confabulation should be part of thorough memory assessment. The examiner should note the severity and frequency of spontaneous confabulation (if present), and should also note the degree of provoked confabulation on memory testing. Provoked confabulation is best assessed by story recall (e.g., Logical Memory from WMS-R). Intrusions on list learning (Buschke, CVLT) may be related to confabulation, but this possibility has not been explored.

Memory assessment should also include evaluation of metamemory. "Metamemory" has been defined as "the knowledge one possesses about the functioning, development, use, and capacities of the human memory system in general, and one's own memory in particular" (Dixon & Hultsch, 1983, p. 682). Memory skills do not exist in a vacuum: a patient's metamemory skills can have major impact on both memory test performance and day-to-day functional abilities. Metamemory should be assessed in two ways. First, patients' test performance should be analyzed for use of memory strategies. A few tests, such as the CVLT, include an analysis of certain strategies. For the most part, however, such assessment must be done informally. As examples, patients may be observed to approach word list learning by repetition of words in immediate memory, followed by recall from LTM; other patients may report use of visual imagery, associations, or other mnemonics; still others may use no strategy at all. Patients' recall of narrative material can also be observed for use of different strategies: attempts at verbatim recall; gist recall followed by attempts to explore LTM for details; recall from immediate memory (the final portion of the narrative) followed by recall from LTM. Certain of these strategies are more effective than others, and the patient's choice of strategy (or failure to use a strategy) reflects cognitive integrity.

A second approach to assessment of metamemory involves interviewing the patient and family about behavior in everyday life. Some patients are adept at circumventing their memory impairment via use of notes, memory aids, calendars, and other strategies. Other patients, although no more demented on cognitive testing, are quite handicapped by their memory loss because of unawareness of their memory deficits and resulting failure to develop effective compensatory strategies. Memory questionnaires are gaining increasing use in evaluating metamemory (e.g., Crook & Larrabee, 1990), and thorough assessment should include such techniques.

CONCLUSION

We have sketched current theoretical conceptions of LTM and have described how these conceptions can be applied to clinical memory assessment. Our knowledge of memory is more advanced than the days of the original Wechsler Memory Scale, which failed to detect subtle memory deficits, confounded the assessment of LTM and of nonmemory skills, and failed to adequately address possible dissociations in memory impairment (Prigatano, 1978). Currently available memory tests are sensitive to mild memory decline, can quantify the severity of memory impairment, and can describe patterns of impaired versus intact skills. Much further development is needed, however, both with regard to theoretical models and clinical assessment tools. The notion of explicit/implicit memory remains vague and the nature of preserved memory skills in amnesia needs to be clearly specified. The relationship between anterograde amnesia and retrograde amnesia is poorly understood and clinical tests of retrograde amnesia are much needed. Claims that qualitative differences exist among amnesic syndromes should be more carefully validated. Procedures for separating memory disorders from perceptual processing deficits need to be developed. The relationship between episodic memory and semantic memory remains to be clarified. The future holds much promise for successfully addressing these issues. In recent years the study of memory has become multidisciplinary, involving contributions by cognitive psychology, clinical neuropsychology, behavioral neurology, and neuroscience, among other disciplines. This confluence of effort has proved productive and should continue to yield insights which increase our understanding of human memory systems.

NOTES

1. Tulving, Hayman, and Macdonald (1991) suggest that the failure of HM to learn new definitions might be attributed to massive interference that would arise when amnesics, in the course of attempting to learn new associations, are forced to produce

responses, many of which would be incorrect. These incorrect responses would interfere with later production of the correct response.

2. Tulving's (1989) most recent theorizing has taken the approach of positing additional memory systems. His current conceptualization includes procedural memory and a perceptual representation system (involved in perceptual priming) in addition to episodic and semantic memory.

3. Some researchers have similarly argued that it is not possible to separate encoding, storage, and retrieval in studies of normal subjects (e.g., Watkins, 1990).

REFERENCES

Andrews, E., Poser, C. M., & Kessler, M. (1982). Retrograde amnesia for forty years. *Cortex*, *18*, 441–458.

Auble, P., Franks, J., & Soraci, S. (1979). Effort toward comprehension: Elaboration of "aha!"? *Memory and Cognition*, *7*, 426–434.

Baddeley, A. (1986). *Working memory*. Oxford: Clarendon Press.

Baddeley, A. & Wilson, B. (1988). Frontal amnesia and the dysexecutive syndrome. *Brain and Cognition*, *7*, 212–230.

Beatty, W. W., Salmon, D. P., Bernstein, N., & Butters, N. (1987). Remote memory in a patient with amnesia due to hypoxia. *Psychological Medicine*, *17*, 657–665.

Blaxton, T. (1989). Investigating dissociations among memory measures: Support for a transfer-appropriate processing framework. *Journal of Experimental Psychology: Learning, Memory, and Cognition*, *15*, 657–668.

Bowers, D., Verfaellie, M., Valenstein, E., & Heilman, K. (1988). Impaired acquisition of temporal information in retrosplenial amnesia. *Brain and Cognition*, *8*, 47–66.

Brooks, D. N. & Baddeley, A. (1976). What can amnesic patients learn? *Neuropsychologia*, *14*, 111–122.

Buschke, H. & Fuld, P. A. (1974). Evaluating storage, retention, and retrieval in disordered memory and learning. *Neurology*, *24*, 1019–1025.

Butters, N. (1984). The clinical aspects of memory disorders: Contributions from experimental studies of amnesia and dementia. *Journal of Clinical Neuropsychology*, *6*, 17–36.

Butters, N. & Cermak, L. S. (1980). *Alcoholic Korsakoff's syndrome: An information processing approach*. New York: Academic Press.

Butters, N., Salmon, D. P., Heindel, W., & Granholm, E. (1988). Episodic, semantic, and procedural memory: Some comparisons of Alzheimer and Huntington disease patients. In R. D. Terry (Ed.), *Aging and the brain*. Raven Press: New York.

Butters, N., Wolfe, J., Grandholm, E., & Martone, M. (1986). An assessment of verbal recall, recognition and fluency abilities in patients with Huntington's disease. *Cortex*, *22*, 11–32.

Cermak, L. (1982). *Human memory and amnesia*. Hillsdale, NJ: Lawrence Erlbaum.

Cermak, L. S., & O'Connor, M. (1983). The anterograde and retrograde retrieval ability of a patient with amnesia due to encephalitis. *Neuropsychologia*, *21*, 213–234.

Cermak, L., & Butters, N. (1973). Information processing deficits of alcoholic Korsakoff patients. *Quarterly Journal of Studies of Alcohol*, *34*, 1110–1132.

Cohen, N. J. (1984). Preserved learning capacity in amnesia: Evidence for multiple memory systems. In L. R. Squire & N. Butters (Eds.), *Neuropsychology of memory* (83–103). New York: Guilford Press.

Cohen, N. J., & Squire, L. R. (1980). Preserved learning and retention of pattern-analyzing skill in amnesia: Dissociation of "knowing how" and "knowing that." *Science*, *210*, 207–209.

Collins, A. M., & Loftus, E. F. (1975). A spreading activation theory of semantic memory. *Psychological Review*, *82*, 407–428.

Corkin, S. (1968). Acquisition of motor skill after bilateral medial temporal lobe excision. *Neuropsychologia*, *6*, 255–265.

Crook, T. H., & Larrabee, G. J. (1988). Interrelationships among everyday memory tests: Stability of factor structure with age. *Neuropsychology*, *2*, 1–12.

Crook, T., & Larrabee, G. J. (1990). A self-rating scale for evaluating memory in everyday life. *Psychology of Aging*, *5*, 48–57.

Delis, D. C., Freeland, J., Kramer, J. H., & Kaplan, E. (1988). Integrating clinical assessment with cognitive neuroscience: Construct validation of the California Verbal Learning Test, *Journal of Consulting and Clinical Psychology*, *56*, 123–130.

Diamond, R., & Rozin, P. (1984). Activation of existing memories in anterograde amnesia. *Journal of Abnormal Psychology*, *93*, 98–105.

Dixon, R. A., & Hultsch, D. F. (1983). Structure and development of metamemory in adulthood. *Journal of Gerontology*, *38*, 682–695.

Freed, D. M., Corkin, S., & Cohen, N. J. (1987). Forgetting in HM: A second look. *Neuropsychologia*, *25*, 461–472.

Fuld, P., Katzman, R., Davies, P., & Terry, R. D. (1982). Intrusions as a sign of Alzheimer dementia: Chemical and pathological verification. *Annals of Neurology*, *11*, 155–159.

Fuster, J. M. (1989). *The prefrontal cortex: Anatomy, physiology, and neuropsychology of the frontal lobes* (2nd ed.). New York: Raven Press.

Gabrieli, J. D. E., Cohen, N. J., & Corkin, S. (1988). The impaired learning of semantic knowledge following bilateral medial temporal-lobe resection. *Brain and Cognition*, *7*, 157–177.

Glisky, E. L., Schacter, D. L., & Tulving, E. (1986). Computer learning by memory-impaired patients. Acquisition and retention of complex knowledge. *Neuropsychologia*, *24*, 313–328.

Goldberg, E., Antin, S. P., Bilder, R. M., Gerstman, L. J., Hughes, J. E. O., & Mattis, S. (1981). Retrograde amnesia: Possible role of mesencephalic reticular activation in long-term memory. *Science*, *213*, 1392–1394.

Goldman-Rakic, P. S. (1987). Circuitry of the prefrontal cortex: Short term memory and the regulation of behavior by representational knowledge. In F. Plum (Ed.), *Handbook of Physiology: Higher Functions of the Brain*. New York: Oxford University Press.

Graf, P., & Schacter, D. L. (1985). Implicit and explicit memory for new associations in normal and amnesic subjects. *Journal of Experimental Psychology: Learning, Memory, and Cognition*, *11*, 501–518.

Graf, P., Squire, L. R., & Mandler, G. (1984). The information that amnesic patients do not forget. *Journal of Experimental Psychology: Learning, Memory, and Cognition*, *10*, 164–178.

Hannay, H. J., & Levin, H. S. (1985). Selective reminding test: An examination of the equivalence of four forms. *Journal of Clinical and Experimental Neuropsychology*, *7*, 251–263.

Hart, S., Smith, C. M., & Swash, M. (1986). Intrusion errors in Alzheimer's disease. *British Journal of Clinical Psychology*, *25*, 149–150.

Hecaen, H., & Albert, M. L. (1978). *Human neuropsychology*. New York: John Wiley & Sons.

Heindel, W. C., Salmon, D. P., Shults, C. W., Walicke, P. A., & Butters, N. (1989). Neuropsychological evidence for multiple implicit memory systems: A comparison of Alzheimer's, Huntington's, and Parkinson's disease patients. *The Journal of Neuroscience*, *9*, 582–587.

Huppert, F. A., & Kopelman, M. D. (1989). Rates of forgetting in normal aging: A comparison with dementia. *Neuropsychologia*, *27*, 849–860.

Huppert, F. A., & Piercy, M. (1978). Dissociation between learning and remembering in organic amnesia. *Nature*, *275*, 317–318.

Jacoby, L. (1983). Remembering the data: Analyzing interactive processes in reading. *Journal of Verbal Learning and Verbal Behavior*, *22*, 485–508.

Jacoby, L., & Dallas, M. (1981). On the relationship between autobiographical memory and perceptual learning. *Journal of Experimental Psychology: General*, *3*, 306–340.

Kimura, D. (1963). Right temporal lobe damage. *Archives of Neurology*, *8*, 48–55.

Kinsbourne, M. (1987). Brain mechanisms and memory. *Human Neurobiology*, *6*, 81–92.

Kinsbourne, M., & Wood, F. (1975). Short term memory and the amnesic syndrome. In D. D. Deutsch & J. A. Deutsch (Eds.), *Short-term memory*. New York: Academic Press.

Kintsch, W., & Buschke, H. (1969). Homophones and synonyms in short-term memory. *Journal of Experimental Psychology*, *80*, 403–407.

Kopelman, M. D. (1985). Rates of forgetting in Alzheimer-type dementia and Korsakoff's syndrome. *Neuropsychologia*, *23*, 623–638.

Kopelman, M. D. (1987). Two types of confabulation. *Journal of Neurology, Neurosurgery, and Psychiatry*, *50*, 1482–1487.

Kramer, J. H., Delis, D. C., Blusewicz, M. J., Brandt, J., Ober, B. A., & Strauss, M. (1988). Verbal memory errors in Alzheimer's and Huntington's dementias. *Developmental Neuropsychology*, *4*, 1–15.

Larrabee, G. J., & Crook, T. H. (1989). Dimensions of everyday memory in Age-Associated Memory Impairment. *Psychological Assessment: A Journal of Consulting and Clinical Psychology*, *1*, 92–97.

Larrabee, G. J., Trahan, D. E., Curtiss, G., & Levin, H. S. (1988). Normative data for the verbal selective reminding test. *Neuropsychology*, *2*, 173–182.

Lashley, K. S. (1963). *Brain Mechanisms and Intelligence: A quantitative study of injuries to the brain*. New York: Dover Publications.

Lezak, M. D. (1983). *Neuropsychological Assessment*. New York: Oxford University Press.

Lhermitte, F., & Signoret, J. L. (1972). Analyse neuropsycholgique et differenciation des syndromes amnesiques. *Revue Neurologique*, *126*, 161–178.

Loring, D. W. (1989). The Wechsler Memory Scale-Revised or the Wechsler Memory Scale-Revisited? *The Clinical Neuropsychologist*, *3*, 161–178.

Loring, D. W., & Papanicolaou, A. C. (1987). Memory assessment in neuropsychology: Theoretical considerations and practical utility. *Journal of Clinical and Experimental Neuropsychology*, *9*, 340–358.

Lowenstein, D. A., Wilkie, F., Eisdorfer, C., Guterman, A., Berkowitz, N., & Duara, R. (1989). An analysis of intrusive error types in Alzheimer's disease and related disorders. *Developmental Neuropsychology*, *5*, 115–126.

MacLeod, C. M. (1989). Word context during initial exposure influences degree of priming in word fragment completion. *Journal of Experimental Psychology: Learning, Memory, and Cognition*, *15*, 398–406.

Mair, W. G. P., Warrington, E. K., & Weiskrantz, L. (1979). Memory disorder in Korsakoff's psychosis: A neuropathological and neuropsychological investigation of two cases. *Brain*, *102*, 749–783.

Mayes, A. R. (1986). Learning and memory disorders and their assessment. *Neuropsychologia*, *24*, 25–39.

Mayes, A. R., & Meudell, P. R. (1984). Problems and prospects for research on amnesia. In L. R. Squire & N. Butters (Eds.), *Neuropsychology of memory*. New York: Guilford Press.

Mayes, A. R., Meudell, P. R., Mann, D., & Pickering, A. (1988). Location of lesions in Korsakoff's syndrome: Neuropsychological and neuropathological data on two patients. *Cortex*, *24*, 367–388.

McAndrews, M., Glisky, E., & Schacter, D. (1987). When priming persists: Long-lasting implicit memory for a single episode in amnesic patients. *Neuropsychologia*, *25*, 497–506.

McGaugh, J. L. (1989). Modulation of memory storage processes. In P. R. Solomon, G. R. Goethals, C. M. Kelley & B. R. Stephens (Eds.), *Memory: Interdisciplinary approaches*. New York: Springer-Verlag.

Meudell, P. & Mayes, A. (1982). Normal and abnormal forgetting: Some comments on the human amnesic syndrome. In A. Ellis (Ed.), *Normality and pathology in cognitive functions*. London: Academic Press.

Miller, E. (1978). Retrieval from long-term memory in presenile dementia: Two tests of an hypothesis. *British Journal of Social and Clinical Psychology*, *17*, 143–148.

Milner, B. (1966). Amnesia following operation on the temporal lobes. In C. W. M. Whitty & O. L. Zangwill (Eds.), *Amnesia*. London: Butterworths.

Milner, B. (1968). Visual recognition and recall after right temporal-lobe excision in man. *Neuropsychologia*, *6*, 191–209.

Milner, B., & Teuber, H. L. (1968). Alteration of perception and memory in man. In L. Weiskrantz (Ed.), *Analysis of Behavioral Change*. New York: Harper & Row.

Mishkin, M., Malamut, B., & Bachevalier, J. (1984). Memories and habits: Two neural systems. In G. Lynch, J. L. McGaugh, & N. M. Weinberger (Eds.), *Neurobiology of learning and memory*. New York: Guilford Press.

Morris, R. G. M., Kandel, E. R., & Squire, L. R. (1988). The neuroscience of learning and memory: Cells, neural circuits and behavior. *Trends in Neurosciences*, *11*, 125–127.

Moscovitch, M. (1982). Multiple dissociations of function in amnesia. In L. S. Cermak (Ed.), *Human memory and amnesia*. Hillsdale, NJ: Lawrence Erlbaum.

Moscovitch, M., Winocur, G., & McLachlan, D. (1986). Memory as assessed by recognition and reading time in normal and memory-impaired people with Alzheimer's disease and other neurological disorders. *Journal of Experimental Psychology: General*, *115*, 331–347.

Ober, B. A., Koss, E., Friedland, R. P., & Delis, D. C. (1985). Processes of verbal memory failure in Alzheimer-type dementia. *Journal of Clinical and Experimental Neuropsychology*, *8*, 75–92.

Nissen, M. J. & Bullemer, P. (1987). Attentional requirements of learning: Evidence from performance measures. *Cognitive Psychology*, *19*, 1–32.

Parkin, A. J., Leng, N. R. C., Stanhope, N., & Smith, A. P. (1988). Memory impairment following ruptured aneurysm of the anterior communicating artery. *Brain and Cognition*, *7*, 231–243.

Petrides, M., & Milner, B. (1982) Deficits on subject-ordered tasks after frontal and temporal lobe lesions in man. *Neuropsychologia*, *20*, 249–262.

Prigatano, G. P. (1978). Wechsler Memory Scale: A selective review of the literature. *Journal of Clinical Psychology*, *34*, 816–832.

Roediger, H., Srinivas, K., & Weldon, M. (1989a). Dissociations between implicit measures of retention. In S. Lewandowsky, J. Dunn, & K. Kirsner (Eds.), *Implicit memory: Theoretical issues*. Hillsdale, NJ: Lawrence Erlbaum.

Roediger, H., Weldon, M., & Challis, B. (1989b). Explaining dissociations between implicit and explicit measures of retention. A processing account. In H. L. Roediger & F. Craik (Eds.), *Varieties of memory and consciousness: Essays in honor of Endel Tulving*. Hillsdale, NJ: Lawrence Erlbaum.

Roman-Campos, G., Poser, C. M., & Wood, F. B. (1980). Persistent retrograde memory deficit after transient global amnesia. *Cortex*, *16*, 509–518.

Rozin, P. (1976). The psychobiological approach to human memory. In M. R. Rosensweig & E. L. Bennett (Eds.), *Neural mechanisms of learning and memory*. Cambridge: MIT Press.

Sanders, H. I., & Warrington, E. K. (1971). Memory for remote events in amnesic patients. *Brain*, *94*, 661–668.

Schacter, D. L. (1987a). Implicit memory: History and current status. *Journal of Experimental Psychology: Learning, Memory, and Cognition*, *13*, 501–518.

Schacter, D. L. (1987b). Implicit expressions of memory in organic amnesia: Learning of new facts and associations. *Human Neurobiology*, *6*, 107–118.

Schacter, D. & Graf, P. (1986). Preserved learning in amnesic patients: Perspectives from research on direct priming. *Journal of Clinical and Experimental Neuropsychology*, *8*, 727–743.

Schacter, D. L., McAndrews, M. P., & Moscovitch, M. (1988). Access to consciousness: dissociations between implicit and explicit knowledge in neuropsychological syndromes. In L. Weiskrantz (Ed.), *Thought without language*. Oxford: Clarendon Press.

Schneider, A. M., & Plough, M. (1983). Electroconvulsive shock and memory. In J. A. Deutsch (Ed.), *The physiological basis of memory*. New York: Academic Press.

Shimamura, A., & Squire, L. (1984). Paired-associate learning and priming effects in amnesia: A neuropsychological study. *Journal of Experimental Psychology: General*, *3*, 556–570.

Shimamura, A. & Squire, L. (1989). Impaired priming of new associations in amnesia. *Journal of Experimental Psychology: Learning, Memory, and Cognition*, *15*, 721–728.

Shindler, A. G., Kaplan, L. R., & Hier, D. B. (1984). Intrusions and perservations. *Brain and Language*, *23*, 148–158.

Smith, M. L., & Milner, B. (1981). The role of the right hippocampus in the recall of spatial location. *Neuropsychologia*, *19*, 781–793.

Speedie, L. J., & Heilman, K. M. (1982). Amnestic disturbance following infarction of the left dorsomedial nucleus of the thalamus. *Neuropsychologia*, *20*, 597–604.

Speedie, L. J., & Heilman, K. M. (1983). Anterograde memory deficits for visuospatial material after infarction of the right thalamus. *Archives of Neurology*, *40*, 183–186.

Squire, L. R. (1981). Two forms of human amnesia: An analysis of forgetting. *Journal of Neurologic Science*, *1*, 635–640.

Squire, L. R. (1982). The neuropsychology of human memory. *Annual Review of Neuroscience*, *5*, 241–273.

Squire, L. R. (1987). *Memory and Brain*. New York: Oxford.

Squire, L. R., & Fox, M. M. (1980). Assessment of remote memory: Validation of the television test by repeated testing during a 7-year period. *Behavior Research Methods and Instrumentation*, *12*, 583–586.

Squire, L. R., & Zola-Morgan, S. (1988). Memory: Brain systems and behavior. *Trends in Neurosciences*, *11*, 170–175.

Strub, R. L., & Black, F. W. (1977). *The mental status examination in neurology*. Philadelphia: F. A. Davis.

Stuss, D. T., & Benson, D. F. (1986). *The frontal lobes*. New York: Raven Press.

Thompson, R. (1983). Neuronal substrates of simple associative learning: Classical conditioning. *Trends in Learning*, *6*, 270–274.

Tulving, E. (1972). Episodic and semantic memory. In E. Tulving & W. Donaldson (Eds.), *Organization of Memory*. New York: Academic Press.

Tulving, E. (1989). Remembering and knowing the past. *American Scientist*, *77*, 361–367.

Tulving, E., Hayman, C., & MacDonald, C. (1991). Long-lasting perceptual priming and semantic learning in amnesia: A case experiment. *Journal of Experimental Psychology: Learning, Memory, and Cognition*, *17*, 595–617.

Tulving, E. & Schacter, D. L. (1990). Priming and human memory systems. *Science*, *247*, 301–306.

Tulving, E., Schacter, D. L., McLachlan, D. R., & Moscovitch, M. (1988). Priming of semantic autobiographical knowledge: A case study of retrograde amnesia. *Brain and Cognition*, *8*, 3–20.

Victor, M., Adams, R. D., & Collins, G. H. (1971). *The Wernicke-Korsakoff syndrome*. Philadelphia: F. A. Davis.

Victor, M., Adams, R. D., & Collins, G. H. (1989). *The Wernicke-Korsakoff syndrome* (2nd ed.). Philadelphia: F. A. Davis.

Von Cramon, D. Y., Hebel, N., & Schuri, U. (1985). A contribution to the anatomical basis of thalamic amnesia. *Brain*, *108*, 993–1008.

Von Cramon, D. Y., Hebel, N., & Schuri, U. (1988). Verbal memory and learning in unilateral posterior cerebral infarction. *Brain*, *111*, 1061–1077.

Warrington, E. K. (1984). Recognition memory test. Odessa, FL: Psychological Assessment Resources.

Warrington, E. K., & Weiskrantz, L. (1968). New method of testing long-term retention with special reference to amnesic patients. *Nature*, *217*, 972–974.

Warrington, E. K. & Weiskrantz, L. (1970). Amnesia syndrome: Consolidation or retrieval. *Nature*, *228*, 628–630.

Warrington, E. K., & Weiskrantz, L. (1973). An analysis of short-term and long-term memory defects in man. In J. A. Deutsch (Ed.), *The physiological basis of memory*. New York: Academic Press.

Warrington, E. K., & Weiskrantz, L. (1978). Further analysis of the prior learning effect in amnesic patients. *Neuropsychologia*, *16*, 169–176.

Warrington, E. K., & Weiskrantz, L. (1982). Amnesia: a disconnection syndrome? *Neuropsychologia*, *20*, 233–247.

Watkins, M. (1990). Mediationism and the obfuscation of memory. *American Psychologist*, *45*, 328–335.

Webster's Vest Pocket Dictionary. (1981). Springfield, MA: Merriam-Webster.

Weiskrantz, L. (1985). On issues and theories of the human amnesic syndrome. In N. M. Weinberger, J. L. McGaugh & G. Lynch (Eds.), *Memory Systems of the Brain: Animal and Human Cognitive Processes*. New York: Guilford Press.

Weiskrantz, L. (1987). Neuroanatomy of memory and amnesia: A case for multiple memory systems. *Human Neurobiology*, *6*, 93–105.

Weiskrantz, L., & Warrington, E. K. (1979). Conditioning in amnesic patients. *Neuropsychologia*, *17*, 187–194.

Whitty, C. W. M., & Zangwill, O. L. (1977). Traumatic amnesia. In C. W. M. Whitty & O. L. Zangwill (Eds.), *Amnesia* (2nd ed.). London: Butterworths.

Wilson, B., & Baddeley, A. (1988). Semantic, episodic, and autobiographical memory in a postmeningitic amnesic patient. *Brain and Cognition*, *8*, 31–46.

Wood, F., Ebert, V., & Kinsbourne, M. (1982). The episodic-semantic memory distinction in memory and amnesia: Clinical and experimental observations. In L. S. Cermak (Ed.), *Human memory and amnesia*. Hillsdale, NJ: Lawrence Erlbaum.

Appendix 7-1 Words for Stem-Completion Priming Test

Set 1: Target words with stems having 10 or more completions in a pocket dictionary (stem is first three letters of each word).

trace	groan	meter	linger
breeze	chance	glaze	regular
cheat	correct	lease	grade
calorie	turban	wither	blaze
unite	venture	broke	recall
mingle	restless	world	treat
thread	expert	proceed	measles
array	frantic	match	pretend
drape	ready	lantern	tension
conspire	prior	string	flare
access	chimp	medal	report
speech	trombone	relay	immune
bring	morning	twine	complete
amber	perspire	termite	divine
truck	apply	monopoly	admire
whine	manger	decide	clover
collect	versus	third	malaria
equip	embroider	beaver	valley
remark	wreath	panda	brass
trick	harbor	theme	marry

Set 2: Five-letter, low-frequency target words having stems with two or more five-letter completions (stem is first three letters of each word).

medic	widow	guilt	snort
pound	stern	squaw	gland
robot	murky	awash	sable
gravy	surly	tiger	gloat
curly	sling	roomy	merit
roach	verse	yearn	tango
swarm	torso	waive	slash
quota	wharf	harsh	perky
troop	pupil	purge	nasal
scald	shunt	knead	tenth
query	tempo	relic	pansy
livid	wrest	sprig	canoe
flask	lunge	drama	scrub
polka	shrug	stray	flint
bland	daily	salve	tonic
plush	weave	satin	brawl
comma	qualm	grope	inept
weigh	cable	prone	swipe
manic	prior	timer	scope
sword	hovel	patio	thump

PART IV
LANGUAGE

8

Anomia: Differentiating Between Semantic and Phonological Deficits

ANDREW W. ELLIS, JANICE KAY, and SUE FRANKLIN

Like many terms in the neuropsychological literature, the term *anomia* can refer, somewhat confusingly, either to a symptom or a syndrome (Benson, 1979; Gainotti, 1987). When it refers to a symptom, it means a difficulty in retrieving words from one's vocabulary which arises as a consequence of brain injury. In this sense, anomia may occur as a component of any form of aphasic language disorder and may coexist with many other language or general cognitive disorders.

When anomia refers to a syndrome, it denotes a neuropsychological condition in which word-finding is the sole (or at least the dominant) result of the brain injury that the patient has sustained. An *anomic aphasic* on this account would be a patient who had problems retrieving words from his or her vocabulary but once retrieved could incorporate them into properly constructed and fluently articulated sentences. Such patients, if they occur in pure form, would be of considerable theoretical importance in demonstrating the separability of the cognitive and neural substrates for word retrieval from those for other aspects of language such as sentence construction (syntax).

Early mentions of anomia (or equivalents such as *amnestic aphasia* or *nominal dysphasia*) in the aphasia literature usually have the syndrome concept in mind (e.g., Bateman, 1890; Potts, 1901). It is interesting to note that the early authors often regarded anomia as more of a memory problem than a language problem. Recent work, in contrast, is often concerned with analyzing the anomic element of the wider language problems of patients who are not in any sense *pure* anomics. As we shall see, there continues to be considerable slippage in the literature between the two conceptually distinct interpretations of anomia (as a symptom and as a syndrome), and we have occasion to use both here (though we endeavour to indicate at any given moment which usage is active). Sometimes we will be discussing patients whose pattern of preserved and impaired abilities approximates to a pure anomia (as syndrome), but more commonly we will be concerned with analyzing the anomic component (as symptom) of the language disorder of a patient with a more generalized language problems.

In common practice, anomia is often demonstrated and investigated by asking patients to name pictures of familiar objects. The term *anomia* is best reserved for patients who can perceive and use objects correctly. Object perception and recognition can be impaired by brain injury, resulting in one of a range of conditions referred to collectively as *agnosias* (see Ellis & Young, 1988, and Coslett and Saffran's discussion in Chapter 13). Agnosic patients fail to recognize seen objects for what they are, but may be able to identify and name them from touch or from verbal description without difficulty. Anomic patients, in contrast, perceive and use objects normally, but experience problems when they try to recall their names. It is important to assess object perception and recognition when testing a putative anomic patient. Suggestions for how to do this will be given in the section on cognitive neuropsychological assessment.

The term *anomia* also suggests a particular problem with the retrieval of nouns such as object names, a misapprehension that may be reinforced by the common use with these patients of object-naming tasks. It is possible that noun use may sometimes be selectively damaged, but noun retrieval problems may more commonly occur in the context of a more general word finding difficulty that afflicts verbs, adjectives and even "function" words as well as nouns.

Anomia appears as a syndrome category in many, though not all, of the aphasia classifications that have been proposed. We have cause to refer from time to time to studies done on groups of anomic aphasics, but in keeping with the currently prevailing view in cognitive neuropsychology, we argue that more is to be learned at this stage by detailed investigations of particular patients with word-finding difficulties than by grouping patients into syndrome categories.

SEMANTIC VERSUS PHONOLOGICAL LEVELS OF BREAKDOWN

Aphasic patients make several different types of error (paraphasia) when attempting to recall and say words. The variety of error types which can be observed suggests that the naming process can break down at a number of levels and for a number of reasons. Two of the levels we are concerned with are semantics and phonology. Semantics refers to the representations of the meanings of words within the brain while phonology refers to the representations of their sound patterns.

Common types of error in response to picture stimuli are semantic and phonological paraphasias. Semantic paraphasias, in which there is a clear meaning relationship between target and response (e.g. noose → "rope"), suggest that while at least some conceptual information about the target has been retrieved, phonological (sound) information about the target has not been successfully accessed. Phonological paraphasias, in which partial information about the sound of the correct target name has been retrieved (e.g. spoon → "/sput/" [spoot]), suggest that conceptual information is available to the patient, and that naming difficulties have arisen at a phonological level involving the retrieval or articulation of the sounds that constitute the word's spoken form.

It is frequently claimed that the causes of naming breakdown differ between patients assigned to different aphasic syndrome categories. For example, reports that "conduction aphasics" demonstrate reliable "tip-of-the-tongue" knowledge, such as first-letter and syllable structure of the sought-after word (Goodglass,

Kaplan, Weintraub, & Ackerman, 1976), have been taken to indicate that naming difficulties in these patients arise at some point in the process of phonological retrieval, rather than, for example, at the stage of picture comprehension. In comparison, Wernicke's aphasics have often been shown to have little useful information about the phonological form of the target word, suggesting that their difficulties arise even before a target phonological word-form has been specified (e.g., Pease & Goodglass, 1980). According to this view, one might expect the nature of error types produced by different aphasia subtypes to differ; with conduction aphasics, for example, generating predominantly phonological errors, and Wernicke's aphasics producing mainly semantic errors (cf. Goodglass, 1981). This straightforward view is wrong, however. Kohn and Goodglass (1985) showed that when the level of severity of naming impairment is controlled across aphasic subgroups, there are no significant differences between the syndrome types in the production of either semantic or phonological paraphasias, though these error categories were the two largest in the total corpus of naming errors (36% and 33%, respectively).

A syndrome label, then, is not necessarily a reliable indicator of the cognitive basis of the difficulty in name retrieval. There is no doubt that different patients can have different cognitive loci of impairments affecting the naming process: the problem is that group studies which use such heterogeneous categories as conduction aphasics and Wernicke's aphasics end up combining patients with different loci of impairment into the same group, and also include many patients whose brain injuries have affected both semantic and phonological processes. The resulting mean values for each group become both uninterpretable and uninformative.

LEVELS OF PROCESSING IN NAMING

A Simple Model

An approach that we, in common with most other cognitive neuropsychologists, have found more useful is one which characterises the naming problems of particular patients with reference to a cognitive psychological model of the naming process. Such a model outlines the different information-processing stages thought to be involved in word retrieval. Armed with a model of this sort, one can relate an individual patient's performance in word finding (e.g., ability to comprehend the meaning of pictures and words, knowledge of phonological forms, types of naming error) to breakdown of one or more components of the model. This approach dates back at least as far as Wernicke (1874), though it has not always been as fashionable as it was then or is again now.

Present-day cognitive neuropsychology does not represent a simple reversion to nineteenth century ways, however. Single case studies now collect much more detailed data on patients than was typically the case a hundred years ago, and those data now have to pass the conventional tests of inferential statistics. It is also becoming possible to translate our diagrammatic models into working computer simulations which may even be "lesioned" to discover whether the symptoms that follow the lesion are those we would predict to occur. We shall not go into the details of such simulations in this chapter. The interested reader is referred to Patterson, Seidenberg, and McClelland (1989) for an illustration of the power of this approach. The point that the sort of model we shall make use of is not just so much handwaving is, however, an important one.

Because so much of the research into anomia has focussed on object (or picture) naming, and because that task is so widely used in clinical assessment, we shall concentrate our subsequent discussion largely upon the act of retrieving the name of a perceived object (so-called "confrontation naming"). If we are concerned with object or picture naming, then a distinction must be drawn between a first stage in which the object is perceived and comprehended for what it represents, and a second stage in which the name for the picture is retrieved. As we noted earlier, impairment to the stage of object perception or comprehension results in agnosia, a condition which must be clearly distinguished from anomia.

Suppose you are shown a picture of a telephone and are asked to name it. Recognition must begin with the formation of an adequate visual description of the object. Telephones are familiar objects, which means that their visual descriptions must be stored permanently within the brain in some form of visual long-term memory. Such long-standing representations have been termed "object recognition units" (Seymour, 1979; Ellis & Young, 1988). Recognizing a picture of a telephone as being a familiar object involves using the visual description created by the picture to activate the long-standing description that is the object recognition unit.

Telephones are complex cultural artifacts which require knowledge if they are to be used successfully. The same applies to natural objects (e.g., knowing which berries are edible and which inedible). A widely (though not universally) held view is that the stage in object recognition after the activation of an object recognition unit is the activation of stored semantic knowledge about the seen object (though Ratcliff and Newcombe, 1982; and Kremin, 1986, have argued for a direct route from object recognition to name retrieval that does not involve the semantic system as an intermediary). In our view, and that of most other accounts of object recognition, an object must not only be perceived correctly, but must be identified and comprehended for what it is if it is to be named. Identification (or "perceptual classification") is the job of the object recognition units. We will not go into detail about theories of the nature of semantic descriptions of objects (see Garnham, 1985), but will simply assert that a semantic system exists in which conceptual, nonverbal information about familiar objects is held (see Allport, 1985).

The final stage of successful object recognition involves retrieving the object's name from memory. Current models hold that names are stored separately from other information about familiar objects, allowing for the mental state in which an object is recognized as familiar and all its uses and properties are known, but the name is either temporarily or permanently inaccessible. We shall use the term "speech output lexicon" to refer to the memory store in which the phonological forms of words, including object names, is held.

In summary, object recognition is thought to involve a series of stages (see Figure 8-1). The object must be perceived adequately and the stored visual description held in the appropriate object recognition unit must be activated. At this stage, the viewer knows only that the object *is* familiar. The next stage involves activating the semantic representation which specifies the object's function, uses, etc. That semantic representation must then be used to select from out of the speech output lexicon the particular phonological word-form that is the object's spoken name. We will assume that this word-form is a sequence of phonemes, a phoneme being a distinctive speech sound in the language. The final stage in successful naming, then, is the articulation of the retrieved word-form.

The semantic system and the speech output lexicon of Figure 8-1 constitute separable cognitive components or modules. Each can be separately impaired, giving rise to differing patterns of symptoms. It is also possible in theory for the components to be intact but for the connections between them to be damaged. The concept of "disconnection" between processes that are themselves intact is well established in neuropsychology (e.g., Geschwind, 1965a, 1965b), though its use is usually confined to situations in which two processing components are completely severed one from the other. More common, perhaps, are cases of "partial disconnection," where there is a fault in the transmission of information or activation from one component to another such that activation succeeds only on some occasions or for some items. We shall discuss below patients whose symptoms suggest that partial disconnection of an intact semantic system from the speech output lexicon.

Benson (1979) commented on how, "Despite more than a century of recognition of word-finding defect as an integral feature of aphasia . . . there has been remarkably little interest in variations of word-finding problems" (p. 297). He went on to draw a distinction between what he called "semantic (nominal) anomia" and "word selection anomia." Gainotti, Silveri, Villa, and Miceli (1986) made a similar distinction between "anomia with lexical comprehension disturbances" and "purely expressive anomia." In addition to their word-finding problems, patients with "semantic anomia" have "difficulty understanding the name when spoken or written; that is, [they have] a defective appreciation of the symbolic value of the word" (p. 305), hence Gainotti et al.'s characterization of this form of disorder as "anomia with lexical comprehension disturbances." Patients with "word selection anomia" will show good comprehension of words they have difficulty retrieving for use in speech. "Thus," Benson writes, "word selection anomia appears to be a one-way defect, an inability to select the correct word from an internal lexicon but with no problem in recognizing (understanding) the meaning of the word when presented by another person" (p. 304). This is Gainotti et al.'s "purely expressive anomia." Benson's (1979) distinction between semantic anomia and word selection anomia corresponds well to the distinction we wish to make between anomia due to impairment to the semantic system and anomia due to disruption of the process of retrieving word-forms from the speech output lexicon.

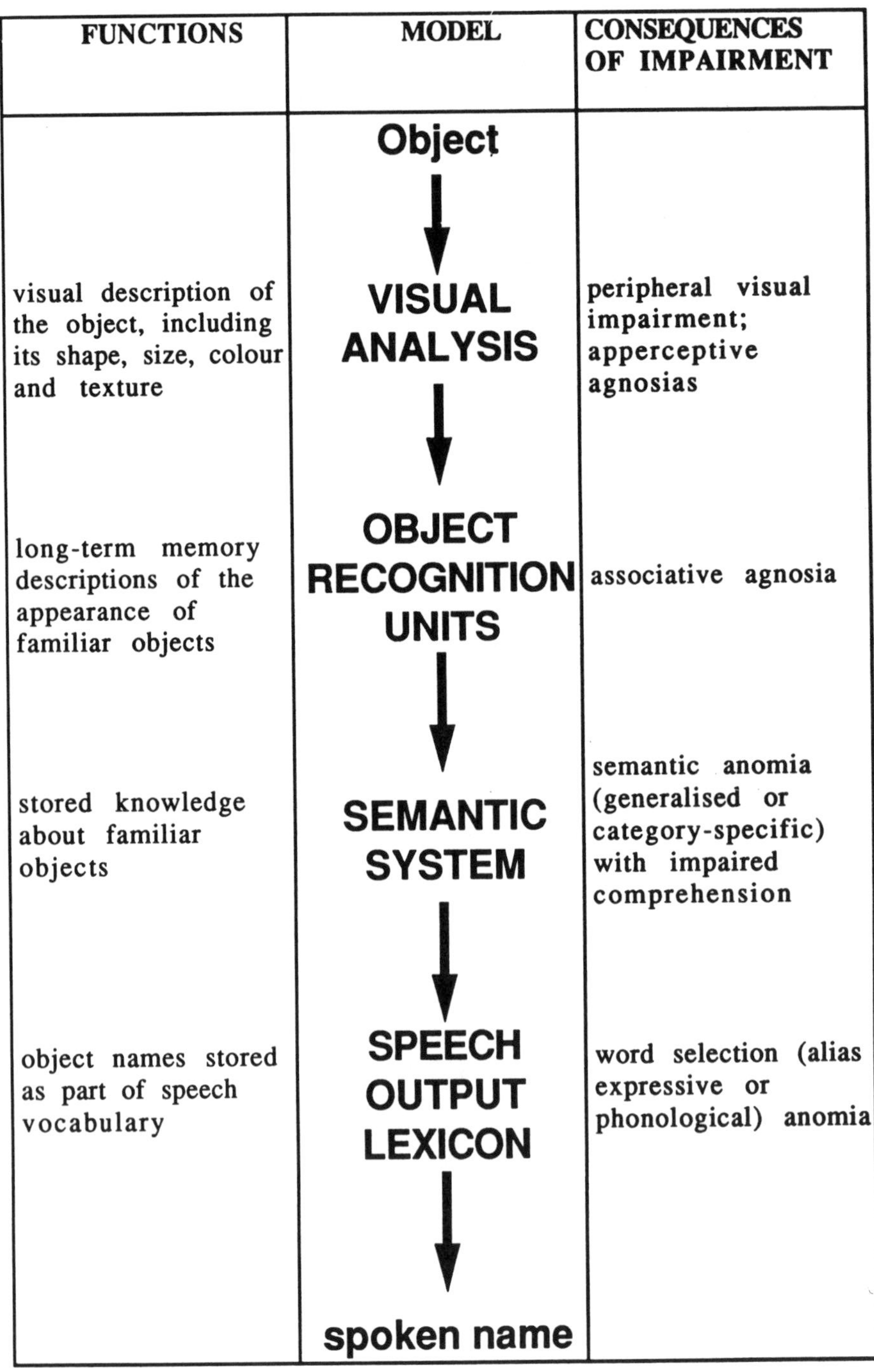

Figure 8-1 A model of object recognition, comprehension, and naming.

SEMANTIC IMPAIRMENTS OF NAMING

Models of word comprehension and production commonly assume that the semantic representations that are activated as the final stage in comprehending a word are the same semantic representations that initiate word retrieval in speech production (see Patterson & Shewell, 1987; Ellis & Young, 1988; Howard & Franklin, 1988; Shallice, 1988a). It is also typically assumed that a common semantic system is involved in the processing of both spoken and written words. Hence, *impairment to the semantic system itself will precipitate difficulties in the comprehension and production of both spoken and written words.* If the damage is to the semantic system, then clinical tests of auditory and written word comprehension, picture comprehension, picture naming (whether oral or written), and picture description will all show evidence of impairment.

A concept becoming increasingly important in cognitive neuropsychology is that of "category specificity." As applied to anomia, this means that a patient may have a word-finding problem that is disproportionately severe for certain categories of word. These may be semantic categories (e.g., greater problems naming living than nonliving objects) or may be syntactic categories (e.g., greater problems naming nouns than verbs). It is important to keep clear the distinction between category specificity and modality specificity. The latter refers to the situation where a patient may be able to name objects presented in one sensory modality (e.g., touch) but not in another (e.g., vision). In this chapter we shall be concerned with category specificity rather than modality specificity.

Category-Specific Semantic Anomia

Patient JBR, a densely amnesic patient reported by Warrington and Shallice (1984), performed extremely poorly on the Peabody Picture Vocabulary Test (with a score of 26). His difficulties were particularly severe where living things were involved, and occurred in naming, comprehending pictures of living things, and defining heard words. JBR's performance on a variety of tests with nonliving things was relatively unimpaired. A similar dissociation between living and nonliving things was also observed in a second patient SBY. The semantic distinction relevant to understanding this dissociation might not be living versus nonliving. Warrington and Shallice (1984) suggest that whereas nonliving things are largely defined by their functional use (e.g., a briefcase is used for holding documents, a suitcase used for holding clothes) rather than by their sensory characteristics (e.g., black, leather), living things are crucially determined by sensory features (e.g., a tiger has striped markings, a leopard is spotted), rather than functional significance. So the underlying distinction may be between objects defined by their sensory properties versus objects defined by their sensory features. This issue has yet to be resolved.

Within the account that we have put forward, one can try to explain these patients' deficits by noting that within a single amodal conceptual system there are subdivisions based on distinct conceptual properties such as functional attributes and sensory qualities and these can be separately impaired (Riddoch, Humphreys, Coltheart, & Funnell, 1988). This is not a view shared by Warrington and Shallice, however (see Shallice 1987; 1988b), who argue for separate, modality-specific semantic systems. Comprehension of pictures, they suggest, depends on access to a pictorial semantic system; while comprehension of words depends on access to a verbal semantic system. Within each of these systems there are subdivisions of conceptual knowledge such as the ones we outlined above. On this account, JBR and SBY would have category-specific impairments in both pictorial and verbal semantic systems. Though it may seem less parsimonious than a single semantic system view for these patients, it may offer an account of other patients who have modality-specific semantic impairments (e.g., the optic aphasic patient JF described by Lhermitte and Beauvois, 1973), and patients who appear to show category-specific difficulties in just one sensory modality (e.g., patient VER reported by Warrington & McCarthy, 1983).

The question of whether cognitive theories should propose one or more than one semantic system—and if more than one, how many—is currently a subject of much debate. In the absence of any resolution, the important point to note is that semantic deficits can be selective and need not cover all aspects of knowledge in a single patient. Impairments differentially affecting the comprehension and naming of some classes of object but not others are now well documented and must be allowed for.

Generalized Semantic Anomia

Patient JCU reported by Howard and Orchard-Lisle (1984) displayed the cluster of difficulties we would expect to arise from a nonspecific impairment to the central semantic system. JCU was a severe "global" aphasic who was extremely poor at picture naming (she could name only 3% of a selection of pictures of familiar objects spontaneously), though she was helped significantly when given the first sound of the target name as a cue (49% of the set could be named with the aid of a phonemic cue). However, it was also easy to induce her to make semantic paraphasias by giving her the first sound of a semantic relative (e.g., given the cue "1" in response to the picture of a tiger, she said "lion"). She spontaneously rejected only 24% of her semantic errors, though she rejected 86% of the unrelated responses she produced (largely perseverations from responses to earlier stimuli). There was no evidence to suggest that there were particular categories of words which caused her more difficulties than others.

Howard and Orchard-Lisle (1984) propose that JCU's problem is that "in addressing the phonological [speech] output lexicon she is using semantic representations that are in some way deficient" (p. 184). That is, her central representations of word meanings in the semantic system are deficient. Although a correct phonemic cue might be sufficient to allow her to select between semantically related alternatives, by the same token, the initial sound of a related word sometimes precipitated a semantic error. Howard and Orchard-Lisle claim that the incomplete semantic representations used in word production were also used in word comprehension. When JCU was shown a picture and asked "Is it an X?" (e.g., shown a picture of a tiger and asked, "Is it a lion?"), she accepted 56% of closely related words as correct, but only 2% of unrelated names proffered by the experimenter.

Gainotti, Silveri, Villa, and Miceli (1986) found that patients who made substantial numbers of semantic errors in naming also showed greater comprehension disturbances than did patients with purely expressive anomia. Gainotti, Miceli, Caltagirone, Silveri, and Masullo (1981) found that a high percentage of semantic errors in naming tasks was associated with poor performance on tasks requiring the comprehension of word meanings. Similar results were obtained by Butterworth, Howard and McLoughlin (1984; see also Gainotti, 1987). This association between semantic errors in naming and poor comprehension is compatible with the suggestion that in many patients an impairment to the semantic system underlies both symptoms.

PHONOLOGICAL IMPAIRMENTS OF NAMING

Category-Specific Word Selection Anomia?

Patient HY of Zingeser and Berndt (1988) was poor at object naming in response to visual input (pictures or real objects), tactile input (felt objects) or object definitions. HY had good comprehension of spoken object names, indicating intact semantic knowledge of words he found hard to retrieve in speaking. His predominant error types were circumlocutions (in which he attempted to demonstrate his recognition of the object by a phrase or sentence) and no responses in which he could not, or would not, attempt a name. He made virtually no phonemic paraphasias. His word finding showed a strong word frequency effect (with common words being more easily recalled than uncommon ones). The category-specific element of HY's anomia lay in the fact that he showed much better retrieval of verbs than of matched nouns, both in spontaneous speech and naming tasks. Repetition of all types of word was excellent, supporting the idea that his word retrieval deficit was due to a difficulty in mapping word meanings (the semantic system) onto spoken word forms (the speech output lexicon).

Patient PC of Semenza and Zettin (1988) showed a selective anomia for objects having proper names (specific persons and places) but had no problems in the auditory comprehension of such words. Repetition of words he had problems retrieving in spontaneous speech was again excellent. HY and PC show different forms of category specificity, but they have in common the fact that word finding was harder for some types of word than others, though comprehension was good for all types. By the logic of our previous arguments, this must mean that the central semantic system is intact in these two patients and that their problem lies in retrieving word-forms from the speech output lexicon. But this must mean in turn that word retrieval (as contrasted with word storage) must be capable of showing category specificity. Zingeser and Berndt (1988) argue that if distinctions between nouns and verbs, living and nonliving objects, objects having proper or common names, and so on are honored in the semantic system—and it is hard to see how language could work if they were not—then the same distinctions might also be honored in the mapping from semantics to the speech output lexicon. If so, then as with central semantic deficits, some patients might have difficulties of a category-specific nature while others could show across-the-board difficulties.

Generalized Word Selection Anomia

The pattern of impaired and intact abilities displayed by patient EST (Kay & Ellis, 1987) is the pattern we would expect to see in a patient with a nonspecific problem in retrieving spoken word-forms from the speech output lexicon. EST's word-finding problems did not appear to be more severe for one category of word than another. In spontaneous speech he tried to circumvent his anomia by replacing difficult words with alternatives which, presumably because of their much higher frequency, he found easier to retrieve (such as "thing" or "stuff"). When obliged to try to retrieve particular words in picture naming tasks his errors were predominantly phonemic paraphasias which often bore a close resemblance to the target word. Shown a picture of a stool, for example, he said "stop, step . . . seat, small seat, round seat, sit on the . . . sit on the stuh, steep, stone . . . it's stole, stay, steet." He called a strawberry a "sumberry" and a balloon a "ballow." EST was occasionally helped by the provision of a phonemic cue indicating the initial sound(s) of a sought-for word, but in many cases such cues were superfluous because he already *knew* what sound a target word began with; it was the rest of the word's sound-form that he could not recall.

Unlike patient JCU of Howard and Orchard-Lisle (1984) described above, EST would not accept the name of a close semantic co-ordinate as the correct picture name and could not be induced to make semantic errors with a misleading phonemic cue. Indeed, he became quite frustrated by a misleading prompt. Given a picture of a baseball bat and the cue, "it's r" (for racquet), he said, "Doesn't begin with that though, does it? It's a b!"

Kay and Ellis (1987) were able to demonstrate across a whole range of comprehension tests that EST's comprehension of object names he could not access in production was well preserved. He was very good, for example, at sorting pictures into semantic categories, even when this could not be done on obvious structural cues (e.g., domesticated vs. wild animals). He also performed within normal limits on picture-picture and word-picture matching tasks.

One characteristic of EST's naming performance, seen also in patient HY of Zingeser and Berndt (1988) who showed a category-specific word selection anomia, was that it was strongly frequency dependent: pictures with common, high-frequency names (e.g., table) were retrieved considerably more reliably than those with less common, low-frequency names (e.g., camel). We shall argue that this pattern can be explained in terms of a *partial disconnection between the semantic system and the speech output lexicon.*

For a cognitive system to work, information (or activation) must be able to pass freely between components of the total system, allowing a representation in one component (e.g., a word meaning in the semantic system) to access an associated representation in another component (e.g., a sound form in the speech output lexicon). Partial disconnection may be thought of as a reduction in the strength of the activation reaching one component from another. In EST's case, this may be a reduction in the strength of activation reaching the speech output lexicon from the semantic system. That activation, though weaker than normal, may be sufficient to permit strongly associated patterns to be accessed, hence EST's ability to recall commonly used (high frequency) words. If the association between meaning and sound form were weaker, as in the case of a very low frequency word, then no useable phonological information may be forthcoming.

The pattern of better recall of high than low frequency words is by no means limited to fairly pure phonological anomics like EST. On the contrary, it is very common in aphasia. Howes (1964) analyzed speech samples from over 60 aphasic patients and reported a consistent shift towards higher frequency words when the frequency distributions were compared with those of non-brain-damaged speakers. This was true of both Broca-type and Wernicke-type aphasics (Type A and B aphasics respectively in Howes's terminology).

Rochford and Williams (1965) found a correlation of 0.79 between the frequency of object names and the naming success of a group of 33 mixed aphasics. They also conducted an experiment in which pair of objects occurred whose names were homonyms (words with the same spelling and sound but different meanings). In each case, one meaning of the pair was substantially more common than the other (e.g., the eye used to see with is more common than the eye of a needle). Although the sound-forms of the homonyms were identical, the aphasics were more successful at recalling the high frequency names. This finding supports our view that frequency exerts its effect at the point where meanings are mapped onto sounds. It is not the frequency of a sound pattern per se that matters, but the frequency with which a sound pattern is associated with a particular meaning.

Kay and Ellis (1987) suggested that one locus of impairment—the connections between the semantic system and the speech output lexicon—might account for both the word frequency effect and the phonological "approximation" errors shown by their patient EST. Since then, however, patients have been reported who show a strong word frequency effect but make few phonological errors (Zingeser & Berndt, 1988; Hirsh, Ellis, & McCloskey, 1990; Miceli, Giustolisi, & Caramazza, 1991). It may be that a second locus of impairment (e.g., damage internal to the speech output lexicon or post-lexical phonemic processes) may be responsible for EST's phonological errors. In concentrating on the semantic system and the speech output lexicon as loci of naming breakdown, we must not forget that naming errors might also arise at stages beyond the lexicon where phonemes are ordered and translated into articulatory commands.

Aphasics are not unique in finding commonly used words easier to retrieve than less commonly used ones. Normal, neurologically intact speakers also show this effect. Pictures with commonly used names are named more rapidly than pictures with less common names (Oldfield & Wingfield, 1965), though the two types of picture differ little in terms of speed of recognizing them for what they are (e.g., Wingfield, 1968). Problems in retrieving little-used words show up most strongly in the "tip-of-the-tongue" state, and there are a number of parallels to be drawn between the behavior of normal speakers in such temporary states and the more permanent condition of anomic aphasics like EST whose problem seems to be an inability to access entries in the speech output lexicon. These parallels are discussed at greater length in Ellis (1985).

Before leaving the topic of word frequency, we should note that words which are frequently used also tend to be words which are acquired early in life. There are exceptions—such words as "manger" or "beanstalk" may be acquired early in life but used relatively infrequently thereafter, while the converse may be true for words specific to a particular profession. Despite such exceptions, the association between age of acquisition and subsequent frequency of use holds generally. Work on object naming in normal subjects indicates that age of acquisition is an important determinant of speed and reliability of word retrieval (Carroll & White, 1973; Gilhooly & Gilhooly, 1979). It is quite possible that age of acquisition also affects word retrieval in at least some aphasic patients (Feyereisen, Van der Borght, & Seron, 1988). If, for example, resistance to brain injury was a function of the total number of times in a person's life that a given meaning had been used to access a given spoken word form from the speech output lexicon, then the combination of frequency and age of acquisition could be a stronger predictor of aphasic naming performance than either factor alone.

COGNITIVE NEUROPSYCHOLOGICAL ASSESSMENT

This section presents some suggestions arising out of the foregoing discussion as to how the nature and level of a particular patient's naming disorder might be assessed. If a naming problem is apparent, then an estimate of the overall level of severity of the impairment could be obtained using a standardized test such as the Boston Naming Test (Kaplan, Goodglass, & Weintraub, 1983) or the Graded Naming Test[1] (McKenna & Warrington, 1983). The Boston Naming Test consists of 60 pictures, ordered from least difficult (bed, tree) to most difficult (protractor, abacus). Patients are allowed up to 20 seconds to make a response, after which a cue may be given to assist naming. The Graded Naming Test consists of 30 pictures, again grading from least to most difficult, though because it is only aimed at assessing adult naming (unlike Boston Naming Test which can also be used with children), the easiest items (kangaroo, scarecrow, buoy) are still not terribly easy, and the most difficult (cowl, tutu, retort) really are difficult.

Both tests allow the patient's overall naming performance to be compared against that of normal control subjects and aphasic patients, but neither allows one to identify the locus of the naming breakdown. At best, the clinician may draw some preliminary inferences from the type of errors made by the patient. Apparent misperceptions (mushroom → umbrella) may indicate an agnosic problem in visual analysis or at the level of object recognition units. Semantic errors could be an indicator of a semantic level disorder, while phonological errors could indicate a disorder in or around the speech output lexicon. Such a provisional diagnosis would need to be evaluated using further tests.

It is important to assess the patient's comprehension of words he or she is unable to retrieve in naming. Deficits within the semantic system (or of access to it) are thought to manifest themselves in semantically-based comprehension problems as well as in anomia. Recognition and comprehension of objects needs to be assessed separately from recognition and comprehension of their spoken names. Object recognition and comprehension might be evaluated using the all-picture version of the Pyramids and Palm Trees test[2] (Howard & Orchard-Lisle, 1984). Here the patient is required to indicate which of two objects belongs with a third object. The test requires that the patient access general semantic knowledge about the objects, because the associations are often *real world* rather than based on category membership. In order to know that a picture of a pyramid belongs with that of a palm tree rather than that of a deciduous tree, the patient must recall the fact that palm trees grow in hot countries like Egypt. A patient who performs satisfactorily on the all-pictures version of Pyramids and Palm Trees clearly recognizes objects and accesses stored semantic knowledge about them. It is still necessary to establish whether the patient understands spoken names that he or she cannot retrieve in speaking. A second version of the Pyramids and Palm Trees test requires the patient to indicate which of two objects matches the spoken name of a third object. Incorrect choices here could indicate semantic difficulties, and because there is only one distractor item (which is always semantically related to the correct response) other possible levels of breakdown cannot be excluded. The combination of all-picture and picture-word versions allows the clinician to distinguish modality-specific disorders affecting just one type of input from a central semantic disorder that will affect performance on all versions of the test.

The Psycholinguistic Assessments of Language Processing in Aphasia (PALPA) Battery (Kay, Lesser, & Coltheart, 1991) contains 60 tests of components of language structure including word and picture semantics.[3] Auditory comprehension of object names is assessed using a 40-item test in which the patient must select one of five pictures to match a heard word. The pictures depict the target word, a close semantic distractor, a more remote semantic distractor, a picture similar in appearance, not function, to the target picture (visual distractor), and an object related in function to the visual distractor. Thus, for the target word "axe," the patient must select from a choice of an axe (target), a hammer (close semantic distractor), a pair of scissors (remote semantic distractor), a flag which in the picture looks like the axe (visual distractor), and a kite (the object related in function to the visual distractor). Patients with perceptual or agnosic problems will tend to make errors involving the visual distractors, while patients with semantic problems will tend to select the semantic distractors on some trials. If there is no obvious pattern to a patient's errors, then any deficit shown by the patient may not be semantic in nature. The possibility of auditory perceptual impairment might be explored at that point.

Semantic difficulties can arise for a variety of reasons, including Alzheimer's disease and other forms of dementia as well as the more focal lesions that can cause aphasia. Dementing patients may show a high incidence of semantic naming errors (Bayles & Tomoeda, 1983). They are often better at providing general rather than specific information about objects (Martin & Fedio, 1983) and are prone to accept related names as correct in a name recognition test (e.g., accepting tiger as correct when shown a picture of a lion; Huff, Corkin, & Growdon, 1986). Hence, when faced with a patient showing semantic errors and/or misselections of semantic distractors in word picture matching, the clinician might be advised to consider the possibility of dementia. Note, though, that semantic problems can also be a feature of aphasic disorder (as in Howard & Orchard-Lisle's patient JCU discussed above; 1984).

Word-finding difficulties occur in most aphasic patients and may form an integral part of some conditions not traditionally regarded as anomic aphasias. This point can be illustrated briefly by reference to patient RD described by Ellis, Miller, and Sin (1983). RD had fluent, paraphasic speech with severely impaired speech comprehension and therefore would, depending on one's scheme, have been classified as a Wernicke's, sensory, receptive, or fluent aphasic. Yet his confrontation naming performance was very similar to that of the anomic aphasic EST discussed above. He made phonological paraphasias that resemble EST's, and he showed a marked frequency effect. Where he differed from EST and other relatively pure phonological anomics is that his spontaneous speech was littered with phonemic paraphasias. Ellis et al., (1983) speculated that this was a consequence of the fact that RD's comprehension deficit prevented him from monitoring and detecting his errors. Hence, they suggested that RD's particular variety of aphasia might be the result of the *combination* of an anomic word-finding impairment with a profound word deafness.

There are no widely available tests for assessing category specificity or the effects of word frequency on naming. There is, however, a very useful set of pictures published by Snodgrass and Vanderwart (1980) which comes complete with norms for such things as object familiarity and name frequency. It is possible to construct matched sets from those pictures to test specific hypotheses. Table 8-1 provides a list of objects from Snodgrass and Vanderwart (1980) whose names are of high, medium, or low frequency of use, and which are matched on syllable length. According to the theory outlined earlier, a patient who performs reasonably well on word-picture matching and makes few semantic errors, but who shows an effect of word frequency is a patient who might be described as showing "word selection anomia," alias "pure expressive anomia." Such a patient should also show reasonably good repetition of words he or she cannot access in naming. Good repetition performance testifies to the integrity of those processes concerned with the storage and articulation of phonemes. Other patients will show particular difficulty in naming longer words, despite the absence of apraxia. This may indicate a general impairment of phonological output, in which case repetition and reading aloud will be as impaired as naming. It is therefore useful to ask the patient to repeat and/or read the same words as have been used to assess naming, so that a direct comparison may be made.

We would emphasize, though, that the goal of a cognitive neuropsychological analysis is to identify the functional locus (or loci) of a patient's deficit(s), not to assign the patient to a syndrome category. There is no reason why semantic and phonological impairments might not be seen in the same patient. Given the indiscriminating nature of natural forms of brain injury, one might even expect that most aphasics who have naming problems will show a combination of semantic and phonological problems. EST, one of the purest "phonological (word selection) anomics" in the (admittedly small) literature, had problems comprehending abstract words, which presumably implicates some damage to the semantic system, and the patients in Gainotti et al.'s (1986) study with "purely

Table 8-1 Sets of Pictures with Names of High, Medium, or Low Frequency, Matched on Syllable Length

High		Medium		Low	
Name	Frequency	Name	Frequency	Name	Frequency
window	119	jacket	33	cannon	7
watch	81	clock	20	stool	8
train	82	fence	30	clown	3
table	198	lemon	18	camel	1
key	88	hat	56	axe	12
house	591	shirt	27	broom	2
horse	117	snake	44	flute	1
heart	173	screw	21	glove	9
hair	148	belt	29	frog	1
hand	431	bird	31	harp	1
glass	99	swing	24	snail	1
door	312	tree	59	sock	4
church	348	cloud	28	grapes	7
book	193	desk	65	comb	6
bottle	76	ladder	19	hammer	9
ball	110	lock	23	leaf	12
arm	94	ear	29	owl	2
knife	76	sheep	23	thumb	10
telephone	86	cigarette	25	butterfly	2
gun	118	cup	45	nut	15

Source: From Snodgrass & Vanderwart, 1980. Frequencies from Kucera & Francis, 1967.

Note: Frequency is defined in terms of number of occurrences per million words of written English. High = >70, Medium = 18–65, Low = 1–15.

expressive anomia" nevertheless made some semantic errors in comprehension and naming. Such terms as "semantic anomia" and "word selection anomia" may have some value as shorthand ways of characterizing patients but are not to be treated as syndrome categories (which cognitive neuropsychology can arguably do without; Ellis, 1987). These terms may be more useful when referring to symptoms which may occasionally occur in isolation but are more likely to be seen in conjunction with a variety of other linguistic and cognitive deficits. By this token, RD (Ellis, Miller, & Sin, 1983) and EST (Kay & Ellis, 1987) may both be said to have manifested "word selection anomia," though in RD's case that was accompanied by a profound auditory word comprehension deficit. While EST had no difficulty perceiving and comprehending the object names, he had great difficulty retrieving in naming or spontaneous speech.

We would also emphasize that a good cognitive neuropsychological analysis cannot be done solely with off-the-shelf tests. The clinician must be prepared to develop additional tests in order to evaluate specific hypotheses concerning the patient's impairment(s). And given the relative youthfulness of the enterprise, the clinician must also be prepared to develop and evaluate hypotheses as to the type of therapy that may work best for a given patient. It would be unwise at this stage to rule out any form of intervention on *a priori* grounds: nevertheless, there are indications in the literature as to the sorts of therapy that may be most effective in treating naming problems.

NAMING THERAPY

Until recently, the efforts of cognitive neuropsychologists have been directed primarily towards understanding something about the nature of the functional impairments underlying different neuropsychological conditions. It is only in the past few years that therapy studies have been designed and executed using cognitive neuropsychological principles (see Coltheart, 1983; Lesser, 1987; Seron & Deloche, 1989; Wilson & Patterson, 1990), and as yet there are few published cognitive neuropsychological studies concerned with the remediation of naming disorders. That said, there is enough in the literature to allow some preliminary conclusions to be drawn and tentative recommendations to be made.

If a patient is failing to retrieve an object name, but is at the same time indicating that he or she knows the word, then providing the initial sound (phoneme) of the target can be a very effective cue in helping to overcome the word-finding block (Podraza & Darley, 1977; Pease & Goodglass, 1978). The evidence suggests, however, that retrieving a word with the aid of a phonemic cue may *not* increase the probability that the patient will be able to retrieve the same word on a subsequent occasion.

Patterson, Purell, and Morton (1983) looked at the ability of patients to name pictures which had earlier been either phonemically cued or repeated. They found that any effects of the phonemic cue disappeared in a matter of minutes. Howard, Patterson, Franklin, Orchard-Lisle, and Morton (1985a, 1985b) contrasted tasks which required phonemic processing with ones which required semantic processing. Repetition only improved naming for a short time. The same effect was found for giving a word which rhymed with the word to be named, or for judging which of two words rhymed (one of the pair corresponding to the picture to be named). By contrast, tasks which required semantic processing improved naming for a much longer period: picture names were still more likely to be retrieved a day after some semantic task using the word had been carried out. The semantic tasks involved hearing the word and selecting the picture from an array of semantically related pictures (e.g., "dog" with pictures dog, cat, rabbit, and mouse); the same task but with the word written down; and a semantic judgment task involving the target word (e.g., "does a dog bark?"). The task was only effective if it was word-specific. Pointing to a picture of an associated word did not facilitate naming.

Howard et al. (1985b) went on to look at the effect of practicing the two types of therapy (semantic and phonological) on patients' naming. The patients, who had long-standing, stable aphasias with good word comprehension, were given two periods of either one or two weeks of daily therapy. Each period of therapy utilized a different set of words, and within each set half the words were given therapy (either three semantic therapies or three phonological therapies) and the other half were just given for naming practice. Another set of words was tested before and after the therapies. For the group of patients as a whole, both types of therapy were effective in improving naming, but the semantic therapies improved performance more quickly, and there was some generalization to untreated items after semantic therapy, which was not true for phonological therapy.

The proposition that semantic therapies will often be more efficient than phonological ones is supported by Cohen, Engel, Kelter, and List's (1979) finding that sentence completions are a more effective therapy for naming than cliché completions. This is based on the premise that clichés will be stored as entire units and do not require semantic processing for completion, whereas a novel, meaningful sentence will need to be processed for its meaning if it is to be completed appropriately. Hence the more semantic processing required in order to access a word, the more benefit is likely to accrue to future attempts at retrieving the same word.

These studies show that naming can be improved by therapy, though there is an important distinction to be made between something which works as an immediate cue, and something which has a longer-lasting therapeutic effect. There is a clear indication that although phonemic cues help resolve immediate word-finding difficulties, semantic therapies have longer lasting effects than do phonological therapies (though the benefits of semantic therapy may be word-specific). Semantic therapies do not benefit all patients equally, however. In the Pease and Goodglass (1978) study, Wernicke's aphasics did not benefit from sentence completions even in the short-term, and in the Howard et al. (1985a;b) study there was some indication that conduction aphasics were less likely to benefit from semantic facilitation.

None of the studies relates therapy to specific cognitive loci of impairment. At the very least, cognitive neuropsychology should allow for a more precise diagnosis of impairment in the individual patient. Scott (1987) describes treatment for a patient who had a central semantic disorder. Using a cognitive neuropsychological methodology, Scott demonstrated that the patient made semantic errors in all modalities. Tasks were then designed which required the patient to demonstrate semantic comprehension, beginning with tasks where only gross semantic knowledge was required, and progressing to finer semantic contrasts. Although naming was not specifically treated, naming performance improved after therapy, presumably because semantic processing had been improved. In contrast, tasks which do not require semantic processing did not improve during the therapy, showing that the observed improvement cannot be attributed to spontaneous recovery.

No single case therapy studies have been reported for patients who appear to have a semantic problem specific to naming. However it seems likely that the studies using word-specific semantic facilitation, such as picture pointing with semantically related foils, semantically-weighted sentence completions or self-generated semantic cues (Berman & Pelle, 1967) will be efficacious with this type of patient. For patients with more general phonological output problems, it may well be that procedures common to dyspraxia treatments (albeit with meaningful stimuli), in terms of beginning with production of shorter strings and progressing to longer words, may be efficacious, since naming in such cases tends to be affected by word length. The naming attempts of conduction aphasics are often characterized by *conduite d'approche* (successive, phonologically related attempts at naming) so, working on the patient's ability to successfully monitor his or her speech may also be important.

These are the best suggestions that can be made at the time of writing on the basis of published studies. It is important, however, to emphasize the preliminary and tentative nature of the conclusions and recommendations. It is likely that future studies will require the modifications of current views. There are, for example, indications that practice in repeating names can sometimes be effective. Franz (1924) practiced object naming repeatedly with two anomic patients. He taught the first patient the names of 60 objects by practising naming 20 objects at a time. When the patient was able to name an object correctly on 7/10 trials, it was discarded and another object was introduced. Each object was then presented for naming a week later to make sure that the name had been learned. This approach appeared to be quite successful with one patient, though the second anomic patient, who was more severely impaired, took 10 weeks of therapy to learn just 15 words. If repeating a word many times is equivalent to increasing its frequency for that patient, then the beneficial effects of repetition might be due to a strengthening of the links between representations of meanings in the semantic system and word forms in the speech output lexicon. If so, then the most beneficial form of practice will involve pairing meanings and word forms (e.g., repeating a name while looking at a picture and actively thinking about the object).

We would note that there is no necessary relationship between theory and therapy. It was known that a bread poultice would help to heal a wound for centuries before penicillin was discovered to be the active ingredient. Hence, a therapy which is known to work should not be frowned upon simply because we do not yet understand why it works. Clinicians should continue to try new approaches to therapy, taking care at the same time to evaluate them with the aid of the methodologies now available. If we are to understand why particular therapies work with particular patients, then outcomes must be related to accurate diagnoses of the cognitive impairment(s) underlying the original word-finding problems. Appropriate therapy will often require detailed assessment of areas of the patient's language other than word finding if an appropriate treatment strategy is to be devised. In the meantime, the best prospects would seem to be offered by a clinical approach that attempts to localize the patient's naming problem within a cognitive framework, such as the one presented here, and that then addresses therapy at improving the defective function.

NOTES

1. The Graded Naming Test (McKenna & Warrington, 1983) is available from NFER-Nelson, Darville House, 2 Oxford Road East, Windsor, Berkshire, SL4 1DF, England, for European orders; and from Nelson Canada, 1120 Birchmount Road, Scarborough, Ontario, M1K 5G4, for North American orders.

2. The Pyramids and Palm Trees Test is available from Dr. David Howard, Department of Psychology, Birkbeck College, University of London, Malet Street, London WC1E 7HX, England.

3. The Psycholinguistic Assessments of Language Processing in Aphasia (PALPA); Kay, Lesser, & Coltheart, in press) is available from LEA Ltd., 27 Palmeria Mansions, Church Road, Hove, East Sussex, BN3 2FA, England.

REFERENCES

Allport, D. A. (1985). Distributed memory, modular systems and dysphasia. In S. K. Newman & R. Epstein (Eds.), *Current perspectives on dysphasia.* Edinburgh: Churchill Livingstone.

Basso, A. (1989). Spontaneous recovery and language rehabilitation. In X. Seron & G. Deloche (Eds.), *Cognitive approaches in neuropsychological rehabilitation.* Hillsdale, NJ: Lawrence Erlbaum.

Bateman, F. (1890). *On aphasia or loss of speech and the localisaton of the faculty of articulate landmark* (2nd ed.). London: J. & A. Churchill.

Bayles, K. A., & Tomoeda, C. K. (1983). Confrontation naming impairment in dementia. *Brain and Language, 19*, 98–114.

Benson, D. F. (1979). Neurologic correlates of anomia. In H. Whitaker & H. A. Whitaker (Eds.), *Studies in neurolinguistics* (Vol. 4). New York: Academic Press.

Berman, M., & Pelle, L. (1967). Self generated cues. *Journal of Speech and Hearing Disorders, 32*, 372–376.

Butterworth, B. L., Howard, D., & McLoughlin, P. J. (1984). The semantic deficit in aphasia: The relationship between semantic errors in auditory comprehension and picture naming. *Neuropsychologia, 22*, 409–426.

Caramazza, A. (1989). Cognitive neuropsychology and rehabilitation: an unfulfilled promise? In X. Seron & G. Deloche (Eds.), *Cognitive approaches in neuropsychological rehabilitation*. Hillsdale, NJ: Lawrence Erlbaum.

Carroll, J. B., & White, N. M. (1973). Word frequency and age of acquisition as determiners of picture-naming latency. *Quarterly Journal of Experimental Psychology, 25*, 85–95.

Cohen, R., Engeł, D., Kelter, S., & List, G. (1979). Kurz- und Langzeiteffekte von Bennenhilfen bei Aphatikern. In G. Peuzer (Ed.), *Studien zur Sprachtherapie.* Munich: Wilhelm Fink.

Coltheart, M. (1983). Investigating the efficacy of speech therapy. In C. Code & D. J. Muller (Eds.), *Aphasia therapy*. London: Edward Arnold.

Ellis, A. W. (1985). The production of spoken words: A cognitive neuropsychological perspective. In A. W. Ellis (Ed.), *Progress in the psychology of language* (Vol. 2). London: Lawrence Erlbaum.

Ellis, A. W., Miller, D., & Sin, G. (1983). Wernicke's aphasia and normal language processing: A case study in cognitive neuropsychology. *Cognition, 15*, 111–144.

Ellis, A. W. (1987): Intimations of modularity, or, the modularity of mind: doing cognitive neuropsychology without syndromes. In M. Coltheart, R. Job, & G. Sartori (Eds.), *The cognitive neuropsychology of language* (Chap. 17). London: Lawrence Erlbaum.

Ellis, A. W., & Young, A. W. (1988). *Human cognitive neuropsychology.* London: Lawrence Erlbaum.

Feyereisen, P., Van der Borght, F., & Seron, X. (1988). The operativity effect in naming: a re-analysis. *Neuropsychologia, 26*, 401–415.

Franz, S. I. (1924). Studies in re-education: The aphasias. *Journal of Comparative Psychology, 4*, 349–429.

Gainotti, G. (1987). The status of the semantic-lexical structures in anomia. *Aphasiology, 1*, 449–461.

Gainotti, G. Miceli, G., Caltagirone, C., Silveri, M. C., & Masullo, C. (1981). The relationship between type of naming error and semantic-lexical discrimination in aphasic patients. *Cortex, 17*, 401–410.

Gainotti, G., Silveri, M. C., Villa. G., & Miceli, G. (1986). Anomia with and without lexical comprehension disorders. *Brain and Language, 29*, 18–33.

Garnham, A. (1985). *Psycholinguistics: Central topics*. London: Methuen.

Geschwind, N. (1965a). Disconnection syndromes in animals and man: I. *Brain, 88*, 237–294.

Geschwind, N. (1965b). Disconnection syndromes in animals and man: II. *Brain, 88*, 585–644.

Gilhooly, K. J., & Gilhooly, M. L. (1979). Age-of-acquisition effects in lexical and episodic memory tasks. *Memory and Cognition, 7*, 214–223.

Goodglass, H. (1980). Disorders of naming following brain injury. *American Scientist, 68*, 647–655.

Goodglass, H. (1981). The syndromes of aphasia: Similarities and differences in neurolinguistic features. *Topics in Language Disorders, 1*, 1–14.

Goodglass, H., Kaplan, E., Weintraub, S., & Ackerman, N. (1976). The 'tip-of-the-tongue' phenomenon in aphasia. *Cortex, 12*, 145–153.

Hirsh, K. W., Ellis, A. W., & McCloskey, M. E. (1990). (1990, July 5–6). *Naming and word frequency: Predicting success but not error type*. Paper presented to the Experimental Psychology Society, Oxford.

Howard, D. (1986). Beyond randomised control trials: The case for effective studies of the effects of treatment in aphasia. *British Journal of Disorders of Communication, 21*, 89–102.

Howard, D., & Franklin, S. (1988). *Missing the meaning*. Cambridge, MA: MIT Press.

Howard, D., & Hatfield, F. M. (1987). *Aphasia therapy: Historical and contemporary issues*. London: Lawrence Erlbaum.

Howard, D., & Orchard-Lisle, V. M. (1984). On the origin of semantic errors in naming: Evidence from the case of a global aphasic. *Cognitive Neuropsychology, 1*, 163–190.

Howard, D., & Patterson, K. E. (1989). Models for therapy. In X. Seron and G. Deloche (Eds.), *Cognitive approaches in neuropsychological rehabilitation*. Hillsdale, NJ: Lawrence Erlbaum.

Howard, D., Patterson, K. E., Franklin, S., Orchard-Lisle, V. M. & Morton, J. (1985a). The facilitation of picture naming in aphasia. *Cognitive Neuropsychology, 2*, 49–80.

Howard, D., Patterson, K. E., Franklin, S., Orchard-Lisle, V. M., & Morton, J. (1985b). The treatment of word retrieval deficits in aphasia: A comparison of two therapy methods. *Brain, 108*, 817–829.

Howes, D. (1964). Application of the word frequency concept to aphasia. In A. V. S. De Reuck & M. O'Connor (Eds.), *Disorders of language*. (Ciba Foundation Symposium). London: Churchill.

Huff, F. J., Corkin, S., & Growdon, J. H. (1986). Semantic impairment and anomia in Alzheimer's disease. *Brain and Language, 28*, 235–249.

Kaplan, E., Goodglass, H., & Weintraub, S. (1983). *Boston Naming Test*. Philadelphia: Lea & Febinger.

Kay, J., & Ellis, A. W. (1987). A cognitive neuropsychological case study of anomia: Implications for psychological models of word retrieval. *Brain, 110*, 613–629.

Kay, J., Lesser, R., & Coltheart, M. (1991). *PALPA: Psycholinguistic assessments of language processing in aphasia*. Hove, England: Lawrence Erlbaum.

Kohn, S. E., & Goodglass, H. (1985). Picture naming in aphasia. *Brain and Language, 24*, 266–283.

Kremin, H. (1986). Spared naming without comprehension. *Journal of Neurolinguistics, 2*, 131–150.

Kucera, H., & Francis, W. N. (1967). *Computational analysis of present-day American English.* Providence: Brown University Press.

Lesser, R. (1987). Cognitive neuropsychological influences on aphasia therapy. *Aphasiology, 1*, 189–200.

Lhermitte, F., & Beauvois, M.-F. (1973). A visual-speech disconnexion syndrome: Report of a case of optic aphasia, agnosic alexia and colour agnosia. *Brain, 97*, 695–714.

Martin, A., & Fedio, P. (1983). Word production and comprehension in Alzheimer's disease: the breakdown of semantic knowledge. *Brain and Language, 19*, 124–141.

McKenna, P., & Warrington, E. K. (1983). *The Graded Naming Test.* Windsor, England: NFER-Nelson.

Miceli, G., Giustolisi, L., & Caramazza, A. (1991). The interaction of lexical and nonlexical processing mechanisms: Evidence from aphasia. *Cortex, 27*, 57–80.

Oldfield, R. C., & Wingfield, A. (1965). Response latencies in naming objects. *Quarterly Journal of Experimental Psychology, 17*, 273–281.

Patterson, K. E., & Shewell, C. (1987). Speak and spell; dissociations and word class effects. In M. Coltheart, R. Job & G. Sartori (Eds.), *The cognitive neuropsychology of language.* Hove and Hillsdale, N.J.: Lawrence Erlbaum Associates.

Patterson, K. E., Seidenberg, M. S., & McClelland, J. L. (1989). Connections and disconnections: Acquired dyslexia in a computational model of reading processes. In R. G. Morris (Ed.), *Parallel distributed processing: Implications for psychology and neurobiology.* Oxford: Oxford University Press.

Patterson, K. E., Purell, C. & Morton, J. (1983). The facilitation of naming in aphasia. In C. Code & D. J. Muller (Eds.), *Aphasia therapy.* London: Edward Arnold.

Pease, D.M., & Goodglass, H. (1978). The effects of cuing on picture naming in aphasia. *Cortex, 14*, 178–189.

Podraza, B. L., & Darley, F. L. (1977). Effect of auditory prestimulation on naming in aphasia. *Journal of Speech and Hearing Research, 20*, 669–683.

Potts, C. S. (1901). A case of transient motor aphasia, complete anomia, nearly complete agraphia and word blindness occurring in a left-handed man; with special reference to the existence of a naming center. *Journal of the American Medical Association, 36*, 1239–1241.

Ratcliff, G., & Newcombe, F. (1982). Object recognition: some deductions from clinical evidence. In A. W. Ellis (Ed.), *Normality and pathology in cognitive functions.* London: Academic Press.

Riddoch, M. J., Humphreys, G. W., Coltheart, M., & Funnell, E. (1988). Semantic system or systems? Neuropsychological evidence reexamined. *Cognitive Neuropsychology, 5*, 3–25.

Rochford, G., & Williams, M. (1965). Studies in the development and breakdown of the use of names. Part IV: The effects of word frequency. *Journal of Neurology, Neurosurgery and Psychiatry, 28*, 407–413.

Schuell, H. M. (1965). *Differential diagnosis of aphasia with the Minnesota Test.* Minneapolis: University of Minnesota Press.

Scott, C. (1987). *Cognitive neuropsychological remediation of acquired language disorders.* Unpublished M. Phil. Thesis, City University, London.

Semenza, C., & Zettin, M. (1988). Generating proper names: A case of selective inability. *Cognitive Neuropsychology, 5*, 711–721.

Seron, X., Deloche, G., Bastard, V., Chasin, G., & Hermand, N. (1979). Word finding difficulties and learning transfer in aphasic patients. *Cortex, 15*, 149–155.

Seron, X., & Deloche, G. (Eds.). *Cognitive approaches in neuropsychological rehabilitation*. London: Lawrence Erlbaum.

Seymour, P. H. K. (1979). *Human visual cognition*. West Drayton: Collier MacMillan.

Shallice, T. (1987). Impairments in semantic processing: Multiple dissociations. In M. Coltheart, R. Job & G. Sartori (Eds.), *The cognitive neuropsychology of language*. London: Lawrence Erlbaum.

Shallice, T. (1988a). *From neuropsychology to mental structure*. Cambridge: Cambridge University Press.

Shallice, T. (1988b). Specialisation within the semantic system. *Cognitive Neuropsychology, 5*, 133–142.

Snodgrass, J. G., & Vanderwart, M. (1980). A standardised set of 260 pictures: norms for naming agreement, familiarity, and visual complexity. *Journal of Experimental Psychology: Human Learning and Memory, 6*, 174–215.

Warrington, E. K., & McCarthy, R. (1983). Category specific access dysphasia. *Brain, 106*, 859–878.

Warrington, E. K., & Shallice, T. (1984). Category-specific semantic impairments. *Brain, 107*, 829–854.

Wernicke, C. (1874). *Der aphasischer Symptomenkomplex: eine psychologische Studie auf anatomischer Basis*. Breslau: Cohn and Weigert. Translated by G.H. Eggert (1977) in *Wernicke's works on aphasia: A sourcebook and review*. The Hague: Mouton.

Wiegel-Crump, C., & Konigsknecht, R. A. (1973). Tapping the lexical store of the adult aphasic: Analysis of the improvement made in word retrieval skills. *Cortex, 9*, 411–418.

Wilson, B., & Patterson, K. E. (1990). Rehabilitation for cognitive impairment: Does cognitive psychology apply? *Applied Cognitive Psychology 4*, 247–260.

Wingfield, A. (1968). Effects of frequency on identification and naming of objects. *American Journal of Psychology, 81*, 226–234.

Zingeser, L. B. & Berndt, R. S. (1988). Grammatical class and context effects in a case of pure anomia: Implications for models of language production. *Cognitive Neuropsychology, 5*, 473–516.

9

The Reading Process and Its Disorders

ARGYE E. HILLIS AND ALFONSO CARAMAZZA

A necessary step in the development of theories about the nature of acquired reading disorders is the formulation of a model of the normal reading process. Such a model provides the basis for characterizing different forms of reading impairment as resulting from particular deformations of the hypothesized structure of the normal reading process. Various considerations are brought to bear in formulating a model of a cognitive process. Minimally, a candidate model must be able to address the computational problem posed by the process of interest; in this case, the problem is to specify how meanings and pronunciations are computed for printed letter strings in a language. In other words, we want to know what cognitive operations are involved in assigning a meaning and pronunciation to a printed word.[1] How, for instance, is the pronunciation /watʃ/ ("watch"), rather than /wætʃ/ (rhyming with "catch") or even /taɪm/ ("time"), selected in response to *watch*? Whereas it might be possible to learn associations between individual letters and speech sounds to assemble acceptable pronunciations in some languages (e.g., Korean, which has a transparent orthography), certainly such a system would not do for reading English. The mechanisms that constitute the process of reading English words must be sufficient to select /lid/ (rhyming with "seed") in response to *lead* in some contexts, and to select /lɛd/ (rhyming with "bed") in response to the same letters in other contexts. What is the structure of the cognitive mechanisms that allow us to assign the pronunciation (and appropriate meaning) /lidɪŋ/ (but not /lɛdɪŋ/ (rhyming with wedding) to *leading* and /lɛdn/ but not /lidn/ to *leaden*? What sorts of mechanisms are required to explain the skilled reader's shift of stress from the first to the second syllable, and shift in vowel pronunciation when a suffix is added to *melody* or *felony* to form *melodious* and *felonious*? These represent just a few of the computational problems in the reading process. Consideration of how these problems might be solved by the cognitive system allows us to propose at least some of the major processing distinctions involved in normal reading. Further refinements will be based on experimental results obtained with normal and reading impaired subjects.

The solution to the computational problem of accessing meanings and pronunciations from letter strings that will be considered here is articulated in terms of an *information processing model*. The principal assumption underlying this class of models is that a cognitive process such as reading involves a series of transformations of mental representations. For example, it might be assumed that one of the computations in the reading process involves transforming a retinotopic representation of a letter array into a stimulus-centered graphemic representation; another assumption may be that a semantic representation is transformed into a phonological representation by accessing a stored phonological description of the word, and so forth. On this view, even very simple cognitive tasks will involve various processing mechanisms each dedicated to a particular aspect of the process as a whole. In the case of reading, the major components of the process are schematically represented in Figure 9-1.

An information processing model of this sort provides a framework in which clinicians can evaluate reading disorders by guiding hypotheses about damage to specific components of the process which may give rise to the observed pattern of performance. This chapter will focus on methods of evaluating disorders of reading by reference to the model of reading shown in Figure 9-1. This model represents a hypothesis about the reading process; and, although it can account for much of the empirical data in the area of reading, it is certainly much too simple (and almost as certainly wrong in some respects). We begin by presenting the theoretical motivation for each of the hypothesized components of the model. Then, patterns of performance by brain damaged patients will be reported and interpreted by hypothesizing damage to specific components of the model.

COMPONENTS OF THE READING PROCESS

The functional architecture of the reading process assumed here is shown in Figure 9-1. A brief description of the hypothesized stages of processing follows.

Visual Processing Mechanisms and the Graphemic Input Buffer

The most basic procedures involved in reading concern visual processing mechanisms: perceiving the identity and location of visual stimuli. The collection of visual features that comprise letters must be distinguished from surrounding visual stimuli and recognized as familiar forms (e.g., the horizontal and vertical lines of an H are seen as a unit), and the relative location of each form must be coded. As in visual processing of other types of stimuli, early stages of word recognition involves the construction of a series of representations which are increasingly abstract (see Seymour, 1979, and Monk, 1985, for further discus-

→

Figure 9-1 Schematic representation of the reading process. The dotted line between the Phonological Output Buffer and the Phonological Output Lexicon represents a proposed interaction between lexical and nonlexical reading mechanisms, rather than a specific transformation. The dotted line between the Phonological Output Lexicon and articulatory mechanisms indicates a speculative proposal that lexico-phonological representations may directly activate "articulatory packages" for familiar words, that do not need to be assembled in the Phonological Output Buffer (cf. Caramazza, Miceli, & Villa, 1986).

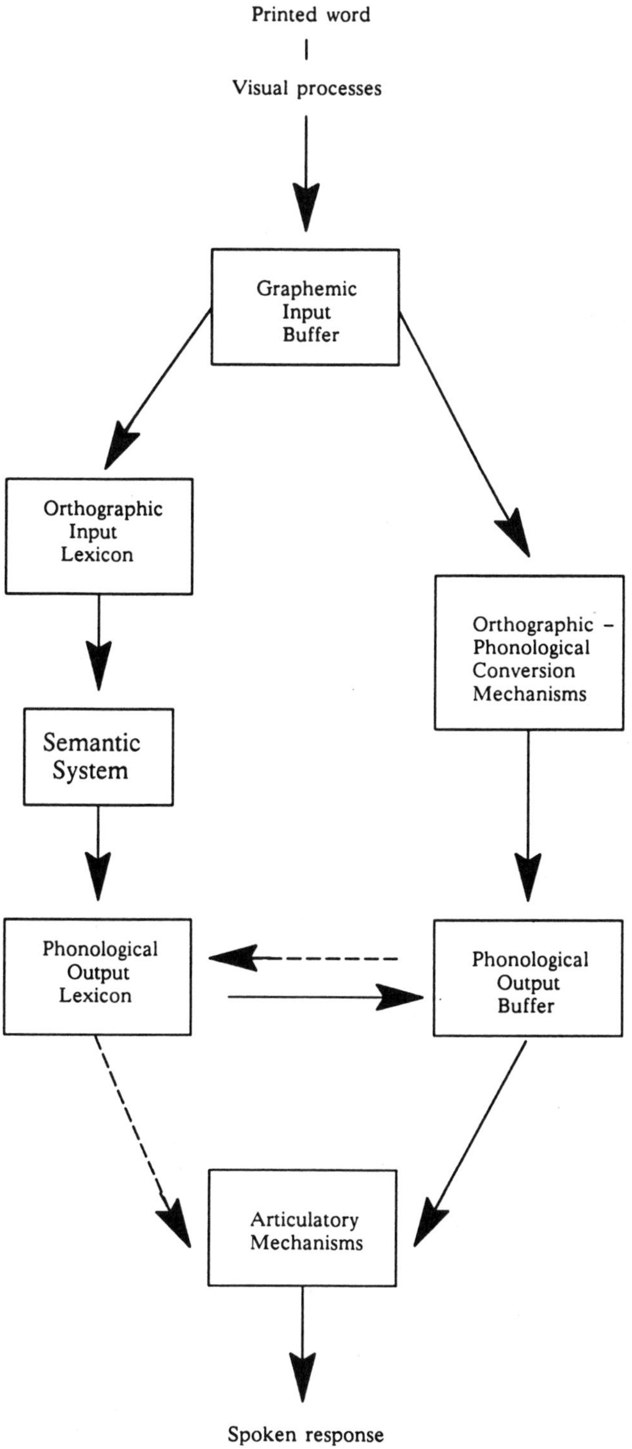
Printed word
Visual processes
Graphemic Input Buffer
Orthographic Input Lexicon
Orthographic – Phonological Conversion Mechanisms
Semantic System
Phonological Output Lexicon
Phonological Output Buffer
Articulatory Mechanisms
Spoken response

sion). Specifically for reading, because it requires that a printed word (say, *chair*) must be recognized as the same word regardless of its font, the combination of visual features that comprise the retinotopic representation of the specific letter shapes of a word must be transformed into a sequence of abstract entities—graphemes—for word recognition. The identity and ordering of graphemes must be retained for further processing, even if the location on the visual field is not. The component of processing in which graphemes are held in sequence is represented in Figure 9-1 as the Graphemic Input Buffer.

The Orthographic Input Lexicon

The generated internal representation of the grapheme sequence corresponding to the stimulus input receives further processing for recognition as a word. Thus, the grapheme sequence for *chair*, but not that for *chare*, would be recognized as a word. Recognizing *chair* requires activation of a stored, lexical-orthographic representation—the series of graphemes that are learned as the word's spelling. The grapheme sequences that constitute familiar words are stored in the Orthographic Input Lexicon. Since these stored, orthographic representations must be accessed by a series of graphemes, it is assumed that combinations of graphemes "activate," to some degree, all of the lexical representations that contain them (McClelland & Rumelhart, 1981). Normally, only the stored unit that corresponds exactly to the grapheme sequence of the encountered letter string will receive sufficient activation to reach "threshold" and become available for further processing. It is further assumed that the rate and ultimate activation of an orthographic representation may depend on how frequently, or how recently, it was accessed, and other factors that determine its "threshold," or degree of activation required for it to be selected from among the competing representations that share many of the same graphemes (Morton, 1969). To illustrate, it is hypothesized that the letter string *w-a-r-t* will activate the orthographic representation *wart* in the input lexicon. Furthermore, the constituent grapheme segments will activate other words in which they appear, so that lexical entries for *war*, *art*, *part*, *want*, *ware*, *tart*, and so forth, would also be activated, but to lesser degree than *wart*. On this view, we would expect that in suboptimal conditions (speeded reading, distorted print, reading while tired, etc.), a word such as *wart*, which occurs relatively infrequently in the language, could be misread as a visually similar, high frequency word like *part*.

An important aspect of the structure of lexical knowledge in the Orthographic Input Lexicon is that it must be organized in such a fashion as to allow productive recognition of affixed words. For example, the reader recognizes *kindness*, but not *kinded* and *warts* but not *wartly*, as familiar words, and can derive their meaning, even the first time the suffixed forms are encountered. While it is not logically impossible that each form is learned separately as an entirely new item, it does not seem likely. Surely, we cannot reasonably suppose that previous knowledge of the meaning of *wart* does not enter into, or indeed is not sufficient for, understanding the word *warts*. Thus, we assume that the lexicon represents information in morphologically decomposed form with constraints on possible combinations of morphemes. One consequence of this assumption is that orthographic representations must be "marked" for grammatical word class to ensure legal combinations of morphemes. So, for example, the stimulus *leading* will activate *lead*-verb (and *leading*-adjective), but not *lead*-adjective; and *warts* is processed as *wart* + plural, rather than *wart* + present, singular.

It is also necessary to propose procedures for distinguishing between morphologically possible, but incorrect forms of words (e.g., *comed*) and correct forms (e.g., *walked*). Although *comed* could be processed and understood as the past tense of *come*, skilled readers would not accept it as a correct word. Further, certain morphologically complex words that have acquired specific meanings that are not transparently derivable from the stem and the affix require independent representation. For example, the meaning of *transmission* of a car cannot be derived solely from *transmit*, as *transmission* of information can be, even though the two meanings clearly originate from the same stem. In light of considerations of this sort, it has been proposed that the lexical access procedure operates both with whole word access units (every learned, legal morphological form; *walk*, *walker*, *walking*, etc.), and with individual morphemes (see Caramazza, Laudanna, & Romani, 1988, for discussion).

In summary, there is a variety of factors, such as the frequency with which a word is encountered, its orthographic and morphological structure, and its grammatical class, that play an important role in lexical representation and access of these representations from the Orthographic Input Lexicon.

The Lexical-Semantic System

In order to compute the meaning of a printed word, information in the Lexical-Semantic System must be addressed by the activated representation from the Orthographic Input Lexicon. On the assumption that language use is a productive process, lexical-semantic mechanisms must allow for both accessing stored meanings of words and for computing new meanings from previously stored information. For instance, it is unlikely that the meanings of *steamboat* and *playground* are learned without reference to their constituent morphemes; and equally unlikely that the meanings of *animal*, *feline*, and *cat* are all acquired and understood independently. Thus, one property of the structure of the semantic system is that it must have some sort of conceptual organization that provides the foundations for perceiving "relatedness" among words. One hypothesis concerning this aspect of the system is that the meanings of conceptually (or taxonomically) related words are linked in such a way as to reflect the degree of relatedness among entries in the system. If we were to assume that activation of an entry in the semantic system could spread to closely related items, we would then have a situation in which the activation of the meaning of a specific entry would automatically result in the activation of related words. Alternatively, semantic representations might consist of a set of features that are shared by related items, so that activating a word's meaning entails activating features common to other items. So, for example, computing the meaning of *tiger* might amount to activating [animal] [feline] [stripes] [wild], and so on, with the result that meanings of *animal*, *feline*, *leopard*, *lion*, *bobcat*, etc. are partially activated. On either account, the activation of the meaning of a word would result in the activation of the meaning of related words. Here we will assume that semantic representations consist of sets of semantic features.

The Phonological Output Lexicon

The semantic representations, once activated, not only form the basis for comprehension, but, in the case of production, also serve to address phonological representations. Although one might wish to postulate direct transcoding from orthographic to phonological representations, the mediation of the semantic component is required at least to account for correct pronunciation of homographs (e.g., *lead*, *read*) in the appropriate contexts. That is, one has to know which meaning of the homograph is intended in order to produce a correct pronunciation.

Activation in the Phonological Output Lexicon of the learned pronunciation of a word should be sensitive to many of the same parameters described for the Orthographic Input Lexicon—including frequency, grammatical class, and morphological structure—and for comparable reasons. Since the input to the Phonological Output Lexicon consists of semantic representations, the processing structure of this mechanism may also be sensitive to semantic parameters. Thus, it is assumed that a semantic representation will activate not only the phonological representation associated with that meaning but also, to some degree, semantically related words. The hypothesis that a semantic representation, say that for *apple*, includes bits of information such as [fruit], [red/yellow], [domestic to United States] and so forth, that jointly serve to define access to the entry /æpəl/ ("apple") in the Phonological Output Lexicon, has implications for the way in which phonological representations are activated. The crucial aspect here is the assumption that individual semantic features in the set that defines the meaning of a word, such as apple, also enter in the definition of other words, such as orange or carrot. This means that a set of semantic features will activate not only the "correct" phonological representation in the Phonological Output Lexicon, but also other phonological representations whose access code shares semantic features with the target entry. Thus, to continue with our example, the semantic representation for apple will not only activate /æpəl/ but also other units that have as part of their access code the features [fruit] (e.g., oranges, bananas . . .), [red/yellow/green] (peppers, traffic lights . . .), and so forth. The degree to which these other units are activated is a function of the degree of overlap in semantic features between the target word and other entries in the lexicon. However, as postulated for other levels of the processing system, only the representation that receives a certain threshold level of activation from the semantic representation actually becomes available for further processing.

Mechanisms for Converting Sublexical Print to Sound

Except for the very earliest processing stage in which an internal series of graphemes is generated from the printed stimulus, the processes described thus far pertain specifically to reading familiar words. What procedures, then, are necessary to pronounce a word that has not been previously encountered? Reading unfamiliar or novel words involves converting constituent grapheme sequences to corresponding sublexical phonological sequences. These sublexical orthography-to-phonology translation procedures will be loosely referred to as orthographic-phonological conversion (OPC), acknowledging that the actual "units" (e.g., graphemes, "functional spelling units" like *th*, syllables, or "rimes") that enter into print-to-sound translation is a matter of considerable controversy (for reviews, see Kay & Bishop, 1987; Patterson & Coltheart, 1987; Patterson & Morton, 1985; Shallice & McCarthy, 1985). More generally, the process of computing a phonological representation for an unfamiliar orthographic string involves mechanisms for parsing (segmenting) the printed string into appropriate units for which there are corresponding phonological units available, for converting each graphemic unit to a phonological unit; and for storing in the Phonological (output) Buffer each converted unit while the remaining orthographic units are processed.

In this section, the functional role of each major component of the reading process has briefly been described. Below we will present patterns of performance by brain-damaged patients that indicate selective damage to the hypothesized components of the reading process. These cases provide the empirical evidence for the existence of each proposed component of the reading process. The methods described for obtaining support for the model are precisely the same methods needed for clear clinical assessment of the underlying reading impairment: Both goals require identifying relatively selective impairment to specific processing components.

In discussing the general architecture of the cognitive system involved in reading, various orthographic and lexical parameters that are assumed to influence processing at each stage became apparent. This information can be exploited by manipulating the relevant dimensions in compiling reading stimuli as one means of probing for the presence or absence of impairment at each level of the process. However, patients' sensitivity to orthographic and lexical dimensions of stimuli is just one factor in determining the nature of their deficit; additional considerations include the distribution of error types and the patients' profile of performance across all lexical tasks (and selected nonlexical tasks, as well). A discussion of the way in which these different sorts of information may be used to identify the possible locus and nature of impairment to the reading process follows.

ANALYSIS OF PATIENT PERFORMANCE

Given the hypothesized functional architecture of the reading system and the qualitatively distinct processing structure proposed for each component, it follows that damage to different loci of the system will result in qualitatively different forms of reading impairment. Thus, for example, damage to the Phonological Buffer is expected to result in a different pattern of performance from that expected for damage to the semantic component. Similarly, damage to, respectively, the Orthographic Input Lexicon and the Phonological Output Lexicon should also result in different forms of reading impairment. There are two classes of factors that determine expectations for particular forms of impairment as a result of damage to a component of the reading process. One set of factors concerns the "kind" of representations that are computed and the manner in which these representations are computed by the component of processing in question. Thus, for example, the fact that the Phonological Output Lexicon involves phonological representations that are activated in parallel, in proportion to the degree of similarity of their access codes, determines the types of impaired performance we expect to find as a result of damage to this component of the system. The other factor determining our expectations about impaired performance as a result of damage to a component of the system concerns the "location" of a cognitive component with respect to other components of the proposed cognitive architecture. So, the fact that the Phonological Output Lexicon takes input from the semantic component is also important in determining the types of performance that are expected to result from damage to the Phonological Output Lexicon. Together, these two hypotheses concerning the Phonological Output Lexicon—that entries with common features in their access codes are activated in parallel and that entries are activated by information from the semantic component—lead to the expectation that disruption at this level might result in the production of semantically related words.

Such expectations about possible forms of impaired performance following selective damage of a single component of the system are relatively straightforward, but the situation is much more complicated in the more commonly encountered cases of damage to more than one component of the system. Inferences from impaired performance to hypotheses about the form of damage to the reading process are usually quite complex, and often speculative. Still, considerable progress has been made in sorting out what aspects of patients' performance are most informative in inferring the locus and nature of damage responsible for reading impairments. The examples that follow are predominantly taken from our laboratory to allow a consistent comparison across subjects with regard to performance on evaluation tools. Clinical characteristics (age, etiology, time post-onset, etc.) of each patient are reported in Appendix 9-1. A portion of the reading data for each patient was obtained by administering the Johns Hopkins University Dyslexia Battery (hereafter, the Dyslexia Battery), compiled by Roberta Goodman and Alfonso Caramazza in 1986. The word lists in this battery are essentially identical to those presented for various spelling tasks in the Johns Hopkins University Dysgraphia Battery (described by Margolin & Goodman-Schulman in Chapter 10 and in Goodman & Caramazza, 1986), with the following exceptions: (1) A list of pseudohomophones, half of which are visually similar to corresponding real words, matched for length in letters to the list of nonhomophones, was added for the Dyslexia Battery; and (2) a list of words in the Dysgraphia Battery, varied according to the probability of correct spelling by applying the most frequent phoneme-to-grapheme conversion rules, is not included in the Dyslexia Battery, because this dimension is not relevant to the reading task. The criteria for stimulus selection for the Dyslexia Battery, and for any assessment of critical factors that determine success in lexical processing, are discussed briefly in the final section of this paper.

Performance on the Dyslexia Battery (which took between 3 and 5 hours to administer, depending on the patient's latency, tendency to self-correct, and so on) provided a sample of errors as well as data regarding the effects of lexicality, grammatical word class, concreteness, and word length in letters. More important, from the pattern of performance on this basic set of word lists, questions specific to each patient's performance were generated. In order to answer questions concerning the source of the patient's errors or the structure of the implicated processing mechanism that would result in the observed pattern, it was most often necessary to develop additional tasks and/or word lists.[2] Each of these tasks will be described in conjunction with the relevant case.

The discussion of cases is organized by error types, since certain errors provide an initial clue as to the possible form of damage to the reading process. However, it will be seen not only that different types of errors can result from damage to a single component of processing, but also that a single error type can result from various sources. Nonetheless, to the extent that a patient exhibits a pattern of performance that is otherwise consistent with a given level of damage, error analyses can provide additional support for the hypothesis.

Semantic Errors

Although any error response that is semantically related to the target word might be labeled a "semantic error," such errors are not informative unless they occur at a rate that verifiably exceeds the level that might be expected by chance if the patient were to be making random lexical errors (see Ellis & Marshall, 1978). In other words, if the patient produced random words when he responded incorrectly, at least some of these errors would be semantically related words. And, of course, such "accidental" semantic errors in this context would not carry the same implications as would semantic errors that constitute the majority of responses produced by the patient. Reading errors that are presumably produced because of their semantic relation to the stimulus can include superordinate responses (e.g., *apple* → "fruit"), coordinate responses (e.g., *apple* → "pear"), subordinate responses (e.g., *apple* → "Macintosh"), and syntagmatically or thematically related words (e.g., *apple* → "pie"; *apple* → "eat").

What sorts of disruption of the reading process might cause such responses? In the model we have considered, its processing structure is such that damage to either the lexical-semantic system or the Phonological Output Lexicon (or both) could result in the production of semantically related oral reading errors. Thus, the production of semantic errors cannot be taken as a sign of a particular form of damage. To identify the specific locus of damage responsible for the production of semantic paralexias further information is needed. Indeed, it can be shown that there are patients whose semantic paralexias result from damage to the lexical-semantic component, and patients whose semantic paralexias result from damage to the Phonological Output Lexicon. Examples follow.

Patients KE (Hillis, Rapp, Romani, & Caramazza, 1990) and RGB (Caramazza & Hillis, 1990) both made frequent semantic errors, a small proportion of which were morphological errors, in oral reading of the Dyslexia Battery stimuli. The predominant sort of error responses by the two patients were remarkably similar: Each made mostly within-category, or "coordinate" semantic

Table 9-1 Performance Across Lexical Tasks (percent of total responses)

	KE		RGB	
	Total errors	Semantic errors	Total errors	Semantic errors
Oral naming	56	34	32	15
Written naming	54	28	81	0
Dictation	58	21	79	0
Oral reading	58	31	31	20
Auditory word-picture matching	58	40	0	0
Printed word-picture matching	63	27	0	0

Stimuli: 144 identical object names/pictures for each task.

errors (e.g., *journal*→ "book") that rarely resembled the target phonologically. Both patients showed substantial effects of grammatical word class, such that nouns were read more accurately than verbs or adjectives, and functors were least correct. Concreteness was also an important factor in reading accuracy: On a list of 21 concrete words and 21 abstract words matched for frequency and word length in letters and syllables, KE read 24% of concrete words and none of the abstract words; and RGB read 71% of the concrete words and 33% of the abstract words correctly. Neither patient was able to read any nonwords other than a few that were both visually similar and homophonic to real words (e.g., *skurt*) correctly read by KE. Only RGB's reading was affected by word frequency (71% vs. 60% correct for high and low frequency words matched on other relevant dimensions). Reading performance alone did not provide clues that distinct deficits gave rise to the two patients' reading errors. However, comparison of performance across other tasks revealed the contrast between the two cases in the nature of the deficit that induced semantic paralexias.

KE made comparable types and rates of semantic errors in all lexical-semantic tasks—oral reading, reading comprehension, auditory comprehension, writing to dictation, written naming, and oral naming (Table 9-1). He made comparable semantic errors in spontaneous speech and writing. Rates of semantic errors for a given category did not vary as a function of modality of input (picture, word, or object) or modality of output (writing, speech, or word/picture matching). Thus, his performance could not be attributed to impairment at the level of input or output mechanisms (e.g., retrieving the phonological representation), but was consistent with the proposal of selective impairment to the semantic system. In contrast, RGB made about the same rate of semantic errors, but only in oral production tasks. He made frequent coordinate semantic errors in oral reading and oral naming, but no errors in comprehension tasks and no semantic errors in written naming or writing to dictation of the same stimuli. His misspelled responses in the writing tasks were recognizable as the target word (e.g., celery → *celry*). The hypothesis of selective damage to the lexical-semantic component could *not* explain RGB's semantic errors restricted to oral production tasks, because a semantic deficit should equally affect comprehension and spelling performance (in the absence of OPC functioning). Thus, his reading difficulty, while symptomatically almost identical to KE's, must reflect damage at a different level of the reading process—the Phonological Output Lexicon.[3] That is, evidence that he understands printed and spoken words and adequately addresses the *Orthographic* Output Lexicon rules out damage to the semantic system as well as to processes assumed to precede this level in naming and other tasks (including reading). Motor programming and articulation mechanisms that operate following activation of an entry in the Phonological Output Lexicon cannot be the source of RGB's semantic errors, if only because his repetition of all words tested was unimpaired. On strictly logical grounds, semantic errors would not be expected to result from articulatory (motor) disorders anyway, unless the patient were to *consciously* select a semantically related word instead of a target word that is expected to present difficulty. In this case, we would expect subjective comments to that effect, at least in fluent speakers like RGB, and synonymic or superordinate errors rather than the more common (in these patients) coordinate errors.

How can the production of semantic errors be explained by appealing to disruption at the level of the Phonological Output Lexicon? In outlining the model adopted here, it was hypothesized that the output lexicons receive input from the semantic system in such a way that a number of semantically related words are partially activated by a particular semantic representation. It follows that if access to semantic information were disrupted so that instead of the target entry a semantically related one were accessed, or the semantic representation itself were damaged so that only partial semantic information were available, the representation that would receive maximum activation in the Phonological (and Orthographic) Output Lexicon could very well be a word semantically related to the target response. This is the explanation we have proposed for KE's performance (see Hillis et al., 1990, for further discussion). In the case of impairment at the level of the Phonological Output Lexicon, we propose that the intact semantic representation activates to varying degrees a set of semantically related phonological representations; and if the target representation is inaccessible as a result of damage, one of the other activated representations, which under normal circumstances would not have received the greatest level of activation, may be produced (see Caramazza & Hillis, 1990, for further discussion). (It should be noted, however, that damage to the Phonological Output Lexicon may take different forms, not all of which would lead to the production of semantic errors. Other forms of disruption at this stage of processing, for example, could result in a "degraded" or partial phonological representation which might be the basis for at least some phonemic paraphasias.)

In summary, there are both theoretical and empirical motivations for postulating a semantic system and a Phonological Output Lexicon as components of the reading process, and for claiming that semantic errors might occur as a result of damage at either of these levels of processing.

Regularization or Phonologically Plausible Errors

If a printed word fails to activate an entry in the Phonological Output Lexicon, for whatever reason (e.g., because it is unfamiliar, or because there is specific damage at any one of the lexical processing stages leading up to the Phonological Output Lexicon), a pronunciation can nonetheless be produced by the application of sublexical print-to-speech conversion mechanisms. The application of the latter procedures in reading words results in "regularization"—as when *come* is pronounced as "comb"—and other phonologically plausible errors—as when, for example, *though* is read as [θ/\f], rhyming with "rough." Plausible but inaccurate oral production of words might be expected to occur whenever there is damage that interferes with normal operation in the lexical subsystem of the reading process. For example, impaired access to the Orthographic Input Lexicon, the semantic system, or the Phonological Output Lexicon might leave only OPC procedures for reading. Although the actual errors that result from each of these loci of damage might be indistinguishable, it is possible to differentiate between the possible sources on the basis of performance on other lexical tasks, as illustrated below.

PS read very poorly following trauma that caused bitemporal brain injury. Other than a highly selective naming deficit (restricted almost entirely to the categories of animals and vegetables; other categories were 90–100% correct), PS showed normal, fluent speech production and normal performance on tests of auditory comprehension, visual perception, memory, and reasoning. His category-specific naming deficit, and implications of this pattern of performance, are described in a separate paper (Hillis & Caramazza, 1991a; see also Basso, Capitani & Laiacona, 1988; Hart, Berndt & Caramazza, 1985; Silveri & Gainotti, 1988; Warrington & McCarthy, 1983 for additional cases of category-specific lexical deficits). Reading and writing deficits were PS's only other persisting neurological sequelae. In oral reading, more than 80% of his errors were phonologically plausible (e.g., *threat*→ [θrit], rhyming with "eat"; *broad*→ [broʊd], rhyming with "road"; the remainder were either "almost plausible" nonwords (i.e., contained one or more implausible phonemes, but represented a general attempt to "sound out" the word; e.g., *rigid*→ [rɪgdə]) or visually similar words (e.g., *learn*→ "leader"). On the Dyslexia Battery, he read high frequency words more accurately than low frequency words (87% vs. 51%), nouns more accurately than adjectives (75% vs. 46%), and concrete words more accurately than abstract words (95% vs. 62%), consistent with impairment to some level of lexical processing. Additional data suggest that when lexical processing failed, PS relied on sublexical, OPC procedures: He correctly read 70% to 80% of low-frequency words with "regular" pronunciations; i.e., words that could be pronounced correctly by applying the most frequent grapheme to phoneme correspondences, whether or not the body of the word (vowel nucleus + subsequent consonants) is consistently or inconsistently given the same pronunciation (e.g., *lake* - regular, consistent or *cord* - regular, inconsistent), compared to 43% accurate reading of low frequency words with exceptional pronunciations—words that contain infrequent grapheme-to-phoneme correspondences (e.g., *word*). It is unlikely that he pronounced words lexically, "by analogy" to other words with the same body, because his reading accuracy was not a function of the number of words with the same body that share the same pronunciation. On lists constructed by Kay and Bishop (1987) to determine the effect of this variable on reading latency, PS's reading accuracy on low frequency words with many "neighbors" (words with the same body and same pronunciation; e.g., *cord, ford, lord, sword*) and on those with few neighbors was 63.0% (17/27) correct and 70.4% (19/27) correct, respectively.[4] Taken together, the results are consistent with the hypothesis that PS read some (especially low frequency) words by applying probabilistic procedures for mapping sublexical orthographic units to phonological segments.

The claim that PS relied on OPC procedures to read aloud does not, however, constitute a hypothesis concerning the level of disruption in his reading system. Localization of his impairment within the proposed functional architecture of reading also required tests of comprehension and naming. PS consistently understood words that he pronounced correctly, as determined by definitions of the words presented in print. On the frequent trials in which he attempted several pronunciations until he arrived at a real word, he was unable to provide a correct definition until he had said the word correctly. For example, the word *talent* elicited: "tablet . . . means pills . . . no, [təl:ɛnt] ("tall" + "lent") . . . talent . . . means something you're good at."[5] Thus, his reading failure must arise prior to comprehension. Also favoring an input impairment as his chief reading problem, PS is very poor at deciding whether or not letter strings are words. In an untimed lexical decision task, he performed at chance (50.4% correct) in rejecting nonwords that included pseudohomophones (e.g., *dawg*), nonhomophones (e.g., *thouth*), nonwords composed of real morphemes (e.g., *chewhood*), and nonwords with real affixes (*preblint, paughtify*). He made errors on all of these types of nonwords.[6] On an "easy," untimed lexical decision task, in which all nonwords were nonhomophonic pseudowords, PS made 17% errors on nonwords.

PS's pattern of performance suggests the hypothesis that he relied on some sort of OPC mechanisms when he failed to access an entry in the Orthographic Input Lexicon. Performance of other patients can be shown to result from application of similar procedures, but due to damage to other components of the reading process. One illustrative case is that of HG, who suffered extensive left parietal and frontal damage seven years prior to testing, resulting in fluent jargon speech and severe impairment in all lexical processing tasks. In many respects, her performance was quite similar to that of patient KE described above; approximately 30% of her responses in repetition, writing to dictation, written naming, auditory word/picture matching and printed word/picture matching were coordinate semantic errors, of the type "cat" produced in response to the stimulus "dog" (for detailed performance see Hillis, 1991). However, she made no such errors in oral reading. Like PS, she appeared to assign a phoneme to each letter or two in the string (e.g., *th* → /təhə/; *gh* → /f/), so that nearly all of her errors in oral reading were phonologically plausible errors.[7] However, unlike PS, she never self-corrected a pronunciation; and her comprehension was virtually unrelated to her oral reading performance. HG read aloud words that she consistently understood (as indicated by correct word/picture matching, gestures and drawings for printed words, written naming and writing to dictation of these items) exactly as she read words that she misunderstood. Thus, HG's performance contrasts with that of PS and similar patients studied by Coltheart, Masterson, Byng, Prior, & Riddoch (1983), who consistently failed to understand words that they mispronounced. A number of other patients have been reported who, like HG, seem to read aloud by converting subword units to speech even when they understand the words, and who also have difficulty retrieving phonological representations in oral naming and spontaneous speech (Deloche, Andreewsky & Desi, 1982; Kay & Patterson, 1985; Kremin, 1985; Margolin, Marcel, & Carlson, 1985). This pattern of performance indicates that the phonologically plausible errors produced by these patients resulted from recruitment of sublexical OPC procedures not (or at least not only) when access to lexical-semantic information was impaired, but when access to an appropriate representation in the Phonological Output Lexicon was impaired.

For some patients the OPC reading system might be recruited when there is a breakdown only, or primarily, at the level of semantics. Performance by another patient, JJ, on various lexical-semantic tasks pointed to selective impairment of semantics in lexical processing. He made comparable semantic errors in written and oral naming and comprehension of printed and spoken words in all categories except animals (which he named and understood much more consistently). The main aspect of performance that was difficult to accommodate within the hypothesis of a category-specific semantic deficit was that JJ read all categories of object names quite well—with 80–100% accuracy, compared to naming performance of 25–65% correct. The puzzling result is that JJ did not make semantic errors in reading names of nonanimals, as did KE. JJ even read passages with less than one error per 100 words, and at a normal rate (83 wpm).

There are at least three possible explanations of JJ's disproportionately accurate reading performance: (1) He reads via application of OPC procedures, at least whenever he fails to activate complete semantic information about the item; or (2) he reads via "direct" connections between orthographic input representations and phonological output representations (the "third, or direct, reading route hypothesis;" see Bub, Cancelliere, & Kertesz, 1985; Patterson, Marshall, & Coltheart, 1985; Schwartz, Saffran, & Marin, 1980); or (3) his selection of output representations is influenced by information (often underspecified) from the semantic system *in conjunction with* information from the OPC system.[8] If the first hypothesis, reading via OPC procedures, were to be correct, we would expect him to be unable to read irregular words that he fails to understand. Indeed, he misread *pint* as [pɪnt] (rhyming with "tint") and *plaid* as [pleɪd] ("played"), and was unable to formulate *any* definition for either. However, JJ also frequently accomplished the unexpected: He accurately read irregular words he did not fully understand. He read correctly 42 words that he mismatched to pictures (of 144 stimuli). At least some of these words were orthophonologically irregular (e.g., *pear*; which he matched to a picture of an orange). Notably, for all of these words, JJ made exclusively within-category semantic errors in the comprehension task, suggesting that he accurately retrieved some semantic information, but not sufficient in quality and/or quantity to reject semantically related picture foils. Thus, semantic information alone could not have adequately supported oral reading; and OPC procedures alone would also not be likely to support correct reading, at least of irregular words.

Could JJ's reading pattern be accounted for by proposing a "third, direct reading route?" If he read in this manner, we would not expect any effects of

Table 9-2 JJ's Reading Performance as a Function of Orthophonological Regularity

	Oral Reading		Comprehension	
	Number Correct	Percent	Number Correct	Percent
Regular, consistent	359/360	(99.7)	107/120	(89.2)
Low frequency	179/180	(99.4)		
High frequency	180/180	(100)		
Regular, inconsistent	175/180	(97.2)	55/60	(91.7)
Low frequency with higher frequency exception	87/90	(96.7)		
High frequency with lower frequency exception	88/90	(97.8)		
Exception words	164/180	(91.1)	54/60	(90.0)
Low frequency	79/90	(87.8)		
High frequency	85/90	(94.4)		
Orthographically "strange"	128/150	(85.3)	43/50	(86.0)
Low frequency	72/90	(80.0)		
High frequency	56/60	(93.3)		

Note: Each list was presented three times for oral reading and once for comprehension; there were 120 different regular words, 60 different regular, inconsistent words; 60 exception words and 50 orthographically strange words, as defined by Seidenberg, Waters, Barnes, & Tanenhaus, 1984.

orthophonological regularity. Discordant with such a prediction, Table 9-2 indicates that JJ's reading was flawless for words that can be correctly pronounced by applying the most frequent grapheme-phoneme correspondences (regular spellings) and have consistently pronounced bodies. He was slightly less accurate in reading regular, inconsistent words (e.g., *five*) and substantially less accurate in reading words with exceptional pronunciations (such as *pint*). Errors on the latter sort of words were primarily phonologically plausible responses, such as "bowel" for *bowl*, and [hʊʃ] (rhyming with push) for *hush*. JJ's attempts to define words that elicited plausible but inaccurate reading errors usually indicated that he had no clue as to their meanings. Similarly, in a synonym matching task JJ selected words that were unrelated to the stimulus only in response to words that elicited phonologically plausible errors in oral reading. Together, these patterns of performance suggest that JJ does use the OPC system to read those words that he does not understand at all. In contrast, all words (exceptional as well as regular) that elicited complete, accurate definitions (e.g., *wool*: "material to cover up the body, to keep it warm; comes from sheep"; *choose*: "to select") were correctly read, presumably via the lexical-semantic system of reading. Thus, his comprehension and oral reading of exceptional words were essentially identical; however, pronunciation exceeded comprehension for regular, consistent words.

Most important for distinguishing among the hypotheses, JJ also correctly read irregular words that apparently addressed partial semantic information; that is, he accurately pronounced irregular words that elicited incomplete definitions or coordinate semantic errors in word/picture matching. For example, he read *watch* correctly, but defined it as "a device for measuring;" and he read *sword* correctly, but defined it as "a weapon . . . I can't recall any more." His definitions of the same words presented auditorily were essentially identical. Perhaps these words were read aloud accurately on the basis of parallel input from the semantic system and the OPC system to the output lexicon. To illustrate, if *sword* addressed a subset of the semantic information (e.g., sufficient to identify it as weapon), it might activate output representations for "gun" and "knife" as well as "sword;" but input from the OPC system might inhibit or "block" the phonologically dissimilar entries, and/or contribute supplementary activation of the correct entry, "sword."

Accordingly, it does not seem to be necessary to postulate whole word spelling-to-sound correspondences to account for JJ's correct reading of irregular words that he does not understand well. But do results from other patients with this pattern of performance require the "direct" reading route? Previously described patients WLP (Schwartz, et al., 1980), HTR (Shallice, Warrington, & McCarthy, 1983), MP (Bub, et al., 1985), and KT (McCarthy & Warrington, 1986) all read fluently and fairly accurately, despite poor comprehension. These cases have provided the strongest evidence for proposing direct correspondences between orthographic and phonological representations of morphemes (see Shallice, 1988, for review of the arguments). Yet, each of these patients read regular words more accurately than irregular words, and at least HTR, KT, and MP (like JJ) read "mildly irregular" words more accurately than "very irregular" words. Only WLP read irregular words reasonably well (95%), but her accuracy declined (to 71%, compared to 85% for regular words) when her semantic and other cognitive functions deteriorated. These findings make it very unlikely that the patients read only by direct morphemic correspondences—which should not be affected by regularity. Shallice (1988) suggests that the patients read aloud via a "broad" phonological route that includes orthophonological translation procedures for various sized units including morphemes (see Shallice & McCarthy, 1985, for a detailed model), and that the regularity effects indicate loss of some spelling-to-sound correspondences, in addition to complete impairment of the semantic reading route. This explanation does not work well for JJ, since it fails to account for his mispronunciation of only the words for which *no* semantic information was available for formulating definitions or selecting (at least related) words in synonym matching. His case suggests that reading can be accomplished by selecting a phonological representation in the output lexicon on the basis of incomplete information from both the semantic system and the OPC system (cf. Hillis & Caramazza, 1991b). Saffran (1985) has similarly proposed that the fact that her patient's phonologically plausible errors and a strong tendency to respond with a word in reading both words and nonwords occurred as a result of activating lexical-phonological representations on the basis of partial information from the OPC system.

Visual Errors

Disruption at any of the numerous stages of visual processing can interfere with accessing the target representation in the Orthographic Input Lexicon. For example, deficits in identifying the form or location of letters, transforming the stimulus-specific forms to abstract, orthographic representations, or "holding" the lexical-orthographic representation in the Graphemic Input Buffer might impede processing of a printed word prior to activating an orthographic representation. Disruptions at any of these stages of input might result in activation of an orthographic representation that shares a subset of letters with the stimulus. These visually similar word errors not infrequently have unshared (incorrect) letters predominantly on one side—usually the side contralateral to brain damage. So, for example, *report* might be read as "export" or "port" by a patient with right hemisphere damage, and read as "repair" or "rep." by a patient with left hemisphere damage.

One potential basis for these contralesional errors is homonomous hemianopia; however, many patients quickly compensate for visual field defects in reading, as in other tasks (Zihl, 1989). Furthermore, patients with reading impairments associated with unilateral attentional deficits, or "hemispatial neglect," are frequently reported to have full visual fields or to make unilateral errors even when words are presented tachistoscopically in the intact visual field (Behrmann, Moscovitch, & Black, 1989; Kinsbourne & Warrington, 1962). Further, the "neglect dyslexic" patient VB, described by Ellis, Flude, & Young (1987) made backward completion errors (e.g., *carry* → "marry") even after naming a red digit to the left of each word. Yet, her errors were eliminated when the page was rotated 90 degrees or when words were spelled aloud to her. Several patients we have studied have shown a comparable pattern. For example, we tested LAB, a right-handed, nonaphasic male, three months after a right anterior parietal infarct that did not reduce his visual field but caused severe left hemispatial neglect (observed in walking, dressing, eating, and so on). He made 33 left-sided errors (*earnestly* → "honestly;" *spoken* → "broken;" *drummer* → "summer" and *thouth* → "south;" *beveal* → "reveal") and only one other error (*nautral* → "natural"), in reading aloud a list of 790 suffixed, prefixed, and unaffixed words and nonwords. He made no left-sided errors and less than 1% errors of any kind, in vertical reading, recognition of oral spelling, and oral spelling of the same words. LAB's pattern of reading, which co-occurred with impaired performance on line cancellation and copying tasks, can be attributed to a spatial attention deficit that results in misperception or reduced processing of visual stimuli that are physically on the "neglected" side.

In contrast to LAB, NG (Hillis & Caramazza, 1990), who was left-handed and had left hemisphere damage with *right* neglect reflected in line cancellation, line bisection and drawing, made reading errors virtually only on the ends of words, which were *not* reduced when words were printed vertically, from right to left, or spelled aloud to her. A total of 96% (210/219) of her errors in normal word reading, 97% (76/78) of her errors in reading vertically printed words and 91% (180/198) of her errors in recognizing words that were spelled aloud to her consisted of additions, deletions, or substitutions of final letters of the word (e.g., *humid* → "human"). Furthermore, types and rates of right-sided errors were comparable in oral spelling, written spelling, and *backward* spelling (where errors were at the beginning of the response). A very similar pattern of errors in reading, vertical reading, and recognition of orally spelled words was reported for HH, a right-handed patient who had a left hemisphere stroke (Hillis &

Caramazza, in press). A total of 93% (239/257) of his errors in normal word reading, 91% (82/90) of his errors in reading vertically printed words and 86% (181/210) of his errors in recognizing orally spelled words occurred on the ends of words. Furthermore, he made the same number and types of errors even after he first named all the letters of the word. So, for example, he read *carry* as "c-a-r-r-y . . . cart." This pattern of responses rules out the possibility that he failed to perceive letters on the right; he perceived and attended to all of the letters, at least at a peripheral level of processing.

The right-sided errors of these two patients were not restricted to lexical tasks. In nonlexical tasks that required identifying the presence of a pair of identical letters in briefly presented nonlexical letter arrays, NG and HH made significantly more errors when the target pair was on the right side than when it was on the left side of the array, irrespective of the location of the array in the visual field. Thus, the results from reading, recognition of orally spelled words, writing, and nonlexical perceptual tasks converge in support of the hypothesis that these two patients are impaired in computation of the internal spatial representations of words and other spatial arrays. That is, NG's and HH's impairments in reading, spelling, and nonlexical tasks can be attributed to a deficit in spatial attention—in the allocation of processing resources across spatial arrays—operating at the level of internal representations. The same type of visually similar word errors made by LAB can also be attributed to a spatial attention deficit—in his case, operating at a more peripheral level, so that only the processing of external spatial stimuli is affected. The fact that "hemispatial neglect" can interfere with reading at these dissociable levels of processing suggests that written words are not only displayed spatially but are also represented spatially in subsequent levels of processing.

These cases underscore a crucial aspect of reading: It involves mechanisms for visual/spatial processing and attention, in addition to lexical, semantic, phonological, and motor processing components. The interaction between processes specific to reading (e.g., the Orthographic Input Lexicon) and more general cognitive mechanisms calls for analysis of reading performance within the context of a wide array of potentially relevant tasks. The number and types of tasks that are relevant depend on the variety of alternative sources of the patient's errors that might account for reading performance. In the case of NG, potential bases of right-sided errors other than the proposed contralesional attentional deficit included impairment of visual acuity, oculomotor control, and visual perception (e.g., field cut). These low-level visual deficits were ruled out by her comparable performance on lexical tasks of vertical reading and recognition of oral spelling. Nonlexical tasks were also needed to assure that her errors result from general attentional mechanisms that interact with reading, rather than to mechanisms specific to the reading process.

In addition to the various unilateral attentional deficits described thus far, other types of attentional impairments can interfere with reading. One type, reported by Shallice and Warrington (1977), is a reduced ability to identify letters, digits, or shapes when they are surrounded by other visual stimuli of the same category. Their two cases showed inability to correctly identify a word's constituent letters following correct reading of the word. This performance was attributed to impaired selection of information that is initially processed "in parallel" for ensuing sequential processing. The behaviorally opposite pattern—impaired word reading after correct serial identification of the component letters—was exhibited by our patient, HH, whose errors confined to the right side for words and nonwords (e.g., *probably* → *p-r-o-b-a-b-l-y* . . . "problems") were attributed to a contralesional disruption in computing the internal, spatial representation at the level of the Graphemic Input Buffer, prior to either activating OPC mechanisms or activating an entry in the Orthographic Input Lexicon. In other cases, letter-by-letter reading has different origins. HR (Rapp & Caramazza, in press), for example, who nearly always read letter-by-letter (and showed the related effect of increased latency of reading as a linear function of word length), was shown to have a more general reduction in visual processing capacity. She was impaired in detecting a target letter briefly presented in an array of three; performance was dependent not only on the absolute position of the letter with respect to the fixation point (more errors on the right, consistent with her right homonymous hemianopia), but also on the relative position of the letter in the array and on the degree of discriminability between the target and the distractors. More revealing was her performance in a visual search task, in which she identified the presence or absence of an X among O's. Unlike the performance of a matched control subject and expectations from the published literature (e.g., Egeth, Jonides, & Wall, 1972), HR's reaction times increased significantly with increased size of the visual array, from 2 to 4 and from 4 to 6 letters. Hence, HR's letter-by-letter reading must be interpreted in the context of a more general perceptual-attentional deficit. The functional impairments of still other patients whose reading is superficially identical to HR's have been ascribed to post-perceptual processes, including transmission of information from a letter analysis stage to a "word-form" or Orthographic Input Lexicon for recognition of words (Patterson & Kay, 1982) or damage to the word-form system itself (Warrington & Shallice, 1980).

So far, we have described patients whose deficits impeded reading, but were not specific to reading. For each of these patients who made visual reading errors, attentional, acuity, or perceptual impairments also affected nonlexical visual and/or spatial abilities. However, it should be noted that visually similar word errors also occur in the absence of problems in any other visuo-spatial tasks. In our reading model, the most likely origin of these visual-orthographic errors is in the activation of representations in the Orthographic Input Lexicon from the string of graphemes computed in the Graphemic Input Buffer.

Performance by patient DJ is consistent with such an impairment in activating representations in the Orthographic Input Lexicon. On the Dyslexia Battery, DJ misread 24/216 words and 33/68 nonwords as visually similar words. He made only one semantic paralexia[9] and no nonword, phonemic errors in response to word stimuli. His visual errors occurred across all letter positions in words: on the right (*pursuit* → "purse," *provide* → "proverb," *feen* → "feet"), on the left (*quaint* → "aint," *excess* → "recess," *herm* → "term"), in the center (*moment* → "movement," *rigid* → "rid") or in more than one position (*vivid* → "avoid;" *haytrid* → "hayride"). Because many of these errors are phonologically similar, as well as visually similar, to the target response, they could result from impairment at the level of the Phonological Output Lexicon, rather than damage to the Input Lexicon. The observed lexical effects on reading performance were consistent with either hypothesis. High frequency words were read more accurately than low frequency words (88% vs. 67% correct, respectively), and accuracy varied across grammatical word classes: He correctly read 93% (26/28) of the nouns, 82% (23/28) of the adjectives, and 71% (20/28) of the verbs, matched for frequency and length; and he correctly read only 50% (10/20) of functors. According to our model of the lexical system, both the Orthographic Input Lexicon and the Phonological Output Lexicon are assumed to have organizational structures that reflect grammatical class information, and both components reflect the influence of word frequency. However, a number of DJ's reading errors, such as those that shared letters with the target but in different relative orders (e.g., *kwine* → "knew"; *phloke* → "polka"), would be difficult to ascribe to an output deficit, since the phonological shape of the response was often very different from that of the target. Evidence consistent with an input basis for DJ's errors comes from two sources: (1) his performance in the easy the "easy" lexical decision task described earlier in which he accepted 11% of nonwords as words; and (2) his definitions of printed words, which indicated that he failed to understand any word that he read aloud incorrectly. Furthermore, he performed normally on verbal naming tasks, such as the Boston Naming Test (Goodglass, Kaplan, & Weintraub, 1983). The latter result provides evidence against the possibility that his visual/phonological paralexias were the result of impairment in accessing phonological representations at the level of the Output Lexicon.

Morphological Errors

Of all the error types discussed, paralexic responses that share a stem or "root" word with the target, such as suffix and prefix deletions, substitutions, or insertions, have perhaps the greatest number of theoretically possible origins. For example, an inflectional error (e.g., *run* → "runs") or derivational error (*run* → "runner") might simply be a form of "semantic error;" i.e., the most available unit among a group of activated units in the output lexicon which is produced either when the semantic information received is deficient (secondary to damage to the semantic system) or when the target form is unavailable (due to damage to the output lexicon). Or, they might occur at input stages, if the visual stimulus is not processed adequately, or if impaired attention disrupts computation of the orthographic representation. Errors of this type could also arise from specific deficits in morphological processing: the mechanisms for parsing or combining morphemes at input, semantic, or output stages of lexical processing. Finally, morphological errors might occur at output levels and reflect the morphological organization of the lexicon. Discriminating among these possibilities can sometimes be virtually impossible, as illustrated by the following studies of FM (Badecker & Caramazza, 1987).

FM made semantic, visual, and morphological paralexias. Derivational and inflectional errors accounted for 17% (680/4171) of his responses (as reported by Gordon, Goodman, & Caramazza, 1987; Caramazza, 1985). There was some basis for rejecting the view that his morphological errors were just one type of visual error: He made many more errors on suffixed words than on pseudosuffixed words (e.g., *corner*; in which the pseudostem, *corn*, is not related to the surface form). However, this result could be explained by the fact that the stem (e.g., *fast*) of a suffixed word (*faster*) is ordinarily more frequent than the suffixed form; while the "stem" of a pseudosuffixed word (e.g., *cent* in *center*) might not be. Comparison of suffixed words with only those pseudosuffixed words in which the pseudostem is more frequent than the surface form showed that FM made more morphological errors (46%) on suffixed words than pseudomorphological errors (e.g., *corner* → "corn"; 17% of responses), but the difference did not quite reach significance. More convincing data contrary to an input deficit were in the form of significantly poorer reading of comparative -*er* adjectives (e.g., *smarter*) than of agentive -*er* nominals (e.g., *teacher*). Although this difference might be attributed to a documented word class effect on FM's reading, such that nouns were read more accurately than adjectives, his error rate on comparative -*er* adjectives also exceeded error rates on adjectives and verbs with embedded nouns of higher frequency than the surface form (e.g., *rustle*). Thus, at least some of FM's morphological errors could not be accounted for by damage at the input level; they must either reflect impairment of specific morphological processing mechanisms at the level of the Orthographic Input Lexicon, or reflect that the Phonological Output Lexicon is organized along morphological principles.

In other cases, morphological errors can be confidently attributed to damage to processes other than morphological processing mechanisms. For example, numerous instances of morphological errors by KE (described above) in reading, naming, writing, and word/picture matching tasks can be accounted for by the proposed semantic impairment. Suffix errors by NG and HH in reading and writing (also discussed above), but never in spontaneous speech or naming, which occurred in the context of other types of letter substitutions, insertions and deletions on the ends of words, can be attributed to their unilateral attentional deficits. Thus, morphologically related error responses can be indicative of disruption to input, output, or semantic components of reading. These various sources can at least sometimes be distinguished by analysis of performance across reading and other types of lexical and nonlexical tasks.

Phonemic and Phonetic Errors

Mispronunciations and misarticulations in reading can also reflect a wide variety of nonlexical output deficits, none of which should be specific to reading tasks. Impairment to the Phonological Output Lexicon or to any of the subsequent mechanisms of motor planning and execution can cause phonemic and/or phonetic errors in reading aloud, as well as in naming, spontaneous speech and repetition. For example, phoneme substitutions or transpositions, such as "dubby" ([dʌb$_{\text{I}}$]) for *buddy*, might reflect impaired activation of the phonological representation or impaired "programming" of the articulatory movements (or "oral-verbal apraxia"). These sources can sometimes be distinguished by effects of lexical variables (e.g., concreteness or word class) on single word reading if words are matched for articulatory complexity, because these lexical factors should not affect motor programming. But, as there are extensive reviews of studies that have been devoted to distinguishing between lexical and motoric sources of individual patients' phonemic errors in speech output, we will not address this issue further (see Wertz, LaPointe, & Rosenbek, 1984, and references therein). It should be noted, however, that phonemic errors might, of course, result from a combination of output problems, or by deficits in components that interface between lexical and articulatory mechanisms. For example, phonemic errors in reading and repeating unfamiliar words can result from damage to the Phonological Buffer—impaired short-term storage of phonological representation during transformation from phonemes to articulatory programs (Bub, Black, Howell, & Kertesz, 1987; Caramazza, Miceli, & Villa, 1986). Furthermore, certain types of phonemic errors (e.g., m/b, p/b), as well as phonetic errors, can also result from various forms of dysarthria—disorders of speech production resulting from neuromuscular impairments in tone, strength, range, speed, and/or timing of the articulators. All of these various types of output problems should be considered in attempting to localize the origin of phonemic and phonetic errors in oral reading.

CONCLUSIONS

From the cases of reading impairment we have briefly discussed, it should be clear that the types of errors made by a patient in reading do not alone allow specification of the locus of impairment within the cognitive processes that underlie reading. Assessing the influence of orthographic and lexical factors on reading performance and evaluating performance on a variety of nonreading tasks are crucial in determining the nature of a reading disorder. A critical assumption of assessment in each case was that damage to a particular cognitive mechanism will affect performance of all tasks that require that mechanism. Thus, for example, unilaterally impaired processing of internal, spatial representations affected both reading and nonlexical, spatial/perceptual processing by NG. Damage to the lexical-semantic system caused semantic errors not only in reading, but also in naming, comprehension, and writing tasks by KE. Damage to the Phonological Output Lexicon caused specific types of mispronunciations in oral reading, oral naming, and repetition by HG. Damage to the Orthographic Input Lexicon, or impairment in identifying units of access, exclusively disrupted reading performance by PS; but all variety of reading tasks including lexical decision were necessarily affected.

We have made no mention of classification of reading disorders, even though there has been a great deal of recent literature in cognitive neuropsychology devoted to discussion of reading impairments in terms of patient categories such as "deep dyslexia," "surface dyslexia," phonological dyslexia," "neglect dyslexia," "letter-by-letter reading," and so on. We have departed from this trend because such arbitrary classifications are not informative with respect to the nature of damage that underlies the reading disorder. Taking one such category as an illustration, the key feature of the so-called syndrome of "deep dyslexia" is the occurrence of semantic paralexias; the following features presumably co-occur in nearly every case (Coltheart, 1980) or are required "by definition" (Morton & Patterson, 1980; Shallice & Warrington, 1980): derivational and visual errors in reading; poor ability to use OPC procedures to read novel words; a substantial effect of grammatical word class on reading accuracy (nouns > adjectives > verbs > functors); and poor reading of abstract words compared to concrete words. We have described a number of patients who made semantic paralexias along with many, but not necessarily all, of the additional characteristics. But for each of our patients, we have proposed a different locus of impairment in the reading process: KE's semantic (and occasional morphological and visual) paralexias and the influence of concreteness and grammatical word class on his reading accuracy stemmed from a lexical-semantic deficit; the same symptoms in RGB, but without visual errors, arose from damage at the level of the Phonological Output Lexicon; DJ's visual and morphological paralexias, as well as his word class effect, can be attributed to damage at the level of the Orthographic Input Lexicon. Similarly, patients PS, JJ, and HG, who each showed the type of oral reading labeled as "Surface dyslexia" (cf. Patterson et al., 1985)—phonologically plausible errors, including regularization of irregular words—had quite different deficits that produced these errors. Even patients who made "neglect dyslexic" errors (confined to one side of words) were shown to be impaired at different levels of processing, resulting in unilateral errors in reading vertical print and in recognition of oral spelling by NG, but not by LAB. The problem with these classification schemes is not, however, that they are empirically inadequate, but that there can be no *a priori* decisions about which aspects of patient behaviors are relevant to postulating the locus at which the reading process is disrupted. All theoretically relevant aspects of performance in language and other cognitive tasks should be considered in determining the level of impairment for every patient (see Caramazza, 1986, for discussion).

CLINICAL USEFULNESS OF A COGNITIVE ANALYSIS OF READING

The previous section was devoted to detailing procedures for identifying an individual dyslexic patient's level(s) of breakdown within the cognitive process of reading. It became obvious that such "diagnoses" are not simple. They often require not only analysis of performance on lengthy measures of reading, but also, in many cases, assessment of performance on other lexical and nonlexical tasks.

In fact, the picture may be even more complicated than in the cases we have described. The subjects we selected for discussion had impairments that were relatively circumscribed to input or output procedures and/or the semantic system. Many patients make errors that reflect damage to both input and output mechanisms (and perhaps, to the semantic system). Given the depth of testing required to satisfactorily identify several loci of impairment, a clinician might wonder if it is worth the effort. Two points should be made. First, the detailed sorts of analyses carried out for many of our patients are not always necessary for developing a fairly clear idea of the sort(s) of damage that lead to a disordered pattern of reading. In each of the cases described above, we had relatively explicit hypotheses concerning the impairment on the basis of performance on the basic Dyslexia Battery which were confirmed by additional studies. Had the subsequent studies, or any observations, invalidated those hypotheses, it would have been necessary to re-evaluate the model that led to them. Thus, reading theories and detailed clinical evaluation techniques develop in synchrony: Current theories guide stimulus selection, and patterns of responses to these stimuli guide further specification of some components of the model. For instance, detailed analyses of reading by NG (who made right-sided errors in reading and recognition of orally spelled words) provided evidence that a *spatial* representation of the stimulus is internally generated prior to accessing a stored representation in the input lexicon. Her case also serves to make the second point: Cognitive analyses of patient performance often create the opportunity for a productive interaction between clinical practice and research. The benefit to researchers—in increasing the understanding of the normal language processes through examination of impaired performance—has been made clear. What is the benefit to the clinician?

Given that the goals of the clinician are diagnosis and/or treatment of patients' disorders, cognitive analyses have one transparent benefit with respect to reading disorders: An informed model of reading provides a framework in which to identify the nature of impaired performance. Initial hypotheses of disruption must be guided by some theory of what is being disrupted. So, the type of model we have discussed, which distinguishes orthographic input from semantic representations, semantic from phonological representations, and so forth, can provide a conceptual framework for specifying the possible origin(s) of the patient's errors. The model also serves to guide the clinician's selection of tasks and stimulus materials needed to evaluate some hypothesis about the possible locus of damage to the reading system. To illustrate, if we wished to confirm a clinical impression that a patient's reading problem was due to damage to the Phonological Output Lexicon, we might begin with the following assessments: (1) comparison of oral reading with comprehension (we would expect difficulty only in the former, since access to semantic information should not be affected by damage later in the reading process); (2) evaluation of reading performance for high frequency versus low frequency words (we would expect more errors on low frequency words, because they are assumed to have higher thresholds of activation in the Phonological Output Lexicon); and (3) comparison of reading familiar words to reading pronounceable nonwords (correct—i.e., plausible—reading of nonwords via OPC procedures should not be affected by damage to the Phonological Output Lexicon).

To document the presence or absence of differences between stimuli that vary along a particular dimension, the different word types must be matched for other possibly relevant dimensions. For instance, identification of a frequency effect requires that low and high frequency words be matched for grammatical class, concreteness, word length, and other parameters that might, according to our theory, influence computations at some level(s) of the reading process. Because measuring the effects of such dimensions often yields clues to the level of impairment, batteries used to "probe" for possible loci of damage in the reading process might include lists of words of different grammatical classes, lists of concrete and abstract words, lists of words with different letter lengths or different phoneme lengths, lists of pronounceable nonwords, and lists of words varying along measures of orthophonological regularity, each counterbalanced for the other variables. However, the stimulus dimensions that we control and evaluate depend not only on the model of reading, but also on the nature of the hypothesized form of reading impairment in an individual patient. A significant effect of word frequency, for example, might help to distinguish damage to the Phonological Output Lexicon from damage to the Phonological Buffer, but not from damage to the Orthographic Input Lexicon, where we would also expect an influence of word frequency. The latter type of distinction would depend primarily on patterns of performance in other lexical tasks (comprehension, lexical decision, naming, and so on). Clearly, then, there is no single set of words, or set of tasks, that will suffice for determining the locus of impairment in the reading process for all patients. Rather, as we have attempted to point out in the cases discussed, observations about each patient's pattern of errors on a variety of lexical and nonlexical tasks, across various types of stimuli, motivate additional questions that must be answered in order to postulate the basis for the patient's reading disorder.

Whereas identification of the underlying problem is directed by the cognitive analysis of performance in a relatively straightforward manner, treatment of the reading problem is not. Even when the clinician is able to confidently specify the patient's reading deficit, the clinical applicability of this "diagnosis" for rehabilitation is not obvious (see Caramazza, 1989, for further discussion). Theories of normal language processing, whether from cognitive neuropsychology or from any other discipline, do not specify how a damaged system might be modified by intervention. The limitations with regard to treatment of reading disorders are threefold: (1) models of reading are silent with respect to issues of recovery, such as which of the components are subject to remediation versus which damaged mechanisms require compensation (see Behrmann & Byng, Chapter 12); (2) even the clearest hypothesis about what should be treated does not automatically determine particular strategies that should improve performance; and (3) factors that underlie the efficacy of particular intervention strategies for specific cases have not been identified.

Nevertheless, even these rather substantial limitations do not undermine the usefulness of identifying what it is about reading that needs to be corrected or circumvented. A number of authors have provided illustrations that a clear hypothesis of the locus of impairment can guide clinical intuitions about the sorts of strategies that should, or should not, facilitate reading performance. For example, Byng and Coltheart (1986) described treatment of a patient EE, who was able to read regular words correctly, but made regularization errors (and corresponding miscomprehension errors) in reading irregular words. By hypothesis, EE was impaired in accessing the orthographc representation of the word, so that he relied on OPC mechanisms for reading aloud. He improved in reading two sets of irregular words, when each set was trained by having him read each word presented with a picture depicting its meaning. Similarly, our case, PS, described above, was also able to learn to read sets of irregular words, which were all homophones, through practice. Training consisted merely of corrected oral reading, followed by presentation of the definition (given auditorily and in print), and writing the word in a sentence. PS improved in spelling, reading, and comprehension of each set of homophones as it was trained; while he remained stable in all three aspects for untrained words that were tested each session. Apparently, practice in reading irregular words (facilitated by a picture or clinician's cues) made those orthographic representations more accessible.[10] In the same vein, for two patients with postulated impairment at the level of the Phonological Output Lexicon (RGB and HW), simply increasing the production of specific sets of words, by supplying phonemic cues to elicit the words in a verbal picture-naming task, improved oral reading of the same words on subsequent occasions. Conversely, cued oral reading practice of a different set of words resulted in improved oral naming of the same items.

Although these "interventions" have been, and are almost bound to be, item-specific, not all rehabilitation methods need be. In fact, prior to teaching homophones, PS's reading accuracy for all types of unfamiliar words and nonwords increased markedly when he was taught contextual rules for pronouncing letters (e.g., that *c* is pronounced /k/ except after i, e, or y) and alternative letter-sound mappings, to "try out" until he pronounced a real word.[11] De Partz (1986) reported similar success with this type of approach for a patient who (unlike PS) made mostly semantic paralexias. Along the same lines, Moss and Gonzalez-Rothi (1987a) reported that "analytic" tasks, such as matching homophones and identifying silent letters, improved a "pure alexic" patient's reading of nonwords and regular words more effectively than "Gestalt" tasks that required rapid semantic or word/nonword decisions (whereas the opposite effects were described for patients who read letter-by-letter; Moss & Gonzalez-Rothi, 1987b; see also Rothi, Goldstein, Teas, Schoenfeld, Moss, & Ochipa, 1986).

Obviously, there is nothing about any of these teaching methods that was uniquely tied to the hypothesized locus of impairment. Any of the tasks mentioned for teaching or reinforcing grapheme to phoneme correspondence might improve some aspects of reading for patients who are impaired in the OPC system *or* who rely more heavily on the OPC system due to damage that impedes lexical or semantic access. Furthermore, the same strategies can produce different types of benefit across patients. For example, teaching contextual constraints and pronunciations of units larger than letters improved PS's oral reading *and* comprehension of print, but did not affect his oral naming or auditory comprehension (which were essentially normal to begin with). In contrast, the same methods improved pronunciation by our patient, HG (who had semantic and lexical output deficits) not only in reading, but also in naming, repetition, and spontaneous speech; but did not affect her reading comprehension (Hillis, 1991). Teaching grapheme-phoneme correspondences can also help certain patients with multiple levels of impairment, even if a functional level of reading by sublexical mechanisms is not reached. For example, reading and naming of one patient (PM) were characterized by frequent semantic, phonemic, and other errors, and both were facilitated by initial phoneme cues. PM improved in accuracy of reading untrained words because she had learned to convert the initial letter to a phoneme, which then served as her own phonemic cue. Presumably, the phonemic cue provided additional activation to an entry in the Phonological Output Lexicon, which was already partially activated by (often incomplete) information from the semantic system (cf. Hillis & Caramazza, 1990).

The cases reported here illustrate that a model of the reading system can provide a framework for identifying processes that might be selectively intact or impaired and alternative systems that might be called upon to compensate for damaged ones. However, such models are not likely to provide the basis for prescriptive treatments (of the sort, "If component X is damaged, use treatment A; if Y is damaged, use treatment B). As noted, many procedures (e.g., training grapheme to phoneme correspondence; establishing word-picture associations) will aid patients with a variety of distinct deficits in the reading process; and patients with the same level of damage might not respond to identical methods. It should also be noted that some of these anecdotally reported improvements in reading performance may not have been directly attributed to the specific treatment procedures but may result from more general effects of intervention, such as practice or increased motivation or confidence.[12] It would, however, be difficult to ascribe improved reading performance by the cases described here to spontaneous recovery, because all of the patients were treated more than a year after their brain damage.

In summary, the primary contributions of cognitive neuropsychology to rehabilitation of acquired dyslexia are quite general: It provides a method of analysis of individual cases, which has led to a functional architecture of the normal reading system and hypotheses regarding the structure of the representations that are computed. In turn, a model allows the clinician to postulate for each patient what it is about reading that needs to be addressed. At this time, rehabilitation depends in large measure on creative, trial and error methods. The crucial point, however, is that developments in clinical practice in the area of acquired reading disorders surely cannot proceed without a reasonably informed theory concerning the nature of the cognitive processes that underlie the task of reading. It has been the aim of this chapter to describe recent efforts to provide such a foundation.

ACKNOWLEDGMENTS

The research was supported in part by grants from the Seaver Institute and NIH grants NS22201 and NS23836 to the Johns Hopkins University. This support is gratefully acknowledged. The authors are also grateful to David Margolin for helpful comments on an earlier draft of this chapter and to the patients who participated in this research.

Notes

1. The clinician may be interested in a number of other cognitive operations involved in reading text, such as processing syntactic structure, sentential semantics, and so on;

but the focus of this chapter will be on the cognitive processes that underlie reading of individual words.

2. The Dyslexia Battery is available upon request from Roberta Goodman-Schulman or Alfonso Caramazza; the supplementary lists are available from Argye E. Hillis.

3. By damage "at the level of" the Phonological Output Lexicon, we remain silent on the issue of whether the damage affects the phonological representations themselves or access to the representations. We have argued elsewhere that degraded representations and impaired access (to representations at any level of lexical processing) are not empirically distinguishable, given the current level of theories (see Caramazza, Hillis, Rapp, & Romani, 1990, for a brief discussion). Therefore, although some of the lexical and/or semantic deficits proposed in this chapter may be explained in terms of impaired representations, they may be as easily interpreted by assuming impaired access to representations or to portions of the representations.

4. It should be noted, however, that the OPC procedures that are applied in any specific case may depend on the probability with which particular graphemic segments are translated into specific phonological segments in all words in the language (not just words with the same body). For example, the probability of producing /æv/ (rhyming with "have") in response to *-ave*, might be a function of the pronunciation of *-ave* in all English words—*avenue*, *raven*, *ravel*, etc. (as well as *have*, *save*, and other words with the same body). Postulating OPC procedures that reflect such probabilities would differ considerably from "analogy" theories such as those proposed by Glushko (1979), Marcel (1980), and Henderson (1985; 1987). Furthermore, such procedures need not be applied in reading familiar and novel words as argued by Seidenberg (1987), for example.

5. The only words that PS understood but failed to articulate correctly were words in the categories of items that elicited errors in picture naming tasks: vegetables and animals. Reading errors on these categories included semantic paralexias and definitions (e.g., *giraffe* → "animal with a long neck . . . kangaroo"). Thus, we assume that reading was disrupted prior to gaining access to semantic information for low frequency words in all categories, but was also disrupted at the level(s) of lexical-semantics and/or the Phonological Output Lexicon for those categories where this second impairment affected oral naming.

6. In contrast to his high false positive rate on nonwords, his error rate was below 10% for words. Although we did not have norms for this task, two other aphasic patients we have tested made less than 10% errors on nonwords, as well as on words, on the same task. In the easy lexical decision task, normal subjects make no errors.

7. With some training in oral naming tasks, HG also produced "regularized" pronunciations of either the correct or semantically related object name. For example, her naming response to a pictured lion was "beer" (bear); and her response in repeating "brush" was [koʊm:b] (a regularization of "comb"). Apparently, she retrieved an orthographic representation, and converted the internal series of graphemes to corresponding phonological sequences. Clearly, this is not the "normal" process of naming, although it incorporates normal components of the naming process. But HG's naming does not suggest that new processes or "routes" were formed as a consequence of her brain damage—we can all produce orthophonologically plausible forms of picture names if asked to do so. For HG, it was the only way she could verbally communicate. Thus, her naming performance provides strong evidence that she was unable to retrieve the correct phonological representations of the names, even when she simultaneously retrieved the appropriate orthographic representations.

8. These three proposals may not be mutually exclusive. All three of the hypothesized mechanisms—independent OPC procedures, direct access to the output lexicon from the Orthographic Input Lexicon, and interaction between information from the semantic

system and from the OPC system (or directly from the Orthographic Input Lexicon)—might exist and could contribute to JJ's accurate oral reading to varying degrees. We have discussed the possibilities as alternative explanations merely for the sake of simplicity. But, of course, we do not want to propose transformations between representations computed at separate levels unless there are strong theoretical or empirical reasons for doing so. So, because we can account for the reported patterns of performance without postulating a direct transformation between the lexicons, we have not included such a route in our model in Figure 9-1.

9. DJ also made functor substitutions in reading, but these were hypothesized to have a different basis from his visual reading errors, because functor errors also constituted the majority of his errors in spontaneous speech and comprehension.

10. However, simply increasing PS's exposure to untrained homophone pairs, which were read daily without reinforcement or correction, did not improve reading accuracy of these words.

11. As expected, this approach did result in some erroneous responses in pronunciation and subsequent comprehension, when there exists a word corresponding to an allowable, but incorrect mapping (e.g., bread → "breed"). However, PS's overall performance on the reading battery improved from about 30% to about 70% accurate following training.

12. However, a functional relationship between the treatment and the change in specific aspects of reading performance was documented in several cases in multiple-baseline treatment studies (e.g., Hillis, 1991; Hillis & Caramazza, in press).

REFERENCES

Basso, A., Capitani, E., & Laiacona, M. (1988). Progressive language impairment without dementia: A case with isolated category-specific naming defect. *Journal of Neurology, Neurosurgery, and Psychiatry*, *51*, 1201–1207.

Badecker, W., & Caramazza, A. (1987). The analysis of morphological errors in a case of acquired dyslexia. *Brain and Language*, *32*, 278–305.

Behrmann, M., Moscovitch, M., & Black, S. E. (1988). *Attentional capacity and selectivity in a subject with neglect dyslexia.* Paper presented at the 26th Annual Meeting of the Academy of Aphasia, Montreal.

Bub, D., Black, S., Howell, J., & Kertesz, A. (1987). Speech output processes and reading. In M. Coltheart, R. Job & G. Sartori (Eds.), *Neuropsychological studies of language.* London: LEA.

Bub, D., Cancelliere, A., & Kertesz, A. (1985). Whole-word and analytic translation of spelling-to-sound in a non-semantic reader. In K. E. Patterson, J. C. Marshall & M. Coltheart (Eds.), *Surface dyslexia.* London: LEA.

Byng, S., & Coltheart, M. Aphasia therapy and research: Methodological requirements and illustrative results. In E. Hjelmquist & L.-G. Nilsson (Eds.), *Communication and handicap: Aspects of psychological compensation and technical aids.* North-Holland: Elsevier Science Publishers, B.V.

Caramazza, A. (1985). Reading and lexical processing mechanisms. Paper presented at symposium, *Recent advances in Cognitive Neuropsychology*, 26th Annual Meeting of the Psychonomic Society, Boston, MA.

Caramazza, A. (1986). On drawing inferences about the structure of normal cognitive systems from the analysis of patterns of impaired performance: The case for single-patient studies. *Brain and Cognition*, *5*, 41–66.

Caramazza, A. (1988). Some aspects of language processing revealed through the analysis of acquired aphasia: The lexical system. *Annual Review of Neurosciences*, *11*, 395–421.

Caramazza, A. (1989). Cognitive neuropsychology and rehabilitation: An unfulfilled promise? In T. Seron & G. DeLoche (Eds.), *Cognitive approaches in rehabilitation* (pp. 383–398). Hillsdale, NJ: LEA.

Caramazza, A., & Hillis, A. E. (1990). Where do semantic errors come from? *Cortex*, *26*, 95–122.

Caramazza, A., Hillis, A. E., Rapp, B., & Romani, C. (1990). The multiple semantics hypothesis: Multiple confusions? *Cognitive Neuropsychology*, *7*, 161–190.

Caramazza, A., Laudanna, A., & Romani, C. (1988). Lexical access and inflectional morphology. *Cognition*, *28*, 297–332.

Caramazza, A., Miceli, G., & Villa, G. (1986). The role of the (output) phonological buffer in reading, writing and repetition. *Cognitive Neuropsychology*, *3*, 37–76.

Coltheart, M. (1978). Lexical access in simple reading tasks. In G. Underwood (Ed.), *Strategies of information processing*. London: Academic Press.

Coltheart, M. (1980). Deep dyslexia: A review of the syndrome. In M. Coltheart, K. Patterson & J. C. Marshall (Eds.), *Deep dyslexia*. London: Routledge & Kegan Paul.

Coltheart, M. (1985). Cognitive neuropsychology and the study of reading. In M. Posner & O. Marin (Eds.), *Attention and performance* (vol. XI). Hillsdale, NJ: LEA.

Coltheart, M., Masterson, J., Byng, S., Prior, M., & Riddoch, M. J. (1983). Surface dyslexia. *Quarterly Journal of Experimental Psychology*, *35a*, 469–495.

De Loche, G., Andreewsky, E., & Desi, M. (1982). Surface dyslexia: A case report and some theoretical implications to reading models. *Brain and Language*, *15*, 11–32.

De Partz, M. P. (1986). Re-education of a deep dyslexic patient: Rationale of the method and results. *Cognitive Neuropsychology*, *3*, 149–177.

Egeth, H., Jonides, J., & Wall, S. (1972). Parallel processing of multielement displays. *Cognitive Psychology*, *3*, 647–698.

Ellis, A. W., Flude, B., & Young, A. (1987). 'Neglect Dyxlexia' and the early visual processing of letters in words and nonwords. *Cognitive Neuropsychology*, *4*, 439–464.

Ellis, A., & Marshall, J. (1978). Semantic errors or statistical flukes? A note on Allport's "On knowing the meaning of words we are unable to report." *Quarterly Journal of Experimental Psychology*, *30*, 569–575.

Glushko, R. J. (1979). The organisation and activation of orthographic knowledge in reading aloud. *Journal of Experimental Psychology: Human Performance and Perception*, *5*, 674–691.

Goodglass, H., Kaplan, E., & Weintraub, S. (1983). *The Boston naming test.* Philadelphia: Lea & Febiger.

Goodman, R., & Caramazza, A. (1986). Dissociation of spelling errors in written and oral spelling: the role of allographic conversion in writing. *Cognitive Neuropsychology*, *3*, 179–206.

Gordon, B., Goodman, R., & Caramazza, A. (1987). Separating the stages of the reading process. Reports of the Cognitive Neuropsychology Laboratory #28. Baltimore, MD: The Johns Hopkins University.

Hart, J., Berndt, R., & Caramazza, A. (1985). Category-specific naming deficit following cerebral infarction. *Nature*, *316*, 338.

Henderson, L. (1985). Issues in the modelling of pronunciation assembly in normal reading. In K. E. Patterson, M. Coltheart & J. C. Marshall (Eds.), *Surface dyslexia*. London: LEA.

Henderson, L. (1987). Word Recognition: A tutorial review. In M. Coltheart (Ed.), *Attention and performance* (vol. XII). London: LEA.

Hillis, A. E. (1991). Effects of separate treatments for distinct components of the naming process. T. Prescott (Ed.), *Clinical Aphasiology* (vol. 19). Austin, TX: Pro-ed, 255–276.

Hillis, A. E., & Caramazza, A. (1990). The effects of attentional deficits on reading and spelling. In A. Caramazza (Ed.), *Cognitive neuropsychology and neurolinguistics: Advances in models of language processing and impairment*. Hillsdale, NJ: LEA.

Hillis, A. E., & Caramazza, A. (1991a). Category specific naming and comprehension impairment: A double dissociation. *Brain* 114, 2081–2094.

Hillis, A. E., & Caramazza, A. (1991b). Mechanisms for accessing lexical representation for output: evidence from a category specific semantic deficit. *Brain and Language* 40, 106–144.

Hillis, A. E., & Caramazza, A. (in press). Theories of lexical processing and theories of rehabilitation. In G. Humphreys & M. L. Riddoch (Eds.). *Cognitive Neuropsychology and Cognitive Rehabilitation*.

Hillis, A. E., Rapp, B. C., Romani, C., & Caramazza, A. (1990). Selective impairment of semantics in lexical processing. *Cognitive Neuropsychology*, *7*, 191–244.

Jeannerod, M. (1987). *Neuropsychological and physiological aspects of spatial neglect* (pp. 183–202). New York: Elsevier Science Publishers.

Kay, J., & Bishop, D. (1987). Anatomical differences between nose, palm, and foot, or the body in question: Further dissection of the processes of sub-lexical spelling-sound translation. In M. Coltheart (Ed.), *Attention and performance* (vol. XII). London: LEA.

Kay, J., & Patterson, K. E. (1985). Routes to meaning in surface dyslexia. In K. E. Patterson, J. C. Marshall & M. Coltheart (Eds.), *Surface dyslexia*. London: LEA.

Kinsbourne, M., & Warrington, E. K. (1962). A variety of reading disability associated with right hemisphere lesions. *Journal of Neurology, Neurosurgery and Psychiatry*, *25*, 334–339.

Kremin, H. (1985). Routes and strategies in surface dyslexia. In K. E. Patterson, J. C. Marshall & M. Coltheart (Eds.), *Surface dyslexia*. London: LEA.

McCarthy, R. A., & Warrington, E. K. (1986). Phonological reading: Phenomena and paradoxes. *Cortex*, *22*, 359–380.

McClelland, J. L., & Rumelhart, D. E. (1981). An interactive activation model of context effects in letter perception: Part I. An account of basic findings. *Psychological Review*, *88*, 357–407.

Margolin, D. I., Marcel, A., & Carlson, N. R. (1985). Common mechanisms in dysnomia and post-semantic surface dyslexia: Processing deficits and selective attention. In K. E. Patterson, M. Coltheart & J. C. Marshall (Eds.), *Surface dyslexia*. London: LEA.

Marcel, A. J. (1980). Surface dyslexia and beginning reading: A revised hypothesis of the pronunciation of print and its impairments. In M. Coltheart, K. Patterson & J. C. Marshall (Eds.), *Deep dyslexia*. London: Routledge & Kegan Paul.

Monk, A. F. (1985). Theoretical note: Coordinate systems in visual word recognition. *Quarterly Journal of Experimental Psychology*, *37A*, 613–625.

Morton, J. (1969). The interaction of information in word recognition. *Psychological Review*, *76*, 165–178.

Morton, J., & Patterson, K. (1980). A new attempt at an interpretation, or, an attempt at a new interpretation. In M. Coltheart, K. Patterson & J. C. Marshall (Eds.), *Deep dyslexia*. London: Routledge & Kegan Paul.

Moss, S., & Gonzalez-Rothi, L. (1987a). Treating a subtype of alexia without agraphia:

A case report. Paper presented to the Annual Convention of the American Speech-Language and Hearing Association, New Orleans, LA.

Moss, S., & Gonzalez-Rothi, L. (1987b). Computerized treatment of alexia without agraphia: A case report. Paper presented to the Annual Conference of the International Neuropsychological Society, Washington, DC.

Patterson, K., & Coltheart, V. (1987). Phonological processes in reading: A tutorial review. In M. Coltheart (Ed.), *Attention and performance* (vol. XII). London: LEA.

Patterson, K. E., & Kay, J. (1982). Letter-by-letter reading: Psychological descriptions of a neurological syndrome. *Journal of Experimental Psychology*, *34A*, 411–441.

Patterson, K. E., Marshall, J. C., & Coltheart, M. (1985). *Surface dyslexia*. London: LEA.

Patterson, K. E., & Morton, J. (1985). From orthography to phonology: An attempt at an old interpretation. In K. E. Patterson, J. C. Marshall & M. Coltheart (Eds.), *Surface dyslexia*. London: LEA.

Prinzmetal, W. (1981). Principals of feature integration in visual perception. *Perception and Psychophysics*, *30*, 330–340.

Rapp, B. & Caramazza, A. (in press). Spatially determined deficits in letter and word processing. *Cognitive Neuropsychology*.

Rothi, L., Goldstein, L. P., Teas, E., Schoenfeld, D., Moss, S., & Ochipa, C. (1986). Treatment of alexia without agraphia: A case report. Paper presented to the Annual Conference of the International Neuropsychological Society.

Saffran, E. (1985). Lexicalization in surface dyslexia. In K. E. Patterson, J. C. Marshall & M. Coltheart (Eds.), *Surface dyslexia*. London: LEA.

Schwartz, M. F., Saffran, E., & Marin, O. S. M. (1980). Fractionating the reading process in dementia: Evidence for word-specific print-to-sound associations. In M. Coltheart, K. Patterson & J. C. Marshall (Eds.), *Deep dyslexia*. London: Routledge & Kegan Paul.

Seidenberg, M. S. (1987). Sublexical structures in visual word recognition: Access units or orthographic redundancy? In M. Coltheart (Ed.), *Attention and performance* (vol. XII). London: LEA.

Seidenberg, M., Waters, G., Barnes, M., & Tanenhaus, M. (1984). When does irregular spelling or pronunciation influence word recognition? *Journal of Verbal Learning and Verbal Behavior*, *23*, 383–404.

Seymour, P. H. K. (1979). *Human visual cognition*. West Drayton: Collier Macmillan.

Shallice, T. (1988). *From neuropsychology to mental structure*. Cambridge: Cambridge University Press.

Shallice, T., & McCarthy, R. (1985). Phonological reading: From patterns of impairment to possible procedures. In K. E. Patterson, J. C. Marshall & M. Coltheart (Eds.), *Surface dyslexia*. London: LEA.

Shallice, T., & Warrington, E. K. (1977). The possible role of selective attention in acquired dyslexia. *Neuropsychologia*, *15*, 31–41.

Shallice, T., & Warrington, E. K. (1980). Single and multiple component syndromes. In M. Coltheart, K. Patterson & J. C. Marshall (Eds.), *Deep dyslexia*. London: Routledge & Kegan Paul.

Shallice, T., Warrington, E. K., & McCarthy, R. A. (1983). Reading without semantics, *Quarterly Journal of Experimental Psychology*, *35A*, 111–138.

Silveri, M. C., & Gainotti, G. (1988). Interaction between vision and language in category-specific semantic impairment. *Cognitive Neuropsychology*, *5*, 677–709.

Spoer, K. T., & Smith, E. E. (1973). The role of syllables in perceptual processing. *Cognitive Psychology*, *5*, 71–89.

Taft, M. (1979). Lexical access via an orthographic code: The Basic Orthographic Syllabic Structure (BOSS). *Journal of Verbal Learning and Verbal Behavior*, *18*, 21–39.

Warrington, E. K., & McCarthy, R. A. (1983). Category specific access dysphasia. *Brain*, *106*, 859–878.

Warrington, E. K., & Shallice, T. (1980). Word from dyslexia. *Brain*, *103*, 99–112.

Wertz, R. T., LaPointe, L. L., & Rosenbek, J. C. (1984). *Apraxia of speech in adults: The disorder and its management.* Orlando: Grune & Stratton, Inc.

Appendix 9-1: Patient Characteristics

Initials	Sex	Age	Education	Occupation at onset	Premorbid Handedness/ Postmorbid*	Diagnosis, Site of Lesion by CT or MRI	Time Post-onset at Time of Testing
DJ	M	28	12	Spice blender	R/L	Left fronto-parietal & temporal infarct	12 months
FM	M	40	12	Truck driver	R/L	Left inferior-posterior frontal lobe, inferior parietal, anterior temporal & lateral basal ganglia infarct	4 years
HG	F	22	12	Student	R/L	Skull fractures & subdural hematomas due to blow to head; damage to left frontal, left temporo-parietal areas & small right parietal area	7 years
HW	F	62	12	Retired saleslady	R	Left occipital infarct, 1982 Left parietal infarcts, 1985	3 years post 2nd stroke
HH	M	57	12	Truck driver	R/L	Left temporal, occipital & thalamic infarct (embolic)	18 months
JJ	M	69	13	Retired expediter	R	Left temporal & basal ganglia infarct	8 months
KE	M	52	18 (MBA)	Corporate executive	R	Left fronto-parietal infarct	6 months
LAB	M	70	8 + GED	Railroad operator	R	Right anterior parital infarct	3 months
NG	F	76	8	Homemaker	L	Left parietal & basal ganglia infarct	8 months
PM	F	50	22 (PhD)	College dean	L	Left inferior frontal, temporal, parietal, basal ganglia	14 months
PS	M	45	12	President of small contracting business	R	Left frontal hematoma evacuation; bitemporal contusions from blow to head	13 months
RGB	M	62	9	Personnel director	R/L	Left fronto-parietal infarct (MCA Occlusion)	5 years

[a]If different from premorbid handedness (due to hemiplegia).

10

Oral and Written Spelling Impairments

DAVID IRA MARGOLIN and ROBERTA GOODMAN-SCHULMAN

CLASSICAL NOTIONS OF DYSGRAPHIA

Carl Wernicke's (1874/1968) prescient and seminal theory of language disorders can be paraphrased as follows: Language disorders are (1) due to impairments of elementary psychic processes, and (2) these processes have specific anatomical substrates. Substituting the word "cognitive" for the word "psychic" transforms these two statements into a reasonably good rendition of the core tenants of contemporary cognitive neuropsychology. Wernicke's assertion that "under no circumstances can a direct path be available from the sense images that form the concept to the motor center, over which the writing movements could be innervated while the sound images were circumvented," (p. 57) does not hold up so well under scrutiny. Translated into the vocabulary of contemporary cognitive psychology, Wernicke's position holds that at least one mandatory step in the information processing cascade subserving written spelling involves phonological processing. This postulate is no longer tenable. Multiple case studies have demonstrated that (at least under certain conditions) semantic processes are sufficient to sustain spelling despite severely impaired phonological processing (Margolin, 1984; Bub & Chertkow, 1988; Ellis, 1989; Patterson, 1989). This more refined view of dysgraphia has rapidly gained widespread acceptance as evidenced by the statement in the most recent edition of a standard neurology textbook (Adams & Victor, 1989, p. 388) that the "writing of a word can be performed either by the direct lexical method of recalling its spelling or by sounding out its phonemes and by transforming them to learned graphemes . . . the phonological method."

AN INFORMATION PROCESSING MODEL OF WRITING AND SPELLING: A STARTING POINT

Margolin (1984) presented an information processing model of writing and spelling based upon analysis of the neuropsychological data available at that time. That model and the key assumptions behind it will be reviewed briefly here. The remainder of the chapter will be devoted to scrutinizing some of the more informative cases which have appeared in the literature since then, and describing a cognitive approach to the clinical assessment of spelling disorders. We will return to this model at the end of the chapter in order to make any changes which are mandated by the new clinical evidence. The dynamic interplay between model building and empirical data reflected in that approach is an essential feature of cognitive neuropsychology. The model helps us to understand a given patient's performance in terms of one or more information processing deficits. At the same time, details of that performance (including a careful error analysis) provide an empirical basis for constraining and refining the model.

Consider the model of single-word spelling presented in Figure 10-1, derived (with some changes in terminology) from Margolin (1984).[1] This model holds that spelling can be accomplished via three qualitatively different and potentially independent ways: nonlexical phonology, lexical phonology, and semantic mediation. The latter two pathways both utilize internal representations of word spellings which are stored in an orthographic output lexicon (an internal spelling dictionary). In contrast, nonlexical spelling is thought to involve segmentation of a whole word or pronounceable nonword into smaller phonological parts and assigning the appropriate letters to those parts. More specifically, one popular theory of nonlexical spelling holds that the whole stimulus is segmented into its component phonemes followed by application of phoneme to grapheme transformations and pronunciation rules (e.g., long vowel after final e) (Baxter & Warrington, 1987; Barry, 1988; Baxter & Warrington, 1988; Goodman-Schulman, 1988); alternative theories will be discussed later.

The spelling pathways used will depend upon the task an individual is engaged in. The semantic pathway must be involved in order for an individual to express thoughts or ideas in writing; the role of the lexical phonological route in that context is less clear. All three pathways can be used in a spelling to dictation task.

After orthographic information is generated (irrespective of the pathway of origin), it is transferred to the orthographic buffer. The orthographic information is held there until it decays or until it undergoes further processing. The orthographic information will then flow along one of two lines depending upon the chosen output modality. Visually based spelling requires activation of a physical letter code; while oral spelling depends upon a name letter code. For the sake of parsimony, and in the absence of any evidence to the contrary, we have assumed that the information retrieved from the physical letter code store is used in all types of visually based spelling, including handwriting, typing, and spelling with preformed letters (e.g., letters displayed on blocks or cards).[2]

Written spelling requires access to stored graphic motor programs which specify the appropriate strokes needed to form each letter. For those who know how to use a keyboard, typing would involve retrieval of typing motor programs. For "hunt and peck" typing and spelling with preformed letters, more generic limb movements (e.g., reaching and pressing) would be utilized. In oral spelling, input from the orthographic buffer would activate the appropriate representations within a phonologically based name letter code, which in turn would activate the articulatory programs needed to speak the corresponding letter names. At the most peripheral level, the graphic or articulatory details are specified (e.g., the muscles to be used and the speed and force of movements) in order

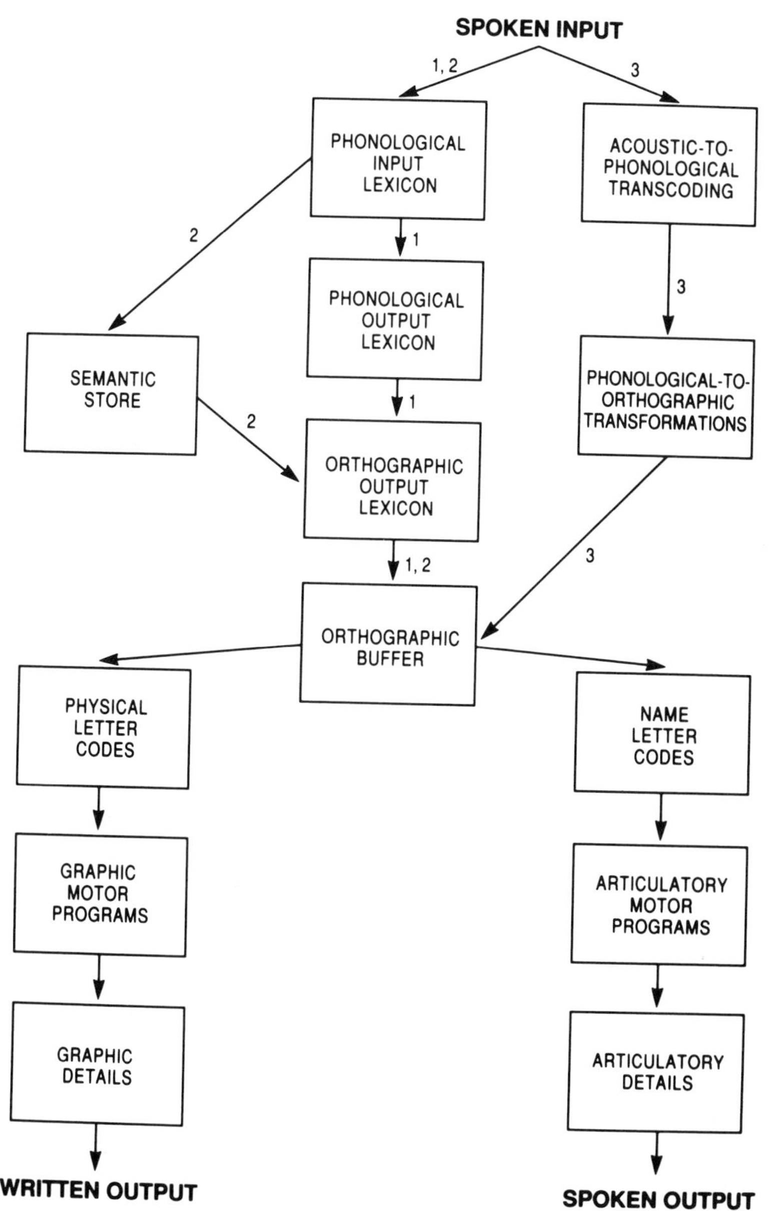

Figure 10-1 An information processing model of spelling (#1 = lexical phonological pathway, #2 = semantic pathway, #3 = nonlexical phonological pathway).

to achieve a written or oral (respectively) instantiation of the specified internal orthographic representations.

TESTING THE MODEL: REVIEW OF THE KEY NEUROPSYCHOLOGICAL EVIDENCE

Apraxic Agraphia

According to the model, a selective deficit of the graphic motor programs would produce a disorder of written letter formation without impairment of letter selection, copying, or other fine-motor movements—an apraxic agraphia.[3] There is now substantial documentation of relatively selective lesions at this level of processing.

In 1986, for example, Baxter and Warrington published a beautifully documented case of a 73-year-old, right-handed man who, despite very impaired handwriting (involving both print and cursive and both upper and lower case), showed flawless copying of letters and normal drawing. Number writing was better than letter writing, and all types of nongraphic praxis were intact. This patient's pattern of performance supports the contention that graphic motor programs (or access to them) can be disrupted without impairing closely related types of movements. Unfortunately, this case did not provide very specific information about the anatomical substrates of graphic motor control since the underlying lesion was a large left-hemisphere parieto-occipital tumor with surrounding edema. As would be expected with such an extensive lesion, there were other cognitive impairments in addition to the agraphia, most notably substantial verbal and visual memory deficits.

The case report by Anderson, Damasio, and Damasio (1990) provided much more useful anatomical data. Their patient was a 58-year-old right-handed woman who was tested 6 and 12 months following surgical resection of a brain metastasis from an adenocarcinoma of the lung. The lesion was localized by CT scan to the posterior, superior, left premotor cortex (Broadmann's area 6), an area that was first linked to writing disorders by Exner in 1881. Anderson et al.'s patient's oral spelling was within normal limits, but her written letters were severely deformed to the point of illegibility. The occasional legible letters were sabotaged by her tendency to write one letter on top of another. Her performance improved substantially when copying letters, and other forms of praxis, including drawing and number writing, were intact.

Coslett, Gonzales-Rothi, Valenstein, and Heilman (1986) described two cases which substantiated further the dissociability between writing and other forms of praxis. Their first patient developed a marked apraxic agraphia along with some impairment of copying letters and drawing. Other types of limb praxis were intact. He was the first reported fully right-handed individual to demonstrate such a dramatic dissociation between writing and most other forms of praxis following a left hemisphere lesion. Unfortunately, more precise anatomical localization was not possible since there were at least four distinct lesions on his CT scan. The dissociation between writing and other forms of praxis can also occur in the reverse direction, as documented by Coslett et al.'s second patient, who had a severe limb apraxia but no apraxic agraphia.

The combination of spared number writing and apraxic letter writing manifested by Anderson et al.'s patient (and less dramatically by Baxter and Warrington's patient) provides compelling documentation of the functional and anatomical autonomy of two categories of praxis with extremely similar perceptual and peripheral motor demands. Documentation of the double dissociation between these two skills was provided by Cossu and Marshall's (1990) case report of an Italian boy who could write cursive letters but was grossly apraxic for writing numbers.

Physical-Letter-Code Agraphia

The physical letter code store is putatively used in all visually based spelling. Theoretically, the physical letter code, "must specify which physical forms are acceptable versions of the letter specified in the orthographic buffer" (Margolin, 1984, p. 469). Until recently, little has been known about how these physical forms are represented or how they are translated into motor commands. Patterson and Wing's (1989) case report has added substantially in this regard. They described a 54-year-old, right-handed man, DK, who developed an apraxic agraphia which was much more severe for lower-case than for upper-case letters. This report complements De Bastiani and Barry's (1986, April) report which described the opposite pattern. Their patient, GB, was a 72-year-old, right-handed woman with a deep left temporo-parietal metastatic tumor. As would be expected, her agraphia was progressive and was associated with other language dysfunction. She preferred to write in lower case script. When instructed to write in capital letters, she would alternate between upper and lower case. As her deficit grew progressively worse, she went through a stage where she "maintained the ability to write in script" and assemble short strings of letters with capital letter blocks, despite the fact that she was "completely unable to write using capital letters." The authors referred to this pattern of deficits as "allographic dysgraphia," reflecting their belief that there was a deficit at the "allographic stage" (Ellis, 1982) which (keeping in mind the limited extent to which either one of these terms has been defined) is equivalent to the physical letter code.

The preceding two patients had very selective disruption of one letter case or the other, but other patterns are possible. De Bastiani and Barry (1989) described a 48-year-old, right-handed man who developed agraphia due to a metastatic tumor involving the left temporal, parietal, and occipital lobes. Only two days of testing were obtained before surgical removal of the tumor, and when first tested after surgery, the patient's writing was "essentially normal." Although he had no weakness or incoordination of the right hand, his writing was "effortful and quite slow." His handwriting problems were multicomponential, including frequent spelling errors and stroke errors consistent with spatial agraphia (which will be described in a later section). The most striking abnormality, however, was his inability to maintain his writing within a particular case. The patient was instructed to write "in normal script," but he usually began each item with an upper-case letter. Judging from the 27 examples provided, his writing consisted of a mixture of cursive and printed forms which alternated between upper and lower case (with no discernable pattern according to the authors). Notably, this patient had "extremely few errors of size or scale," consistent with the hypothesis (as reflected in our model) that letter shape is controlled by cognitive processes which are separate from the cognitive processes which control the size or speed of writing.

The aforementioned cases not withstanding, disruption of the physical letter code need not affect the ability to maintain the proper case (upper vs. lower), or style (print vs. script), of writing. Goodman and Caramazza's (1986b) patient, MW was tested 13 months after a left hemisphere stroke. He produced letter substitution errors in written spelling which resulted in phonologically implausible errors (e.g., chair → chait). No such errors were made in oral spelling.[4] This dissociation between written and oral spelling is indicative of a problem beyond the orthographic buffer, which would localize it to the physical letter code or more peripheral. The fact that written letters were well formed and easily legible means that the lesion was central to the graphic motor pattern stage. We are thus able to localize the site of the lesion to the physical letter code or to the transfer of information between the orthographic buffer and the physical letter code.

Despite the fact that MW made letter substitution errors, information about case and style was efficiently processed. Specifically, MW's letters were well formed in both upper and lower case; and in both print and cursive, he used the appropriate case in written narratives (e.g., capitalizing at the beginning of a sentence and for proper nouns), and he easily transcribed across case in letter copying tasks. Combining MW's performance with the data from the other patients discussed in this section provides compelling evidence that at least three dissociable elements are needed in order to successfully translate orthographic information into the form of a physical letter code. Namely, reading out the abstract letter identity, reading out the case assignment, and reading out the style assignment. Furthermore, the impairment within each element can be selective (e.g., for lower case but not upper or vice versa, for script but not print or vice versa, for some letters but not others).

Transitional Agraphia

Based upon the spelling model in Figure 10-1, what type of agraphia would be predicted to result from a lesion which disconnects (functionally if not anatomically) the physical letter codes from the graphic motor programs without disturbing either of these two stores of information themselves? Oral spelling will be spared, and letters will be well formed, but written letter selection will be impaired. Other types of visually based spelling, like spelling with preformed letters, will be intact. In other words, the pure syndrome of physical letter code-graphic motor program disconnection would result in a spelling disorder confined to written spelling. Margolin (1984) proposed the term "transitional agraphia" for this syndrome to emphasize its intermediate position between the central and the peripheral agraphias. At that time, no detailed descriptions of patients whom fit the pattern of transitional agraphia had been reported. In the interim, there have been several well-documented cases which support the validity of transitional agraphia as a distinct clinical entity (Kapur & Lawton, 1983; Crary & Heilman, 1988; Black, Behrmann, Bass, & Hacker, 1989; Friedman & Alexander, 1989).

The most thoroughly documented case report is by Black et al. (1989). Their patient, MP, was an 80-year-old man who was rendered aphasic from a left parieto-occipital hemorrhage. His oral and typewritten spelling were unimpaired and his handwriting was very legible. In contrast, his handwritten spelling was severely impaired. Lexical variables (i.e., orthographic regularity, wordness, part of speech) did not influence his performance but letter frequency did. Black et al. lucidly describe (pp. 272–273) how they used these data in order to localize MP's functional deficit to the point at which information is transferred from the physical letter code (allographic conversion system in their terms) to the graphic motor pattern store. Despite the frequent spelling errors, MP's written words contained the same number of letters as the target word 77% of the time. This provides additional documentation in support of the conclusion that the specification of the number of letters in a word can be preserved despite the loss of other orthographic information (Margolin, 1984, p. 468).

Friedman and Alexander (1989) tested their patient, GV, 18 months after a stroke which involved the left medial frontal region including the genu and anterior body of the corpus callosum, as shown by CT scan. His speech was sparse but there were "no significant deficits" in grammar, word-finding, comprehension, or repetition, and oral spelling was "excellent." He was originally right-handed, but his residual motor problems were too severe to permit assessment of written spelling ability for that hand. His left-handed writing was characterized by well-formed, clearly legible letters. He correctly wrote 58% of letters to dictation and 23% of high frequency concrete nouns. There was no detailed analysis of written spelling errors, but two of the three errors shown in the paper show partial preservation of lexical orthography (and a hint that there was a relative sparing of initial graphemes) (avenue → averur, building → bluk). He could match orally presented letter names with letter blocks with 96% accuracy and his spelling of words with letter blocks (68% correct) far exceeded his written spelling ability. Unfortunately, an error analysis of his letter-block spelling was not provided.

Kapur and Lawton (1983) reported the case of a 54-year-old woman who was left-handed for writing but "she did use her right hand for some activities."[5] The past medical history was relevant for a 14-year history of epilepsy. In July, 1980, she presented with a two-year history of "difficulty in writing." Despite a severe dysgraphia she had "no significant speech or reading deficit." A CT scan showed a left occipital mass which was thought to be a glioma. Detailed neuropsychological testing was not begun until October, 1981.

She performed at or near ceiling on small samples of letter copying, oral spelling, and plastic-letter spelling. The data provided for error analysis is quite small but very intriguing. The only figure shows what is apparently her attempt to write letters of the alphabet to dictation, presumably written with her left hand (which was dominant for writing), although it is stated that her performance was actually slightly better with her right hand. The salient feature of her dysgraphia was the production of reasonably well-formed, predominantly legible, but incorrect letters (e.g., B → S, K → Y). In writing letters to dictation, she scored 7/26 correct; all but four were recognizable letters. Each letter of the alphabet was dictated once, but the 22 recognizable letters represented only 11 different letters of the alphabet. Several letters (S, U, E, Y) were written more than once (although never consecutively). According to the criteria put forth by Warrington and Shallice (1979) and Shallice (1987), this patient's restricted corpus of correctly produced letters is consistent with a description of the physical letter code itself, as opposed to a disconnection between the physical letter code and the graphic pattern. If the disruption in this patient was at the level of the physical letter code store, however, why was plastic-letter spelling preserved? This dilemma is somewhat overstated and contrived since the Shallice and Warrington criteria are quite controversial (Humphreys, Riddoch, & Quinlan, 1988) and the data from the Kapur and Lawton case were very limited. However, this analysis illustrates how comparison of empirical neuropsychological data with predictions made by existing models gradually leads to progressively more veridical models of cognitive functions.

Crary and Heilman's (1988) 56-year-old, right-handed (personal communication, May, 1989) patient had an acute agraphia following a left parietal hemorrhage. The agraphia was characterized mainly by poor written spelling with slow but very legible letter formation and good oral spelling. These characteristics were indicative of a problem within the physical letter code or in the transfer of information between that code and the graphic motor pattern. The fact that spelling improved quite a bit (83% correct) with letter blocks, supports the latter interpretation. Through a series of visual imagery tasks (e.g., describing the shape of letters from memory) the authors show that this patient had a deficit of visual image formation. They attributed their patient's dysgraphia to damage to the "graphemic area" which they conceptualize as containing, "representations that are responsible not only for guiding the skilled movements required to write, but also for recognizing the physical features of letters." In their schema the graphemic area would thus subserve the function of both the physical letter code and the graphic motor pattern, but that postulation is difficult to reconcile with the dissociation between written spelling and letter-block spelling which they themselves reported. Other recent reports also argue for a role of visual imagery in visually-based spelling (Levine, Mani, & Calvanio, 1988; Friedman & Alexander, 1989).

The Orthographic Buffer

There have also been major advances in our understanding of the next most central stage in spelling, the orthographic buffer. It has been hypothesized that selective damage to the orthographic buffer would lead to a spelling disorder which is independent of output modality and equal for words and nonwords (Margolin, 1984, pp. 468). At that time, only one relevant case report was available (Selnes, Zuben, Risse, & Levy, 1982), but the data were too limited to determine if he met all of the aforementioned criteria. A series of subsequent papers by Caramazza and colleagues, describing four patients, has substantially refined our understanding of the role of the orthographic buffer (graphemic buffer in their terms) in spelling (Miceli, Silveri, & Caramazza, 1985; Caramazza, Miceli, Villa, & Romani, 1987; Hillis & Caramazza, 1989).

According to Caramazza et al. (1987) the orthographic buffer is a working memory system which temporarily stores abstract letter identities (graphemic representations) in a spatial format until they are transcoded into one or another output forms, or until they decay. Based upon that definition, they extended Margolin's criteria for an orthographic buffer deficit as follows: Spelling performance is independent of task (e.g., writing to dictation, written naming, narrative writing), lexical variables (e.g., concreteness, imagability, word class, or frequency), or orthographic regularity. On the other hand, spelling should be sensitive to word length and show a decrement in performance in a delayed letter-copying task. In addition, spelling errors should reflect decay of information about individual graphemes and/or their position in the spatial sequence of letters. Specifically, errors should include transpositions (e.g., pluse for pulse), deletions (e.g., digt for digit), insertions (e.g., lendge for ledge), and substitutions (e.g., muric for music). Note that all of these errors are visually similar to the target word, but many are phonologically implausible nonword responses. More complex distortions can often be recognized to be combinations of simple error forms. The error lifd for the target field, for example, consists of a transposition (if for fi), deletion (e) and location change (l moved from 4th to 1st position). The cases reported by Caramazza and colleagues did indeed demonstrate all of these error types.

Both substitution errors and transposition errors preserve the number of letters in the target word, providing additional evidence of the robustness of numerical specification. The frequent occurrence of transposition errors in some patients (e.g., Caramazza et al., 1987; Lesser, 1990) provides additional documentation in support of another pattern of dissociation—selective loss of information about letter order with preserved specification of both the number of letters and the letter identities (Margolin, 1984, p. 469).

This concept of an orthographic buffer deficit has received support from other authors as well (Posteraro, Zinelli, & Mazzucchi, 1988), but some aberrant data has not yet been accounted for. Consider for example, the patient CB reported by Pate and Margolin (1990). This man with mixed handedness (right-handed for writing and ambidextrous for most other actions) suffered a stroke in June, 1988, at age 64. He died of chronic respiratory and cardiac problems seven weeks later; autopsy showed a small bland infarct limited to the posterior portion of the left inferior frontal gyrus and adjacent inferior-rolandic region (including parts of Broca's area). Although he was severely aphasic in all domains immediately after his stroke, CB's language comprehension and speech production rapidly improved (to the lower limits of normal). There was no incoordination or weakness; all letters were written with his right hand and were well formed and easily legible. In contrast, there was a severe disorder of both written and oral spelling which was evident in all spelling tasks including narrative writing, spelling to dictation, and spelling the names of pictured objects. The discrepancy between spelling and other language functions was striking. On the

Boston Naming Task (Kaplan, Goodglass, & Weintraub, 1983) for example, he provided the correct oral name for 77% of the stimuli and read aloud 85% of the written names correctly. In contrast, he provided the correct written name for only 7% of the stimuli.

In all types of spelling tasks, his errors were almost always visually similar responses (e.g., house → houes, blood → bloob) and there was a strong inverse relationship between stimulus length and probability of correctly spelling words to dictation. These findings point to a deficit at the level of the orthographic buffer. On the other hand, when writing to dictation, CB was much more accurate when writing real words than nonwords. In addition, highly imagable and orthographically regular words were written more accurately than poorly imagable or orthographically irregular words respectively. Other patients have been reported who also partially fulfill the requirements for an orthographic buffer deficit but show a word-over-nonword advantage in spelling (Caramazza et al., 1987; Lesser, 1990).

Pate and Margolin (1990) proposed two possible explanations for the influence of lexical variables in spelling in patients who otherwise fit the orthographic buffer deficit profile. Their first account maintains the fundamental characteristics of the spelling model which we have been discussing,[6] but postulates that lexical and semantic information are used to refresh the memory trace for words in the graphemic buffer. That would account for the word-nonword advantage and the imagability effect. Alternatively, more recently developed "connectionist," "neural network," or "parallel distributed processing" models can be invoked. This class of model portrays a given skill, such as spelling, as the product of complex patterns of excitatory and inhibitory connections among large numbers of simple processing elements or nodes (loosely patterned after networks of neurons in the human brain). The neural network models emphasize the complex multilevel, bidirectional, and simultaneous interactions which take place among processing elements (see Rumelhart & McClelland, 1988 and McClelland & Rumelhart, 1988 for an introduction) and thus provide one plausible account for the variable patterns of lexical influences on spelling found across patients. A neural network model of spelling would thus readily account for the lexical influences seen in CB's spelling performance.

Figure 10-2 shows Pate and Margolin's preliminary sketch of how such a model might operate. In this sketch, each group of nodes (which constitute a processing level) contains a distinct type of information which differs qualitatively across the levels. The top level contains concept nodes which would be roughly analogous to the semantic store in the standard model. The concept of a cake is shown in visual form for the sake of convenience; the format or formats in which information is stored in semantic memory is an open issue in cognitive neuropsychology (see Shallice, 1988, pp. 291–297). The concept nodes interact with both the orthographic and phonological associates of that concept. This information becomes progressively more output-modality specific as an overt response is prepared. All of the connections shown here are excitatory, but interlevel connections between unrelated nodes would be inhibitory (e.g., between the concept cake and the word elevator). Furthermore, intralevel (within one group of nodes) connections are always inhibitory (McClelland & Rumel-

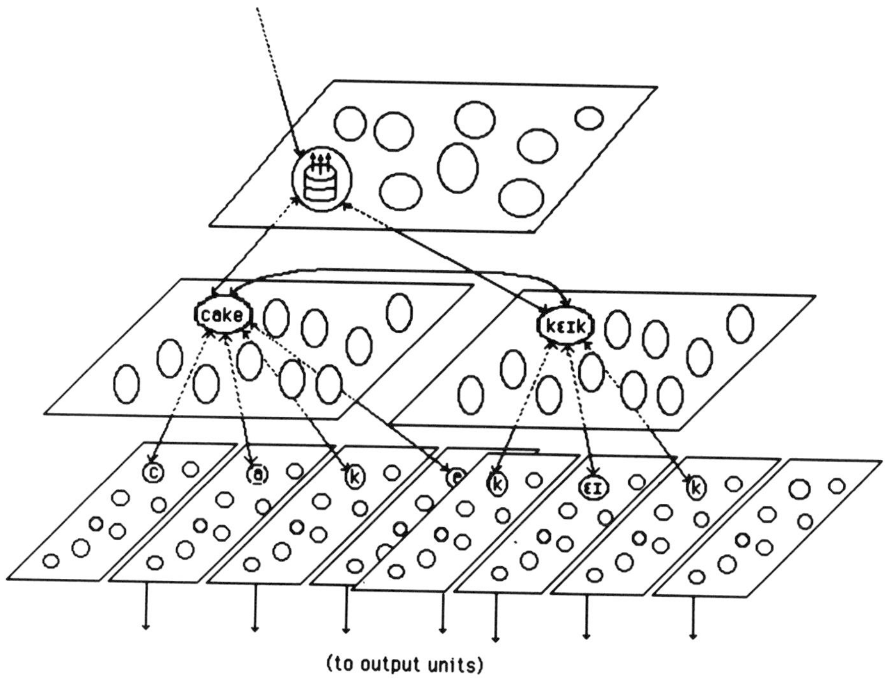

Figure 10-2 Neural network sketch of spelling (with interlevel semantic to orthographic associations shown on the left and semantic to phonological associations on the right).

hart, 1981, p. 379). The sum of excitatory and inhibitory inputs to a node determines the momentary level of activation of that node. The pattern and strength of activation of nodes throughout the system determines the ultimate output (and input since this is a bidirectional process). Later on we will develop one version of how a neural network model could account for how information in the orthographic buffer activates the appropriate corresponding representations in the physical letter code and discuss possible applications for neural network models in cognitive rehabilitation.

CB's performance also challenges traditional notions of how short-term memory buffers function. It is commonly believed that such buffers have a finite number of slots or places which determines the upper limits of their information processing capacity. Applying this characteristic to the orthographic buffer would lead to the prediction that a buffer impairment would result in a well-defined ceiling on the number of letters that could be accurately processed. This was not the case for CB; the number of letters which he produced correctly increased in a monotonic but nonlinear fashion as the number of letters in the target word was increased from four to seven.

Lesser's (1990) case report provides a different sort of challenge to our model. Her patient, CS, produced quantitatively and qualitatively different errors in written and oral spelling. Written spelling was by far the more severely impaired and was influenced by lexical status (words were less impaired than nonwords) but not by orthographic regularity. Oral spelling was influenced by orthographic regularity, but not by lexical status. Lesser concluded that there were separate output buffers subserving written and oral spelling. The relevance of this case to the orthographic buffer is unclear, however, since some of CS's written spelling errors were considerably more gross than would be expected from disruption of the orthographic buffer alone (e.g., nervakmann for drinking, lui for funnel, hand for easel). These errors implicate disruption of phonological and semantic input to the orthographic buffer. Differences in the way these higher-order processes are activated by oral as opposed to written spelling tasks is an alternative (to the two-buffer hypothesis) explanation for the discrepancy in spelling seen in the two modalities. While this controversy cannot be definitively resolved based upon current data, Lesser's buffer-deficit explanation is weakened by the fact that her patient did not show a significant word length effect in oral spelling.

Spatial Agraphia

Acquired disorders of sensory information processing have been linked to a form of writing disturbance referred to as spatial agraphia (Hecaen, Penfield, Bertrand, & Malmo, 1956) or afferent agraphia (Lebrun, 1976). Most commonly seen in patients with nondominant parietal lobe lesions, spatial agraphia is characterized by legible letters and preserved spelling. Some letters, particularly those which include sequences of repeated strokes, such as M, W, and E, may show overrepetition of otherwise appropriate letter strokes. Additional changes are appreciated when looking at more extended writing samples. Typically, there is progressive widening of the page margin contralateral to the side of the lesion and deviation of the line of writing off the horizontal. It has been suggested that all of these components of spatial agraphia can be accounted for on the basis of acquired perceptual and attentional deficits. Specifically, the widened margin could be due to neglect of that side of visual space, the deviation of the writing off the horizontal could be due to difficulty in judging the proper spatial orientation of lines, and the over-repetition of letter strokes may reflect loss of perceptual feedback which is believed to be important in keeping track of the number of strokes which have already been executed (Margolin & Wing, 1983; Margolin & Binder, 1984; Margolin, 1984).

Ellis, Young, and Flude's (1987) detailed case report of patient VB led to an important refinement in this perceptual/attentional account of spatial agraphia. VB was originally left-handed but was compelled by her school teachers to use her right hand for writing. Following "a series" of strokes beginning at age 77, she was left with a left homonymous hemianopsia, left-sided hemiplegia, hemisensory loss, and left-sided visual and tactile neglect. In addition to the previously mentioned symptoms of spatial agraphia, VB's errors included omissions of both letter strokes and whole letters and failure to go back in order to complete letters (e.g., cross "t"s, or dot "i"s or "j"s). Ellis provided cogent evidence that the margin widening and the failure to complete letters was due to neglect. The letter and stroke omissions and repetitions, on the other hand, were thought to be due to problems using perceptual (visual and proprioceptive) feedback which were not indicative of neglect. This conclusion was based in large part upon the presence of a serial position effect (more errors at the beginning of the word than at the end) for the letter completion errors but not for the omissions or repetitions.

It is not immediately apparent how to reconcile Ellis et al.'s appealing account with the data presented in Hartman, Griggs, & Vishwanat's (1985) brief case report. This right-handed, 69-year-old patient developed a spatial agraphia following a right hemisphere stroke. His agraphia was manifested almost solely by prominent overrepetition of letters. While he sometimes neglected to cross "t"s and dot "i"s, he was "able to maintain appropriate margins and straight lines throughout all writing tasks." Unfortunately, it is not stated whether the patient had sensory neglect or not.

Given the pervasive influence of attention on cognitive function, it is not surprising that disorders of attention have been implicated in more central types of dysgraphia as well. Some patients with right hemisphere lesions have more difficulty spelling the initial letters of words than the terminal letter (Baxter & Warrington, 1983; Hillis & Caramazza, 1989), while some patients with left hemisphere lesions show the reverse pattern (Hillis & Caramazza, 1989; Caramazza & Hillis, 1990). Operating from the premise that orthographic information is held in some type of internal visual display (e.g., an "inner screen," Baxter & Warrington, 1983, p. 1077) during one or more stages of information processing (the orthographic buffer in particular), these cases of "neglect dysgraphia" have been attributed to a unilateral neglect of (or hemi-inattention to) the part of this display contralateral to the lesion (Baxter & Warrington, 1983; Hillis & Caramazza, 1989; Caramazza & Hillis, 1990).

Central Agraphia

In the last five years, several well-documented case reports have helped to confirm the three-pathway hypothesis of spelling which we have been advocating here and have provided additional details regarding the functional dynamics of the lexical and nonlexical pathways (Goodman & Caramazza, 1986a; Patterson, 1986). The terminology used to describe these more central disorders of spelling parallels the cognitively based descriptions of reading disorders. "Surface" or ("lexical") dysgraphia refers to spelling dominated by the nonlexical pathway, "phonological" dysgraphia refers to the selective loss of the nonlexical pathway, and "deep" (or "phonemic") dysgraphia refers to spelling dominated by the semantic pathway. A less commonly encountered syndrome, "semantic" (or "direct") dysgraphia, refers to spelling dominated by the lexical phonological pathway.

The performance of Goodman and Caramazza's (1986a) 24-year-old patient, JG, addressed issues pertaining to nonlexical spelling processes. JG developed a profound difficulty in spelling following head trauma (see the upcoming section on clinical assessment for additional details). She made many errors when spelling read words; these almost always produced plausible nonwords (e.g., crisp → krisp, priest → preast). In contrast, her nonword spelling was 100% successful (a pure surface agraphia). A detailed analysis of JG's writing errors showed that her phoneme-to-grapheme selections were influenced by previously learned lexical information (e.g., the probability of the target word, the syllabic position of the phoneme, and the surrounding phonemes). In other words, her nonlexical spelling still carried the legacy of the lexical influences which were at play during the learning of the grapheme-phoneme correspondence rules, even after the lexical spelling systems were profoundly disrupted.

The performance of an 8-year-old Italian boy, TA, described by Cossu and Marshall (1990) also strongly supports the proposition that the nonlexical spelling system can function successfully with little or no help from the other spelling routes. Despite his severe mental retardation (verbal IQ = 53, performance IQ = 50) he developed excellent reading and writing skills. He was able to write over 90% of nonwords correctly (even up to 9 phonemes).

There is still a considerable controversy regarding the specifics of the phoneme-to-grapheme transformation process. Experts disagree, for example, on the size of the orthographic segment which the nonlexical phonological system is capable of processing (e.g., phoneme, biphoneme, morpheme), the most valid way of defining orthographic ambiguity, and how phoneme-to-grapheme transformations and correspondence rules are initially established (Baxter & Warrington, 1987; Barry, 1988; Baxter & Warrington, 1988; Goodman-Schulman, 1988).

Baxter and Warrington's (1985) case report addressed issues concerning the functional characteristics of lexically based spelling. Their patient, GOS, suffered a large left temporo-parietal intracerebral hemorrhage at age 66. Subsequently, she had a severe phonological agraphia; she could not accurately spell any nonwords that exceeded two letters in length. Her spelling of words was above average, but she showed a word class effect. Nouns were written more accurately than adjectives, which in turn were spelled better than verbs or functors. The authors provided important new information by demonstrating that the advantage of nouns over verbs persisted when the lexical variable of concreteness was controlled for. This finding is evidence that different grammatical classes of words are processed differentially at one or more of the information-processing stages subserving spelling.

This conclusion is strengthened by Patterson and Shewell's (1987) patient, GA, who also showed better written spelling ability for content words than for function words. GA, however, showed a reversal of this pattern in all tasks involving spoken output (i.e., spontaneous speech, repetition, and oral naming). This discrepancy between written and oral output impacts upon the active debate over whether writing and speaking depend upon common or separate central semantic and phonological mechanisms. The fact that many (if not most) patients make similar errors in written naming, oral naming, and reading aloud has been used as evidence to support the argument that a common cognitive deficit underlies all these language deficits (Allport & Funnell, 1981), but GA's performance seriously challenges that hypothesis.

Even more compelling evidence against the common deficit hypothesis comes from patients who show important differences in performance even within a single output modality. Allport and Funnell's (1981) patient, AL, showed a content-word-over-function-word-advantage in oral reading but she showed a function-word-over-content-word-advantage in spontaneous speech. On the other hand, Caramazza, Hillis, Rapp, and Romani (1990) and Hillis, Rapp, Romano, and Caramazza (1990) have provided detailed arguments in favor of a common semantic system shared by all lexical processes. It is clear that mapping out the functional complexities of these language subsystems will continue to challenge cognitive neuropsychologists for a long time to come.

Several recent publications have substantiated the existence of a discrete lexical-phonological pathway as postulated by Margolin (1984). Patterson (1986) described her patient, GE, in great detail; this case report is an excellent example of the cognitive neuropsychological approach. GE, a right-handed man, worked as a senior administrative officer for local government until he suffered an extensive left middle cerebral artery stroke and possible right hemisphere ischemia secondary to a pituitary tumor hemorrhage. Neuropsychological testing was begun two months later and continued for three months. Residual neurological problems included a dense right hemiplegia and a dense global aphasia. His written expression (he could now only write with his left hand), similar to his speech production, was severely impaired. It was noted, however, that his ability to write words to dictation was dramatically better than both his oral output and his written output in other tasks. GE's ability to write words to dictation was not influenced by word class (content vs. function word) or orthographic regularity; he correctly spelled 68–79% of the words. He spelled dictated nonwords correctly about one-third of the time. The lack of word class effect and his poor ability to communicate in writing indicate that the semantic pathway was not the primary mediator of GE's writing. The lack of regular-over-irregular word advantage, and the poor nonword spelling, indicate that GE's spelling was not primarily subserved by the nonlexical phonological pathway. That leaves the lexical phonological pathway as the likely candidate for the main mediator of GE's spelling to dictation.

One simple but powerful technique for documenting that spelling is generated by the lexical phonological route is the use of nonhomographic homophonic word pairs (e.g., ate-eight). Since both members of these pairs sound the same they cannot be successfully disambiguated by means of the lexical phonological route alone—input from the semantic system is required. Patients who are spelling predominantly by means of the lexical phonological pathway should thus have more difficulty with spelling homophones than with spelling other words. Results of the initial homophone spelling task supported the hypothesis that GE was relying on the lexical phonological pathway. He wrote between 0% and 10% of homophones correctly, and some of his errors consisted of the correctly spelled other member of the homophone pair. Using a different set of 80 homophones, the experimenter took special care to have GE listen to the disambiguating sentence before he began to write the dictated homophone. With that procedure his success rate rose to 84%! In a third task, a subset of these 80 homophones were dictated but the disambiguating sentence was designed to rely, as much as possible, on syntactic information alone (e.g., "the flag *blew*," "the flag was *blue*," "she told him his *right*," "she told him to *write*"). His performance fell off drastically. It appears that with special effort, GE could utilize the semantic pathway but that under less constrained conditions the better preserved lexical phonological pathway provided the dominant influence.

Rapcsak and Rubens (1990) described a 58-year-old, right-handed, college-educated man who was rendered aphasic by a left frontal intracerebral hemorrhage. His written spelling to dictation was normal or near normal for regular words, irregular words, functors, and nonwords, but substantially impaired for homophones even though a disambiguating sentence was provided (e.g., spell *sea* as in "the sea is stormy today"). He was correct on 57% of the trials; all of his errors consisted of the correctly spelled alternative homophone. The preservation of nonword spelling is indicative of an intact nonlexical phonological route similar to patients with "surface" dysgraphia. His ability to spell irregular words, however, and the disproportionate difficulty with homophones are not compatible with "surface" dysgraphia and implicate the influence of a lexical phonological or "direct," or "third" (Patterson, 1986) route.

Roeltgen, Rothi, and Heilman (1986) described a heterogeneous group of five patients with aphasia secondary to stroke who all had relative (to other language functions) preservation of spelling to dictation. Oral spelling was analyzed in four of the five patients (because motor difficulties interfered with their written spelling) and written spelling was tested in the remaining patient. The unifying characteristics of this group were: Limited ability to spell homophones correctly (mean = 43% correct), errors were frequently (mean = 31%) the correctly spelled alternative homophone, homophone spelling accuracy was influenced by word frequency but not by orthographic regularity. These findings are consistent with reliance predominantly on the lexical phonological route for spelling. Ability to use the nonlexical pathway varied considerably across the patients. The authors proposed the term "linguistic semantic" agraphia to describe the loss of semantic influences in writing evident in these patients. Those that are fond of syndrome labeling might want to call this "transcortical" agraphia in analogy to "mixed transcortical" aphasia in which the salient feature is relatively preserved speech repetition which occurs with little or no semantic mediation (Benson, 1985, pp. 34–35). In light of this analogy, it is interesting to note that all of Roeltgen et al.'s (1986) "semantic" agraphia patients had lesions in locations which have been associated without transcortical aphasia in other patients.

Patients with dementia of the Alzheimer's type (DAT) are another source of information regarding the effects of lexical and semantic deficits on spelling. Language dysfunction, including agraphia, is now a well recognized consequence of DAT (Faber-Langendoen et al., 1988; Horner, Heyman, Dawson, & Rogers, 1988; Rapcsak, Arthur, Blicklen, & Rubens, 1989; Margolin, Pate, Friedrich, & Elia, 1990). The progressive loss of semantic memory is one of the salient clinical features in DAT (Weingartner, Grafman, Boutelle, Kaye, & Martin, 1983; Morris & Kopelman, 1986; Bayles & Kaszniak, 1987, pp. 291–292); this semantic memory loss would be predicted to lead to a progressive deterioration of the semantic pathway for spelling. Residual spelling performance would thus depend upon the integrity of the lexical phonological and nonlexical phonological pathways. As a group, the 11 DAT subjects studied by Rapcsak et al. (1989) were able to spell orthographically regular words and nonwords better than orthographically irregular words, pointing to loss of both the semantic and lexical phonological pathways with resultant pathological reliance on the nonlexical pathway. That conclusion is supported by the predominance of phonologically plausible errors in this group. The patient with dementia reported by Baxter and Warrington (1987) showed a similar pattern.

Theoretically, some DAT subjects' spelling performance should parallel the reading performance of dementia patients who are able to read both orthographically irregular and regular words despite an apparent inability to comprehend those words—a pattern indicative of loss of the semantic route and preservation of the lexical phonological route. One DAT patient, WLP, showed the aforementioned profile in both reading (Schwartz, Saffran, & Marin, 1980), and in spelling, although far less data were reported for spelling (Schwartz, Marin, & Saffran, 1979, pp. 297–300). The data reported consisted of spelling 60 homophones (30 pairs) presented in each of three contexts, a semantic triad (e.g., priest—pope—*nun*), a limited syntactic context (e.g., a *nose*), and a full sentence (e.g., she *blew* out the candles on her cake). WLP did significantly better in the full sentence and limited syntactic context than in the semantic triad, supporting the interpretation that her spelling was not primarily dependent upon semantic information. Similarly, Lesser's (1989) patient, TF, with multi-infarct dementia showed partial preservation of both nonlexical phonological and lexical phonological spelling along with severe impairment of the semantic route.

ANATOMICAL CONSIDERATIONS

The precise anatomical localization of spelling-related cognitive processes remains elusive. Lesions in patients with "lexical" agraphia have ranged from ipsilateral (to the dominant hand) parieto-occipital infarcts (Gonzales-Rothi, Roeltgen, & Kooistra, 1987) to contralateral pre-central gyrus lesions (Rapcsak, Arthur, & Rubens, 1988). Lesions in patients with "nonlexical" (phonological) agraphia, "semantic" agraphia, "orthographic buffer" agraphia, "transitional" agraphia, "physical letter code" agraphia and "apraxic" agraphia have also occurred in diverse anatomical locations.

Our knowledge of the anatomical substrates of the more peripheral aspects of writing is based mainly on extrapolation from studies of motor control in a broader context. For example, disorders of the extrapyramidal nervous system (e.g., Parkinson's disease) primarily disrupt the control of force of movement (including the amount of force and its distribution to particular anatomical sites) while disorders of the cerebellum primarily disrupt the timing of movements (Hallett & Khoshbin, 1980; Marsden, 1982; Paillard, 1982; Margolin & Wing, 1983; Wing, Keele, & Margolin, 1984; Keele, Cohen, & Ivry, 1990).

Selecting the motor effector to be used in writing is another potentially dissociable element in executing the motor program. Writing produced by anatomically different muscle groups (e.g., hand, elbow, shoulder, foot) can have a very similar physical appearance (Marsden, 1982, p. 535; Keele et al., 1990, pp. 89–90), implying that they are controlled by a common set of graphic motor programs. If that extrapolation is correct, then effector selection would have to occur after the graphic motor program stage.

THE MODEL REVISITED

Starting with the most peripheral components, we will review changes in the spelling model which are mandated by neuropsychological material which has come to light over the last six years. These changes are illustrated in Figure 10-3 which stops at the orthographic buffer level. Insufficient data is available at the present time to warrant a revised model of more central processing components.

In 1984, Margolin (p. 470) postulated that the graphic code translates information from graphic motor program into specific neuromuscular instructions. In order to do so, "a number of decisions must be integrated at this stage including which muscle groups will be used, the amount of force to be applied, and the speed of writing." This hypothesis has been supported by the clinical and neuroanatomical data described in the preceding sections. Accordingly, three subcomponents of the graphic code are designated in the revised model (Figure 10-3): Timing specification, effector selection, and force regulation. Controlling force and timing will determine the absolute size and relative size (scale) of letters. Factors influencing these three variables are in large part pragmatic ones (e.g., the type of writing surface, the size of the writing surface, the writing instrument, the distance from which the letters will be read).

Our understanding of the physical letter code has improved substantially in the past six years. It now appears that specifying the physical form which a letter will take necessitates selecting the abstract letter identity, the case (upper or lower), and the style (print or cursive) of writing. The patterns of impaired performances exhibited by various patients show that each of there qualitatively different types of information can be disrupted selectively, and the model has been modified accordingly.

The orthographic buffer has been modified in response to data which indicates that at least three qualitatively different types of information are stored there—the abstract letter identities which constitute the correct spelling for a target word or nonword, the proper order of these letters, and the number of letters required. Data has been reviewed previously (Margolin, 1984, p. 468) which indicates that specification of the number of letters required also influences more peripheral stages of information processing, such as the graphic motor programs. It is not yet clear how far down the information processing cascade these three distinct types of information exert independent influences. As far as specifying the correct number of letters is concerned, Black et al.'s (1989) patient showed selective preservation of that information up to the level of input to the graphic motor programs. Some patients with apraxic agraphia demonstrate that the same selective preservation of the number of letters (often just distorted approximations of letters) persists at least as far peripherally as output from the graphic motor program (Geschwind & Kaplan, 1962; Roeltgen & Heilman, 1983).

Recent cases have substantiated the existence of independent lexical phonological, semantic, and nonlexical pathways in spelling. The wide variety of performance patterns (in terms of the relative influence of each of these pathways) seen in patients with deficits at the level of, or central to, the orthographic

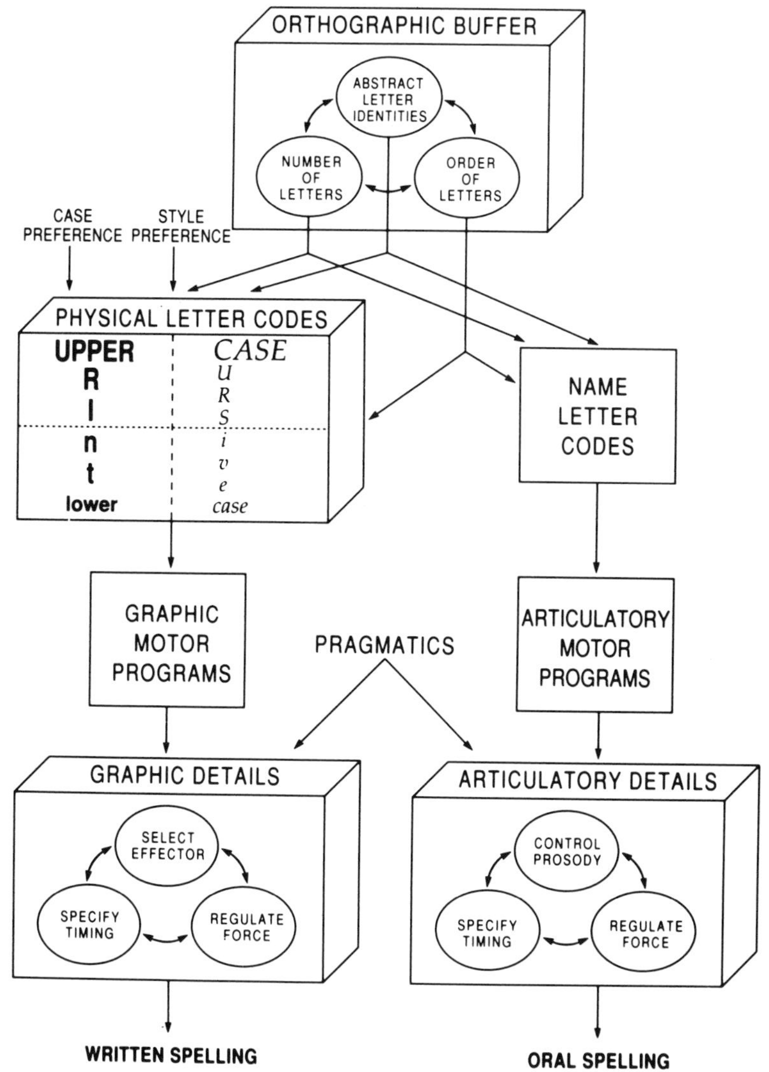

Figure 10-3 Revised model of spelling—the orthographic buffer and beyond.

buffer, indicates that these pathways can retain a high degree of interaction even when one or more of them are partially disrupted. Neural network models provide both a conceptual framework and computational tool for clarifying the details of these interactions. Figure 10-4 illustrates a fanciful attempt to show how one might begin to apply neural network modelling principles to spelling performance.

This figure focuses on the part of the model dealing with the specification and selection of a given letter in the physical letter code. We have concluded from the patient evidence that there are three qualitatively different inputs into the physical letter code: abstract letter identity as specified by the orthographic buffer, case selection, and style selection. Consider the processes involved in

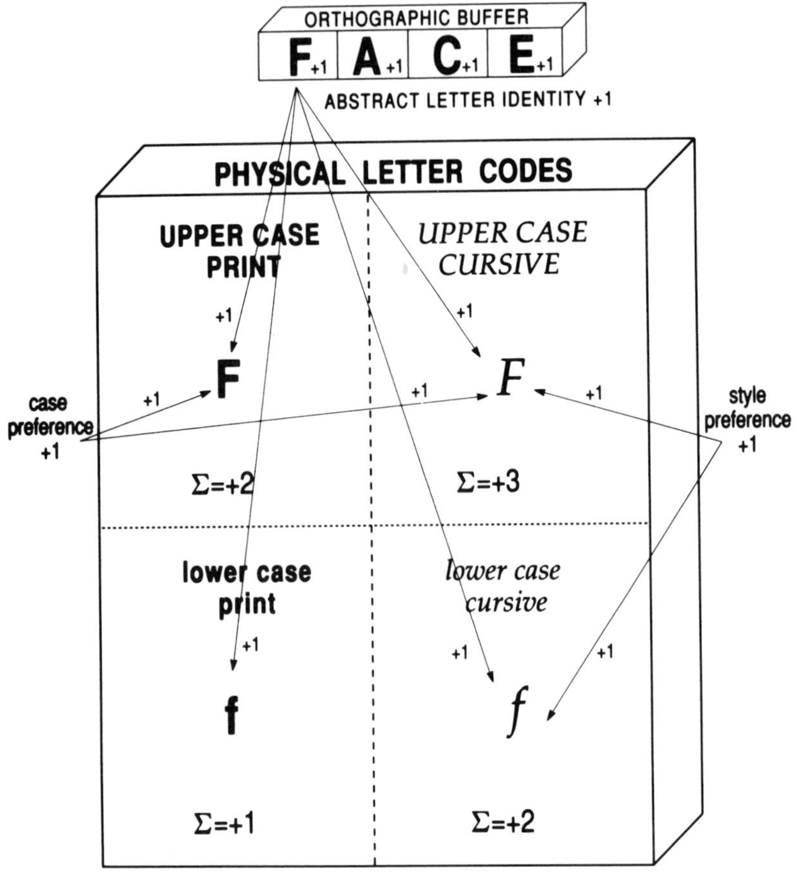

Figure 10-4 Neural network sketch of the orthographic buffer-physical letter code interface.

writing an upper-case cursive *F*. The output from the orthographic buffer effects four nodes, one in each of the four case and style combinations which represent the letter *F*. This would result in +1 units of activation in each of the cells for the letter *F*. The case selection process would provide +1 units of activation to both of the upper case *F*s, and the style selection would produce +1 units of activation for each of the cursive *F*s. The net result would be lower-case printed *F* = +2, and upper case cursive *F* = +3. The oversimplification becomes obvious when one considers the fact that representations are presumably receiving facilitation from multiple levels in the hierarchy as well as inhibition from other letter nodes at the same level of the hierarchy. This conceptualization leads to the prediction that qualitatively different errors should occur depending upon the case and style being used to write a given letter. If we are correct in assuming that the physical letter code is represented in some type of visual format, then the degree of activation of other letters should be proportionate to their visual similarity to the target. The physical resemblance between letters will vary depending upon the case and style being used. The capital cursive *F* resembles the letter *E*. A lower case cursive *F* on the other hand resembles a lower case cursive *P*. Such models have the benefit of lending themselves to computer simulations. Computational models provide investigators with the potential for producing "lesions" at will and observing the resultant behavioral "deficits." If such deficits do not match the types of errors produced by human patients, then the modeler must go back to the drawing board. To date, such lesions have been imposed upon only extremely simplified simulations of cognitive processes (Wood, 1978; 1982; Hinton & Sejnowski, 1986).

CLINICAL ASSESSMENT

In natural settings, patients will rarely, if ever, be evaluated for spelling disorders without first undergoing some type of more general mental status testing. The examiner will thus have some idea of the patient's cognitive strengths and weaknesses prior to focussing on the spelling disorder. On the other hand, spelling is not emphasized in the most widely used screening mental status instruments, and it is possible for even a fairly severe spelling disturbance to go undetected if the examiner relies solely on those instruments.

This pitfall can be avoided by having the patient provide a short written narrative. An open-ended instruction will be suitable for some patients (e.g., write a paragraph about whatever you want), but many subjects require a more focussed instruction (e.g., write a description of the weather today). This task will be sufficient to detect all but the most subtle or circumscribed spelling disorders (e.g., limited to nonword spelling or to a particular case or style). Such a paragraph should provide a sufficient sample of various parts of speech to detect lexical agraphia. Apraxic agraphias should be immediately apparent regardless of the lexical characteristics of the words produced. If a more quantitative assessment of written narrative is desired, the Written Proficiency Scale (WPS) (Horner et al., 1988) can be used. In the WPS, written narrative is evaluated along five dimensions: organization, vocabulary, grammar, spelling, and mechanics. A rating is assigned for each dimension according to a five-point ordinal scale (ranging from normal to severe deficiency). The WPS is applicable to any extended written narrative, such as a written description of the "Cookie Theft" picture from the Boston Diagnostic Aphasia Examination (Goodglass & Kaplan, 1983).

A Spelling Battery

In this section, we describe a spelling battery, the Johns Hopkins University Dysgraphia Battery (hereafter referred to as the Battery; Goodman & Caramazza, 1985) that was developed within the framework of the information-processing model of spelling described in this chapter. The composition of the battery, as well as the classification scheme used for error analyses, is outlined in Appendix 10-1 (for more detail, see Goodman, 1986; copies of the battery are available from Dr. Goodman-Schulman).

Briefly, this screening battery was constructed to discriminate among lexical, nonlexical, and post-orthographic or post-graphemic (involving the orthographic buffer or more peripheral processing steps) influences on spelling. The primary task involves writing words and nonwords to dictation. Words vary along lexical dimensions (i.e., part of speech, word frequency, concreteness), and nonlexical dimensions (i.e., word length, word probability). In addition to the variables assessed in the writing to dictation tasks, other spelling tasks in the battery include written spelling to picture confrontation, oral spelling, and direct and delayed copy transcoding. The pictures in the confrontation task are for noun concepts only. For direct copy transcoding, the patient has the word or nonword stimulus in view at all times while writing, and for delayed copy transcoding, the patient views the stimulus, covers it, and immediately writes the stimulus from memory. For both forms of copying, lower-case stimuli are to be transcoded into upper-case print, and vice versa. Similarly, print versus script can be evaluated. Analysis of the patient's pattern of performance on the battery allows the clinician to discriminate among deficits to the major subsystems of spelling, that is, to localize patterns of impairment to underlying lexical, nonlexical, or post-graphemic processes (or any combination thereof). As the following comparison of two cases demonstrates, a careful analysis of the pattern and distribution of errors produced on each task is also an important part of the assessment.

Brief Case Reports

This assessment was performed in 1985 when MO, a right-handed woman, was 58 years old (Goodman, 1986; Goodman & Caramazza, 1986c). In 1978, she experienced a subarachnoid hemorrhage due to a ruptured middle cerebral artery aneurysm. Five days later, she had neurosurgical treatment (wrapping of the aneurysm). CT scan revealed a left anterior temporal lobe infarct (presumably secondary to vasospasm) and the residual aneurysm. Prior to this event, this high-school educated woman had been employed as an executive secretary and was reportedly facile with reading, writing, and spelling. In 1984, MO revealed characteristics of fluent aphasia in her verbal expressive and auditory receptive processing (Figure 10-5). Oral reading at the single-word level was intact; however, but MO produced some errors at the sentence level (e.g., "The *lawyer* closing argument *convince* him" for "The lawyer's closing argument convinced him").

JG, a 24-year-old right-handed female, sustained a head injury due to a fall in September 1983. She had a high school education, was employed as a hair stylist, and her reading and writing skills were within normal limits prior to the accident. The initial CT scan revealed a small intracerebral hematoma in the left temporoparietal region. A second CT scan, performed in November 1983, showed resolution of the hemorrhage and residual loss of brain tissue in the left temporoparietal area.

JG was evaluated from November 1984, through May 1985; her spoken language and auditory comprehension were within normal limits (Figure 10-6). She had some difficulty reading, particularly for nonwords. Her reading performance is described in more detail elsewhere (Goodman & Caramazza, 1986a).

Patient's Name **MO** Date of rating **November 1984**

Rated by **RG-S**

APHASIA SEVERITY RATING SCALE

0. No usable speech or auditory comprehension.
1. All communication is through fragmentary expression; great need for inference, questioning, and guessing by the listener. The range of information that can be exchanged is limited, and the listener carries the burden of communication.
2. Conversation about familiar subjects is possible with help from the listener. There are frequent failures to convey the idea, but patient shares the burden of communication with the examiner.
3. (circled) The patient can discuss almost all everyday problems with little or no assistance. Reduction of speech and/or comprehension, however, makes conversation about certain material difficult or impossible.
4. Some obvious loss of fluency in speech or facility of comprehension, without significant limitation on ideas expressed or form of expression.
5. Minimal discernible speech handicaps; patient may have subjective difficulties that are not apparent to listener.

RATING SCALE PROFILE OF SPEECH CHARACTERISTICS

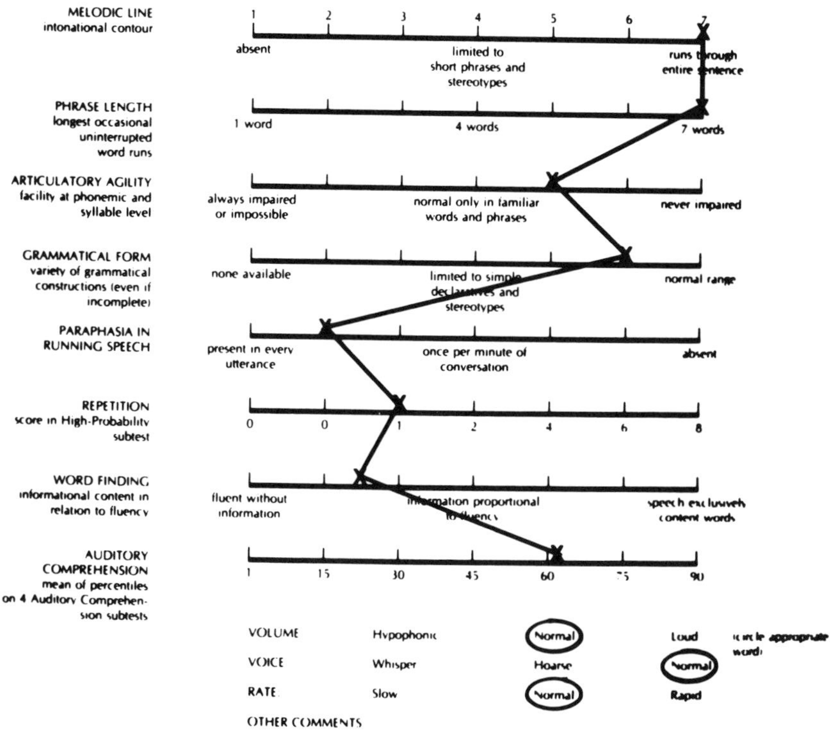

MELODIC LINE intonational contour — 1 2 3 4 5 6 7 — absent; limited to short phrases and stereotypes; runs through entire sentence

PHRASE LENGTH longest occasional uninterrupted word runs — 1 word; 4 words; 7 words

ARTICULATORY AGILITY facility at phonemic and syllable level — always impaired or impossible; normal only in familiar words and phrases; never impaired

GRAMMATICAL FORM variety of grammatical constructions (even if incomplete) — none available; limited to simple declaratives and stereotypes; normal range

PARAPHASIA IN RUNNING SPEECH — present in every utterance; once per minute of conversation; absent

REPETITION score in High-Probability subtest — 0 0 1 2 4 6 8

WORD FINDING informational content in relation to fluency — fluent without information; information proportional to fluency; speech exclusively content words

AUDITORY COMPREHENSION mean of percentiles on 4 Auditory Comprehension subtests — 1 15 30 45 60 75 90

VOLUME Hypophonic (Normal) Loud (circle appropriate word)

VOICE Whisper Hoarse (Normal)

RATE Slow (Normal) Rapid

OTHER COMMENTS

Figure 10-5 BDAE rating scale—MO. (Reprinted from Goodglass, H., & Kaplan, E. (1983). *The assessment of aphasia and related disorders*, (2nd ed.). Philadelphia: Lea & Febiger.)

Patient's Name **JG** Date of rating **November 1984**

Rated by **RG-S**

APHASIA SEVERITY RATING SCALE

0. No usable speech or auditory comprehension.
1. All communication is through fragmentary expression; great need for inference, questioning, and guessing by the listener. The range of information that can be exchanged is limited, and the listener carries the burden of communication.
2. Conversation about familiar subjects is possible with help from the listener. There are frequent failures to convey the idea, but patient shares the burden of communication with the examiner.
3. The patient can discuss almost all everyday problems with little or no assistance. Reduction of speech and/or comprehension, however, makes conversation about certain material difficult or impossible.
4. Some obvious loss of fluency in speech or facility of comprehension, without significant limitation on ideas expressed or form of expression.
5. (circled) Minimal discernible speech handicaps; patient may have subjective difficulties that are not apparent to listener.

RATING SCALE PROFILE OF SPEECH CHARACTERISTICS

	1	2	3	4	5	6	7
MELODIC LINE intonational contour	absent			limited to short phrases and stereotypes			runs through entire sentence
PHRASE LENGTH longest occasional uninterrupted word runs	1 word			4 words			7 words
ARTICULATORY AGILITY facility at phonemic and syllable level	always impaired or impossible			normal only in familiar words and phrases			never impaired
GRAMMATICAL FORM variety of grammatical constructions (even if incomplete)	none available			limited to simple declaratives and stereotypes			normal range
PARAPHASIA IN RUNNING SPEECH	present in every utterance			once per minute of conversation			absent
REPETITION score in High-Probability subtest	0	0	1	2	4		8
WORD FINDING informational content in relation to fluency	fluent without information			information proportional to fluency			speech exclusively content words
AUDITORY COMPREHENSION mean of percentiles on 4 Auditory Comprehension subtests	1	15	30	45	60	75	90

VOLUME:	Hypophonic	Normal (circled)	Loud	(circle appropriate word)
VOICE:	Whisper	Hoarse	Normal (circled)	
RATE:	Slow	Normal (circled)	Rapid	

OTHER COMMENTS:

Figure 10-6 BDAE rating scale—JG. (Reprinted from Goodglass, H., & Kaplan, E. (1983). *The assessment of aphasia and related disorders*, (2nd ed.). Philadelphia: Lea & Febiger.)

Table 10-1 Relative Performance of MO and JG in Written Spelling (% correct)

	Words (N = 34)	Nonwords (N = 34)
MO	67	0
JG	65	100

Written language expression was the most difficult section by far on the BDAE. Even though copy transcoding was intact, oral and written spelling of single words and sentences was impaired. Her major complaint was that she now produced two types of spelling errors; one type consisted of responses that sounded like the words she was trying to write but were not "real" words, the other type consisted of word substitutions that sounded like the words she intended to write but which had the "other meaning." Examples of these errors provided by JG and family members indicated that she was referring to phonologically plausible errors (e.g., writing "kach" for "catch") and homophone confusion errors (e.g., writing "pear" instead of "pair"). Her spelling performance was quite stable during those seven months of testing. She used her right hand in all writing tasks.

MO and JG are both impaired in written and oral spelling of dictated words. Both patients show a significant advantage of high frequency over low frequency words in spelling. In addition, MO shows a significant effect of part of speech (nouns better than verbs and adjectives) and concreteness (higher better than lower). However, the two patients differ markedly in their ability to spell nonwords. While JG can spell nonwords quite well, MO is completely unable to do so (Table 10-1). One plausible explanation for this differential performance is that JG has much better access to the nonlexical pathway than MO. According to the logic which we have developed so far, this differential access should be detectable via an error analysis. Specifically, MO should not produce any phonologically plausible errors whereas JG should. As was expected on the basis of her inability to spell any nonword accurately, MO produced no phonologically plausible errors and in fact produced a large number of "Don't know" response stating that she knew the word but just couldn't "get the spelling out." For JG, on the contrary, the overwhelming majority (97–100%) of her errors when spelling words to dictation were phonologically plausible renditions of the target stimuli (e.g., fabric → phabrick; curtain → kirtin).

Additional testing beyond the battery is required for thorough assessment of patients with more peripheral dysgraphias. In order to distinguish between the different forms of visually based spelling disorders; for example, (e.g., disruption at the level of the physical letter code versus the graphic motor patterns) forms of visually based spelling other than handwriting should be assessed. This is typically done by providing some type of preformed letters (e.g., Scrabble blocks or flash cards) for spelling to dictation. In cases of apraxic agraphia, the clinician should determine if the apraxia is limited to writing or if it is more pervasive. To this end, drawing and copying of geometric figures and executing various transitive and intransitive gestures is tested. In this way, one can detect

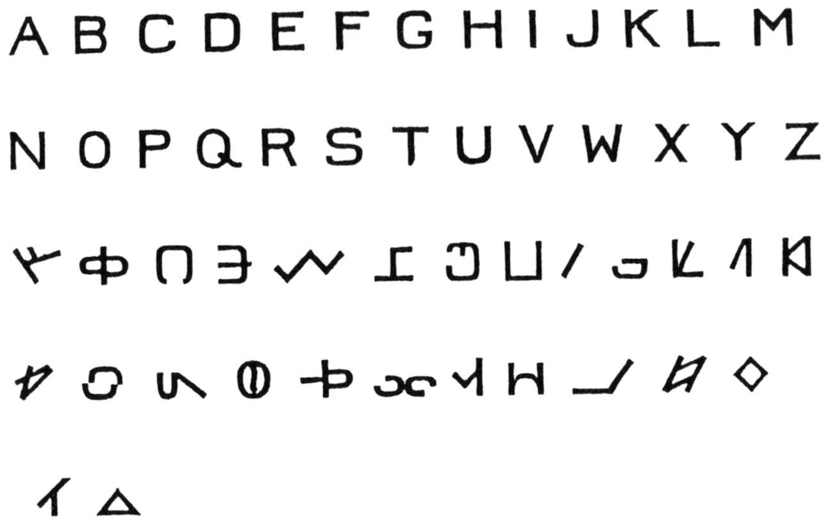

A B C D E F G H I J K L M

N O P Q R S T U V W X Y Z

Figure 10-7 Letters and derived nonletters for copying tasks. (Reprinted with permission from Brown, J. W., Piasetsky, E., & Chobor, K. L. (1986). Writing, drawing and praxis in aphasia. *Journal of Neurolinguistics*, 2, 91–101. © Pergamon Press.)

the occasional patient in whom apraxic agraphia occurs without any other form of apraxia (Roeltgen & Heilman, 1983; Baxter & Warrington, 1986).

There are some intriguing gaps in our knowledge of the relationship between writing letters based upon internal representations and copying letters. It has been postulated that patients with apraxic agraphia should be able to copy letters normally unless there is an additional neurological impairment, such as a constructional apraxia or visual perceptual deficit (Margolin, 1984). However, at least one patient has been reported to have a deficit in copying letters despite preservation of the ability to copy geometric figures (Gersh & Damasio, 1981). If this dissociation is verified, it will necessitate a refinement in our cognitive model of handwriting since the model will have to include dissociable systems for copying letters as opposed to other visual forms. The set of stimuli prepared by Brown, Piasetsky, and Chobor (1986) are particularly well suited for investigating the relationship between letter and nonletter copying. The set consists of 26 nonsense forms, each one created by rearranging the strokes of one letter of the alphabet (Figure 10-7).

Recent data from case reports strongly suggest that some testing of visual imagery be included in a comprehensive assessment of agraphic patients, particularly those whose errors bare a close visual relationship to the target (Crary & Heilman, 1988; Levine, Mani, & Calvanio, 1988; Friedman & Alexander, 1989). Crary and Heilman (1988) provided the most fully developed strategy for the evaluation of imagery function. In one of their more widely used tasks subjects describe the physical characteristics of letters from memory (e.g., which direction capital block letters open or if the letter is composed of straight lines, curved lines, or both).

THEORY-DRIVEN REHABILITATION STRATEGIES

Even when the clinician has a clear idea of what went awry with the spelling system, it is not so evident how to "fix it." In other words, an understanding of the functional deficits in spelling does not automatically translate into a practical solution for the problem (Caramazza, 1989; Behrmann & Byng, Chapter 12). At this point in the history of cognitive neuropsychology, the impact of information processing models on therapy is modest. The information processing approach emphasizes the qualitatively different ways in which a given task may be impaired. This orientation lends theoretical support for certain intuitive approaches to therapy. In attempting to remediate lexical spelling impairments, for example, it makes sense from the cognitive standpoint to focus on the retraining of words, and not on individual letters. Thus, if the disruption to the orthographic output lexicon results in the inaccessibility of low-frequency words relative to high frequency words (as has been described earlier in this chapter), attempts to relearn the spelling of a select, and functionally important, set of words may be more productive than concentrating on writing individual letters. Drills of a select set of words that a patient deems useful in his/her everyday activities will hopefully lower the threshold for accessing these words in the orthographic output lexicon, resulting in an increase in the patient's functional vocabulary.

In contrast, a disruption of the physical letter code would be approached in a very different fashion. Retraining of a set of words is quite inappropriate since the disruption is at the individual letter level. On the contrary, drills for which the patient writes individual letters, then two letters at a time, three letters at a time, and so forth, has face validity.

There are a number of current reports addressing therapeutic issues in spelling from a theoretical orientation (see Hatfield, 1983; Hatfield & Patterson, 1984; Schechter, Bar-Israel, Ben-Nun, & Bergman, 1985; Byng and Coltheart, 1986; Behrmann, 1987; Behrmann and Herdan, 1987; Goodman-Schulman, Sokol, Aliminosa, & McCloskey, 1988, 1990; Hillis-Trupe, 1988; Behrmann & Byng, Chapter 12). Hatfield (1983) and Hatfield and Patterson (1984), for example, described an approach to retraining spelling of function words in a patient, BB, who showed signs of "deep" dysgraphia (e.g., had great difficulty writing function words, substituted one function word for another, and made semantic errors for content words). The therapy approach, which yielded "satisfactory improvement," focussed on word meaning and whole-word spelling. Spellings of content words were used to re-teach spellings of homophonic (or near-homophonic) function words (e.g., inn, in; Ron, on). For example, the phrases "Holiday Inn" and "The string is *in* the cup" were paired. The procedure of first writing the content word and then extracting the function word from this content word was eventually "internalized" or omitted entirely.

More recently, Behrmann (1987; also see Behrmann & Byng, Chapter 12) described a homophone retraining study for a patient who showed a pattern of performance suggestive of disruption at the level of the orthographic output lexicon in the face of intact nonlexical spelling processes. There was significant improvement in trained homophone writing which lasted for at least five weeks.

There was no significant improvement in spelling untrained homophone writing—implying that there was a specific benefit of training and not just spontaneous improvement. On the other hand, there was also improvement in spelling untrained irregular words. Clearly, the relationship between applying rehabilitation techniques targeted to specific functional deficits to the spelling system and, subsequent improvement in performance, is not well established. Hillis-Trupe (1988) nicely summarizes the current state of affairs when she says that she has a "high level of optimism regarding how much chronically aphasic patients can improve in spelling, and a reluctant pessimism regarding how much we can learn about the underlying mechanisms of treatment."

Our conclusions are somewhat more optimistic. A better understanding of the cognitive components of the spelling system and how they interact should lead to development of more refined assessment tools to be used in the differential diagnosis of these disorders. It is expected that practical model driven treatment strategies will ultimately follow.

ACKNOWLEDGMENTS

This work was supported by the Department of Veterans Affairs Research and Development Service. Drs. Debra Sue Pate and Steven Keele provided constructive review of the manuscript. Cynthia Meyer and her staff provided excellent medical library support and Sheryl Carter provided excellent secretarial support.

NOTES

1. There is also a substantive change. In 1984, Margolin chose to finesse the controversial issue of whether there were separate input and output phonological and orthographic lexicons or a unitary phonological and a unitary orthographic lexicon (p. 461). This issue is still controversial, but the weight of the evidence now supports the existence of two separate lexicons for each modality (Margolin, 1991).

2. Disorders of typewritten spelling will not be dealt with further in this review due to the paucity of new neuropsychological data.

3. The ambiguous term, pure agraphia, has been applied to this disorder by those who define pure as without other types of apraxia, but allow for other types of cognitive deficits (e.g., aphasia). We would reserve this term for patients who have no other higher-cortical dysfunction (see note 5).

4. There were phonologically plausible errors in both oral and written spelling.

5. This report is a good example of the problems with the use of the term "pure" agraphia. She is described as having pure dysgraphia by virtue of the fact that there was "no significant speech or reading deficit" on the BDAE. However, she was suffering from a brain tumor, and on the WAIS-R she had a Verbal IQ of 85, a Performance IQ of 65 and a Full-Scale IQ of 75 which the authors admit, "represent a significant generalized drop from her premorbid intellectual level." This included a "marked impairment" on the Block Design subtest.

6. This model is representative of information processing models which have dominated cognitive psychology and cognitive neuropsychology over the last 15 years. These

"box-and-arrow" models assert that information flows in a hierarchical fashion one step at a time. While such models have usually paid little attention to the time course of information flow, the usual implication is that the influence of one level of information stops as soon as the next level is activated. The effects of lexical variables (i.e., wordness, imageability, orthographic, regularity) in patients with orthographic buffer deficits militate against that view.

REFERENCES

Adams, R. D., & Victor, M. (1989). *Principles of neurology* (4th ed.). New York: McGraw-Hill.

Allport, D. A., & Funnell, E. (1981). Components of the mental lexicon. In H. C. Longuet-Higgins, J. Lyons, & D. E. Broadbent, (Eds.), *The psychological mechanisms of language*. London: The Royal Society.

Anderson, S. W., Damasio, A. R., & Damasio, H. (1990). Troubled letters but not numbers. *Brain*, *113*, 749–766.

Barry, C. (1988). Modelling assembled spelling: Convergence of data from normal subjects and "surface" dysgraphia. *Cortex*, *24*, 339–345.

Baxter, D. M., & Warrington, E. K. (1983). Neglect dysgraphia. *Journal of Neurology, Neurosurgery, and Psychiatry*, *46*, 1073–1078.

Baxter, D. M., & Warrington, E. K. (1985). Category specific phonological dysgraphia. *Neuropsychologia*, *23*, 653–666.

Baxter, D. M., & Warrington, E. K. (1986). Ideational agraphia: A single case study. *Journal of Neurology, Neurosurgery, and Psychiatry*, *49*, 369–374.

Baxter, D. M., & Warrington, E. K. (1987). Transcoding sound to spelling: Simple or multiple sound unit correspondence? *Cortex*, *23*, 11–28.

Baxter, D. M., & Warrington, E. K. (1988). The case for biphoneme processing: A rejoinder to Goodman-Schulman. *Cortex*, *24*, 137–142.

Bayles, K. A., & Kaszniak, A. W. (1987). *Communication and cognition in normal aging and dementia*. Boston: College-Hill Press.

Behrmann, M. (1987). The rites of righting writing: Homophone remediation in acquired dysgraphia. *Cognitive Neuropsychology*, *4*, 365–384.

Behrmann, M., & Herdan, S. (1987). The case for cognitive neuropsychological remediation. *The South African Journal of Communicative Disorders*, *134*, 3–9.

Benson, D. F. (1985). Aphasia. In K. M. Heilman & E. Valenstein (Eds.), *Clinical neuropsychology*, (2nd ed., chapter 2). New York: Oxford.

Black, S. L., Behrmann, M., Bass, K., & Hacker, P. (1989). Selective writing impairment: Beyond the allographic code. *Aphasiology*, *3*, 265–277.

Brown, J. W., Piasetsky, E., & Chobor, K. L. (1986). Writing, drawing and praxis in aphasia. *Journal of Neurolinguistics*, *2*, 91–101.

Bub, D., & Chertkow, H. (1988). Agraphia. In F. Boller & J. Grafman (Eds.), *Handbook of neuropsychology, Vol. 1* (Chapter 21). New York: Elsevier.

Byng, S., & Coltheart, M. (1986). Aphasia therapy research: Methodological requirements and illustrative results. In E. Hielmquist and L. B. Nilsson (Eds.), *Communication and handicap. Aspects of psychological compensation and technical aids*. Amsterdam: North Holland.

Caramazza, A. (1989). Cognitive neuropsychology and rehabilitation: An unfulfilled promise? In X. Seron & G. Deloche (Eds.), *Cognitive approaches in neuropsychological rehabilitation* (chapter 12). Hillsdale, NJ: Erlbaum.

Caramazza, A., & Hillis, A. E. (1990). Levels of representation, coordinate frames, and unilateral neglect. *Cognitive Neuropsychology*, *7*, 391–445.

Caramazza, A., Hillis, A. E., Rapp, B. C., & Romani, C. (1990). The multiple semantics hypothesis: Multiple confusions? *Cognitive Neuropsychology*, *7*, 161–190.

Caramazza, A., Miceli, G., Villa, G., & Romani, C. (1987). The role of the graphemic buffer in spelling: Evidence from a case of acquired dysgraphia. *Cognition*, *26*, 59–85.

Coslett, H. B., Gonzalez-Rothi, L. J., Valenstein, E., & Heilman, K. M. (1986). Dissociations of writing and praxis: Two cases in point. *Brain and Language*, *28*, 357–369.

Cossu, G., & Marshall, J. C. (1990). Are cognitive skills a prerequisite for learning to read and write? *Cognitive Neuropsychology*, *7*, 21–40.

Crary, M. A., & Heilman, K. M. (1988). Letter imagery deficits in a case of pure apraxic agraphia. *Brain and Language*, *34*, 147–156.

De Bastiani, P., & Barry, C. (1986, April). *After the graphemic buffer: Disorders of peripheral aspects of writing in Italian patients.* Paper presented at the joint meeting of the Experimental Psychology Society and the Societa Italiana cli Neuropsicologica, Padova, Italy.

De Bastiani, P., & Barry, C. (1989). A cognitive analysis of an acquired dysgraphic patient with an "allographic" writing disorder. *Cognitive Neuropsychology*, *6*, 25–41.

Ellis, A. W. (1982). Spelling and writing (and reading and speaking). In Ellis, A. W. (Ed.), *Normality and pathology in cognitive functions* (Chapter 4). London: Academic Press.

Ellis, A. W. (1989). Modelling the writing process. In G. Denes, C. Semenza, P. Bisiacchi, & E. Andreewsky (Eds.), *Perspectives on cognitive neuropsychology* (Chapter 20). London: Erlbaum.

Ellis, A. W., Young, A. W., & Flude, B. M. (1987). "Affarent dysgraphia" in a patient and in normal subjects. *Cognitive Neuropsychology*, *4*, 465–486.

Exner, S. (1881). Untersuchungen iiber die Lokalisation der Funktionen in der *Grosshirnrinde des Menschen*, Wein: W. Braumuller.

Faber-Langendoen, K., Morris, J. C., Knesevich, J. W., La Barge, E., Miller, J. P., & Berg, L. (1988). Aphasia in senile dementia of the Alzheimer type. *Archives of Neurology*, *23*, 365–370.

Friedman, R. P., & Alexander, M. (1989). Written spelling agraphia. *Brain and Language*, *36*, 503–517.

Gersch, F., & Damasio, A. (1981). Praxis and writing of the left hand may be served by different callosal pathways. *Archives of Neurology*, *38*, 634–636.

Geschwind, N., & Kaplan, E. (1962). A human cerebral disconnection syndrome. *Neurology*, *12*, 675–685.

Gonzalez-Rothi, L. J., Roeltgen, D. P., & Kooistra, C. A. (1987). Isolated lexical agraphia in a right-handed patient with a posterior lesion of the right cerebral hemisphere. *Brain and Language*, *30*, 181–190.

Goodglass, H., & Kaplan, E. (1983). *The assessment of aphasia and related disorders*, (2nd ed.). Philadelphia: Lea & Febiger.

Goodman, R. A. (1986). *Patterns of acquired dysgraphia: Evidence for a model of the normal spelling system.* Doctoral dissertation. The University of Maryland, College Park, MD.

Goodman, R. A., & Caramazza, A. (1985), *The Johns Hopkins University dysgraphia battery.* Baltimore, MD: The Johns Hopkins University.

Goodman, R. A., & Caramazza, A. (1986a). Aspects of the spelling process: Evidence from a case of acquired dysgraphia. *Language and Cognitive Processes, 1*, 263–296.

Goodman, R. A., & Caramazza, A. (1986b). Dissociations of spelling errors in written and oral spelling: The role of allographic conversion in writing. *Cognitive Neuropsychology, 3*, 179–206.

Goodman, R. A., & Caramazza, A. (1986c). Phonologically plausible errors: Implications for a model of the phoneme-grapheme conversion mechanism in the spelling process. In G. Augst (Ed.), *New trends in graphemics and orthography* (pp. 300–325). Berlin: Walter de Gruyter.

Goodman-Schulman, R. A. (1988). Orthographic ambiguity: Comments on Baxter & Warrington. *Cortex, 24*, 129–135.

Goodman-Schulman, R. A., Sokol, S. M., Aliminosa, D., & McCloskey, M. (1988). *Remediation as a modeling tool: Evidence from acquired dysgraphia.* The Annual Convention of the American Speech-Language-Hearing Association, Boston, MA.

Goodman-Schulman, R. A., Sokol, S. M., Aliminosa, D., & McCloskey, M. (1990, October). *Remediation of acquired dysgraphia as a technique for evaluating models of spelling.* Presented at the meeting of the Academy of Aphasia, Baltimore, MD.

Hallett, M., & Khoshbin, S. (1980). A physiological mechanism of bradykinesia. *Brain, 103*, 301–314.

Hartman, D. E., Griggs, S. J., & Vishwanat, B. (1985). Dysgraphia after right hemisphere stroke. *Archives of Physical Medicine and Rehabilitation, 66*, 182–184.

Hatfield, F. M. (1983). Aspects of acquired dysgraphia and implications for reeducation. In C. Code and D. J. Muller (Eds.), *Aphasia Therapy*. London: Edward Arnold.

Hatfield, F. M., & Patterson, K. E. (1983). Phonological spelling. *Quarterly Journal of Experimental Psychology, 35A*, 451–468.

Hatfield, F. M., & Patterson, K. E. (1984). Interpretation of spelling disorders in aphasia. Impact of recent developments in cognitive psychology. In F. C. Rose (Ed.), *Advances in neurology, vol. 42: Progress in aphasiology* (pp. 183–192). New York: Raven Press.

Hecaen, H., Penfield, W., Bertrand, C., & Malmo, R. (1956). The syndrome of apractagnosia due to lesions of the minor cerebral hemisphere. *Archives of Neurology and Psychiatry, 75*, 400–434.

Hillis, A. E., & Caramazza, A. (1989). The graphemic buffer and attentional mechanisms. *Brain and Language, 36*, 208–235.

Hillis, A. E., Rapp, B. C., Romani, C., & Caramazza, A. (1990). Selective impairment of semantics in lexical processing. *Cognitive Neuropsychology, 7*, 191–244.

Hillis-Trupe, A. E. (1988). *Treatment of acquired writing disorders.* Mini-seminar presented at the meeting of the American Speech-Language-Hearing Association, Boston, MA.

Hinton, G. E., & Sejnowski, T. J. (1986). Learning and relearning in Boltzmann machines. In D. E. Rumelhart & J. L. McClelland (Eds.), *Parallel distributing processing: Vol. 1 Foundations* (Chapter 7). Cambridge, MA: MIT.

Horner, J., Heyman, A., Dawson, D., & Rogers, H. (1988). The relationship of agraphia to the severity of dementia in Alzheimer's disease. *Archives of Neurology, 45*, 760–763.

Humphreys, G. W., Riddoch, M. J., & Quinlan, P. T. (1988). Cascade process in picture identification. *Cognitive Neuropsychology, 5*, 67–103.

Kaplan, E., Goodglass, H., & Weintraub, S. (1983). *Boston naming test.* Philadelphia: Lea & Febiger.

Kapur, N., & Lawton, N. F. (1983). Dysgraphia for letters: A form of motor memory deficit? *Journal of Neurology, Neurosurgery, and Psychiatry, 46*, 573–575.

Keele, S., Cohen, A., & Ivry, R. (1990). Motor programs: Concepts and issues. *Attention and performance XIII: Motor representation and control*, (Chapter 3). In M. Jeannerod (Ed.), Hillsdale, NJ: Lawrence Erlbaum.

Lebrun, Y. (1976). Neurolinguistic models of language and speech. In H. Whitaker and H. A. Whitaker (Eds.), *Studies in neurolinguistics, Vol. 1* (pp. 1–30). New York: Academic Press.

Lesser, R. (1989). Selective preservation of oral spelling without semantics in a case of multi-infarct dementia. *Cortex*, *25*, 239–250.

Lesser, R. (1990). Superior oral to written spelling: Evidence for separate buffers? *Cognitive Neuropsychology*, *7*, 347–366.

Levine, D. N., Mani, R. B., & Calvanio, R. (1988). Pure agraphia and Gerstmann's syndrome as a visuospatial-language dissociation: An experimental case study. *Brain and Language*, *35*, 172–196.

Margolin, D. I. (1984). The neuropsychology of writing and spelling: Semantic, phonological, motor, and perceptual processes. *Quarterly Journal of Experimental Psychology*, *34A*, 459–489.

Margolin, D. I. (1991). Cognitive neuropsychology: Resolving enigmas about Wernicke's aphasia and other higher cortical disorders. *Archives of Neurology*, *48*, 751–765.

Margolin, D. I., & Binder, L. (1984). Multiple component agraphia in a patient with atypical cerebral dominance: An error analysis. *Brain and Language*, *22*, 26–40.

Margolin, D. I., Pate, D. S., Friedrich, F. J., & Elia, B. (1990). Dysnomia in dementia and in stroke patients: Different underlying cognitive deficits. *Journal of Clinical and Experimental Neuropsychology*, *12*, 597–612.

Margolin, D. I., & Wing, A. (1983). Agraphia and micrographia: Clinical manifestations of motor programming and performance disorders. *Acta Psychologica*, *54*, 263–283.

Marsden, C. D. (1982). The mysterious motor function of the basal ganglia: The Robert Wartenberg Lecture. *Neurology*, *32*, 514–539.

McClelland, J. C., & Rumelhart, D. E. (1981). An interactive model of context effects in letter perception: Part 1. An account of basic findings. *Psychological Review*, *88*, 375–407.

McClelland, J. C., & Rumelhart, D. E. (1988). *Explorations in the microstructure of cognition, Volume 2: Psychological and biological models*. Cambridge, MA: MIT Press.

Micelli, G., Silveri, M., & Caramazza, A. (1985). Cognitive analysis of a case of pure dysgraphia. *Brain and Language*, *25*, 187–196.

Morris, R. G., & Kopelman, M. D. (1986). The memory deficits in Alzheimer's type dementia: A review. *Quarterly Journal of Experimental Psychology*, *38A*, 575–602.

Paillard, J. (1982). Apraxia and the neurophysiology of motor control. *Philosphical Transactions of the Royal Society of London*, *B298*, 111–134.

Pate, D. S., & Margolin, D. I. (1990, May). *Disruption of the spelling system: Evidence for interlevel interaction*. Poster presented at the meeting of the American Academy of Neurology, Miami Beach, FL. *Neurology*, *40* (Suppl. 1), 241, 1990.

Patterson, K. (1986). Lexical but not nonsemantic spelling? *Cognitive Neuropsychology*, *3*, 341–367.

Patterson, K. (1989). Acquired disorders of spelling. In G. Denes, C. Semenza, P. Bisiacchi, & E. Andreewsky (Eds.), *Perspectives on Cognitive Neuropsychology*. London: Erlbaum.

Patterson, K., & Shewell, C. (1987). Speak and spell: Dissociations and word-class effects.

In M. Coltheart, G. Sartori, & R. Job (Eds.), *The cognitive neuropsychology of language* (pp. 273–294). London: Erlbaum Associates.

Patterson, K., & Wing, A. M. (1989). Processes in handwriting: A case for case. *Cognitive Neuropsychology*, *6*, 1–23.

Posteraro, L., Zinelli, P., & Mazzucchi, A. (1988). Selective impairment of the graphemic buffer in acquired dysgraphia: A case study. *Brain and Language*, *35*, 274–286.

Rapcsak, S. Z., Arthur, S. A., Bliklen, D. A., & Rubens, A. B. (1989). Lexical agraphia in Alzheimer's disease. *Archives of Neurology*, *46*, 65–68.

Rapcsak, S. Z., Arthur, S. A., & Rubens, A. B. (1988). Lexical agraphia from focal lesion of the left precentral gyrus. *Neurology*, *38*, 1119–1123.

Rapcsak, S. L., & Rubens, A. B. (1990). Disruption of semantic influence on writing following a left prefrontal lesion. *Brain and Language*, *38*, 334–344.

Roeltgen, D. P., & Heilman, K. (1983). Apractic agraphia in a patient with normal praxis. *Brain and Language*, *18*, 35–46.

Roeltgen, D. P., Rothi, L. G., & Heilman, K. M. (1986). Linguistic semantic agraphia: A dissociation of the lexical spelling system from semantics. *Brain and Language*, *27*, 257–280.

Rumelhart, D. E., & McClelland, J. L. (1988). *Explorations in the microstructure of cognition, Volume 1: Foundations.* Cambridge, MA: MIT Press.

Schechter, I., Bar-Israel, J., Ben-Nun, Y., & Bergman, M. (1985). The phonemic analysis as a treatment method in dysgraphia patients. *Scandanavian Journal of Rehabilitation Medicine*, Suppl. *12*, 80–83.

Schwartz, M. F., Marin, O., & Saffran, E. (1979). Dissociations of language function in dementia, a case study. *Brain and Language*, *7*, 277–306.

Schwartz, M. F., Saffran, E. M., & Marin, O. S. M. (1980). Fractionating the reading process in dementia: Evidence for word-specific print-to-sound associations. In M. Coltheart, K. Patterson, & J. C. Marshall (Eds.), *Deep dyslexia* (Chapter 12). London: Routledge & Kegan Paul.

Selnes, O. A., Zubens, A. B., Risse, G. L., & Levy, R. S. (1982). Transient aphasia with persistent apraxia. *Archives of Neurology*, *39*, 122–126.

Shallice, T. (1987). Impairments of semantic processing: Multiple dissociations. In M. Coltheart, G. Sartori, & R. Job (Eds.), *The cognitive neuropsychology of language* (Chapter 5). London: Erlbaum.

Shallice, T. (1988). *From neuropsychology to mental structure.* Cambridge: Cambridge University.

Warrington, E. K., & Shallice, T. (1979). Semantic access dyslexia. *Brain*, *102*, 43–63.

Weingartner, H., Grafman, J., Boutelle, W., Kaye, W., & Martin, P. R. (1983). Forms of memory failure. *Science*, *221*, 380–382.

Wernicke, C. (1968). The symptom complex of aphasia. (Trans.) *Boston Studies in the Philosophy of Science*, *4*, 34–97. (Original published 1874.)

Wood, C. C. (1978). Variations of a theme on Lashley: Lesion experiments of the neural model of Anderson, Silverstein, Ritz, & Jones. *Psychological Review*, *85*, 582–591.

Wing, A. M., Keele, S., & Margolin, D. I. (1984). Motor disorder and the timing of repetitive movement. *Annals of the New York Academy of Science*, *423*, 183–192.

Wood, C. C. (1982). Implications of simulated lesion experiments for the interpretation of lesions in real nervous systems. In M. A. Arbib, D. Caplan, & J. C. Marshall (Eds.), *Neural models of language processes.* New York: Academic Press.

Appendix 10-1 Johns Hopkins University Dysgraphia Battery

I. Primary Tasks

A. Writing to dictation

Subsets of stimuli postulated to assess lexical processes:

1. Grammatical word class
2. Word concreteness
3. Word frequency

Subsets of stimuli postulated to assess nonlexical and post-graphemic processes:

1. Nonwords
2. Probability of phoneme-grapheme conversion mappings
3. Word length

B. Oral spelling

II. Associated Tasks

C. Written spelling to picture confrontation

D. Written picture description

E. Copy transcoding

1. Direct copy transcoding
2. Delayed copy transcoding

III. Error Coding

Each response error is analyzed and placed into one of the following error categories:

1. Phonologically Plausible Errors (PPE)

Example Stimulus	Example Response
curtain	kirtin
chorus	courress
fabric	phabrick
surface	cerfiss

2. Spelling Errors

a. Substitutions (e.g., 'adgice' for ADVICE)
b. Deletions (e.g., 'adice' for ADVICE)
c. Transpositions (e.g., 'adevic' for ADVICE)
d. Additions (e.g., 'adtvice' for ADVICE)
e. Multiple

3. Visually/Phonologically Similar Word Responses

Example Stimulus	Example Response
ship	shop
work	worst
relate	delete

4. Semantic Errors

Example Stimulus	Example Response
fish	boat
preacher	minister
wonderful	fantastic

Appendix 10-1 *(Continued)*

5. Semantic or Visually Similar Word Responses

Example Stimulus	Example Response
coat	cloak
reach	catch
dinner	liver

6. Visual-to-Semantic Errors

Example Stimulus	Example Response	(inferred visual error)
cap	dog	(cat)
dump	stupid	(dumb)
true	bush	(tree)

7. Morphologically Related Errors

Example Stimulus	Example Response	Error Type
run	running	Inflectional
entertain	entertainment	Derivational

8. Function Word Substitutions

Example Stimulus	Example Response
your	mine
this	because
she	him

9. Function Word Substitution or Visually Similar Word Response

Example Stimulus	Example Response
mine	me
she	her
could	should

10. Homophone Confusions

Example Stimulus	Example Response
suite—a group of connected rooms	sweet
ate—having eaten something	eight
nun—a religious woman	none

11. Partial Responses, or Gaps

Example Stimulus	Example Response
partial	pa _ _ _ _
response	res _ _ _ _
counts	co _ nt

12. "Don't Know" Responses

13. Miscellaneous Errors

11

Processes, Breakdowns, and Remediation in Developmental Disorders of Reading and Spelling

DAVID P. ROELTGEN and PENNI BLASKEY

Developmental disorders of written language are usually divided into the disorders labeled developmental dyslexias and contrasted with those disorders labeled developmental dysgraphias. The first group includes those developmental abnormalities that lead to difficulty with reading. Most models of developmental dyslexia have primarily addressed difficulties with oral reading, although some have also addressed difficulties with reading comprehension. However, all of these models primarily address linguistic components of reading. The second group of disorders in this dichotomy are the developmental dysgraphias. In contrast to the approach to the developmental dyslexias, models that address the developmental dysgraphias have frequently divided the dysgraphias into two groups. These groups include disorders dealing with the linguistic components, those cognitive systems necessary for correct word and letter choice (spelling), and the motor components, those cognitive systems necessary for the correct formation of letters (handwriting). This chapter will be limited to linguistic disorders: reading and spelling.

Multiple models have been used in analysis of the linguistic breakdown of developmental disorders of reading, spelling, or both. However, most of these models have been applied to developmental dyslexia. Two methods frequently used for developing these models have been (1) use of a computerized descriptive analysis that groups subjects based on neuropsychological profiles (Fletcher & Satz, 1985) and (2) clinical observations and inference to form groups with similar strengths and weaknesses (Mattis, French, & Rapin, 1975). These models have predominantly emphasized the association of the subject's other neuropsychological strengths and weaknesses with reading disability, rather than categorizing the reading or spelling disability based on analysis of the actual reading and spelling performance by the subjects. Such approaches have received considerable criticism (Siegel, 1988) because of their approach, an emphasis on associated findings, and lack of analysis of the cognitive deficits that lead to the poor performance. An alternative approach is to start with a model, and on its basis perform linguistic analysis of reading samples, and in the case of developmental agraphia, writing samples. This information can then be used in an attempt to understand what significant cognitive properties may be preserved or impaired. One study of this type was that by Boder (1973) who described three types of dyslexia: dysphonetic (impaired sound-symbol integration), dyseidetic (impaired visual gestalt), and mixed dysphonetic-dyseidetic (a combination). A similar study that was limited to developmental dysgraphia was that by Sweeney and Rourke (1978). They found differences between two groups of children, one was phonetically accurate and one was not. Other studies, with special emphasis on whether or not the children read and/or spelled phonetically have also examined children's linguistic abilities (Campbell, 1985; Frith, 1985; Snowling, Stackhouse, & Rack, 1986; Temple, 1986).

Such detailed analyses of behavior have been used, as described in other portions of this book, for developing behavioral models based on information processing systems. These models can be used to evaluate the specific behaviors in children with developmental disorders of written language. In addition, the models can be used to develop and evaluate remediation schemes that have a basis in cognitive function and dysfunction.

In this context, this chapter is an attempt to briefly contrast two differing frameworks as they apply to linguistic disorders of written language (reading and spelling). In describing these frameworks or approaches, both theoretical background and empirical evidence related to those frameworks will be discussed. Using these frameworks as background, a cognitive neuropsychological approach to assessment will be described. This will be followed by case discussions that will illustrate certain features of the models, highlight assessment issues and generate discussion regarding remediation.

COGNITIVE FRAMEWORKS APPLICABLE TO DEVELOPMENTAL DYSLEXIA AND DEVELOPMENTAL LINGUISTIC DYSGRAPHIA

The cognitive approach to linguistic disorders of written language examines reproducible patterns of performance on selected cognitive tasks designed to delineate cognitive breakdowns. It also uses error analysis designed to examine the same cognitive features. This approach is used in order to better develop the understanding of the cognitive systems underlying the normal development and a better understanding of their breakdown in developmental dyslexia. There is a controversy within the group of studies that use this approach. Some investigations, and the models from which they are derived, fall within a framework that stresses the similarity between acquired and developmental disorders, implying similar cognitive substrates for reading and spelling in adults and children. In addition, this framework incorporates the position that in children with normally developing reading and spelling, the cognitive functions necessary for these abilities develop relatively independently of one another. Furthermore, this framework also implies that in children with reading or spelling impairment these functions still develop relatively independently of one another. Such models utilize relatively independent modules that are capable of developing normally when other written language modules are not developing normally (Marshall, 1987).

The alternative position is a framework that stresses dissimilarity between the disrupted cognitive substrates in children with developmental disorders of writing language and adults with acquired disorders of written language (Baddeley & Logie, 1988). Supporters of this position argue that the apparent similarity between acquired and developmental disorders is secondary to the limited patterns of deficit that can be found, given the behaviors (reading and spelling) that are being measured. They further argue that rather than independent modules, the cognitive mechanisms of written language consist of sequentially dependent systems, and that the normal development of certain systems is dependent on the normal development of other systems. For example, Frith (1985, 1986) and Morton (1987) argue that the normal development of highly skilled, automatic reading (what they term orthographic reading) is dependent on the normal development of a phonologic letter-by-letter or phoneme-by-phoneme stage of development of reading and spelling development (what they term alphabetic).

Developmentally Independent Systems

Previous chapters in this book have provided detailed descriptions of processing models which explain reading and spelling in normal and brain-damaged adults. Caramazza and Hillis (Chapter 9) have provided a multiple system model for reading with descriptions of the clinical syndromes that have been used to first develop, then refine, and support the model. This model postulates that three dissociable systems or routes subserve reading: sublexical phonological, lexical phonological, and semantic. The application of a multiple system or route reading model to children with developmental disorders provide a framework that can be used to assess children, develop more specific models, and perhaps plan remediation.

Those who argue that the models of adult reading should be applied to developmental disorders of reading cite as evidence the finding of developmental dyslexic and dysgraphic disorders in children that are qualitatively similar to acquired dyslexic and dysgraphic disorders in adults. For example, developmental phonological dyslexia, developmental surface dyslexia, developmental semantic dyslexia (called hyperlexia), and developmental deep dyslexia have been described. It is argued that the child with one of these reading disorders who has difficulties with one or more of the systems or routes shows an overreliance on the remaining systems. It is also implied, though rarely explicitly stated, that an abnormality of one system or route will not preclude the normal development and use of the alternate systems or routes.

Difficulty with phonological reading (and usually accompanying difficulty with phonological spelling) has been extensively studied. It has been suggested by some authors that this difficulty is the hallmark of developmental dyslexia. Such difficulty has been termed developmental phonological dyslexia (Snowling et al., 1986; Siegel & Faux, 1987; Siegel, 1986). Children with this disorder have difficulty reading nonsense words as their striking feature. However, most of these children have a more generalized dyslexia in the sense that they have impaired real-word reading as well. Therefore, it has been argued by those who support the use of adult models that the phonological system is important during the normal acquisition of literacy (Marshall, 1987). This would also further suggest that there is a close relationship between the development of those systems important for phonological processing and those systems important for real word processing.

Overrreliance on the phonological system or route, with difficulties in the direct or lexical route and the semantic route has been termed developmental surface dyslexia. It has been described in some children and is characterized by relatively good reading of regular words and nonsense words accompanied by difficulty reading irregular words. The irregular words tend to be regularized (i.e., island as /aIs' lænd/[iceland]). In children who have this type of difficulty their ability to access semantics tends to be tied to the regularization of the response. Marshall (1987), for example, describes the reading of bristle (with a silent t) as being read as Bristol, a town in England.

Impairment of the semantic system or route, (along with a spared lexical phonological system) acquired semantic alexia in adults, has been described in detail in children with a certain form of reading disorder, hyperlexia. Children with this difficulty usually have some ability to read nonsense words (use of the sublexical phonologic system). Their most striking feature is a superb ability to read real words that are both regular and irregular, despite being unable to access or utilize the meaning of these words (Glosser, Roeltgen, & Friedman, 1991; Welsh, Pennington, & Rogers, 1987). Two such children will be described in the case studies section.

Lastly, insofar as the use of the adult model as a framework for assessing developmental disorders is concerned, is the syndrome of developmental deep dyslexia. Children who have difficulty reading nonsense words (evidence of impairment of the sublexical phonologic system) and who make semantic paralexias have been described. Siegel (1985) described six children who showed reading behaviors consistent with this diagnosis.

Implicit in the use of adult models in attempts to understand developmental dyslexia is the use of similar models for understanding developmental dysgraphia. Such a model of spelling is described in the chapter by Margolin and Goodman-Schulman. As with the models of reading, these models of spelling usually include three systems: a sublexical phonological system, a direct or lexical (or orthographic) system, and a semantic system. Similar to that found in the reading models, these systems are thought to function in parallel. Such a model predicts at least three types of acquired and developmental disorders of spelling, including acquired and developmental phonological dysgraphia, acquired and developmental surface or lexical dysgraphia, and acquired and developmental semantic dysgraphia. The acquired disorders are discussed previously in this volume. In adults with developmental spelling impairment, the first two developmental disorders have been described by Roeltgen and Tucker (1988) who described two groups of adults with developmental spelling impairments. The first group, subjects with developmental phonological dysgraphia, spelled regular and irregular words equally well but had difficulty spelling nonsense words. On a

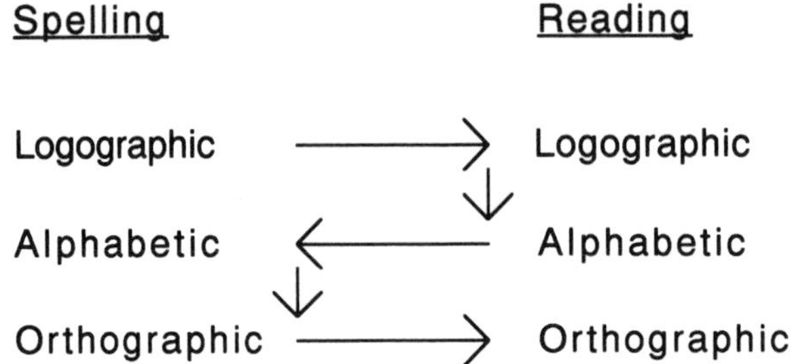

Figure 11-1 A model of the development of normal literacy (after Frith, 1985, 1988).

quantitative (analysis of variance) and qualitative analysis (multidimensional scaling) utilizing performance on real (orthographically regular and irregular) and nonsense words, this group of subjects was indistinguishable from patients with acquired phonological dysgraphia. The second group of subjects was described as having developmental lexical dysgraphia. These subjects spelled the nonwords well but had difficulty spelling orthographically irregular words relative to orthographically regular words. On analysis this group was similar to a group of subjects with acquired lexical agraphia. These authors concluded that the adult models of acquired spelling might be applicable to developmental disorders. However, because this study was limited to adults, there are concerns regarding whether its conclusions can be generalized to children.

Developmentally Dependent Systems

In contrast to the use of adult models with systems of modules applied to specific cognitive functions, is a framework that emphasizes developmental acquisition of abilities in which each of the sequential acquisitions is dependent upon the normal acquisition of previous abilities. Frith (1985, 1986) has proposed a model of the development of normal literacy that encompasses three basic stages: logographic, alphabetic, and orthographic (Figure 11-1). These three stages are thought to be applicable to both reading and spelling.

The first stage is the logographic stage. This stage is described as that stage of reading when there is an instant recognition of familiar words, using salient graphic features but largely ignoring letter order. Although Frith does not explicitly indicate what she means by salient graphic features, there are certain features implied by her descriptions and those of Snowling and colleagues (1986). Perhaps the most likely important features are major (initial and visually distinctive, ascending and descending) consonants. It is thought that there is an important visual component and that phonological factors that may be present are only minimally utilized. In addition, it is thought that context and pragmatics are highly utilized and that guessing is common. Logographic reading would be that ability to read the letters STOP in the context of an eight-sided red sign. In contrast, those same letters presented out of the context of the eight-sided red sign would not be read correctly. It is Frith's contention that logographic reading precedes logographic writing. Furthermore, logographic writing is thought to be one of the first examples of a "sight vocabulary" (Morton, 1987). It is

Morton's opinion that these words are learned from copying. Frequently the responses are not recognizable and are usually not perfect copies.

The second stage is the alphabetic stage. At this stage the reader is thought to use individual phonemes and graphemes and their correspondences. This stage is described as being analytic or letter-by-letter and systematic, utilizing grapheme-by-grapheme or phoneme-by-phoneme decoding. In the alphabetic system, letter order and phonology are thought to be extremely important in the developing reader and speller for pronouncing and spelling novel and nonsense words. Frith explicitly states that the alphabetic writing system should replace logographic writing and that it should precede alphabetic reading. This alphabetic writing system is very dependent upon phonemic segmentation. It is argued that with the initial acquisition of this system, words that may have been correctly read by the child in the logographic phase are now incorrectly written (Morton, 1987), because the child is using alphabetic spelling according to the Frith model. Frith has argued that the understanding of grapheme/phoneme representations are influenced by the existence of phoneme/grapheme rules that were developed or are being developed during the alphabetic writing stage. Morton suggests that the initial phase of alphabetic reading has little in the way of semantic access because of the lack of feedback to the semantic system, but with development it gains better access.

The final stage, orthographic, is described as a level of processing that yields instant analysis of words by orthographic units without phonological conversion. As such, it utilizes a letter code at a level more abstract that the visual match (logographic) and less analytic or letter-by-letter than the alphabetic stage. Ideally the orthographic units coincide with morphemes or other sublexical but nonphonologic representations. It is argued by Frith that the normal acquisition of orthographic reading stage is dependent upon the normal development of the alphabetic systems. Furthermore, Morton (1987) argues that the progress to the orthographic stage is an almost automatic consequence of the interaction of reading, linguistic knowledge, and other cognitive processes, as long as the alphabetic stages are mastered. Orthographic spelling is similarly thought to depend both on the normal development of the alphabetic systems as well as development of orthographic reading.

In addition to the sequential model of Frith (1985, 1986), Marsh and colleagues (1981) and Seymour and MacGregor (1984) have proposed models using a similar sequential framework. However, their models do not require that the normal development of one stage be dependent on the normal development of a preceding stage.

Most of the details postulated by these sequential models await empirical support. The best method to assess them would be detailed longitudinal data of both normally developing readers and children with developmental dyslexia, dysgraphia or both. Only rarely have longitudinal studies been performed. However, the few longitudinal studies available as well as certain nonlongitudinal studies do allow examination of certain features of these models.

Stuart and Coltheart (1988) used a longitudinal study to examine early acquisition of reading in an attempt to test the early stages of these sequential models. They argued that their data supported the position that initial reading

Table 11-1 Children Taught With and Without Emphasis on Phonics

Results for Grades 1–3

	A (n = 16)	*B (n = 18)*
Age	7.9	7.4
LAC	70.9[c]	48.9[c]
WRAT-R/Sp	2.8	2.4
NW-Sp	46.9[b]	25.4[b]
WRAT-R/Rd	3.0	2.4
NW-Rd	44.8[a]	29.9[a]

Results for Ages 6–8

	A (n = 12)	*B (n = 17)*
Grade	1.2	1.5
LAC	75.9[c]	47.6[c]
WRAT-R/Sp	2.2	2.6
NW-Sp	38.7[b]	22.7[b]
WRAT-R/Rd	2.3	2.2
NW-Rd	36.4	28.5

Note: Results comparing assessment of two groups of school children. Group A: children from the school emphasizing phonics. Group B: children from the school using a whole word approach. (WRAT-R: Wide Range Achievement Test—Revised [Jastak & Wilkenson, 1984], NW: nonword performance from the Battery of Linguistic Analysis for Writing and Reading [Roeltgen, 1989].)
[a]$p < .1$.
[b]$p < .01$.
[c]$p < .001$.

in many normal readers was related to phonological (or in Frith's words, alphabetic) skills and was not logographic. In contrast, other authors have argued from their results that, although phonological processing skills may predict skill in reading, initial word recognition has an important logographic component (Seymour & Elder, 1986).

In this context, Roeltgen and Fonteyne (1990) studied two groups of normally developing school children (Table 11-1). One group was taught with an emphasis on phonics, including frequent spontaneous writing using "creative" spelling (spelling words as they sound), and one group was taught using a "whole word" visual approach without phonics. Although both groups had equal achievement levels, consistent with their ages and grades, there was a significant difference between their phonological processing ability, especially in the younger children. These children differed both on nonword ability and on a nonlinguistic test of phonological processing, involving segmentation and phonological translation, the Lindamood Test of Auditory conceptualization (LAC) (Lindamood & Lindamood, 1979). Furthermore, errors from both groups were analyzed using an error analysis designed to examine phonological accuracy (Roeltgen, personal communication, 1991). The readers from both groups with lower achievement made many more nonphonological or logographic errors than did readers with higher achievement. Lastly, the group taught by the whole word method made more logographic errors (errors consistent with a logographic approach) than did the group taught by the phonics method. These results support the contention that although phonological processing skill highly predicts reading acquisition

Table 11-2 Nonword Reading Compared to Nonword Spelling

Results

Group	Achievement Level
Group I	Sp or Rd < Gr 1
Group II	Sp and Rd = Gr 1–2B (Sp or Rd)
Group III	Sp and Rd = Gr 2B, M, E
Group IV	Sp and Rd = Gr 2/3 mixed
Group V	Sp and Rd = Gr 3, Gr. 3/4 mixed, Gr 4
Group VI	Sp and Rd = Gr 4/5–Gr 6/7
Group VII	Sp and Rd = Gr 6/7

Means for Nonwords by Group

	Sp	*Rd*		*Sp*	*Rd*
I	5.8	1.0	IV	52.8	54.4
II	16.6	14.8	V	47.7	60.9
III	34.6	33.6	VI	72.0	75.3
			VII	86.0	87.3

Note: Results for Subjects grouped by Achievement (To assess for Alphabetic Spelling preceding Alphabetic Reading). Groups I–III vs. IV–VII (All S): ANOVA Interaction $p < .03$. Achievement determined by grade equivalent score from the WRAT-R. B: beginning, M: middle, E: end.

ability, a logographic approach accounts for at least a portion of initial word recognition.

Roeltgen and Fonteyne (1990) also examined the prediction made by the Frith model that alphabetic spelling precedes alphabetic reading. This would predict better nonword performance when spelling than reading in children at lower achievement levels. Roeltgen and Fonteyne combined both groups of children and examined their nonword spelling and reading ability. They found that in comparing lower achieving (younger age and earlier grade) children (less than third grade achievement) with higher achieving children, there was a group by task interaction (Table 11-2). This result is consistent with Frith's proposal that alphabetic spelling drives alphabetic reading at low achievement levels in normally developing children.

Other studies have examined later stages of Frith's model. Frith described a group of adolescents with unexpectedly poor spelling but relatively good reading. Their performance was consistent with relatively good phonological (or in Frith's terminology, alphabetic) ability. Frith argued, based on these and other data, that good readers/poor spellers had normal phonological processing but impaired orthographic processing, especially at the final stage of linguistic acquisition, the stage important for good spelling ability.

Although previous data on studies of developmental phonological and lexical agraphia (Roeltgen and Tucker, 1988) clearly delineate two groups, and Frith's data argue for a specific category of good readers/poor spellers, recent data have led us (Blaskey & Roeltgen, 1990) to believe that the conclusions regarding the existence of two distinct spelling types of developmental disorders may be an oversimplification. We have recently studied a group of adolescents who produced a wide range of reading and spelling abilities, in order to examine adolescents who might be classified as good readers/poor spellers. In addition, the study was designed to examine the relationships among written language achievement, ability to read and spell regular and irregular words and phonological ability. This group of subjects had a range of IQ scores that were, for the most part, above average. Selected examples of these subjects are presented later in this chapter. Although the results formed a continuum, eight of the subjects performed relatively well on reading and performed poorly on spelling, filling the category of "good readers/poor spellers." On the same set of spelling tests that were previously given to subjects in Roeltgen and Tucker's study, this group of subjects performed in a manner almost identical to the subjects with developmental lexical agraphia as described by Roeltgen and Tucker (good nonword spelling and better performance on spelling orthographically regular compared to irregular words, 1988). However, there was variability among this group of adolescent subjects. One subject had reading ability that was similar to that found in a group of 12 age-matched controls, but the others did not. Therefore, there was only one subject who completely fulfilled the criteria of having normal reading, poor spelling, and normal phonological ability. The seven other subjects had relatively good reading for their age and education (standard scores on word identification of 95–109) but had reading results at least one standard deviation less than the normal control subjects. This finding is similar to that of Frith (1979) who found that good readers who were poor spellers read more slowly than good readers who were good spellers. Six of Blaskey and Roeltgen's seven poor-spelling subjects also read nonwords less well than the control subjects. These results suggest that adolescents who have impairment in the orthographic system for spelling (as defined by impaired spelling performance and a regular-irregular word difference), may also have mild impairment in the alphabetic (phonological) system. Therefore, Blaskey and Roeltgen concluded that a strong version of the Frith model, requiring normal alphabetic performance in adolescents with good reading and poor spelling, is inconsistent with the data. However, if the Frith model is viewed as a continuum, in which the development of better orthographic ability depends on continuing improvement in alphabetic ability, then the data are consistent with the model. The model can therefore be viewed in the following manner: Orthographic function is dependent on the development of a functional alphabetic system. With a moderate, though not normal degree of alphabetic ability, a moderate degree of orthographic reading ability, as measured by word identification of regular and irregular words, follows. In turn, development of orthographic spelling ability follows, but does not develop fully unless there is full and normal development of the alphabetic reading and spelling stage and orthographic reading.

Data such as those described here neither directly support nor refute either framework for viewing the development of linguistic processes. However, models such as Frith's that emphasize the development of stages that are dependent on previous stages, provide testable hypotheses and offer a possible conceptualization that acknowledges interactive and interdependent development of brain systems.

ASSESSMENT

The debate regarding whether the modular developing (or independently developing systems) framework or the sequential acquisition framework better explains the normal and abnormal development of linguistic written language skills is important theoretically and may have importance for approaches to written language instruction and remediation. However, it might be best to consider both frameworks (Baddeley, Logie, & Ellis, 1988), especially when considering methods of assessment. Only with assessment of each of the important cognitive processes can a better understanding of normal and abnormal acquisition of reading and spelling ability be developed.

Before proceeding with the detailed discussion of the methods used to analyze specific linguistic systems, it is important to briefly review those general aspects of cognitive and reading ability necessary for adequate description of the subject or subjects being tested. Classically, the diagnosis of developmental dyslexia has frequently rested upon discrepancy criteria. A discrepancy analysis contrasts a child's reading ability, frequently measured as a standard score on an achievement test, with his or her general cognitive ability, as measured by a standard IQ measure. If a significant difference, defined arbitrarily, but usually approximately a 15-point difference, is found, a child is classified as dyslexic. However, multiple studies have questioned this position. Stuart and Coltheart showed that IQ scores were significant predictors of reading age only for the very earliest achievement (1988). Later levels of achievement were predicted not by IQ but by phonological ability. They therefore suggested that more intelligent children, when not capable of phonological analysis, will have more strategies available for memorizing printed words to which they are exposed than will less intelligent children. However, this advantage is soon rapidly outweighed by the development of phonological understanding. A different approach to the same question was used by Scott (1987). He showed that poor readers with average or above average intelligence (developmental dyslexics) had the same pattern of phonological impairment as poor readers with less than average IQ (traditionally classified as slow learners) and that phonological impairment rather than IQ predicted reading ability. In addition, Blaskey and Roeltgen showed that adolescents with average or above average IQ may have a range of performance on reading and spelling assessment, and that the degree of impairment is related to phonological ability. An additional larger scale study was that by Siegel (1988) who performed a meta-analysis of data from several studies that included 250 reading disabled and 719 non-reading disabled (normally achieving) individuals. She showed that language and short-term memory processes were deficient in the learning disabled children, independent of IQ level, and that IQ level did not predict ability to perform on other cognitive processes important for written language. She therefore concluded that intelligence test scores do not appear to be relevant to the diagnosis of reading disability and that there was no justification for the discrepancy criteria in the definition of reading disability. She further stated that detailed analyses of specific skills and information processing abilities were more important for analysis of developmental dyslexia than scores on intelligence tests.

Although discrepancy criteria do not appear to be important for diagnosis of developmental dyslexia or developmental dysgraphia, standard achievement test scores do provide useful information. It is necessary to obtain general measures of reading and spelling ability that are independent of the specific instruments used to measure the cognitive processes that underlie the general ability being evaluated. For example, although the WRAT-R does not provide the type of cognitive assessment provided by word lists described later in this chapter, it does provide a standardized and independent measure of single word reading and spelling ability. In addition to the WRAT-R, there are other standard assessment tools that measure reading and spelling. However, as Voeller (personal communication, 1990) has described, the standard published assessment tools were not designed in the context of linguistic processing models and therefore do not help assess them.

Assessment of Specific Cognitive Processes

Utilizing the frameworks described previously, one of the authors (DPR), has developed a series of tests designed to examine those features of written language processing proposed by the various models.

Based on these models certain linguistic features are important for analysis and others are important to be kept constant because they may influence the outcome. The first major distinction is that between nonwords and the real words. Nonwords are important for analyzing the subject's ability to perform phonological (or alphabetic) analysis and output of written material. Real words are important for analysis of other factors including the effects of word class, degree of imagability, degree of orthographic regularity (as it compares to the phonology of the stimulus), degree of phoneme-grapheme ambiguity (between the stimulus and response), and semantic ability. Variables for which control is needed include the age of acquisition, the frequency of occurrence and the length of the stimuli.

For the nonwords important features include the complexity of the stimulus (one to one phoneme-grapheme or grapheme-phoneme correspondences, as compared to blends and diphthongs), the length of the stimulus and the similarity of the stimulus to real English words. This last feature may include pseudohomophones (e.g., fone), nonwords that clearly reflect English orthography (e.g., kalt) and nonwords that have "illegal" orthography or represent letter combinations that do not exist in real English words (e.g., kwaj).

The examination of the effect of word class is important for assessing phonological and deep dyslexias and dysgraphias (Beauvois & Dereousne, 1979; Shalice, 1981; Roeltgen, Sevush, & Heilman, 1983; Roeltgen & Heilman, 1985; Roeltgen, 1985). In examining word class, comparisons can be made among nouns, verbs, adjectives, and function words (Baddeley, Logie, & Ellis, 1988) or more simply between nouns and function words, the two groups of words that usually show the largest difference.

The examination of the effect of the degree of imagability is important for those disorders described as "deep" (dyslexia and dysgraphia; Bub & Kertesz, 1980; Coltheart, 1980; Roeltgen et al., 1983). Published or unpublished measures of imagability can be used to establish ratings. For both this feature and the previous one, limited data are available regarding their relationships to developmental disorders. However, a further discussion of them is available in the chapters on acquired disorders of reading and spelling.

Orthographic regularity and phoneme-grapheme ambiguity are thought to be important for examining the direct, lexical, or orthographic systems. Differences between performance on regular and irregular words has been described as being important in the diagnosis of surface dyslexia and surface or lexical dysgraphia, both in adults and children (Beauvois & Derouesne, 1981; Hatfield & Patterson, 1983; Margolin, 1984; Roeltgen, 1985; Roeltgen & Heilman, 1985; Baddeley et al., 1988). The degree of orthographic regularity or irregularity is usually operationally defined, as will be discussed later in this chapter. Ambiguity of pronunciation in a response to a spoken stimulus (such as reflected by the k sound (/k/) in cotton) is also thought to be important for analysis of the orthographic, lexical, or direct systems or routes in spelling but not reading (Roeltgen, 1985; Roeltgen & Heilman, 1984; Hatfield & Patterson, 1983). Ambiguity is operationally defined as the extent to which multiple letters may represent a single sound. In the above example, the k sound (/k/) may be represented by both the letter "k" and the letter "c" without violating cotton's phonology. Ambiguity can be divided into words of relatively low ambiguity (e.g., charm) or high ambiguity (e.g., cotton). Words of relatively low ambiguity are those for which there is only one acceptable American English spelling for a given phonology. Words of relatively high ambiguity are those for which there are two or more sounds (phonemes) that have more than one spelling that will provide the correct pronunciation. In the above example, the k (/k/) sound and the schwa (/ə/) sound may be spelled in more than one way, yet still yield the correct pronunciation (e.g., kotton and cottin).

Semantic ability is one additional area that is emphasized by the various models. Reading comprehension tests and analysis of errors are two ways that semantic ability has been assessed in reading. The assessment of semantic output in writing with the use of homophones is thought to be important both for lexical agraphia (Roeltgen & Heilman, 1984) and semantic agraphia (Roeltgen, Rothi, & Heilman, 1986).

The control variables listed previously have all been described as influencing written language ability and need to be addressed in assessing children's reading and spelling ability. For the age of acquisition, not only are there empirical data demonstrating this influence, but common sense would also indicate that words not learned until eighth grade have limited use when given to first and second graders. However, the means of measurement of the age of acquisition may vary. Some studies have utilized for development of their test instruments adult ratings as to whether words were acquired during early grades or later grades (Baddeley et al., 1988). Other studies have utilized the list of words grouped by the usual time of introduction into the elementary school curriculum (Roeltgen, 1989). Similarly, what would to be a simple matter, word frequency, may also be more complicated in terms of developing a test instrument for children. The frequency data of Thorndike and Lorge (1944) have had wide usage, both in adult and children's studies (Roeltgen, Sevush, & Heilman, 1983; Roeltgen

& Heilman, 1984; Baddeley et al., 1988). However, this list published in 1944 may not reflect current word frequency, and the higher frequency word comparisons are blurred by the lack of distinction for words that occur at frequencies above 50 per million. Both of these issues can be resolved by the use of the frequency counts developed by Francis and Kucera (1982). However, even with this source, there remains a major issue that is unaddressed and that is the frequency of words at different child ages or grade levels. Data on this clearly indicate that at one age, the frequency of a word may be strikingly different than at a different age. For example, "grow" has a frequency in third grade level material of 494 (per 1 million words) but a frequency of 47 in ninth grade material. In contrast, "type" has a frequency of 16 in third grade material but a frequency of 168 in ninth grade material (Carrol, Davies, & Richman, 1971). This information suggests that it might be necessary to rank words by their frequency at a given grade rather than by their general frequency, especially if that frequency is obtained from studies of adult reading materials. The last control variable, length, can be measured by the number of letters, syllables, morphemes or all three.

In addition to the word types and the variables for which control is needed, methods for comparison across different age groups need to be developed. Unlike the analysis of acquired dyslexia and dysgraphia where it might be possible to assume a certain base line reading and spelling competence prior to the disorder, such a base line assumption in children is heavily dependent upon the age and grade at which the children are examined.

One of the authors (DPR) has developed a test battery that attempts to address these experimental and control variables. The initial version was designed for assessment of adults and was termed the Battery of Linguistic Analysis for Writing and Reading (Roeltgen, Cordell, & Sevush, 1984; Roeltgen & Heilman, 1985). The BLAWR list was used by Roeltgen and Tucker (1988) for their study of developmental phonological and lexical agraphia in adults. The tests in this battery include nonwords and real words. There are four lists of pronounceable nonwords, each containing 10 one-syllable (e.g., *nid*, *fosh*, *mab*), and 10 two-syllable nonwords (e.g., *homfis*, *lodar*, *blumpkin*). The lists are all of relatively equal difficulty. This is to allow repeat assessments of a single subject without incurring a learning effect. The real word lists include matched sets of nouns and function words, words of high and low imagery, words that are either of regular or irregular orthography, words with ambiguous spelling relative to their pronunciations, and homophones.

There are three sets of nouns and function words, each containing 20 nouns (e.g., arm, chair and gold) and 20 function words (e.g., why, who and much). For each list the words are matched for length in letters, syllables, and morphemes as well as frequency. Two of the lists are matched by frequency using Thorndike and Lorge (1944), and the third list is matched using frequency data of Kucera and Francis (1967). All three sets of nouns and function words are of relatively equal difficulty.

For the comparison of words of high and low imagery, imagery ratings published by Paivio, Yuille, and Madigan (1968) were used. Words of high imagability include those with a rating of 6 or above, and those of low imagability include those rated as 4 or below. Each of the three sets contains 10 words of high (e.g., city, book, and child) and 10 words of low imagery (e.g., fate, law, and idea), and at each set they are matched for frequency (Kucera & Francis, 1967), length in letters, syllables, and morphemes and frequency of orthographically irregular words. The three sets are of gradually increasing difficulty.

For the groups of words that compare orthographically regular and irregular words, there are also three lists of increasing difficulty. The first two lists contain 20 regular and irregular words matched for length in letters, syllables, and morphemes, imagability (Paivio et al., 1968), frequency (Kucera & Francis, 1967) and word class (all are nouns). A word was considered regular if it could be spelled by an algorithmic (letter-by-letter), sound-to-letter method and read by a letter-to-sound conversion (e.g., moment, letter, nutmeg). With the exception of words with double vowels (e.g., speech, green), a word was considered irregular if it could not be spelled or read by an algorithmic (letter-by-letter) method (e.g., jealousy, marriage, glacier). Words were included only if they were irregular for both spelling and reading.

There are two lists of differing difficulty for the words of varying ambiguity. The first list contains 10 words of low ambiguity (e.g., hotel, charm, and anger), 10 words of medium ambiguity (e.g., green, temple, and speech) and 10 words of high ambiguity (e.g., city, breeze, and cotton), and the second list contains 10 words of low ambiguity, 10 words of medium-low ambiguity, 10 words of medium-high ambiguity, and ten words of very high ambiguity. For both lists, all groups of words are matched for the same variables as are the orthographically regular and irregular words.

The homophones list consists of 100 words containing homophonic dyads and triads with sentences containing the stimulus word to use for disambiguating the meaning of the stimulus. All of the homophones are listed as orthographically regular, orthographically irregular and relative high or low frequency as defined previously by Roeltgen, Rothi and Heilman (1986).

Although this battery has been of use in analyzing adults, including adults with developmental disorders (Roeltgen & Tucker, 1980) and contains important features for analysis of selected linguistic deficits, its use in children is severely limited by the lack of control for age of acquisition and frequency at specific grade or age levels. Also, for certain lists, length and complexity precludes the use of those lists with any children younger than approximately sixth grade level. In order to address this difficulty, an extension of the BLAWR to younger ages was developed, leading to the BLAWR-Children's Version (BLAWR-CV) (Roeltgen, 1989). On this test the nonwords range from two-phonemes and one syllable to multiple phonemes and four syllables in length. At each level (two phoneme, three phoneme and four phoneme one syllable nonwords, etc.) there are two groups. The first consists of nonwords with simple one-to-one phoneme-grapheme or grapheme-phoneme translation, such as *nud* (three phoneme), *kalt* (four phoneme) or *akvin* (two syllable). The second consists of consonant clusters such that there is one more grapheme than phoneme or blends, such as *zang* (three phoneme), *ferd* (four phoneme with a blend), *tharp* (four phoneme), or *uthvam* (two syllable with a blend). There are also a series of nonwords with stressed (long) vowels with simple consonant forms (e.g., *mebe*), complex consonant forms (e.g., *clape*) and two syllables (e.g., *imbebe*). There are a total of 80 one syllable nonwords, including 20 with stressed vowels. There are 24 two syllable nonwords, 10 three syllable nonwords and 10 four syllable nonwords. Most studies performed by the authors to date have used the one and two syllable stimuli.

For each of the real word groups in the BLAWR-CV, there are sets of increasing difficulty containing 10 words of each type (i.e., 10 nouns and 10 function words). The lists include nouns and function words, words of high and low imagery, orthographically regular and irregular words, words of high and low ambiguity and homophones. For each set of comparisons (i.e., 10 nouns and 10 function words), the block of words have gradually increasing difficulty as defined by decreasing frequency, increasing length in letters, syllables and morphemes, increased number of compound forms, and later age of acquisition (Thomas, 1974). The frequency determinations were made using the data of Carroll et al. (1971) and reflect the frequency of a given word at approximately its age of acquisition. Word lists were also matched for other variables when appropriate, including degree of orthographic regularity and ambiguity for nouns and function words; word class, degree of orthographic regularity and imagability for words of low or high ambiguity; word class, degree of orthographic regularity and ambiguity for words of high and low imagery; and word class, imagability, and degree of ambiguity for words of different orthographic regularity. Imagery ratings were obtained from van der Veur (1975), and words of high imagery averaged 5 or above and words of low imagery averaged 3 or lower. Criteria for other variables was the same as that used for the BLAWR.

The use of the BLAWR and the BLAWR-CV is described in the case studies that follow later in this chapter. These tests, although unpublished, are available from the first author.

In addition to tests included in the BLAWR and the BLAWR-CV, other assessment tools can be helpful in delineating the linguistic processing involved in the normal and abnormal development of reading and spelling. The types of nonwords used can be modified so as to stress an algorithmic phonologic process. Such a task would use those nonwords that do not conform to the usual patterns of English orthography (e.g., *kwaj*). Alternatively, nonwords can be used that examine whether there is a greater likelihood that the reading or spelling was performed by analogy with real words or by a letter-by-letter process. For example, in assessing spelling, a stimulus such as /wIs'tʃəf/ can be used and one can note whether the response reflects a translation at the phoneme-by-phoneme level producing "wischif," or whether there is a level of processing at a greater than letter level producing "wischief" as an analogy with mischief. For reading, stimuli such as *tave* can be used to determine whether the subject produces a "regular" pronunciation such as would be found with "save" or an irregular pronunciation such as would be found with "have."

Other tests that have been developed have been used in an attempt to assess the level of orthographic ability. These tasks include proof reading, as described by Ormrod (1985), letter cancellation within words, as described by Frith (1979), and morphological tests, such as adding prefixes and suffixes to real and nonwords, as described by Scholes (unpublished test). Unfortunately, insufficient data regarding the meaningfulness of these tests in children are available.

In addition to single word reading and spelling, an important aspect of analysis in determining linguistic processing is qualitative error analysis. Error analysis has been utilized in multiple studies (Holmes & Pepper, 1977; Temple, 1986; Sweeney & Rourke, 1978; Snowling et al., Stackhouse & Rack, 1986; Stuart & Coltheart, 1988; and recently in our studies, Roeltgen, unpublished manuscript). The major focus of all these studies is an attempt to delineate the type of processing or type of processing breakdown as demonstrated by the quality of the error.

Our error analysis distinguishes four types of errors at the word level. The first error type includes responses designated as phonologically accurate. Such responses are those responses that are identical to the phonology of the stimulus (e.g., "woch" for watch or "bilt" for built [written]) or reflect an over-reliance on phonological rules (e.g., "/seid/" (sade) for said [read]). Phonologically acceptable responses are the second error type. These responses contain letter or phoneme changes that fulfill certain criteria that suggest good phonological processing (e.g., "srprise" for surprise [written] or "/glaI'tʃər/" (glacher) for glacier [read]). The standard for classification within this group was developed from two criteria. First, we analyzed the productions from normal children with good phonological processing ability for their age and determined what errors were produced frequently. Second, we operationally defined certain criteria as being phonologically acceptable, based on similar acoustic properties between the response and the stimulus. This approach was an outgrowth of previous studies (Read, 1975; Snowling, 1982). Combined errors are the third type. These are errors with any number of acceptable phonologic changes but contain one component that differs from the stimulus in such a way that it is not phonologically acceptable (e.g., "equiment" for equipment [written] or "/pær tik eIp/" (partikape) for participate, [read]). Logographic errors are the fourth error type. These are errors that are phonologically inaccurate relative to the stimulus by at least two phonemes and usually contain a physical resemblance to the stimulus word (e.g., "maragitidy" for majority [written] or /di veIs/ (devise) for decisive [read]). An example of the use of this error analysis follows in the case report on developmental dyslexia.

REMEDIATION

Although extensive time, money, and effort have been used for remediating children with reading and spelling problems, only limited data are available regarding the efficacy of the various programs available. Based on the data that suggested a relationship between impaired phonological ability and impaired reading, Bradley and Bryant (1983) showed that reading proficiency could be improved with increased phonological awareness. In this context, multiple remediation techniques have been developed, emphasizing phonological ability. Two of these approaches include the Orton-Gillingham technique (Cox, 1985), one that emphasizes sound blending techniques, as well as instructions in rules and patterns governing spelling, and the Glass Analysis Program for Decoding. Glass (1976) has designated a structure program that emphasizes word families in words ranging from simple to complex (including multiple syllabic words) such as the use of "at" in mat and attic. Although these methods emphasize phonics, they, as well as other commonly used techniques, also frequently incorporate one or more other approaches, including kinesthetic feedback, whole language involvement and multisensory involvement, to greater or lesser degrees. These generalized approaches to remediation appear designed to capture the multiple possibilities by which a child may learn to read or spell. In a review of the paucity of data regarding the efficacy of remediation in dyslexia, Lovett and colleagues emphasized the fact that most evidence is anecdotal, or from poorly designed studies without control populations or lacks adequate statistical assessment. In this context, a study by Lovett and colleagues (Lovett, Ransby, Hardwick et al., 1989) is one of the first to show that use of a decoding skills program and an oral and written language skills program both improved reading and spelling performance in a group of dyslexic children, compared to children remediated with a classroom survival skills program. However, the effects from the decoding skills program were more generalized than those from the oral and written language program. What is uncertain, however, is whether their remediation technique is applicable to all subjects, or whether the possible heterogeneity of dyslexia is important in predicting outcome. In a recent abstract, Lovett and colleagues (Lovett, Benson, & Olds, 1990) suggested that the response to remediation could be predicted by pretest language assessment, verbal IQ and performance IQ, but these variables accounted for only a limited amount of posttest variance. They further suggested that dyslexia should be approached from the point of view of a continuum rather than a subtype model.

The results from these limited studies raise questions as to the relationships among performance, processing impairments, and remediation. Even given the results of Lovett and colleagues, it is still not at all clear whether individually guided remediation plans based on cognitive processing models will or will not have an impact on the overall outcome following remediation. Consequently, detailed discussion of these relationships awaits study.

CASE STUDIES

The following case studies are designed to illustrate certain issues. First, they have been chosen to help illustrate the cognitive neuropsychological approach to assessment of children's reading and spelling. In doing this, there are examples of different ages of children and different patterns of reading ability, including advanced, delayed, and average. In addition to the issue of assessment, an attempt has been made to discuss the subjects studied in the context of the theoretical frameworks presented earlier. Lastly, a brief discussion of the approach to remediation is included.

Developmental Dyslexia

This case is a 10-year-old male in the third grade who at 7½ years was evaluated by his public school without a diagnosis being made. He was retained after the second grade because of deficient reading skills and was referred for evaluation because of poor reading, spelling, and writing performance. His full scale IQ was 103 and his verbal naming ability, verbal memory, and visual perceptual ability were all average for his age. On two separate tests of reading and spelling (the Wide Range Achievement Test-Revised) (Jastak, 1984) and the Woodcock-Johnson Psycho-Educational Battery (1977), he performed at the early second grade level with standard scores of 68 (reading) and 71 (spelling) (WRAT) and 84 (reading) 78 (written language; Woodcock-Johnson). These scores are consistent with the diagnosis of developmental dyslexia, based on both the traditional discrepancy formula as well as performance compared to his age and grade. Table 11-3 lists his performance on the Lindamood Test of Auditory Conceptualization (LAC) and the Battery of Linguistic Analysis for Writing and Reading—Children's Version (BLAWR-CV) along with a summary from a group of achievement-matched controls. One additional comparison is helpful. For a group of 10-year-old normally achieving children (age-matched controls), error analysis on a group of 10 children indicated that they produced less than 2% logographic errors on reading; rare, if any, logographic errors on spelling; less than 6% combined errors for writing, and less than 8% combined errors for reading.

Analysis of these data reveal certain interesting features of developmental dyslexia. First, the phonological ability of this particular developmental dyslexic is quite similar to that of a group of achievement matched controls based on the results of the LAC and the pattern of performance of regular and irregular words. However, the performance on spelling and reading of nonwords is less than the mean score of the achievement matched controls but within two standard deviations. Furthermore, the frequency of non-phonological type errors (combined and logographic) is similar to that in the achievement matched controls as well. Clearly, normal achievement-matched children and this dyslexic child at this level of phonological ability use a certain degree of phonologic attack, accounting for the difference in performance on regular and irregular words and the frequency of phonological type errors. In addition, however, when comparing this dyslexic child to a group of children who are almost age-matched rather than achievement-matched, this child has less phonological ability. Ten-year-old children produce rare logographic errors and have nonword reading and spelling ability that is greater than 70% correct on the nonwords from the BLAWR-CV.

Note that this child made one semantic error in reading. However, given that it was the only semantic error from a corpus of over 80 real word errors, it is probably of limited significance and probably does not support the diagnosis of developmental deep dyslexia. In addition to semantic errors and difficulty with nonwords, subjects with deep dyslexia usually also have a word class effect and an effect of imagery. This dyslexic subject had none of those features for either reading or spelling. The mean differences on these tasks, with the excep-

Table 11-3 Developmental Dyslexic Compared to Controls

	Developmental Dyslexic		Achievement Matched Controls (n = 6)	
Age	$10^{10/12}$		8	
Grade	3		1–2	
LAC	54[a]		49[a]	
BLAWR-CV (% correct)				
Spelling				
Regular	55		50	
Irregular	35		36	
Reg-Irreg.	20		14	
Nouns	45		62	
Function words	40		58	
High imagery	50		41	
Low imagery	50		32	
Reading				
Regular	67		79	
Irregular	37		50	
Reg-Irregular	30		29	
Nouns	83		86	
Function words	67		67	
High imagery	65		53	
Low imagery	40		50	
Nonwords (n = 92)				
Spelling	26		35	
Reading	26		33	
Error Analysis on real words (%)	*Sp*	*Rd*	*Sp*	*Rd*
Phonological	82	41	78	59
Combined	15	32	12	11
Logographic	3	23	4	29
Other	0	4[b]	6	1

Note: Comparison of a typical developmental dyslexic with achievement matched controls. LAC: Lindamood Test of Auditory Conceptualization.
[a]Early first grade level.
[b]including one semantic error (huge read as giant).

tion of reading high and low imagery words, were similar to those from the control subjects. Even on reading high and low imagery words, the subject did not differ from the control subjects because the standard deviation for the difference between these word groups is 21. These results illustrate the importance of control data. Based merely on analysis of matched lists of nouns and function words and words of high and low imagery, there are apparent effects of word class and imagability. However, the effects are no greater than those seen in normal children.

The results from this developmental dyslexic are compatible with the Frith model to the extent that there is impaired phonological ability for both reading and spelling (alphabetic impairment) and, as measured by overall poor achievement, a poorly developed orthographic system. Alternatively, the results could be explained utilizing a modular framework or one with independently developing systems by ascribing deficits to a sublexical phonologic system (accounting for poor nonword performance) and to the direct or lexical system, accounting for impaired real word performance. In other words, these data are consistent with either hypothesis.

Hyperlexia

Hyperlexia has been defined as a reading ability that is precocious and uninstructed and emerges during the early preschool period (Welsh et al., 1987). It is frequently described in children with developmental abnormalities, including autism and hyperactivity. However, an accepted definition for hyperlexia is that it reflects ability to recognize words that is better than the ability to comprehend reading material or better than other levels of verbal functioning. Not all subjects described as hyperlexic have had clear evidence of cerebral dysfunction (Aram & Healy, 1988).

The two cases described here are examples of the extremes under which hyperlexia may present. The first description is that of a child who is clearly cognitively gifted and the second is that of a child who is clearly cognitively impaired as well as hyperactive.

The gifted hyperlexic began reading at approximately three years old at the time he told his mother he wanted to learn to read. At the time of testing, he had received no formal reading instruction, and his parents noted that they rarely read to him at home because they were usually too busy. As seen in Table 11-4, the child falls in the very superior range of general intelligence and his oral word vocabulary reading comprehension ability are above his age and grade level. However, he has reading recognition (single word oral reading ability) at the late fifth grade level with a standard score greater than 155 (the highest standard score listed on the WRAT-R). On an additional test, the Woodcock Reading Master Test-Revised, he had a word identification grade equivalent of 7.4. Based on these results, he can be classified as hyperlexic, despite his gifted status. In comparing his performance with achievement matched controls, his phonological ability is close to or slightly less than theirs, in that his LAC is slightly less and his nonword spelling is slightly less. However, these differences are probably not meaningful. As with previously described subjects with good phonological ability, he also showed differences between his ability to process orthographically regular and orthographically irregular words. Again, these results are similar to that seen in normal control subjects.

The mentally retarded, hyperactive hyperlexic is similar, in regard to these features, to most previously described hyperlexics. His parents noted that at age 3½ he had remarkably developed oral reading ability which continued to improve until the time of testing, when he was six years old. By history, he showed delays in all developmental milestones, and on examination he had an attention deficit disorder, hyperactivity, and mild to moderate mental retardation, as expressed in his full scale IQ (51). He was unable to perform the LAC or provide any oral or written spelling. However, his written word identification was greater than would be expected given his age and education, which included no previous formal and minimal informal reading instruction.

This hyperlexic was also found to be similar to normal achievement matched

Table 11-4 Performance by Hyperlexics

	Gifted Hyperlexic	Achievement Matched Controls (n = 6)	Retarded Hyperlexic	Achievement Matched Controls (n = 7)
Age	6	10	6	8
Grade	K	4	K	2
IQ	145	–	50	–
WRAT				
Sp: Grade, SS	5E, >155	5	a	2M–3E
Rd:	4E, >155	4	3B, 135	3B
LAC	75[b]	86[c]	a	79[b]
BLAWR-CV (% correct)				
Spelling				
Regular	55	64	a	66
Irregular	15	39	a	42
Reg-Irregular	40	25		24
Reading				
Regular	87	91	85	82
Irregular	70	59	50	66
Reg-Irregular	17	32	35	16
Nonwords				
Spelling	63[d]	72[d]	a	60[e]
Reading	78[d]	75[d]	47[e]	52[e]
Comprehension				
Words	grade 3	–	f	–
Sentences	grade 2	–		–
PPVT(SS)	130	–	57	–

Note: Comparison of two hyperlexics with achievement matched controls.
[a]Unable to perform.
[b]Mid third grade level.
[c]Mid fourth grade level.
[d]n = 92.
[e]n = 60[f]68% of words that he comprehended aloud were comprehended when he read. No words were comprehended that he could not read aloud.

control subjects for those phonological tests on which he could be examined, including reading of nonwords and regular and irregular difference in reading real words.

These two very different case samples provide further evidence of the important relationship of achievement in written word recognition and phonological ability. Similar to that seen in the child with delayed written word recognition (developmental dyslexia), these children, with advanced written word recognition ability, had phonological processing skills similar to those found in a group of control subjects with the same degree of achievement.

Case studies from the Blaskey and Roeltgen (1990) Adolescent Study

Case 1

This control subject was typical of the 12 control subjects who were classified by their teachers as good readers and good spellers and had reading results no lower than one year less than their grade level. At the time of testing this 13-year-old girl had just completed the seventh grade, and was an A student. She

Table 11-5 Performance by Adolescents

	Case 1	Case 2	Case 3	Case 4	Case 5	Normal Controls $n = 12$
Age	13	16	14.5	14.2	15	12–14.5
Grade	8	11	10	7	8	7–8
WRAT (SS)						
Spelling	112	95	98	75	77	113
Reading	146	119	105	95	77	125
LAC	99	99	75	93	39	94 ± 11
BLAWR						
Real words						
Spelling						
Reg	98	94	88	84	60	95 ± 6
Irreg	86	82	72	58	50	82 ± 8
(R-I)	12	12	16	26	10	12 ± 6
Reading						
Reg	97	100	96	90	82	99 ± 1
Irreg	90	98	90	67	66	93 ± 4
(R-I)	7	2	6	23	16	6 ± 4
Nonwords						
Spelling	82	89	58	79	46	70 ± 9
Reading	95	93	67	86	46	91 ± 5

Note: Selected subjects from the Blaskey & Roeltgen (1990) study of adolescents with poor spelling. SS: standard score. Control subject results: mean ± 1 standard deviation.

had always enjoyed reading and composing stories. Spelling skills had been excellent, and she had recently won the spelling bee for her junior high school. Test results indicated that her Full Scale IQ was 135, and her reading and spelling were above grade level. The results from her testing are listed in Table 11-5. She has excellent phonological ability based on her LAC and her ability to read and spell nonwords. On the remainder of the tests, she predominantly showed a ceiling effect.

Case 2

This subject, a 16-year-old eleventh grade boy was referred for testing because he was a slow reader and had spelling deficits that were noted by his parents and teacher. He appeared to be underachieving in school, as he was very bright (Full Scale IQ 128) but only achieving C's. He stated that he enjoyed reading subject matter of interest to him, but had difficulty with reading when not actively involved with the subject. His test results (Table 11-5) are very similar to the control group, with one exception. His standard score on the WRAT-R spelling subtest was more than one standard deviation below the mean of the control group subjects. Thus, despite excellent phonological processing skills as found on the LAC and nonword reading and spelling, he is not quite at the level of the good reader/good speller control group. What he appears to lack is a well functioning orthographic system, that cognitive system described by Frith as the orthographic stage and delineated in the modular models as the lexical system. Unfortunately, it is difficult to test this hypothesis, as there are no tests currently in use that convincingly measure orthography. However, given the normal performance on other tests and the low performance on overall spelling ability, the results are consistent with an impairment in what might be variously called the orthographic, direct or lexical system, similar to that described by Roeltgen and Tucker (1988). The possibility of spelling remediation was discussed with this subject and his parents. Because his problem was so mild, it was decided that a better option was to use a computer with a spell check program rather than invest the time required to undertake a structured spelling program such as the Orton Gillingham program, with an emphasis on higher level skills, such as prefixes, roots, and suffixes.

Case 3

This subject, a 14½-year-old tenth grade girl, was referred for testing due to problems with foreign language. She had always been an excellent student in school until the year of referral, when she began having difficulty in her French class, particularly in the area of vocabulary. Although spelling has always been a weak area for her, it never interfered with her maintaining excellent grades. Her parents blamed the spelling problems on the fact that there were frequent family moves during her early elementary grades, and they assumed that she just missed specific instruction due to varying curricula. It was not until the year of evaluation that a teacher made the possible connection between the spelling and foreign language problems. On assessment this subject's Full Scale IQ was 131. The striking finding from this evaluation was the clear difficulty with phonology, despite grade level reading skills. Her reading skills, however, were not comparable with the control subjects, because her WRAT reading was almost two standard deviations below the mean. In addition her reading was less than expected given her grade education and IQ. Her spelling demonstrated even greater weaknesses, and was more than one year below her current grade placement based on the WRAT. This was confirmed on spelling the regular and irregular real words from the BLAWR on which her total performance was one standard deviation below the mean. On testing of phonological ability, she was more than one standard deviation below the mean in comparison to the control group on the LAC and more than five standard deviations below the mean on reading of nonwords (67%, in comparison to the control group mean of 91.3%). She had a similar difficulty when asked to spell nonwords (58% spelled correctly compared to the mean of 69.8% for the control group). If overall reading and spelling ability are measures of the relative intactness of the orthographic or lexical system, then it is possible to conclude that this system was only mildly dysfunctional. However, phonological or alphabetic ability was more dysfunctional. Therefore, she appeared to have a fairly good orthographic system despite poor phonology. Her performance appears to be contrary to Frith's model that states that good phonology is needed for good orthography. In addition, it appears that her performance is an exception to the generalization that phonology is the best predictor of achievement. These data are more consistent with a descriptive diagnosis of phonological dyslexia and phonological dysgraphia because she had performance consistent with dysfunction of the phonological systems for reading and spelling and relative sparing of the lexical or direct systems. The subject would be an excellent candidate for a structured remediation program in order to improve her spelling skills. In addition, given her poor performance on phonological tasks and her difficulty with foreign language, a phonics program to increase her overall phonological concentualization might be helpful.

The results from this subject, demonstrating relatively good but clearly not normal orthography (based on her achievement being less than control subjects) in the context of relatively poor phonology are of interest. As noted previously, this is in apparent contradiction to the usual pattern. Such a case illustrates the clear heterogeneity among individuals in their ability to acquire written language. It is possible that this subject was able to compensate for relatively poor phonology, perhaps on the basis of the varying instruction described by her parents, by making use of her superior intelligence. However, in spite of her compensation, she was still relatively weak in all areas of written language.

Case 4

This 14-year-old boy had just completed the seventh grade for the second time at the time of testing. He repeated the seventh grade due to a combination of academic problems and family stressors during his first time in seventh grade. He had a history of struggling throughout the elementary grades, with written language problems predominating. Academic struggling is a common history for children presenting for a diagnostic evaluation in seventh grade. Testing revealed that his Full Scale IQ was 124. From the results listed on Table 11-5, this subject was not achieving at expected levels in either reading or spelling. His reading was greater than two standard deviations below the mean, and his spelling was greater than three standard deviations below the mean. His pattern of functioning appears to be quite different from the previous subject. His phonological abilities do not appear to be impaired, relative to the controls, as they are all at or within one standard deviation of the mean. There is a striking difference between this subject's reading and spelling of orthographically regular compared to irregular real words. For both, his differences were greater than two standard deviations from the mean obtained from the control subjects. This subject appears to fulfill the criteria of lexical agraphia as described by Roeltgen and Tucker (1988). In addition, he appears to fulfill the criteria for lexical or surface dyslexia. According to the Frith model, he appears to have a well developed phonological stage, but a poorly developed orthographic stage for both reading and spelling. Again, because there are no good tests of orthography, it is difficult to more fully assess this area. A remedial approach that would be appropriate for this subject is the Glass Analysis for Decoding (Glass, 1976). This program seeks to develop the orthographic structure of words through repeated chunking of word segments. The emphasis would be on those words with irregular patterns. In addition, spelling remediation would follow the same approach with irregular word patterns. Other techniques that might be helpful would be any method that emphasized parts of words such as letter groups and morphemes, including roots, derivations, and inflections.

Case 5

This 15½-year-old eighth grade boy was referred for evaluation by his learning disabilities team in school. This team had been providing instructional assistance to him throughout most of his school career. Except for a D in Spanish, he maintained A's and B's in school, throughout the school year during which he was referred. Testing revealed that his Full Scale IQ was 119. His reading and spelling scores were four standard deviations or more below the mean obtained from the control subjects. He was delayed on measures of phonology, including the LAC and nonwords. These results are similar to Frith's poor readers who are poor spellers and would appear to be consistent with the pattern of linguistic deficit seen in those children traditionally labeled as having developmental dyslexia. If his results are compared to the control subjects listed on Table 11-4 with achievement in the fourth to fifth grade range (this subject's achievement level), it can be appreciated that his phonological performance is also less than a group of achievement matched control subjects. Preferred remediation for this subject would be a combination of the Glass analysis for Decoding, followed by a more structured phonetic approach such as the Orton Gillingham program.

It is important to contrast the performance of this subject with that of the 10-year-old developmental dyslexic previously described. The 10-year-old developmental dyslexic had phonological performance similar to a group of achievement-matched control subjects. In contrast, this 15½-year-old developmental dyslexic had phonological performance that was less than a group of achievement matched controls. This contrast examplifies two areas of current debate among investigators in this field. First, do children with developmental dyslexia have phonological impairment that is more than expected given their level of achievement (disordered reading) or do they have phonological ability that is equal to what is expected given their level of achievement (delayed reading). The results from these subjects would suggest that in some cases there is a true disorder of reading and in other cases a possible delay. The second area of debate is a downward extension of the first. Do young children with this problem continue to fall further and further behind their peers as they grow older? Although the differences seen in comparing these two developmental dyslexic children with their peers suggest that the answer may be "yes," such a question can only be adequately answered by longitudinal studies.

Summary of Case Studies

The purpose of the case studies has been four fold. The first purpose has been to provide examples of children and adolescents with developmental differences in reading ability, including both impaired and exceptional children as well as adolescents with good reading and poor spelling. These children have been presented in the context of an assessment that utilizes cognitive neuropsychological principles applied to developmental linguistic disorders of written language (developmental dyslexia and dysgraphia). A second purpose has been to supply single case support for the commonly held principle that there is a very strong relationship between the degree of phonological or alphabetic ability, and the ability to read and spell, and that this relationship holds for children with normal developmental acquisition of these abilities and children with impaired or exceptional acquisition.

Also, these case studies have been presented to illustrate, in part, the study of adolescents by Blaskey and Roeltgen (1990) that emphasizes the continuum of disability within the realm of developmental dyslexia and dysgraphia, and to further emphasize the need for detailed analysis of processing abilities to better understand how children learn to read and spell.

Lastly, these studies help to provide some background to the controversy regarding the two previously described approaches to developmental disorders, relatively independent modules and sequentially dependent systems. Unfortunately, neither the data supplied here, nor studies previously published provide a clear answer to this controversy. However, a review of the available data suggests that in order to explain at least some of the data, it is necessary to utilize a model of systems that are not completely independent in their function. However, only with longitudinal data will it be possible to determine if they are truly sequentially dependent.

ACKNOWLEDGMENTS

This study was supported in part by NIH Clinical Investigator Award NS01364 (Dr. Roeltgen) and Biomedical Research Support Grant No. 2 S07 RR05413-27 to Hahnemann University. The authors thank the teachers, students, and Drs. O. V. Wheeler and L. Heimowitz, principals, of the Ridgeway School, Columbia, MO and the Finletter School, Philadelphia, PA for their cooperation and help. They also thank Bari Searles for manuscript preparation.

REFERENCES

Aram, D. M., & Healy, J. M. (1988). Hyperlexia: A review of an extraordinary word recognition. In: L. K. Obler & D. Fein (Eds.), *The Exceptional Brain*. New York: Guilford Press.

Baddeley, A. D., Logie, R. H., & Ellis, N. C. (1988). Characteristics of developmental dyslexia. *Cognition*, *29*, 197–228.

Beauvois, M. F., & Derouesne, J. (1981). Lexical or orthographic agraphia. *Brain*, *104*, 21–49.

Beauvois, M. F., & Derouesne, J. (1979). Phonological alexia: Three dissociations. *Journal of Neurology, Neurosurgery and Psychiatry*, *42*, 115–124.

Blaskey, P., & Roeltgen, D. P. (1990). Mild phonological (alphabetic) impairment in children who are good-readers and poor-spellers. *Journal of Clinical and Experimental Neuropsychology*, *12*, 100.

Boder, E. (1973). Developmental Dyslexia: A diagnostic approach based on three atypical reading-spelling patterns. *Developmental Medicine and Child Neurology*, *15*, 663–687.

Bradley, P., & Bryant, L. (1983). Catagorizing words and learning to read: a causal connection. *Nature*, *301*, 419–421.

Bub, D., & Kertesz, A. (1980). Deep agraphia. *Brain and Language*, *17*, 146–165.

Campbell, R. (1985). When children write nonwords to dictation. *Journal of Experimental Child Psychology*, *40*, 133–151.

Carrol, J. B., Davies, P., & Richman, B. (1971). *American heritage word frequency book*. Boston: Houghton Mifflin Company.

Coltheart, M. (1980). Deep dyslexia: A right hemisphere hypothesis. In M. Coltheart, K. E. Patterson & J. C. Marshall (Eds.), *Deep dyslexia*. London: Routledge & Kegan Paul.

Cox, A. R. (1985). Alphabetic phonics: An organization and expansion of Orton-Gillingham. *Annals of Dyslexia*, *35*, 187–198.

Fletcher, J. M., & Satz, P. (1985). Cluster analysis and the search for learning disability subtypes. In B. P. Rourke (Ed.), *Neuropsychology of Learning Disabilities*. New York: Guilford.

Francis, W. N., & Kucera, H. (1982). *Frequency analysis of English usage: Lexicon and grammar*. Boston: Houghton Mifflin.

Frith, U. (1979). Reading by eye and writing by ear. In P. A. Kolers, M. Wrolstad & H. Bouma (Eds.), *Processing of Visual Language*. New York, Plenum Press.

Frith, U. (1985). Beneath the surface of developmental dyslexia. In K. E. Patterson, J. C. Marshall, & M. Coltheart (Eds.), *Surface dyslexia*. Hillsdale, NJ: Erlbaum.

Frith, U. (1986). A developmental framework or developmental dyslexia. *Annals of Dyslexia*, *36*, 69–81.

Glass, G. (1976). *Glass analysis for decoding*. Garden City, NY: Easier to Learn, Inc.

Glosser, G., Roeltgen, D. P., & Friedman, R. (1991). Hyperlexia: A case of reading without meaning. *Journal of Clinical and Experimental Neuropsychology*, 13, 54.

Hatfield, K., & Patterson, K. E. (1983). Phonological spelling. *Quarterly Journal of Experimental Psychology*, *35A*, 451–468.

Holmes, D. L., & Peper, R. J. (1977). An evaluation of the use of spelling error analysis in the diagnosis of reading disabilities. *Child Development*, *48*, 1708–1711.

Jastak, S., & Wilkinson, G. S. (1984). *Wide-Range Achievement Test-Revised*. DE: Jastak Associates, Inc.

Kucera, H., & Francis, W. N. (1967). *Computational analysis of present to-day American English*. Providence: Brown University Press.

Lindamood, C. H., & Lindamood, P. C. (1979). *Lindamood Auditory Conceptualization Test*. TX: DLM Teaching Resources.

Lovett, M. W., Benson, N. J., & Olds, J. (1990). Individual difference predictors of outcome in the treatment of developmental dyslexia. *Journal of Clinical and Experimental Neuropsychology*, *12*(1), 98.

Lovett, M. W., Ransby, M. J., Hardwick, N., Johns, M. S., & Donaldson, S. A. (1989). Can dyslexia be treated? Treatment-specific and generalized treatment effects in dyslexic children's response to remediation. *Brain and Language*, *37*, 90–121.

Margolin, D. I. (1984). The neuropsychology of writing and spelling: Semantic, phonological, motor, and perceptual processes. *The Quarterly Journal of Experimental Psychology*, *36A*, 459–489.

Marsh, G., Friedman, M., Welsh, V., & Desberg, P. (1981). A cognitive developmental theory of reading acquisition. In G. E. MacKinnon & T. G. Waller (Eds.), *Reading Research, Advances in Theory and Practice* (Vol. 3). New York: Academic Press.

Marshall, J. C. (1987). *Reading modules and developmental disorders*. Paper presented at the From Neurons to Reading Symposium. Florence.

Mattis, S., French, J. H., & Rapin, I. (1975). Dyslexia in children and young adults: Three independent neuropsychological syndromes. *Developmental Medicine and Child Neurology*, *17*, 150–163.

Morton, J. (1987). *An information processing account of reading acquisition.* Paper presented at From Neurons to Reading Symposium. Florence.

Omrod, J. E. (1985). Proofreading "The Cat in the Hat:" Evidence for different reading styles of good and poor spellers. *Psychological Reports*, *57*, 863–867.

Paivio, A., Yuille, J. C., & Madigan, S. A. (1968). Concreteness, imagery and meaningfulness values for 925 nouns. *Journal of Experimental Psychology Monograph*, *76* (Supp.) 1–25.

Read, C. (1975). Lessons to be learned from the preschool orthographer. In E. H. Lenneberg & E. Lenneberg (Eds.), *Foundations of language development—A multidisciplinary approach* (Vol. 2). New York: Academic Press.

Roeltgen, D. P. (1985). Agraphia. In K. M. Heilman & E. V. Valenstein (Eds.), *Clinical Neuropsychology*. New York: Oxford.

Roeltgen, D. P. (1989). The battery of linguistic analysis for writing and reading-children's version. *Journal of Clinical and Experimental Neuropsychology*, *11*, 57.

Roeltgen, D., Cordell, C., & Sevush, S. (1984). A battery of linguistic analysis for writing and reading. *The INS Bulletin.*

Roeltgen, D. P., & Fonteyne, N. (1990). Examination of phonological or alphabetical ability in normal young children, and an analysis of the Firth Model. *Journal of Experimental Clinical Neuropsychology*, *12*, 97.

Roeltgen, D. P., & Heilman, K. M. (1984). Lexical agraphia, further support for the two system hypothesis of linguistic agraphia. *Brain*, *107*, 811–827.

Roeltgen, D. P., & Heilman, K. M. (1985). Review of agraphia and proposal for an anatomically-based neuropsychological model of writing. *Applied Psycholinguistics*, *6*, 205–230.

Roeltgen, D. P., Rothi, L. G., & Heilman, K. M. (1986). Linguistic semantic agraphia. *Brain and Language*, *27*, 257–280.

Roeltgen, D. P., Sevush, S., & Heilman, K. M. (1983). Phonological agraphia: Writing by the lexical-semantic route. *Neurology*, *33*, 733–757.

Roeltgen, D. P., & Tucker, D. M. (1988). Developmental phonological and lexical agraphia in adults. *Brain and Language*, *35*, 287–300.

Scott, M. (1987). *Examining the reading and spelling skills in slow learners: Frith's model of developmental dyslexia.* Unpublished doctoral dissertation, University of Missouri, Columbia.

Seymour, P. H. K., & Elder, L. (1986). Beginning reading without phonology. *Cognitive Neuropsychology*, *3*(1), 1–37.

Seymour, P. H. K., & MacGregor, C. J. (1984). Developmental dyslexia: A cognitive experimental analysis of phonological, morphemic and visual impairments. *Cognitive Neuropsychology*, *1*(1), 43–83.

Shallice, T. (1981). Phonological agraphia and the lexical route in writing. *Brain*, *104*, 412–429.

Siegel, L. S. (1986). Phonological deficits in children with a reading disability. *Canadian Journal of Special Education*, *2*, 45–54.

Siegel, L. S. (1988). Evidence that IQ scores are irrelevant to the definition and analysis of reading disability. *Canadian Journal of Psychology*, *42*, 201–215.

Siegel, L. S., & Faux, D. (in press). Acquisition of certain features of English in normally achieving and disabled readers. *Reading and Writing.*

Snowling, M. (1982). The spelling of nasal clusters by dyslexic and normal children. *Spelling Progress Bulletin*, *22*, 13–18.

Snowling, M., Stackhouse, J., & Rack, J. (1986). Phonological dyslexia and dysgraphia—A developmental analysis. *Cognitive Neuropsychology*, *3*, 309–339.

Stuart, M., & Coltheart, M. (1988). Does reading develop in a sequence of stages? *Cognition*, *30*, 139–181.

Sweeney, J. D., & Rourke, B. P. (1978). Neuropsychological significance of phonetically accurate and phonetically inaccurate errors in younger and older retarded spellers. *Brain and Language*, *6*, 212–225.

Temple, C. M. (1986). Developmental dysgraphia. *The Quarterly Journal of Experimental Psychology*, *38A*, 77–110.

Thomas, V. (1974). *Teaching spelling, Canadian word lists and instructional spelling.* Calgary: Gage Educational Publishing Limited.

Thorndike, E. L., & Lorge, I. (1944). *The teacher's word book of 30,000 words.* New York: Teacher's College Press.

van der Veur, B. (1974). Imagery ratings for 1,000 frequently used words. *Journal of Educational Psychology*, *67*, 44–56.

Welsh, C. W., Pennington, B. F., & Rogers, S. (1987). Word recognition and comprehension skills in hyperlexic children. *Brain and Language*, *32*, 76.

Woodcock, R. W., & Johnson, M. B. (1987). *Woodcock-Johnson Psycho-Educational Battery.* Allen, TX: DLM Teaching Resources.

12

A Cognitive Approach to the Neurorehabilitation of Acquired Language Disorders

MARLENE BEHRMANN and SALLY BYNG

In recent years, we have witnessed the emergence of a series of remediation studies sharing a set of common assumptions. Chief among these assumptions is that these studies analyze acquired language disorders in terms of information-processing models of normal cognitive functioning and then devise a treatment program to rehabilitate the damaged components of the cognitive apparatus. These treatment studies are associated with the emerging discipline of cognitive neuropsychology which, in turn, has its roots in experimental cognitive psychology. Cognitive neuropsychology assumes that the architecture of the cognitive processing system is made up of functionally independent components or modules (the modularity hypothesis) which together comprise the cognitive system that subserves a particular ability such as language or memory. Whereas all the components function adequately in normal people, they are susceptible to discrete disruption following brain damage (the fractionation hypothesis). Even though a single component of the system may be selectively impaired through brain damage, the remainder of the processing system continues functioning in its routine fashion with the exclusion of the contribution of the affected component (the subtraction hypothesis; see Caramazza, 1986, 1989; Howard & Patterson, 1989).

The role of the clinician, then, in using this approach as a basis for rehabilitation, is to identify the locus of the damaged component first. Therapy is then directed to treating the underlying cognitive deficit from which the disorder arises rather than simply treating the presenting symptoms. If, for example, the patient is unable to repeat a sentence, and the deficit is diagnosed as one of short-term memory, instead of merely requiring the subject to practice repetition (which might lead to improvement), therapy would be directed to enhancing the patient's memory capacity. In other words, in such an approach, the analysis of the disorder suggests which cognitive aspects of the deficit need to be the focus of treatment, allowing the clinician to focus in on the primary deficit. This type of analysis does not necessarily suggest what the exact nature of the treatment should be, but it constrains the type of intervention procedure one might possibly undertake.

The information-processing models used to determine the source of the underlying deficit include separate boxes or modules for discrete cognitive processes. The boxes correspond to representations of knowledge and/or procedures while the arrows connecting the boxes reflect the transmission of or access to this knowledge. These models share many features in common with the classical *diagrams* devised by people such as Wernicke, Lichtheim, and Bastian in the nineteenth century. There is, however, a critical distinction between the diagrams of the present and those of the past. Whereas the diagram makers assumed a neuroanatomical substrate for each "box" or "cerebral center," cognitive processing models have remained neutral on the issue of neuroanatomical localization. Current diagrammatic box-and-arrow representations serve as a guide in the search for the crucial functional (and not structural) deficit underlying impaired performance. The search for the core deficit is critical since a surface symptom may arise from a number of possible underlying sources. For example, a disturbance in confrontation naming may be the product of a fundamental impairment in the semantic system, or it may arise from difficulty accessing the correct phonological form of the word, or it may be the result of a peripheral articulatory disturbance. Clearly, treatment of the naming disturbance will be markedly different in all these cases. The primary aim of this form of rehabilitation, then, is to ensure that treatment is tailored to address the underlying deficit.

Along with the primary assumptions concerning the organization of cognitive processes, several other more practical and methodological considerations have become characteristic of remediation based on an information-processing approach. Many of these assumptions relate to research practice, since it is here where the discipline originally received its impetus. We will argue, however, that these considerations can be incorporated easily into clinical practice and if done, allow measurement of the efficacy of rehabilitation.

Most of the remediation studies based on information-processing models take as their focus single subjects (Bruce & Howard, 1987; Byng, 1988; de Partz, 1986; Hillis & Caramazza, 1987; Jones, 1986; see also Seron and Deloche, 1989; Wilson, 1987; for several examples). Because brain-damaged subjects are typically so heterogeneous, the results of group studies convey limited information (Caramazza, 1986, 1989). The averaging of data from individual subjects reflects the functioning of an *average* cognitive system, but this is not very enlightening since it blurs the distinction between qualitatively different individual systems. Based on the limitations of group studies, Caramazza and McCloskey (1988) and McCloskey and Caramazza (1988) have suggested that single-patient studies represent the only appropriate methodology for drawing inferences about cognition based on observations of brain-damaged patients (see Caplan, 1988; Bub & Bub, 1988; for differing opinions). The question of single versus group studies continues to generate lively debate in the neuropsychological literature. It seems to us, however, that the need to focus on a single subject is particularly relevant in the case of treatment where individual needs and differences between patients are so great. In addition, in order to understand which particular forms of treatment suit which particular types of patients, the approach to therapy must be more specific and focused. Instead of working with a group of subjects, the intact and defective components of the language system of a single subject are analyzed in great detail and a therapy program is then tailored to meet this subject's needs.

The traditional classification schema (such as Broca's and Wernicke's aphasia, alexia with agraphia, and alexia without agraphia) which are used extensively in clinical practice are qualitatively different from this kind of approach. For the most part, the existing taxonomies, while helpful in demarcating broad behavioral divisions, are not specific enough to be able to define and localize the defective cognitive component (Marshall, 1986; Schwartz, 1986). These broad schema do not elucidate the structure of the cognitive disorder (Caramazza, 1984, 1986), and therefore cannot guide and inform a therapeutic regime. Moreover, although the literature contains many examples of ready-made exercises or training schemes which accompany the classical taxonomies, the ease and rapidity of implementing any intervention should not be confused with its efficacy (Seron & Deloche, 1989).

An alternative strategy, adopted by those working within a cognitive framework, is to interpret each individual case with reference to an explicitly articulated model of cognitive functioning, concentrating on variables which are known to affect normal performance, for example, psycholinguistic variables such as frequency or imageability of words. A detailed understanding of the *nature* of the disorder, not only the *severity*, provides the basis for rational, theoretically driven therapy.

A further characteristic of this approach is the incorporation of some principles of experimental methodology into its implementation. Methodological design, for example, using a test-treat-test (or ABA longitudinal/time-series design) has allowed researchers and clinicians to determine the efficacy of the intervention procedure and to establish a functional relationship between the treatment and the change in the treated behavior. While these methodological practices are clearly imperative in research practice, they are also valuable clinically. They enable the clinician to interpret the outcome of treatment from a firm, statistical basis and to determine whether any significant behavioral change occurred. In addition, they allow for comparison of two treatment techniques within the same subject and facilitate examination of generalization of treatment to untreated items, modalities, and tasks. Furthermore, a systematically controlled remediation procedure allows the clinician to attribute any observed change in behavior to a cause. The linking of outcome and cause is particularly useful for determining whether the improvement in performance was the result of nonspecific effects such as spontaneous recovery or increased motivation, or whether the change was a direct consequence of the intervention program (see Coltheart, 1985; for further discussion).

For the most part, the rehabilitation studies using this cognitive approach have been carried out in controlled laboratory settings; hence, this way of thinking has not yet found its way into routine clinical practice. The goal of this chapter is to demonstrate that analyzing the individual's underlying cognitive deficit with reference to an explicit multicomponent processing model readily lends itself to clinical practice. We believe that, in turn, the widespread use of such a framework will yield additional theoretical insights which will benefit theory and therapy alike.

In this chapter, we have chosen to discuss the rehabilitation of single-word processing disorders, cutting across both input and output modalities (expression and comprehension of single words) and across the auditory and visual channel. The acquired language disorders (particularly reading and writing) have received considerable attention within the theoretical formulation described above and models to account for normal and impaired processing are probably most explicit in this domain. The idea of a cognitively oriented approach to language rehabilitation is not a novel one. Even in his early work, Luria (1963, 1973) attempted to establish a link between neuropsychological disorders, a cognitive psychological framework, and rehabilitation procedures. This view has increased in popularity more recently owing to the evolution of specific models in cognitive psychology. Although our focus in this chapter is restricted to acquired language disorders, the principles, which we will illustrate, are equally applicable to other cognitive domains such as picture and object recognition or calculation.

Just as rehabilitation studies have spun off from the increase in cognitive psychology research, so has there been a reciprocal benefit for theory as a result of therapy studies. Theory has benefitted from therapy by the acquisition of converging theoretical evidence, adding to our understanding of cognitive processes in normal subjects. In addition, these studies provide the opportunity to address certain issues which cannot be easily illuminated by more typical case studies (Howard & Patterson, 1989). If theoretically driven, therapy studies may serve as a means of checking and constraining the development of theoretical models. For example, if the outcome of therapy is such that it could not have been predicted by the model or if components which are theoretically distant and distinct from the treated component also show improvement posttreatment, the formulation of the model necessarily requires reevaluation. In this way, therapy is a source of confirmatory (or contradictory) evidence for models of normal cognitive processing (Howard & Patterson, 1989).

The organization of this chapter will take the following form. The first section sets out the fundamental notions which underlie a cognitive approach to neurorehabilitation. Following that, we describe and schematically sketch a basic well-accepted (although grossly oversimplified) model of single-word processing. The next section presents single case studies which illustrate the principles of rehabilitation and outline the therapy program. The final section summarizes the chapter and offers some concluding remarks.

WHAT ARE THE BASIC PRINCIPLES?

As mentioned previously, the central concern in this form of treatment is the analysis of the patient's deficit in terms of clearly articulated architectures of information processing. Appropriate treatment can only be instituted when the nature and degree of the deficit is understood (Byng, Kay, Edmundson, & Scott, 1990). The clinician adopts a series of hypotheses about the source of the underlying cognitive deficit and proceeds, on the basis of elimination and converging evidence, finally to locate the critical locus of impairment. Pretherapy assessment is theoretically motivated by the model and draws on a series of measurements, some standardized and others constructed to test out a specific ability. Initially, observation of the patient motivates the selection of tasks for assessment of the patient. Thus, observations of spontaneous interactions and conversational language produce the initial hypotheses for an astute clinician. Fine-grained analysis of performance follows. It is perhaps in this area (and possibly only in this area, according to Caramazza, 1989) that cognitive approaches have the most to offer—a logical and rational enquiry into the disorder increases the probability of success of remediation. Once the hypothesis about the nature of the underlying deficit has been formulated, the treatment objectives are specified. These should be neither too broad nor too narrow (Coltheart, 1983) and should focus on a specific linguistic function, for example, the production of verbs.

Jones and Byng (1989) set out a guideline for the series of steps in therapy. They suggest that these steps are followed:

i. Choose and justify a therapy strategy on the basis of the hypothesis you have about the nature of the deficits.
ii. Design tasks to implement the strategy.
iii. Form a hierarchy of treatment tasks, with criteria for moving from one level to the next.
iv. Design a method to measure both the initial problem as well as the other untreated deficits.
v. Implement therapy.
vi. Measure the outcome of treated and untreated functions.
vii. Re-evaluate the outcome of therapy in the light of previous hypotheses.

The exact therapy procedure employed depends largely on the nature of the deficit. An important notion to bear in mind when designing intervention, however, is whether knowledge is lost or degraded from the system. It may be the case that the knowledge or representations remain intact but that the deficit prevents access to this knowledge. Therapy follows different routes depending on whether the information is abolished from the system or not (Howard & Patterson, 1989). If information or representations are lost or abolished, direct reteaching or restoration of the missing information is suitable (also see Luria, 1973). Reorganization or reconstitution therapy also aims at reteaching the missing knowledge. Rather than directly teaching the information, some alternative process is employed so that teaching takes place from a medium of strength through to an area of weakness. Finally, facilitation (or stimulation) is optimal when the information exists but is not accessible. Here, the knowledge is not taught but the existing representations are reactivated for access.

With regard to the actual techniques or therapy tasks, the information-processing method of analysis remains neutral as it does not provide a specific theory of therapy. The creativity and clinical acumen of the therapist is just as important in this approach as in any other and critically contributes to the success of the program. The choice of which tasks to use depends, in part, on the type of problem as well as variables concerning the patient such as age, interest, cultural background, and so forth. Importantly, the tasks used in this form of rehabilitation are not unique to this approach and already exist in the practitioner's repertoire. Tasks such as matching, using external aids, repeating, and completion could all be employed in this therapy. Other therapeutic considerations such as grading tasks in terms of difficulty and establishing appropriate response criteria operate as they do in any form of therapy. The post-therapy evaluation is unique to this approach. It is here where several critical measures are obtained. For example, post-therapy measures provide an indication for any change in performance on the treated function.

In addition, these measures allow the clinician to determine what gave rise to the observed change in behavior. Conceivably, the change in behavior could be attributable to various causes, some of which are more general—for example, an increase in the patient's motivation—and some of which are specific, for example, the direct result of the intervention program. If post-therapy performance on a number of behaviors improves, it is reasonable to conclude that spontaneous recovery or increased motivation were responsible. If, however, the change in performance is restricted to the behavior being treated, it is more likely that the improvement is a direct and specific result of the therapy program.

Another important measure obtained post-therapy concerns the extent of generalization—the clinician evaluates whether there has been any transfer from therapy stimuli to other untreated items, modalities, or tasks. While the ideal outcome would be to observe widespread generalization, even item-specific change is an acceptable outcome, reflecting benefit from therapy. The post-intervention testing, then, is a critical stage in the estimation of the effectiveness of the intervention program.

The first step in establishing efficacy is to demonstrate an improvement in the patient's performance after therapy. Once this has been done, the clinician attempts to draw a causal link between therapy and outcome, thereby excluding other nonspecific contributing factors and attributing the patient's improvement to the therapy program. In order to draw these conclusions and carry out this evaluation, the appropriate methodology must be in place from the initiation of remediation.

Multiple pretherapy baseline measurements taken at several points prior to the onset of therapy ensure that the deficit is stable. Any change observed later, therefore, cannot be attributed to fluctuations or to spontaneous recovery of the deficit itself. To distinguish between general and specific causes of change in behavior, we need to take pretherapy measurements across several cognitive functions, only one of which will be treated. Measurements of these alternative behaviors, which must be unrelated to the deficit under consideration, are taken both before and after therapy.

For example, if therapy is directed at treating single-word oral reading, assessment of comprehension of sentences or object recognition may be undertaken. If post-therapy testing reveals positive changes in these unrelated and untreated behaviors, it would not be legitimate to conclude that any improvement in single-word reading is due to therapy. A more feasible interpretation would be that some nonspecific factor produced changes across the board. If, however, the change was only observed in the treated function, then drawing a functional relationship between the change and the therapy plan would be legitimate.

One way of measuring transfer or generalization is to use a cross-over therapy design (McReynolds & Kearns, 1982). Using this procedure to assess item generalization, one would randomly assign the corpus of matched stimuli to two groups prior to therapy, treating one group first (A) and then "crossing over" and treating items in the second group (B). To obtain an estimate of generalization to untreated items, then, one may take interim measures prior to crossover. If therapy is useful, improvement in group A items should be observed. Any improvement observed in the as-yet untreated items (B), at this stage, clearly indicates transfer or generalization from the treated items (A), since group B items have not yet been treated. Following crossover, further improvement of group B items should now be evident since by this stage, they have received specific attention.

A further manipulation which provides information about the relative efficacy of different therapy procedures (as well as of item generalization) would be to crossover therapy procedures in addition to crossover of stimulus sets. Here, one procedure might be initiated and its effectiveness evaluated prior to the crossover point when the second procedure would be introduced. Interim evaluation, taken at crossover point, demonstrates the efficacy of procedure A as well as generalization to procedure B and post-therapy evaluation measures the added effectiveness of procedure B.

The use of statistical tests in single-case designs to measure change from one occasion to another is still controversial. While some argue that demonstrations of clinical significance are sufficient (and more meaningful than statistical test results), others have suggested that statistical tests help in ruling out changes in behavior which are spurious or produced by chance. Nonparametric analyses which do not rely on a normal distribution are most frequently used in single-case studies. Tests such as the Wilcoxon, Chi-squared, or some specific implementation of them (McNemar's test, Fisher exact test) and Cochran's Q, for example, are used to estimate whether the observed change in performance post-therapy is significantly different from the behavior expected if chance alone were operating (see Siegel, 1956). If the results could not have been produced by chance alone or are not simply a random fluctuation produced by noise in the data, then we conclude that posttherapy behavior is statistically different from pretherapy behavior. Statistical significance, however, is not the only measure of change. Results which are statistically significant do not necessarily mean that clinical improvement has taken place. Similarly, clinically significant results may not reach levels of statistical significance. Ideally, then, both clinical and statistical significance should result from a treatment (Wilson, 1987).

In the following section, the above clinical and practical principles will be illustrated using three single cases, each selected to exemplify a different aspect of language processing. The three patients all show single-word deficits which can be analyzed and described with respect to a model of normal word processing. The first two subjects received therapy for deficits manifesting in impairments of written language, while the final subject was treated for deficits in the access to or representation of semantic knowledge. We have chosen these cases to demonstrate the fine-grained dissociations between narrowly-defined linguistic abilities and to show how treatment was formulated to remediate the underlying source of the disorder.

SIMPLIFIED MODEL OF SINGLE-WORD PROCESSING

Many information-processing models of single-word processing exist, most of which share the same general architecture but differ in details (for example, Coltheart, 1987; Shallice, 1988). We have chosen one such model taken from Patterson and Shewell (1987) which we think adequately sketches the components central to our discussion. In this model (see Figure 12-1), initial processing of input is conducted separately for auditory and visual information. Since our concern here is with visual information (and indeed there exist more data describing this component), we will restrict our discussion to the processing of visual information. In the case of a previously seen written word, preliminary orthographic analysis (e.g., parsing into letter features) is conducted, after which an abstract code is assigned to the letters so that letters of the same type are given the same code. For example, the letters "A" and "a" are given the same identity; case and style are superfluous. This information is transmitted to the orthographic input lexicon which stores orthographic word forms for words encountered previously, and it is here that the word is recognized. Access to meaning is obtained from the cognitive or semantic system and pronunciation is obtained in the phonological output lexicon for reading aloud. In the case of unfamiliar words which have no prior lexical entry and for which the pronunciation cannot be directly addressed, the incoming information is transmitted through a second route which employs a rule-based conversion procedure which operates on segments smaller than the whole word—that is, subword level orthographic-to-phonological conversion. This system assigns graphemes to their phonological counterparts, the phonemes. These subword segments are later synthesized and held in a response buffer to be assembled for pronunciation. This dual route theory of word processing, inspired by cognitive psychologists working with normal readers, accounts for the reading of words which are both regular and irregular in their spelling-sound correspondences. Words which have not been encountered previously cannot be read lexically (i.e., pronunciation cannot be directly addressed) and are thus subject to the nonlexical conversion procedure or assembled pronunciation. Additionally, irregular words cannot be processed via this conversion procedure as the output will be incorrect and therefore must necessarily be read using the lexical routine. For example, if an irregular word such as island is subjected to subword orthographic-phonological conversion, it would be read aloud as "*izland*." Word-specific lexical information is therefore necessary to read irregular words correctly. This dual-route theory has been the subject of much heated debate. One reason for the controversy is that it cannot account for those cases who can read irregular words aloud but who have not proceeded via the semantic system and thus, cannot comprehend what they have read. To remedy this situation, a third route, in which the visual input lexicon makes direct contact with the phonological output lexicon has been

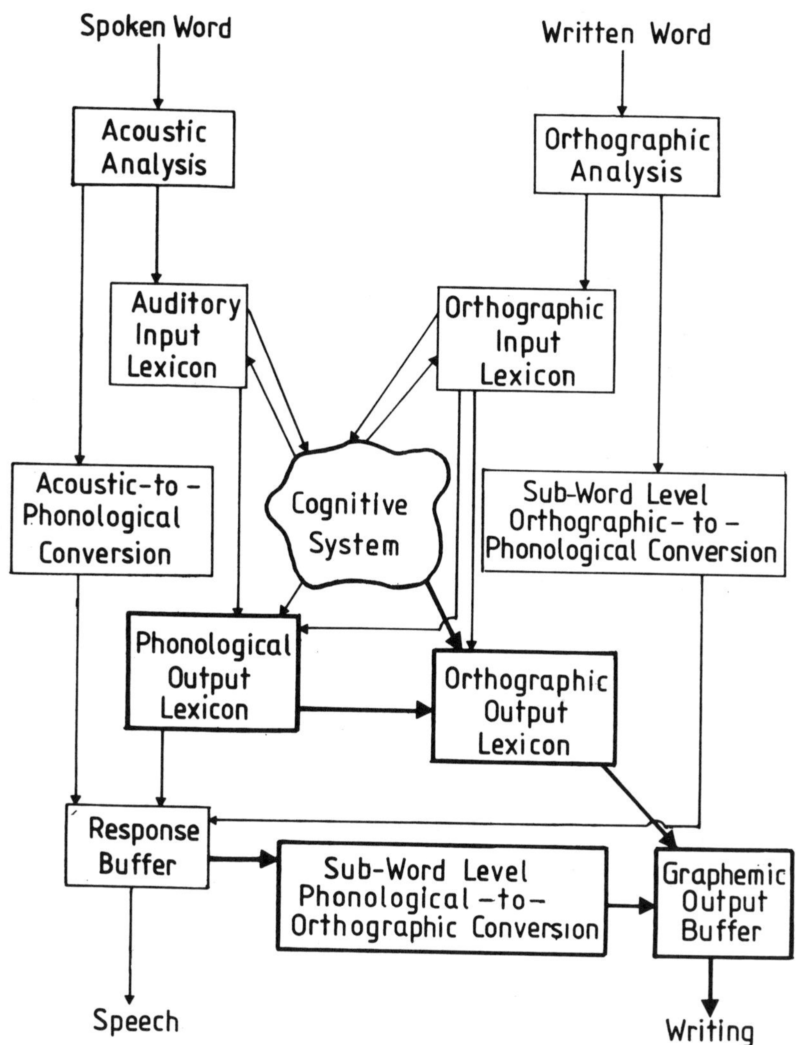

Figure 12-1 A simple model of single word processing. (Reprinted with permission from Patterson, K. & Shewell, C. (1987). The cognitive neuropsychology of language. London: Lawrence Erlbaum.)

proposed (Schwartz, Saffran, & Marin, 1980). Even more recently, it has been suggested that a single reading route can account for processing of both regular and irregular words (Seidenberg & McClelland, 1989; Patterson, Seidenberg, & McClelland, 1989). For the purposes of this paper, we have elected not to become embroiled in the active controversy. Since the dual-route model is the most explicit of all formulations at this stage, we have chosen to stick with it although we recognize that varying theoretical alternatives do exist.

The dual-route theory described here has also been proposed to account for writing. Two independent routes, capable of handling somewhat different input, have been proposed as the mechanism underlying writing (Ellis, 1982; 1984; Margolin, 1984; Margolin & Goodman-Schulman, Chapter 10.), The one route, known as the lexical route, is used for writing words which have existing entries. It may be used for writing both regular and irregular words but is essential for irregular words which do not have regular spelling-sound correspondences. The second route which is nonlexical employs sound-spelling (phonological-orthographic) correspondence rules to assemble the orthography of the output for words which have not been encountered previously. This latter route only operates successfully for words which obey regular phoneme-grapheme correspondences. A third, direct but nonsemantic route has also been suggested for writing (Patterson, 1986), analogous with the third lexical but nonsemantic reading route.

Double dissociations between two routes of the dual-route model have been described in the literature. Some individuals show preservation of one (but not the other) of the two routes following brain damage, while other individuals show the reverse pattern in which the second (but not the first route) may be preserved. This dissociation has provided support for the functional autonomy of the two independent routes. Patients who show an impairment of the direct lexical route read nonwords and regular words relatively well but fail to read irregularly spelled words. These patients are termed "surface dyslexic" (if the deficit appears in reading) or "surface dysgraphic" (if the deficit manifests in writing). Deficits of the nonlexical route, on the other hand, give rise to "phonological dyslexia" or "phonological dysgraphia." Here, patients can read or write regular and irregular words well but fail on novel words or nonwords which demand the use of phoneme-grapheme conversion rules. For more detailed discussion of the two routes and the ensuing neuropsychological deficits, see Coltheart (1985, 1987), Ellis (1982, 1984), Margolin (1984), and Margolin & Goodman-Schulman, Chapter 10. The first two cases we discuss demonstrate impairments in the use of the lexical route, resulting in reliance on subword level conversion. The restoration of the impaired lexical procedure is the focus of therapy in reading in one case and in writing in the second.

TREATMENT FOR READING AND WRITING DEFICITS

Case 1: The Treatment of Surface Dyslexia

Background

The reading deficit discussed below is a case of surface dyslexia (Byng & Coltheart, 1988; Coltheart & Byng, 1989). As discussed, it is inadequate and inappropriate to consider all reading deficits alike when operating within the information-processing framework. Instead, the problem may originate in entirely different loci for two seemingly similar patients and therefore detailed testing is necessary to make clear the locus of the deficit.

EE, a 40-year-old left-handed postal worker, was admitted to hospital following a head injury sustained by falling off a ladder. A right temporoparietal craniotomy and evacuation of an acute subdural hematoma and intracerebral hemorrhage was performed. A complicated recovery course ensued during which EE received both speech therapy and physiotherapy. Approximately six months after the accident,

EE's reading was tested in detail. On oral reading, he made many errors to irregularly spelled words but not to regularly spelled words, indicative of surface dyslexia.

The impairment in using any form of lexical access for reading was further confirmed in a homophone matching task in which EE was required to decide whether or not a pair of words were identical in pronunciation. EE was able to perform this task for regularly spelled words and nonwords but not for irregular words. Unless EE had pronounced a word correctly, he was unable to understand it, so his reading impairment affected both his comprehension and oral reading. EE's error responses were mostly regularizations; i.e., phonologically plausible alternatives for the target, for example, PINT → /pint/ (as in mint) and FLOOD → /flu:d/ (as in food). The presence of regularization errors suggest that EE was relying on the nonlexical phonological procedure for reading and was converting graphemes into their corresponding phonemes according to subword rules.

Therapy

Stage I: Irregular words containing two consecutive vowels. Prior to the onset of therapy, EE was able to read correctly only 5 out of 24 irregular words containing the letter sequence "ough" (words such as plough or dough). A crossover therapy design was used, treating 12 words first (group 1), testing the generalization to the 12 untreated words (group 2) and then treating the group 2 words. Treatment consisted of linking the orthography of the item to its phonology using a mnemonic aid or picture to represent the word (for example, a drawing of a tree to represent bough) and to link the referent to the word form in the orthographic input lexicon. The rationale for this therapy was that the nonlexical route should not be the focus of therapy, because reading by this route would not enable EE to read and understand words with irregular spellings or homophones. Instead, the therapy attempted to restore the representations of written words and to reinforce the use of the lexical route via semantics through linking the orthography with its meaning. Therapy continued for five weeks with one session per week. At each session, EE would read aloud all group 1 and group 2 words without the mnemonic aids. Between therapy sessions, EE would practice the group 1 words, using the mnemonic aids to ensure that his responses to the words were correct. He practised the words every day and was reminded to use the pictures to help remember the pronunciation of the word if he misread it. The interim measures, taken prior to crossover, consisted of EE reading aloud all the words without the mnemonic aids. The results revealed a specific effect of therapy. The group 1 words improved from pretherapy to interim testing, and there was some generalization to the untreated group 2 items. When group 2 became the focus of therapy, further improvement was noted in these items. At the end of this stage of therapy, all 24 words were read correctly, and this improvement was still observed a year later.

Stage II: High-frequency irregular words. Before the onset of the second stage, EE read aloud 485 of the most frequent words from the Kučera and Francis (1967) list on two occasions, separated by a week. The rationale for using this list was that these words represented those that EE would come across most often in everyday reading tasks. Performance was equally poor on both occasions. The 54 words that were read incorrectly on both occasions were then divided into two groups. A crossover design was used again—only the first half (treated or T) but not the second (untreated or U) were treated. Treatment still involved linking a mnemonic symbol to the meaning of the word but this time, instead of using a picture, a small symbol was incorporated into the orthography of the word. For example, for the word *work*,

Table 12-1 Proportion of Words Correctly Read by EE in Stages II and III of Therapy

	Pretreatment		Posttreatment	
	Pretest 1	Pretest 2	Posttest 1	Posttest 2
Stage II				
Treated words	.19	.44	1.00	.96
Untreated words	.47	.44	.85	.74
Stage III				
Treated words	.45	.63	1.00	.96
Untreated words	.48	.52	.78	.70

Source: Reprinted from Coltheart & Byng (1989). By permission of Lawrence Erlbaum.

an envelope was drawn attached to the final *k*. This was considered to be functionally relevant to EE, given his occupation as a postman. Similarly a picture of Big Ben was drawn onto the final t in the word *government*. The purpose of such symbols was to act as a link to semantics which would then assist in the retrieval of the appropriate pronunciation. It also served to focus attention on the word and to discourage EE from attempting to sound out the components, a strategy which usually resulted in an incorrect pronunciation. The mnemonic symbols were written in a different color ink from the word in order not to interfere with the orthographic form or shape of the word. At posttest four weeks after therapy, when the words were presented without the mnemonic symbols, the T words showed significant improvement. Generalization was also noted as the U words had improved although not to as great a degree as the treated words. Since spontaneous recovery could not account for the change in behavior, because the deficit was stable before therapy (no difference in performance across the two pretherapy sessions), a specific effect of therapy was demonstrated.

Stage III: Irregular words lower in frequency. In the final stage of therapy, EE read the next 388 words from the Kučera and Francis (1967) list. Of these, 101 were incorrectly read and became the target for therapy. Fifty-one formed the T group, while the other 50 formed the U group. Two pretreatment and two post-treatment sessions were conducted, and therapy consisted of the same mnemonic procedure described above. The results of this phase were identical to the previous stage. There was a significant change in T words from pre- to post-therapy and there was also some generalization to the U group.

A summary of EE's performance in Stages II and III of therapy is presented in Table 12-1. It is clear from this table that there was change from pre- to post-therapy in both stages of the therapy program.

Discussion

The purpose of the three rehabilitation stages was to restore the functioning of the whole-word or lexical semantic routine by reestablishing the lexical representations for irregular and also frequently occurring words. The outcome was beneficial as treated items were learned in all stages, and furthermore, some generalization to untreated items occurred. The change in EE's behavior could not be ascribed to spontaneous recovery or practice effects—the deficit was stable before therapy and there is no reason to think that random fluctuations in performance were being observed. The functioning of the lexical route for word reading was restored to some extent through the intervention.

Case 2: Treatment of Surface Dysgraphia

Background

The discrepancy between the lexical and the nonlexical route was also observed in the next subject, although in this case it was mainly restricted to the writing (not reading) of irregular words, a deficit known as "surface dysgraphia" (Behrmann, 1987; Behrmann & Herdan, 1987).

CCM, a 53-year-old high-school educated woman with a left temporoparietal lesion (following a middle cerebral artery infarct) displayed the typical pattern associated with surface dysgraphia. On average, she wrote 79% of regular words correctly to dictation but only wrote 32% of irregularly spelled words correctly, reflecting a highly significant effect of regularity in writing. The majority of her errors were phonologically plausible, for example CHIEF → *cheef* and SHOES → *shuse*, suggesting that she was using subword level conversion procedures for translating phonology into orthography. Neither imageability, length nor word class affected her writing performance significantly. CCM's reading was well preserved with accuracy scores around 90% for all except low-imageability words for which she obtained 71% accuracy.

Therapy

Like the previous therapy designed for EE, CCM's therapy was directed at improving her use of the lexical procedure (via semantics) to access word-specific orthographic representations which are critical for irregular words. Therapy was divided into two stages, the first using homophones and the second using nonhomophonic irregular words. The purpose of using homophones is to ensure that therapy taps into the lexical-to-semantic route; homophones necessarily require direct lexical mediation since the phonological or spoken form is ambiguous with respect to the written representation. In other words, in writing to dictation there is no way to determine the orthography of /seil/ without having recourse to some context or semantic disambiguation to specify whether it is spelled *sale* or *sail*. The ambiguity is only resolvable through specification in the semantic system, and access to the lexical route is thereby guaranteed.

Stage I: Treatment of homophones. Prior to the onset of therapy, CCM wrote 49% (68/138) of the homophones correctly (dictated individually with context added to allow disambiguation). Therapy was conducted on a weekly basis over a period of six weeks. A total of 50 homophones, all of which were incorrectly written pretherapy, were randomly selected for treatment (the T group). The homophones were always taught in pairs, even if one member was correctly written pretherapy, so that the co-members could be contrasted orthographically and phonologically. As far as possible, homophones sharing a common feature (for example, the spelling pattern -a-e as in sale/sail and hare/hair) were taught together. An average of eight new homophones were taught in each session.

As in the treatment of surface dyslexia described previously, therapy aimed to reestablish the orthographic representation of the word. Therapy techniques involved linking the word-specific orthography with a pictorial representation to reinforce the direct link between the word, its meaning, and its written form. Initially, each homophone was written on a card and paired with the corresponding picture to provide the correct meaning. The spoken form was also provided. The second member of the homophone pair was then introduced together with its picture. The two written forms were contrasted and the differences in meaning were pointed out.

CCM was encouraged to distinguish between the two written forms and to memorize the differences. The written words were shuffled, and CCM was required to match them to their pictorial representations. Following this, the words were removed and CCM had to write the homophone word corresponding to the picture. Thereafter, the words were dictated to her along with a disambiguating definition, and she wrote them in her homework book without the aid of the pictures. This procedure was repeated for each homophone pair. Home practice was also designed to link the phonology with the orthography via semantic disambiguation. CCM completed a series of forced-choice tasks matching pictures and words (and checking the backs of the cards to see if the match was correct) as well as writing the homophone in response to the picture (checking the back of the picture to determine whether the response was correct). She also performed a sentence completion task in which she had to select the correct word from the homophone pair (for example, "After Christmas the shops have a big . . . (sale/sail).")

Post-therapy testing, conducted after a delay of two weeks, showed a significant difference in the accuracy of homophone writing (from 49% pretherapy to 67% post-therapy averaged over four pre- and post-therapy testing sessions; Cochran Q test 13.4, $p < .01$). In addition, CCM tended not to write nonword responses as she had done prior to intervention. Instead, her errors consisted of the opposite member of the pair. This change in error type provides additional evidence for the fact that CCM had shifted to a lexical strategy.

Efficacy and specificity of therapy was demonstrated by the overall improvement on treated homophones and no change on other unrelated cognitive functions. For example, on the Test for Reception of Grammar (Bishop, 1982), CCM scored 67/80 pre-therapy and 69/80 post-therapy, reflecting no significant change in performance. Generalization of improved spelling was observed to untreated irregular words (from 32% to 67% post-therapy), but there was no significant difference in her writing of untreated homophones (0/20 pre-therapy and 2/20 post-therapy). This result was unexpected and puzzling. If access to the lexical route was improved, one would have expected carry-over to both untreated irregular and homophone words. Since this was not the case and only irregular words were significantly better, it was suggested that perhaps homophone writing required item-specific attention, and that semantic disambiguation was necessary for each individual pair.

Stage II: Treatment of irregular words. A new baseline was taken before the second phase of therapy was instituted. CCM wrote 450 words drawn from the Kučera and Francis corpus and divided into frequency bandwidths (frequencies 69975–580 per million, 574–330 per million, and 329–231 per million). These words were written over a period of three weeks. Overall, CCM wrote 80% of them correctly, and there was no difference in her performance across sessions, reflecting stability of the deficit. The incorrectly written words were divided into two groups, matched in terms of frequency. The first group of 44 words (T) was taught over a period of two weeks (two sessions per week), and then interim testing was carried out to determine the generalization to the as-yet-untreated group of 42 words (U), following which the words from U were taught (now group U + T). The therapy techniques used at this stage were similar to those in Stage I. Whole-word processing was stressed through linking the orthographic word form with a semantic referent (usually represented as a picture), and nonlexical strategies were deemphasized. Copying and writing to dictation formed part of the home program exercises as did dictionary work in which CCM looked up the target in a dictionary, copied it and its meaning into her own homemade dictionary. Interim testing (following therapy on Group T) showed a significant improvement on Group T (χ^2 = 38, $p < .001$) and also on Group U (χ^2 = 23, $p < .001$), suggesting generalization to untreated items as had been found in EE's therapy for reading of irregular words. Post-therapy testing of all the words revealed a significant improvement in behavior following intervention since T and U + T items improved from 0% of words pre-therapy to 79% post-therapy. Furthermore, spelling on the words from Group T showed no decay post-therapy compared to the interim measure, indicating retention of learning even after a month had elapsed. There was also no significant difference on her performance on the Test of Receptive Grammar before and after treatment, indicating no widespread or generalized effects but rather a specific effect of therapy on CCM's writing skills.

Discussion

The results of both the homophone and the irregular word treatment were encouraging, showing stabilization of the treated forms and some (although not total) carry-over to untreated items. Assessment of CCM's ability to comprehend sentences revealed no change after Stage I or Stage II of therapy. This provides support for the hypothesis that the observed change in performance was not directly attributable to a nonspecific factor (like spontaneous recovery or increased motivation) as this might have resulted in change in all aspects of functioning rather than simply in the domain under consideration. The treatment program illustrates that it is indeed possible to retrain writing through a whole-word technique and to restore the functioning of the direct lexical procedure. A replication of this study, using a patient showing similar deficits to CCM, conducted by Morris (1989) reveals results considerably like those reported for CCM. This finding is encouraging, and additional replications of all the therapy studies are urgently needed.

TREATMENT FOR LEXICAL SEMANTIC AND OUTPUT DEFICITS

To obtain the meaning of the single word, either read or written, one needs to access the entry in the cognitive system (Figure 12-1). This necessarily requires connections between the input (orthographic and auditory lexicons) and output lexicons (orthographic and phonological) and the cognitive system. In reading for meaning then, once the item has been processed visually and orthographically, it addresses the semantic representation associated with that form. If this item is now to be pronounced or written (after meaning is obtained), the entry in the phonological output lexicon or the orthographic output lexicon must be accessed.

In comparison to other aspects of the dual-route theory of reading and writing, our knowledge of the semantic system is rudimentary. A clinician faced with a patient with deficits in this system is in a rather awkward position. The model is not explicitly articulated, and yet it is supposed to guide the assessment and rehabilitation. The solution we have adopted is to work within the existing model and hopefully, to add to its refinement.

In this section, we will not discuss the gaps and controversies in the models of the semantic system (see Riddoch, Humphreys, Coltheart, & Funnell, 1988; Shallice, 1988). Instead, we will show that insights into the functioning and breakdown of this system are still possible given this obviously simplified theoretical framework. At this point, we are concerned only with the semantic system and the phonological lexicon and with the communicating arrow between them. Simply put, the semantic system (considered for our purposes to be a central mechanism common to all input and output modalities such as words, pictures, and objects) is a pool of semantic features from which detailed knowledge about the referent/concept and its relationship to other referents/concepts may be obtained. Semantic items are attached to their whole word phonological form in the phonological output lexicon. The phonological form is accessed prior to the selection and synthesis of the necessary phonemes.

There are several critical theoretical concepts regarding the organization of the central semantic system which are incorporated into processing models. Warrington and her colleagues, for example, have suggested that the semantic system is organized into fine-grained categories in which items are grouped according to category membership (Warrington & McCarthy, 1983, 1987; Warrington & Shallice, 1984). Double dissociations between categories such as abstract and concrete words have been reported as well as fractionations within the broad category of concrete words itself (Howard & Franklin, 1988). Warrington and Shallice (1984), for example, found a disproportionate impairment of their subjects' ability to define animal, plant, and food names compared with object names. Dissociations of this type led them to postulate a distinction between animate and inanimate items although this dichotomy has been contested recently (Warrington & McCarthy, 1987). Of importance to us is the fact that dissociations between semantic categories do exist, and this has implications for therapy. Another issue which has clinical significance is the proposal that within each category, meaning is accessed from general superordinate knowledge to more specific, subordinate attributes. Patients with focal lesions as well as those with Alzheimer's disease have been observed to correctly assign words to a broad semantic field based on superordinate features. These same patients, however, are unable to make finer, more precise semantic discriminations (Allport, 1983; Bub, Black, Hampson, & Kertesz, 1988; Martin & Fedio, 1983). These results suggest that the semantic system is organized in a hierarchical fashion with specific attributes being more vulnerable to damage compared with more general attributes. Any therapy program which is designed to exploit the inherent structure of the semantic system must necessarily take these issues into account.

Deficits affecting the central semantic system, which can be observed in any medium of language, are usually explained as an abolition of meaning (or its degradation) or the failure to access the existing, intact knowledge. The latter explanation is consistent with a facilitation or reactivational therapy approach; whereas the former suggests that either the meanings need to be retaught or a compensatory strategy should be adopted. To illustrate the application of these theoretical and therapeutic concepts, we provide an example of a subject with problems in the comprehension of single words. In this case, the deficit is attributable to a fundamental problem in the cognitive or semantic system, pervading all modalities. The following therapy study was designed to restore, as far as possible, semantic representations in the central cognitive system.

Case 3: Treatment of a Central Semantic Deficit

Background

The treatment of semantic deficits within a cognitive framework is particularly problematic given that there is no single agreed-upon model of semantic processing and that our theoretical understanding of this domain is limited. The purpose of the therapy procedure, as discussed previously, has wider implications than improving the patient's use of lexical semantic knowledge, although clearly this is of paramount importance from a clinical perspective. Therapy studies may enhance understanding of the semantic system and provide insight into the manner in which information is stored in this system. The therapy program discussed here was constructed to exploit the theoretical viewpoint that semantic knowledge is stored in specific categories and that damage might affect some categories selectively (Behrmann & Lieberthal, 1989). The assumption adopted was that the semantic system is structured categorically and that if therapy results were inconsistent with this, the underlying assumption might well be challenged. More specifically, the rationale behind the treatment plan was to show that if treatment of items within a single category showed generalization within that category alone and not to items of other categories, this would provide support for the view that the semantic system is divided into independent, discrete categories (as suggested by Warrington & McCarthy, 1983, 1987; Warrington & Shallice, 1984).

CH, a 57-year-old, English-speaking male was admitted to hospital in May 1984 following a middle cerebral artery infarct involving the frontal, temporal, and parietal lobes as well as the internal capsule. This therapy study was initiated approximately two years after his stroke. CH was globally aphasic with almost no expressive output aside from a string of vowels and varying intonation. He was also severely limited in comprehension, even at the single-word level; although he seemed to follow gesture and simple conversations. It was decided that the first priority for his treatment was to improve his comprehension of single items.

On preliminary pretesting, CH performed particularly poorly on tests requiring semantic knowledge. He seemed to be able to compute a relatively broad but crude semantic representation but was unable to access a precise definition of the stimulus as observed on three different tests, the Funnell test (1983), the Coughlan and Warrington Auditory Picture Vocabulary test (1978), and an Odd-Man-Out test.

The Funnell test requires the patient to decide which of two choices matches with the target; for example, for the target *glove*, the close condition choices are *sock* and *mitten*, and in the case of semantically distant foils, the choices are *sock* and *plate*. The Coughlan and Warrington task (60 items) also requires that a choice be made between wide and narrow distractor items. The patient is required to indicate which of two alternatives is synonymous with the target. For example, for the target *serene*, the choices are *rope* and *calm* (wide or distant choice); while for the target *vacant*, the narrow or close choices are *empty* or *open*. Both the Funnell and the Coughlan and Warrington tests were presented once with spoken and once with written stimuli, but the auditory version of the Funnell test was terminated when CH became exasperated and frustrated. The results of these tests showed that CH was able to choose one of two items which was synonymous with a target when the items were semantically distant but not when they were closer in meaning. The Odd-Man-Out task required CH to indicate which of three items was semantically distant from the other two; for example *day*, *food*, and *night*. Sixty trials were run and CH performed at chance level, confirming the impairment in semantic processing.

Prior to the implementation of therapy, baseline performance was established using a category sorting task including items from six categories (animals, body parts, colors, transport, furniture, and food). The items for the first three categories were taken from Warrington and Shallice (1979); the items from the last three categories were generated expressly for this study. Half the items were high frequency while the other half occurred less often than 20 times per million. This task was presented first with both spoken words and then in written form. CH was required to indicate in which category the target belonged. The categories were signaled with pictures and written words.

There was no difference in performance depending on modality of presentation, providing tentative evidence for a central, rather than modality-specific, semantic deficit. There was, however, a significant difference in performance depending on category ($\chi^2 = 92.2$, $p < .01$), with animals categorized most easily (63/80), and body parts (4/40) and furniture (3/34) being more difficult to categorize. There was no overall effect of frequency of occurrence of the items. This pretherapy test was administered over three sessions (one-third of the items per session presented auditorily and a different third presented visually), forming a primary baseline. There was no difference in performance across the three sessions, suggesting that the deficit was stable and that CH was performing at an equal level over time.

Therapy

The aim of therapy in this study, as in the other studies, was to improve performance of the deficient component. In the case of CH, the major aim was the restoration of the semantic representation of single lexical items. The assessment of the specific consequences of the intervention program and the amount of generalization to untreated items was also critical to the program. The working hypothesis regarding the organization of the semantic system was that if knowledge was indeed stored according to categorical specificity, transfer might occur to untreated items within a single category but not to items in other categories.

Three categories were randomly selected for treatment (treated categories [TCs]): transport, body parts, and furniture); while the other three were untreated categories (UCs): animals, colors, and food). Within the TCs, two groups of items were formed, one to be treated (T), and one to act as an untreated control (U). The two groups contained an equal number of items correctly and incorrectly classified prior to therapy. Fifteen one-hour therapy sessions were conducted (five sessions per category) with two primary goals: to teach meaning at a general level of description, i.e., at the superordinate level and to teach item-specific details of the T words leading to precise identification of these items. The progression from generic to specific meanings is in keeping with the view that access to the semantic system is top-down with information ranging from superordinate to progressively more detailed attributes of the items.

The therapy procedure involved describing to CH the semantic properties common to all the items in the category being treated. Individual items were then introduced one-by-one in both printed and spoken form and a connection between the referent and the label was established using a picture and the verbal identifier. Exercises consisted of matching the label and referent under a variety of conditions. Following this, more specific tasks were undertaken emphasizing the semantic features of the individual items. CH was required to pick out from an array the target item that corresponded to the semantic cue provided. For example, for the item *bus*, the initial cue was "in the category transport, this object has four wheels and is driven on land" (foils: airplane and boat). At a later stage in therapy, the cue was modified to "in the category transport, this object has four wheels, is driven on land

Table 12-2 Correct Categorization of Treated and Untreated Categories on Pre-, Intra, and Post-Therapy Measures

Category	Pre-Therapy	Intra-Therapy	Post-Therapy
	Treated category (TC)/Treated items		
Transport	8/20	20/20	20/20
Body parts	2/20	20/20	18/20
Furniture	2/20	20/20	18/20
Treated category (TC)/Untreated items			
Transport	6/20		7/20
Body parts	0/20		13/30
Furniture	1/20		2/20
Untreated category (UC)			
Colors	10/40		9/40
Animals	63/80		57/80
Food	7/40		21/40

Source: Reprinted from Behrman and Lieberthal. By permission of the British Journal of Disorders of Communication.

and carries many passengers" (foils: airplane, boat and car). As CHs comprehension was so limited, all cues were given several times over and nonverbal gestures and pantomime accompanied the input. Even though the cue described here is complex, CH appeared to comprehend the gist and could act upon it. Home program work included a dictionary exercise (locating entry in a child's dictionary and reviewing the critical item and category features). Matching new pictures of the treated referents to verbal labels also formed part of the home program.

Interim measures were taken after the completion of each category (three interim measures) and consisted of a category sorting task of both T and U of the current treated category as well as items from the remaining TCs and UCs. After the completion of therapy, the outcome measures included a repetition of the original category sorting task using all stimuli administered over three sessions. The pretherapy semantic testing (Funnell, Coughlan and Warrington, and Odd-Man-Out test) was also repeated.

CH showed no significant difference in performance across the three post-therapy sessions (although minimal fluctuation was noted) but overall performance on the pre-therapy category sorting task was significantly different from post-therapy. The results of the pre-, intra-, and post-therapy category sorting task is shown in Table 12-2.

As is evident from this table, the results revealed that all T items of all TCs were sorted significantly better at post-therapy than they had been pre-therapy. Even the T items from the first TC (transport) were still sorted well 10 weeks later, reflecting the stabilization of the newly acquired information. Generalization from T to U items within each TC was also observed overall. However, a breakdown of the scores suggest that this carry-over was restricted to body parts and transport and not to furniture. The change in performance on items in UCs was not significant pre- versus post-therapy, and a breakdown in scores shows that some generalization occurred with food but not with animals or colors. The improvement on treated items in treated categories with transfer to untreated items in two treated categories and carryover to only one of the three untreated categories presents a perplexing outcome. The fact that improvement was noted on the untreated category, food, is consistent with interpretations which suggest that functional salience is a critical factor in determining performance. Furthermore, the fact that carry-over to untreated items in treated categories was not widespread suggests that some spillover is possible but that item-specific retraining may be necessary to ensure more global generalization in such a severely impaired patient.

Performance on the other post-therapy semantic tasks reveals significant change in some areas but not in others. Significant change was observed on the wide choice (distant distractors) of Coughlan and Warrington's Auditory Choice Vocabulary Test ($\chi^2 = 9.09, p < .01$) but not on the narrow choice items nor on the Coughlan and Warrington test. In other words, CH's performance on tasks requiring broad semantic knowledge had improved, although he was still unable to access precise and specific knowledge about untreated items. One positive outcome of therapy was that the effect of treatment was not material-specific; i.e., there was some generalization, and improved use of semantic knowledge was apparent. The fact that carry-over to UCs was limited to "food" supports the view that the semantic system is organized in fine-grained categorical fashion (Warrington & McCarthy, 1983 1987; Warrington & Shallice, 1979; 1984). Items sharing class membership benefitted more from the treatment of their co-members than did items in UCs. Another significant implication of these findings was that general or superordinate knowledge is acquired more readily than specific knowledge. Thus, broad, but not precise, definitions are improved during the therapy process. This supports the claim that semantic representations are ordered and reinstated in order of specificity (Warrington & McCarthy, 1987). The results of this study also suggest that the reacquisition of semantic knowledge may mirror the order of initial acquisition in children. The developmental literature has repeatedly showed that the attainment of full semantic specification is gradual, acquired only through systematic differentiation of broader concepts into narrower details (Clark, 1973, 1975).

The final goal of therapy was to demonstrate that the change in performance was directly attributable to the intervention program. In this study, a sentence comprehension test (the Test for Reception of Grammar, Bishop, 1982), administered pre- and post-therapy revealed no significant change in behavior. Since syntactic comprehension bears no theoretical relationship to lexical semantics, one would not expect to see change in this behavior after therapy. The fact that syntactic comprehension was equal pre- and post-therapy suggests that the benefits of therapy were probably restricted to the domain being treated (single-item comprehension). This finding is particularly relevant in narrowing down the possible causes of change in CH's behavior. It suggests that the positive outcome is not attributable to nonspecific factors but rather to the intervention program per se.

Discussion

The results of this therapy study proved positive in many respects. Comprehension of treated items showed change as did some untreated items. No change was observed on an unrelated behavior and thus, the effects of therapy were considered to be specific. The specificity of the results also have bearing on a theory of the organization of the semantic system. Superordinate knowledge showed improvement, supporting a hierarchical theory of semantic representations and the pattern of carry-over coincides with categorical organization of the system. Lexical items sharing class membership showed more improvement than unrelated items. The CH case study demonstrates that despite the fact that no model of semantic processing is universally accepted, adopting a cognitive approach to the deficit is valuable in that it provides a logical and rational basis for evolving a therapy procedure. Furthermore, the outcome of the therapy may constrain future theorizing on the structure of the semantic system.

SUMMARY OF THERAPY STUDIES

The outcome of all the therapy studies described in this chapter proved to be positive for specific aspects of language and, importantly, the change in behavior was specifically ascribed to the intervention procedure. This is especially relevant at present when the utility of intervention for acquired language disorders is being debated (Meikle et al., 1979; David, Enderby, & Bainton, 1982). Although we have only described therapy for remediating language disorders occurring at the single-word level, there are some current studies which adopt a similar approach to domains other than this. Byng (1988), for example, described the use of an information-processing theory for the assessment and remediation of two subjects with sentence processing disorders. These subjects, who exhibited deficits in relating sentence form and meaning in sentence comprehension and production, both showed significant gains after therapy. The observed change in behavior was shown to be specific to tasks related to the therapy and like the single word therapy studies, was also shown to be a direct outcome of the therapy program.

The approach we have laid out here seeks to guide remediation through a model-driven analysis of intact and defective cognitive components. With regard to therapy techniques traditionally employed in aphasia, this is somewhat of a novelty. For the most part, in recent years, the predominant rehabilitation procedures for acquired language disorders have been inspired by the traditional aphasia taxonomies. These classification schema, however, rely heavily on neuroanatomical distinctions while depending less on behavioral interpretations. The cognitive approach to neurorehabilitation outlined here takes as its starting point a detailed and thorough analysis of behavior. It is argued that working from an in-depth analysis of the deficit, therapy is more rational, specific, and efficient. Using this approach then not only increases the probability of success at this level, it also provides evidence of the specific effects of the intervention procedure. One of the major thrusts in aphasia therapy today is not only to show that procedures work but, furthermore, to attempt to determine whether specific patients benefit from specific therapies. Because the cognitive approach described here places so much emphasis on individualized treatment and in-depth analysis of patient's strengths and weaknesses, much information on the "what, when, and for whom of aphasia treatments" (Kitselman & Wertz, 1985) may be gradually accumulated.

ACKNOWLEDGMENTS

We are grateful to David Margolin for his constructive suggestions.

REFERENCES

Allport, D. A. (1983). Language and cognition. In R. Harris (Ed.), *Approaches to language*. London: Pergamon Press.

Behrmann, M. (1987). The rites of righting writing: Homophone remediation. *Cognitive Neuropsychology*, *4*, 3, 365–384.

Behrmann, M., & Herdan, S. (1987). The case for cognitive neuropsychological remediation. *The South African Journal of Communication Disorders*, *34*, 3–9.

Behrmann, M., & Lieberthal, T. (1989). Category-specific treatment of a lexical semantic deficit: A single case study of global aphasia. *British Journal of Communication Disorders*, *24*, 281–299.

Bishop, D. (1982). *The test for reception of grammar*. Abingdon, Axon: Thomas Leach.

Bruce, C., & Howard, D. (1987). Computer-generated phonemic cues: An effective aid for naming in aphasia. *British Journal of Disorders of Communication*, *22*, 191–201.

Bub, D., Black, S. E., Hampson, E., & Kertesz, A. (1988). Semantic encoding of pictures and words: Some neuropsychological observations. *Cognitive Neuropsychology*, *5*, 1, 27–66.

Bub, J., & Bub, D. (1988). On the methodology of single case studies in cognitive neuropsychology. *Cognitive Neuropsychology*, *5*, 5, 565–582.

Byng, S. (1988). Sentence processing deficits: Theory and therapy. *Cognitive Neuropsychology*, *5*, 629–676.

Byng, S., & Coltheart, M. (1988). Aphasia therapy research: Methodological requirements and illustrative results. In E. Hjelmquist & L. G. Nilsson (Eds.), *Communication and handicap*. North Holland: Elsevier.

Byng, S., Kay, J., Edmundson, A., & Scott, B. (1990). Aphasia tests reconsidered. *Aphasiology*, *4*, 1, 67–91.

Caplan, D. (1988). On the role of group studies in neuropsychological and pathopsychological research. *Cognitive Neuropsychology*, *5*, 5, 535–548.

Caramazza, A. (1984). The logic of neuropsychological research and the problem of patient classification in aphasia. *Brain and Language*, *21*, 9–20.

Caramazza, A. (1986). On drawing inferences about the structure of normal cognitive systems from the analysis of patterns of impaired performance: The case for single patient-studies. *Brain and Cognition*, *5*, 41–66.

Caramazza, A. (1989). Cognitive neuropsychology and rehabilitation: An unfulfilled promise. In X. Seron & G. Deloche (Eds.), *Cognitive approaches in neuropsychological remediation*. London: Erlbaum.

Caramazza, A., & McCloskey, M. (1988). The case for single-patient studies. *Cognitive Neuropsychology*, *5*, 5, 517–528.

Clark, E. V. (1973). What's in a word? On the acquisition of semantics in his first language. In T. E. Moore (Ed.), *Cognitive development: The acquisition of language*. New York: Academic Press.

Clark, E. V. (1975). Knowledge context and strategy in the acquisition of meaning. In D. P. Dato (Ed.), *University round table on language and linguistics*. Washington, DC: Georgetown University Press.

Coltheart, M. (1983). Aphasia therapy research: A single case study approach. In C. Code & D. J. Muller (Eds.), *Aphasia Therapy*. London: Edward Arnold.

Coltheart, M. (1985). Cognitive neuropsychology and the study of reading. In O. S. M. Marin & M. I. Posner (Eds.), *Attention and performance XI*. Hillsdale, NJ: Erlbaum.

Coltheart, M. (1987). The functional architecture of language. In M. Coltheart, R. Job,

& G. Sartori (Eds.), *The cognitive neuropsychology of language*. London: Lawrence Erlbaum.

Coltheart, M., & Byng, S. (1989). A treatment for surface dyslexia. In X. Seron & G. Deloche (Eds.), *Cognitive approaches in neuropsychological rehabilitation*. London: Lawrence Erlbaum.

Coughlan, A. K., & Warrington, E. K. (1978). Word-comprehension and word-retrieval in patients with localised cerebral lesions. *Brain, 101*, 163–185.

David, R. M., Enderby, P., & Bainton, D. (1982). Treatment of acquired aphasia: Speech therapists and volunteers compared. *Journal of Neurology, Neurosurgery and Psychiatry, 45*, 957–961.

de Partz, M.-P. (1986). Re-education of a deep dyslexic patient: Rationale of method and results. *Cognitive Neuropsychology, 3*, 149–177.

Ellis, A. W. (1982). Spelling and writing (and reading and speaking). In A. W. Ellis (Ed.), *Normality and pathology of cognitive functions*. London: Academic Press.

Ellis, A. W. (1984). *Reading, writing and dyslexia: A cognitive analysis*. London: Erlbaum.

Funnell, E. (1983). Phonological processes in reading: New evidence from acquired dyslexia. *British Journal of Psychology, 74*, 159–180.

Hillis, A. E., & Caramazza, A. (1987). Model-driven remediation of dysgraphia. In R. Brookshire (Ed.), *Clinical Aphasiology*. Minneapolis, MN: BRK Publishers.

Howard, D., & Franklin, S. (1988). *Missing the Meaning*. Cambridge, MA: MIT Press.

Howard, D., & Patterson, K. E. (1989). Models for therapy. In X. Seron & G. Deloche (Eds.), *Cognitive approaches in neuropsychological rehabilitation*. London: Erlbaum.

Jones, E. V. (1986). Building the foundations for sentence production in a non-fluent aphasic. *British Journal of Disorders of Communication, 21*, 1, 63–82.

Jones, E. V., & Byng, S. (1989). The practice of aphasia therapy: An opinion. *College of Speech Therapists Bulletin*, May.

Kitselman, K. T., & Wertz, R. T. (1985). The treatment of aphasia. In J. K. Darby (Ed.), *Speech and language evaluation in neurology: Adult disorders*. Orlando: Grune and Stratton.

Kučera, H., & Francis, W. N. (1967). *Computational analysis of present-day American English*. Providence: Brown University Press.

Luria, A. R. (1963). *Restoration of function after brain injury*. New York: McMillan.

Luria, A. R. (1973). *The working brain*. New York: Basic Books.

Margolin, D. I. (1984). The neuropsychology of writing and spelling: Semantic, phonological, motor and perceptual processes. *The Quarterly Journal of Experimental Psychology, 36*, 459–489.

Marshall, J. (1986). The description and interpretation of aphasic language disorder. *Neuropsychologia, 24*, 5–24.

Martin, A., & Fedio, P. (1983). Word production and comprehension in Alzheimer's disease: The breakdown of semantic knowledge. *Brain and Language, 19*, 124–141.

McCloskey, M., & Caramazza, A. (1988). Theory and methodology in cognitive neuropsychology: A response to our critics. *Cognitive Neuropsychology, 5*, 5, 583–623.

McReynolds, L. V., & Kearns, K. (1982). *Single subject studies in communication disorders*. Baltimore: University Park Press.

Meikle, M., Wechsler, E., Tupper, A., Benenson, M., Butler, J., Mulhall, D., & Stern, G. (1979). Comparative trial of volunteers and professional treatment of dysphasia after stroke. *British Medical Journal, 2*, 87–89.

Morris, C. (1989) (unpublished manuscript). The rites of righting writing: A replication.

Patterson, K. E. (1986). Lexical but nonsemantic spelling? *Cognitive Neuropsychology*, *3*, 341–367.

Patterson, K., Seidenberg, M., & McClelland, J. L. (1989). Connections and disconnections: Acquired dyslexia in a computational model of reading processes. In R. G. M. Morris (Ed.), *Parallel distributed processing: Implications for psychology and neurobiology*. Oxford: Oxford University Press.

Patterson, K., & Shewell, C. (1987). Speak and spell: dissociations and word-class effects. In M. Coltheart, R. Job, & G. Sartori (Eds.), *The cognitive neuropsychology of language*. London: Erlbaum.

Riddoch, M. J., Humphreys, G. W., Coltheart, M., & Funnell, E. (1988). Semantic system or systems? Neuropsychological evidence re-examined. *Cognitive Neuropsychology*, *5*, 1, 3–26.

Schwartz, M. (1986). What the classical aphasia categories can't do for us and why. *Brain and Language*, *21*, 3–8.

Schwartz, M., Saffran, E., & Marin, O. S. M. (1980). Fractionating the reading process in dementia: Evidence for word-specific print-to-sound associations. In M. Coltheart, K. Patterson & J. C. Marshall (Eds.), *Deep Dyslexia*. London: Routledge & Kegan Paul.

Seidenberg, M., & McClelland, J. L. (1989). A distributed, developmental model of word recognition and naming. *Psychological Review*, *96*, 523–568.

Seron, X., & Deloche, G. (1989). Introduction. In X. Seron & G. Deloche (Eds.), *Cognitive approaches in neuropsychological rehabilitation*. Hillsdale, NJ: Erlbaum.

Shallice, T. (1988). *From neuropsychology to mental structure*. New York: Cambridge University Press.

Siegels, S. (1956). *Nonparametric Statistics for the Behavioral Sciences. New York*: McGraw-Hill Book Co.

Warrington, E. K., & McCarthy, R. (1983). Category specific access dysphasia. *Brain*, *106*, 859–878.

Warrington, E. K., & McCarthy, R. (1987). Categories of knowledge. *Brain*, *110*, 1273–1296.

Warrington, E. K., & Shallice, T. (1979). Semantic access dyslexia. *Brain*, *102*, 43–63.

Warrington, E. K., & Shallice, T. (1984). Category specific semantic impairments. *Brain*, *107*, 829–853.

Wilson, B. (1987). Single-case experimental designs in neuropsychological rehabilitation. *Journal of Clinical and Experimental Neuropsychology*, *9*, 5, 527–544.

PART V

OTHER DOMAIN-SPECIFIC DISORDERS

13

Disorders of Higher Visual Processing: Theoretical and Clinical Perspectives

H. BRANCH COSLETT and ELEANOR M. SAFFRAN

In view of the many types of visual information available to the human perceiver—color, form, movement, location, depth, object identity—and the number of discrete cortical areas involved in visual processing (at least 20), it is not surprising that the disorders of visual perception encountered in clinical practice are many and varied. Although some of these impairments are rare, the clinical phenomenology is so compelling and the theoretical implications so significant that these disorders warrant close examination.

A convenient starting point in the assessment of disorders of visual perception comes from the realization that vision provides two critical types of information: the *identity* of objects and the *location* of those objects relative to the viewer. Each of these types of information may be selectively impaired by brain injury (e.g., Newcombe & Russell, 1969).

Failure to recognize an object is designated "visual object agnosia." This term is generally applied to patients who exhibit a modality-specific impairment in visual object recognition which is not attributable to language deficits or elementary sensory disorders such as brightness discrimination or visual feature registration. As will be discussed in detail below, the disorders designated as "visual object agnosias" include a wide variety of visual processing deficits which presumably arise at a number of different stages in visual processing. For this reason, Teuber's oft-cited definition (1968) of agnosia as "a normal percept stripped of its meanings" may be appropriate for some patients with visual deficits but does not adequately characterize many of the visual deficits commonly considered to be agnosic.

Impairment in the ability to appreciate object location was termed "visual disorientation" by Holmes (1918). Similar disorders have been reported as "imperception," "Balint's syndrome," "simultanagnosia," and "visuospatial" disorders.

In this chapter we provide a brief historical overview of visual agnosia and visuospatial impairments. We also outline a model of visual processing motivated by recent anatomic and physiologic investigations in monkeys as well as experimental studies of visual perception in human subjects. We attempt to demonstrate that this model provides a coherent account of some (though not all) disorders of visual processing. In addition, we present data from two case studies to illustrate the clinical utility of the approach.

HISTORICAL OVERVIEW

Perhaps the first neurological account of an acquired disorder of visual processing was provided in Hughlings Jackson's (1876) report of a patient with a large tumor in the posterior portion of the right hemisphere. This patient was unable to find his way in familiar places, failed to recognize familiar people and places, and was unable to dress himself. Jackson suggested that the posterior right hemisphere was critical for visual memory and recognition.

Shortly thereafter, Munk (1878) reported that bilateral ablation of the upper convex surface of the occipital lobes of dogs produced an intriguing condition characterized by a profound impairment in visual recognition but not an inability to "see." Thus, Munk's dogs were able to negotiate their environment without difficult but were unable to recognize their masters and failed to respond appropriately to visual stimuli such as threat or food. Munk termed this condition "mindblindness" (*Seelenblindheit*) and attributed it to a loss of visual "memory images." Subsequently, several investigators (e.g., Wilbrand, 1887; Lissauer, 1890) reported patients who were unable to recognize people or objects despite relatively preserved visual acuity.

Lissauer (1890) provided one of the first and, ultimately, the most influential theoretical account of human disorders of visual recognition. In his insightful discussion of the mechanisms underlying deficits in visual recognition, Lissauer argued for a distinction between processes mediating *perception* and those mediating the *association* between the percept and stored information. Thus, according to Lissauer's two-stage model of visual processing, an *apperceptive* visual deficit was attributable to a failure of early visual processes to generate an adequate internal representation of the visual stimulus. An *associative* deficit, in contrast, was characterized by a preserved ability to generate an accurate internal representation of the stimuli but an inability to link the representation to stored information derived from previous experience with the object. Following Lissauer, apperceptive and associative impairments have traditionally been distinguished on the basis of the patient's ability to copy visually presented stimuli: "apperceptive agnosia" is characterized by an inability to copy whereas "associative agnosia" is associated with a preserved ability to produce an accurate drawing of a stimulus which the patient is unable to identify.

Lissauer's (1890) nosology remains the most frequently cited account of visual object agnosia. We will argue below that although this distinction offers a useful starting point for clinical assessment, the simple two-stage model cannot account for the variety and specificity of the visual impairments encountered by the clinician.

At approximately the same time that disorders of visual object recognition were first described, a number of investigators reported a very different pattern of visual deficits characterized by the preserved ability to identify objects but a failure to appreciate object size, location, or distance. Badal (1888), for example, reported a woman with preserved central visual acuity who was able to name letters, words, and objects but was unable to read text because she got lost on the page. Similar cases were described by a number of investigators (e.g., Dunn, 1895; Foerster, 1890).

Gordon Holmes (Holmes, 1918; Holmes & Horrax, 1919) provided perhaps the most detailed and insightful descriptions of patients with disorders of visual attention and spatial localization. In order to provide a richer understanding of the nature of these impairments, excerpts from Holmes' description of a patient with a missile injury involving the bilateral parietal lobes are presented below (Holmes, 1918; Case 1). It should be noted that the patient's visual acuity was normal (6/6 O.U.) and his visual fields full except for an "amblyopia" in the right inferior quadrant extending to approximately 20° from the fixation point.

> He presented no trace of visual agnosia—that is, inability to recognize and distinguish by their visible characters objects he could see. From the first, too, he recognized ordinary symbols, as the plus, subtraction and the multiplication signs, an arrow pointing direction, etc. He was also able to recognize letters, and to read. . . .
>
> Throughout the whole time he was in hospital his most striking symptom was his inability to take hold of or touch any object with accuracy, even when it was placed in the line of vision. When a pencil was held up in front of him he would often project his arm in a totally wrong direction, as though by chance rather than by deliberate decision, or more frequently he would bring his hand to one or other side of it, above or below it, or he would attempt to seize the pencil before he had reached it, or after his hand had passed it. When he failed to touch the object at once he continued groping for it until his hand or arm came into contact with it, in a manner more or less like a man searching for a small object in the dark. . . .
>
> Another prominent symptom was his inability to determine, or at least recognize correctly, the relative positions of objects within his field of vision. . . . The most remarkable errors were made when he was asked to say which of two objects was the nearer to him; even when they were separated by 10 to 15 cm., at a distance of a half a meter from his eyes he made many mistakes. The explanation he offered was "I can only look at one object at a time." . . . When his finger was moved from one to the other, he could, however, recognize their relative positions at once.
>
> If left alone, he quickly deviated from the direction in which he wished to go, and ran into objects even though he was aware they were present. When, for instance, he was asked to walk between two rows of beds, he frequently turned to the right or to the left and stumbled up against one. . . Even when urged to keep his eyes to the ground and avoid obstacles, he often did not succeed; he repeatedly ran with considerable force against a wall or into a large red screen which stood in the ward.
>
> Although there was no ocular palsy, for several weeks after his injury he was frequently unable to move his eyes to order in any direction, though he understood fully what was required of him, and even after three months he often made mistakes or succeeded only after several attempts. When on one occasion he was not asked to look upwards toward the ceiling, he pointed correctly to it with his hand, but moved his eyes first to the right, then to the left, and finally downwards. His eyes were, however, always turned accurately towards an unexpected noise made to one side of him. (pp. 452–455)

Additional patients exhibiting a similar constellation of symptoms were described by Holmes (1918), Riddoch (1917), Balint (1909) and Hecaen and Ajuireguerra (1954) and Benson, Davis, and Snyder (1988). Balint's description of a patient who was unable to voluntarily direct his gaze to visually presented targets, impaired in reaching out and grasping visually presented targets and unable to see more than one object at a time has been particularly influential; these deficits, termed "psychic paralysis of gaze," "optic ataxia," and "simultanagnosia," respectively, represent the core features of Balint's syndrome. (The term "simultanagnosia" was, in fact, coined by Wolpert (1924) in his description of a patient who exhibited letter-by-letter reading and an ability to recognize or interpret a complex array despite a normal ability to identify single items in the array.)

No recapitulation of the history of impairments in visual processing would be complete, however, without mention of the investigators who have denied the very existence of visual agnosia as a specific impairment of recognition. Thus, for example, whereas Munk (1878) described the behavior of his dogs by writing "the dog sees but does not understand," Pavlov (1927) argued that the phenomenon was better described as "the dog understands but does not see sufficiently well." Perhaps the most forceful and influential critic of the concept of visual agnosia was Eberhard Bay (1953) who contended that the phenomena considered under the rubric of "visual agnosia" were caused by disorders of primary sensory disturbance, often complicated by dementia or other deficits in higher cognitive functions. This argument was based in part on data from a patient with an "agnosia" who exhibited impairment in the measures such as the time taken for registration of visual stimuli or the time required for a visual stimulus to fade (*funkionswandel*). The force of this argument was weakened, however, by Ettlinger's (1957) demonstration that some patients with visual processing impairment and dementia who do not exhibit visual agnosia exhibited abnormalities similar to those described by Bay. More recently, Bender and Feldman (1972) resurrected the claim that visual agnosia is attributable to a combination of deficits in primary visual function in conjunction with deficits in memory, attention, and general intellectual function.

While it is essential to consider the possible contribution of low level visual deficits to high level perceptual disorders, the strong positions taken by Bay (1953) and others cannot simply be attributed to caution. They reflect, rather, a skeptical view of the reality of higher level processing operations—an implicit belief that object recognition is *given*, as it were, in the output of the full array of visual feature analyzers. We will attempt to show below that adequacy of low-level visual processing is not sufficient for recognizing objects and locating them in space. It will also emerge from this discussion that a strict classification of visual disorders as sensory, perceptual, and agnosic is not compatible with the characteristics of the visual processing system as they are emerging in current research.

RECENT ADVANCES IN THE UNDERSTANDING OF VISUAL PROCESSING

Although the two-stage model of visual processing proposed by Lissauer has provided a useful starting point for the clinical assessment of disorders of visual processing, subsequent investigations have demonstrated the inadequacy of this simple model. Recent anatomic and physiologic research indicates, for example, that visual input is processed in small number of separate streams. Starting at the retina, two distinct anatomical pathways deal with different forms of visual information (color and movement, for example); this segregation is maintained at the lateral geniculate and the visual cortex where the pathways become further differentiated (see DeYoe & Van Essen, 1988; see also Figure 13-1). Furthermore, in contrast to traditional accounts which assume an exclusively hierarchical mode of visual processing in which visual input is subjected to successively "higher" levels of analysis, recent work has shown that visual information is processed not only in a serial but in a *parallel* fashion. Several lines of evidence support this claim. Anatomic and physiologic investigations in primates, for example, have demonstrated that at least 20 cortical areas are involved in visual processing; many of these regions contain complete topographic maps of the visual field and, perhaps most significantly, many are thought to process different aspects of vision. For example, on the basis of anatomic and physiologic data, area V4 is thought to be particularly important for the processing of color and shape whereas MT may be critical for the processing of movement (and stereopsis).

Additional evidence for parallel processing of visual information also comes from the domain of cognitive psychology; numerous investigations have shown, for example, that when normal subjects are asked to search a visually presented array for a stimulus which differs from distractors by a single parameter (e.g., an X in an array of Os), the stimulus "pops out" of the field of distractors in as little as 10 msec. regardless of the number of distractors or dimensions of the array (Sagi & Julesz, 1985; Treisman & Souther, 1985). This finding has been interpreted as evidence that the processing of single visual features is performed in parallel over the entire array (or visual field).

In the present context, probably the most compelling evidence for parallel streams of visual processing comes from demonstrations by Gross et al. (1972), Pohl (1973), and Mishkin and colleagues that *what* and *where* are processed independently by different cortical systems. (See Ungerleider & Mishkin, 1982, for a review.)

Information about object identity—the *what* in vision—is processed primarily by occipitotemporal cortex. Gross (1973), for example, reported that bilateral ablation of inferior temporal cortex in monkeys causes a severe impairment in the ability to make visual discriminations learned prior to surgery as well as a deficit in the postoperative learning of visual discriminations. Subsequently, destruction of inferior temporal cortex or disconnection of this region from striate cortex was shown to cause deficits on a variety of discrimination tasks including those involving hue, brightness, two-dimensional patterns and three-dimensional objects (Ungerleider & Mishkin, 1982). These monkeys, it should be noted, are not impaired on tasks requiring a discrimination of the location of visually presented objects.

Ablation of occipitoparietal cortex, in contrast, causes the opposite pattern of deficits; following bilateral ablation of parietal lobe, monkeys may perform normally on object discrimination tasks but exhibit a gross deficit on tasks assessing visuospatial function. One test that has been profitably employed to

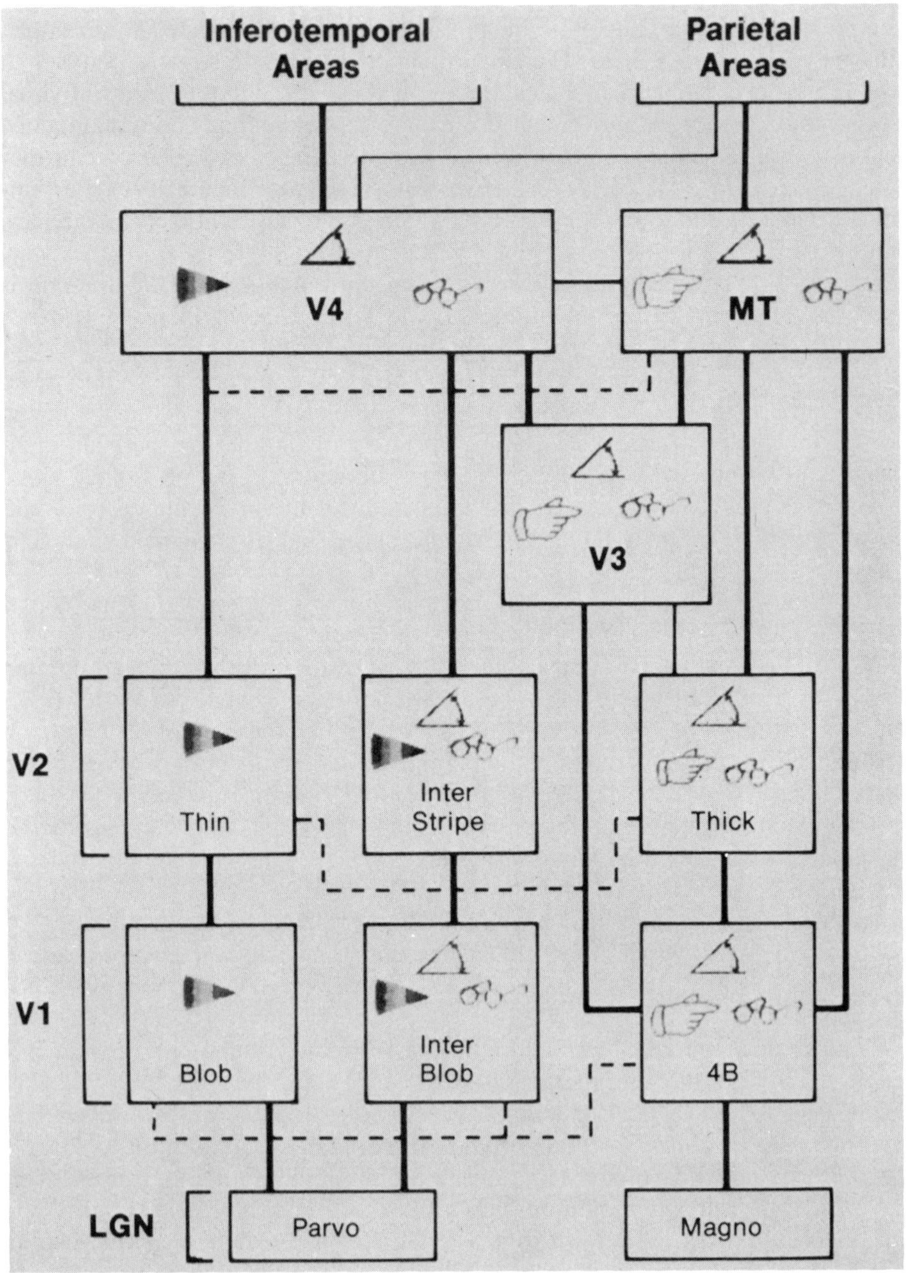

Figure 13-1 Schematic diagram of the anatomical connections and neuronal selectivities of early visual areas in the macaque monkey. Key: LGN = lateral geniculate nucleus,

investigate the processing of spatial information in monkeys following destruction or disconnection of the posterior parietal cortex is the "landmark" test in which monkeys are shown a tray with two food wells and a distinctive object such as a striped cylinder which is closer to one food well; after the object is removed, the animal is rewarded for identifying the food well to which it had been closest. After ablation of the occipitoparietal cortex, these monkeys are profoundly impaired on this task. Bilateral posterior parietal lobe lesions have also been reported to impair performance on other visuospatial tasks including cage finding (Sugishita et al., 1978) and route finding (Petrides & Iversen, 1979).

The results of electrophysiologic investigations are, for the most part, consistent with behavioral studies following cortical ablations. Thus, for example, visually responsive neurons in the inferior temporal cortex have been found to have very large receptive fields, most of which include portions of both visual fields and all of which include the fovea. Information regarding location is apparently not conserved in this stream of visual processing; as pointed out by Gross and Mishkin (1977), however, this type of processing does provide for the ability to recognize an object across a wide range of spatial locations.

Visually responsive neurons in the posterior parietal cortex have quite different characteristics. These neurons have, in general, smaller receptive fields with less representation of the ipsilateral visual field and more extensive representation of the peripheral visual field. According to one estimate (Ungerleider & Mishkin, 1982), the receptive fields of over 60% of posterior parietal neurons do not include the fovea. Lastly, in contrast to inferior parietal neurons which may require complex stimuli for full activation, most posterior parietal neurons respond maximally to simple stimuli such as a point of light (Robinson, Goldberg, & Stanton, 1978).

More recently, Livingstone and Hubel (1987) have proposed that the input to the object recognition system ("what") comes from the parvocellular neurons of the lateral geniculate, whereas the localization pathway may depend on input from the magnocellular division of the lateral geniculate.

---

parvocellular and magnocellular divisions. Divisions of V1 and V2: blob = cytochrome oxidase blob regions; interblob = cytochrome oxidase-poor regions surrounding the blobs; 4B = lamina 4B; thin = thin cytochrome oxidase strips; interstripe = cytochrome oxidase-poor regions between the thin and thick strips; thick = thick cytochrome oxidase strips; V3 = visual area 3; V4 = visual area 4; MT = middle temporal area. Areas V2, V3, V4, and MT have connections to other areas not shown here; heavy lines indicate robust primary connections and thin lines denote weaker, more variable connections. Dotted lines represent observed connections that require additional verification. Icons: triangle = tuned and/or wavelength selectivity; angle symbol = orientation selectivity; spectacles = binocular disparity selectivity and/or strong binocular interactions; pointing hand = direction of motion selectivity. (Reprinted with permission from *Trends in Neuroscience*, Vol 2, DeYoe, E. A. & Van Essen, D. C. Concurrent processing streams in monkey visual cortex, 1988, Elsevier.)

A MODEL OF VISUAL PROCESSING

Based on these various lines of evidence as well as other data that will be considered below, we have developed a model of visual processing that can serve as a framework for the investigation and interpretation of the visual disturbances that result from brain lesions in man. The model, which is depicted in Figure 13-2, postulates the following stages and processes:

Visual Feature Maps

As noted above, detailed physiologic and anatomic investigations in animals have demonstrated that as many as 20 discrete cortical areas receive visual information, several of which appear to operate in parallel as analyzers of specific visual "features" such as color, line orientation, spatial frequency and movement (Maunsell & Newsome, 1987; DeYoe & Van Essen, 1988). Converging evidence for parallel processing of basic attributes of the visual array comes from psychological experiments of the kind referred to earlier (e.g., the "pop-out" effect demonstrated by Treisman and her colleagues [Treisman & Souther, 1985; Treisman & Gelade, 1980]). This parallel or "preattentive" form of processing is thought to proceed automatically and to provide a set of maps specific to each visual feature which identify the spatial location(s) of that feature; preattentive processing would generate, for example, maps of the location of angles, colors, vertical lines, and so on (Sagi & Julesz, 1985; Robertson, chapter 4).

Visual Analog Representation (VAR)

Although the visual feature maps collectively provide sufficient data to assemble a veridical image of the visual environment, "seeing" requires two types of integrative processes: the integration of information across feature maps, which results in the conjoining of features as a function of location; and integration across arrays as a function of similarity to yield surfaces. The integration of visual feature information is a capacity-limited process that requires "selective attention." Thus, search for feature combinations (e.g., a red X in a field of blue Xs and red Os) does not show the "pop-out" effect characteristic of search for individual features; search is serial rather than parallel, and dependent on the number of elements in the array. Under conditions where attentional capacity is limited (for example, by an auxiliary task), the observer is at risk of perceiving "illusory conjunctions" of visual features (e.g., angle and color) actually present at different loci in the array. Treisman and Schmidt (1982) reported, for example, that when asked to identify black digits flanking three colored letters, normal subjects often reported incorrect combinations of letters and colors, reporting a pink T when a pink S and a yellow T had, in fact, been present. Selective attention deployed over a limited area of the visual field is, in other words, the glue that binds the separately analyzed visual features together.

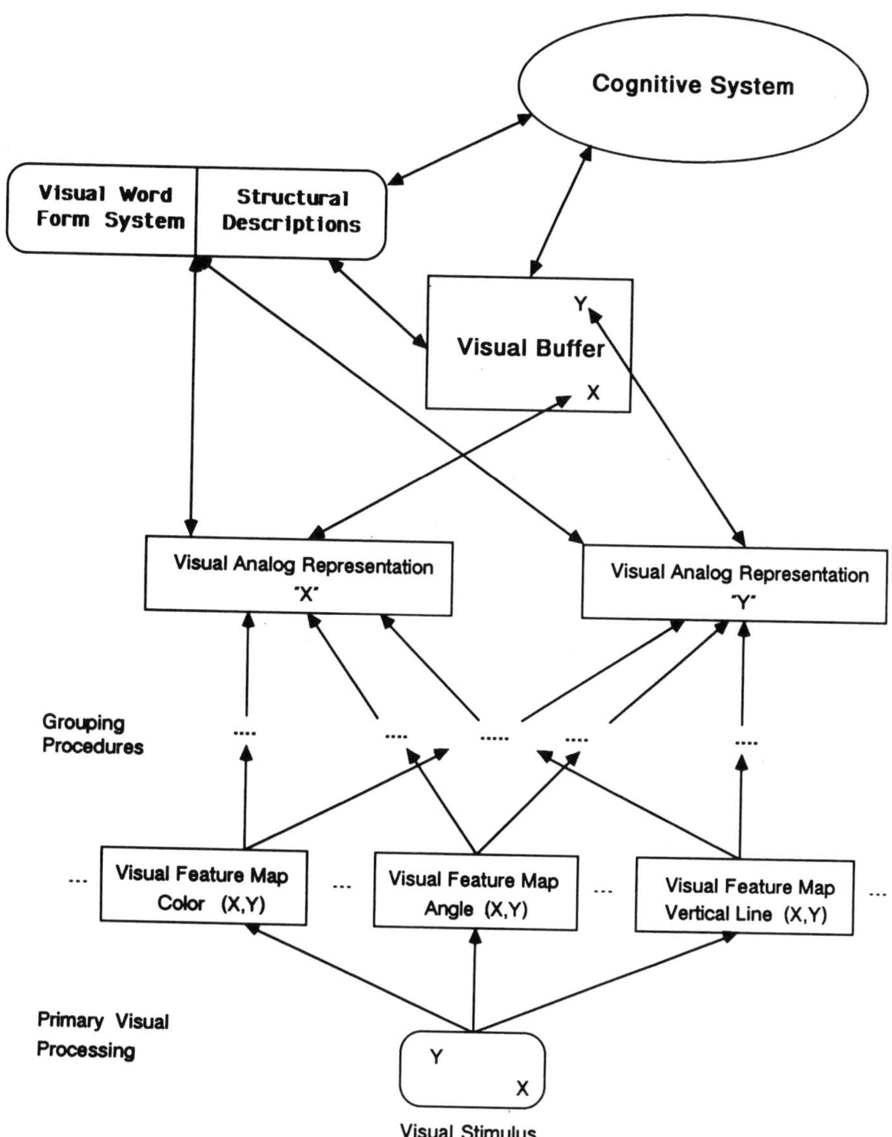

Figure 13-2 A schematic diagram of the proposed model of visual processing.

Feature integration results in the generation of a retinotopic (that is, eye position and fixation-dependent) map in which coherent regions of the array are represented as surfaces, and attributes such as depth and orientation are encoded. We call this representation the VAR, a term that has been used to designate a level of processing that provides a precise but transient encoding of the information in a briefly presented visual display (DiLollo & Dixon, 1988; Irwin & Youmans, 1986). Results of psychological experiments indicate that the VAR decays over a 150–300 msec. interval and is susceptible to visual masking

(Irwin & Youmans, 1986). The VAR, which is recomputed for each fixation, provides the input to object and word recognition systems ("structural descriptions" and "visual word forms," respectively).

As noted above, this integrated representation is achieved under the influence of "selective attention" deployed over a restricted region of the visual field. When confronted with a novel visual display, the visual system must first determine the site to which attentional capacity should initially be directed. A number of investigators have described visual processing mechanisms which may help guide the initial deployment of selective attention; we have designated these mechanisms "grouping procedures." Prinzmetal and colleagues (Prinzmetal & Banks, 1976; Prinzmetal, 1981), for example, have demonstrated that visual feature integration is influenced by the principles developed by Gestalt psychologists. There is also evidence to suggest that the deployment of selective attention is slowed by the presence of other elements in the array. Thus, data from Kahnemann, Treisman, and Burkell (1983; also Treisman, Kahneman, & Burkell, 1983) demonstrate that the presence of a nonverbal distractor significantly alters the time required to read a single word. The cost associated with the distractor suggests that most or all visual stimuli are, at least briefly, analyzed.

To achieve an integrated representation, attentional capacity must be deployed serially across the array (e.g., Treisman & Gormican, 1988); this entails shifting the attentional spotlight from one locus to another, in itself a complicated process (Posner, Cohen, & Rafal, 1984; Posner, Walker, Friedrich, & Rafal, 1984).

Structural Descriptions and the Visual Word Form System

We use the term "structural descriptions" to refer to stored representations of objects; following Marr (1982), we assume that object recognition requires a stable representation which is independent of viewpoint. Thus, these representations are "object-centered" in that they are described with reference to an *object-based* rather than a viewer-centered coordinate system. On our view, object recognition entails the matching of integrated visual feature information represented at the visual buffer (see below) to a structural description and the subsequent activation of the semantic information linked to that structural description.

In the real world, of course, familiar objects may be viewed from many different perspectives. To account for the ability to recognize objects across these transformations, it is necessary to postulate a procedure for transposing the multitude of depictions of an object to a representation which may activate a structural description. Such a procedure, which will be discussed later in this chapter, provides for the phenomenon of "object constancy."

Visual Buffer

A more stable representation of the visual environment is built up at the level of the visual buffer which stores information about object location. The buffer is a viewer-centered map of locations which binds visual information (the current display at the VAR) to structural descriptions. Information in the visual buffer, which persists over seconds (Phillips, 1974; Irwin & Youmans, 1986; Kroll, Parks, Parkinson, Bieber, & Johnson, 1970), accumulates over several fixations and is not susceptible to visual masking. We hypothesize that conscious perception of the visual environment normally involves articulation of the VAR with the corresponding region of the visual buffer; while it is the representation of surfaces in the VAR that is explicitly "visible," it is the information bound to it in the buffer that enables interpretation of the visual input, localizes it with respect to the observer, and serves as the basis for action. The binding of information across these structures is a function of selective attention.

Although this model is essentially an information-processing account of visual function, we believe it to be consonant with current knowledge of the anatomy and physiology of vision. Thus, we suggest that visual feature maps are dependent on distinct regions of striate and prestriate visual cortex which, recent work suggests, are differentiated both functionally and anatomically; thus, for example, features such as color and angle appear to be processed by areas that receive differential input from the magnocellular and parvocellular streams (Livingstone & Hubel, 1987; Maunsell & Newsome, 1987). A number of lines of evidence suggest that "selective attention," which plays a major role in the model described above and has been demonstrated to influence neuronal responsiveness at a number of cortical loci (e.g., V4; Moran & Desimone, 1985), may be dependent on portions of the thalamus including the pulvinar and nucleus reticularis (Jones, 1985; see LaBerge & Brown, 1989). The latter structure, which has a lateral inhibitory network and connections with the thalamic relay nuclei, has been described as having physiologic properties which could subserve the role of selective attention. A number of investigators including Watson, Valenstein, & Heilman (1981) and Crick (1984) have proposed that this structure facilitates the integration of information across cortical regions, a function we have identified as selective attention. Although there is anatomic evidence demonstrating reciprocal connections between the lateral, medial, and inferior pulvinar nuclei and multiple areas of visual cortex, the role of the pulvinar in visual selective attention is not clear (Jones, 1985). It should be noted, however, that unilateral injections of the GABA-inergic drugs into a subnucleus of the pulvinar may produce an attentional deficit in the contralateral visual field (Peterson, Robinson, & Morris, 1987).

The neural basis of the shift of visual selective attention has been investigated by Posner and colleagues. On the basis of data from patients with degenerative disorders affecting the midbrain (progressive supranuclear palsy) as well as lesions of the parietal lobes, these investigators assert that the movement of visual selective attention may be dependent on midbrain structures such as the superior colliculus whereas the ability to disengage selective attention may be impaired by parietal lobe lesions (Posner, 1989).

The anatomic underpinnings of the VAR and the visual buffer are less clear, possibly because these computationally distinct levels of processing are dependent on input from multiple cortical regions. Given the clinical data (briefly described above; see below) and evidence from monkeys that the processing of what and where may be subserved by different visual cortices, one might expect the visual buffer to be critically dependent on the integration of information from both visual streams. The model described above assumes that selective attention provides the linkage between the what and where systems. In this context it is interesting to note that Andersen, Essick, and Siegel (1985) have argued that neurons in area 7a exhibit properties that suggest a mechanism for generating an egocentric rather than retinotopic representation of space; as one of the critical features of the putative visual buffer is that it is organized in an egocentric fashion, we would speculate that this area may, in part, provide the anatomic substrate for the visual buffer. Lastly, it should be noted that recent data demonstrate interconnections between structures in the what and where stream (e.g., V4 and MT; see DeYoe & Van Essen, 1988; Livingstone & Hubel, 1987); these connections may permit the integration of information from these streams and may represent part of the anatomic instantiation of selective attention.

Nosology of Visual Processing Disorders

The processing model and its anatomical substrate, to the extent that we know it, provide a new conceptual framework for categorizing the various disorders of visual processing that have been described in the literature. It follows, for example, from both functional and anatomical considerations that there are likely to be disturbances involving single visual features, such as color or movement; that other disorders should reflect failure in the integration of feature information; and that there should be a variety of other disturbances reflecting impairment to memory stores (structural descriptions), spatial maps (visual buffer), and the attentional capacity that we have postulated as the mechanism that binds these disparate forms of information.

Impairments in Visual Feature Processing

In the present context, visual features include attributes of a visual stimulus such as line orientation, length, color, luminance, closure, curved/straight, intersection and convergence (Treisman & Gormican, 1988). Disorders of visual feature processing have rarely been described, probably because these deficits are frequently associated with visual field deficits and are often considered "sensory" rather than "agnosic." Perhaps the best example of a deficit of this type is achromatopsia.

Achromatopsia

Achromatopsia is an acquired disorder of color perception characterized by a loss of ability to discriminate between colors. Although the disorder may be associated with visual field defects, prosopagnosia or acquired dyslexia in some patients, it is crucial to note that an inability to recognize and discriminate between colors may occur *in the absence* of impairments in the ability to appreciate other forms of visual information, such as shape or depth.

The severity of the impairment is variable, presumably reflecting the size and location of the lesion(s) causing the disorder. Some patients complain of a complete absence of color, stating that the world looks like a "black and white TV;" whereas other patients note only a loss of color clarity or vibrancy which does not prevent the patient from distinguishing between colors. Stimuli presented in the affected portion of the visual field are often described as "dirty" "washed out," or "blackish." Damasio and colleagues (1980), for example, report that one of their patients with achromatopsia complained that all the draperies in her home were "dirty;" she had them cleaned only to find that they looked no better for her efforts.

Achromatopsic defects may involve a portion of the visual field, a hemifield or the entire visual field. Lesions of the inferior occipitotemporal cortex may, for example, produce achromatopsia restricted to a single visual field; lesions of this region on the right may be associated with a left hemiachromatopsia in the absence of other readily identifiable behavioral deficits; similar lesions in the left hemisphere may present with pure alexia if the lesion extends into the paraventriculuar white matter or with a superior right quadrantanopia with inferior hemiachromatopsia if the lesion involves the optic radiations or inferior portions of visual cortex (Damasio & Damasio, 1983).

Most patients with full-field achromatopsia exhibit additional visual perceptual disorders. Pearlman, Birch, and Meadows, (1979), for example, described a patient with right and left superior quadrantanopias and achromatopsia in the preserved inferior quadrants who also exhibited prosopagnosia and topographical disorientation. Other investigators have reported prosopagnosia (Damasio et al., 1980) and visual object agnosia in association with achromatopsia.

Achromatopsia is, in most instances, attributable to vascular lesions in the distribution of the posterior cerebral artery which involve the inferior occipitotemporal cortex while sparing, at least in part, the optic radiations and the calcarine cortex. From the original report of acquired achromatopsia by Verrey (1888) to the present, pathologic investigations of patients with this disorder have revealed damage to the fusiform (or medial occipitotemporal) and lingual gyri in the hemisphere contralateral to the affected portion of the visual field, or in the case of whole-field achromatopsia, in both hemispheres (e.g., Verrey, 1888; Mackay & Dunlop, 1899). CT scans from patients with this disorder have demonstrated similar lesions (Albert, Reches, & Silverberg, 1975a; Pearlman et al., 1979; Meadows, 1974; Green & Lessel, 1977; Damasio et al., 1980). Occasionally, however, the disorder has been observed with lesions in other sites; Damasio, for example, has observed achromatopsia with lesions of the white matter of the occipitotemporal region as well as lesions of the superior occipital lobe (Damasio, 1987).

As described briefly above, recent investigations of the anatomy and physiology of the primate visual system suggest that color information is processed by the parvocellular division of the lateral geniculate, the "blob cells" of the primary visual cortex (V1), and the cells of the "thin stripes" in V2. A higher visual area, V4, has been demonstrated to contain a preponderance of color-selective cells, prompting some investigators to speculate that the lingual and medial occipitotemporal gyri represent the human analogue of V4. Recent investigations, however, have demonstrated that most cells in this region are also highly selective for stimulus form, suggesting that form and color are processed together within V4 (Desimone & Schein, 1987). In light of the fact most patients with achromatopsia do *not* exhibit impairments in form discrimination, the hypothesis that the lingual and medial occipitotemporal gyri represent the human analogue of V4 remains quite speculative.

In this context, brief mention should be made of the phenomenon of dyschromatopsia, a disorder characterized by a perversion of color vision. In this condition, color perception may be preserved but distorted as if the patient is viewing the environment through a tinted filter. As pointed out by Meadows (1974), the fact that two patients developed this phenomenon as their achromatopsia resolved suggests that this disorder is closely related to achromatopsia; interestingly both patients exhibited altitudinal visual field defects suggesting that they suffered from inferior occipital or occipitotemporal lesions (Critchley, 1965; Rondot, deRecondo, Ribadeau, & Dumas, 1967).

There are other disorders that involve color information ("color agnosia" or "color anomia"); as in achromatopsia, such patients are unable to name colors, but their ability to *discriminate* between colors is unaffected. These disorders will be discussed later in this chapter.

LATER STAGES IN OBJECT RECOGNITION

The Visual Analog Representation

On the model of visual processing described above, the VAR is the level of representation at which visual feature information is integrated under the influence of selective attention. Impairment at this level, therefore, would be expected to cause a failure of object recognition in association with normal visual feature registration. Since this putative level of representation has not been incorporated in previous accounts of visual processing disorders, we are unable to identify patients whose deficits can be reliably attributed to a deficit at this level. One previously described disorder which may be attributable to an impairment at this level is described below.

Impaired Processing of Shape

Normal vision requires that information about edges, orientation, length (or, more generally, spatial parameters) be integrated with other types of visual feature information to generate shapes. As accurate information about stimulus shape would appear to be a prerequisite for object identification, failure to process this information accurately might be expected to be associated with visual object agnosia. In fact, several agnosic patients have been described whose deficit may be attributable to a failure to generate accurate form information.

One such patient, a 25-year-old man who suffered from carbon monoxide poisoning, was reported by Benson and Greenberg (1971) and Efron (1968). Although the patient exhibited a profound impairment in visual object recognition, careful examination of his vision revealed that many aspects of visual processing were normal or nearly so. His visual fields were normal except for a minimal constriction (although his performance was apparently somewhat erratic). Visual acuity was difficult to assess but appeared to be at least 20/100 ou. As demonstrated by the ability to discriminate between hues differing by as little as 7–10 mμ, his color perception was normal. He discriminated differences in luminance of as little as 0.1 log units, a performance which is only marginally impaired relative to controls. Lastly, he could detect movement normally and his performance on flicker fusion and spatial summation tasks was only mildly impaired.

Thus, the patient performed quite accurately on many tests requiring that he make judgments about single attributes of objects. He was profoundly impaired, however, when the task required that he make a judgment about the shape of two stimuli. For example, while he correctly indicated that a triangle and circle were identical in hue, he was unable to determine if the stimuli were the same shape. This phenomenon was, perhaps, most graphically illustrated on a task in which he was asked to indicate if two black silhouette stimuli matched for reflectance and size were the same shape. He performed poorly, indicating on some trials, for example, that a square and a long thin rectangle (that is, the long and short edges of the rectangle differed by a factor of eight) matched for area were identical in shape. Although the patient exhibited several other types of visual deficit including a visual search impairment, a relative deficit in the appreciation of location and distance to stationary objects, the authors (and subsequent investigators) attributed the patient's visual object agnosia to his failure to derive an accurate representation of shape from visual feature information. Somewhat similar patterns of impairment were reported for two additional patients who suffered carbon monoxide poisoning (Adler, 1944, 1950; Campion & Latto, 1985; Campion, 1987). Although the lack of information about the processing of visual features such as line length and angle make the interpretation of these data difficult, we believe these data to be consistent with the hypothesis that these patients suffered from a deficit at the VAR.

Impairments in Structural Descriptions

The VAR provides the input to object and word recognition systems ("structural descriptions" and "visual word forms," respectively). Object "recognition" can occur only if the information displayed in the VAR activates a stored entry in the catalog of familiar forms.

Failure to recognize an object despite normal visual processing to the level of the VAR can occur for a number of reasons. First, a patient may fail to recognize an object because of an inability to *access* preserved structural descriptions. Although we are unaware of any well-studied patients whose performance is attributable to this type of deficit, it is possible to specify the pattern of performance which would be predicted of such a patient. As the patient would have achieved an integrated representation, one might expect the patient to be able to copy drawings of real and imaginary objects. Furthermore, one would expect the copies to be executed in slavish fashion; one would not expect to see corrections or modifications in the output (e.g., adding a missing hand when copying a drawing of a person) which would suggest the influence of stored information about object structure. Additionally, such patients should not only be impaired in the explicit identification of objects but would be expected to perform poorly on an object/nonobject test in which the subject is asked to discriminate between drawings of real objects such as a hammer and nonobjects generated by altering a depiction of a real object or combining component parts of real objects such as a head of a hammer and the handle of a saw (Riddoch & Humphreys, 1987; see below).

Patients with normal visual processing to the level of the VAR may also be impaired in object recognition because of a *loss* of structural descriptions. Although such a deficit may, of course, be difficult to distinguish from a failure to access structural descriptions, there are several criteria which may serve to distinguish these disorders. Patients with deficits in visually-based access to preserved structural descriptions may be expected (in the absence of motor or other impairments) to draw objects from memory whereas patients in whom information about object structure is lost would not be expected to be able to do this. Sartori and Job (1988) recently reported a patient who was impaired in naming pictures of exemplars of certain semantic categories (including animals, fruits, and vegetables). He was impaired on a variety of tasks assessing the integrity of structural descriptions including object/nonobject decision tests and drawing from memory. Interestingly, he was also impaired on tests requiring the retrieval of visual attributes of objects from memory. The investigators suggested that the pattern of performance was consistent with an impairment at the level of structural descriptions.

Impairments in Object Constancy

Familiar objects are quickly and effortlessly recognized even when viewed from very different perspectives. A coffee cup, for example, may be viewed from the bottom when encountered in a dishwasher, from below when situated on a high shelf or from directly overhead when placed in a sink or on a table. In spite of the obvious fact that the same cup seen from these perspectives will give rise to very different representation of features and surfaces at the VAR, normal subjects have little difficulty in identifying the coffee cup. The ability to recognize that an object is identical across view shifts may be termed object constancy.

Several investigators have demonstrated that object constancy may be impaired by brain damage. Warrington and Taylor (1973), for example, asked patients with focal brain injury to name two sets of 20 pictures: one set of pictures depicted the object from a "prototypical" or usual perspective, while the other set included pictures of the same objects taken from what the investigators considered to be a nonprototypical or unusual perspective. They found that patients with lesions involving the posterior portion of the right hemisphere were impaired in naming the objects depicted in the unusual view photographs but not in the usual view photographs. Subsequently, Warrington and Taylor (1978) performed an experiment in which subjects were shown two pictures, one a usual view of an object and the other an unusual view of the same or a different object. Subjects were asked to indicate if the pictures were of the same or different objects. They found that subjects with damage to the posterior portion of the right hemisphere were more impaired than patients with left hemisphere lesions.

More recently several researchers have investigated the mechanisms by which object constancy is achieved (Layman & Greene, 1988; Humphreys & Riddoch, 1984; Riddoch & Humphreys, 1986). There are at least two mechanisms which may contribute to this ability. First, the individual's catalog of structural descriptions may be searched for a match for the viewer-centered, retinotopically mapped representation at the VAR; if no match is found, the retinotopically mapped representation may be transformed by means of procedures such as coding of the relations between local features relative to object's principal axis (Marr, 1982) or a mental rotation process similar to that described by Shepard and others (e.g., Shepard & Metzler, 1971). Second, matching across view shifts might be accomplished by the identification of distinctive or salient visual features (e.g., the handle of a cup, the spokes of a wheel) which are relatively invariant across changes in perspective.

Humphreys and Riddoch (1984; Riddoch & Humphreys, 1986) have presented data from five subjects impaired in matching across view shifts which suggest that, indeed, both mechanisms may be relevant. Four of their patients, all with right posterior hemisphere lesions, were particularly impaired with stimuli in which the principal axis had been foreshortened, suggesting that the patients were unable to generate a representation of an object relative to its principal axis; these data are consonant with the computational model of Marr and Nishihara (1978) according to which a structural description is determined relative to its principal axis. In contrast to the patients with right hemisphere lesions, the fifth patient (HJA) was more impaired on stimuli in which the principal distinctive feature was obscured, suggesting that he relied upon distinctive feature information to achieve object constancy (however, see Shallice, 1988, for a critique of this interpretation).

Warrington and James (1986) also investigated the effects of foreshortening on object recognition in patients with right hemisphere lesions. These investigators employed an apparatus which projected shadows to the object to form a single stereoscopic shadow image. In one condition, objects were slowly rotated around their vertical axis so that they became progressively easier to identify; in a second condition, objects were rotated around their horizontal axis. Controls and subjects with right hemisphere lesions were asked to identify the object at the smallest possible angle of rotation. The latter subjects were impaired relative to controls in both conditions. Of particular interest here, however, is the finding that patients with right hemisphere lesions did not benefit from the initial presentation of information about the principal axis of the object. According to Warrington and James (1986), these data do not support the Marr-Nishihara account of object recognition but are consistent with their postulate that objects are represented as a hierarchy of sets of distinctive features.

Lastly, it is interesting to note that stored information about an object's form assists in matching stimuli across view shifts. Layman and Greene (1988), for example, found that normals and subjects with unilateral hemisphere lesions were on some occasions unable to name unusual views of familiar objects; they responded more accurately, however, when asked to match the *same* unusual view to one of two prototypical views of familiar objects. These data are consistent with subjects' anecdotal reports that the presence of the prototypical view assisted the identification of stimuli which they had previously been unable to identify. Although semantic information may also facilitate matching across view-shifts by means of top-down processes, such information does not appear to be necessary for matching across view shifts as demonstrated by Warrington (1975) who reported data from three patients with dementia who were unable to explicitly identify some objects but were able to reliably match usual and unusual views of the same object. When shown a prototypical view of a ping-pong paddle after having failed to name the unusual view of the same object, one of Warrington's patients informed her that he had already said that he couldn't identify the pictured stimulus.

Thus, at this point the relative contributions of these and perhaps other mechanisms to the phenomenon of object constancy remain unclear.

Impairments in Access to Semantic Information

Object recognition requires the activation of stored semantic information. Failure to activate this information either because of an impairment in access to semantics or a disruption of the semantic store itself may result in what Lissauer (1890) termed an "associative" visual agnosia. A number of patients with this type of processing deficit have been described (Rubens & Benson, 1971; Taylor & Warrington, 1971; Benson, Segarra, & Albert, 1974; Newcombe & Ratcliff, 1974; Albert et al., 1975a, 1975b; Mack & Boller, 1977). In light of these and other case descriptions, there is little doubt about the existence of a condition which fits Teuber's classical (but restrictive) definition of agnosia as "perception stripped of its meaning" (Teuber, 1968).

According to traditional usage, associative agnosia is distinguished by the ability to copy or to match to sample visually presented stimuli which the patient cannot name. There is reason to believe, however, that this criterion may not reliably distinguish between patients whose deficits affect processing up to and including access to structural descriptions and those which impair activation of semantic information. Consider, for example, the cognitive demands imposed by copying; as noted by Ratcliff and Newcombe (1982), there are at least two potential mechanisms by which a visual stimulus may be copied. The first is a slavish, line-by-line procedure by which the reproduction is gradually compiled. On the model of visual processing described previously, information displayed at the VAR might be sufficient for this type of copying. Slavish or piecemeal copying has, in fact, been described by a number of investigators. Alternatively, copying may be performed by an "object-based" procedure in which a structural description activated by perceptual information serves as the template for copying. These procedures should be empirically distinguishable; patients who copy in a piecemeal fashion may copy real and nonobjects equally well and would not be expected to have difficulty, for example, copying "impossible" figures. In contrast, patients who copy by means of an "object-based" procedure might be expected to perform better with real objects; these patients might also correct inaccuracies (e.g., an upside down nose in a picture of a face) in stimuli which they could not identify. To our knowledge empirical data which might distinguish between these putative types of copying are not available. In this context, the major point to be made is that performance on simple tasks such as copying or matching to sample do not permit one to reliably infer the level(s) at which processing is impaired.

As the impairment in associative agnosia is thought to reflect an impairment in access to or the loss of semantic information, one might expect patients with this disorder to perform normally on tests of object constancy; a number of patients described as having associative agnosia have, in fact, been demonstrated to perform normally on at least some tasks involving matching across view shifts (Taylor & Warrington, 1971; Warrington, 1975; see also Humphreys & Riddoch, 1987).

Although there is a clear conceptual distinction between disorders of *access to* as compared to *loss of* semantic information, in practice it has proven difficult to distinguish between these types of processing deficits (Humphreys, Riddoch, & Quinlan, 1988; Shallice, 1988). One well-studied patient (JB) whose deficit appears to involve access to semantic information was recently reported by Humphreys and Riddoch (1987; Humphreys et al., 1988). JB was impaired in naming visually presented objects after a left hemisphere contusion and subdural hematoma. He exhibited a right homonymous hemanopia but performed well on a variety of other visual tasks in his good left visual field. JB performed relatively well on tasks assessing object constancy as well as object/nonobject tasks assessing the integrity of structural descriptions; thus, he performed as well as controls on a task in which he was asked to discriminate between drawings of real objects and drawings generated by combining parts of objects drawn from the same semantic category to generate a nonobject. He was impaired, however, on tasks assessing access to semantic information from visual as compared with verbal input; for example, the patient made more errors in response to specific questions about chickens when shown a picture of the bird as compared to the condition in which the name was provided auditorily. These and other data were interpreted as evidence for an impairment in visually based access to semantic information.

Loss of Semantic Information

Finally, a visual object recognition deficit may, in principle, be caused by a loss of semantic information. Such a patient might fail to recognize a comb, for example, because stored information about the attributes, uses, and associations of a comb have been lost. Warrington (1975) reported three patients with progressive dementia whose performance, she argues, may be explained on this basis. These patients were impaired in object (and word) recognition despite relatively normal language, memory and "visual and perceptual" functions. These patients performed well, for example, on tests of shape discrimination, figure-ground discrimination, and matching across view shifts.

Marin et al. (1983) reported a patient with probable Pick's disease whose impairments were also attributed to a loss of semantic information. At a point in her illness at which she was profoundly impaired in the production and comprehension of speech, this patient continued to perform well on a variety of visual perceptual tasks. For example, the patient was able to copy words and designs; she produced an exact copy of the sentence BiRdS ArE PReTtY, using upper and lower case letters as in the original. The patient was also able to match letters, drawings, photographs, and coins on the basis of visual information. In contrast, she was grossly impaired on all tasks involving semantic judgments; she was, for example, unable to sort pictures according to semantic categories or categorize coins as a function of value.

Recently, Warrington and Shallice (1979) and Shallice (1988) have proposed that disorders of semantic access may be distinguished from loss of semantic representation by a number of criteria. One consequence of a loss of semantic information, according to these investigators, is response consistency; thus, for example, on this argument, loss of semantic information pertaining to hammers would be manifested by consistently poor performance on questions pertaining to hammers. A second factor which several authors have considered to be evidence of loss of semantic information is reduced efficacy of semantic priming or cueing (Nebes, Martin, & Horn, 1984; Shallice, 1988). A third prediction of the semantic loss hypothesis, according to Warrington and Shallice (1979; also see Warrington, 1975), is that more specific (or subordinate) information will be impaired first, whereas superordinate information will be relatively preserved. Although the adequacy of these criteria remains controversial, Chertkow and Bub (1990) recently reported data from 10 patients with presumed Alzheimer's disease demonstrating the co-occurrence of these three phenomena. These investigators found a significant correlation between performance on tests of naming pictures and pointing to named pictures in an array of foils drawn from the same semantic category. Additionally, they found that their demented patients were significantly more impaired on questions probing subordinate as compared to superordinate level semantic information. In light of these data as well as findings from other investigators, we believe that some neuropsychological deficits including picture naming and pointing to named pictures may be attributable to a loss of semantic information.

IMPAIRMENTS AT THE VISUAL BUFFER

As described briefly above, the visual buffer stores information about object location. Information is represented in egocentric rather than retinotopic coordinates and persists over seconds, permitting information from multiple fixations to be integrated into a map of the visual environment. We hypothesize that object identity is not explicitly marked in the visual buffer; rather, the locations of objects are marked by "tokens" which are linked to structural descriptions, on the one hand, and information in the VAR on the other. In one sense, then, the visual buffer may be regarded as the "where" system, while the structural descriptions provide information about "what". The integration of the two systems so critical for normal vision is provided by the linkages between place tokens and structural descriptions.

In this section we will discuss two distinct types of impairment in the visual buffer. We suggest that the first, termed "spatial disorientation" by Holmes (1918, 1919), is characterized by a disruption of the spatial map or buffer itself. The clinical phenomena encountered in patients with this type of disorder are described by Holmes in the excerpt quoted earlier in the chapter. It should be emphasized that for many of these patients, single objects are recognized normally, suggesting that the processes (and brain structures) culminating in activation of structural descriptions are intact. In contrast to this preserved function, however, these patients may be utterly incapable of locating a previously (correctly perceived) object. These patients may, for example, be unable to point or walk to an object at which they are gazing, unable to direct their gaze to an object and unable to indicate the spatial relationships between two or more objects which they have correctly identified. These deficits are not likely to be attributable to a motor impairment or confusion because many of these patients are able to point to or direct their gaze to named body parts (which can, of course, be located without vision) quickly and accurately.

A second type of impairment to be considered in this context is a disorder in simultaneous form perception, often termed "simultanagnosia." Patients of this type may be unimpaired in the recognition of single objects but have difficulty identifying more than a single object in an array. On the basis of a recent, extensive evaluation of a patient with this disorder, we postulate that this disorder is attributable to limited capacity to form or maintain multiple linkages between structural descriptions and locations marked at the visual buffer. In order to illustrate the general approach to the investigation of visual processing disorders and to demonstrate the utility of single case investigations, data from this patient will be described in some detail later in this chapter.

OTHER DISORDERS OF VISUAL PROCESSING

In this section we briefly discuss a number of additional visual processing disorders; as the underlying processing impairment has not been well established for most of these disorders, we have elected not to attempt to emulate Procrustes by insisting that they be considered within the theoretical framework which motivates this chapter.

Color Anomia and Color Agnosia

As noted above, achromatopsia is a disorder of color perception in which patients lose the ability to discriminate between colors. The condition is symptomatic in the sense that these patients are typically aware of their perceptual deficit. In this section we describe several quite different disorders of color processing; these disorders differ from achromatopsia in that patients are typically unaware of the deficit and color perception, as assessed by the Ishihara plates or Farnsworth-Munsell tests, is normal or nearly so.

Historically, there has been a great deal of confusion about these disorders. Some investigators have employed the designation "color agnosia" (e.g., Hecaen & Albert, 1978), while others have referred to the same patterns of performance—and in some instances, the same patient—as "color anomia" (e.g., Oxbury, Oxbury, & Humphrey, 1969). In the following brief discussion, we suggest that a distinction be drawn between these disorders. Thus, for example, we reserve the term "color anomia" for a condition characterized by the inability to name visually presented colors, usually, but not always, in association with an auditory comprehension deficit for color names as demonstrated by an impairment in pointing to a named color (see Goodglass, Klein, Carey, & Jones, 1966). A variety of explanations for color anomia have been offered. Perhaps the most influential account has been the "disconnection" theory proposed by Geschwind and Fusillo (1966; see also Geschwind, 1965). These investigators reported a 58-year-old man with pure alexia who was able to name objects and ideograms but not colors. This patient was able to match colors and sort visually presented color patches according to hue, suggesting that he did not suffer from a defect in color perception. Additionally, he was able to state the usual color of familiar objects (e.g., a banana). Autopsy revealed that the patient had suffered an infarction involving the left calcarine cortex, the posterior third of the corpus callosum, and the left hippocampus.

Geschwind and Fusillo (1966) reasoned that, as a consequence of the left occipital infarction, primary visual information did not reach the left hemisphere; additionally, the lesion of the splenium of the corpus callosum prevented visual information processed in the normal right hemisphere from reaching the left hemisphere. Thus, the result of these lesions was a "disconnection" of the left hemisphere language centers from visual information. The preserved ability to name objects was attributed to the fact that the visual image of objects activated additional somesthetic associations in the parietal lobe. As most of the body of the corpus callosum was not infarcted, it was further assumed that the somesthetic information was transmitted to the left hemisphere language centers by callosal fibers which crossed anterior to the infarction.

Although this account may provide a reasonable explanation for some cases of color anomia, the disconnection hypothesis does not account for the data from all patients. Davidoff and Ostergaard (1984), for example, recently reported a patient who was able to point to named colors but unable to name colors. On the basis of a series of elegant experiments, they concluded that the deficit was attributable to a short-term memory deficit which was specific to color.

On our usage, "color agnosia" refers to a modality independent impairment in the ability to associate objects and their color. These patients are similar to patients with color anomia in that color *perception* is normal and they perform poorly on "visual-verbal" tasks in which verbal information (e.g., a color name) must be produced in response to a visual stimulus (e.g., a color). They differ from color anomics, however, in that they are impaired on tasks requiring the retrieval of color information on the basis of *verbal* information. Thus, patients with color agnosia perform poorly when asked to provide the color of a named object (e.g., "what color is a lime?").

Patients with what we term color agnosia have been reported by a number of investigators (e.g., Stengel, 1948; Oxbury, Oxbury, & Humphrey, 1969, Case 2). Kinsbourne and Warrington (1964), for example, described a patient with normal visual fields and color perception who was unable to point to or name colors, could not provide the color appropriate to an object and could not select the appropriate color marker with which to draw an object. Additionally, the patient was impaired on tasks involving the acquisition of associations between color and object names but was able to acquire verbal associations in which color names were not involved. A similar case was reported by Oxbury et al. (Case 2, 1969) who attributed this impairment to a "color aphasia akin to a comprehension deficit" (p. 856). Although these investigators included this disorder under the rubric of "color anomia," they clearly distinguished the disorder from the visual modality-specific disorder secondary to a disconnection between visual input and the left hemisphere structures subserving language.

Loss of Stereopsis and Depth Perception

Stereopsis refers to the procedures by which depth is computed from binocular visual information. As a consequence of the separation of the eyes, objects in the visual environment give rise to two-dimensional projections which differ slightly in their location on the retina. This retinal "disparity" information is processed at the level of the cortex and ultimately gives rise to a perception of depth.

The physiologic basis for stereopsis remains poorly understood despite a number of recent advances in the field. Several investigators have recorded from neurons in area 17 (V1) of primates which are responsive to stereoscopic input (that is, they exhibit disparity tuning). Estimates of the proportion of such cells exhibiting disparity tuning are quite variable, ranging from a small minority (Hubel & Wiesel, 1970) to 84% of cells (Poggio & Fischer, 1977). Hubel and Livingstone (1987) have recently demonstrated that cells in the "thick stripes" (as defined by cytochrome oxidase staining) in area 18 (V2) are primarily concerned with stereopsis. Cells responsive to stereoscopic information have also been identified in MT, a "higher" visual area also involved in the perception of movement.

Although rare, profound impairments in stereoscopic vision have been reported as a consequence of brain injury (e.g., Birkmayer, 1951; Hecaen & de Ajuriaguerra, 1954; Holmes & Horrax, 1919; Riddoch, 1917). The case described by Holmes and Horrax (1919) is particularly instructive. This patient sustained a missile injury to the superior parieto-occipital lobes bilaterally resulting in an inability to appreciate depth. This patient mistook a cardboard box which was 18 inches square and 8 inches deep for a flat piece of cardboard and expressed surprise when he was able to put his hand into the box; a flight of steps was described as "a number of straight lines on the floor" (p. 398). The patient also exhibited an inferior horizontal hemianopia and an impairment in spatial orientation (see below). Riddoch's patient (1917) exhibited a similar pattern of impairment. Less dramatic deficits ranging in severity from clinically significant impairments (e.g., Michel, Jeannerod, & Devic, 1965; Symonds, 1945) to an asymptomatic deficit in stereoacuity (Paterson & Zangwill, 1944) have been reported more frequently (see also Holmes, 1918; Symonds, 1945; Cole, Schutta, & Warrington, 1962).

In a recent review, Danta et al. (1978) noted that most patients (27/46) with impairments in stereopsis exhibit clinical evidence of bihemispheric involvement. When observed in patients with unilateral hemispheric lesions, most investigators have reported that these deficits are more frequently associated with damage to the right hemisphere. Carmon and Bechtoldt (1969) and Benton and Hecaen (1970), for example, both reported that right hemisphere lesions produced greater impairment on a stereoscopic tests using random letter stereograms. Similarly, Danta et al. (1978) assessed stereopsis in 26 patients with right and 28 patients with left hemisphere lesions with two different tasks. They found that 69% of patients with right but only 27% of patients with left hemisphere lesions performed abnormally on at least one task. It should be noted, however, that not all investigators have reported an association between right hemisphere lesions and an impairment in stereopsis (e.g., Rothstein & Sacks, 1972). Additionally, investigations with normals by Julesz and colleagues (1976) demonstrated no differences on tests of stereopsis in the right and left visual fields. Thus, although some data suggest that the right hemisphere is "dominant" for stereopsis, this issue has not been resolved.

At this juncture, it is worth emphasizing that the perception of depth is a complex phenomenon which is presumably dependent on the derivation and subsequent processing of information about retinal disparity at multiple levels in the visual system. This complexity is illustrated by the following observations. Several investigators have reported that many patients perform inconsistently on tasks assessing stereopsis. Danta, Hinton, & O'Boyle (1978), for example, found that of the 23 patients with unilateral brain lesions who performed abnormally on at least one of their two tasks assessing stereopsis, only 9 (39%) were abnormal on both. Similar inconsistency was reported by Birkmayer (1951) who assessed stereopsis using four standard tests.

Also of interest in this context is the observation that impairments in stereopsis may be associated with lesions involving a variety of anatomic structures, many of which are outside the primary visual pathway or occipital lobes (Danta et al., 1978).

Lastly, a number of interesting and unanticipated dissociations in performance have been reported in patients with brain injury. Thus, for example, Symonds (1945) reported a patient who was able to fuse stereoscopically presented images of a landscape yet was not able to determine the relative depth of elements in the picture. Similarly, Danta et al. reported that 10 of their subjects were able to fuse stereoscopically presented stimuli yet were unable to discriminate the depth of the fused image. Kramer (1970) reported a patient who apparently had normal stereoscopic vision but lost the ability to perceive depth and perspective in drawings and pictures, presumably because he was unable to use perspective, occlusion, and other types of information which underlie monocular depth perception. Clearly, much remains to be learned about stereopsis and its breakdown in patients with cerebral lesions.

Impaired Perception of Movement

As evidenced by such diverse activities as the ability to hit a pitched ball or negotiate a crowded highway on foot or in a car, normal vision provides quite reliable and precise information about the location, speed, and trajectory of moving objects. Recent investigations in monkeys as well as data from patients with brain injury suggest that this capacity may be relatively selectively impaired. Newsome and Pare (1988), for example, reported that ibotenic acid-induced lesions of area MT in monkeys may cause a substantial deficit in the ability of the animals to appreciate movement in the absence of a discernible effect on spatial contrast sensitivity.

Patients with relatively selective deficits in movement perception are quite rare (Goldstein & Gelb, 1918; Pötzl & Redlich, 1911). The most striking example of this phenomenon was reported by Zihl, VonCramen, & Mai (1983) who described a 43-year-old woman who developed a profound deficit in the ability to appreciate movement after bilateral posterior cerebral infarctions. This patient experienced difficulty perceiving movement in all three dimensions. When attempting to fill a cup, for example, she noted that the fluid appeared to be frozen or "like a glacier;" she did not know when to stop pouring because she could not appreciate the change in the fluid level in the cup. She was uneasy in busy or crowded environments because "people were suddenly here or there but I have not seen them moving." Formal assessment of her ability to appreciate movement revealed that perception of movement in depth was essentially abolished; she could perceive direction of movement at low velocities (below 10°/s) up to 15° of eccentricity but in the peripheral fields could only discriminate between moving and stationary stimuli. Additionally, she did not perceive normal visual after-effects.

In contrast to this profound deficit in the perception of movement, other aspects of visual processing were preserved. For example, visual fields, visual acuity, stereopsis (as tested with the Titmus and TNO tests) and color discrimination were normal. Critical flicker fusion, a measure of the ability to discriminate between a constant and flickering light source, was also normal. The deficit was restricted to the visual domain as indicated by the fact that she correctly indicated the direction of movement of tactile stimuli. On the basis of CT scan data, the investigators argue that the deficit in movement perception is attributable to bilateral lesions involving the lateral temporo-occipital cortex, a localization not inconsistent with data from monkeys.

In this context, mention should also be made of the phenomena of "visual static agnosia." In direct contrast to the patients described above, Botez and colleagues (1965) reported two patients whose performance on visual object and letter identification tasks was facilitated by movement. Thus, for example, letter identification was assessed in three conditions: static presentation of letters varying in size and case, with slow movement of the stimulus, and with tracing of the letter. They found that both patients performed very poorly indeed with static stimuli, were improved when the letters were slowly moved, and performed almost perfectly when the letters were traced. Interestingly, both patients performed equally well whether the letters were traced over a blank background or over a static letter; the lack of interference from the static letter suggests that this form was not represented. Movement also facilitated the recognition of objects, faces, and pictures.

A similar pattern of performance was demonstrated by the patient with "visual form agnosia" described by Benson and Greenberg (1971). Although unable to identify Xs and Os presented on a motionless paper, he reliably identified the same stimuli when the paper was moved slowly. Additionally, he was able to identify these stimuli when permitted to watch them being slowly drawn.

Unfortunately, little information is available regarding the anatomic substrate for this disorder. One patient described by Botez et al. (1965) had apparently suffered bihemispheric infarctions. The second patient was examined after a left occipital resection for treatment of an angioma; this patient was said to exhibit general intellectual impairment and "hyperemotivity" suggesting dysfunction in brain regions remote from the left occipital lobe. The patient of Benson and Greenberg (1971) had suffered carbon monoxide poisoning. Lastly, a patient with a similar pattern of performance reported by Horner and Massey (1986) was noted to have multiple, bihemispheric infarcts.

Prosopagnosia

Prosopagnosia is an acquired disorder of visual facial recognition characterized by an inability to recognize familiar faces or to learn new faces. While these patients state that all faces are unfamiliar or unrecognizable, they are often able to use cues such as voice, gait, body habitus, or distinctive personal features such as a beard to identify familiar people. In most cases, prosopagnosic patients are immediately aware of their deficit and seek medical attention. We have seen one patient, for example, who consulted his doctor after noting one morning that the face he was shaving did not appear to be his own! We have also observed patients who were so unnerved by their deficit that they successfully hid it for several weeks.

It is important to note that the deficit in prosopagnosia is not attributable to an inability to process the visual information depicted in a face; these patients, for example, may be able to match faces across view shifts, distinguish between well-formed and distorted faces, identify facial components (e.g., nose) and derive certain types of generic information (e.g., gender) about the depicted individual. Rather, the deficit appears to be attributable to the fact that the face does not activate the full-range of stored information pertinent to the depicted individual.

Recent investigations of some prosopagnosic patients, however, have revealed that faces do activate certain types of stored information without awareness. Bauer (1984), for example, recorded electrodermal responses from a prosopagnosic patient while he viewed faces of famous people and family members; a list of five names was provided and the patient was asked to indicate which of the names was appropriate to the face. While performing at chance in matching the faces and names, the patient generated electrodermal responses on trials in which the names were appropriate to the face. Thus, although the patient stated that all of the faces were unfamiliar and could provide no explicit information relevant to the faces, there was psychophysiological evidence of "recognition." Additional psychophysiologic evidence of recognition without awareness was reported by Tranel and Damasio (1985). More recently De Haan and coworkers have demonstrated evidence of covert recognition of faces using a variety of behavioral tests (De Haan, Young, & Newcombe, 1987).

Although the impairment in facial recognition is, of course, the sine qua non of prosopagnosia, these patients also exhibit an impairment in the identification of specific examplars of other categories of objects. Thus, while prosopagnosics are not impaired in the identification of objects at a generic level, they may be grossly impaired in the recognition of specific exemplars of a category. PH, for example, reliably distinguished pictures of cars from other types of stimuli yet was unable to identify the makes of cars. (De Haan, Young, & Newcombe, 1987) Similarly, Bornstein (1963) reported that after becoming prosopagnosic, an ornithologist lost the ability to distinguish between different birds.

Prosopagnosia is typically but not invariably associated with bilateral lesions which involve the inferior occipital or occipitotemporal cortex or subjacent white matter (Landis, Regard, Bliestle, & Kleihues, 1988). The lingual and/or fusiform gyri are frequently damaged. In light of the location of the lesions associated with prosopagnosia, it is not surprising that a variety of other deficits such as alexia, achromatopsia, and visual field deficits may be observed in these patients.

The nature of the processing deficit(s) underlying prosopagnosia has not been established. Given the differences in the anatomic substrate and behavioral deficits exhibited by patients with this disorder, one must, of course, consider the possibility that a number of different processing deficits may underlie the clinical syndrome of prosopagnosia. Consonant with the postulate that prosopagnosia is attributable to a failure to activate the full range of stored information normally evoked by a face, Young and De Haan (1988) have recently suggested that the covert recognition displayed by prosopagnosics may reflect the operation of a partially isolated face recognition system. An alternative possibility is that the disorder is attributable to a disruption or "pruning" of the structural descriptions for faces; the loss of information about particular facial features such as the contour of the nose or the prominence of the chin, for example, may be sufficient to prevent full activation of a specific structural description, thereby preventing explicit recognition of the face. On this hypothesis, "implicit" recognition may be attributed to subthreshold activation of a structural description.

In this context, it is interesting to note that recent electrophysiologic investigations in monkeys have demonstrated that many neurons in the inferior temporal cortex respond maximally to faces; although many face selective neurons exhibit greater responses to particular faces, most of these cells show little sensitivity to a variety of other factors such as size, color, spatial frequency, content, or position within their receptive field (Perett et al., 1984, 1985; Rolls, 1984, Desimone et al., 1984). One might speculate that a disruption (but not elimination) of this population of face sensitive neurons could cause a failure to evoke the full range of stored information normally associated with a face. Additional data from well-studied prosopagnosic patients will be necessary to evaluate these and other hypotheses.

Finally, it should be noted that a severe disorder in face recognition is encountered in patients with obvious object agnosia and may also be associated with alexia (e.g., Newcombe et al., 1989). These patients may be impaired on tasks such as the unusual views test suggesting that the disturbance in face recognition may be attributable to lower level processing deficits than those that give rise to isolated impairments in face recognition. Consistent with this hypothesis, Newcombe et al. (1989) reported one patient (MS) with visual agnosia and prosopagnosia who failed to demonstrate evidence of covert face recognition. Although there is certainly precedent to regard these patients as prosopagnosic, we believe that the term should be reserved for those patients with deficits in face recognition without other symptomatic visual processing deficits.

Anton's Syndrome

Anton's syndrome is a disorder in which patients with profound visual loss explicitly deny their visual deficit. The disorder, originally described by Dejerine and Vialet (1893) and Von Monakow (1897), is typically associated with vascular lesions of the occipital cortex bilaterally. The disorder has been reported in association with head injury (Teuber et al., 1960) and anoxia (Barnet et al., 1970). In our experience, the disorder has been encountered most frequently in the postpartum and postoperative states. Although the disorder may be long lasting when caused by cortical infarction, in other contexts, the deficits are often transient with gradual resolution of visual disturbance over the course of days or weeks.

Many patients with this disorder insist that their vision is normal; even when confronted with evidence to the contrary (e.g., walking into stationary objects, failure to identify a family member), these patients will typically attribute the mishaps to factors such as poor lighting or the absence of their glasses. Anton's syndrome may also be associated with memory impairment as well as a confusional state.

EXAMINATION OF VISUAL PROCESSING

As illustrated by the penetrating analyses provided by investigators such as Holmes and Riddoch, careful and thorough clinical assessment of patients with visual processing deficits may provide important insights into a patient's impairment and contribute to the understanding of visual processing mechanisms as well. Performance on tasks purporting to probe high-level visual processes, for example, may be influenced by a variety of factors not directly relevant to vision. Thus, for example, a general cognitive impairment causing a memory deficit or an inability to comprehend task demands may seriously prejudice the evaluation of visual processing. Language disorders may interfere with evaluation of visual function for a number of reasons. Not only may language comprehension deficits render the patient unable to understand the task at hand, but the anomia often associated with left hemisphere lesions may complicate the interpretation of tasks requiring verbal output. The latter issue is often particularly troublesome in a clinical setting; consider, for example, the response "trunk" produced in response to a picture of a tree. Such an error might be generated by a variety of processing impairments including (but not restricted to) a perceptual deficit such as simultanagnosia, a semantic deficit resulting in the substitution of a word related in meaning to the target, or a phonologic deficit characterized by the production of errors which are similar in sound to the target.

Fortunately, the confounding effects of these variables can be minimized with appropriate testing. Examination of reasoning and problem solving, for example, may provide useful information about the patient's general cognitive function. As object naming provides the most direct and accessible information about visual recognition, naming should be carefully assessed in an effort to distinguish visual processing deficits from an anomia; as will be discussed below, visually based object recognition impairments should be distinguishable from linguistically based errors by a number of criteria. Perhaps most importantly, object naming deficits attributable to visual deficits would be expected to be modality-specific whereas linguistically based naming deficits would not. Thus, in contrast to an anomic patient, for example, an agnosic patient would be expected to perform relatively well on tests of naming to definition ("What is the name of the utensil with which one eats soup?") or palpation. Analysis of the naming errors may in many instances be of assistance. Errors in which the name of a visually similar object is substituted for the target (e.g., the response "cigar" to a picture of a pen) would suggest that the impairment was visually based; whereas a response which was phonologically similar, for example, to the target would suggest that the error was attributable to dysfunction within the language domain.

Visual processing may also be assessed by tasks employing nonverbal responses. Patients may be asked, for example, to match a picture to one of an array of objects, to make judgments (e.g., same-different, larger-smaller) about objects or pictures or to point to named or pictured objects. A word of caution is appropriate regarding the interpretation of tasks employing a reaching or pointing response (e.g., pointing to a named object); optic ataxia, or misreaching under visual guidance, may be associated with a variety of disorders of visual processing. We have encountered patients, for example, who made frequent errors on tasks requiring a manual response when the targets were close together but performed quite well when the spacing between the objects was increased. Accuracy of motor responses should be carefully evaluated in all patients, particularly if vision is to be assessed with manual responses.

Although the focus of this chapter has been "higher" disorders of visual processing, it is clear that the clinical assessment of a patient with visual processing disorders should include the evaluation of the entire visual system. Information about visual acuity, visual fields and what we have termed "visual features" (e.g., color, line, orientation) is indispensable to the assessment of visual processing deficits. Care must be exercised, however, in the interpretation of this information as "higher level" visual deficits may influence performance on routine clinical tests putatively assessing basic visual properties. Consider, for example, the assessment of the visual fields, whether performed at the bedside by confrontation, using perimetry or by means of an automated system. Although this task is often thought to be trivially easy, a number of alert, intelligent, and cooperative patients have been reported who exhibit inconsistent performance on visual field evaluations. There are a number of possible explanations for this observation. One important but rarely controlled factor concerns the extent to which the patient fixes attention on the central target. We have observed patients, for example, in whom the plotted "visual field" was significantly influenced by this variable. When asked to concentrate on the fixation point, such patients may appear to have quite narrowed fields (or even "tunnel vision"); yet when asked to maintain their eye position constant but not to concentrate on the fixation point the visual fields were normal. The problem here would seem to be narrowing of the attentional field, not a visual field deficit per se.

Another factor which may confound the interpretation of the visual field examination is the extent to which the targets move. Riddoch noted in 1917 that some patients detect moving targets more reliably than static ones; yet in practice the extent to which targets move varies widely as a function of the examiner and the technique. Thus, we believe that it is quite likely that the inconsistencies noted in visual field testing may, at least in some instances, be attributable to a failure to control for factors such as movement and the deployment of visual attention.

One should note that the confounding effects of higher level visual deficits may be manifest on other tests of visual processing. We have encountered patients with deficits in integrating visual feature information, for example, who were thought to have an impairment in color processing because of an inability to name the numbers on the Ishihara plates. In fact, these patients were not impaired in color processing per se but were unable to integrate the shape information displayed on the plates to identify the stimulus. The major point to be made in this context is that because visual processing mechanisms are complex and highly interactive, performance on even seemingly straightforward tests of visual function may be influenced by a variety of factors. In light of this complexity, we believe that converging evidence is desirable when evaluating visual function. Thus, for example, a consistent pattern of performance on the Ishihara plates, hue discrimination (e.g., Farnsworth D-15 Panel), and pointing to named colors would strongly support the diagnosis of achromatopsia; whereas an impairment on only one of the tests might be attributable to dysfunction of a qualitatively different capacity (e.g., language, feature integration).

Finally, in light of the important distinction between covert and overt information processing, the evaluation of patients with visual processing deficits should incorporate tasks in which patients are required to respond even if they insist that they are "guessing." Using forced-choice tasks assessing word and object recognition, for example, we as well as a number of other investigators have been able to demonstrate that certain patients process visual information much more reliably than would be suggested by their performance on tasks requiring explicit identification of a target (e.g., Coslett & Saffran, 1989).

Table 13-1 provides a brief list of some of the tasks which may be useful in the evaluation of visual disorders. The putative levels of visual processing tapped by these tasks are also indicated in Table 13-1. One should note, however, that as processing in the visual system is assumed to be highly interactive, we do not claim that deficits on these tasks are necessarily specific to any putative level of processing. Impaired performance on an unusual views test, for example, does

Table 13-1 Assessment of Visual Functions

Assessment Target	Nature of Testing	Example of Task	Reference
I. General Assessment			
A. Perception of complex arrays			
1. Scenes	Verbal description	BDAE "Cookie Theft"	Goodlgass & Kaplan, 1972
2. Nonobject arrays	Match-to-sample	Benton Visual Form Discrimination Test	Benton et al., 1983
3. Reading of text	Oral reading of paragraphs		
B. Perception of single objects			
1. Visual identification	Naming of line drawings	Boston Naming Test	Kaplan et al., 1983
	Naming of objects[a]	Real objects	
	Visual matching	Match drawing to object	
2. Naming via tactile input[a]	Naming to palpation	Real objects	
	Naming to verbal description	Description naming	
3. Naming to description[a]			Coughlan & Warrington, 1978
C. Perception of faces			
1. Familiar faces	Identification of famous faces	Facial recognition test	Albert et al., 1980
2. Unfamiliar faces	Identity matching	Benton Facial Recognition Test	Benton et al., 1983
D. Perception of words and letters	Oral reading of single words	Single words, one word at a time	
	Letter naming	Single letters, one letter at a time	
II. Basic visual functions			
A. Acuity	Standard acuity testing		
B. Visual fields	Standard visual field testing		
C. Color perception	Standard color vision testing	Farnsworth D-15 Panel	
D. Stereoscopy		Titmus Fly Test	
E. Eye movements	Neurologic exam		

continued on next page

Table 13-1 *(Continued)*

Assessment Target	Nature of Testing	Example of Task	Reference
III. Processing at the visual feature level			
A. Line			
1. Parallel ("preattentive") processing	Detection as a function of array size	Detection of "Q" in array of "O's"	Treisman & Souther, 1985 Robinson, Ch. 4
2. Orientation	Discrimination of line orientation	Detection of \ in array of /'s	Sagi & Julesz, 1985
3. Length	Discrimination of line length		Taylor & Warrington, 1973
B. Color	See II.C above		
C. Movement	Movement detection		Zihl et al., 1983
IV. Integrative processing (VAR)			
A. Attentional requirements for feature integration	Detection of feature conjunctions	Detection of "O" in an array of "Q's"	Treisman & Souther, 1985
	Formation of illusory conjunctions	Detection of colored letters	Treisman & Schmidt, 1983
B. Grouping of visual features	Effect of array regularity	Detection of inverted T	Humphreys et al., 1985
C. Figural integration	Shape discrimination		Warrington & James, 1967
V. Structural descriptions			
A. Integrity of structural descriptions	Recognition of object shapes	Object/nonobject discrimination	Riddoch & Humphreys, 1987
B. Object constancy	Matching of non-canonical to canonical view	Matching across view shifts	Warrington & Taylor, 1978
VI. Semantic knowledge			
A. Category	Recognition of category membership	Sorting and matching tasks	Coslett & Saffran, 1989
B. Function	Recognizing similarity of function	Functional similarity test	Warrington & James, 1967

C. Characteristics	Identifying characteristics of objects	Sorting according to characteristics	Chertkow & Bub, 1990
VII. Visual buffer			
A. Capacity	Ability to process multi-item array	Speed of identification of 1 vs. 2 items	Coslett & Saffran, 1991
B. Location			
1. Relative location of two objects	Discriminating relative location	Position discrimination test	Warrington & Taylor, 1978
2. Location of single object	Discriminating absolute location	Pointing task *Priming of location in detection task	Eriksen & Yeh, 1985

[a]Needed only in case if impairment of preceding task.

not provide unequivocal evidence of a deficit in the procedures by which object constancy is achieved. Inferences regarding the nature of the visual processing impairment(s) exhibited by a patient must be based on the *pattern* of performance on a wide range of tasks rather than the data from a single test.

In the final section of this chapter, we summarize two recent case studies performed in our laboratory; the details of these evaluations are available elsewhere. In this context, the brief descriptions of the evaluations are intended only to illustrate an approach to the analysis of visual processing disorders.

Patient CB: Evaluation of a Patient with Optic Aphasia

In 1889, Freund described a patient with a right homonymous hemianopia who was unable to name visually presented objects yet could name objects from touch. He attributed this impairment to a disconnection between the preserved right occipital lobe and the left hemisphere speech areas and designated this disorder "optic aphasia." More recently a number of investigators (Margolin, Friedrich, & Carlson, 1985; Lhermitte & Beauvois, 1973; Riddoch & Humphreys, 1987) have convincingly demonstrated that the clinical syndrome of optic aphasia as described by Freund does, in fact, exist; the interpretation of these deficits, however, remains controversial. Certain investigators, citing the frequently reported observations that these subjects use objects appropriately in a naturalistic context and can demonstrate the gesture appropriate to an object they can not name, have concluded that object recognition is preserved and that the impairment involves accessing the object's name (Larrabee et al., 1985). Others (Bauer & Rubens, 1985) have argued that optic aphasia is best considered a mild form of visual agnosia. In the following, we describe the investigation of a patient with optic aphasia.

The patient was a 67-year-old male laborer with an 11th grade education who noted the sudden onset of confusion and right-sided weakness. He also stated that he could not see clearly and was noted by family members to bump into stationary objects on his right. His past medical history was significant for a mild left hemiparesis which lasted for approximately one month and resolved two years prior to his admission. The clinical diagnosis on admission was a left occipital lobe ischemic infarction.

When first examined by the authors 24 days after admission, the patient was noted to be alert and cooperative but oriented only to person and place. The general neurological examination revealed a dense right homonymous hemianopia as well as a minimal spastic hemiparesis on the left and a mild spastic hemiparesis on the right. He exhibited mild pyramidal clumsiness of the left hand and severe clumsiness of the right hand. He also demonstrated optic ataxia with the right hand. Sensory examination was normal. Deep tendon reflexes were brisk bilaterally with a right-sided preponderance. No cerebellar deficit was noted. His gait was remarkable for bilateral leg spasticity, right greater than left. A Babinski sign was elicited on the right. Speech was fluent and well articulated with normal prosody and information content. Auditory comprehension and repetition were normal. Naming of pictures and visually presented objects was grossly impaired. He correctly named only one item ("yoke") on the 60-item Boston Naming Test (Kaplan et al., 1983). He failed to name any of 25 visually presented real objects. Most errors on these tasks bore no clear semantic, phonologic or visual relationship to the stimulus (e.g., "scissors"—"clock," "volcano"—"pillar"). For only one item was there a suggestion of visually based error ("stethoscope—microphone").

Naming of palpated objects, in contrast, was quite good. With his eyes closed, the patient was able to name 23 of the 25 (92%) objects which he had been unable to name with visual input. A clear semantic relationship between stimulus and response was discernible in both of his errors (paperclip > "holds things together;" pipe > "cigarette, ashtray"). When asked to name the same objects by means of palpation but with his eyes open, the patient's performance deteriorated markedly.

Reading was profoundly impaired. The patient read no words and named not a single letter correctly. His errors bore no evident relationship to the target.

A CT scan performed three weeks after the stroke revealed a left occipital infarction with involvement of the left forceps major and extension into the posterior limb of the internal capsule; a lacune in the posterior limb of the internal capsule on the right was also visualized.

Analysis of the Deficit

The patient therefore demonstrated an inability to identify objects presented visually, as well as a right homonymous hemianopia. The preservation of naming via the tactile modality ruled out a linguistic deficit as the basis for the naming impairment. While clearly not "blind" in the left visual field, the status of his visual functions remained to be determined.

We began the examination of the patient's visual functions with an object decision task, in which he had to determine whether a drawing depicted a real or imaginary object. Good performance on this task would establish that the patient could achieve an adequate percept of the object (or, to use the classical terminology, that he did not have an apperceptive agnosia); it would also indicate that stored structural descriptions of objects were relatively intact. Failure on this task would point to a visual processing deficit, or possibly to a disturbance involving structural descriptions.

We used for this purpose a test modeled after a task developed by Riddoch and Humphreys (1987). The patient was asked to discriminate drawings of real objects from nonobjects constructed by making composites of two objects. All of the nonobject stimuli were generated by combining portions of two objects drawn from the same semantic category; for example, nonobjects included the head of a chicken on the body of a turtle and the head of a hammer mounted on the handle of a pair of pliers. Each drawing was individually presented for an unlimited period, and the subject was simply asked to say yes if the pictured item was familiar. The patient correctly rejected all nonobjects and correctly accepted 29 of 30 real objects. He erred with the drawing of a snail.

Further investigation confirmed the inference, drawn from the patient's good performance on this task, that visual processing operations per se were relatively intact. the patient performed well on a test of shape discrimination, as well as on a range of tests designed to assess lower level visual functions.

Matching Across View Shifts

The recognition of a familiar object is, except under unusual circumstances, independent of the perspective from which it is viewed; normal subjects, for example, immediately recognize a bucket whether viewed from the side, top or bottom. The most parsimonious explanation for this ability is that we store canonical object representations along with a system which maps viewpoint-dependent visual information onto an "object-centered" or perspective-independent representation (Marr, 1982). If this account is correct, the mapping procedures may be critical to object recognition and therefore of interest with respect to our patient.

To determine whether our patient's impaired object naming might reflect an inability to use viewpoint-dependent visual information to access a canonical stored representation, he was asked to match pictures of objects taken from a different perspective. Stimuli for this test included three pictures of each of 33 different objects; for each object, pictures were taken from "standard" (that is, prototypical), "familiar" (less typical but readily recognized), and "odd" (unusual) views. The patient's task was to match each of the 99 pictures to the "standard" view of the same object. For each of the 99 trials, the patient was given one of the stimulus pictures and asked to place the picture next to the picture of the same object on an answer sheet on which standard views of three visually similar objects were glued. The patient correctly matched all of the standard and familiar views and 29 of 33 of the "odd" views, a performance which is within normal limits for his age.

Semantic Processing

The next series of investigations, in which the patient was asked to sort pictures and drawings according to semantic criteria, was undertaken to determine if the patient could access semantic information relevant to the visual representations.

In the first test, the patient was asked to distinguish drawings of animals from other objects. He was instructed not to attempt to name the stimulus but to place the drawings of animals in one pile and all other drawings in another pile. He performed the task flawlessly.

Second, the patient was asked to distinguish between drawings of edible and inedible objects. In addition to drawings of foods (e.g., an apple), the items included drawings of items used in food preparation (e.g., pot, ladle) as well as inedible objects which had no obvious semantic link to food (e.g., a hammer). The semantically related foils were included to assess the specificity of the semantic information retrieved; impairment in semantic access or disruption of semantic networks might be expected to be associated with a confusion between items which are edible and items which are employed in the preparation of edible items. The patient was asked to sort the drawings as described above. He correctly sorted 29 of 30 items; he misclassified a drawing of a pot.

The patient also performed well on a categorization task in which he was asked to match a photograph to another photograph of a "standard' exemplar which was a prototypical member of the category. The exemplars varied in their typicality for the category; for example, airplanes included helicopters, early model planes, and advanced military aircraft as well as standard planes. The patient correctly categorized 61 of 63 (97%) of the photographs; both errors occurred with photographs rated by normal subjects as atypical members of the category. This performance is within the normal range.

Thus, the patient performed quite well on a variety of tests of picture categorization. One interpretation of these data is that the patient was able to directly access semantic information from visual information. Alternatively, one might propose that the visual information contained in the object images is sufficient to permit categorization of the drawings in the absence of full semantic specification. thus, on this hypothesis, the ability to categorize a picture of a lion, for example, may reflect not the access to a full semantic entry indicating (in part) that the animal is a large carnivore which lives in Africa but to a generic "animal" visual object representation which indicates that the object has a head, eyes, mouth, and four extremities (see Riddoch & Humphreys, 1987). In an effort to exclude the latter possibility, two additional experiments were performed in which correct sorting could not be performed on the basis of visual feature alone but required access to object-specific semantic information.

In the first test, which was modeled after the functional similarity test of Warrington and Taylor (1978), the patient was shown three pictures and asked to point to the two objects which were similar in function or "served the same purpose." As the stimuli were selected so that the functionally similar objects were visually dissimilar and the foil was judged to be more visually similar to one of the semantically related objects than was the other semantically related object (e.g., a button, a zipper, and a coin), good performance on this task is not readily explained by the hypothesis that the subject categorized objects on the basis of basic visual features common to most members of a semantic category.

The patient was correct on 29 of 32 trials (91%); all three errors resulted from the selection of the two visually related stimuli. Normal controls 60 and older scored from 27 to 31 correct with a mean of 30. Thus, the patient performed normally on this task.

The patient's normal performance on this task, together with the data from the semantic categorization tasks, indicates that the patient has access to semantic information appropriate to a visually presented object. Additionally, the ability to determine that visually dissimilar objects perform the same function suggests that the patient was not relying on information available at the level of a visual object representation or structural description.

Many theories about the organization of the semantic domain propose that semantic information is hierarchically represented (e.g., Warrington, 1975); it is postulated that superordinate information regarding, for example, the semantic class of a hammer (e.g., a tool) is accessed prior to subordinate (e.g., ball-peen vs. claw) or associative (e.g., often used with a nail) information. If this is true, one might postulate that the patient is able to successfully perform the categorization and functional similarity tests described above by accessing only superordinate semantic information; as naming is thought to require access to a complete semantic entry, the inability to name the objects which were successfully classified might be attributed to an inability to access the full semantic entry.

To test this hypothesis, an experiment was performed in which the patient was required to make semantic judgments on the basis of associative as opposed to categorical information. In this experiment, three objects were placed before the subject, and he was asked to indicate which two of the objects were associated or "went together." On one trial, for example, a cup, knife and fork were placed before the patient. The patient performed perfectly.

Collectively, the results of these investigations suggest that the patient's failure to name visually presented objects cannot be attributed to impaired early visual processing, failure to match visual information to stored structural descriptions, or impaired access to semantic information. In particular, the normal performance on the functional similarity and semantic association tests provide compelling evidence that the patient was able to access detailed semantic information relevant to visually presented objects. Thus, these data suggest that the patient's naming impairment cannot be attributed to a failure of object recognition. Rather, the naming deficit reflects an inability to access the lexicon on the basis of semantic information derived from visual input. This hypothesis is presented in graphic form in Figure 13-3.

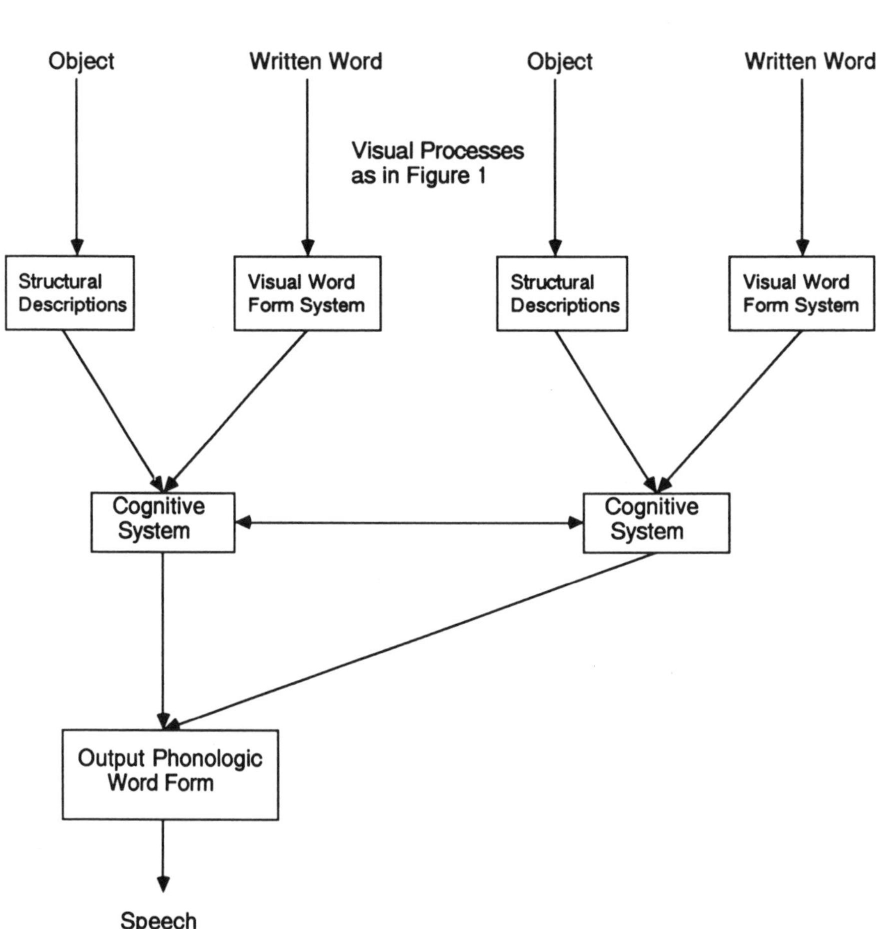

Figure 13-3 A schematic diagram of a model of naming which incorporates right and left hemisphere semantic systems.

Patient BP: Evaluation of a Patient with Simultanagnosia

The patient was a 67-year-old, right-handed woman who noted a transient episode of mild word-finding problems and reading difficulties followed two years later by a right parietal stroke resulting in neglect of the left body and environment.

When first examined by the authors four months after the right hemisphere infarction, the patient's major complaint was that her environment appeared fragmented. Although she saw individual items clearly, they appeared to be isolated, and she could not discern any meaningful relationship among them. She stated, for example, that she could find her way in her home (in which she had lived for 25 years) with her eyes closed but she became confused with her eyes open. On one occasion, for example, she attempted to find her way to her bedroom by utilizing a large lamp as a landmark; while walking toward the lamp, she fell over her dining room table. Although she enjoyed listening to the radio, television programs bewildered her because she could only "see" one person or object at a time and, therefore, could not determine who was speaking or being spoken to. She reported watching a movie in which, after hearing a heated argument, she noted to her surprise and consternation that the character she had been watching was suddenly sent reeling across the room, apparently as a consequence of a punch thrown by a character she had never seen. Although she was able to read single words effortlessly, she stopped reading because the "competing words" confused her. She was uanble to write as she claimed to be able to see only a single letter. Thus, when creating a letter she saw only the tip of the pencil and the letter under construction and "lost" the previously constructed letters. She recognized objects depicted in large and small drawings equally well.

Finally, the patient's ability to generate visual images was assessed. She was asked to describe the floor plan and contents of her home. Although she often offered adequate descriptions of specific items (e.g., "a long low sofa with a gold brocade and clear plastic cover"), she was unable to indicate the locations of household items relative to landmarks such as doors or walls; when asked to imagine that she was standing in the living room and looking into the dining room, she stated that she simply couldn't "picture" it. She was unable to describe the route she had used for many years to walk from her home to the nearby market.

Neurologic examination at that time revealed her to be alert and oriented. Cranial nerve examination revealed a corrected visual acuity of 20/40 ou. and normal ocular movements; strength, reflexes, sensation, and coordination were normal. Automated perimetry demonstrated normal visual fields. Examination of higher nervous system functions revealed no intellectual impairment except for her visual information processing deficit. She exhibited a profound dressing impairment; she was unable to put on a single item of clothing without assistance. She also exhibited mild optic ataxia with the left hand. She could, however, reach quickly and accurately with her right hand in right and left hemispaces.

MRI scan performed two years after the onset of symptoms revealed a small, discrete left temporo-occipital infarct as well as an infarct on the right involving the posterior portions of the right middle and superior temporal gyri and extending into the supramarginal and angular gyri as well as small portions of the lateral occipital lobe.

Although the patient performed normally on tasks that required identification of single objects, she had difficulty on tasks that involved multiple-object arrays. Thus, while she performed normally in recognizing single objects presented at brief (40 msec) exposures, she was dramatically slower than normals to recognize a second object in a tachistoscopic display. BP required two seconds for a task that controls performed in 75 ms. Similar restrictions applied in word identification; the patient read single words at 40 ms. exposures, but required one second to reliably read pairs of unrelated words. The patient was markedly impaired in reporting strings of letters that did not correspond to words. With 75 msec stimulus exposure, she correctly identified only 4 of 30 four-letter strings which were visually similar to real words (e.g., "MOND") and 0 of 30 letter-strings with unusual or illegal letter sequences (e.g., "GRNT"). Errors included the substitution of visually similar real words and trials on which she reported only one or two letters. She reported seeing "nothing" on approximately 20% of trials with nonwords.

She also performed poorly on tasks requiring that she judge relationships between elements in the same array or compare two separate arrays. Thus, she performed at chance on the dot localization task (Warrington & Rabin, 1970) in which the subject is presented with two squares one with a dot placed in and one with a dot placed near the center, and asked to indicate in which square the dot is centered. She was also at chance (5 of 16) on Benton's visual form discrimination task (Benton, Hamsher, Varney, & Spreen, 1983), in which the subject is asked to match a target array containing several geometric stimuli to one of four arrays. Finally, she was impaired on visual search tasks such as the Trail Making Test (Reitan, 1958) in which the subject is asked to draw lines connecting a series of numbered circles.

Analysis of the Deficit

This patient's deficit appeared to reflect a restriction on the number of discrete elements that she was able to identify in multi-term arrays. Further examination of the patient focussed on the level of processing at which such a deficit could arise. The model allows several possibilities: (1) Although the observations that the patient's visual fields are full and that object recognition is independent of object size suggest that the disorder is not attributable to a local failure to register visual feature information, these tasks do not assess the capacity for processing of visual information in parallel across the visual field. It is conceivable, for example, that a patient could perform normally on visual field tests, which involve detection of a single luminance point anywhere in the visual field, yet fail in tasks (like scene recognition) in which it is necessary to monitor information displayed at multiple sites in the field. (2) One possible explanation for the limitation on the number of items that can be identified is that the patient is unable to accurately and rapidly shift selective attention from one portion of the visual array to another. Such a deficit would lead to disorganized and ineffective serial search of the stimuli resulting in a failure to process all of the targets in the array. On a behavioral level, such a deficit might be manifested as poor scanning of the visual array with a tendency to identify only a portion of the objects in view. Impaired scanning of a visual array with a tendency to report the same object more than once was, in fact, observed in our patient and has been frequently reported in patients with simultanagnosia (Luria, 1959; Hecaen & de Ajurigeurra, 1954). (3) Yet a third possibility is a general slowing in the rate of visual processing, which would be expected to reduce the number of items that could be identified in complex arrays. Kinsbourne and Warrington (1962) and Levine and Calvanio (1978) have, in fact, demonstrated an impairment in the speed of visual processing in patients with disorders of recognition of simultaneously presented objects. (4) Finally, it is possible that the deficit reflects a limitation on the capacity of the visual buffer.

To examine the first possibility, a limitation to parallel processing of features across complex arrays, we used a modified version of a paradigm reported by Sagi and Julesz (1985). The test of preattentive processing involved the detection of one or more lines differing in orientation from the diagonal lines in the array; as targets differ from the background lines by virtue of a single visual feature—that is, orientation—this task can be performed without the integration of visual feature information and is therefore a test of preattentive function. Stimulus exposure duration was reduced until the patient responded correctly on 75% of 144 trials. The patient performed normally on this task, indicating that she was able to register visual feature information presented simultaneously at different sites in the visual field.

Next we examined the second possibility described above, that the patient was unable to accurately and rapidly shift selective attention from one portion of the visual array to another. To examine the patient's ability to shift visual attention from one site to another in the visual field we used a paradigm developed by Posner and colleagues (Posner et al., 1984). In this task, the patient was asked to respond as quickly as possible to a target (a diamond) presented in one of two locations. Prior to each trial, a cue was provided which directed the patient's attention to the eventual site of the target (valid condition) or to another location (invalid or neutral conditions). With this paradigm normal subjects are typically quicker to respond to a target presented in the location to which their attention has been summoned by the preceding cue. Alternatively expressed, reaction times are longer when subjects' attention is cued to one location but the target is presented at a different location.

If the mechanism controlling the shift of selective attention from one target to another is impaired, one might expect to observe a greater than normal cost on invalid trials. Thus, for example, if the subject were impaired in "disengaging" attention from the incorrectly cued site, as has been reported in patients with parietal lobe lesions (Posner et al., 1984), one might expect that reaction times on invalidly cued trials would be substantially longer than reaction times on validly cued trials. The difference between RTs on invalid and valid trials has been termed the "validity effect." Similarly, if the patient was impaired in the movement of selective attention (Coslett, Saffran, & Fitzpatrick, 1988), one might also expect a greater-than-normal cost on invalid trials.

BP exhibited no difficulty learning the task and, in fact, performed well. While she showed larger validity effects than the normal control under some conditions, she did not demonstrate the consistently large validity effect for targets in the contralateral field that is typical of neglect patients (Posner et al., 1984); moreover, she showed substantially smaller effects of invalid cues than many of the brain-damaged subjects of Posner et al. (1984) who, like our patient, did not manifest significant neglect. Given her unexceptional performance on this task, relative to that of other brain-damaged patients who do not demonstrate comparable perceptual abnormalities, it is difficult to attribute her impaired processing of complex arrays to a deficit in the mechanism which shifts the spotlight of selective attention from one site in the visual field to another.

Another study focussed on the possibility that the restriction on the number of items that could be identified reflected a general slowing of visual processing. Although we demonstrated that our patient was able to identify single objects as accurately as controls with brief (unmasked) stimulus presentation, it could be argued that this task is not a particularly sensitive index of high level recognition procedures. We therefore tested the patient's ability to make semantic judgments about rapidly presented words. More specifically, the patient was asked to indicate if one of a series of four rapidly presented words was a member of a designated semantic category (e.g., an animal). Each word was presented for 50 ms. and was immediately replaced by the succeeding word. She was asked to indicate if a target word was present and, if possible, to read the word aloud. The patient performed flawlessly on this task, and reported it to be "effortless."

She explicitly identified every target word in all three blocks and produced no false positive errors.

Collectively, the results of these studies argued against a deficit in low level processing operations as the source of the simultanagnosic impairment. Were multiple items, in fact, being processed to a high level, though not with awareness?

Our patient's simultanagnosia was most dramatically demonstrated by her inability to identify two objects at exposures more than 20 times those required to identify a single stimulus of the same type. In a variety of studies with normal subjects, object and word recognition has been shown to be facilitated by semantic priming; that is, presentation of a semantically related item prior to or along with the target (e.g., Meyer and Schvaneveldt, 1975). In another set of experiments, we sought to determine whether the patient's ability to identify both words or objects in a two-item display could be influenced by the relationship between the two items. Demonstration of a priming effect would indicate that multiple items were being processed to a high level.

In the first experiment, the patient was asked to read aloud briefly presented pairs of unrelated and related words. The latter took two forms: words which were semantically associated ("deer elk") and words which could be combined to generate a compound word (e.g., "news paper"). She correctly identified both words on 25 of 30 (87%) trials with potential compounds, 21 of 30 trials (70%) with semantically associated words and 10 of 30 (33) trials with unrelated words. On 31 trials she correctly identified only one word and, in fact, claimed to have seen only one word. Performance with potential compound and associated words was significantly better than with unrelated words.

These and other data from similar experiments with word and picture stimuli demonstrate that the patient's ability to identify simultaneously presented stimuli is significantly improved if the stimuli are semantically related. These data reinforce the conclusion that the limitation does not arise at early levels of visual processing; both stimuli are available to high level recognition processes.

What, then, is the nature of the patient's limitation in multiple item perception? We argued earlier that the evidence obtained in Experiments 1 and 2 indicates that parallel processing of visual features is normal in our patient. Though we have not directly assessed the integrity of the VAR, the ease of recognition of single objects and words implies that integrative processes at this level are essentially normal. We assume that the buffer, qua viewer-centered spatial map, is not itself impaired; if it were, we would expect to see gross failures of orientation in visual space, which were not evident in our patient (cf. Holmes, 1918). Thus, unlike patients described by Holmes and others (Badal, 1888; Balint, 1909; Riddoch, 1917), having targeted an object, she could reach for it without difficulty with her right hand, and she could navigate adequately in space (except, as noted earlier, for the problem of unattended obstacles in her path).

We propose that the patient's deficit is attributable to a limitation in the attention-requiring process by which sites marked in the buffer are linked to structural description or word form information. On the account described above, "seeing" involves the articulation of stored information with information linked to specific sites in the visual buffer. An inability to maintain the linkages—that is, a failure to keep more than one structural description in registration with the appropriate site in the buffer—would result in an inability to see more than one object at a time.

This account of the patient's deficits also provides an explanation for the semantic priming effects. When two stimuli are related, activation from semantic/conceptual systems results in feedback to the structural description (or word form entry), which in turn feeds back to reinforce the weak binding site at the buffer. Consider, for example, the stimulus "deer elk"; in this situation, the identification of the word "deer" would serve to activate related information in the semantic/conceptual system, including, presumably, the node for "elk." Feedback from the semantic/conceptual system to the word form system would serve to activate both entries, thereby facilitating the process by which linkages between entries in the word form system and sites in the visual buffer are maintained.

Most patients with spatial disorientation or Balint's syndrome have had bilateral parietal lobe lesions; indeed, on the basis of autopsy data and inferences from the sites of entry and exit wounds, Holmes (1918, 1919) argued that damage to the angular and supramarginal gyri is particularly likely to cause these disorders. Hecaen and Ajuriaguerra (1954) reported four patients with Balint's syndrome, two of whom also had evidence of frontal lobe damage. On the basis of these patients, they argued that frontal lobe lesions may contribute to the disorder. The absence of frontal lobe lesions in many patients with these symptoms suggests, however, that frontal lobe damage may contribute to the overall clinical picture but does not play an important role in the genesis of these disorders.

Although, as noted above, visual disorientation and Balint's syndrome in their full form appear to require bilateral lesions, Riddoch (1935) has reported visual disorientation restricted to the contralateral visual field in two patients suffering from left parietal gliomas. While recognizing the potential hazards of localizing the effects attributable to an infiltrating tumor, it is worth noting that in both cases the tumor involved the angular and supramarginal gyri.

A final point of interest concerns possible subtypes of simultanagnosia. Although the term was introduced in the description of a patient with a posterior left hemisphere lesion, most patients with prominent simultanagnosia exhibit bilateral parietal damage. The visual processing disorder exhibited by patients with unilateral and bilateral lesions may, however, be distinguishable. Patients with simultanagnosia secondary to unilateral, dominant hemisphere lesions in whom speed of processing has been assessed have consistently exhibited a slowed rate of visual information processing (Kinsbourne & Warrington, 1962; Levine & Calvanio, 1978). Our patient, whose dominant hemisphere infarct was relatively small, exhibited no such impairment. Thus, we speculate that the disorder in simultaneous form perception associated with unilateral, dominant hemisphere lesions may be, at least in part, attributable to a slowing of information processing, while the disorder associated with bilateral lesions may be secondary to a limitation in attentional capacity at the visual buffer.

REFERENCES

Adler, A. (1944). Disintegration and restoration of optic recognition in visual agnosia. *Arch. Neurol. Psychiat*, *51*, 243–259.

Adler, A. (1950). Course and outcome of visual agnosia. *Journal of Nervous and Mental Disease*, *111*, 41–51.

Albert, M. L., Reches, A., Silverberg, R. (1975a). Hemianopic color blindness. *Journal of Neurosurgery and Psychiatry*, *38*, 546–549.

Albert, M. L., Reches, A., Silverberg, R. (1975b). Associative visual agnosia without alexia. *Neurology*, *25*, 322–326.

Albert, M. S., Butters, N., & Brandt, J. (1980). Memory for remote events in alcoholics. *Journal of Studies on Alcoholism*, *41*, 1071–1081.

Andersen, R. A., Essick, G. K., and Siegel, R. M. (1985). The encoding of spatial location by posterior parietal neurons. *Science*, *230*, 456–458.

Badal, J. (1888). Contribution a l'etude des cecites psychiques: Alexie, agraphie, hemianopsie inferieure, trouble du sens de l'espace. *Archives d'Ophthalmologie 8*, 97–117.

Balint, R. (1909). Seelenlähmung des "Schauens", optische Ataxie, räumliche Störung der Aufmerksamkeit. *Monatsschrift fur Psychiat. Neurol.*, *25*, 51–81.

Barnet, A. B., Manson, J. I., & Wilner, E. (1970). Acute cerebral blindness in childhood: Six cases studied clinically and electrophysiologically. *Neurology*, *43*, 1147–1156.

Bauer, R. M. (1984). Autonomic recognition of names and faces in prosopagnosia: A neuropsychological application of the Guilty Knowledge Test. *Neuropsychologia*, *22*, 457–470.

Bauer, R. M., & Rubens, A. R. (1985). Agnosia. In K. Heilman & E. Valenstein (Eds.), *Clinical neuropsychology* (pp. 187–242). New York: Oxford.

Bay, E. (1953). Disturbances of visual perception and their examination. *Brain*, *76*, 515–550.

Bender, M. D., & Feldman, M. (1972). The so-called "visual agnosias." *Brain*, *95*, 173–186.

Benson, D. F., Segarra, J., & Albert, M. L. (1974). Visual agnosia-prosopagnosia. *Archives of Neurology*, *30*, 307–10.

Benson, D. F., Davis, J., & Snyder, B. D. (1988). Posterior cortical atrophy. *Archives of Neurology*, *45*, 789–793.

Benson, D. F., & Greenberg, J. P. (1971). Visual form agnosia. *Archives of Neurology*, *20*, 82–89.

Benton, A. L., Hamsher, K. deS., Varney, N. R., & Spreen, O. (1983). *Contributions to neuropsychological assessment: A clinical manual*. New York: Oxford University Press.

Benton, A. L., & Van Allen, M. W. (1973). *Test of facial recognition*. Neurosensory Center Publication 287. Ames, IA: University of Iowa.

Benton, A. L., & Hecaen, H. (1970). Stereoscopic vision in patients with unilateral cerebral disease. *Neurology*, *20*, 1084–1088.

Birkmayer, W. (1951). *Hirnverletzungen*. Vienna: Springer-Verlag.

Bornstein, B. (1963). Prosopagnosia. In L. Halpern (Ed.), *Problems of dynamic neurology*. New York: Grune and Stratton.

Botez, M. I., Serbanescu, T., & Vernea, I. (1965). Visual static agnosia with special reference to literal agnosic alexia. *Neurology*, *5*, 1101–1111.

Campion, J., & Latto, R. (1985). Apperceptive agnosia due to carbon monoxide poisoning: An interpretation based on critical band masking from disseminated lesions. *Behavioral Brain Research*, *15*, 227–240.

Campion, J. (1987). Apperceptive agnosia: The specification and description of constructs. In G. W. Humphreys & M. J. Riddoch (Eds.), *Visual object processing: A cognitive neuropsychological approach.* Hove and London: Lawrence Erlbaum Associates.

Carmon, A., & Bechtoldt, H. P. (1969). Dominance of the right cerebral hemisphere for stereopsis. *Neuropsychologia*, *7*, 29–39.

Chertkow, H., & Bub, D. (1990). Semantic memory loss in dementia of Alzheimer's type. *Brain*, *113*, 397–417.

Cole M., Schutta, H. S., Warrington, E. K. (1962). Visual disorientation in homonymous half-fields. *Neurology*, *12*, 257–263.

Coslett, H. B., Saffran, E. M., & Fitzpatrick, E. (1988). Impaired movement of selective attention in neglect. *Journal of Clinical and Experimental Neuropsychology*, *10*, 21. (Abstract)

Coslett, H. B., & Saffran, E. M. (1989). Evidence for preserved reading in 'pure alexia.' *Brain*, *112*, 327–359.

Coslett, H. B., & Saffran, E. M. (1991). Simultanagnosia: To see but not two see. *Brain*, *114*, 1523–1545.

Coughlan, A. K., & Warrington, E. K. (1978). Word-comprehension and word-retrieval in patients with localised cerebral lesions. *Brain*, *101*, 163–185.

Crick, F. (1984). Function of the thalamic reticular complex. The searchlight hypothesis. *Proceedings of the National Academy of Science*, *81*, 4586–4590.

Critchley, M. (1965). Acquired anomalies of colour perception of central origin. *Brain*, *88*, 711–724.

Damasio, A. R., Yamada, T., Damasio, H., Corbet, J., & McKee, J. (1980). Central achromatopsia: Behavioral, anatomic and physiologic aspects. *Neurology*, *30*, 1064–1071.

Damasio, A. R., & Damasio, H. (1983). Anatomical basis of pure alexia. *Neurology*, *33*, 1573–1583.

Damasio, A. R. (1987). Disorders of complex visual processing: Agnosias, achromatopsia, Balint's syndrome and related difficulties of orientation and construction. In M. Mesulam (Ed.), *Principals of behavioral neurology*. (pp. 259–288). Philadelphia: F. A. Davis.

Danta, G., Hilton, R. C., & O'Boyle, D. J. (1978). Hemisphere function and binocular depth perception. *Brain*, *101*, 569–589.

Davidoff, J. B., & Ostergaard, A. L. (1984). Colour anomia resulting from weakened short-term colour memory. *Brain*, *107*, 415–431.

DeHaan, E. H. F., Young, A. W., & Newcombe, F. (1987). Face recognition without awareness. *Cognitive Neuropsychology*, *4*, 385–415.

Dejerine, J., & Vialet, N. (1893). Sur un cas de cécité corticale. *Competes Rendus de Seances de la Societe de Biologie et de Ses Filiales*, *11*, 983, 1893.

Desimone, R., Albright, T. D., Gross, C. G., & Bruce C. (1984). Stimulus selective properties of inferior temporal neurons in the macaque. *Journal of Neuroscience*, *4*, 2051–2062.

Desimone, R., & Schein, S. J. (1987). Visual properties of neurons in area V4 of the macaque: Sensitivity to stimulus form. *Journal of Neurophysiology*, *57*, 835–868.

DeYoe, E. A., & Van Essen, D. C. (1988). Concurrent processing streams in monkey visual cortex. *Trends in Neuroscience*, *11*, 219–226.

DiLollo, V., & Dixon, P. (1988). Two forms of persistance in visual information processing. *Journal of Experimental Psychology: Human Perception, and Performance*, *14*, 671–681.

Dunn, T. D. (1895). Double hemiplegia with double hemianopsia and loss of geographic centre. *Transactions of the College of Physicians of Philadelphia*, *17*, 45–56.

Efron R. (1968). What is perception? *Boston Studies in the Philosophy of Science*, *4*, 137–173. New York: Humanities Press.

Eriksen, C. W., & Yeh, Y. Y. (1985). Allocation of attention in the visual field. *Journal of Experimental Psychology: Human Perception and Performance*, *11*, 583–597.

Ettlinger, G. (1957). Sensory deficits in visual agnosia. *Journal of Neurology, Neurosurgery, and Psychiatry*, *19*, 297–307.

Freund, S. (1889). Zur ueber optische aphasie und seelenblindheit. *Arch Psychiatr. Nervenkr.*, *20*, 276–297, 371–416.

Geschwind, N. (1965). Disconnection syndromes in animals and man. *Brain*, *88*, 237–294, 585–644.

Geschwind, N., Fusillo, M. (1966). Color-naming defects in association with alexia. *Archives of Neurology*, *15*, 137–146.

Goldberg, M. E., & Bruce, C. J. (1985). Cerebral cortical activity associated with the orientation of visual attention in the rhesus monkey. *Vision Research*, *25*, 471–481.

Goldstein, K. M., & Gelb, A. (1918). Psychologische Analysen hirnpathologischer Falle auf Grund von Untersuchungen Hirnverletzter. *Zeitschrift fur die Neurologie and Psychiatrie*, *41*, 1–142.

Goodglass, H., Klein, B., Carey, P., & Jones, K. (1966). Specific semantic word categories in aphasia. *Cortex*, *2*, 74–89.

Goodglass, H., & Kaplan, E. (1972). *The assessment of aphasia and related disorders*. Philadelphia: Lea and Febiger.

Green, G. J., & Lessell, S. (1977). Acquired cerebral dyschromatopsia. *Archives of Ophthalmology*, *95*, 121–128.

Gross, C. G. (1973). Inferotemporal cortex and vision. *Progress in Physiologic Psychology*, *5*, 77–123.

Gross, C. G., & Mishkin, M. (1977). The neural basis of stimulus equivalence across retinal translation. In S. Harned, R. Doty, J. Jaynes, L. Goldberg & G. Krauthamer (Eds.), *Lateralization in the nervous system* (pp. 109–122). New York: Academic Press.

Gross, C. B., Rocha-Miranda, C. E., & Bender, D. B. (1972). Visual properties of cells in infratemporal cortex of the macaque. *Journal of Neurophysiology*, *35*, 96–111.

Head, H. (1920). Aphasia and kindred disorders of speech. *Brain*, *43*, 87–165.

Hecaen, H., & de Ajuriaguerra, J. (1954). Balint's syndrome (psychic paralysis of visual fixation) and its minor forms. *Brain*, *77*, 373–400.

Hecaen, H., & Albert, M. (1978). *Human neuropsychology*. New York: John Wiley.

Holmes, G. (1918). Disturbances of visual orientation. *British Journal of Ophthalmology*, *2*, 449–68, 506–516.

Holmes, G., & Horrax, G. (1919). Disturbances of spatial orientation and visual attention with loss of stereoscopic vision. *Archives of Neurology and Psychiatry*, *1*, 385–407.

Horner, J., & Massey, E. W. (1986). Dynamic spelling alexia. *Journal of Neurology, Neurosurgery, and Psychiatry*, *49*, 455–457.

Hubel, D. H., & Weisel, T. N. (1970). Cells sensitive to binocular depth in area 18 of the macaque monkey cortex. *Nature* (London), *225*, 41–42.

Hubel, D. H., & Livingstone, M. S. (1987). Segregation of form, color, and stereopsis in primate area 18. *Journal of Neuroscience*, *7*, 3378–3415.

Humphreys, G. W., Riddoch, M. J. (1984). Routes to object constancy: Implications from neurological impairments of object constancy. *Quarterly Journal of Experimental Psychology*, *36A*, 385–415.

Humphreys, G. W., Riddoch, M. J., & Quinlan, P. T. (1985). Interactive processes in perceptual organization: Evidence from visual agnosia. In M. I. Posner & O. S. M. Marin (Eds.), *Attention and performance XI*. Hillsdale, NJ: Lawrence Erlbaum.

Humphreys, G. W., & Riddoch, M. J. (1987). *To see but not to see: A case study of visual agnosia*. London: Lawrence Erlbaum.

Humphreys, G. W., Riddoch, M. J., & Quinlan, P. T. (1988). Cascade processes in picture identification. *Cognitive Neuropsychology*, *5*, 67–103.

Irwin, D. E., & Youmans, J. M. (1986). Sensory registration and informational persistence. *Journal of Experimental Psychology: Human Perception and Performance*, *12*, 343–360.

Jackson, J. H. (1876). Case of large cerebral tumour without optic neuritis and with left hemiplegia and imperception. *Royal Ophthalmological Hospital Reports*, *8*, 434–444.

Jenkins, J. J. (1970). The 1952 Minnesota word association norms. In L. Postman & G. Keppel, Eds. *Norms of word association*. New York: Academic Press.

Jones, E. G. (1985). *The thalamus*. New York: Plenum Press.

Julesz, B., Breitmeyer, B., & Kropel, W. (1976). Binocular disparity dependent upper lower hemifield anisotropy and left right hemifield isotropy as revealed by dynamic random dot stereograms. *Perception*, *5*, 129–141.

Kahneman, D., Triesman, A., & Burkell, J. (1983). The cost of visual filtering. *Journal of Experimental Psychology: Human Perception and Performance*, *9*, 510–522.

Kaplan, E., Goodglass, H., & Weintraub, S. (1983). *Boston Naming Test*. Philadelphia: Lea & Febiger.

Kinsbourne, M., & Warrington, E. K. (1962). A disorder of simulaneous form perception. *Brain*, *85*, 461–486.

Kinsbourne, M., Warrington, E. K. (1963). The localizing significance of limited simultaneous form perception. *Brain*, *86*, 697–702.

Kinsbourne, M., & Warrington, E. K. (1964). Observations on color agnosia. *Journal of Neurology, Neurosurgery, and Psychiatry*, *27*, 296–299.

Kramer, F. (1970). Uber eine partielle Storung der optischen Tiefenwahrnehmung. *Monatschrift fur Psychologie und Neurologie*, *22*, 189–202.

Kroll, N. E. A., Parks, T.E., Parkinson, S. R., Bieber, S. L., and Johnson, A. L. (1970). Short-term memory while shadowing: Recall of visually and aurally presented letters. *Journal of Experimental Psychology*, *85*, 220–224.

Kroll, J. F., & Potter, M. C. (1984). Recognizing words, pictures and concepts: A comparison of lexical, object, and reality decisions. *Journal of Verbal Learning and Verbal Behavior*, *23*, 39–66.

Kucera, H., & Francis, W. N. (1967). *Computational analysis of present-day American English*. Providence, RI: Brown University Press.

LaBerge, D., & Brown, D. (1989). Attentional operations in shape identification. *Psychological Review*, *96* 101–124.

Landis, T., Regard, M., Bliestle, A., & Kleihues, P. (1988). Prosopagnosia and agnosia for noncanonical views. *Brain*, *111*, 1287–1297.

Larrabee, G. J., Levin, H. S., Huff, F. J., Kay, M. C., & Guinto, F. C. Jr. (1985). Visual agnosia contrasted with visual-verbal disconnection. *Neuropsychologia*, *23*, 1–12.

Layman, S., & Greene, E. (1988). The effect of stroke on object recognition. *Brain and Cognition*, *7*, 87–114.

Levine, D. N., & Calvanio, R. (1978). A study of the visual defect in verbal alexia-simultanagnosia. *Brain*, *101*, 65–81.

Lissauer, H. (1890). Ein fall von Seelenblindheit nebst einem Beitrag zur Theorie derselben. *Archiv fur Psychiatrie und Nervenkrankheiten*, *21*, 22–70.

Livingstone, M. S., Hubel, D. H. (1987). Psychophysical evidence for separate channels for the perception of form, color, movement and depth. *Journal of Neuroscience*, *7*, 3416–3468.

Lhermitte, F., & Beauvois, M. F. (1973). A visual-speech disconnection syndrome. *Brain*, *96*, 696–714.

Luria, A. R. (1959). Disorders of "simultaneous perception" in a case of bilateral occipitoparietal brain injury. *Brain*, *83*, 437–449.

Luria, A. R., Praudina-Vinarskaya, E. N., Yarbus, A. L. (1963). Disorders of ocular movement in a case of simultanagnosia. *Brain*, *86*, 219–228.

Mack, J. L., & Boller, F. (1977). Associative visual agnosia and its related deficits: The role of the minor hemisphere in assigning meaning to visual perceptions. *Neuropsychologia*, *15*, 345–349.

MacKay, G., & Dunlop, J. C. (1899). The cerebral lesions in a case of complete acquired colour-blindness. *Scott. Med. Surb. J.*, *5*, 503–512.

Margolin, D. I., Friedrich, F. J., & Carlson, N. R. (February, 1985). *Visual agnosia-optic aphasia: Continuum or dichotomy*? Presented at the Meeting of the International Neuropsychological Society, San Diego, CA.

Marin, O. S. M., Glenn, C. G., & Rafal, R. D. (1983). Visual problem solving in the absence of lexical semantics: Evidence from dementia. *Brain and Cognition*, *2*, 285–311.

Marr, D. (1982). *Vision*. San Francisco: W. H. Freeman Co.

Marr, D., & Nishihara, H. K. (1978). Representation and recognition of the spatial organization of three-dimensional shapes. *Proceedings of the Royal Society of London B*, *200*, 269–294.

Maunsell, J. H. R., & Newsome, W. T. (1987). Visual processing in monkey extrastriate cortex. *Annual Review of Neuroscience*, *10*, 363–401.

Meadows, J. D. (1974). The anatomic basis of prosopagnosia. *Journal of Neurology, Neurosurgery, and Psychiatry*, *37*, 489–501.

Meyer, D. E., Schvaneveldt, R. W., & Ruddy, M. G. (1975). Loci of contextual effects on visual word recognition. In P. M. Rabbitt & Dornic (Eds.), *Attention and Performance V* (pp. 98–118). New York: Academic Press.

Michel, F., Jeannerod, M., & Devic, M. (1965). Trouble de l'orientation visuelle dans les trois dimensions de l'espace. *Cortex*, *1*, 441–466.

Moran, J., & Desimone, J. (1985). Selective attention gates visual processing in the extrastriate cortex. *Science*, *229*, 782–784.

Mountcastle, V. B., Lynch, J. C., Georgopoulos, A., Sakata, H., & Acuna, C. (1975). Posterior parietal association cortex of the monkey: Command function from operations within extrapersonal space. *Journal of Neurophysiology*, *38*, 871–908.

Mountcastle, V. B., Anderson, R. A., & Motter, B. C. (1981). The influence of attentive fixation upon the excitability of the light sensitive neurons of the posterior parietal cortex. *Journal of Neuroscience*, *1*, 1218–1245.

Munk, H. (1878). Weitere Mittheilungen zur Physiologie der Grosshirnrinde. *Archiv fur die Anatomie und Physiologie*, *2*, 161–178.

Nebes, R. D., Martin, D. C., Horn, & L. C. (1984). Sparing of semantic memory in Alzheimer's disease. *Journal of Abnormal Psychology*, *93*, 321–330.

Neisser, U. (1967). *Cognitive psychology*. New York: Appleton-Century-Crofts.

Newcombe, F., & Russell, W. R. (1969). Dissociated visual perceptual and spatial deficits in focal lesions of the right hemisphere. *Journal of Neurology, Neurosurgery, and Psychiatry*, *32*, 73–81.

Newcombe, F., Ratcliff, G. (1974). Agnosia: A disorder of object recognition. In F. Michel and B. Schott (Eds.), *Les Syndromes de Disconnexion Calleuse chez L'homme*. Colloque International de Lyon.

Newcombe, F., Young, A. W., & De Haan, E. H. F. (1989). Prosopagnosia and object agnosia without covert recognition. *Neuropsychologia*, *27*, 179–191.

Newsome, W. T., & Pare, E. B. (1988) A selective impairment of motion perception following lesions of the middle temporal visual area (MT). *Journal of Neuroscience*, *8*(6), 2202–2211.

Oxbury, J., Oxbury, S., & Humphrey, N. (1969). Varieties of colour anomia. *Brain*, *92*, 847–860.

Paterson, A., & Zangwill, O. L. (1944). Disorders of visual space perception associated with lesions of the right cerebral hemisphere. *Brain*, *67*, 331–358.

Pavlov, I. P. (1927). *Conditioned reflexes*. London: Oxford.

Pearlman, A. L., Birch, J., & Meadows, J. C. (1979). Cerebral color blindness: An acquired defect in hue discrimination. *Annals of Neurology*, *5*, 253–261.

Perenin, M. T., & Vighetto, A. (1988). Optic ataxia: A specific disruption of visuomotor mechanisms. *Brain*, *111*, 643–674.

Perett, D. I., Smith, P. A. J., Potter, D. D., Mistlin, A. J., Head, A. S., Milner, A. D., & Jeeves, M. A. (1984). Neurons responsive to faces in the temporal cortex: Studies of functional organization, sensitivity to identity and relation to perception. *Human Neurobiology*, *3*, 197–208.

Perett, D. I., Smith, P. A. J., Potter, D. D., Mistlin, A. J., Head, A. S., Milner, A. D., & Jeeves, M. A. (1985). Visual cells in the temporal cortex sensitive to face view and gaze direction. *Proceedings of the Royal Society of London, Series B*, *223*, 293–317.

Peterson, S. E., Robinson, D. L., & Morris, J. D. (1987). Contributions of the pulvinar to visual spatial attention. *Neuropsychologia*, *25*, 97–105.

Petrides, M., & Iversen, S. D. (1979). Restricted posterior parietal lesions in the rhesus monkey and performance on visuospatial tasks. *Brain Research*, *161*, 63–77.

Phillips, W. A. (1974). On the distinction between sensory storage and short-term visual memory. *Perception and Psychophysics*, *16*, 283–290.

Poggio, G. F., & Fischer, B. (1977). Binocular interaction and depth sensitivity in striate and prestriate cortex of behaving rhesus monkey. *Journal of Neurophysiology*, *40*, 1392–1405.

Pohl, W. (1973). Dissociation of spatial discrimination deficits following frontal and parietal lesions in monkeys. *Journal of Comparative and Physiological Psychology*, *82*, 227–39.

Posner, M. I., Walker, J. A., Freidrich, A. J., & Rafal, R. D. (1984). Effects of parietal lobe injury on covert orienting of visual attention. *Journal of Neuroscience*, *4*, 1863–1874.

Posner, M. I., Cohen, Y., & Rafal, R. D. (1982). Neural systems control of spatial orienting. *Philosophical Transactions of the Royal Society of London B*, *298*, 187–198.

Posner, M. I. (1989). Structures and function of selective attention. In T. Boll & B. K. Bryant (Eds.), *Clinical Neuropsychology and Brain Function*. Washington, DC: American Psychological Association.

Postman, L. (1970). The California norms: Association as a function of word frequency. In L. Postman & G. Kleppel (Eds.), *Norms of Word Association*. New York: Academic Press.

Pötzl, O. (1928). Die optisch-agnostischen Storungen. Leipzig and Vienna: Franz Deuticke.

Pötzl, O., & Redich, E. (1911). Demonstration eines Falles von bilateraler Affektion beider Occipitallapen. *Weiner Klinsche Wochenschrift*, *24*, 517–518.

Prinzmetal, W., & Banks, W. P. (1976). Configurational effects in visual information processing. *Perception and Psychophysics*, *19*, 361–367.

Prinzmetal, W. (1981). Principles of feature integration in visual perception. *Perception and Psychophysics*, *30*, 330–340.

Ratcliffe, G., Newcombe, F. (1982). Object recognition: Some deductions from the clinical evidence. In A. W. Ellis (Ed.), *Normality and Pathology in Cognitive Function*. London: Academic Press.

Reitan, R. M. (1958). Validity of the Trail Making Test as an indicator of organic brain damage. *Perceptual and Motor Skills*, *8*, 271–276.

Riddoch, G. (1917). Dissociation of visual perception due to occipatal injuries with special reference to appreciation of movement. *Brain*, *40*, 15–57.

Riddoch, G. (1935). Visual disorientation in homonymous half-fields. *Brain*, *58*, 376–382.

Riddoch, M. J., & Humphreys, G. W. (1986). Neurological impairments of object constancy: The effects of orientation and size disparities. *Cognitive Neuropsychology*, *3*, 207–224.

Riddoch, M. J., & Humphreys, G. W. (1987). Visual object processing in optic aphasia: A case of semantic access agnosia. *Cognitive Neuropsychology*, *4*, 131–185.

Robinson, D. L., Goldberg, M. E., & Stanton, G. B. (1978). Parietal association cortex in the primate: Sensory mechanisms and behavioral modulations. *Journal of Neurophysiology*, *41*, 910–932.

Rolls, E. T. (1984). Neurons in the cortex of the temporal lobe and in the amygdala of the monkey with responses selective for faces. *Human Neurobiology*, *3*, 209–22.

Rondot, P., de Recondo, J., Ribadeau Dumas, J. L. C. (1976). Visuomotor ataxia. *Brain*, *100*, 355–376.

Rosch, E. (1975). Cognitive representations of semantic categories. *Journal of Experimental Psychology: General*, *104*, 192–233.

Rothstein, T. B., & Sacks, J. G. (1972). Defective stereopsis in lesions of the parietal lobe. *American Journal of Ophthalmology*, *73*, 281–284.

Rubens, A. B., & Benson, D. F. (1971). Associative visual agnosia. *Archives of Neurology*, *24*, 304–316.

Sagi, D., & Julesz, B. (1985) "Where" and "What" in vision. *Science*, *228*, 1217–1219.

Sartori, G., & Job, R. (1988). The Oyster with Four Legs: A neuropsychological study on the interaction of visual and semantic information. *Cognitive Neuropsychology*, *5*, 105–132.

Schneider, W., & Shiffrin, R. M. (1977). Controlled and automatic human information processing: I. Detection, search and attention. *Psychological Review*, *84*, 1–66.

Shallice, T. (1988). *From neuropsychology to mental structure*. Cambridge: Cambridge University Press.

Shepard, R. N., & Metzler, J. (1971). Mental rotation of three-dimensional objects. *Science*, *171*, 701–703.

Snodgrass, J. C., & Vanderwart, M. A. (1980). Standardized set of 260 pictures: Norms for name agreement, image agreement, familiarity and visual complexity. *Journal of Experimental Psychology: Human Learning and Memory*, *6*, 174–215.

Stengel, E. (1948). The syndrome of visual alexia with color agnosia. *Journal of Mental Science*, *94*, 46–58.

Sugishita, M., Ettlinger, G., & Ridley, R. M. (1978). Disturbance of cage finding in the monkey. *Cortex, 14*, 431–438.

Symonds, C. P. (1945). Discussion on the ocular sequelae of head injuries. *Trans. of the Ophth. Soc. of the UK, 65*, 3–19.

Taylor, A., & Warrington, E. K. (1971). Visual agnosia: A single case report. *Cortex, 7*, 152–164.

Taylor, A., & Warrington, E. K. (1973). Visual discrimination in patients with localized cerebral lesions. *Cortex, 9*, 82–93.

Teuber, H. L. (1968). Alteration of perception and memory in man. In L. Weiskrantz (Ed.), *Analysis of Behavioral Change*. New York: Harper and Row.

Teuber, H. L., Battersby, W., & Bender, M. B. (1960). *Visual field defects after penetrating missile wounds of the brain*. Cambridge, MA: Harvard University Press.

Tranel, E., & Damasio, A. R. (1985). Knowledge without awareness: An autonomic index of facial recognition by prosopagnosics. *Science, 228*, 1453–1454.

Treisman, A., & Gelade, G. (1980). A feature integration theory of attention. *Cognitive Psychology, 12*, 97–136.

Treisman, A., & Schmidt, H. (1982). Illusory conjunctions in the perception of objects. *Cognitive Psychology, 14*, 107–141.

Treisman, A., & Souther, J. (1985). Search asymmetry: A diagnostic for preattentive processing of separable features. *Journal of Experimental Psychology: General, 114*, 285–310.

Treisman, A., Kahneman, D., & Burkell, J. (1983). Perceptual objects and the cost of filtering. *Perception and Psychophysics, 33*, 527–532.

Treisman, A., & Gormican, S., (1988). Feature analysis in early vision: Evidence for search asymmetries. *Psychological Review, 95*, 15–48.

Tyler, H. H. (1968). Abnormalities of perception with defective eye movements (Balint's syndrome). *Cortex, 4*, 154–171.

Ullman, S. (1984). Visual routines. *Cognition, 18*, 97–159.

Ungerleider, L. G., & Mishkin, M. (1982). Two cortical visual systems. In D. J. Ingle, M. A. Goodale, & R. J. W. Mansfield, (Eds.), *Analysis of visual behavior*. Cambridge, MA: MIT Press.

Verrey, D. (1888). Hemiachromatopsie droite absolute. *Archives de Ophthalimologie* (Paris), 8, 289–300.

Von Monakow, C. (1897). *Gehirnpathologie*. Vienna: Nothnagel.

Warrington, E. K. (1975). Selective impairment of semantic memory. *Quarterly Journal of Experimental Psychology, 27*, 635–657.

Warrington, E. K., & James, M. (1967). Disorders of visual perception in patients with localized cerebral lesions. *Neuropsychologia, 5*, 253–266.

Warrington, E. K., & James, M. (1986). Visual object recognition in patients with right hemisphere lesions: Axes or features. *Perception, 15*, 355–366.

Warrington, E. K., & Rabin, P. (1970). Perceptual matching in patients with cerebral lesions. *Neuropsychologia, 8*, 475–487.

Warrington, E. K., & Taylor, A. M. (1973). The contribution of the right parietal lobe to object recognition. *Cortex, 9*, 152–164.

Warrington, E. K., & Taylor, A. M. (1978). Two categorical stages in object recognition. *Perception, 7*, 695–705.

Warrington, E. K., & Shallice, T. (1979). Semantic access dyslexia. *Brain, 102*, 43–63.

Watson, R. T., Valenstein, E., & Heilman, K. M. (1981). Thalamic neglect: Possible role of the medial thalamus and nucleus reticularis in behavior. *Archives of Neurology, 38*, 501–506.

Wilbrand, H. (1887). *Die Seelenblindheit als Herderscheinung und ihre Beziehungen zur Homonymen Hemianopsie*. Wiesbaden: Bergmann.

Wolpert, I. (1924). Die Simultanagnosie: Storung der gesamtauffassung. *Zeitschrift fur die gesamte Neurologie und Psychiatrie*, *93*, 397–413.

Young, A. W., DeHaan, E. H. F. (1988). Boundaries of covert recognition in prosopagnosia. *Cognitive Neuropsychology*, *5*, 317–336.

Zihl, J., Von Cramon, D., & Mai, N. (1983). Selective disturbance of movement vision after bilateral brain damage. *Brain*, *106*, 313–340.

14

Assessment of Acquired Dyscalculia

PAUL MACARUSO, WALTER HARLEY, and
MICHAEL McCLOSKEY

Clinical techniques for assessment of cognitive dysfunction have traditionally focussed on language and perceptual deficits, at the expense of impairments in other cognitive domains. One area that has received scant attention is *dyscalculia*, the class of deficits affecting number comprehension, number production, and calculation. For instance, of the more than 600 tests and subscales treated in Lezak's (1983) extensive handbook of neuropsychological assessment, only three are described as useful for assessment of dyscalculia. In this chapter we describe theoretically grounded assessment procedures that have emerged from our research on number-processing and calculation deficits.

GOALS OF ASSESSMENT

Assessment of cognitive deficits resulting from brain damage may be undertaken for a variety of reasons. Until recently, such assessment was often carried out in order to assist in localization of lesions. With advances in neuroimaging technology, however, the role of neuropsychological assessment in lesion localization is no longer a primary one (Lezak, 1983). Assessment of acquired cognitive disorders may also be undertaken by researchers interested in learning more about cognition or brain/cognition relationships. For the practicing clinician, however, the principal goal in assessing a patient's cognitive functioning is usually to provide a basis for advising the patient and others (e.g., family members, the patient's physician) about the nature and severity of deficits, the probable impact of these deficits on the patient's life, and the prospects for rehabilitation. If efforts at remediation are undertaken, assessment results may also be used to monitor the progress of these efforts.

From the clinical perspective, the motivation for assessing number-processing and calculation skills is straightforward: these skills are important for functioning in everyday life. Many job categories, from store clerk to stock trader, require the ability to comprehend and produce numbers, and to perform simple calculations. Furthermore, numerical abilities are implicated in a wide range of everyday activities, such as reading prices in a store, using the telephone, addressing letters, or writing checks. Thus, in any patient who may return to at least some degree of normal functioning, number-processing and calculation abilities merit assessment.

APPROACHES TO ASSESSMENT

From the cognitive information-processing perspective, acquired cognitive disorders reflect damage to one or more components of a previously normal cognitive system. On this view, assessment of cognitive functions such as number processing and calculation should involve (1) the selection of tasks to probe systematically the various cognitive mechanisms underlying the to-be-assessed functions; and (2) the use of the task results to infer for each of these mechanisms whether it is intact or impaired and, if impaired, the nature of the impairment. Clearly, an important prerequisite for this sort of assessment is an explicit model of the processing mechanisms underlying the to-be-assessed function. In the absence of such a model, one has no firm basis for characterizing the set of cognitive processes that should be assessed, for deciding what tasks might serve to probe these processes, or for inferring the status of the processes from performance on the tasks. In the extreme, absence of a theoretical framework leads to what might be called "task-oriented" assessment, in which a series of tasks is chosen on pretheoretical grounds, and diagnoses are stated simply as a list of task results (e.g., the patient is impaired in reading numbers aloud, intact in writing numbers to dictation, etc.).

Model-based assessments are superior in several respects to task-based diagnoses. In addition to being more detailed and more systematic, model-based assessments provide a means for generalizing to tasks other than those which have been specifically tested. For example, a task-oriented approach offers no grounds for predicting whether a patient who shows impairment in reading numbers aloud will also be impaired in production of numbers in spontaneous speech. Given, however, a model that specifies the cognitive mechanisms involved in number-reading and spontaneous number production, and assessment techniques that identify the underlying deficit(s) responsible for impaired number-reading performance, clear predictions about spontaneous number production can be made.

Thus, model-based assessments are far more useful than task-based assessments for purposes of advising patients and others about the nature of deficits, the likely impact of these deficits, and prospects for rehabilitation. For example, a clinician may wish to counsel patients about situations in which they may encounter difficulty, and about ways to compensate for these difficulties. Given a task-based diagnosis, advice can be offered only about situations involving the specific tasks that were administered. A diagnosis stated in terms of underlying cognitive mechanisms, however, provides a basis for more useful advice. For example, given a diagnosis of selective impairment to the mechanisms responsible for production of number words in spoken form, the patient might be advised that he or she may be likely to experience difficulty whenever he or she says numbers aloud (e.g., giving an address over the phone), but should have no trouble in understanding numbers, or in writing numbers in digit or word form. Further, the patient might be advised to write rather than speak numbers whenever possible, and to request confirmation of the correct numbers when spoken production is necessary.

With respect to remediation, a model-based diagnosis identifies the specific cognitive processes that should be targeted, and provides a basis for selecting tasks that involve these processes (including tasks not administered during assessment). For example, given the diagnosis of a selective impairment in spoken number production, the clinician may be confident that any task involving spoken production of numbers is a legitimate exercise for a program of remediation, and that any other task is unlikely to prove helpful. In contrast, task-based diagnoses suggest only that practice might be given with the particular assessment tasks that showed impaired performance.

METHODS OF ASSESSMENT

Traditional methods for assessment and classification of dyscalculia, while not entirely atheoretical, have typically not been based upon explicit models of the cognitive mechanisms underlying number comprehension, number production, and calculation. Perhaps the most widely adopted system for classifying forms of dyscalculia is that of Hecaen, Angelergues, and Houillier (1961). The Hecaen et al. formulation distinguishes three types of dyscalculia: (1) *number alexia/agraphia*—impaired calculation resulting from deficits in reading or writing numbers; (2) *spatial dyscalculia*—impaired calculation resulting from spatial processing deficits; and (3) *anarithmetia*—disruption of calculation ability per se. This classification system appropriately categorizes impairments in terms of disruption to cognitive abilities presumed to be implicated in normal calculation (i.e., number reading/writing abilities, spatial processing ability, calculation ability). Unfortunately, however, the postulated normal abilities are not clearly specified. Hence, it is uncertain what role these abilities play in particular calculation tasks, or what specific types of impaired calculation performance would be expected to result from their disruption.

Given the absence of an explicit theoretical framework, it is perhaps not surprising that no standard techniques for assessment of number-processing and calculation disorders have emerged from dyscalculia research. Subscales of several standardized tests, including the Wechsler Adult Intelligence Scale (WAIS; Wechsler, 1955), the Wechsler Adult Intelligence Scale—Revised (WAIS-R; Wechsler, 1981), the Wide Range Achievement Test (WRAT; Jastak & Jastak, 1965), and the Peabody Individual Achievement Test (PIAT; Dunn & Markwardt, 1970), are sometimes used in assessment of calculation disorders. However, these tests are not designed to probe systematically the various cognitive processes implicated in calculation, or to determine the specific nature of an impairment. Moreover, each of the tests has additional shortcomings that limit its usefulness for assessing dyscalculia. For instance, the arithmetic subscales of the WAIS and WAIS-R contain only 14 items, of which the first two are rarely administered; the WRAT is difficult to use with some patients because of its small typeface and limited room for responses; and the PIAT uses a multiple-choice format, making analysis of errors somewhat difficult (Lezak, 1983).

Several researchers (e.g., Benton, 1963; Levin, 1979; Levin & Spiers, 1985; Lezak, 1983; Luria, 1966) have discussed additional sets of tasks that may be useful in assessment of dyscalculia. However, these tasks typically have not been discussed in the context of an explicit model. Hence, as in the case of the standardized tests, it is unclear whether the tasks are sufficient to probe each of the cognitive mechanisms implicated in number-processing and calculation, how the results should be interpreted, and so forth.

In this chapter we described assessment and classification methods based on a model of the cognitive mechanisms underlying number comprehension, number production, and calculation. We first describe the model and then discuss methods for inferring the status of the various mechanisms specified in the model. Finally, we illustrate applications of these methods by discussing three patients studied in our laboratory.

The assessment procedures focus on assessment of number-processing and calculation skills that are important in everyday life. In particular, we assess comprehension and production of positive integers (and 0) in digit and word form, as well as simple addition, subtraction, and multiplication. Thus, we do not consider negative numbers, decimals, fractions, algebra, and so forth. Also, our discussion is limited to a cognitive level of analysis; we do not address issues concerning the neural substrata of the various cognitive mechanisms.

A COGNITIVE MODEL OF NUMBER PROCESSING AND CALCULATION

Figure 14-1 presents a cognitive model of number processing and calculation proposed by McCloskey, Caramazza, and Basili (1985). Building upon earlier attempts to characterize forms of dyscalculia in terms of disruption to normal number-processing and calculation mechanisms (e.g., Cohn, 1961; Hecaen et al., 1961; Henschen, 1925; Grewel, 1952, 1969), the model provides a more detailed description of the normal mechanisms, and therefore supports specific, theoretically-motivated characterizations of deficits. (See McCloskey et al., 1985, for further discussion of the relation of their model to earlier analyses of dyscalculia.)

At the most general level the model draws a distinction between the *number-processing system* and the *calculation system*. The number-processing system comprises cognitive mechanisms implicated in number comprehension and production, whereas the calculation system consists of cognitive mechanisms specifically involved in calculation.

The Number-Processing System

The number-processing system is assumed to comprise functionally independent *number comprehension* and *number production* subsystems. Within each of these subsystems a further distinction is drawn between components for processing *Arabic numbers* (i.e., numbers in digit form, such as 362), and components for

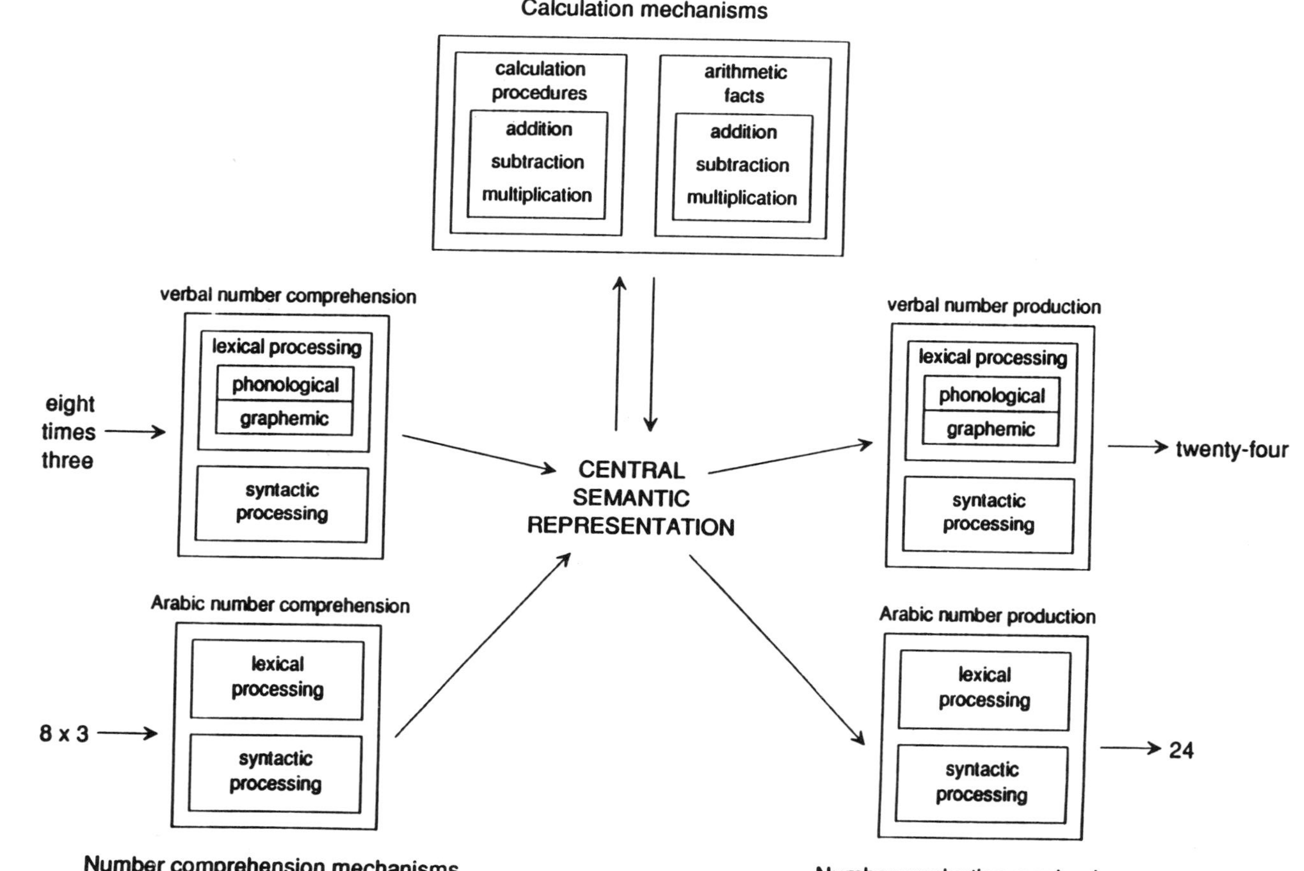

Figure 14-1 A model of the cognitive number-processing and calculation mechanisms.

processing *verbal numbers* (i.e., numbers in the form of words, such as *three hundred sixty-two*).[1]

Number Comprehension

The number comprehension components serve to translate Arabic or verbal number inputs into internal semantic representations for use in subsequent cognitive processing. Thus, for example, reading prices on products in a department store implicates the Arabic number comprehension component; whereas listening to basketball scores on the radio involves spoken verbal number comprehension.

Within the Arabic and verbal number comprehension components, a distinction is drawn between *lexical* and *syntactic* processing mechanisms. Lexical processing involves comprehension of the individual elements in a number (e.g., the digit 3 or the word *three*); whereas syntactic processing involves analysis of the relations among elements (e.g., word order) to produce an internal semantic representation of the number as a whole. Finally, within the lexical processing components for verbal number comprehension, the model distinguishes between phonological processing mechanisms for comprehension of spoken number words and graphemic processing mechanisms for comprehension of written number words. For example, in comprehension of the spoken verbal number "six hundred twelve," phonological lexical processing mechanisms would first generate semantic representations of the individual words *six*, *hundred*, and *twelve*. Syntactic processing mechanisms would then use these representations, in conjunction with information about word order, to generate an internal representation specifying a number made up of 6 hundreds, 1 ten, and 2 ones. The syntactic processing would involve, among other things, determining that the word *six* was followed by the "multiplier" word *hundred* (which multiplies by 100 the value of the immediately preceding word), and hence that the number includes 6 hundreds.

Number Production

Arabic and verbal number production components serve to translate internal semantic representations of numbers into sequences of digit or word representations for output. For example, giving one's address over the telephone requires the mechanisms for spoken verbal number production, and writing a check involves both Arabic and written verbal number production mechanisms.

As in the case of the number comprehension components, the Arabic and verbal number production components are divided into *lexical* and *syntactic* processing mechanisms. The role of syntactic processing in number production is to generate a plan for production of a number. The plan, or *syntactic frame*, specifies in abstract form the appropriate sequence of digits (in the case of an Arabic number) or words (in the case of a verbal number) to be produced. Lexical processing mechanisms then act to retrieve the individual elements specified in the syntactic frame. For spoken verbal numbers lexical processing involves retrieval of phonological number-word representations from a phonological output lexicon, while for written verbal numbers graphemic number-word representations are retrieved from a graphemic output lexicon. For Arabic numbers lexical processing involves retrieval of graphemic representations of the appropriate digits. The retrieved phonological or graphemic representations are then processed by more peripheral output mechanisms, leading ultimately to production of a spoken or written response.[2]

For example, if the verbal number production component received a semantic representation specifying a number made up of 8 ten-thousands and 4 hundreds, syntactic processing mechanisms would generate an abstract syntactic frame indicating that the to-be-produced verbal number comprises the tens word for the quantity 8, followed by the multiplier word *thousand*, followed by the ones word for the quantity 4, followed by the multiplier word *hundred*. Lexical processing mechanisms would then retrieve the phonological number word representations /eighty/, /thousand/, /four/, and /hundred/.[3] (For more detailed discussion of lexical and syntactic processing in number production, see McCloskey, Sokol, & Goodman, 1986.)

The Calculation System

Performing arithmetic calculations requires, in addition to the cognitive processes for number comprehension and production, cognitive processes that are specific to calculation. In particular, the McCloskey et al. (1985) model distinguishes among cognitive mechanisms for (1) comprehension of operation symbols or words, (2) retrieval of arithmetic facts, and (3) execution of calculation procedures.

Operation Symbol/Word Comprehension

For arithmetic problems in which the operations are specified in symbol form (e.g., 9 + 4) processing of the operation symbol (e.g., +) is assumed to yield an internal representation of the to-be-performed operation. Similarly, for problems in which the operations are specified verbally (e.g., "nine plus four") the operation is identified through processing of the operation word (e.g., plus).

Arithmetic Fact Retrieval

The model assumes that for each arithmetic operation the so-called "table facts" (e.g., $5 + 4 = 9$, $8 - 5 = 3$, $9 \times 6 = 54$) are stored directly in memory, and that single- or multidigit calculation involves retrieval of these stored facts. Thus, for example, solving the problem 58×6 requires retrieval of the facts $6 \times 8 = 48$ and $6 \times 5 = 30$.

Execution of Calculation Procedures

Performing multidigit calculations requires the use of calculation procedures that specify the sequence of steps to be followed in solving a problem (e.g., in solving a multidigit multiplication problem, start at the rightmost column, retrieve the product of the digits in this column, write the ones digit of the product at the bottom of the column, carry the tens digit, if any, and so forth). The model postulates a separate procedure for each arithmetic operation.

Empirical Evidence Bearing on the Model

These assumptions about the functional architecture of the cognitive number-processing/calculation mechanisms are supported by patterns of performance observed in brain-damaged patients (for reviews, see Caramazza & McCloskey, 1987; McCloskey & Caramazza, 1987; McCloskey et al., 1985). At the broadest level several researchers have reported dissociations between number processing and calculation (e.g., Cohn, 1961; Grewel, 1969; Hecaen et al., 1961; McCloskey et al., 1985; Warrington, 1982). Within the realm of number processing, dissociations have been found between number comprehension and production (e.g., Benson & Denckla, 1969; Singer & Low, 1933), between Arabic and verbal number processing (e.g., Berger, 1926; McCloskey & Caramazza, 1987), and between lexical and syntactic processing (e.g., Benson & Denckla, 1969; Singer & Low, 1933; McCloskey & Caramazza, 1987). Within the calculation domain, dissociations have been reported between arithmetic fact retrieval and execution of calculation procedures (e.g., McCloskey et al., 1985; Sokol & McCloskey, 1991; Warrington, 1982), and between comprehension of operation symbols and other calculation abilities (Ferro & Botelho, 1980). Examples of some of these dissociations will be evident in our discussion of case studies.

ASSESSMENT OF NUMBER-PROCESSING AND CALCULATION ABILITIES

In this section we describe the procedures used in our laboratory for assessment of acquired dyscalculia. These procedures are designed to determine for each of the processing mechanisms specified in the model whether the mechanism is intact or damaged and, in the case of damaged mechanisms, the nature and extent of the damage. Although we undertake assessment for research purposes, the procedures we follow are for the most part suitable for clinical application.

Before we describe our assessment procedures, three points need to be made. First, we do not offer a simple cookbook approach to assessment of dyscalculia. In our view adequate diagnosis of impairments cannot usually be accomplished by administering a fixed set of tasks and examining the resulting profile of scores. One must consider not only the patient's overall performance on each task, but also the types of items on which errors occurred and the nature of the errors. Further, it is often necessary to follow up administration of an initial battery of tasks with additional testing designed specifically to clarify the nature of impairments uncovered by the initial tasks.

Second, we present our assessment methods not as a set of procedures to be followed exactly, but rather as an example of how one may proceed in a theory-based assessment of dyscalculia. The particular tasks we discuss are ones we have found useful in probing the cognitive mechanisms underlying number-processing and calculation abilities. However, these tasks are not the only ones that could be used; in many instances a variety of different tasks might be chosen to probe the same underlying mechanisms.

Third, our discussion focuses on deficits resulting from disruption of the cognitive number-processing/calculation mechanisms discussed in the preceding section. However, impaired performance on number-processing and calculation tasks may also result from perceptual, motor, or other general cognitive deficits. For example, a patient with an articulation deficit is likely to perform poorly on any task requiring spoken responses; similarly, a working memory deficit may lead to impaired performance on tasks in which information must be held temporarily in memory. Thus, the possibility of perceptual, motor, or general cognitive dysfunctions must be considered in interpreting results from number-processing and calculation tasks. In many instances the nature of a patient's errors may suggest, or argue against, a deficit of this sort. For example, an articulation deficit is likely to be responsible if a patient produces unintelligible spoken responses in saying numbers aloud, but not if the patient produces clearly-articulated but incorrect number words (e.g., "two" produced in place of "six"). Specific assessment of perceptual and motor processes and of general cognitive functions such as attention and working memory can of course also provide relevant evidence.

Our assessment of a patient's number-processing and calculation abilities involves three phases. First, in a brief interview with the patient or other informant (e.g., a relative) we gather information about the patient's premorbid and post-onset number and mathematics skills. Second, we administer a dyscalculia test battery designed to probe the various number-processing and calculation mechanisms specified in the cognitive model. Because the battery is designed to probe a variety of different cognitive mechanisms (e.g., Arabic and verbal number comprehension and production mechanisms, mechanisms for arithmetic fact retrieval and execution of calculation procedures in addition, subtraction, and multiplication), a substantial number of tasks are included. As a consequence, the number of items per task is necessarily limited. Given this limitation, conclusions drawn from results on the battery are usually tentative. Hence, in the final assessment phase, we administer follow-up tasks to clarify ambiguous results from the test battery and to probe in greater detail the nature of the impairments uncovered by the battery.

Premorbid and Post-Onset Skills

In the initial interview we request information about the patient's mathematics education, as well as his or her premorbid and post-onset use of numbers on the job and at home (e.g., balancing a checkbook, completing tax returns). Information about any known premorbid or post-onset difficulties with numbers or mathematics is noted. For example, school records, if available, many aid in determining whether the patient experienced any premorbid difficulties in arithmetic. The information about premorbid abilities is important for assessing whether any of the patient's current number-processing or calculation difficulties could have resulted from developmental disabilities or lack of premorbid training. The information about post-onset status may point to areas that deserve special attention in testing. For example, if the patient reports particular difficulty in saying numbers, special attention may be directed toward assessing spoken verbal number production.

I. NUMBER PROCESSING TASKS

Magnitude Comparison

Arabic Numbers
Spoken Verbal Numbers
Written Verbal Numbers

Transcoding Numbers

Input Form		Output Form
Arabic	--->	Spoken Verbal
Spoken Verbal	--->	Written Verbal
Spoken Verbal	--->	Arabic
Arabic	--->	Written Verbal
Written Verbal	--->	Spoken Verbal
Written Verbal	--->	Arabic

II. CALCULATION TASKS

Operation Symbol and Word Comprehension

Operation Symbol Comprehension
Operation Word Comprehension

Written Arithmetic

Addition
Subtraction
Multiplication

Oral Arithmetic

Addition
Subtraction
Multiplication

Figure 14-2 Outline of the dyscalculia test battery.

The Dyscalculia Test Battery

The next step in the assessment process is the administration of the dyscalculia test battery.[4] The battery is divided into two sections, a number-processing section and a calculation section. Figure 14-2 summarizes the organization of the battery.

The battery may be administered to patients varying widely in severity of impairment. Whereas many patients will be able to perform all of the tasks (although perhaps with high error rates), some patients may be unable to give interpretable responses on one or more tasks. Thus, it may occasionally be necessary to omit some tasks. For example, in a patient with a severe auditory comprehension deficit it may be necessary to omit tasks involving aural presentation of stimuli. Even when some tasks must be omitted, however, useful information can usually be obtained from results on other tasks. Of course, as in any neuropsychological testing, some patients (e.g., Alzheimer's patients in advanced stages of the disease) may be so severely impaired that meaningful results cannot be obtained.

The amount of time required to administer the battery depends upon the nature and severity of the patient's deficits. In our experience the battery typically takes from one to three hours to complete, and we often present it over two test sessions. Both the task themselves and the items within each task are arranged with the aim of providing the patient with a mixture of easy and more difficult items.

The Number-Processing Section

The battery's number-processing section probes comprehension and production of Arabic, spoken verbal, and written verbal numbers. Two types of tasks are presented: *magnitude comparison* tasks, and *transcoding* tasks. In the magnitude comparison tasks the patient judges which of two numbers (e.g., 3,077 vs. 3,057) is larger. These tasks probe number comprehension. In the transcoding tasks the patient converts numbers from one form to another (e.g., Arabic stimulus 4,601, written verbal response *four thousand six hundred one*). These tasks probe both number comprehension and number production. Each task contains an initial practice item followed by 20 test items. Further, in each task half of the test items involve single-digit (tasks with Arabic stimuli) or single-word (tasks with verbal stimuli) numbers, and the remaining half involve multidigit/word numbers. The single-digit/word items (e.g., 6 or *six*) primarily require lexical processing, whereas the multidigit/word items (e.g., 3,080 or *three thousand eighty*) require both lexical and syntactic processing. Examples of items from each task are presented in Figure 14-3.

Magnitude Comparison Tasks

Arabic Magnitude Comparison. Two Arabic numbers are presented (e.g., 2 vs. 5; 83,497 vs. 84,398), and the patient points to the larger number. This task probes comprehension of Arabic numbers.

Spoken Verbal Magnitude Comparison. Two verbal numbers are presented in spoken form (e.g., "three" vs. "seven;" "six hundred twenty-four" vs. "six thousand twelve"), and the patient indicates which is larger. This task probes comprehension of spoken verbal numbers. How the patient should respond in this task is a somewhat vexing issue—there are no written stimuli to which the patient can point, and for several rather obvious reasons it is advisable to avoid spoken responses like "the first number" or "the second number." In the method we have devised, a piece of paper with two squares drawn one above the other is placed between the patient and the tester. While reading the first number,

DYSCALCULIA BATTERY: NUMBER-PROCESSING SECTION

	Item	Correct Response
Magnitude Comparison Tasks		
Arabic numbers	108 150	Point to '150'
Spoken verbal numbers	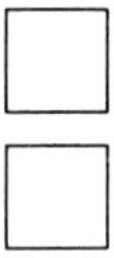 ☐ "fifty" ☐ "fifteen"	Point to square representing "fifty"
Written verbal numbers	eleven thousand eighteen three hundred eighty-five	Point to 'eleven thousand eighteen'
Transcoding Tasks		
Arabic to spoken verbal numbers	190	"one hundred ninety"
Spoken verbal to written verbal numbers	"nineteen"	nineteen
Spoken verbal to Arabic numbers	"four thousand fifty-seven"	4,057
Arabic to written verbal numbers	5	five
Written verbal to spoken verbal numbers	ninety-two	"ninety-two"
Written verbal to Arabic numbers	three thousand twenty-four	3,024

Figure 14-3 Examples of test items from the number-processing section of the dyscalculia test battery.

the tester points to the top square; while reading the second number, the tester points to the bottom square. The patient responds by pointing to the square corresponding to the larger number.

Written Verbal Magnitude Comparison. Two written verbal numbers are presented (e.g., thirteen vs. twenty; three thousand four hundred vs. eight thousand one), and the patient points to the larger number. This task probes comprehension of written verbal numbers.

Transcoding Tasks

On these tasks the patient is asked to perform the six possible conversions among Arabic, spoken verbal, and written verbal numbers. On tasks involving written

Transcoding Tasks

On these tasks the patient is asked to perform the six possible conversions among Arabic, spoken verbal, and written verbal numbers. On tasks involving written verbal responses the patient is asked to spell out the number words, whereas on tasks involving Arabic responses the patient is asked to write the numbers in digit form.

Transcoding Arabic Numbers to Spoken Verbal Numbers. Arabic numbers (e.g., 36) are presented visually, and the patient reads each number aloud (e.g., "thirty-six"). This task probes comprehension of Arabic numbers and production of spoken verbal numbers.

Transcoding Spoken Verbal Numbers to Written Verbal Numbers. Verbal numbers (e.g., "sixteen") are dictated, and the patient writes each number in verbal form (e.g., *sixteen*). This task probes comprehension of spoken verbal numbers and production of written verbal numbers.

Transcoding Spoken Verbal Numbers to Arabic Numbers. Verbal numbers are dictated (e.g., "eight thousand two hundred seventeen"), and the patient writes each number in Arabic form (e.g., 8,217). This task probes comprehension of spoken verbal numbers and production of Arabic numbers.

Transcoding Arabic Numbers to Written Verbal Numbers. Arabic numbers are presented visually (e.g., 503), and the patient writes each number in verbal form (e.g., five hundred three). This task probes comprehension of Arabic numbers and production of written verbal numbers.

Transcoding Written Verbal Numbers to Spoken Verbal Numbers. Written verbal numbers (e.g., nine thousand thirty-nine) are presented, and the patient reads each number aloud (e.g., "nine thousand thirty-nine"). This task probes comprehension of written verbal numbers and production of spoken verbal numbers.

Transcoding Written Verbal Numbers to Arabic Numbers. Written verbal numbers (e.g., one hundred forty-six) are presented, and the patient writes each number in Arabic form (e.g., 146). This task probes comprehension of written verbal numbers and production of Arabic numbers.

Interpretation of Results

Examination of the patient's pattern of performance across the magnitude comparison and transcoding tasks provides a basis for conclusions about the status (intact or impaired) of the various Arabic and verbal number comprehension and production mechanisms. Interpretation of performance requires consideration not only of overall level of performance on each task, but also the nature of the items on which errors occurred, and (in the case of transcoding tasks) the nature of the errors themselves.

Space does not permit a detailed discussion of each of the possible forms of disruption to the cognitive number-processing mechanisms. Hence, in this section we illustrate how to interpret results from the number-processing tasks by considering the performance pattern expected to result from damage to one of the number-processing mechanisms. Then, in a later section on case examples we discuss some additional types of number-processing deficits. (For further discussion of number-processing impairments, see McCloskey & Caramazza, 1987; McCloskey et al., 1985; McCloskey, Sokol, Goodman-Schulman, & Caramazza, 1990.)

Consider a hypothetical patient who presents with the following pattern of results: (a) excellent performance on all three magnitude comparison tasks; (b) impaired performance on the written-verbal-to-Arabic and spoken-verbal-to-Arabic transcoding tasks; and (c) excellent performance on the remaining transcoding tasks. The impaired transcoding tasks collectively involve comprehension of written verbal numbers, comprehension of spoken verbal numbers, and production of Arabic numbers. Thus, the results for these tasks suggest that one or more of these processes may be disrupted.

The results from other tasks can narrow down the possibilities. The patient's intact performance on magnitude comparison tasks for spoken and written verbal numbers suggests that mechanisms for comprehension of spoken and written verbal numbers are intact. This possibility is further supported by intact performance in spoken-to-written-verbal transcoding (which requires comprehension of spoken verbal numbers), and in written-to-spoken-verbal transcoding (which requires comprehension of written verbal numbers). Given the assumption of intact verbal number comprehension, the patient's impaired performance on the two verbal-to-Arabic transcoding tasks suggests an impairment in Arabic number production.

Examination of the specific performance pattern on the impaired transcoding tasks may provide further evidence bearing on this interpretation. If the impaired performance on both the spoken-verbal-to-Arabic and written-verbal-to-Arabic transcoding tasks reflects the same underlying deficit (i.e., an Arabic number production deficit), then the patient's performance pattern should be similar across tasks. That is, although the patient will inevitably show some variation in performance across the two tasks, the poor performance should nevertheless be constrained by the fact that it reflects damage to the same underlying mechanism(s). Thus, one would expect the overall level of performance, the types of items on which errors occur, and the nature of the errors to be roughly the same for the two tasks.

The patient's performance pattern on the tasks showing impairment can also offer insights into the nature of the impairment. Suppose the following pattern was observed on both tasks: (a) excellent performance for stimuli requiring single-digit responses, and (b) impaired performance for stimuli requiring multidigit responses, with errors in which the individual nonzero digits are correct, but the response is of the wrong order of magnitude. An error pattern of this sort is illustrated in Table 14-1 with written-verbal-to-Arabic transcoding results from our patient ES (who also had other number-processing and calculation deficits.) This type of error pattern suggests that the Arabic number production deficit primarily involves syntactic processing. The patient's consistent produc-

Table 14-1 Examples of ES's Performance in Transcoding Written Verbal Numbers to Arabic Numbers

Stimulus	Response
seven	7
four	4
three	3
eight	8
six	6
two hundred thirty-seven	2037
seven thousand forty	7,4
forty thousand seven	40.7
four hundred thirty-seven thousand	40370
sixty-seven thousand	67,
seven hundred eighty	7008

tion of correct nonzero digits implies that lexical processing mechanisms for Arabic number production are intact; that is, the patient can retrieve the appropriate digit representations. However, syntactic processing in Arabic number production is disrupted: the patient is impaired in assembling the digits into the appropriate representation of the number as a whole.

Suppose that instead of the specific error pattern described above, the patient made errors for both single- and multidigit responses, and further that the erroneous responses were consistently of the correct order of magnitude but included incorrect digits substituted for one or more of the correct digits (e.g., stimulus *two hundred twenty-one*, response 215). This pattern of results would suggest disruption of lexical processing in Arabic number production. That is, the errors appear to result from a deficit in retrieving the appropriate digit representations for production of the written response. In the above example, the patient apparently retrieved a graphemic representation of the digit 1 in place of a representation of the correct digit 2, and a 5 in place of a 1. (This example is from Benson & Denckla, 1969, who describe a patient with lexical processing impairments in Arabic and verbal number production.)

The Calculation Section

The second section of the dyscalculia test battery probes calculation mechanisms. This section includes *operation symbol and word comprehension* tasks, *written arithmetic* tasks, and *oral arithmetic* tasks. Each task includes an initial practice item followed by test items that vary in number across tasks. Examples of items from each task are provided in Figure 14-4.

Operation Symbol and Word Comprehension Tasks

Operation Symbol Comprehension. This task comprises nine items probing comprehension of the operation symbols +, −, and ×. For each item an operation name (e.g., addition) is presented visually and aurally. Three single-digit arithmetic problems with identical operands but different operation symbols are then presented visually (e.g., 9 × 4, 9 − 4, 9 + 4), and the patient's task is to point

DYSCALCULIA BATTERY: CALCULATION SECTION

Operation Symbol and Word Comprehension Tasks	Item	Correct Response
Operation symbol comprehension	subtraction 6 + 2 6 x 2 6 - 2	Point to '6 - 2'
Operation word comprehension	addition "nine times six"	"No"

Written Arithmetic Tasks	Item	Correct Response
Addition	752 + 978	1 1 752 + 978 1730
Subtraction	86 - 37	7 ~~8~~6 - 37 49
Multiplication	30 x 84	30 x 84 120 2400 2520

Oral Arithmetic Tasks		
Addition	"five plus eight"	"thirteen"
Subtraction	"seventeen minus nine"	"eight"
Multiplication	"six times three"	"eighteen"

Figure 14-4 Examples of test items from the calculation section of the dyscalculia test battery.

to the problem corresponding to the specified operation (in the above example, 9 + 4). The operation name is presented in both spoken and written form to minimize the possibility that observed errors reflect failure to comprehend the operation name instead of failure to comprehend the operation symbols.

Operation Word Comprehension. This task consists of 12 items probing comprehension of the spoken operation words "plus," "minus," and "times." For each item an operation name (e.g., multiplication) is presented visually and aurally. A single-digit arithmetic problem (e.g., "six minus three") is then dictated and the patient indicates whether or not the problem corresponds to the specified operation name. This task uses a yes/no procedure rather than the multiple-choice method used in the symbol comprehension task in order to avoid errors that might result from difficulties in retaining three dictated problems in memory. Further, 12 instead of nine items are presented because the likelihood of being correct by chance is higher with the yes/no procedure, and hence more items are needed to ensure that a mild deficit will be detected.[5]

Written Arithmetic Tasks

These tasks probe retrieval of arithmetic facts and execution of calculation procedures. Problems are presented in Arabic form, and the patient writes responses in Arabic form. All problems are presented in the standard manner with their operands arranged vertically (see Figure 14-4). Addition, subtraction, and multiplication are tested in separate tasks. In each task, 20 problems are presented. Half are simple problems that can be solved by retrieval of a basic arithmetic fact (e.g., $6 + 8 = 14$, $14 - 5 = 9$, $7 \times 9 = 63$); the remaining half are complex problems that require execution of calculation procedures as well as arithmetic fact retrieval. The complex problems vary in their procedural complexity (e.g., whether or not they require carrying or borrowing).

Written Addition. This task probes retrieval of addition facts (e.g., $7 + 4 = 11$), and execution of the addition procedure.

Written Subtraction. This task probes retrieval of subtraction facts (e.g., $8 - 3 = 5$), and execution of the subtraction procedure.

Written Multiplication. This task probes retrieval of multiplication facts (e.g., $7 \times 7 = 49$), and execution of the multiplication procedure.

Oral Arithmetic Tasks

These tasks probe retrieval of arithmetic facts. Problems are presented aurally (e.g., "eight plus three"), and the patient says the answer aloud. Addition, subtraction, and multiplication are tested separately, with 10 problems presented in each task. All items are simple problems that can be solved by retrieval of the appropriate arithmetic fact.

Oral Addition. This task probes retrieval of addition facts (e.g., $5 + 8 = 13$).

Oral Subtraction. This task probes retrieval of subtraction facts (e.g., $9 - 7 = 2$).

Oral Multiplication. This task probes retrieval of multiplication facts (e.g., $9 \times 4 = 36$).

Interpretation of Results

Operation Symbol and Word Comprehension Tasks. For the most part, interpretation of performance on these tasks is straightforward. However, if impaired performance is observed, the possibility must be considered that the errors reflect impaired comprehension of the operation names (e.g., addition) and not the operation symbols or words (e.g., +, plus). This possibility may be discounted if impairment is evident on only one of the two tasks (because both tasks require comprehension of the operation names).

Arithmetic Tasks. Both the written and oral arithmetic tasks require number comprehension and production processes as well as calculation-specific processes. The written arithmetic tasks require comprehension and production of Arabic numbers, and the oral arithmetic tasks involve comprehension and production of spoken verbal numbers. (The required processing is largely lexical in all cases.) Thus, results from the number-processing tasks that probe Arabic and spoken verbal number processing must be taken into account in interpreting the arithmetic results. (Conversely, results from the arithmetic tasks may shed additional light on the status of these number-processing mechanisms.)

It should be noted that lexical processing deficits in Arabic or spoken verbal number processing do not usually render results from the arithmetic tasks uninterpretable. First, some types of arithmetic errors (e.g., the procedural errors discussed below) are not readily interpretable as resulting from number-processing deficits; these errors are diagnostic of impairments to calculation mechanisms even in the presence of impaired number processing. Second, interpretation of performance on some arithmetic tasks may be unaffected by a number-processing deficit. For example, if processing of spoken verbal numbers is impaired but Arabic number processing is intact, then interpretation of the oral arithmetic results will be complicated by the number-processing impairment, but interpretation of the written arithmetic results will not.

Deficits in operation symbol or word comprehension must also be considered in interpreting arithmetic task results, but these deficits are rather unlikely to affect performance. The arithmetic problems are blocked by operation (i.e., addition, subtraction, and multiplication are each tested separately), and the tester informs the patient of the operation to be performed for each block. Thus, processing the operation symbol or word for each problem is not required, and therefore an operation symbol or word comprehension deficit should not usually lead to errors on the arithmetic tasks. It is also worth noting that only errors of a particular type (i.e., errors in which the answer is correct for another operation, such as $8 \times 5 = 13$) are even potentially attributable to an operation symbol or word comprehension deficit.

Having noted these potential complications, let us now consider how to infer the status of calculation mechanisms from the arithmetic task results. As in the discussion of the number-processing tasks, we will not consider all possible forms of impairment. Rather, we develop a single example in this section, and then present another form of calculation impairment in the section on case examples. (For further discussion of calculation deficits, see Caramazza & McCloskey, 1987; McCloskey et al., 1985; Warrington, 1982).

As in the case of the number-processing results, interpretation of calculation results requires examination of performance across tasks, and of the specific pattern of performance within each task (i.e., the types of problems on which errors occur, and the types of errors that occur). Consider, for example, the following set of findings: (1) excellent performance on Arabic and spoken verbal number-processing tasks; (2) excellent performance on simple written and oral arithmetic problems; and (3) impaired performance on complex written arithmetic problems. (Recall that the complex problems are not presented in the oral arithmetic tasks.)

Complex arithmetic problems require Arabic number comprehension and production, retrieval of arithmetic facts, and execution of calculation procedures. Hence, impaired performance on these problems could potentially result from disruption to any one or more of these processes. However, the patient's excellent performance on Arabic number-processing tasks and on the simple written arithmetic problems argues against an impairment in Arabic number comprehension or production. Further, excellent performance on simple written and oral arithmetic problems (e.g., 6×7) suggests that arithmetic fact retrieval is intact. Taken together, these findings point to a procedural impairment affecting addition, subtraction, and multiplication.

Further evidence bearing on this interpretation may be obtained by examining the nature of the errors on the complex problems. Specifically, the errors should be interpretable in terms of disruption of calculation procedures, and not in terms of impaired fact retrieval. Procedural impairments may take many forms, as illustrated by the performance of four patients shown in Figure 14-5. (For further discussion of these and other procedural deficits, see McCloskey et al., 1985.) For the multiplication problem in Figure 14-5A, the patient failed to shift the second row of partial products one column to the left. (Note, however, that the patient retrieved the correct multiplication facts.)[6] Figure 14-5B depicts a procedural impairment in which the patient fails to separate retrieved products into ones and tens digits, so that the tens digit, can be carried. Rather, entire retrieved products (i.e., 10, 20, 5) are simply written down. Figure 14-5C illustrates a similar impairment in addition. Finally, as Figure 14-5D illustrates, the calculation procedures may be drastically disrupted. In this example, the patient is grossly impaired in organizing the steps of the multiplication procedure, and in arranging the retrieved products.

Deficits in arithmetic fact retrieval should yield somewhat different patterns of results. In the section on case examples we consider a deficit of this sort studied extensively in our laboratory.

Follow-Up Testing

In discussing interpretation of test battery results, we considered examples involving isolated deficits, for purposes of making the interpretive logic clear. Often, however, patients present with multiple deficits, leading to impaired performance on many different tasks, and thereby complicating interpretation of results on the battery. Further, as we have already noted, the number of items on each of the battery tasks is limited, so that results may be equivocal

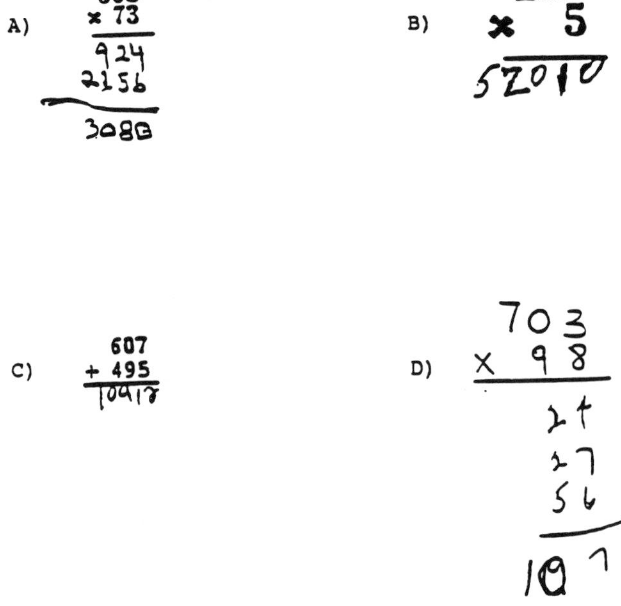

Figure 14-5 Examples of errors in execution of calculation procedures.

with respect to whether the patient shows impairment, the nature of the impairment, and so forth. Thus, conclusions drawn from battery results are usually tentative. In order to draw more definitive conclusions, we often find it necessary to follow up the battery with further testing. The follow-up work typically involves additional testing with one or more tasks from the battery, using stimulus lists developed specifically to probe for certain types of impairments. In some instances we may employ tasks not included on the battery to obtain further evidence bearing on the nature of the patient's deficits. The case examples discussed in the next section illustrate the role of follow-up testing in our assessment of number-processing and calculation deficits.

CASE EXAMPLES

In this section we exemplify the assessment procedures outlined above by discussing three patients tested in our laboratory. For each patient we also comment upon implications of our diagnosis for the development of strategies for therapy.

Patient PS: Impaired Arithmetic Fact Retrieval

PS is a right-handed woman who suffered a left-hemisphere cerebrovascular accident (CVA) in 1985 at the age of 38. Arteriograms revealed an intracranial bleed resulting from either an arterial venous malformation (AVM) or small aneurysm. As a consequence of her CVA, PS retains right-sided weakness and rather severe verbal dysfluency. PS has a B.S. in finance and, prior to her CVA, worked as a financial planner and seller of securities. She was tested for an eight-month period from January through August 1987. In the initial interview she indicated that she had a particular aptitude for mathematics and enjoyed playing "mental math games." It seems likely, then, that her premorbid calculation abilities were at least within the normal range.

PS was tested with an earlier version of the dyscalculia test battery described in the preceding section.[7] On the number-processing section, PS performed quite well overall (although responses on tasks requiring spoken verbal number production were slow and halting due to her verbal dysfluency, and she made a few syntactic errors in processing large numbers on transcoding tasks).

On the calculation section of the battery PS's performance suggested an impairment in retrieval of multiplication facts. She made no errors on the operation symbol and word comprehension tasks, and also performed well on written and oral addition and subtraction problems. On the multiplication tasks, however, she had more difficulty. In written multiplication she responded incorrectly to only one of 12 problems (writing 48 for 6 × 7), but on three of the problems she was able to arrive at the correct answer only by calculating products through successive addition. For example, she solved the problem 8 × 5 by adding five 8's. On complex written problems PS executed the multidigit multiplication procedure flawlessly, although her fact retrieval impairment was apparent. For example, in solving the problem 78 × 26, she computed 6 × 8 and 6 × 7 by successive addition. In oral multiplication PS erred on one of the four problems, and resorted to successive addition for two of the remaining three.

Thus, the most notable aspect of PS's performance on the dyscalculia test battery was her apparent difficulty in retrieval of multiplication facts. In follow-up testing we sought additional evidence bearing on this tentative diagnosis (see Sokol & McCloskey, 1991, for a more detailed discussion). Although our testing was far more extensive than would be necessary for purposes of clinical assessment, the general approach would be appropriate for a clinician evaluating a patient similar to PS.

The follow-up testing had three specific goals. The first was to collect additional data concerning PS's number-processing abilities, to ensure that her difficulties with multiplication did not result from lexical processing deficits in number comprehension or production. In pursuit of this goal, we administered several transcoding tasks involving stimuli in the range 0 through 99. PS's performance was excellent on all of the tasks, confirming the original conclusion that the number comprehension and production skills required for solving multiplication problems were intact.

The second goal of the follow-up testing was to probe further the nature and extent of the apparent fact retrieval impairment. Toward this end we presented PS with the 100 single-digit multiplication problems (i.e., 0 × 0 through 9 × 9) in each of 23 blocks of trials. The results supported the initial diagnosis that PS was impaired in multiplication fact retrieval: PS erred on 20% of the problems. Most of her errors were either *omissions*, in which she failed to give a response (we did not allow her to solve problems by successive addition in the follow-up testing), or *operand* errors, in which her incorrect answer was correct for a problem sharing an operand with the presented problem (e.g., 9 × 5 = 54, in which the erroneous answer is correct for 9 × 6).[8]

Table 14-2 presents PS's error rate on each of the individual problems. The rows in the table represent the first operand in the problem, and the columns represent the second operand. For example, the entry in row 4 column 9 indicates that PS's error rate was 74% for the problem 4 × 9. It is apparent from the table that PS's

Table 14-2 Percentage of Errors for PS on Individual Multiplication Problems

First Operand	Second Operand 0	1	2	3	4	5	6	7	8	9
0	0	43	43	48	39	39	48	39	39	35
1	39	13	0	4	0	0	0	4	0	0
2	39	0	0	0	0	0	9	4	0	4
3	39	0	0	30	4	0	4	0	13	9
4	39	0	0	4	52	4	9	4	17	74
5	43	4	0	0	0	4	9	17	26	30
6	48	0	0	4	4	26	0	30	13	9
7	39	4	0	0	13	9	52	78	52	83
8	39	0	0	9	17	22	9	26	61	0
9	43	0	0	17	83	22	26	91	0	100

fact retrieval impairment was not uniform over the set of multiplication facts. Rather, her error rate was very high for some facts (e.g., 7 × 7, 7 × 9) and very low for others (e.g., 7 × 5, 8 × 9). This nonuniformity of impairment, which we have found to be characteristic of patients with arithmetic fact retrieval deficits, is significant for the clinician considering remediation of a fact retrieval impairment. Given that fact retrieval impairments often affect only a subset of the facts for an operation, retraining all table facts will typically not be necessary. If assessment has been sufficiently thorough to identify the impaired and spared facts, remediation can be targeted at just those facts that show impairment. Of course, the clinician may also want to include a few problems on which the patient has no difficulty in order to minimize frustration or fatigue.

Our final goal in follow-up testing of PS was to evaluate the tentative conclusion that her multiplication deficit was limited to fact retrieval, and did not involve execution of the multiplication procedure. Hence, we presented PS with a large number of multidigit multiplication problems. Although she erred on nearly half of these problems, virtually all of the errors were straightforwardly interpretable as resulting from her fact retrieval impairment. Figure 14-6 presents an example of a multidigit problem in which PS made two operand errors in fact retrieval (i.e., 4 × 9 = 32, and 9 × 9 = 72).

In contrast to the fact retrieval errors, PS made virtually no errors in execution of the multiplication procedure. She consistently carried out the appropriate single-digit multiplications (although not always successfully) in the correct order. Further, she dealt appropriately with the retrieved products (e.g., writing the ones digit and carrying the tens digit), and added partial products in the correct manner. Thus, the results for the multi-digit problems provided additional evidence of a fact retrieval

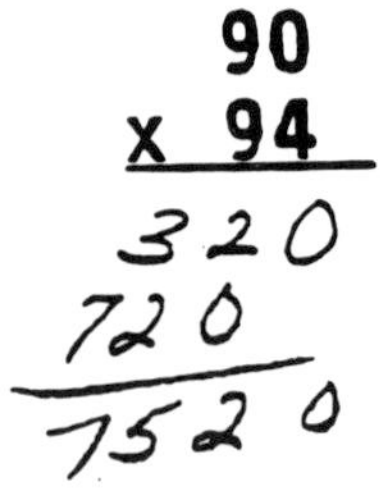

90
x 94
320
720
7520

Figure 14-6 An example of PS's multidigit multiplication performance, illustrating impaired fact retrieval and intact execution of calculation procedures.

impairment, and also confirmed the original conclusion that PS was intact in execution of the multiplication procedure.

Implications for Therapy. Vague and general classifications such as "anarithmetia" provide little specific guidance for the clinician attempting to arrive at an appropriate strategy for therapy. In contrast, a detailed diagnosis formulated within an explicit theoretical framework clearly delineates the impaired processes toward which attempts at remediation should be targeted, and also identifies intact processes that need not be addressed in therapy. For example, the diagnosis we have arrived at for patient PS (i.e., impaired arithmetic fact retrieval, with the deficit principally affecting certain multiplication facts) suggests that remediation efforts should be focussed on the impaired facts, and need not address comprehension or production of Arabic numbers, or the procedures for carrying out multidigit calculations. Thus, as mentioned above, a clinician encountering a patient like PS might consider retraining the specific facts that show impairment. (In our limited attempts at this sort of remediation we have found that some patients can relearn the facts, and retain them indefinitely.) Alternatively, the patient could be advised to use a calculator whenever he or she needs to solve problems involving impaired operations. Given that the patient shows intact comprehension and production of Arabic numbers, he or she should have little difficulty entering numbers into a calculator, reading off the answers, or writing them down.

Patient HY: Impairments in Spoken Verbal Number Production

For PS the follow-up evaluation primarily involved additional testing with tasks included on the battery. For the second patient we discuss, however, the follow-up testing involved not only tasks from the battery, but also some additional tasks devised specifically to evaluate hypotheses developed on the basis of results from the battery.

HY is a right-handed man who suffered a left-hemisphere CVA in December 1981, at the age of 66. CT scans revealed an intracerebral hemorrhage of the left temporal and parietal lobes, obliteration of the left lateral ventricle, and intraventricular bleeding with minimal midline shift to the right. HY was tested for a six-month period from April through September 1984. At this time his speech was fluent, although he had some word-finding difficulties that were apparent in conversation and in formal testing. Tests of general language skills also revealed difficulties in reading and writing, but relatively intact auditory comprehension skills. HY and members of his family report that his reading, writing, and number-processing skills were excellent prior to his stroke.

HY's performance on the dyscalculia test battery suggested several mild to moderate deficits in number processing and calculation. In this discussion we focus on one of the number-processing deficits, which was revealed by HY's poor performance on the Arabic-to-spoken-verbal transcoding task. His errors on this task were mainly lexical substitutions, in which an incorrect word was produced in place of the correct word (e.g., 5 read as "seven"; and 26,370 read as "twenty-*eight* thousand three hundred and seventy").

The errors HY made on the Arabic-to-spoken-verbal transcoding task could result from lexical processing deficits in Arabic number comprehension, verbal number production, or both. However, other results from the dyscalculia test battery suggested that HY's comprehension of Arabic digits was intact. In particular, he performed without error on the Arabic magnitude comparison task. Hence, it was

Table 14-3 Examples of HY's Lexical Substitution Errors in Arabic-to-Spoken Verbal Transcoding

Stimulus	Response
5	*seven*
1	*five*
17	*thirteen*
29	*forty*-nine
317	three hundred *fourteen*
902	nine hundred *six*
5,450	five thousand four hundred *seventy*
14,840	*sixteen* thousand eight hundred forty
30,260	thirty thousand two hundred *fifty*

tentatively concluded that his transcoding errors reflected a verbal number production deficit. In particular, our hypothesis was that HY generated correct semantic representations from the Arabic stimulus numbers, but that a deficit in retrieval of phonological number word representations from the phonological output lexicon led to the occasional retrieval of incorrect number-word representations (e.g., /eight/ instead of /six/ in the case of 26,370 read as "twenty-*eight* thousand . . ."). Three sets of follow-up tasks were presented to evaluate this hypothesis. (See McCloskey et al., 1986, for more details about this study.)

First, HY was tested with additional Arabic-to-spoken-verbal transcoding tasks. His performance confirmed the initial results from the battery; that is, HY produced errors that were predominantly lexical substitutions (although his error rate was somewhat lower than on the battery). Examples of his errors are presented in Table 14-3.

Second, HY was presented with several tasks that required comprehension of Arabic digits, to test the hypothesis that his digit comprehension was intact. In one task individual digits were presented, and HY selected the corresponding number of plastic chips from a pile (e.g., given 9, select nine chips from the pile). A second task involved matching of Arabic and written verbal numbers (e.g., from the set 19, 4, 14, 16 choose the number that matches *fourteen*; or from the set *fifteen*, *four*, *thirty*, *forty*, select the number that matches 40). Third, HY was shown simple addition or subtraction problems in Arabic form with correct or incorrect answers (e.g., 4 + 9 = 13, 14 − 6 = 7) and was asked to indicate for each problem whether the presented answer was correct or not. HY's performance on all of these tasks was excellent, supporting the initial conclusion that his comprehension of Arabic digits was intact.

The third set of tasks presented in follow-up testing constituted additional tests of HY's spoken verbal number production. In one task simple addition problems were presented, and HY was asked either to say the answer aloud, or write the answer in Arabic form. He made more errors for spoken than for written responses. Given the assumption that the spoken and written response tasks involve the same cognitive mechanisms except in the response production stage, the higher error rate for spoken responses points to a specific problem in spoken verbal number production. A second task involved transcoding written verbal numbers to spoken verbal numbers or to Arabic numbers (e.g., stimulus *fifteen*, response "fifteen" or 15). As in the addition task HY made more errors for spoken than for written responses, again suggesting a deficit in spoken verbal number production. Finally, HY was asked to give spoken or written (Arabic) responses to general knowledge questions with numerical answers (e.g., "How many eggs are in a dozen?"). Once again, he made more errors for spoken responses. In all of the tasks, HY's errors were interpretable as lexical substitutions. For example, in response to the question "How many days are in a year?" HY wrote 365 but said "three hundred *forty-two*."

Taken together, the results of the follow-up testing provide strong support for the conclusion that HY suffers from a lexical processing deficit in spoken production of verbal numbers. Specifically, in retrieving phonological representations of to-be-spoken number words, he occasionally retrieves the wrong representation, resulting in lexical substitution errors.

Implications for Therapy. Given this specific diagnosis, attempts at remediation or compensation could be targeted at the identified impairment. In particular, HY might be given practice on various tasks involving spoken production of number words, in hope that his retrieval of phonological number-word representations would thereby be improved. Further, HY might be advised that whenever he says number words aloud, he may produce number words other than those he intends to say. Thus, he might be encouraged to express numeric information (e.g., his telephone number, his address, the time of day) in Arabic rather than spoken verbal form whenever possible. If it is necessary for HY to convey numeric information in spoken form (e.g., over the telephone), he should monitor his output carefully, and perhaps also have the information repeated back to him. (Because his comprehension of spoken verbal numbers is, at most, only slightly impaired, he should be able to recognize whether the number he said is in fact the number he intended to say.)

Patient RH: Multiple Impairments

The last patient we discuss, RH, presented with several severe deficits in number processing. For this patient the challenge was to determine whether any of the cognitive number-processing mechanisms were intact. (RH also exhibited calculation impairments which will not be considered here.)

RH is a left-handed man who underwent a left parietal/temporal craniotomy resulting in subtotal resection of a low grade astrocytoma in October 1980, at the age of 35. Postoperative examination revealed significant right hemiparesis with expressive and receptive aphasia. In January 1988, RH was reexamined after complaining of increasing right-sided weakness and cognitive dysfunction. A CT scan revealed recurrence of the astrocytoma. Because of the size of the tumor, surgery and radiation therapy were ruled out in favor of chemotherapy. At this time RH was found to be alert and oriented to person, place, and time, but suffered from expressive aphasia with mild short-term memory and concentration difficulties.

Prior to the onset of his illness, RH, a college graduate, worked as a chemical officer in the United States Army. He reported that before his illness he experienced no difficulty with numbers. In our laboratory RH was tested from October 1987 through February 1989. Formal assessment of language skills revealed severe dysgraphia in addition to difficulties in oral expression, auditory comprehension, and reading.

On the dyscalculia test battery RH performed poorly on most of the number-processing tasks. He responded incorrectly to at least 50% of the items in each of the transcoding tasks, providing errors for most of the stimulus numbers larger than one hundred. For example, in the spoken-verbal-to-Arabic transcoding task, RH wrote 64,400 in response to the stimulus "six thousand thirty." Overall, results on the transcoding tasks suggested severe syntactic processing deficits as well as some lexical processing impairments. However, given that RH showed poor performance on all transcoding tasks, it was difficult to localize the impairments to particular number comprehension or production mechanisms.

Although results on the transcoding tasks seemed to suggest that all of RH's number comprehension and production mechanisms might be disrupted, a more careful examination of these results—as well as of the results from the magnitude comparison tasks—suggested that one or more of the number-processing mechanisms might be spared. On the written-verbal-to-Arabic transcoding task, RH responded correctly to the stimulus numbers below one hundred (e.g., *fourteen*, response 14). Further, his errors for larger numbers were either failures to respond, or syntactic errors. These results suggest that RH's lexical processing in comprehension of written verbal numbers and in production of Arabic numbers may be largely intact. Consistent with the hypothesis of largely intact comprehension of individual written number words, RH performed well on the written verbal magnitude comparison task. He did not err on any of the single-word comparisons, but did make a few errors on comparisons involving large-number stimuli (for which syntactic processing is required). Finally, RH made no errors on the Arabic magnitude comparison task, suggesting intact comprehension of Arabic numbers.

We decided to focus our follow-up investigation on RH's lexical processing abilities. As with PS and HY, our testing was more extensive than would be necessary for purposes of clinical assessment (and also more selective, in that we did not pursue his syntactic deficits). In the follow-up phase we tested RH on 12 transcoding tasks using stimuli in the range 0 through 99. The 12 tasks comprised all possible conversions among spoken verbal numbers, written verbal numbers, Arabic numbers and numbers in the form of dots. For dots stimuli and responses, numbers were represented by two columns of dots, a TENS column and a ONES column. The tester presented a dots stimulus number by pulling strips of paper from TENS and ONES envelopes to reveal the appropriate number of dots. For example, the stimulus number 58 was indicated by pulling out five dots from the TENS envelope and eight dots from the ONES envelope. Similarly, for dots responses, RH pulled out the paper strips to reveal the desired number of dots.

Results from the follow-up transcoding tasks were quite informative. First, RH performed quite well in transcoding written verbal numbers to dots or Arabic numbers. These results support the hypothesis that RH is largely intact in comprehension of individual written number words. The data also provided evidence of intact lexical processing in Arabic number production: in addition to his good performance in written-verbal-to-Arabic transcoding, RH performed well in transcoding dots to Arabic numbers. Finally, RH's excellent performance in transcoding Arabic numbers to dots suggested intact lexical processing in Arabic number comprehension.

The follow-up testing also clarified RH's lexical processing deficits. He showed moderately impaired performance on all transcoding tasks involving production of spoken verbal numbers, including those tasks in which comprehension of the stimuli had been shown to be largely intact. His errors took the form of lexical substitutions (e.g., stimulus 27, response "twenty-*eight*"), suggesting that RH, like HY, was impaired in retrieving phonological number word representations from the phonological output lexicon. RH also performed poorly on all transcoding tasks involving comprehension of spoken verbal numbers, including those tasks in which production of the responses had been shown to be largely intact, suggesting a lexical processing deficit in comprehension of spoken verbal numbers. Finally, RH had extreme difficulty on all transcoding tasks requiring production of written verbal numbers, regardless of the stimulus form. As in the spoken verbal production tasks, his errors in written production were lexical substitutions (e.g., stimulus 50, response *five*), suggesting a severe impairment in retrieval of graphemic number word representations from the graphemic output lexicon.

Implications for Therapy. In helping someone cope with multiple impairments in number-processing skills, a clinician may want to share with the patient information about the forms of numbers he or she should encounter the least difficulty in processing. For example, a patient similar to RH could be advised to ask others to relate numeric information in Arabic (or written verbal) form rather than in spoken verbal form. Likewise, the patient could be instructed to provide numeric information in Arabic rather than in spoken or written verbal form. The patient could be warned about the difficulty he or she may experience communicating numbers over the telephone, and about the mistakes he or she might make in writing number words (e.g., on a check). That is, the patient's productions may contain correctly spelled or articulated number words that are not the words he or she is trying to convey (e.g., the patient might write *seven* for *seventy*). Finally, attempts at remediation might be undertaken for those number-processing abilities most important to everyday functioning (e.g., spoken verbal number comprehension and production), although it is unclear how successful such attempts would be.

Concluding Remarks

Although dyscalculia has been recognized as a possible consequence of brain damage at least since the beginning of this century (e.g., Lewandowsky & Stadelmann, 1908; Henschen, 1925), techniques for assessment of dyscalculia have remained underdeveloped. The method we have outlined in this chapter is based upon an explicit model of the cognitive number-processing/calculation system, and aims at assessing the status of the various processing mechanisms specified in the model. The method involves the administration of a dyscalculia test battery to arrive at a tentative diagnosis, and then follow-up testing to confirm and elaborate the initial assessment. Although this procedure requires a substantial investment of time and effort, the payoff is a specific, theoretically-grounded diagnosis that provides a basis for development of remediation and compensation strategies targeted directly at the impaired processes. Thus, the time and effort put forth in assessment may be recouped many times over in increased efficiency (and, one would hope, effectiveness) of therapy.

ACKNOWLEDGMENTS

The research discussed in this chapter was supported by NIH grant NS21047. Paul Macaruso was supported by NRSA traineeship grant MH18215. We thank Donna Aliminosa for her assistance in testing patients and for her helpful comments. Patient RH died shortly after completion of the testing described above; we wish to express our special gratitude for his willingness to participate in this research.

NOTES

1. We use the term *verbal numbers* to refer to numbers in the form of words, whether they are in spoken or in written form. *Spoken verbal numbers* and *written verbal numbers* refer to verbal numbers that are in spoken and in written form, respectively.

2. In referring to verbal number comprehension and production components we do not intend to imply that the mechanisms for processing numbers in word form are necessarily separate from the mechanisms for processing language in general; this remains an open question. Thus, the lexical processing mechanisms responsible for retrieval of phonological number-word representations from a phonological output lexicon may well be the same mechanisms that retrieve phonological representations of other words. The approach we adopt is to characterize cognitive mechanisms in terms of the role these mechanisms play in number processing and calculation, leaving open the question of whether some of the mechanisms are also involved in other cognitive processing.

3. For convenience, we use words enclosed in slashes (e.g., /eighty/) to indicate phonological representations.

4. Copies of the test battery are available from Michael McCloskey, Department of Cognitive Science, The Johns Hopkins University, Baltimore, MD 21218.

5. We test comprehension of spoken operation words because arithmetic problems presented in spoken verbal form (e.g., "eight times five") are included on the test battery, and are occasionally encountered in everyday life. Given, however, that arithmetic problems in written verbal form (e.g., *eight times five*) are not included on the test battery, and are rarely encountered in everyday life, we do not test comprehension of written operation words.

6. In the Hecaen et al. (1961) classification scheme this impairment would probably be classified as a spatial dyscalculia, because the alignment of digits is incorrect. Note, however, that the impairment probably does not stem from a general spatial processing deficit that renders the patient unable to align digits. The columns of digits are perfectly aligned; the alignment is simply inappropriate.

7. The earlier version of the battery, which was used to test all three of the patients we discuss in this section on case examples, had fewer items than the current version, and also differed in some other minor respects.

8. We have found omission and operand errors to be common among patients with arithmetic fact retrieval deficits. Other types of errors that may also be observed include *operation* errors, in which the response is correct for a different arithmetic operation, as in $8 \times 7 = 15$; and *nontable* errors, in which the response is a number that is not among the answers in the table for the operation being tested, as in $8 \times 4 = 38$.

REFERENCES

Benson, D. F. & Denckla, M. B. (1969). Verbal paraphasia as a source of calculation disturbance. *Archives of Neurology*, *21*, 96–102.

Benton, A. L. (1963). *Assessment of number operations*. Iowa City: University of Iowa Hospitals, Department of Neurology.

Berger, H. (1926). Ueber Rechenstorungen bei Herderkrankungen des Grosshirns. *Archiv fur Psychiatrie und Nervenkrankheiten*, *78*, 238–263.

Caramazza, A., & McCloskey, M. (1987). Dissociations of calculation process. In G. Deloche & X. Seron (Eds.), *Mathematical disabilities: A cognitive neuropsychological perspective.* Hillsdale, NJ: Lawrence Erlbaum.

Cohn, R. (1961). Dyscalculia. *Archives of Neurology, 4,* 301–307.

Dunn, L. M., & Markwardt, F. C. (1970). *Manual for the Peabody Individual Achievement Test.* Circle Pines, MN: American Guidance Service.

Ferro, J. M., & Botelho, M. A. S. (1980). Alexia for arithmetic signs. A cause of disturbed calculation. *Cortex, 16,* 175–180.

Grewel, F. (1952). Acalculia. *Brain, 75,* 397–407.

Grewel, F. (1969). The acalculias. In P. J. Vinken & G. Bruyn (Eds.), *Handbook of clinical neurology.* Amsterdam, North Holland.

Hecaen, H., Angelergues, R., & Houillier, S. (1961). Les varietes cliniques des acalculies au cours des lesions retrolandiques: Approche statistique du probleme. *Revue Neurologique, 105,* 85–103.

Henschen, S. E. (1925). Clinical and anatomical contributions on brain pathology. *Archives of Neurology and Psychiatry,* W. F. Schaller (trans.), *13,* 226–249 (Originally published in 1919).

Jastak, J. F., & Jastak, S. R. (1965). *Manual for the Wide Range Achievement Test.* Wilmington, DE: Guidance Associates of Delaware.

Levin, H. S. (1979). The acalculias. In K. M. Heilman & E. Valenstein (Eds.), *Clinical neuropsychology.* New York: Oxford.

Levin, H. S., & Spiers, P. A. (1985). Acalculia. In K. M. Heilman & E. Valenstein (Eds.), *Clinical neuropsychology.* New York: Oxford.

Lewandowsky, M., & Stadelmann, E. (1908). Ueber einen bemerkenswerten Fall von Hirnblutung und uber Rechenstorungen bei Herderkrankung des Gehirns. *Zeit. fur Neurol. Psychiat., 2,* 249–265.

Lezak, M. D. (1983). *Neuropsychological assessment.* New York: Oxford.

Luria, A. R. (1966). *Higher cortical functions in man* (B. Haigh, trans.). New York: Basic Books.

McCloskey, M., & Caramazza, A. (1987). Cognitive mechanisms in normal and impaired number processing. In G. Deloche & X. Seron (Eds.), *Mathematical disabilities: A cognitive neuropsychological perspective.* Hillsdale, NJ: Lawrence Erlbaum.

McCloskey, M., Caramazza, A., & Basili, A. G. (1985). Cognitive mechanisms in number processing and calculation: Evidence from dyscalculia. *Brain and Cognition, 4,* 171–196.

McCloskey, M., Sokol, S. M., & Goodman, R. A. (1986). Cognitive processes in verbal-number production: Inferences from the performance of brain-damaged subjects. *Journal of Experimental Psychology: General, 115,* 307–330.

McCloskey, M., Sokol, S. M., Goodman-Schulman, R. A., & Caramazza, A. (1990). Cognitive representations and processes in number production: Evidence from cases of acquired dyscalculia. In A. Caramazza (Ed.), *Advances in cognitive neuropsychology and neurolinguistics.* Hillsdale, NJ: Lawrence Erlbaum.

Singer, H. D., & Low, A. A. (1933). Acalculia (Henschen): A clinical study. *Archives of Neurology and Psychiatry, 29,* 476–498.

Sokol, S. M., & McCloskey, M. (1991). Cognitive mechanisms in calculation. In R. Sternberg & P. A. Frensch (Eds.), *Complex problem solving: Principles and mechanisms.* Hillsdale, NJ: Lawrence Erlbaum.

Warrington, E. K. (1982). The fractionation of arithmetical skills: a single case study. *Quarterly Journal of Experimental Psychology*, *34*, 31–51.

Wechsler, D. (1955). *Wechsler Adult Intelligence Scale. Manual*. New York: Psychological Corporation.

Wechsler, D. (1981). *WAIS-R manual.* New York: Psychological Corporation.

15

New Strategies for Studying Higher Level Motor Disorders

HOWARD POIZNER and JOHN F. SOECHTING

The study of the neural bases of motor behavior provides a special window into higher brain functions. Motion has played an important role in the evolution of the brain, and it is becoming apparent that sensory and motor systems are fundamentally interdependent, so that analysis of motor behavior is essential to the understanding of sensory as well as motor systems (Edelman et al., 1984; Gelfand, Gurfinkel, Tsetlin, & Shik, 1971). There are parallel as well as serial aspects to the processing operations which underlie the production of a movement. Currently, these processing operations are poorly understood, and the study of human subjects with motor disorders can help to uncover the specialized processing operations that different parts of the central nervous system perform. Studies of human limb movements which are not restricted to a single joint are of recent vintage (Georgopoulos, 1986), and even less is known in the way of quantitative descriptions of the motor deficits of patients with motor disorders. This situation has resulted in part from the difficulty of tracking and analyzing movement in three-dimensional space. Without such quantitative methods for analyzing and measuring movement in three-dimensional space it can be extremely difficult to deduce the nature of the processing operations that must be performed. This chapter presents some new strategies for investigating the nature of the breakdown in motor control in subjects with diseases affecting the motor systems of the brain. Recent technological advances in movement analysis make possible new investigations of brain function for motor behavior. We present these techniques and illustrate their use through three-dimensional analysis of the movement breakdown of a subject with limb apraxia (although the approach is applicable to understanding a wide range of clinical disorders of movement). Finally, we simulate portions of these experimental data by implementing a model of the trajectory formation process and "lesioning" component processes of the model. Before turning to these new ways of studying motor disorders we briefly consider selected aspects of the motor systems of the brain as they relate to upper limb control.

The motor system, like the visual system, is organized to process information in both a hierarchical and parallel fashion. It is clear that cortical motor areas stand in hierarchical relation to limb muscles. However, different motor control systems may work in parallel in distributed systems, each adding a particular property to the controlled piece of movement (Wiesendanger, 1981). The particular computations that the different motor systems perform, however, are not well understood.

THE MOTOR SYSTEMS OF THE BRAIN

The brain contains multiple systems whose coordinated activity regulates motor functioning. Three major central structures participate in controlling movement: cortical motor areas, basal ganglia, and cerebellum. These systems are bilaterally symmetric with nearly identical structures in the left and right cerebral hemispheres.

Motor Cortex

The motor cortex (or "primary motor cortex") is located in the precentral gyrus. Electrical stimulation of a small area of cortex leads to contraction of individual muscles (and their synergists) and some of the efferents from motor cortex have been shown to make monosynaptic connections with alpha motor neurons (Fetz & Cheney, 1980). Electrophysiological recordings of cortical activity in alert animals have demonstrated correlations of the discharge with parameters of the movement (Evarts, 1967; Humphrey, 1986), One important parameter which appears to be represented in motor cortical activity is the direction of the movement in three-dimensional space (Georgopoulos, Schwartz, & Kettner, 1986), although a correlation with load direction has also been demonstrated (Kalaska, Cohen, Hyde, & Prud'homme, 1989). Primary motor cortex receives important projections from other cortical areas including somatosensory cortex, and the supplementary motor area and premotor cortex. These latter areas are located anteriorly to the primary motor area on the medial and lateral aspects of the hemisphere, respectively.

Secondary Motor Cortex

Supplementary motor area and premotor cortex (secondary motor cortex) are involved in motor control of a higher order. Both seem important for motor preparation and sensory guidance of movement (Fox, Fox, Raichle, & Burde, 1985; Wiesendanger et al., 1973; Wise, 1984). Lesions to the supplementary motor area cause deficits in bimanual coordination (Brinkman, 1981), and a transient poverty of internally generated contralateral limb movements, and if in the left hemisphere, to speech (Damasio & Van Hoesen, 1980). Studies of local cerebral blood flow in humans shows selective activation of supplementary motor cortex for complex movements and for movements not actually executed but only imagined (Roland et al., 1980a, 1980b; 1982). These findings suggest an important role of the supplementary motor area both in the internal preparation for complicated motor acts and for the sensory guidance of movement based on somatosensory feedback. Lesions to the left supplementary motor area also cause limb apraxia in man (Watson, Fleet, Rothi, & Heilman, 1986).

Premotor cortex, like the supplementary motor area, seems important for the preparation of movement, the guidance of movement sequences, and the changing of motor programs based on sensory information, primarily visual (Roland et al., 1980a, 1980b; Wise, 1984; Rizzolatti, 1987). Two additional motor structures do not project directly to the spinal cord motor neurons—the basal ganglia and the cerebellum, which act as subcortical regulators of motor activity. These structures provide feed-forward and feedback loops with cortical motor areas, producing distributed, parallel motor processing.

Basal Ganglia

The basal ganglia are a collection of grey matter located deep in the cerebral hemispheres (the caudate, putamen, and globus pallidus) and in the upper brainstem (the subthalamic nuclei and the substantia nigra). They receive motor instructions from the cortex and their output is closely coded to movement (DeLong & Georgopoulos, 1981; Marsden, 1982). Damage to the basal ganglia may be associated with lack of movement, slowness of movement initiation or execution, or involuntary movements. Parkinson's disease provides a human model of basal ganglia dysfunction (Marsden, 1982). Patients with Parkinson's disease seem to be unable to predict and preprogram the end position of their hands following a rapid ballistic arm movement (Flowers, 1975, 1976). Instead, they are restricted to a "closed-loop" form of control, having to visually monitor their arm movements.

Hallett and Khoshbin (1980) proposed that patients with Parkinson's disease cannot make large amplitude ballistic movements because they cannot initiate sufficient force of muscle contraction to move the arm rapidly to a required point of aim. Loss of force control is supported by Margolin and Wing (1983) from studies of handwriting of subjects with Parkinson's disease, and alterations in the use of a gestural language in a deaf signer (Poizner et al., 1988). These latter data also suggest that the force control problem in Parkinson's disease may be related to maintaining or programming forces over time.

Cerebellum

The cerebellum, like the basal ganglia, receives inputs from primary and secondary motor cortex as well as from nonmotor cortex. However, the cerebellum also receives sensory inputs from the periphery. The cerebellum is strategically located and connected to obtain information about where the body, muscles, and joints are in space and how they are moving (Stein, 1986). Its output by way of the thalamus to motor cortex allows feedback of its processing of this information to motor cortex. Unifying principles of cerebellar function, like basal ganglia function, have remained elusive (Brooks & Thach, 1981). However, the cerebellum appears to have an important predictor function by comparing control signals from cortical motor structures, which specify intended motor responses, with afferent signals resulting from the consequencers of those responses. The cerebellum may then modify movements as they deviate from intended trajectories and modify central programs to correct for movement deviations as well (Ghez & Fahn, 1985; Stein, 1986). Indeed, the main route by which visual information reaches the motor cortex does not run through the cerebral cortex, but passes through the cerebellum (Stein, 1986). Damage to the cerebellar hemisphere produces a characteristic loss of coordination due to disruption of muscle synergies. Movements become decomposed into component parts that are made with errors of force, velocity, amplitude, and timing (Holmes, 1939).

Patients with cerebellar damage show a coarse and irregular tremor during voluntary movement which becomes increasingly prominent as the patient attempts to terminate the movement at a particular point. The patient may also be unable to brake (and stop) the movement at a desired point, either overshooting or undershooting the intended goal (Holmes, 1939). Recent evidence also indicates that patients with lesions to the lateral cerebellum have impairments both in the production of movement timing and in the perceptual discrimination of small temporal intervals, implying a central role of the cerebellum in timing (Ivry & Keele, 1989).

Parietal Lobe

The posterior parietal areas of cortex appear to be one of the main processing stages for the sensorimotor transformations required to produce movement. Lesions of these areas lead to attentional deficits including the neglect of the contralateral part of space and to difficulties in reproducing the spatial relationships among objects (Andersen, 1989). There are also errors in localizing targets in space which cannot be attributed to a motor impairment. Electrophysiological studies show that these areas receive a strong input from the primary visual areas of cortex, and several stages in the processing of visual information have been detailed (Andersen, 1989). Andersen and Zipser (1988) have recently provided evidence that one of the operations performed by neurons in Area 7a of parietal cortex is a coordinate transformation of visual information from a retinotopic to a craniotopic frame of reference.

In man, lesions in the left posterior parietal cortex cause apraxia (Heilman, 1979; Heilman & Rothi, 1985). Apraxia is an impairment of the execution of learned, skilled movements, in subjects with intact afferent and efferent systems. The incorrect performance cannot be explained by weakness, incoordination, impaired perceptual systems, inattentiveness or lack of cooperation (Heilman & Rothi, 1985; Geschwind & Damasio, 1985). This definition implies that the movements are learned, and thus that apraxia is a disorder of the high level control of the execution of certain classes of movement. Its study can help inform us about cerebral organization in relation to movement.

The Problem of Accurate Measurement

It is clear that the various motor systems of the brain perform different operations whose coordinated activity allows smooth, integrated motor behavior. However, the nature of these operations has been difficult to investigate, in large part due to the difficulty of measuring and analyzing movement in three-dimensional space. One simply cannot uncover precise patterns of timing and spatial relations in three-dimensional trajectories from observation or from viewing of videotaped recordings. However, just such precise information on the temporal and spatial trajectory variables is essential for uncovering the processing operations performed by the central motor systems of the brain. As the noted neurologist Gordon Holmes recognized long ago, "One of the great disadvantages which clinical investigations suffer is difficulty in recording and measuring observations accurately by such methods as physiologists employ" (Holmes, 1939, p.10). It is our view that the study of motor function through the quantitative, three-dimensional computer-graphic analysis of patients with selective damage to the major central motor systems could prove most valuable in refining models of the neural basis of motor control. Without such methods of movement analysis, many issues can only be attacked in a qualitative rather than quantitative manner, and models of motor control are deprived of such potentially important information as patterns of movement displacement, velocity, and acceleration over time. We have recently developed powerful new techniques for three-dimensional spatial trajectory tracking, and computer-graphic analysis of movement (Poizner, Wooten, & Salot, 1986; Jennings & Poizner, 1988).

CASE STUDY

METHODS: Three-Dimensional Movement Tracking and Computer-Graphic Analysis

Traditional methods of movement measurement have utilized video recording or high-speed cinematography. In these methods, the positions of multiple markers on the image from a camera are digitized frame by frame by a human operator. This is a notoriously laborious and error-prone procedure (Woltring, 1984). Furthermore, the use of a single camera provides only two-dimensional information; the use of multiple cameras presents problems of camera synchronization. We have developed a new system for automated movement measurement that offers high spatial and temporal resolution for tracking up to eight moving body segments in three-dimensional space (Poizner, Wooten, & Salot, 1986).[1]

Three-Dimensional Data Acquisition

Figure 15-1 presents the main hardware components of our system and shows the positioning of 4 LEDs on the major joints of a subject's arm. The main hardware components consist of optoelectronic cameras and amplifying electronics, together with an analog to digital converter (Data Translation DT-2801; United Detector Technology, Op-Eye 5 system); specially built LED drive electronics that pulse and time multiplex up to eight LEDs under computer control; and an IBM-PC microcomputer. The cameras are optoelectronic and directly sense the position of infrared emitting diodes (LEDs). An optical lens focuses light from an LED onto a detector plate (a lateral effect photodiode). The spot of light generates four output currents on the photodiode that are proportional to the position of the spot on the detector surface. The four output currents are

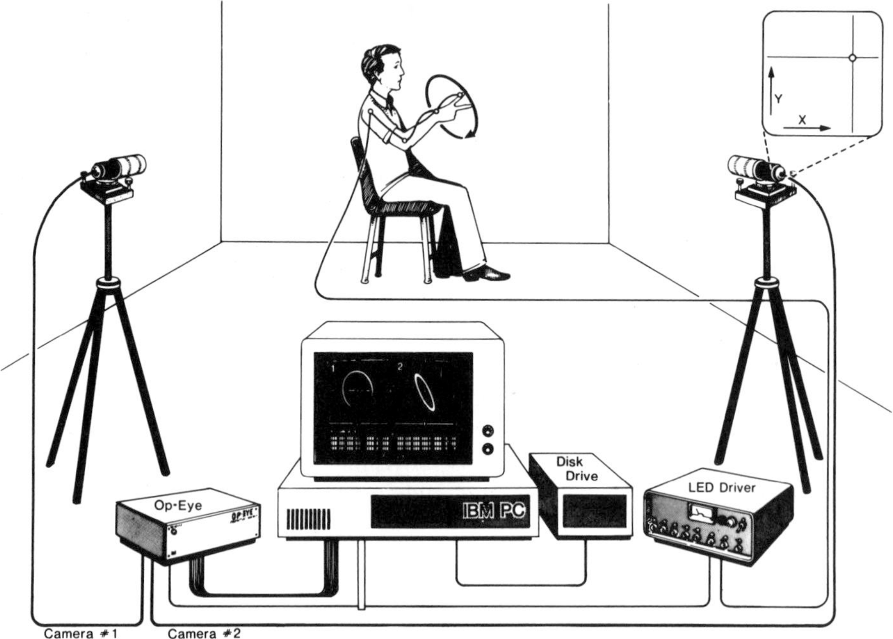

Figure 15-1 Three-dimensional movement monitoring system. The main hardware components and the positioning of the LEDs on a subject is shown. (Reprinted with permission from Poizner, Wooten, & Salot (1986). *Behavior Research Methods, Instruments, & Computers, 18,* 427–433. Computergraphic modeling and analysis: A portable system for tracking arm movements in three-dimensional space, Psychonomic Society, Inc.)

then amplified by the amplifying electronics and digitized to 12 bit (1 part in 4096) resolution. The microcomputer synchronizes the digitizing of the camera outputs with the flashing of the LEDs. Each of the four LEDs is sampled at 100 Hz.

Digital Data Processing

The data from each camera are first corrected for lens and electronic distortion by making use of a prior calibration procedure that involved the exhaustive placement of target diodes at known locations across the field of view of each camera. In order to remove high-frequency noise, the data from each camera are low-pass filtered with a modified Butterworth filter using a cutoff frequency of 8 hz. The three-dimensional coordinates of each joint are then calculated from the two cameras by triangulation, utilizing knowledge of relative camera position and orientation. Finally, the three-dimensional coordinates are differentiated twice for calculation of the tangential velocity and acceleration of each joint of the arm over time.

Computer-Graphic Reconstruction

Movement trajectories are reconstructed in three dimensions on a computer-graphics system so that they can be interactively manipulated and dynamically displayed, including real-time rotation, translation, scaling, and clipping. The interactive control and three-dimensional visualization of the digitized movements allow separate analyses of various temporal and spatial characteristics of segments of the movement trajectory (Jennings & Poizner, 1988). Trajectories are graphically edited to remove extraneous portions at the beginning and ending of the movement related to the subject's raising his hand to the initial position and dropping his hand after the movement was completed. When gestures involve rhythmic movement repetition, movements are segmented into individual repetition cycles. Subjects were not instructed to produce any specific number of cycles of movement, but the number of such cycles actually produced varied from 2 to 14 across movements and subjects.

To illustrate the application of these techniques to the analysis of motor disorders, we present a case study of a subject with apraxia. Portions of this work have been previously reported (Poizner, Mack, Verfaellie, Rothi, & Heilman, 1990; Poizner, Soechting, Bracewell, Rothi, & Heilman, 1989; Poizner, Figel, Rothi, & Heilman, 1990). This case was seen at the University of Florida in collaboration with Leslie Rothi and Kenneth Heilman.

Subject

BH is a 47-year-old right-handed male who was hospitalized with the abrupt onset of aphasia. On examination, BH had severe impairment of language function with little or no language output and very poor comprehension. He was originally diagnosed as having severe global aphasia and mild dysarthria. At that time there was no significant limb or oral apraxia noted. There was a right supranuclear facial palsy and mild weakness of the right extremities. The remainder of his examination was normal.

Shortly after his admission to the hospital, the patient developed rapidly progressive right hemiplegia despite anticoagulation therapy with heparin. A CT scan indicated no evidence of hemorrhage but showed a rather large area of infarction. The patient's hospital course was marked by continued severe neurological deficits; he could not move his right arm or leg and was globally aphasic. He was then transferred to a rehabilitation center for continued rehabilitation. BH received treatment at that facility for approximately two months. At the time of evaluation at the Gainesville VA Medical Center, he was five months post-onset and diagnosed as having severe Broca's aphasia. The tests reported here were performed 16 months post-onset. An MRI scan performed more than three years after his stroke indicated a large perisylvian lesion in the left hemisphere involving the frontal, temporal, and parietal lobes. His right hemisphere was intact. His performance was mildly apraxic on the Florida Praxis Screening Test. Five neurologically intact subjects, matched for age and sex with the Apraxic BH, served as control subjects. All subjects were right-handed.

Procedure

Four learned, skilled movements were selected for three-dimensional movement analysis: roll up a car window (WIND), erase a blackboard (ERASE), carve a turkey (CARVE), and unlock a door (KEY). These movements are drawn from a particular subclass of learned, skilled movements, namely, transitive movements, which are movements that require the limb to work in concert with an external object, such as a tool or instrument. Transitive movements are more severely affected in apraxia than are intransitive movements, which are learned communicative gestures that do not require tool or instrument manipulation (Haaland & Flaherty, 1984; Heilman & Rothi, 1985). To minimize cues, subjects were asked to produce each gesture to verbal command, without the tool (e.g., knife) or object of the tool's action (e.g., turkey) being present. To obtain measures of movement variability, each gesture was replicated four times. All subjects performed the movements with their nondominant left hand. The subjects' left hand was used, since it was ipsilateral to the side of the lesion for Apraxic BH, and thus would not be affected by weakness or incoordination due to primary motor deficit.

Qualitatively, Apraxic BH's movements were clumsy and appeared poorly coordinated. For example, on the gesture CARVE, he moved his arm medially to laterally, "wrapping" the movement around his body, instead of smoothly coordinating elbow flexion and extension with shoulder flexion and extension to produce movement in the sagittal plane. Likewise, the spatial paths of all of his gestures were highly disorganized, although characteristic aspects of the target gestures remained apparent. While qualitative movement descriptions of this sort are informative, the quantitative analysis of the breakdown of the movement kinematics (patterns of displacement, velocity, and acceleration over time) can provide insight into the control procesess that may be disrupted in apraxia. Understanding the nature of these control processes should help refine our understanding both of apraxia and of cerebral control of movement. Kinematic analyses of movement abnormalities of the apraxic subject in spatial orientation, in joint coordination, and in space-time relations will be discussed.

Results

1. Impaired Spatial Orientation of Movement

Figure 15-2 presents the changes in the position of the hand over time in the gesture CARVE for a control subject and for Apraxic BH. Position changes in the sagittal, vertical, and horizontal dimensions are shown. The movement of the control subject had largest components in the sagittal and vertical dimensions, and very small movement amplitude in the horizontal dimension. In contrast, the movement of Apraxic BH had its largest component in the horizontal direction, reflecting an improper direction of the movement axis. Furthermore, the movement lacked the smooth, oscillatory pattern of that of the control subject. Indeed, the one dimension which did show rhythmic oscillation in the movement of Apraxic BH, vertical position change, increased value over the course of the movement indicating that Apraxic BH continually raised the height of his hand as he moved laterally across his body in the horizontal plane.

The use of improper spatial orientation is evident in the reconstructed motions of the arm for a control subject and Apraxic BH performing the gesture CARVE (Figure 15-3). The images show the sequential positions of the arm and hand in three-dimensional space during the course of the movement. Figure 15-3 clearly shows Apraxic BH's impaired control of the direction of the movement axis. Whereas the control subject orients the movement in the sagittal plane, Apraxic BH orients the movement laterally, in the horizontal plane.

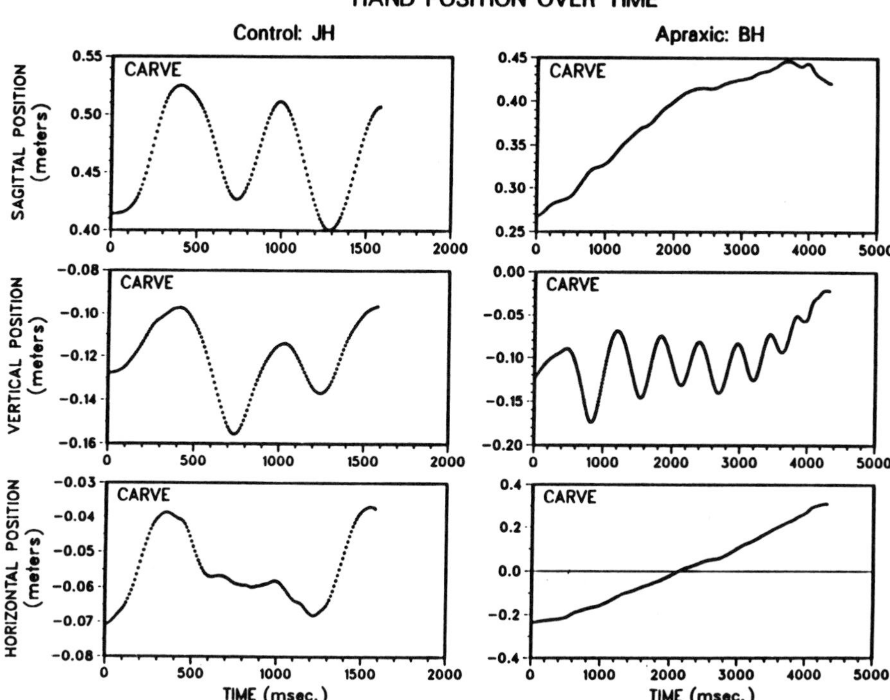

Figure 15-2 Hand position over time for the gesture CARVE for a control subject and for Apraxic BH. Changes in position are displayed for sagittal, vertical, and horizontal dimensions. Apraxic BH improperly orients the movement in space, and lacks the smooth, sinusoidal motion of the control subject.

To capture the spatial orientation of the plane of motion and changes in that orientation during the movement, the best-fitting plane of motion of the hand trajectory for CARVE was computed for Apraxic BH and all control subjects. This best-fitting plane of motion was computed for each replication of the gesture and for each movement repetition cycle within a given gesture. To quantitatively specify the plane's orientation in three-dimensional space, the direction perpendicular to each plane was calculated. These directional vectors for each movement replication and repetition cycle are presented in Figure 15-4.

To display the three-dimensional structure, the vectors are shown from four views: an enlarged side view, and smaller views from the top, front, and side of the motion. Figure 15-4 shows that in the control subjects, these vectors lie predominantly in the frontal plane, reflecting hand motion in the sagittal plane. The spread of vectors seen from the front reflects a downward component of the movement plane. Apraxic BH, in contrast, has major vector components in the sagittal direction. Thus, in Apraxic BH the motion was predominantly in the frontal plane, reflecting lateral and downward movement. The sagittal and lateral components of the movement statistically differed between the control subjects and Apraxic BH [$t(72) = 10.6$, $p < .001$, and $t(72) = 11.3$, $p < .001$

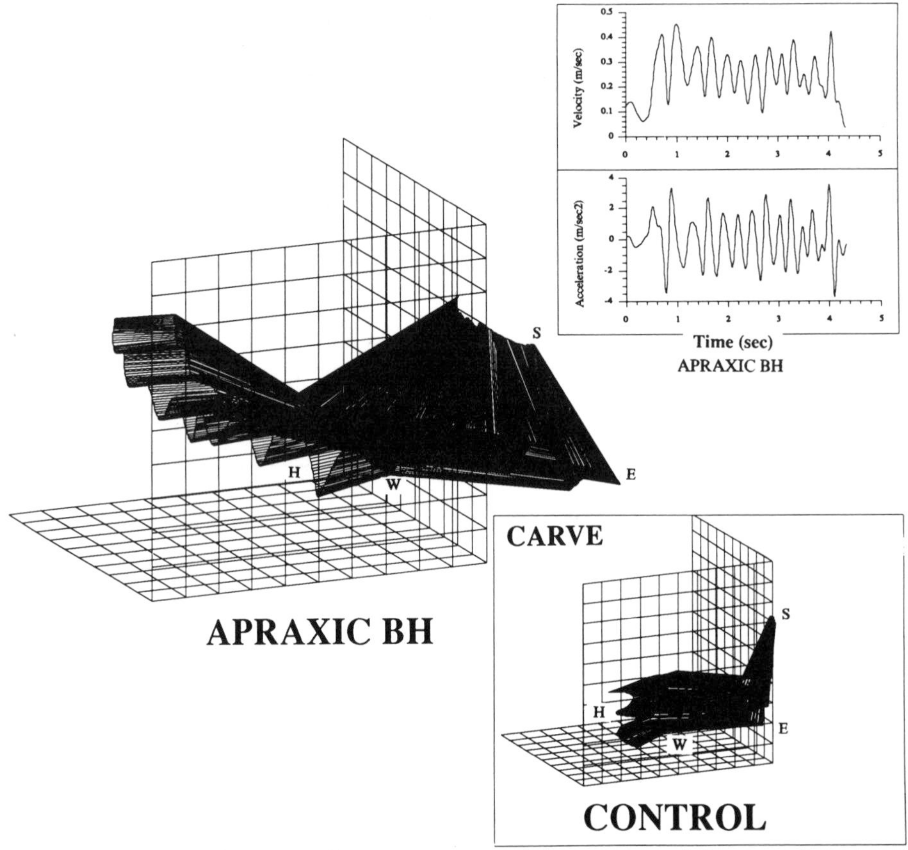

Figure 15-3 Three-dimensional reconstructions of the motions of the arm of a control subject and Apraxic BH performing the gesture CARVE. The entire sequence of hand and arm positions during the course of the movement is shown. The trajectories are embedded three dimensional grids composed of squares that are 5 cm. on a side, calibrating for absolute displacement. The apraxic and control trajectories are viewed from the same angle. Note the impaired orientation of the movement axis in the Apraxic BH. S, shoulder; E, elbow; W, wrist; H, hand.

for the gesture CARVE; $t(91) = 5.8, p < .001$, and $t(91) = -4.1, p < .001$ for the gesture ERASE].

Thus, control over the impaired direction of the movement axis is impaired in Apraxic BH. This impaired movement control is also reflected in the inappropriate addition of movement axes by the apraxic subject. For example, Figure 15-5 presents the reconstructed movement of a control subject and of Apraxic BH for the gesture WIND. The control subject shows smooth circular movement repeated about a well-defined center point. In contrast to the control subject, Apraxic BH produces repeated circular movement paths, but constantly changes their amplitudes and spatial orientations.

While the movements of Apraxic BH are variable and highly disorganized (cf. Figure 15-2), the basic structure of both the WIND and CARVE movements

PLANE NORMALS: CARVE

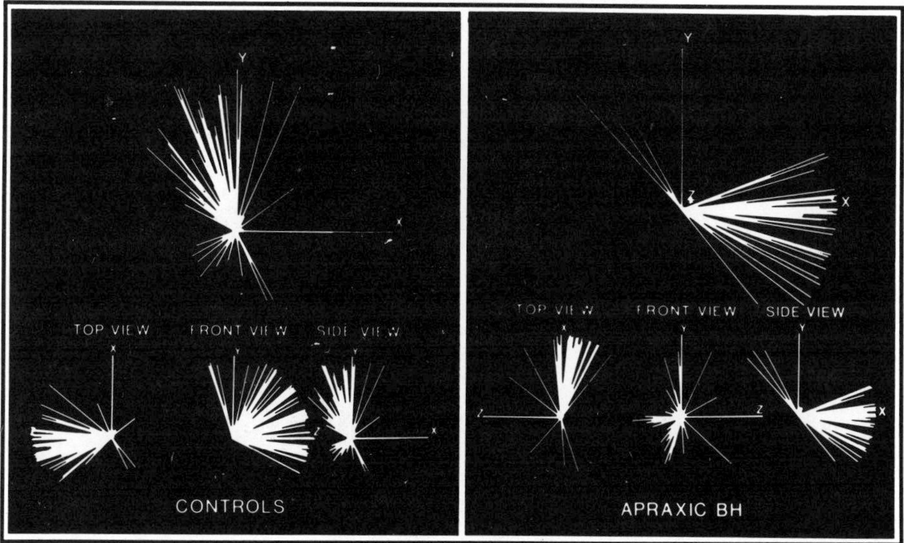

Figure 15-4 Direction vectors perpendicular to the best fitting plane of motion for the hand trajectory in the gesture CARVE are shown across movement replications and repetition cycles within a given movement for all subjects. All vectors have been converted to a unit length of 1. These vectors describe the orientation of the plane of motion and show the disruption in the control of planar orientation in Apraxic BH. (Reprinted with permission from *Brain, 113*, Poizner, H., Mack, L., Verfaellie, M., Rothi, L., & Heilman, K., Three-dimensional computergraphic analysis of apraxia: Neural representations of learned movement, 1990, Oxford University Press.)

is preserved. One can recognize the to-and-fro motion of carving in Figure 15-3 and the circular motion in Figure 15-5 which characterize the movements of normal controls. In both cases, however, the spatial orientation of the movement is not preserved, and cycle-to-cycle variations of the movement are much greater than that of control subjects. Furthermore, unlike control subjects who exhibit smooth, sinusoidally varying hand velocity profiles, Apraxic BH's hand velocity is much more irregular, lacking smooth, sinusoidal variation in timing (Figure 15-5).

2. Decoupling of Normal Space-Time Relations

Movement trajectories may be described in terms of their spatial path and the time sequence along that path. A strict relationship exists between these two movement attributes: hand velocity is tightly coupled to a spatial aspect of the trajectory, namely, its curvature, or degree of bending (Viviani & Terzuolo, 1982; Morasso, 1983). This relationship is not due to any physical law, but rather has been related to a control process by which complex trajectories are planned through proportional control of velocity and curvature (Viviani & Terzuolo, 1982). This space-time coupling breaks down in apraxia. Figure 15-6 presents the temporal course of hand velocity and radius of curvature for a control subject

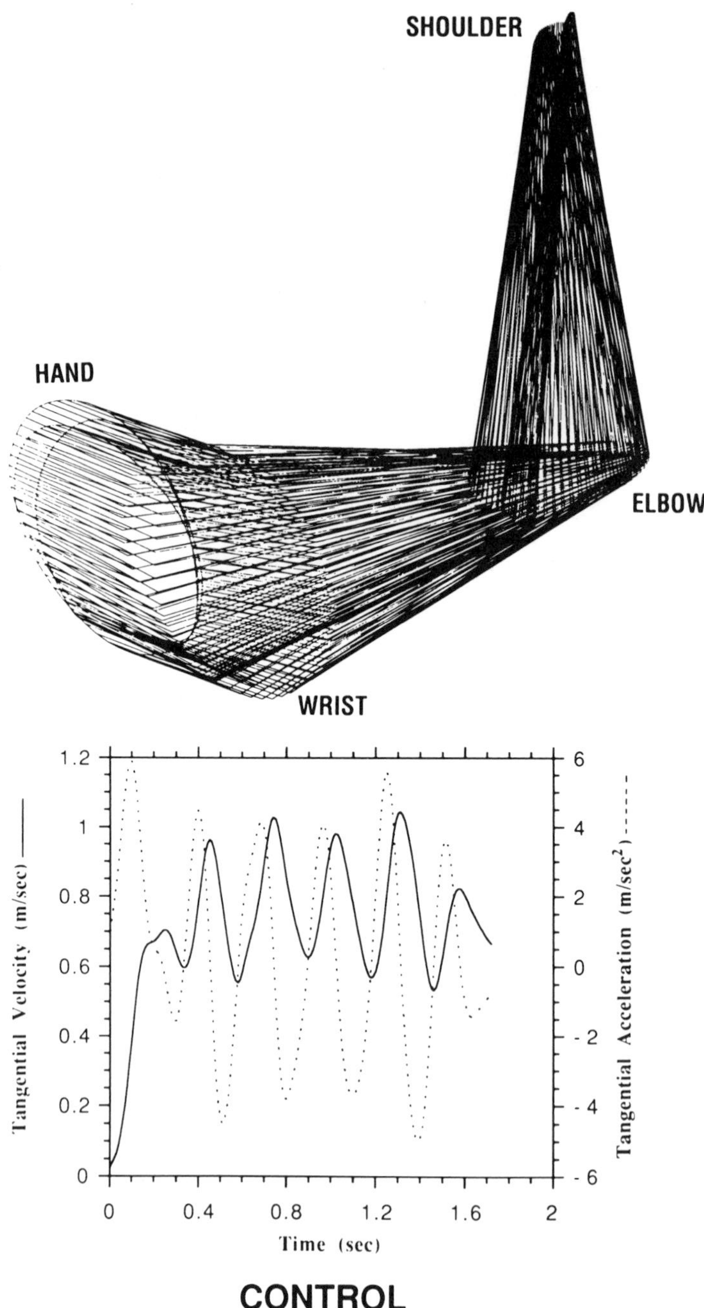

Figure 15-5 Three-dimensional reconstructions of the motions of the hand and arm of a control subject and Apraxic BH performing the gesture WIND. Tangential velocities and accelerations are also presented. Note searching behavior of Apraxic BH, and the irregular velocity profile.

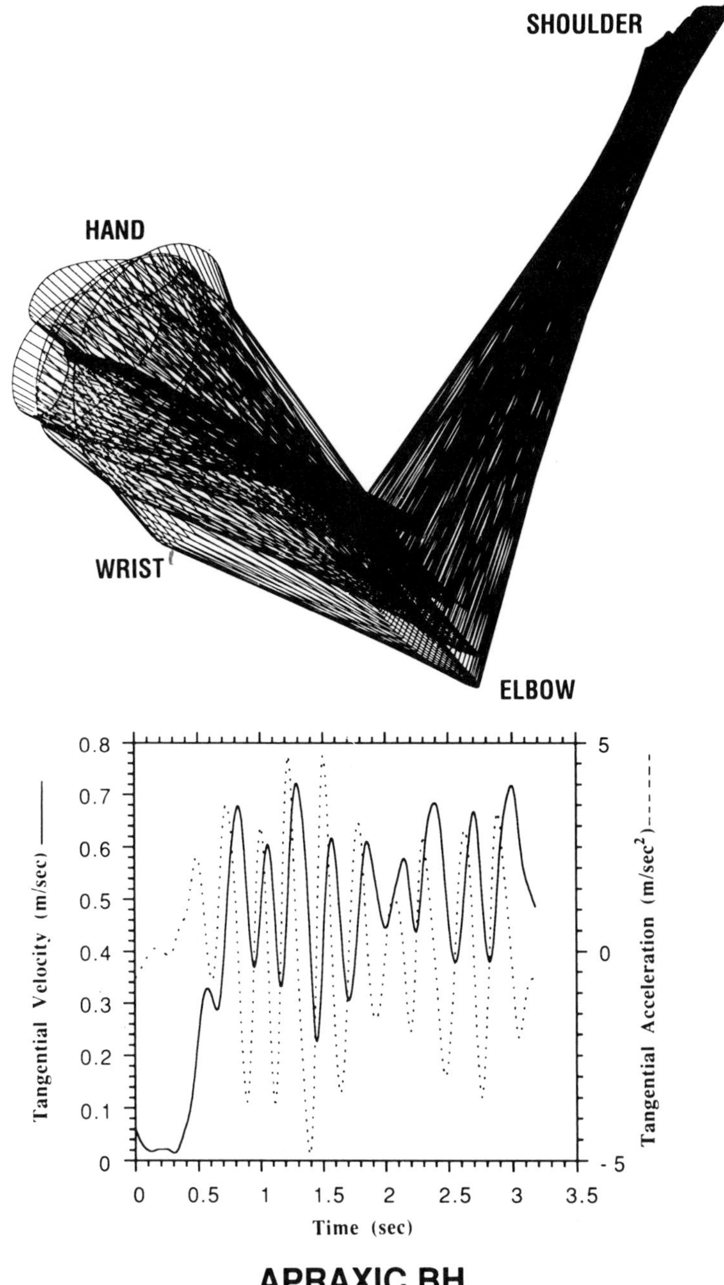

Figure 15-5 *(Continued)*

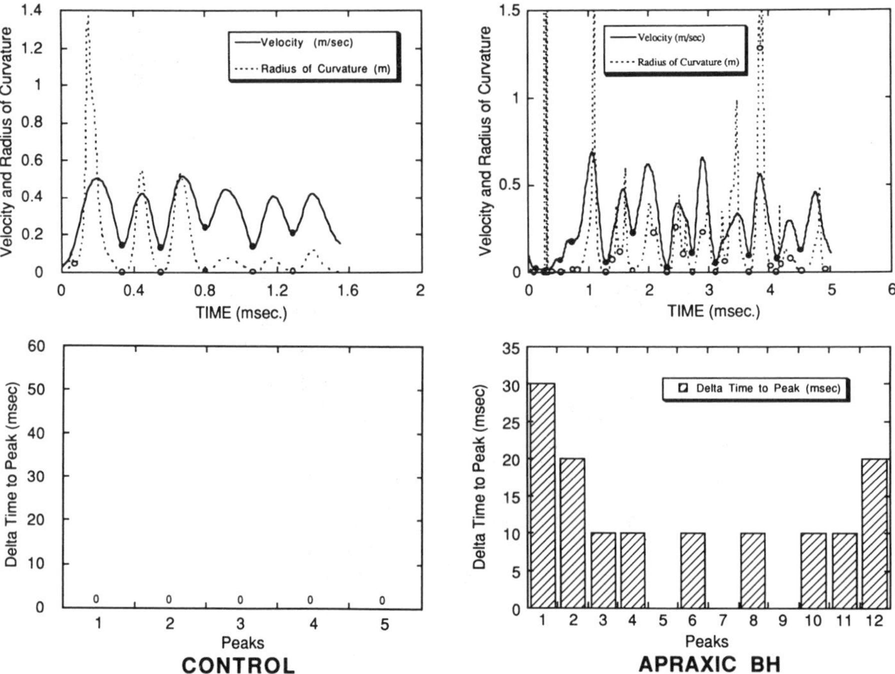

Figure 15-6 Velocity-curvature decoupling in the movement of Apraxic BH. Tangential hand velocity and radius of curvature are plotted in the upper panels. Time correspondences between velocity minima and radius of curvature minima are plotted in the lower panels.

and for Apraxic BH performing the gesture CARVE. (Radius of curvature, the inverse of curvature, is plotted rather than curvature, so that it may be plotted on the same axis as velocity.)

Figure 15-6 shows that for the control subject, there is a strict correlation between velocity and curvature: as velocity increases, curvature decreases. Further, the figure shows that this relationship is decoupled in Apraxic BH. To capture the linkage between the curves, a computer algorithm was written to locate and mark velocity minima and radius of curvature minima. The filled circles in the figure mark these minima. The times of occurrence of the velocity minima were noted, and the difference in time between each velocity minimum and the nearest radius of curvature minimum was computed. These time differences are plotted in the lower panel. Whereas the time correspondence between minimum velocity and peak curvature was almost perfect for control subjects, there was substantial lack of such correspondence in Apraxic BH [for the gesture CARVE, $t(138) = 5.3$, $p < .001$; for the gesture ERASE, $t(159) = 5.7$, $p < .001$].

Computer-Graphic Modeling

One way in which we can gain insight into the control processes that may be disrupted by apraxia (or other motor disorders) is by simulating the movement abnormalities of these disorders that we uncover by three-dimensional trajectory analysis. We have begun preliminary simulations of movement abnormalities in apraxia, in collaboration with Terry Figel, by implementing a graphic model based on aspects of the underlying trajectory formation process. The motor system contains hierarchies in terms of planning and movement specification. A basic outcome of studies of complex trajectories, varying from handwriting to drawing to three-dimensional scribbling in the air, has been that the velocity profile of the hand shows a very stereotyped segmentation, having very clearly defined bell-shaped segments (Morasso, 1981; 1983; Morasso & Tagliasco, 1986). This segmentation of velocity has been taken to indicate that complex trajectories are planned in terms of independent trajectory segments which are centrally represented in terms of motor shape (e.g., size, curvature, direction); each trajectory segment is associated with a bell-shaped velocity profile.

Based on kinematic analyses of three-dimensional movement trajectories, Morasso and his colleagues (Morasso & Mussa Ivaldi, 1982; Morasso & Tagliasco, 1986) have proposed a model of the underlying trajectory formation process, which expresses in a formal way, the spatiotemporal structure underlying motor representations. The model is space oriented rather than joint or muscle oriented; that is, the hypothesized mechanism of trajectory formation is based on controlling the trajectory of the hand in space, independent of actual joint and muscle patterns. Based on experimental data, Morasso et al. (1982; 1986) propose that the trajectory formation process seems to result from a sequence of discrete motor commands and a smoothing mechanism that overlaps in time movement segments generated by each discrete command. The model of trajectory formation consists of two different levels: a level of representation of the planned trajectory in terms of discrete motor primitives, characterized by spatial and timing parameters, and a level of activation and synchronization of these abstract representations whereby smooth trajectories are formed through appropriate temporal overlap of the motor primitives (see Morasso & Mussa Ivaldi, 1982; Morasso & Tagliasco, 1986, for a more detailed description).

Morasso and his colleagues have validated the model through the match of simulated and experimental data in such diverse motor acts as point-to-point movements and handwriting, and they provide an explicit computational framework for the implementation of the model (Morasso, 1983; Morasso & Mussa Ivaldi, 1982; Morasso & Tagliasco, 1986). The approach uses methods from computational geometry and computer graphics (Faux & Pratt, 1979) for generating composite curves derived from a chain of curved segments which have been joined in a smooth way. These methods are used since they imply segmentation in a natural way, and might provide a biologically feasible computational mechanism (Morasso & Tagliasco, 1986).

We have implemented the basic segment specification and chaining capabilities of the model interactively on our computer-graphics system. Typical attributes of both control and apraxic subjects were extracted to produce apraxic and control profiles. In this model, movement of the hand, not of all joints, is simulated. In our implementation of the model, a finite set of control points is used to specify a sequence of strokes (motor primitives). This generates a somewhat discontinuous initial trajectory. A B-spline method is then used to fit a cubic polynomial to the boundaries supplied by the control points. Each control point is now related to a corresponding bell-shaped curve. Four such bell-shaped

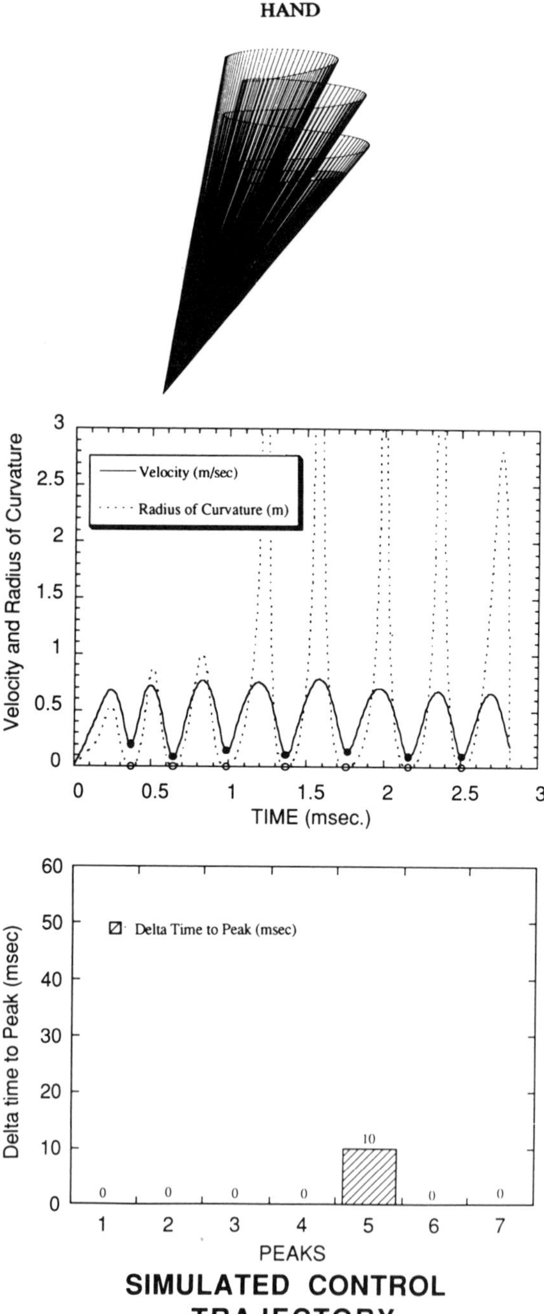

Figure 15-7 Simulated hand trajectories of a control subject and an apraxic subject. The upper panels present the simulated trajectories, the middle panels, the resultant velocity and radius of curvature profiles, and the lower panels, the time correspondences between velocity minima and radius of curvature minima. Note that the simulations capture the velocity-curvature decoupling observed in the trajectories of Apraxic BH.

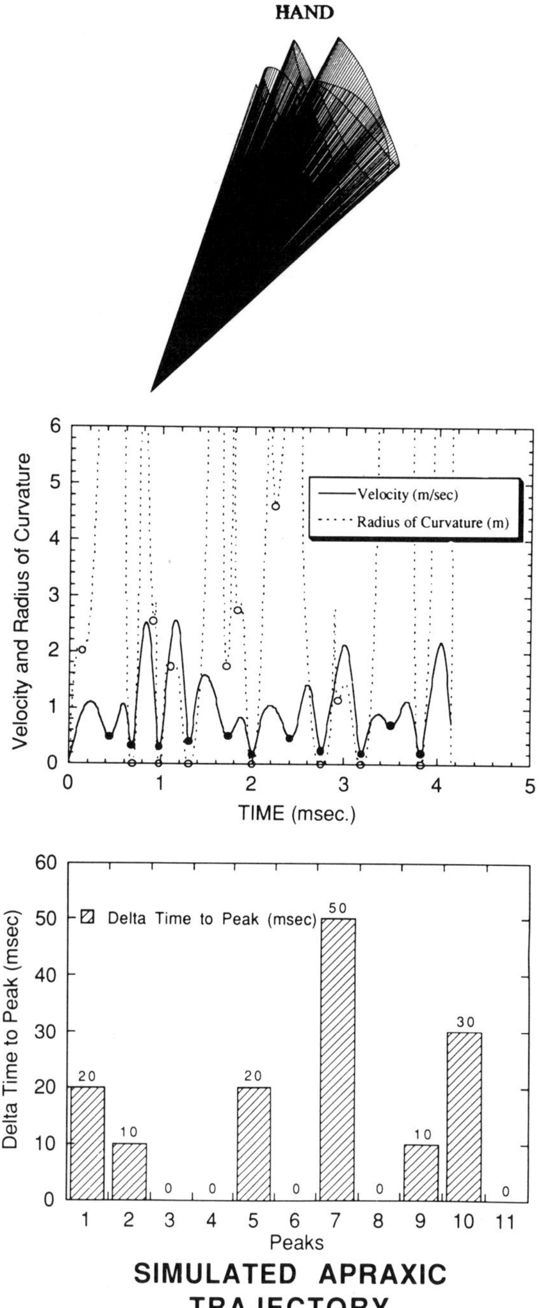

Figure 15-7 *(Continued)*

curves are active at any point in time and provide weighted functions to determine fitted points. Based on relationships provided by Morasso (1983) and Morasso and Tagliasco (1986), six B-spline bell functions correspond to each second of real time. Given the conversion to real time, the kinematic properties of the simulated trajectories can then be computed. Hand trajectories for the gesture CARVE of control subjects were accurately simulated using this method (see Figure 15-7). Figure 15-7 presents reconstructed motions of the hand trajectories (not of all joints of the arm), velocity and curvature patterns, and the resultant velocity-curvature coupling. The simulated trajectory of the control subject has properly patterned spatial structure, shows a smooth, sinusoidally varying velocity profile, and, indeed, the expected coupling between velocity and curvature.

We have begun simulating our finding that the coupling that normally occurs between spatial and temporal trajectory attributes (i.e., between velocity and curvature) is disrupted in apraxia. The model that we are using has proven realistic enough that this space-time coupling emerges as an implicit consequence of the structure of the model (Morasso & Mussa Ivaldi, 1982). We have observed that the decoupling of spatial and temporal attributes of the movements of the apraxic subjects do not occur at random points in the trajectories, but rather at points in which the movement is least smooth, that is, at points of local irregularities in the velocity profile. We have attempted to simulate this potentially important finding by specifically interfering with the joining together and synchronization in time of the movement segments. Delays were introduced to temporally offset a small percentage of the B-spline curves. The simulated trajectories that resulted are presented in the right hand panels of Figure 15-7. The reconstructed hand trajectory captured certain aspects of the movement abnormalities of the apraxic subject. The path of the hand shows variation in spatial orientation across cycles of movement and the velocity profile does not sinusoidally vary, but has many irregularities and local minima and maxima. Importantly, the coupling between velocity and curvature is no longer maintained in the simulated trajectory of the apraxic subject. These simulations, while preliminary, support a model of the trajectory formation process in which discrete movement segments are temporally overlapped and suggest that aspects of the movement breakdown in apraxia can result from small disturbances in the temporal organization of these segments.

Impaired Joint Coordination

Thus far, we have described the deficits in terms of the spatiotemporal characteristics of the displacement of the distal end point of the arm. This displacement results from angular motion at the shoulder and elbow joints, and since there are more degrees of freedom of motion at these joints (at least three at the shoulder and one at the elbow) than there are degrees of freedom at the end point, different combinations of shoulder and elbow motion can result in the same displacement at the wrist. Therefore it is of interest to describe the differences between normal motor behavior and that of the Apraxic BH in terms of joint kinematics as well.

In addition to making spatial orientation errors, the spatial trajectory of an apraxic's limb when making a pantomine is often incorrect (Rothi et al., 1988). This error in spatial path may be related to incorrect joint use or poor joint coordination. To examine the apraxic subjects' relative use of proximal versus distal joints in their movements, we ask whether the apraxic subjects may be attempting to control their distal musculature via their proximal. The gesture "unlock a door' provides a good starting point for this analysis. The control subjects generate the twisting portion of the movement distally from the elbow. Figure 15-8 presents reconstructed movements of the arm in this gesture for a control subject and for Apraxic BH. The control subject shows a small elbow displacement, in contrast to Apraxic BH who exhibits a very large elbow displacement.

The twist portion of each movement was graphically edited out so that it could be analyzed directly. To determine the degree to which the movement was generated at the shoulder as opposed to the elbow, the maximum displacement of the hand and elbow was measured. If the movement is distally generated, there should be larger hand than elbow movement. If the movement is proximally generated at the shoulder, there should be an opposite pattern. Figure 15-9 presents the maximum displacement of the hand and the elbow, across trials, for a control subject and for Apraxic BH.

Figure 15-9 shows that the control subject has substantially larger hand than elbow displacements across movement replications. In contrast, Apraxic BH shows exactly the opposite pattern. To quantify the relative displacements of hand and elbow movement, the ratio of hand-to-elbow displacement for the twist portion of the movement was calculated for each trial, for each control subject and for Apraxic BH. The mean hand-to-elbow displacement ratio for the control subjects was 1.86, indicating almost twice as much hand as elbow movement. The mean ratio for Apraxic BH, however, was .73, reflecting greater elbow than hand motion. Apraxic BH's mean ratio was significantly different from that of the control subjects [$t(20) = 2.2$, $p < .05$]; indeed there was no overlap in the two ratio distributions. These data indicate that whereas the control subjects were generating the movement distally from a point axis at the elbow, Apraxic BH was generating it proximally at the shoulder.

Evidence from a detailed investigation of the joint kinematic patterns of normal subjects is in accord with the hypothesis of a segmentation of complete movement into discrete units of motion. Soechting and Terzuolo (1987) found such segmentation when they asked subjects to draw figures such as stars and figure-8's. During each segment, motion at the wrist was confined to one plane, the modulation in the yaw and elevation angles of the upper arm and forearm was close to sinusoidal, and there was characteristic phase relations among these angles, depending on the plane of wrist motion. These features of normal limb motion are also disrupted in the apraxic subject. The angular orientation of the upper arm and of the forearm was calculated, as was the angle of flexion and extension of the elbow. The parameters chosen are defined in Figure 15-10. They are: theta and beta (the angular elevation) and eta and alpha (yaw) of the arm and forearm. Angular elevation is measured in a vertical plane relative to the vertical and yaw in the horizontal plane relative the the anterior direction.

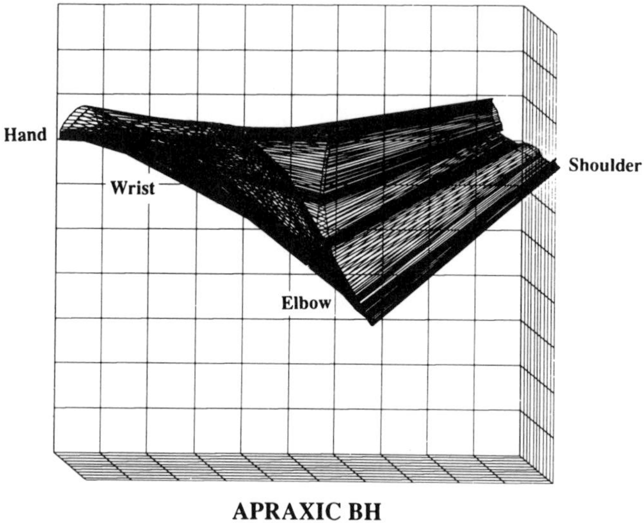

APRAXIC BH

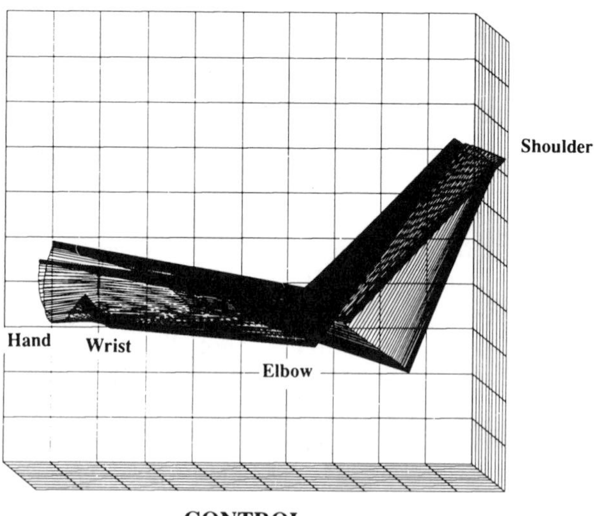

CONTROL

Figure 15-8 Three-dimensional reconstructions of the motions of the hand and arm of a control subject and Apraxic BH performing the gesture KEY. Note large displacement of the elbow by the apraxic as compared to the control subject.

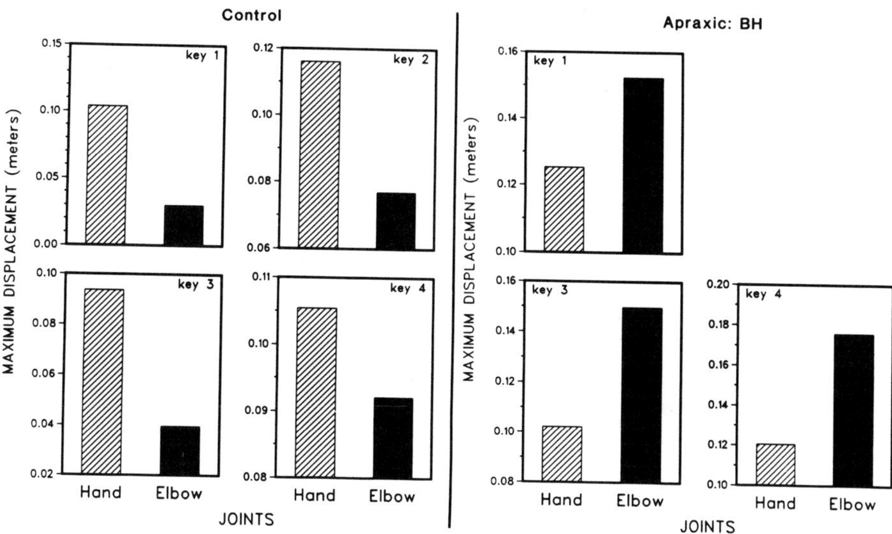

Figure 15-9 Maximum displacements of the hand and elbow across trials for the twist portion of the gesture KEY of a control subject and Apraxic BH. Apraxic BH shows larger elbow than hand displacements in contrast to the control. (Reprinted with permission from *Brain, 113*, Poizner, H., Mack, L., Verfaellie, M., Rothi, L., & Heilman, K., Three-dimensional computergraphic analysis of apraxia: Neural representations of learned movement, 1990, Oxford University Press.)

These angles were identified previously psychophysically as the preferred coordinate system for the recognition of the orientation of the arm in space (Soechting & Ross, 1984).

Figure 15-11 presents the variation in these arm angles over time together with the spatial trajectories of the gesture CARVE for a control subject and for Apraxic BH. Figure 15-11 shows that Apraxic BH's joint motions were less sinusoidal than that of the controls, and that the relative amplitudes of certain arm angles were apportioned differently from that of the control subject. For example, eta and alpha, motions of the upper arm and forearm in the horizontal plane, increased over somewhat large ranges for Apraxic BH, but varied sinusoidally over much smaller ranges for the control subject. In contrast, the control subject showed larger and more sinusoidal variation in elbow flexion and extension (phi) than did Apraxic BH. In order to quantify the relations among amplitudes for the arm angles, the angles were first segmented. In this step, an initial set of boundary positions were defined to break up the arm angle functions into short segments that can be fit with sine waves. A computer algorithm then moved the segment boundaries to the left and to the right along the time axis to reduce the error of the fit of sine waves to the data. This error reduction procedure was performed iteratively by gradually reducing the time interval over which a given boundary was adjusted. In this manner, the algorithm narrowed in on the segment boundaries that maximized the fit of sine waves to the data.

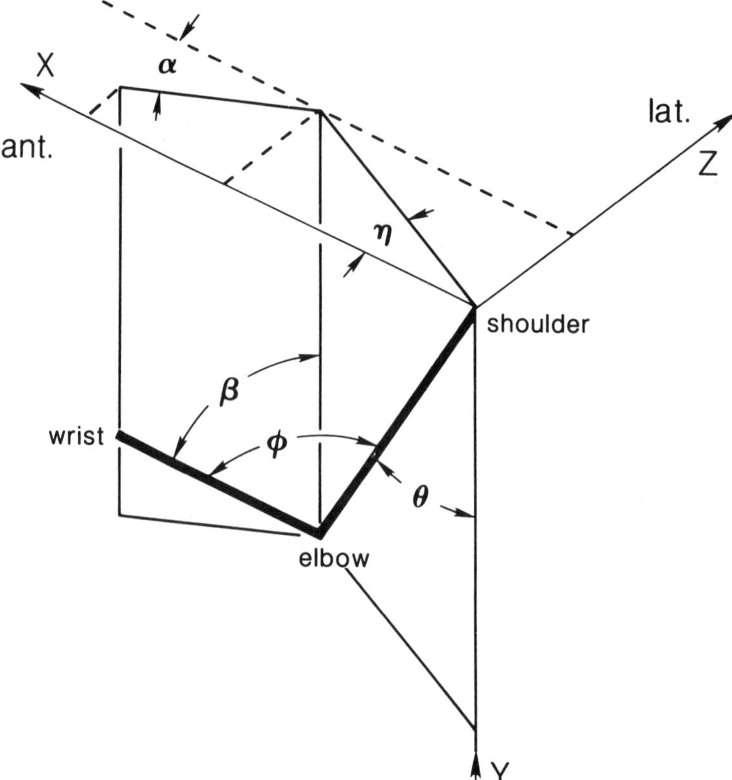

Figure 15-10 Parameters used to define the angular orientation of the arm. The angles theta and beta present the angular elevation of the arm and forearm and are measured in a vertical plane relative the the vertical (*Y*) axis. The yaw angles eta and alpha are measured in the horizontal plane from the anterior (*X*) direction. (Reprinted with permission from *Neuroscience, 13,* Soechting, J. F., & Ross, B., Psychophysical determination of coordinate representation of human arm orientation, 1984, Pergamon Press Ltd.)

Within a segment, all the fitted sine waves were required to have the same period, but could vary in amplitude and phase across the arm angles (see Soechting, 1983; Soechting & Ross, 1984; Soechting, Lacquaniti, & Terzuolo, 1986). The vertical lines in the bottom panels of Figure 15-11 represent the positions of the computed segment boundaries. The fit of the sine waves to the arm angle data was quite good as seen by the match of the fitted curves (dotted lines) and actual data (solid lines) in Figure 15-11.

With the data fitted with sine waves, relative amplitudes of the arm angles could be calculated. Figure 15-12 presents a histogram of the relative amplitudes of two arm angles, forearm yaw to elbow flexion and extension, across segments for all replications of the gesture CARVE for Apraxic BH versus that for all five control subjects. Ratios of arm angles are taken to normalize for differences in arm size and in absolute size of movements. Arrows in Figure 15-12 indicate median ratios. Figure 15-12 shows that the control subjects had a median amplitude ratio less than .4, indicating that the control subjects had much greater flexion and extension at the elbow than displacement of the forearm in the horizontal plane. Figure 15-12 further shows that Apraxic BH had just the opposite pattern, with median forearm yaw to elbow flexion and extension ratios greater than one. Thus, for the gesture CARVE as for KEY, Apraxic BH avoided distal movement at the elbow, relying instead on proximally generated movement at the shoulder.

SUMMARY AND CONCLUSIONS

We have presented a detailed description of transitive arm movements performed by an apraxic subject as an example of the possibilities afforded by a three-dimensional analysis of learned skilled movements. Since the nature of the motor deficits attendant to apraxia (as well as other movement disorders) is not known, we have analyzed these movements from a variety of perspectives: the spatial characteristics of the wrist motion, the coupling between the spatial and the temporal characteristics of the movement, and relationships between the wrist trajectory and the joint angular motions at the shoulder and elbow which determine the wrist trajectory.

Each of these analyses are predicated on one central assumption: that learned, skilled movements such as the ones described in this paper are generated by putting together, in the appropriate sequence and with the proper temporal relationship, a series of simpler subunits or movement segments. This assumption appears to be appealing intuitively, since it would permit the acquistion of a larger repertoire of skilled movements without making excessive demands on the amount of memory needed to represent them, much as is the case for speech. While this idea is difficult test critically, it has been applied successfully in the past to model skilled arm movements in normal subjects (Morasso, 1983; Soechting & Terzuolo, 1987). Here we show that this assumption also provides a useful starting point in analyzing the movement deficits in brain damaged patients, and may help us better understand the nature of their motor programming deficits.

While the performance of the apraxic subject was highly disorganized and clearly different from normal, it is also clear that the movements he produced were not random. Some aspects of normal movement are apparent in each case: the to-and-fro motion in "carve," the oscillatory motion in "wind," and the twisting motion in "key." What is lacking, in part, in each case is an ability to control precisely the spatial orientation of the wrist trajectory. Thus, in carving a turkey Apraxic BH has produced a trajectory which sweeps medially to laterally, rather than being confined to the sagittal plane, and in the gesture "wind", the plane of motion changes substantially from segment to segment. These deficits are apparent as well when the movement is described in terms of the changes in joint angles (Figure 15-12). In "carve," Apraxic BH generates the sweeping motion of the hand by changing the yaw angles of the arm (eta) and forearm (alpha) and significant use of elbow flexion and extension (phi), in contrast to the sinusoidal modulation seen in normals. When the task so demands ("key"), he is unable to stabilize the proximal (shoulder joint).

An analysis of the spatiotemporal aspects of the movement (relationship

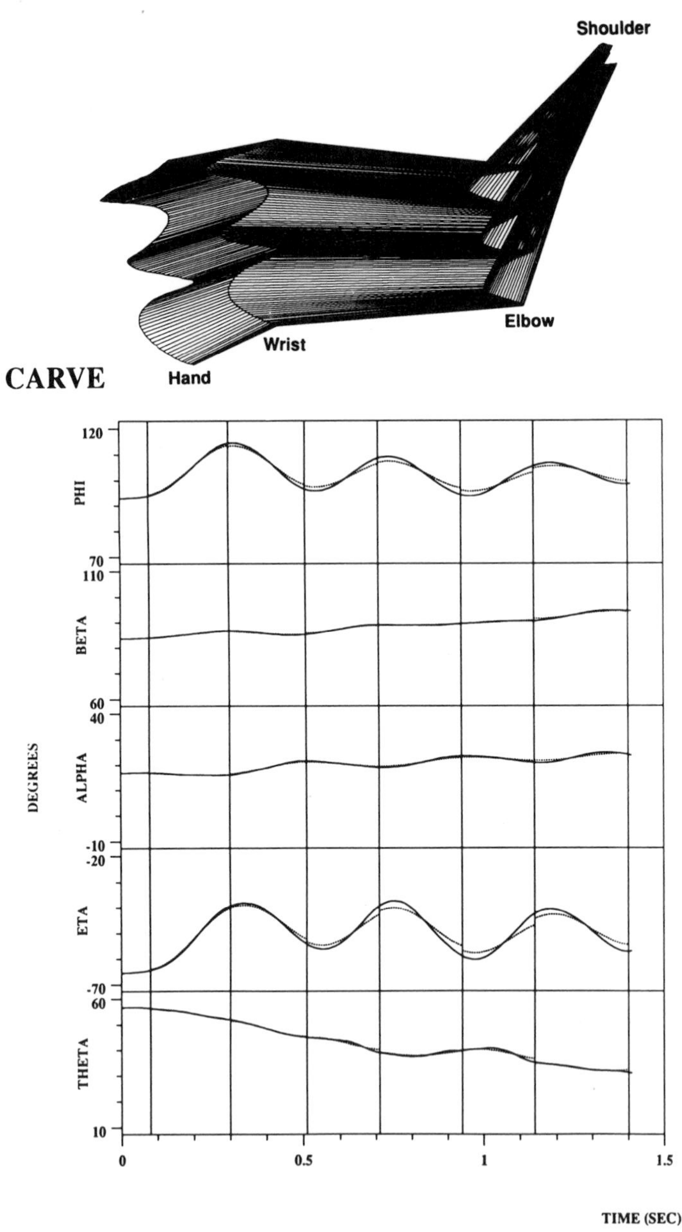

Figure 15-11 Reconstructed trajectories for the gesture CARVE for a control subject and for Apraxic BH are shown in the upper panel. For clarity, every other sampled arm position is shown in the reconstructed trajectory of Apraxic BH. Variation of arm angles over time is shown in the lower panel. Vertical lines define computed segment boundaries for the movements over which sine waves were fit to the data. The solid lines represent the data, and the dotted lines the fitted curves. Note the good match between the data and the fitted curves.

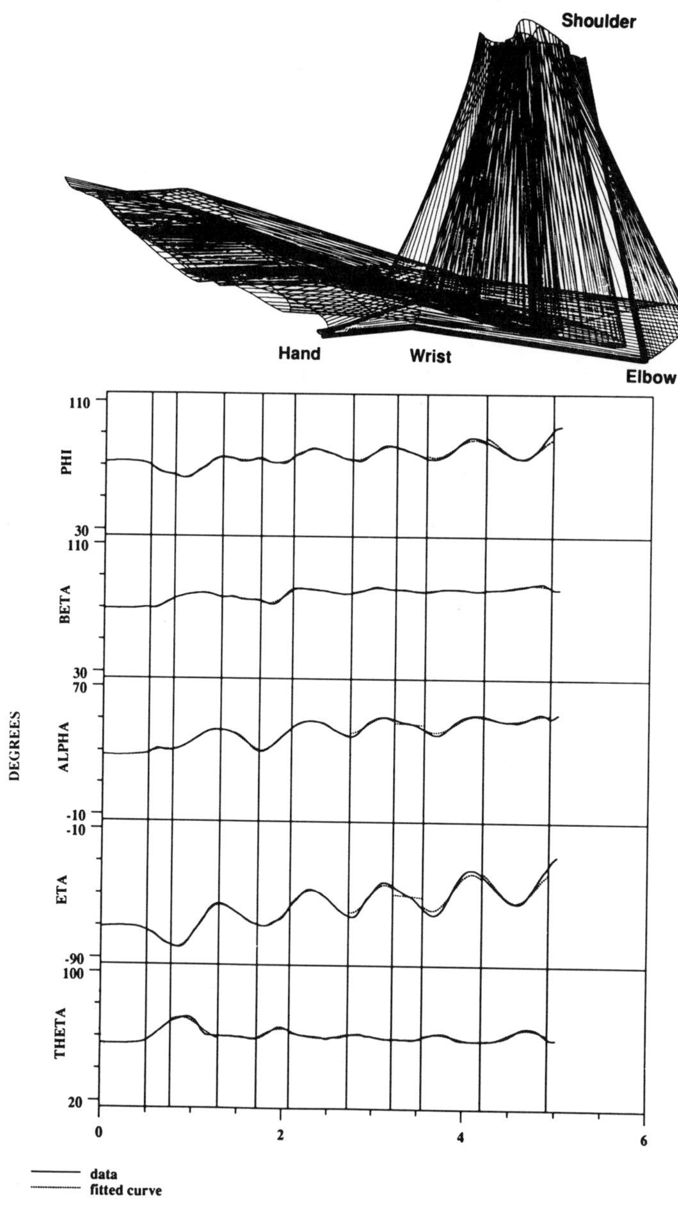

APRAXIC BH

Figure 15-11 *(Continued)*

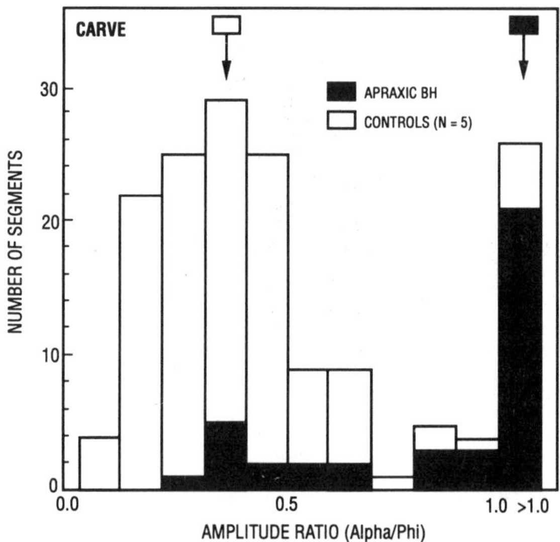

Figure 15-12 Relative amplitudes of forearm yaw to elbow flexion and extension, across all segments and replications of the gesture CARVE for Apraxic BH versus the control subjects. Arrows provide median amplitude ratios. Note that Apraxic BH apportions the arm angles in different relative amplitudes than the control subjects.

between hand speed and curvature) revealed deficits in this aspect of the motion as well. The coupling that normally occurs between velocity and curvature may serve to simplify the programming and representation of movement, since these spatial and temporal characteristics can be coded in a single representation (Lacquaniti, 1989). The decoupling of velocity and curvature shown by Apraxic BH shows that this relationship cannot be a physical law. Rather, this decoupling seems to be due to a fractionation of the representations of movement, consistent with a model of apraxia in which the movement execution deficits derive from destruction of visuokinesthetic spatial representations of learned movement (Heilman & Rothi, 1985). The simulation studies presented here indicated that the decoupling between speed and curvature could result if successive movement segments were not joined together in the proper manner.

To summarize then, our analysis of the performance of the apraxic subject suggests that individual segments of the movement were not oriented properly in space and that they may also not have been joined together properly. Such a deficit could arise if the subject had a spatial plan of movement which was incompletely or inappropriately specified. Such a spatial plan of movement would include parameters such as the amplitude of the movement at the wrist, the plane in which it was to be performed and the path the movement was to take, as well as the speed and the frequency with which it was to be performed. However, these same deficits could also arise if the spatial plan of movement were normal but the rules used to effect the movement were deficient or incomplete. Such rules are needed to translate the plan of the movement into the details of angular motion at each of the joints of the arm, and into the pattern of activation of each of the arm's muscles. Since Apraxic BH showed joint-specific deficits, being more impaired in the use of distal than proximal joints, as well as spatiotemporal deficits in hand trajectories, this apraxic subject appears to have deficits both in spatial planning (representation), and in transforming such plans into the proper kinematic patterns.

The methodology we have presented for studying apraxia provides a quantitative rather than just a qualitative analysis, and can help us begin to measure quantitatively the breakdown in motor programming in apraxia and in other motor disorders. Such analyses should not only advance our understanding of the neural basis of motor behavior, but also should serve as a useful clinical tool in evaluating motor disorders. For example, these procedures should allow the early detection of movement disorders which might otherwise go undetected until the disorder was more advanced. They should also allow discovery of new subclassifications of disorders that might otherwise remain unrecognized. Moreover, these methods should allow development of a reliable method for measuring the effects of drug or surgical treatment of diseases which affect the motor systems of the brain. Finally, the better we understand the nature of a disorder, the better we can design therapies to remediate it. By applying these methods to apraxia and other neural disorders of movement, we can begin to provide a new perspective on neural processes underlying spatial planning and movement execution.

ACKNOWLEDGMENTS

This work was supported in part by National Institutes of Health Grants NS 28665, and NS 25149, and by National Science Foundation Grant BNS-9000407 to Rutgers University. Dr. Kenneth Heilman and Dr. Leslie Rothi are collaborators in our studies of apraxia. We thank Dr. Mark Kritchevsky for helpful comments on the review of the motor systems.

NOTE

1. Commercial systems such as the WATSMART system of Northern Digital, Inc. use a similar principle of position sensing and provide excellent capabilities for three-dimensional data acquisition. The address of Northern Digital, Inc. is 403 Albert Street, Waterloo, Canada, N2L3V2.

REFERENCES

Andersen, R. A. (1989). Visual and eye movement functions of the posterior parietal cortex. *Ann. Rev. Neurosci.*, *12*, 377–403.

Andersen, R. A., & Zipser, D. (1988). The role of the posterior parietal cortex in coordinate transformations for visual-moor integration. *Canadian Journal of Physiology*, *66*, 488–501.

Brinkman, C. (1981). Lesions in supplementary motor area interfere with a monkey's performance of a bimanual coordination task. *Neuroscience Letters*, *27*, 267–270.

Brooks, V. B., & Thach, W. T. (1981). Cerebellar Control of Posture and Movement. In J. M. Brookhart, V. B. Mountcastle, V. B. Brooks & S. R. Geiger (Eds.), *Handbook of Physiology: The Nervous System, Vol. II, Motor Control* (pp. 877–946). Bethesda, MD: American Physiological Society.

Damasio, A., & Van Hoesen, G. W. (1980). Structure and function of the supplementary motor cortex. *Neurology*, *30*, 359.

DeLong, M. R., & Georgopoulos, A. P. (1981). Motor fnctions of the basal ganglia. In V. B. Brooks (Ed.), *Handbook of Physiology—The Nervous System, Vol. II, Motor Control, Part 2*. Bethesda, MD: American Physiological Society.

Edelman, G. M., Gall, W. E., & Cowan, W. M. (Eds.) (1984). *Dynamic Aspects of Neonatal Function*. New York: John Wiley & Sons.

Evarts, E. V. (1967). Representation of movements and muscles by pyramidal tract neuron of the precentral cortex. In M.D. Yahr & D.P. Purpura, (Eds.), *Neurophysiological basis of normal and abnormal motor activities* (pp. 215–250). Hewlett, NY: Raven Press.

Faux, I. P., & Pratt, M. J. (1979). *Computational geometry for design and manufacture*. Chichester: Ellis Horwood (John Wiley & Sons).

Fetz, E. E., & Cheney, P. D. (1980). Post-spike dacilitation of forelimb muscle activity by primate corticomotoneuronal cells. *Journal of Neurophysiology*, *44*, 751–772.

Flowers, K. A. (1975). Ballistic and corrective movements on an aiming task: Intention tremor and Parkinsonian movement disorders compared. *Neurology*, *25*, 413–21.

Flowers, K. A. (1976). Visual 'Closed-Loop' and 'Open-Loop' Characteristics of Voluntary Movements in Patients with Parkinsonism and Intention Tremor. *Brain*, *99*, 269–310.

Fox, P. T., Fox, J. M., Raichle, M. E., & Burde, R. M. (1985). The role of cerebral cortex in the generation of voluntary saccades: A positron emission tomographic study. *Journal of Neurophysiology*, *54*, 348–369.

Gel'fand, I. M., Furfinkel, V. S., Tsetlin, M. L., & Shik, M. L. (1971). Some problems in the analysis of movements. In I. M. Gel'fand, V. S. Gurfinkel, S. V. Fromin & M. L. Tsetlin (Eds.), *Models of the structural-functional organization of certain biological systems* (pp. 329–345). Cambridge, MA: MIT Press.

Georgopoulos, A. P. (1986). On reaching. *Annual Review of Neuroscience*, *9*, 147–170.

Georgopoulos, A. P., Schwartz, A. B., & Kettner, R. E. (1986). Neural coding of movement direction. *Science*, *233*, 1416–1419.

Geschwind, N., & Damasio, A. R. (1985). Apraxia. In J. A. M. Frederiks, (Ed.), *Handbook of Clinical Neurology*, *Vol. 1, 45*, (pp. 423–432).

Ghez, C., & Fahn, S. (1985). The Cerebellum. In E. Kandel & J. H. Swartz (Eds.), *Principles of Neural Science* (pp. 502–522). New York: Elsevier.

Haaland, K. Y., & Flaherty, D. (1984). The different types of limb apraxia errors made by patients with left or right hemisphere damage. *Brain and Cognition*, *3*, 370–384.

Hallett, M., & Khoshbin, S. (1980). A physiological mechanism of bradykinesia. *Brain*, *103*, 301–314.

Heilman, K. M. (1979). Apraxia. In K. M. Heilman & E. Valenstein (Eds.), *Clinical Neuropsychology* (pp. 159–185). New York: Oxford.

Heilman, K. M., & Rothi, L. J. G. (1985). Apraxia. In K. M. Heilman & E. Valenstein (Eds.), *Clinical Neuropsychology, Ed. 2* (pp. 131–147). New York: Oxford.

Holmes, G. (1939). The cerebellum of man. *Brain*, *62*, 1–31.

Humphrey, D. R. (1986). Representation of movements and muscles within the primate precentral motor cortex: Historical and current prospective. *Federal Proceedings*, *45*, 2687–2699.

Ivry, R. I., & Keele, S. W. (1989). Timing functions of the cerebellum. *Cognitive Neuroscience*, *1*: 134–150.

Jennings, P., & Poizner, H. (1988). Computergraphic modeling and analysis II: Three-dimensional reconstruction and interactive analysis." *Journal of Neuroscience Methods*, *24*, 45–55.

Kalsaka, J. F., Cohen, D. A. D., Hyde, M. L., & Prud'homme, M. (1989). A comparison of movement direction-related versus load direction-related activity in primate motor cortex, using a two-dimensional reaching task, *Journal of Neuroscience*, *9*, 2080–2102.

Lacquaniti, F. (1989). Central representations of human limb movement as revealed by studies of drawing and handwriting. *Trends in Neurosciences*, *12*, 287–291.

Margolin, D. I., & Wing, A. M. (1983). Agraphia and micrographia: Clinical manifestations of motor programming and performance disorders. *Acta Psychologica*, *54*, 263–283.

Marsden, C. D. (1982). The mysterious motor function of the basal ganglia. *Neurology*, *32*, 514–539.

Morasso, P. (1981). Spatial control of arm movements. *Experimental Brain Research*, *42*, 223–227.

Morasso, P. (1983). Three-dimensional arm trajectories. *Biological Cybernetics*, *48*, 187–194.

Morasso, P., & Mussa Ivaldi, F. A. (1982). Trajectory formation and handwriting: A computational model. *Biological Cybernetics*, *45*, 131–142.

Morasso, P., & Tagliasco, V. (Eds.) (1986). *Human movement understanding: From computational geometry to artificial intelligence*. Amsterdam: North Holland.

Poizner, H., Kritchevsky, M., O'Grady, L., & Bellugi, U. (October 1988). Disturbed prosody in a Parkinsonian signer. Academy of Aphasia, Montreal.

Poizner, H., Mack, L., Verfaellie, M., Rothi, L., & Heilman, K. (1990). Three-dimensional computergraphic analysis of apraxia: Neural representations of learned movement. *Brain*, *113*, 85–101.

Poizner, H., Soechting, J. S., Bracewell, M., Rothi, L. J., & Heilman, K. M. (1989). Disruption of hand and joint kinematics in limb apraxia. *Society for Neuroscience Abstracts*, *15*, 481.

Poizner, H., Figel, T., Rothi, L. J., & Heilman, K. M. (1989). Timing deficits in limb apraxia. *Journal of clinical and experimental neuropsychology*, *12*, 89.

Poizner, H., Wooten, E., Salot, D. (1986). Computergraphic modeling and analysis: A portable system for tracking arm movements in three-dimensional space. *Behavior Research Methods, Instruments, & Computers*, *18*, 427–433.

Rizzolatti, G. (1987). Functional organization of inferior area 6. In G. Bock, M. O'Connor & J. Marsh, (Eds.), *Motor areas of the cerebral cortex* (pp. 171–186). Chichester: Wiley (Ciba Foundation Symposium 132).

Roland, P. E., Larsen, B., Lassen, N. A., & Skinhoj, E. (1980a). Supplementary motor area and other cortical areas in organization of voluntary movements in man. *Journal of Neurophysiology*, *43*, 118–136.

Roland, P. E., Meyer, E., Shibaski, T., Yamamoto, Y. L., & Thompson, C. J. (1982). Regional cerebral blood flow changes in cortex and basal ganglia during voluntary movements in normal human volunteers. *Journal of Neurophysiology*, *48*, 467–478.

Roland, P. E., Skinhoj, E., Lassen, N. A., & Larsen, B. (1980b). Different cortical areas in man in organization of voluntary movements in extrapersonal space. *Journal of Neurophysiology*, *43*, 137–150.

Rothi, L. J. G., Mack, L., Verfaellie, M., Brown, P., & Heilman, K. M. (1988). Ideomotor apraxia: Error pattern analysis. *Aphasiology*, *2*, 381–388.

Soechting, J. F. (1983). Kinematics and dynamics of the human arm. *Laboratory of Neurophysiology Report*, Minneapolis, MN: University of Minnesota.

Soechting, J. F., Lacquaniti, F., & Terzuolo, C. A. (1986). Coordination of arm movements in three-dimensional space. Sensorimotor mapping during drawing movement. *Neuroscience*, *17*(2), 295–311.

Soechting, J. F., & Ross, B. (1984). Psychophysical determination of coordinate representation of human arm orientation. *Neuroscience*, *13*, 595–604.

Soechting, J. F., & Terzuolo, C. A. (1987). Organization of arm movements. Motion is segmented. *Neuroscience*, *23*, 39–52; 53–61.

Stein, J. F. (1986). Role of the cerebellum in the visual guidance of movement. *Nature*, *323*, 217–221.

Viviani, P., & Terzuolo, C. (1982). Trajectory Determines Movement Dynamics. *Neuroscience*, *7*(2), 431–437.

Watson, R. T., Fleet, W. S., Rothi, L. G., & Heilman, K. M. (1986). Apraxia and the supplemental motor area. *Archives of Neurology*, *43*, 787–792.

Wiesendanger, M. (1981). Organization of secondary motor areas of cerebral cortex. In J. M. Brookhart, V. B. Mountcastle, V. B. Brooks & S. R. Geiger (Eds.), *Handbook of Physiology, Vol. II, Motor Control, Part 2*. Bethesda, MD: American Physiological Society.

Wiesendanger, M., Seguin, J. J., & Kunzle, H. (1973). The supplementary motor area: A control system for posture? In R. B. Stein, K. C. Pearson, R. S. Smith & J. B. Redford (Eds.), *Control of posture and locomotion* (pp. 331–346). New York: Plenum.

Wise, S. P. (1984). The nonprimary motor cortex and its role in the cerebral control of movement. In G. M. Edelman, W. E. Gall & W. M. Cowan (Eds.), *Dynamic aspects of neocortical function* (pp. 525–556). New York: John Wiley & Sons.

Woltring, H. J. (1984). On methodology in the study of human movement. In H. T. A. Whiting (Eds.), *Human motor actions–Bernstein reasessed*. Amsterdam, Elseiver.

16

Neuropsychological Rehabilitation of Musicians and Other Artists

TEDD JUDD

How can we use what we currently know about neuropsychology in general and neuropsychology of the arts in particular to help brain-damaged artists? Perhaps the most important thing we can do is to not assume that we know very much. Considerable literature exists on the effects of brain damage on musical (Critchley & Henson, 1977; Judd, 1988; Marin, 1982; Wertheim, 1969) and artistic (Gardner, 1982; Schweiger, 1988) abilities. Likewise, there is a fairly large literature on the uses of music and art modalities as therapy in rehabilitation from brain injury (Anderson, 1977; Gaston 1968; *The Journal of Art Therapy; The Journal of Music Therapy*). There is also considerable writing on the general process of rehabilitation from brain injury (Prigatano, 1986; Sohlberg & Mateer, 1989; Uzzell & Gross, 1986). However, very little has been written about methods of facilitating the recovery of musical and artistic abilities in brain damaged musicians and artists (Nagler & Lee, 1987). Furthermore, there is relatively little research on the ecological validity of our methods of neuropsychological assessment (Hart & Hayden, 1986), and even less with respect to the arts.

This chapter is a summary of personal clinical observations and experiences in attempting to facilitate the recovery of special talents in musicians and artists who have sustained brain damage. While most of my experience is with musicians and graphic artists, I expect that much of what I have to say will also apply to writers, film makers, dancers, crafts people, and others working in creative media. Throughout this paper I will refer to all of these people by the generic term "artists".

The neuropsychological rehabilitation of artistic abilities is ideally just one component of a fully integrated rehabilitation program. Most aspects of such a program need not be specially adapted to accommodate the artist. The proper assessment and treatment of the artistic abilities themselves, however, often require creativity which builds upon but extends beyond standard assessments. This challenge is perhaps most keenly felt in the rehabilitation disciplines of neuropsychology, occupational therapy, therapeutic recreation, and speech pathology. Ideally the entire rehabilitation team can be called upon to address specifically the artistic needs. Several recent symposia (Roehmann & Wilson, 1988; the annual Medical Problems of Musicians and Dancers Symposium at the

Aspen Music Festival) and a new journal (*Medical Problems of Performing Artists*) have addressed the recently developed subspecialty of medicine for performing artists.

COGNITIVE NEUROPSYCHOLOGY OF MUSIC

Music is quite possibly the art which has received the most attention from cognitive psychologists and neuropsychologists alike. It also appears to be in this realm that the most progress has been made. Nevertheless, even in music it is still premature to attempt to advance any but the crudest of cognitive neuropsychological models (Judd, 1988). Two recent and excellent books reviewing psychomusicology (Dowling & Hardwood, 1986; Sloboda, 1985) do not contain models except within specialized areas such as the cognitive representation of pitch. Lerdahl and Jackendoff[1] (1983) have made the most successful attempt to date to produce a generative grammar for tonal music. This work has not yet been adequately developed through cognitive psychomusicology to allow for its practical application in clinical neuropsychology.

Shuter-Dyson and Gabriel (1982, p. 72) have produced a preliminary cognitive model of musical abilities. They first differentiate auditory, kinesthetic, and visual factors at both the sensory and perceptual levels. At the perceptual level they also add in a perceptual speed factor. Still within the realm of music, they make the familiar distinction between short-term and long-term memory. At the next level of organization, they distinguish between fluid and crystallized musical abilities. Crystallized abilities are stored knowledge of music and overlearned or automatized musical activities. Fluid musical abilities are those which require flexibility or adaptation in the application of musical knowledge and skills in the present. Above this level, they speak of a general musical organization ability related to general intelligence. They have made preliminary attempts to decribe how individual differences in musical ability relate to this model (pp. 82–84). For example, the highly talented musician would have developed exceptional skills in all of these areas except at the sensory level. The musical, retarded savant would have normal or exceptional perceptual and memory skills for music, but impairments in general intelligence and fluid musical abilities. This model can be regarded as a useful preliminary heuristic, incorporating many familiar neuropsychological distinctions.

For the purposes of relating music to other clinical neuropsychological concepts, it may be most useful to turn to a framework proposed by Gardner (1983). Gardner divides many of the cognitive functions that are usually delineated in a clinical neuropsychological report into "horizontal" and "vertical" functions. The "horizontal" functions include attention, memory, executive functions (initiation, planning, executing plans, error correction, judgment, etc.), and emotions. They are "horizontal" because changes or impairments in any of these will tend to affect all of the vertical functions fairly equally. The "vertical" functions include language, mathematics, visuospatial functions, music, kinesthetic skills, and two types of social skills. These are Gardner's "intelligences" in his theory of multiple intelligences, and also correspond roughly to Fodor's

(1983) mental modules. These "vertical" functions may be fairly separably impaired with localized cortical damage.

One cannot press this framework too far and expect it to serve without many exceptions. For example, localized cortical damage can produce somewhat module-specific or modality-specific impairments in attention and memory, as with unilateral inattention. It is also possible to split the functions further, subdividing language functions into expressive and receptive, for example, or dividing memory into procedural and declarative. Other special skills can also be added to the framework, such as the wine taster's art. Nevertheless, this framework will serve the purposes of this chapter.

Most people who have difficulties with music due to brain damage do not have a specifically musical deficit. Instead they may have impairments in attention or memory or visual perception or kinesthetic skills that affect some aspects of their musical behavior. The cognitive model needed to plan rehabilitation for these patients, then, will not be just a specifically musical model; more general neuropsychological models of cognitive processes, such as Gardner's (1983) model described above or that of Luria (1966) are also relevant.

A number of schema have been proposed for describing the component skills of musical activities (Feuchtwanger, 1930; Marin, 1982; Seashore, 1938). In spite of considerable research, however, these schema have not yet received full empirical support. Factor analytic studies of normals have usually focussed on music perception of Western tonal music. These studies suggest separate factors of pitch discrimination, tonal memory, rhythmic abilities, and comprehension of complex relationships such as harmony and form (Shuter-Dyson & Gabriel, 1981). Neuropsychological case studies lend some support to these dissociations. Music perception and production can be somewhat dissociated in brain damaged patients, and rhythm can be dissociated from pitch-timbre relationships. Music reading functions can be impaired separately from other musical skills, but other visual functions including language reading are usually also impaired (Benton, 1977; Judd, 1988; Marin, 1982).

Among those components of musical abilities with some empirical basis, the more complex pitch-timbre capacities, tonal memory, and the comprehension of harmony and form appear most likely to be at the core of "musical intelligence" (Judd, 1988; Serafine, 1988; Shuter-Dyson & Gabriel, 1981). Rhythmic abilities are also critical musical skills, but they are also shared with other kinesthetic skills such as dance. Clearly, however, musical activities also involve many other skills both "horizontal" and "vertical."

In the absence of well developed and tested general cognitive models of neuropsychology or of specific artistic skills it may be necessary at times to generate ad hoc models for the purposes of assisting an impaired artist. Suppose we have a patient, for example, who has difficulty singing "Happy Birthday" with a crowd of people. The crude model given in Figure 16-1 can help us to figure out where this activity may have gone wrong. For example, we can test the auditory system by inquiring from the patient about changes in hearing abilities, by audiometry, and by testing basic functions such as pitch discrimination either informally or with commercially available educational tests of musical abilities (e.g. Gordon, 1965; Seashore 1960). We can test vocal production

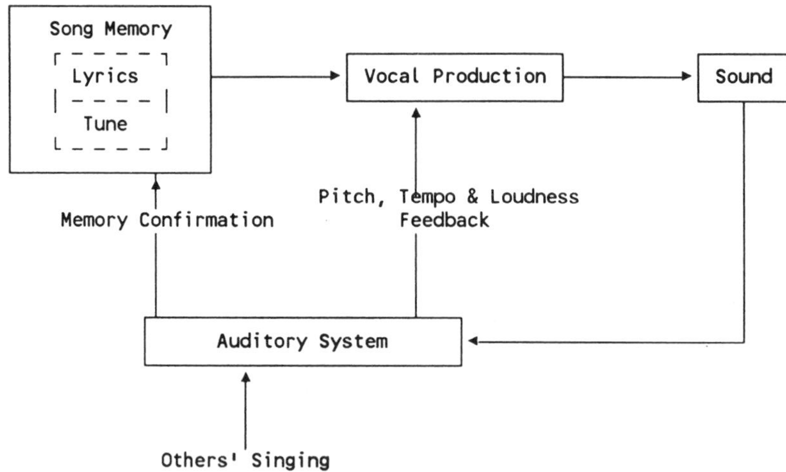

Figure 16-1 Ad hoc model of processes involved in group singing of a familiar song.

by asking the patient and others about any changes they have noticed in the patient's voice and by having the patient sing alone. We can test song memory by asking them to sing "Happy Birthday," and we can look at the separate components by having them hum the melody and then recite the words. We can further test song memory by singing it ourselves, introducing intentional errors, and asking if they were detected. We can check the ability to adapt to other's singing by asking that the patient sing along with us. We can check this feedback loop in an alternative way through musical repetition tests.

Without adequate knowledge of neuropsychology, however, such a model could lead us astray. For example, all of these systems could be reasonably intact, yet the patient's failure may have come from impaired attention. Or it may have been thrown off by having to figure out how to insert the proper name into the song. Or the particular circumstance of the singing may have induced reflex crying or some other emotional reaction making it impossible to sing. Finally, the patient may have been "impaired" in a technical sense, yet their singing may have been entirely acceptable personally in the particular social circumstances, and so there may be no disability to rehabilitate.

MUSIC AND LANGUAGE

A brief comparison of music and language will also help to define the neuropsychological nature of music. For most of the history of neuromusicology, music has been viewed as a sort of special case of language, and terms like "musical aphasia" (Edgren, 1895) and "the musical language" (Dupre & Nathan, 1911) were common. The metaphor has often obscured more than it illuminated, however. Attempts were made to find forms of *amusia* (acquired musical deficits) corresponding to each of the aphasia syndromes in a system of aphasia syndromes that we are coming to find less and less useful. Rather than arguing that music

Table 16-1 Music and Language: Similarities and Differences

Similarities	
Uniquely and universally human vocal-auditory communication system	
Transformational grammar structure	
Categorical perception of basic elements	
Can be written and read	
Differences	
Language	*Music*
Typically turn-taking among communicators	Typically simultaneous participation
Typically spontaneous and improvised	Typically preset (memorized or read)
Relatively homogeneous distribution of ability in the population	Relatively heterogeneous distribution of abilities & skills in the population
Semantics	Emotional significance
	Use of scale, use of beat, & use of instruments

is or is not a language, I will quickly review major similarities and differences between music and language. These are summarized in Table 16-1.

Similarities

So far as we know music and language are both uniquely and universally human forms of vocal-auditory communication (Sloboda, 1985). Challenges to the unique claim come primarily from attempts to teach language to apes, and from bird song and whale song which show a number of music-like properties.[2] The claim of universality applies not to all humans (since many individuals lack minimal musical understanding, and there are, after all, aphasics and congenitally non-verbal people who are quite human), but to all human cultures. This claim has not been seriously challenged in the ethnomusicology literature. Although typically auditory, language certainly is not necessarily auditory, as in sign languages and writing. The same may be true of music, but this claim must await more careful evaluation of the nature of the sometimes excellent musical performance of the deaf (Cleall, 1983; Edwards, 1974; Hood, 1977), and perhaps studies of the mental processes of composers (Sloboda, 1985).

Mental representations of language and music are hierarchial and can be described by generative grammars. The argument for generative grammars for language is classic (Chomsky, 1957). The most convincing case so far for a generative grammar structure to music has been made by Lerdahl and Jackendoff (1983). It may be this characteristic that makes both language and music universally and uniquely human. Understanding the ways in which music has a transformational grammar may help us to understand the cognitive and neurological underpinnings of this process, as well as aspects of cerebral plasticity and development. Neurologically normal individuals who have not developed music are fairly common and give us a wide selection of natural experiments with which to study cerebral plasticity and the development of transformational grammarlike cognitive processes (Judd, 1988). Neurologically normal individuals who have not developed language, by contrast, are extremely rare.

While music and language may share a formal structure of cognitive representation, they do not always share a cortical structure of cognitive representation. This is perhaps most clearly demonstrated by several cases of aphasic composers who continued their craft (Bouillaud, 1865; Judd, Gardner, & Geschwind, 1983; Luria, Tsvetkova, & Futer, 1965), as well as a nonaphasic composer with right hemisphere damage who lost some but not all aspects of his craft (Judd, 1988).

Although speech and singing share the vocal apparatus, cortical control of those functions appears to diverge in many cases. Nonfluent aphasics who can sing have been frequently observed, and loss of singing with preserved speech has also been reported (Botez & Wertheim, 1959; Mann, 1898). Similarly, there have been dissociations of language and music perception reported with unilateral temporal lobe lesions (Marin, 1982).

In certain experimental contexts, it has been found that stimuli which differ slightly from one another along some particular dimension are not perceived as slightly different along a continuum but are perceived as belonging to distinct categories ("categorical perception").[3] This is true for many speech consonants (Harnad, 1987), for the bowed versus plucked sound of a string instrument (Cutting & Rosner, 1974), for musical chords (Locke & Kellar, 1973), and for musical intervals (Burns & Ward, 1982). It may also be true for rhythmic intervals (Sloboda, 1985).

Both language and music can be written and read. These graphic symbol systems representing sounds and the actions needed to produce them have many features in common, but they also typically differ greatly in the forms of representation used, the functions of the notational systems, and the neurological substrates serving them (Judd, Gardner, & Geschwind, 1983).

Differences

Although both language and music have many uses, their typical uses are quite different. The prototype of language use is conversation, two or more people saying things to each other, taking turns, in a spontaneous and improvised way. While a prototype example of music is perhaps less clear, it more likely involves several people making music at once with a song or piece or structure predetermined and memorized (or read). The prototype of language use readily lends itself to an information-processing approach which looks at how a message is sent from one person to another.

The prototype of music can be less readily analyzed in this way. Each participant is both a sender and receiver of messages more or less simultaneously, and each mostly already knows what the message is. Transferring information often is not the major point of the activity. With increasing stratification of society and with the electronic age, this prototype of musical activity has become less common (Lomax, 1968). The roles of sender and receiver have become more specialized. Most of the studies of the psychology and neuropsychology of music have incorporated the concept of separate roles of sender and receiver, and an information-processing approach has dominated (Dowling & Harwood, 1986). In this approach, the typical experiment in music perception plays unfamiliar quasimusical acoustic stimuli to subjects and tries to determine what differences they can discriminate or what similarities, groupings, or structures they perceive. The typical experiment in music production studies the relationship between the musician's intended production and the acoustic result.

This approach has produced many valuable results but it is limited in scope. When this paradigm predominates it advances unstated implications that the acoustic signal of music conveys a message, and that when we have cracked the code we will understand the true meaning of the music. To take this one step further, when we have a computer that can take an acoustic performance of a piece of music and transform it into a musical score and then a Schenkerian[4] analysis of that score and back again, the job will be done. This paradigm seeks explanations for musical phenomena in characteristics of the individual. It seeks to explain why music is the way it is based on the nature of the auditory, motor, nervous, and cognitive systems.

A complementary but under-utilized approach is to look at the communication and social functions of music to see how they have influenced music's cognitive and acoustic properties. This approach can begin with the simultaneity and predetermination of the prototypical musical event as described above which distinguishes musical communication from language. From this perspective it appears likely that music has developed fixed scales and rhythmic beats as mechanisms of coordination and memory which facilitate the simultaneity of music making. Research from this perspective explores the social and communicative functions of music (Blacking, 1976; Lomax, 1968) and the processes of keeping the beat, staying in tune, and memorizing music (Sloboda, 1988).

The simultaneity of musicmaking is also of potential neuropsychological significance. In my experience, patients with difficulty initiating, particularly aphasics, can often sing well with others but not alone, a feature of music which has been exploited in melodic intonation therapy for aphasia (Sparks, Helm, & Albert, 1974). By contrast, patients with self-monitoring difficulties, most notably those with right frontal damage, may sing alone reasonably well, but may be unable to match pitch or tempo when singing with others. These same patient groups are also likely to differ in their ability to respond to the pragmatics and social norms of conversation. The aphasics may be able to indicate the proper place to respond, while the patients with poor monitoring may talk excessively, interrupt, and in other ways derail the conversation.

Both the information processing and the social communication perspectives are needed in approaching the rehabilitation of the neuropsychologically impaired musician. The information processing perspective can help to identify the deficits and strengths (*how* the patient does music), while the social communication approach can help identify the priorities and alternatives for rehabilitation (*why* the patient does music).

The major purpose of language is semantics or the communication of ideas or meaning. A corresponding main purpose for music is much less clear. Perhaps the primary component is communication of emotion. But that communication is not simply conveying information from one person to another, as if a piece of music were a very inefficient way for a composer or performer to say to an audience, "I feel joy, pain, fear, anger, etc." Rather, it is also more experiential, as if the message is, "Here is what it feels like; you feel it, too," or, "We are doing joy together." Thus, music's emotional signficance takes many forms, which have been categorized as index, icon, and symbol (Dowling & Harwood, 1986), or as formal and referential (Meyer, 1956). Since psychologists and music theorists have not yet made much progress in measuring these various forms of musical meaning, the neuropsychologist's work in this area must necessarily remain largely subjective for the moment.

RESEARCH ON THE CLINICAL NEUROPSYCHOLOGY OF THE ARTS

Music

There is an extensive research literature on the clinical neuropsychology of music which extends back more than a century (see Benton, 1977; Judd, 1988; Marin, 1982; Ustvedt, 1937; and Wertheim, 1969 for reviews). Briefly stated, the major findings of this literature are:

1. The lateralization of musical skills is quite variable and appears to depend upon the type of skill, the individual's experience, training and handedness, and unknown variables.
2. Specific acquired impairments of musical abilities from focal damage are frequently but not always dissociated from acquired impairments of language and other abilities.
3. Receptive and expressive musical abilities can be somewhat dissociated by focal lesions.
4. Lesions in the inferior posterior frontal lobe, especially on the right, often impair pitch in singing.
5. Temporal lobe lesions, particularly on the right, sometimes impair music perception and memory.
6. Certain aspects of music learning appear to involve procedural memory and are dissociated from anterograde amnesias for declarative memory.
7. Damage just about anywhere in the brain can produce impairments in some musical activities, usually in ways typical of the nonmusical effects of a lesion in the given area.
8. Exceptional musical memory appears to be a fairly reliable companion to exceptional musical skill.

The literature also suggests the possibility that the parts of the brain used in any particular musical task may depend upon the nature of the task, the individual's level of expertise in different types of skills, and the strategies employed. The literature makes clear that there are many different types of musical activities and that there are multiple valid strategies or approaches for carrying out most of these activities. While many musical activities are highly complex and probably employ maximum capacities of many different areas of the brain, and are thus quite fragile to brain injury, the variety of strategies and approaches available suggest that the skilled musician can often find alternative or compensatory approaches to many musical tasks. The clinical conclusions of all of this are that it is very hazardous to attempt to predict musical impairments on the basis of known lesion sites or from the results of a standard neuropsychological assessment.

Other Arts

Drawing is a standard part of most neuropsychological assessments (Kimura & Faust, 1987; Lezak, 1983). Nevertheless, the neuropsychology of advanced graphic arts is less well developed, consisting mostly of case studies (Alajouanine, 1948; Ball, 1983; Gardner, 1982; Jung, 1974; Schweiger, 1988; Wapner, Judd, & Gardner, 1978; Zaimov, Kitov, & Kolev, 1969). From these cases some obvious conclusions emerge. Visual perceptual impairments such as those resulting from right parietal occipital lesions (Schweiger, 1988), left neglect (Jung, 1974), and visual agnosia (Wapner, Judd, and Gardner, 1978), significantly impair expression in the graphic arts. Nevertheless, in each of these cases the resilience of artistic abilities through compensating skills was also evident. For example, the visual agnosic was able to use his retained abilities in the principles of representational drawing to copy, with fair accuracy, objects and drawings he was unable to recognize. Similarly, Schweiger's patient with visual spatial impairments was able to direct projects in fashion design in spite of an inability to draw in three dimensions, and Jung's artist with left neglect continued painting in an expressionistic style, albeit mostly on the right side of the canvas. Thus, as with music, there is much individual variation, and there are many compensatory strategies. It is therefore also hazardous to predict artistic impairments based on lesion locus and the results of standard neuropsychological assessments.

The neuropsychology of other arts is even less well developed. Creative writing, for example, will obviously be compromised by aphasia (Alajouanine, 1948). Theatrical skills have also received scant attention, although some of this may have to do with our lack of knowledge, until recently, of the neuropsychology of emotional communication (Ross, 1981). It is because of this lack that I present the following brief account of the experiences of a prominent man of the theater, although this is based only on observations of his performances, newspaper reviews, and personal conversations with him and not on clinical interviews or examinations.

Joseph Chaikin is an actor, director, playwright, and founder of the Open Theatre in New York. Among his many other honors he received an Obie Award for lifetime accomplishment. During open heart surgery in 1984, Chaikin suffered a stroke, leaving him with a persistent mild to moderate Broca's aphasia. Although he is able to recall the lines from parts he has played in the past, it is much more difficult for him to memorize new lines now. He is not able to deliver memorized material fluently whether old or new; he now reads his lines. In this way he is able to give a stunning performance. In the play "Struck Dumb," about his aphasia, which he co-authored with playwright Jean-Claude Van Itallie, he was able to make full use of tone of voice, timing, facial expression, and gesture. One critic wrote:

> The aphasia limits Chaikin's rhythm patterns; the effort of speech puts unusual stress on the beginnings of phrases. This rhythm could defeat a lesser actor, but Chaikin gives it an incantatory power. Using the vocal options open to him, he creates an oral world that envelopes and compels . . .
>
> The aphasia, if anything, has increased the mystery, the mischievous quality of Chaikin's presence. He has even adapted his jokes to a kind of shorthand, and his eyes and face fill in the expressive details far better than mere words ever could: "My doctors say . . . I say . . . poetry better than . . . sentences." (Hulbert, 1987).

Chaikin continues to teach and direct, now using more demonstration and less explanation. He has been able to collaborate on writing in an improvised process in which he and his co-author hammer out material on a word processor. Often Van Itallie suggests an expression of Chaikin's experience, and Chaikin then accepts, rejects, or modifies it.

Interestingly, Chaikin reported that, for the first two years after his stroke he experienced the increased crying or reflex crying common to stroke patients (Green, McAllister, & Bernat, 1987). Prior to his stroke, he had not developed the capacity to cry on demand which some actors have developed. After his stroke, he discovered that he was able to do this, although he did not choose to use it in his acting. Prior to his stroke, Chaikin had learned American Sign Language for use in the theatre. After his stroke, he found that he was aphasic for Sign as well as for spoken language. Chaikin's triumphant return to acting and directing is literally a dramatic demonstration of the neuropsychological dissociation of language from emotional communication (apparently mediated primarily by the right hemisphere, Ross, 1981). His performance in "Struck Dumb" communicates as much about the rehabilitation of artists as any article can.

We have seen that, for music and other arts, neither cognitive psychology nor clinical neuropsychology has yet produced either well-developed models of music or other arts or consistent empirical findings that could provide a solid foundation for rehabilitation. Nevertheless, these disciplines do provide general techniques as well as models and consistent empirical findings for related areas of skill which, when applied with sensitivity and creativity, can allow us a reasonable approach to the neuropsychological rehabilitation of musicians and other artists.

ASSESSMENT

Artistic History

Good assessments begin with thorough history taking, and this is particularly true for artistic abilities. An attempt should be made to determine not only *what* the patient's artistic activities were, but also *how* and *why* they were done.

What?

In determining *what* the patient's art is, it is important to know not only the patient's strongest or most characteristic artistic activities but also the breadth of the patient's work. Knowledge of the range of media and styles that the patient can work in can be very valuable in finding the most appropriate channels for rehabilitation efforts. There is no point in attempting an exhaustive typology of artistic endeavors here, since it would inevitably be incomplete, and since such a checklist would be far inferior to a directed clinical interview. Outlining the major dimensions of inquiry may, however, be an aid to the clinician. For musicians it is important to determine at least the instruments played (including voice), and whether there is skill at music reading, playing by ear, improvising, composing, arranging, conducting, critiquing, and/or teaching. For graphic artists, one should determine the media worked in (charcoals, oils, various sculpting materials, etc.), the subjects treated, and whether there is skill in teaching and/or critiquing. For writers, it will be important to know at least the forms used (prose, poetry, scripts, essays, etc.). In practice, for most patients the questions "What do you do (as an artist, musician, writer, etc.)?" and "What else do you do?" will probably suffice.

How?

The question of *how* involves styles, skill levels, settings, and habits. Artists will usually readily tell you about their *style* and teach you what you need to know about it, but often the artist may be an unreliable informant with regard to their own skill level. Formal markers such as arts education and commercial success are often only loosely associated with level of skill. It is therefore best to obtain examples of premorbid work whenever possible, and to consult other sources such as reviews of the patient's work and the observations of family members and artistic colleagues.

The artistic setting can, at times, be important to artistic rehabilitation, just as the work or home setting is important in other areas of rehabilitation because of wheelchair accessibility, distractions, appropriate equipment, etc. Examples are given below in the Fixed Approaches and Shifts in Style sections. In some cases a studio or rehearsal visit may be justified.

The artist's habits or approaches to the art can also give clues to approaches to rehabilitation. For example, does a musician read music, play by ear, and/or improvise? Does the artist work from a model, photographs, or imagination? Does the writer work systematically in a quiet environment for a certain time each day, or in spontaneous bursts of frenzied creativity?

Why?

It is especially important to determine *why* the artist engages in art. To understand what some of the motivations are is to understand better what is to be rehabilitated. At a minimum it is useful to know how the patient's art functions as a personal or emotional expression, as a personal identity, as recreation, as a career, and as a social activity.

Reviewing the reasons for doing/making art after a brain injury can sometimes lead the artist to take stock of the meanings of life in light of the injury.

Sometimes the need which artistic activity filled can be better met in a nonartistic way after the brain injury. Or sometimes the art can even take on a more important role as a substitute for something else. Assal (1973) reported a case, for example, of a bureaucrat who developed Wernicke's aphasia who then turned his amateur music into a career.

A proper historytaking can be psychotherapeutic in itself. It can be a life review of what is important and what is not important, of what may need to be rehabilitated and what may need to be grieved, and of what options remain.

Testing

In most cases conventional neuropsychological testing can provide a foundation for artistic testing. Neuropsychological test results, along with information from other rehabilitation team members, interview information, and behavioral observations, can be sources of hypotheses about artistic impairments. For example, a musician with the "horizontal" impairment of new learning deficits for verbal and visual spatial material secondary to anoxia might be hypothesized to have new learning deficits for musical material, as well. This patient can then be tested informally by having the patient attempt various musical activities, with special attention to the ability to learn new musical material. A patient with a "vertical" impairment such as an anomia might be expected to have difficulty in talking about music or art, but might be hypothesized to have no difficulties in doing those activities when language is not involved.

In the arts, as in other areas of neuropsychology, one of the corollaries of Murphy's Law[5] (Fox, 1982) and its reverse often apply. The corollary is: "If it goes right in the lab, it will go wrong in the field," and the reverse is "If it goes wrong in the lab, it will go right in the field." Particularly because our tests of executive function are not yet well refined, it is not uncommon to find that patients who do well on our tests do poorly in practical settings. This is why neuropsychologists in rehabilitation settings have learned that it is often wise to defer to nurses, occupational therapists, family members, and home visits on issues such as safety, ability to be left alone, and ability to drive. The reverse situation most often arises with elderly patients who function well in their familiar setting and routines, but adapt poorly to the neuropsychology laboratory. Other examples of the limits of ecological validity in neuropsychological testing are found in Hart and Hayden (1986).

It is for this reason that neuropsychological testing provides hypotheses and not answers about patient functioning in other settings. An artistic example comes from Wapner, Judd, & Gardner (1977). Our initial expectation had been that this artist's visual agnosia would have rendered him almost completely impaired as an artist. This was essentially true for drawing to command without models present. Yet he was sometimes quite accurate in copying drawings and drawing real objects with models present, even when he could not even recognize the model. A musical example comes from Judd (1988). Because a church organist, Case CE, was able to resume her work after two bilateral cingulotomies, one might expect that music is not affected by this surgery. However, the patient KM had a great deal of difficulty learning new folk songs following cingulotomy, apparently due to impairment in learning complex procedures, a result of this surgery which was also demonstrated on nonmusical neuropsychological tests. CE presumably did not experience difficulties in her performance, because she was able to read her music and did not need to memorize it.

In the strictest sense there are no formal standardized neuropsychological tests of any artistic abilities. That is, there are no tests of any form of specifically artistic ability designed from a neuropsychological perspective, normed on an artistic population, and validated with a population of brain-damaged artists. It is also unlikely that there will be such tests in the foreseeable future, given the wide variety and level of artistic skills, the relatively small number of people that possess a common set of skills, and the high cost of test development. There are some tests of artistic component skills, particularly tests of drawing and of various musical skills, which have been developed mostly for educational purposes. These have been standardized on normal populations and in some instances on artists and musicians (see Shuter-Dyson & Gabriel, 1982, for a review of music tests). These can be useful in neuropsychology in some specific cases and for some specific hypotheses. However, we need to be careful not to see everything as a nail just because we have a hammer. These tests do not give a neuropsychologically thorough review of musical abilities.

Several authors have outlined schemes for neuromusicological examinations (Dorgeuille, 1966; Jellinek, 1956; Marin, 1982; Ustvedt, 1937; Wertheim, 1969). These schemes, although differently organized, cover basically the same sets of skills. All together they include about 75 different tasks or skill areas to be tested. These include diverse activities such as sight reading, whistling, improvising, taking musical dictation, tuning an instrument, etc. These schemes were derived mostly with research in mind. They are useful to the clinician either as a source of ideas for alternative ways of exploring a problem or hypothesis, or as a systematic approach to the patient when hypotheses are lacking, but most are too lengthy and cumbersome for practical clinical use.

The screening tests outlined in Table 16-2, derived from the research batteries just mentioned, provide a useful starting place for the clinician. It is prudent to tape record the testing. When problems are encountered on any of these tasks they can be further explored using the above batteries, commercially available tests (Shuter-Dyson & Gabriel, 1981), or improvised tasks and activities.

Another approach, with possibly more clinical utility, is to view the artistic assessment as a collaboration between the neuropsychologist and the patient/artist. This is almost a necessity because even the most broadly educated neuropsychologist is unlikely to be familiar with the intricacies of skill and the wide variety of artistic endeavors present in the general community. For example, my neuropsychological caseload in the past few years has included a high school music teacher, a contemporary composer, a jazz guitarist, a rock singer, a folk singer, a fabric artist, a wood sculptor, a fine arts teacher, an oil painter, and a blacksmith.

A collaborative exploration of the artists' impairments and residual strengths can proceed from hypothesis testing as described above. It can also proceed by asking the artist to do what they typically do in their art. This means they will

Table 16-2 Music Screening Tests for Neurologically Impaired Musicians

I. Performance of Choice
The musician is asked to perform a typical piece from their repertoire by their choice on the instrument of choice (or voice) and in their usual manner (from memory, reading, improvised, alone or with others if possible, etc.).

II. Preparing a Piece
The musician is asked to begin preparing a new piece of their choice in their usual manner.

III. Vocal Expression
- A. The musician is asked to sing familiar songs named by the examiner, singing alone and also singing along with the examiner.
- B. The musician is asked to sing short, unfamiliar melodies by imitation.

IV. Rhythmic Expression
- A. The musician is asked to reproduce rhythmic patterns tapped on a table.
- B. The musician is asked to repeat rhythmic patterns tapped on a table, keeping time with the examiner's tapping.

V. Reading and Writing (when appropriate to the musician's background)
- A. The musician is asked to copy a simple musical text.
- B. The musician is asked to transcribe a dictated melody.
- C. The musician is asked to sight-read musical texts both singing and on their usual instrument.

VI. Perception
The musician is asked to comment on an unfamiliar recording of a performance in a familiar style, identifying instruments, structures, themes, quality of performance, etc. as appropriate to their background.

use their own instruments or materials, subject matter, and possibly setting, rather than simply attempting tasks imposed by the examiner.

When problems are encountered, these can be explored by breaking down the artistic process into its component skills. The artist will often have a reasonably good conceptualization of the component skills derived from their own training. This exploration can also lead to the discovery of strengths and compensatory strategies. For example, I worked with a graphic artist who had a marked hand tremor following a stroke. When he attempted sketching with me we discovered that his tremor moved in a vertical direction, so that horizontal lines were sinusoidal, while vertical lines were straight. He learned to compensate for this by rotating the paper so that he was always drawing vertical lines, except for a few places where he consciously used the product of the tremor to produce a particular effect.

Many artistic skills, particularly in the performing arts, require continual practice to be kept in peak form. The patient who has been forced to abandon their practice because of a neurologic illness or who has become discouraged by failures and has given up art for a period of time may need opportunity to

Table 16-3 Artistic Problem-Oriented Treatment Plan

Artistic Problem	Components	Plan
Impaired technique	Impaired attention	Practice (slow)
	Lack of practice	Practice
	Anxiety	Relaxation training education & reassurance
Unable to improvise with others	Distractibility	Play along with records at home, alone
	Anxiety	Recognize when tension builds, stop and relax; continue supportive counseling
Unable to play jobs at clubs	Distractibility	Avoid high pressure, noisy clubs
	Anxiety and perplexity	Continued relaxation training and supportive counseling
	Subtle executive function and social skills impairments	Practice playing with good friends at home, check social perception & judgement with good friends and in counseling

Note: T.M., a jazz guitarist and pianist with a mild head injury.

practice before an accurate evaluation can be carried out. In some instances they may also need help figuring out how to practice. Indeed, as with many other neurologically impaired skills, it may take months of practice and rehabilitation before we can even begin to guess just how much recovery may ultimately be possible (Baird, 1986).

The Treatment Plan

In the neuropsychological artistic intervention, as with any other psychological assessment and treatment, there is often a blurring of the point when assessment ends and treatment begins. There are often elements of treatment going on during assessment. Conclusions and plans arrived at during assessment are often later modified based on information which has emerged during treatment. Nevertheless, there is usually a point in this process when the major formulation of the case and treatment plan takes place. This formulation can begin with each artistic problem or complaint and identify its neuropsychological basis in sensory, motor, and cognitive impairments, personality changes, and emotional reactions. Alternatively, the artistic consequences of each identified neuropsychological change can be described. A plan can then be formulated for each problem area based on the nature of the problem, the patient's desires, and the available resources. These two similar approaches can fit into the models of the problem oriented medical record and also the process specific approach to cognitive rehabilitation (Sohlberg & Mateer, 1989). Abbreviated examples of both of these approaches to formulation of the same case are given in Tables 16-3 and 16-4 from the following case:

Case

TM is a 32-year-old jazz guitarist referred for neuropsychological assessment of a mild head injury. He had a college education in music and played both guitar and

Table 16-4 Neuropsychological Problem-Oriented Treatment Plan

Neuropsychological Problem	Artistic Consequences	Treatment Plan
Impaired attention	Difficulty practicing Difficulty playing with others Difficulty playing in clubs	Progressive attention training beginning with simple, memorized or read material at home alone, moving to more complex material, to playing with records, to playing with friends, to playing in quiet clubs, to playing in noisy clubs
Anxiety/perplexity	Fear of practicing & performing Fear of loss of art & livelihood Fear of going crazy	Head injury education, supportive counseling, relaxation training with hierarchial reintroduction to fear-producing situations
Subtle executive function and social skills impairments	Gullibility in business dealings Alienating band members and clientele Fear of failure	Practice with friends at home Check on social perceptions and judgment with friends & counselor, Continued supportive counseling including role playing situations

piano. He was well versed in music theory and was skilled at reading, but his preferred and most lucrative musical activity was playing jazz guitar by ear in small groups. He was not able to earn his entire living with this, but it was the career he identified with, while he viewed other jobs such as gas station attendant as necessary to support his music. His musical jobs were usually in late-night, noisy, crowded, jazz clubs. He often played with pick-up groups rather than one steady band. His music also constituted a major part of his social life.

In interviews, he complained of difficulty concentrating, memory problems, impaired guitar technique, a great deal of anxiety about having lost his musical abilities, feelings of insecurity, and social gullibility. He was afraid to see any but his closest friends for fear that he would embarrass himself.

Neuropsychological testing revealed mild impairments in attention, psychomotor speed, and new learning abilities, as is typical of mild head injuries and consistent with his complaints. It was hypothesized that these accounted for his impaired technique, and that his anxiety and perplexity were quite natural reactions to his losses. This hypothesis was tested by having him bring in his guitar and play. His playing was, indeed, inaccurate with many wrong notes, loss of flow, and awkwardness. Moreover, it was clear that he was trying very hard to play as fast as possible and was very anxious about his difficulties. Self-deprecating statements were common.

Screening testing did not reveal any difficulties in auditory perception, dexterity, or coordination. When TM was instructed in relaxation and asked to play more slowly, his playing again became accurate and musical. It was felt, therefore, that the hypothesis was adequate to account for his difficulties and a short-term goal of restoring his technique was set. I instructed him to go home and practice the scales and arpeggios in all keys, gradually increasing his speed as long as he maintained his accuracy. In a few weeks he had re-established his technical competence on the instrument.

At this point he complained that his restored technique was useless, because he could not jam (improvise) with other musicians. He said that he could not attend to what they were playing and play what he wanted to play in a coordinated fashion.

I hypothesized that this was also a manifestation of anxiety and impaired attention. We set a new goal for him to be able to return to jamming. Relaxation training and supportive counseling were continued. I instructed him to go home and put on tapes of music that he liked to play with at slow tempos and simply play the chords. He was then to add embellishments and running lines gradually, but only as long as he felt secure that he was staying with the music he was playing with. Within a few weeks he had returned to jamming with the tapes, including his accustomed fancy technical embellishments.

At this point he complained that it was still difficult to jam with others, and he was frightened of playing in the clubs. He found the atmosphere stressful and distracting. I hypothesized that the impaired attention and anxiety again contributed to this, along with subtle impairments of executive functions and social skills. We set the final goal of returning to the clubs and this was approached with supportive counseling and education and a gradual approximation to the setting of the clubs. He first joined small groups of friends jamming in their apartments where there were fewer distractions and less pressure. At this same time he began a solo afternoon job playing "space music" in a quiet restaurant. This allowed him to experience the pressure of a job and public performance without as much distraction and without the demands of playing in a group. The "space music" format uses slower tempos and also has considerable structural freedom making it easier to cover up mistakes. Eventually he began sitting in with his friends for a few pieces at their club jobs, at first playing only back-up guitar and not taking solos. Eventually he returned to his regular performance practices.

This case illustrates an integration of the patient's particular artistic background and goals and his emotional needs with a musical adaptation of conventional cognitive rehabilitation techniques for attention (Sohlberg & Mateer, 1989). Hypotheses about the deficits and the interventions themselves were conceived in the clinic and tested and implemented in the field. In this instance the patient's musical disabilities were the neuropsychological impairments which most interfered with his life. Nevertheless, they could be accounted for by more general, "horizontal," neuropsychological impairments and did not involve specifically musical skills.

A MODEL FOR INTERVENTION

The decision of whether to treat an artistic impairment deserves perhaps more attention than the decision of whether to treat other cognitive impairments, since artistic activities are often viewed as more optional and the emotional and social implications of treatment can be quite complex for the patient. The decision tree in Figure 16-2 represents one possible approach for the clinician to the artistic patient with a neuropsychological complaint. This decision tree guides the clinician in ruling out depression, lack of information about potential for artistic recovery, denial, and anosognosia (lack of awareness of deficits) as barriers to treatment. The decision tree then asks the clinician to collaborate with the patient to prioritize treatment goals, hypothesize a list of impairments underlying the artistic difficulties, test those hypotheses by formulating and implementing compensation or retraining strategies for each impairment, and inte-

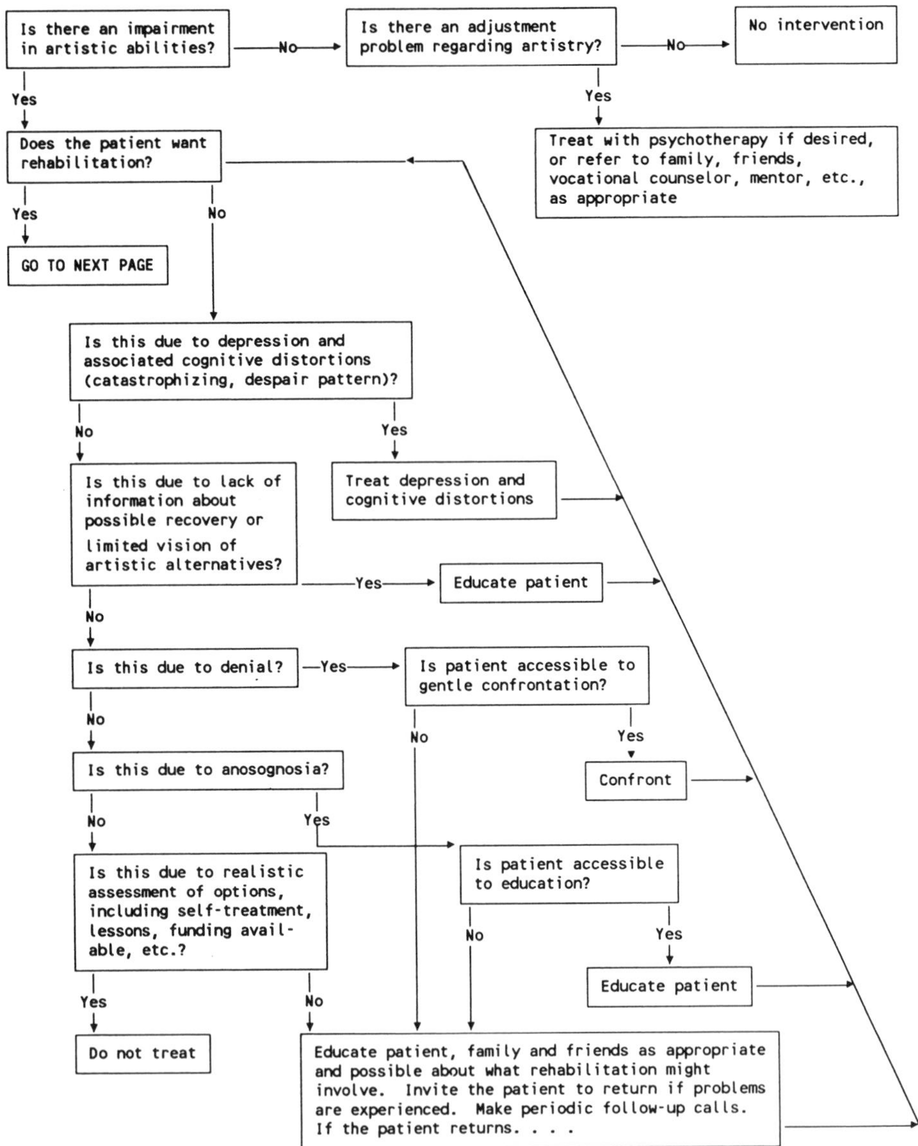

Figure 16-2 (*a*) Artistic rehabilitation decision tree. (*b*) artistic rehabilitation decision tree: assessing and treating the willing, neuropsychologically impaired artist.

grating this intervention plan with other rehabilitation providers and community resources.

Types of Intervention

The evaluation process itself, particularly the part of the process which explores the specific artistic skills, can sometimes be the main intervention. Providing

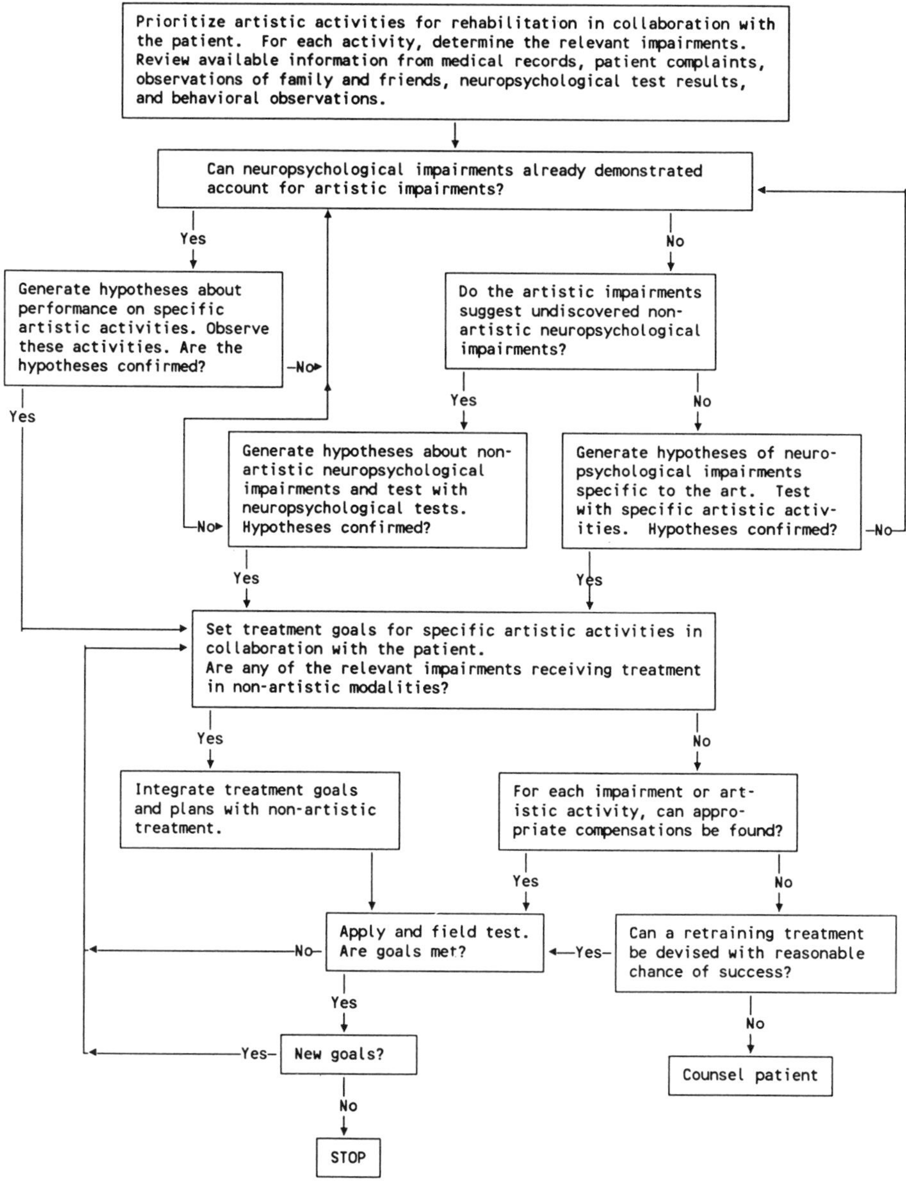

Figure 16-2 *(Continued)*

the patient with an emotionally safe and supportive environment in which to explore artistic skills and deficits may be sufficient to allow grieving for losses, finding their best compensations and adaptations, and continuance of artistic life. The assessment can also lead to education about the nature of the deficits and recommendations for appropriate adaptations. The neuropsychologist is also in a natural position to help the artist deal with the emotional consequences of the impairments, the loss and grief, the change in self-image, and the change in perspective on life. Sometimes these changes can be harnessed for considerable personal growth and artistic expression, as discussed below.

With a mature artist the most pragmatic approach to rehabilitation is probably to try to find out what aspects of the art are most critical, how those aspects can best be salvaged, and what adaptations or alternative approaches may be used. In some instances critical skills may be retrainable following models of physical, occupational, and cognitive therapy. My experience in these areas suggests, however, that we cannot expect standard therapeutic protocols to generalize to artistic abilities. Rather, the retraining approach should be adapted to the specific skills to be relearned. It may be possible to redirect the developing artist within or even outside the field of endeavor to media of expression which most effectively cultivate their new constellation of strengths.

There are many varied and specific types of disabilities that can affect artistic abilities. Furthermore, there is a large variety of creative modalities and related skills (Judd, 1988), and artists tend to be unconventional individuals. Their social and emotional adjustment may be out of the ordinary, and they may have unusual philosophies and strategies for approaching everyday as well as artistic tasks and endeavors (Ostwald, 1987). However, there are also emotional reactions, attempts to adapt, and appropriate interventions that appear to be both common to and specific to most brain-damaged artists.

The Despair Pattern

The artist, whether professional or amateur, often has a much deeper personal identification with their talent than most people have with their careers. Any threat to that sensitive talent (such as through brain damage) can therefore be perceived as a severe threat to ego and personal identity. Any diminution at all in highly refined artistic skills may be regarded as devastating and as having destroyed the entire skill.

A brain-damaged artist not uncommonly will try, as soon as possible after their illness or injury, to test for the preservation of artistic abilities. For example, Dr. Samuel Johnson, the seventeenth century British man of letters, awoke one night to discover that he had had a stroke and composed a prayer in Latin verse as a self test of his intellectual skills (Critchley, 1971). Brain-damaged artists will often test themselves with their most ambitious or difficult undertakings. If there is any loss of ability, the reaction may be despair and total abandonment of skill. This is especially true if they come from a highly competitive environment where technical virtuosity is prized.

This unhappy outcome can be diminished or eliminated altogether by educating the patient about this despair pattern. This is more effective if it is done before the self test but can also be effective afterwards. It is helpful to empathize with their concern about whether their artistic abilities have been affected. It should be stated that the artist will almost certainly experience difficulties initially, but this does not necessarily indicate what the final outcome will be. It can be helpful to give her the perspective of the long time frame of recovery, the artistof the possibilities for rehabilitation (outlined below), and realistically optimistic stories of the recoveries and/or adaptations of other artists.

Fixed Approaches

Artists can often develop elaborate fixed systems in their approach to their creative endeavors which can even take on an obsessive/compulsive or ritualistic quality. Some musicians, for example, will insist on certain meals and clothing and lengthy warm-up exercises before a performance, and will feel unsettled if these are not available. Brain damage can interrupt some of these patterns in ways which do not directly affect the special abilities themselves, but which are perceived by the artist to affect it. For example, I once saw a young painter with lupus erythematosus which resulted in excessive fatigue. She had been in the habit of painting landscapes in an expressive style. Her routine was to pack up her equipment, drive to the setting, carry her equipment out into the field, and stand while she painted. She painted large canvases and had always completed them in a single session. When she no longer had the stamina to do this, she felt that she could no longer be an artist and, in fact, had not painted for several months when I first saw her.

This type of difficulty can often be overcome by stripping away the nonessential parts of the fixed pattern. In this case, I instructed the painter to go back to the studio, and sketch small still lifes while sitting down. When she got tired she was to interrupt the work and come back and complete it later. By following these instructions she was able to rediscover her own talent and to find adaptations that worked for her. She also experienced some recovery in stamina and went on to graduate school in fine art.

Shift in Style

Many artists find a shift in their style following their illness or injury. Sometimes this is due to a direct psychological effect, an emotional reaction to the trauma of the injury or illness. Often it is a more direct consequence of the brain damage. This shift in style is not always an impairment. Sometimes it is an improvement or simply a change in taste. For example, I once saw a painter and teacher who experienced mild diffuse brain damage due to an air embolus to the brain. She found that her visual perception had changed. She used to look at a scene and analyze it according to the proper way to depict it on the canvas according to the laws of perspective and so forth. Following her injury, she was able to look at a scene and see it without regard to the actual objects that were there, but rather as blotches of color. She described it as if the entire scene were represented on a plate of glass in front of her. She was then able to paint those blotches of color directly as she saw them. This sometimes gave the objects in her paintings a new and intriguing ambiguity. She found herself shifting from her previous insightful portrait work to more impressionistic landscapes which, for whatever reason, sold better.

She also found a shift in her teaching style. Previously her classes had been full of noise and activity and she would move rapidly around the studio commenting in passing on many students' work. Following her injury she found that she was distractable. She insisted that her classes be silent. She would move slowly from one student to another, spend considerable time studying each student's work, and give a detailed commentary. She found that some students preferred her old style and some her new. It was a matter of taste, a shift in style, which was neither good nor bad.

A second example, more directly related to an impairment, comes from Kathy Morris, a singer who was the subject of the nonfiction novel, *Seizure*, by Charles Mee (1978). Ms. Morris had a tumor removed from her left temporal lobe and recovered her ability to sing. At the end of the television movie based on the novel, the real Kathy Morris sings a song that she wrote after the removal of the tumor. This song clearly reflects the mild anomic aphasia which she had experienced following surgery. The lyrics contain few concrete content words. It is a good song, however, and the word-finding difficulties reflected in the lyrics give it an ambiguity common in popular songs which makes it easy for many people to project their own situation and feelings onto it.

The artist may need help in appreciating that a shift in style can be an opportunity to explore new areas of self expression. They should be encouraged to discover the new self, rather than trying to recapture and relive the old.

Relearning

Artists who encounter difficulties with their skills following a brain injury may need to go through a process of relearning. Essentially, this can be thought of as a greatly condensed redoing of the original learning process. The artist goes back to the most complex of the basic skills that they can still reliably do and works forward from there towards their previous level of competence, for example, as with TM, the jazz guitarist discussed above.

In many ways relearning parallels the process of rehabilitation in other areas. Skilled artists typically have spent many years developing their own skills largely independently. They often know quite a bit about the process of retraining themselves and frequently have the self-discipline and motivation to do so (Baird, 1986). They often, however, need guidance and encouragement. At times it may be possible to work collaboratively with a teacher in guiding the artist's relearning process.

Such guidance can draw from cognitive rehabilitation. For example, the jazz guitarist, TM, described previously went through a process which closely parallels attention process training (Sohlberg & Mateer, 1989). Initial goals had to do with improving sustained attention and increasing efficiency and speed, while maintaining accuracy. Later, the attentional nature of the task became more selective as more complex musical material was selected. The focus then shifted to divided attention as the guitarist began to work on jamming. Finally, he returned to the distracting environment of playing in clubs.

Similar processes can be envisioned in work with graphic artists. Here, where speed is often less critical, it may be necessary to provide some assistance with executive functions (Sohlberg & Mateer, 1989), for example, in helping the artist to replan the sequence of an approach to an artistic project, breaking it down into steps. The component skills can then be attended to and retrained as necessary. The theory of cognitive rehabilitation for executive functions (Sohlberg and Mateer, 1989) will apply here, but the theory of the structure of the component skills will probably need to come from the artist's own training. It is often best to take the artist back through the familiar sequence of their own training, although at a different pace than their original training.

Adaptations

Brain-damaged artists often encounter significant impairments in their abilities which will not yield to overcoming despair patterns, breaking out of fixed approaches, accepting any cognitive restructuring implicit in a shift in style, or relearning. It is often necessary to consider adaptations which may allow them to continue their art or some aspect of it. Sometimes the adaptations can be mechanical (Chadwick & Clark, 1979; Kurth, 1987; Nagler & Lee, 1987). The jazz saxophonist, Rasaan Rolland Kirk, adapted his saxophones for one-handed playing following a stroke which left him paralyzed on the left side (Giddins, 1978). A composer I worked with who had visual difficulties due to a left occipital lobe stroke was able to continue his composing in part because I provided him with staff paper with wide lines (Judd, Gardner, & Geschwind, 1983). Braille music notation is another adaptation of a mechanical nature. Musicians accustomed to performing without notation might find themselves relying more on notation and written lyrics should they develop memory deficits.

Other adaptations may involve greater adjustments in what aspects of the art are attempted and how. Beethoven, Smetana, and Fauré each continued and even intensified their composing when they became deaf though they withdrew from performance and conducting (Hood, 1977). Count Geza Zeichy in the 19th century and Paul Wittgenstein in the 20th were wealthy pianists who lost their right arms and commissioned works from eminent composers of the day for piano left hand (Lorenzeu & Jokl, 1974). Cyril Smith suffered a stroke and paralysis of the left side and continued a concert piano career as documented in his autobiography, *Duet for Three Hands* (1958). A list of literature for piano one hand and three hands is available from the U.S. Library of Congress, Services for the Blind and Physically Handicapped, Music Division.

The composer with a right hemisphere stroke described earlier (Judd, 1988) was no longer able to compose, but did continue a successful teaching career. He continued to conduct, although he found that he needed to avoid music with mixed meters because he had difficulty shifting from one meter to another. He also wrote a textbook of music theory. In these ways he was able to continue and even expand upon these aspects of his multifaceted musical career that he was still capable of, while abandoning or scaling back and adapting the impaired aspects.

Starr and Phillip (1970) described a patient with a profound anterograde amnesia for declarative material (he could not learn new information). He was nevertheless able to participate in his institution's band through his preserved procedural learning of music. Similarly, I had a patient, a former high school music teacher, who was residing in a nursing home due to profound anterograde amnesia and impaired executive functions resulting from an anterior communicating artery aneurysm. In spite of these deficits, he sang regularly in a church choir, which he was able to do because he could read the music.

Sometimes adaptations involve adjustments where parts of the artist's abilities are emphasized and other parts are de-emphasized or avoided. I once saw a blacksmith a year after his closed head injury who had mild deficits in concentration, planning, and problem solving. He reported that when everything was running smoothly when he was doing production work on products he had designed earlier, he could be as fully productive as he had been prior to his injury. However, if something broke or went wrong, such as running out of certain supplies, or being distracted by phone calls, he found it much harder to figure out what was wrong and fix it or to pick up again where he had left off. He also found that he still had new ideas for products, but had lost some of his artistic touch in bringing the projects to completion. Therefore, he worked at decreasing the distractions in his work environment and doing more production work and less creative work.

Similarly, an artist who worked in fabric constructions found that she had greater difficulty in concentrating on creating and carrying to completion new projects in the first months following a mild head injury. She therefore used much of her recovery period to finish up a number of backlogged projects which involved somewhat more routine operations (rather like production work). She also had to structure her time and pace this work more carefully because of marked fatiguability.

Sometimes a disability can provide an unexpected focus and enhancement of artistic abilities. For example, the composer Smetana remarked on the effects of the isolation brought on by his deafness, "I have completed in these three years of deafness more than I had otherwise done in ten" (Large, 1970).

Recovery Time

As with most people recovering from brain damage, the artist needs to be given a time perspective on what to expect. They need to be educated that the recovery process can continue for a year or two and even longer (Baird, 1986). They need to be reminded to avoid attempting to do too much too soon in returning to work and previous commitments. In particular, they should avoid commitment to any deadlines or performances until they have clearly reestablished and demonstrated their capabilities. At the same time, recovery is an active not a passive process. There needs to be active working on skill recovery and no expectation that the simple passage of time will bring them back. Even with no impairment, the skilled artist can often experience a loss of performance due to lack of practice resulting from hospitalization and lengthy illness.

Using Art To Recover

For most people, an injury or illness resulting in brain damage is a major life event producing many emotional reactions and requiring much adjustment. Many artists are able to use their art to help them through this emotional adjustment. Their art can be used to explore and express their experiences and to communicate them to others. It is sometimes helpful to direct the artist in this way, reframing the experience as, in part, an opportunity and inspiration. Indeed, the artistic exploration of the meanings and manifestations of the disability may be the only practical artistic alternative in some cases, for example, for a physically disabled dancer or actor. The artist may in this way not only achieve a new personal adjustment, but perhaps even help others in their adjustments to disabilities and other challenges in ways that we, as clinicians, can perhaps only dream of. Examples range from the 17th century English poet John Milton's sonnet about his blindness, "When I consider how my light is spent," to the New York actor, Joe Chaikin's play, "Struck Dumb," about his aphasia (described above), to May Sarton's journal, *After the Stroke* (1988), to the quadriplegic cartoonist, John Callahan's autobiography, *Don't Worry, He Won't Get Far on Foot* (1988).

CONCLUSIONS

The neuropsychological rehabilitation of artists ideally involves an integrated understanding of the role of the art in the patient's life and personality, the art itself and its social context, processes of physical and cognitive rehabilitation, and the emotional process of adjustment to brain damage. When some of these are lacking it is probably best to bring them into the picture through consultation with others. Artists are often helped in their attempts to adjust by the opportunity to see examples of others who have adjusted, either clinical or historical examples, many of which have been described in this paper. It is also helpful to present these patients with the challenge to their creativity of finding ways to continue to express themselves through their art in spite of their disabilities. This cognitive reframing of the disability as a creative and emotional challenge can give hope for the resilience of the person who is an artist.

NOTES

1. Lerdahl and Jackendoff (1983) have given a formal description of the structure of tonal music. This description is stated by means of well-formedness rules which describe permissible structures, and preference rules which describe likely structures. These rules describe the groupings of musical events within a piece and the hierarchical relationships among the groups (represented by tree structures). To the extent that empirical data are available, their rules are reasonably well supported by the findings of perceptual and cognitive psychology of music.

2. If these challenges ultimately succeed they will increase our knowledge of language and music and of their underlying cognitive structures, but they will not make music and language any less interesting or less similar.

3. For example, it is possible to generate sounds electronically that sound like "pa." By altering one dimension of this sound (called the voicing onset time) a similar electronic sound is perceived as "ba." People (and some animals) are very good at perceiving very small differences in voicing onset time when they make the difference between hearing the sound as "pa" and as "ba," but they are not nearly as good at distinguishing the same degree of difference in voicing onset times for sounds that are all perceived as "ba" or for sounds that are all perceived as "pa." Because perception is keener across categories than it is within categories this is called "categorical perception."

4. Heinrich Schenker is a music theorist currently favored by psychomusicologists (e.g., Lehrdahl & Jackendoff, 1983; Sloboda, 1985).

5. Murphy's Law is, "If anything can go wrong, sooner or later it will."

REFERENCES

Alajouanine, T. (1948). Aphasia and artistic realization. *Brain*, *71*, 229–241.

Anderson, W. (1977). *Therapy and the arts: Tools of consciousness*. New York: Harper & Row.

Assal, G. (1973). Aphasie de Wernicke sans amusie chez un pianiste. *Revue Neurologique*, *129*, 251–255.

Baird, C. M. (1986). A pianist's techniques of rehabilitation. *Medical Problems of Performing Artists*, *1*, 128–130.

Ball, M. (1983). Lyrical abstract expressionism. *Artweek*, 5–7.

Benton, A. L. (1977). The amusias. In M. Critchley and R. A. Henson (Eds.), *Music and the brain*. (pp. 378–397). Springfield: Charles C. Thomas.

Blacking, J. (1976). *How musical is man?* London: Faber.

Botez, M. I., & Wertheim, N. (1959). Expressive aphasia and amusia following right frontal lesion in a right-handed man. *Brain*, *82*, 186–202.

Bouillaud, J. B. (1865). Sur la faculte due langage articule. *Bulletin de l'Academie de Medicine*, *30*, 752–755.

Burns, E. M., & Ward, W. D. (1982). Intervals, scales, and tuning. In D. Deutsch (Ed.), *The Pychology of Music*, (pp. 241–270). San Diego: Academic Press.

Callahan, J. (1988). *Don't worry, he won't get far on foot*. New York: Random House.

Chadwick, D., & Clark, C. (1979). *Clinically adapted instruments for the multiply handicapped*. Westford, MA: Modulations, Inc.

Chomsky, N. (1957). *Syntactic structures*. The Hague: Mouton.

Cleall, C. (1983). Notes on a young deaf musician. *The Psychology of Music*, *11*, 101–102.

Critchley, M. (1971). *Aphasiology*. London: Arnold.

Critchley, M., & Henson, R. A. (Eds.) (1977). *Music and the brain: Studies in the neurology of music*. London: William Heineman Medical Books.

Cutting, J. E., & Rosner, B. S. (1974). Categories and boundaries in speech and music. *Perception and Psychophysics* *16*(3), 564–570.

Dorgeuille, C. (1966). *Introduction a l'etude des amusies*. Paris: These.

Dowling, W. J., & Harwood, D. L. (1986). *Music cognition*. San Diego: Academic Press.

Dupre, E., & Nathan, M. (1911). *Le language musical: Etude medico-psychologique*. Paris: Alcan.

Edgren, I. (1895). *Amusie (musikalische Aphasie)*. Deutsche Zeitschrift fur Nervenheilkung, *6*, 1–64.

Edwards, E. M. (1974). *Music education for the deaf*. South Waterford, ME: Merriam-Eddy.

Feuchtwanger, E. (1930). *Amusie*. Berlin: Springer.

Fodor, J. A. (1983). *Modularity of mind: Faculty psychology*. Cambridge, MA: MIT Press.

Fox, P. D. (1981). The contributions of Edsel Murphy to the understanding of the basic laws of psychology. *Australian Psychologist*, *16*, 438–439.

Gardner, H. (1982). *Art, mind, and brain: A cognitive approach to creativity*. New York: Basic Books.

Gardner, H. (1983) *Frames of mind: The theory of multiple intelligences*. New York: Basic Books.

Gaston, E. T. (1968). *Music in therapy*. New York: Macmillan.

Giddins, G. (1978, June 12). Last ride on the Kirkatron. *Village Voice*, p. 62.

Gordon, E. (1965). *Musical aptitude profile*. Boston: Houghton Mifflin.

Green, R. L., McAllister, T. W., & Bernat, J. L. (1987). A study of crying in medically and surgically hospitalized patients. *American Journal of Psychiatry*, *144*, 442–447.

Harnad, S. (1987). *Categorical perception*. Cambridge University Press.

Hart, T., & Hayden, M. E. (1986). The ecological validity of neuropsychological assessment and remediation. In B. Uzzell & Y. Gross, Eds., *Clinical Neuropsychology of Intervention* (pp. 21–50). Boston: Nijhoff.

Hood, J. D. (1977). Deafness and music appreciation. In M. Critchley & R. A. Henson (Eds.), *Music and the brain* (pp. 378–397). Springfield: Charles C. Thomas.

Hulbert, D. (1987, November 20). The death and life of Joseph Chaikin. *The Atlanta Journal-The Atlanta Constitution*.

Jellinek, A. (1956). Amusia. *Folia Phoniatrica*, *8*, 124–149.

Judd, T. (1988). The varieties of musical talent. In L. K. Obler & D. A. Fein (Eds.), *The exceptional brain: The neuropsychology of talent and special abilities*. New York: Guilford Press.

Judd, T., Gardner, H., & Geschwind, N. (1983). Alexia without agraphia in a composer, *Brain*, *106*, 435–457.

Jung, R. (1974). Neuropsychologie und Neurophysiologie des konturund Formschens in Zeichnung und Malerei. In H. H. Wieck (Ed.), *Psychopathologie Musischen Gesaltungen*. Stuttgart and New York: Praeger.

Kimura, D., & Faust, R. (1987). Spontaneous drawing in an unselected sample of patients with unilateral cerebral damage. In D. Ottoson (Ed.), *Duality and unity of the brain* (pp. 114–146). Wenner-Gren Center International Symposium Series, Macmillan Press.

Kuath, R. H. (1987). Portrait of a unique instrumentalist. *Medical Problems of Performing Artists*, *7*, 29–30.

Large, B. (1970). *Smetana* (p. 266). London: Duckworth.

Lerdahl, F., & Jackendoff, R. (1983). *A generative theory of tonal music*. Cambridge, MA: MIT.

Lezak, M. (1983). *Neuropsychological assessment*. Oxford: Oxford University Press.

Locke, S., & Kellar, L. (1973). Categorical perception in a non-linguistic mode. *Cortex*, *9*(4), 355–369.

Lomax, A. (1968). *Folk song style and culture*. Washington, DC: American Association for the Advancement of Science.

Lorenzen, H., & Jokl, E. (1974). Piano music for the one-handed with remarks on the role of art in rehabilitation. *American Corrective Therapy Journal*, *28*, 11–23.

Luria, A. R. (1966). *The higher cortical functions in man*. New York: Basic Books.

Luria, A. R., Tsvetkova, L. S., & Futer, D. S. (1965). Aphasia in a composer. *Journal of the Neurological Sciences*, *1*, 288–292.

Mann, L. (1898). Casuistische Beitrage zur Hirnchirurgie und Hirnlokalisation. *Monatschrift fur Psychiatrie und Neurologie*, *4*, 369–378.

Marin, O. (1982). Neurological aspects of music perception and performance. In D. Deutsch (Ed.), *The psychology of music* (pp. 453–477). New York: Academic Press.

Mee, C. (1978). *Seizure*. Philadelphia, Evans.

Meyer, L. (1956). *Emotion and meaning in music*. Chicago: University of Chicago Press.

Nagler, J. C., & Lee, M. H. M. (1987). Use of microcomputers in the music therapy process of a postviral encephalitic musician. *Medical Problems of Performing Artists*, *2*, 72–74.

Ostwald, P. F. (1987). Psychotherapeutic strategies in the treatment of performing artists. *Medical Problems of Performing Artists*, *2*, 131–136.

Prigatano, G. (1986). *Neuropsychological rehabilitation after brain injury* Baltimore: Johns Hopkins University Press.

Roehmann, F. L., & F. R. Wilson, (Eds.). (1988). *The biology of music making*. St. Louis, MO: MMB Music, Inc.

Ross, E. D. (1981). The aprosodias: Functional-anatomic organization of the affective components of language in the right hemisphere. *Archives of Neurology*, *38*, 561–569.

Sarton, May. (1988). *After the stroke: A journal*. New York: Norton.

Schweiger, A. (1988). A portrait of the artist as a brain-damaged patient. In L. K. Obler & D. A. Fein (Eds.), *The exceptional brain: The neuropsychology of talent and special abilities*. New York: Guilford Press.

Seashore, C. E. (1938). *The psychology of music*. New York: McGraw Hill.

Seashore, C. E. (1960). *Seashore measures of musical talents* (rev. manual). New York: The Psychological Corp.

Serafine, M. L. (1988). *Music as cognition: The development of thought in sound*. New York: Columbia University Press.

Shuter-Dyson, R., & Gabriel, C. (1981). *The psychology of musical ability* (2nd ed.). London and New York: Methuen.

Sloboda, J. A. (1985). *The musical mind: The cognitive psychology of music*. Oxford: Oxford University Press.

Sloboda, J. A., (Ed.). (1988). *Generative processes in music*. Oxford: Clarendon Press.

Smith, C. (1958). *Duet for three hands*. London: Angus & Robertson.

Sohlberg, M. M., & Mateer, C. A. (1989). *Introduction to cognitive rehabilitation*. New York: Guilford.

Sparks, R., Helm, N., & Albert, M. (1974). Aphasia rehabilitation resulting from melodic intonation therapy. *Cortex*, *10*, 347–359.

Starr, A., & Phillips, L. (1970). Verbal and motor memory in the amnestic syndrome. *Neuropsychologia*, *8*, 75–88.

Ustvedt, H. J. (1937). Uber die Untersuchung der musikalischen Functionen bei Patienten mit Aphasie. *Acta Medica Scandanivica*, Suppl. 86.

Uzzell, B., & Gross, Y. (1986). *Clinical neuropsychology of intervention*. Boston: Nijhoff.

Wapner, W., Judd, T., & Gardner, H. (1978). Visual agnosia in an artist. *Cortex*, *14*, 343–364.

Wertheim, N. (1969). The amusias. In P. J. Vinken and G. W. Bruyn, (Eds.), *Handbook of clinical neurology*, vol. 4. Amsterdam: North Holland.

Zaimov, K., D. Kitov, & N. Kolev. (1969). Aphasie chez un paintre. *Encephale*, *68*, 377–417.

PART VI
CONCLUSIONS

17

Neuroimaging and Cognitive Function

BETH A. OBER, BRUCE R. REED, and WILLIAM J. JAGUST

Neuroscience investigations of the relationships between brain and behavior have been advanced considerably by the advent of techniques for the visualization of the brain in living humans. Prior to this era, inferences about brain structure and function were largely drawn from studies of the neurological examination, the use of neurosurgical procedures, and autopsy correlations. Techniques such as cerebral angiography and pneumoencephalography, while providing structural information about the brain, are highly invasive and yield poorly resolved spatial information. Electrophysiologic studies, while providing high temporal resolution information about brain physiology, remain limited with regard to spatial resolution.

The modern era of neuroimaging began with the application of x-ray computed tomography (CT), allowing the *in vivo* imaging of brain structure in humans. Information pertinent to brain-behavior relationships gained from CT studies has largely been of a correlational nature, with inferences drawn about localization of function as a result of extrapolation from studies of humans with brain lesions. Such information, in conjunction with earlier autopsy, clinical neurological, and neurosurgical data, have formed the basis of much of our current understanding of brain-behavior relationships.

More recently, magnetic resonance imaging (MRI) has provided an additional tool for studying brain structure. Because of particular advantages relating to image processing, resolution, and contrast sensitivity (see below), this technique allows more accurate description of lesions as well as normal brain structures than does CT.

The use of physiological imaging techniques such as positron emission tomography (PET) and single photon emission computed tomography (SPECT), as well as ^{133}Xe regional cerebral blood flow (rCBF) measurement, allow the external detection of radiotracers which image cerebral functions such as blood flow and metabolism. The investigations of relationships between such indices of regional cerebral function and cognition have utilized correlational methods adapted from studies of lesioned patients using anatomic imaging, as well as stimulation or activation studies which are uniquely suited to these new modalities. This chapter will review the contributions of both traditional anatomic imaging techniques and newer techniques for imaging brain function to the study of normal and abnormal human cognition.

Our goal for this chapter is to provide clinical neuropsychologists with a selective and critical overview of the ever-increasing literature on the relationships between normal and abnormal cognitive function on the one hand and structural and functional neuroimaging on the other hand (with consideration of both correlational and stimulation studies of brain function). First, we briefly review the techniques used in structural and functional neuroimaging and their methodological limitations, which have important consequences for inferring specific brain-cognitive relationships. We then provide an overview of the various types of investigations which relate neuroimaging to cognitive functions, with an emphasis on the limitations inherent in each type of investigation. Next, we briefly discuss the limitations in our current knowledge of specific cognitive functions. Each of the next four sections of the chapter focuses on one of the following "cognitive realms:" attention, memory, language, and visuospatial processes (including mental imagery). For each of these areas of cognitive function, we review neuroimaging studies which either have attempted to correlate neuroimaging findings with some aspect of cognition or which have studied regional cerebral activity (usually in normal subjects) as a function of cognitive task. We have been very selective in our choices of studies to present in each of the subsections on neuroimaging-cognition relationships. Whenever possible, we selected studies in which the cognitive functions under study were derived from a reasonably well-described cognitive model, or at least in which the cognitive functions being investigated were relatively specific ones. Thus, we have left out the numerous studies that relate neuroimaging data to very general cognitive functions (such as overall memory ability as assessed, for example, by the Wechsler Memory Scale), to traditional neuropsychological syndromes (e.g., Broca's aphasia, Wernicke's aphasia), or to performance on a "compound" cognitive task such as verbal fluency (the timed generation of exemplars from a given letter or semantic category; this task entails multiple attentional skills and retrieval from semantic memory in addition to language production skills). After the review of neuroimaging-cognition studies for each of the "cognitive realms," we review the steadily increasing number of studies relating neuroimaging data to cognitive dysfunction in dementia, particularly in Alzheimer's disease. In the final section of the chapter we offer some concluding remarks about the study of neuroimaging-cognition relationships, make some suggestions for future research in this area, and discuss the relevance of this type of research for the clinical neuropsychologist.

OVERVIEW OF NEUROIMAGING TECHNIQUES

Structural Imaging—CT and MRI

Until recently, CT has been the procedure utilized by both clinicians and researchers to image anatomic features of the brain. This technique utilizes tissue interactions with x-rays, transmitted through the patient's brain from an external source, to produce a three-dimensional image of brain structure. The intensity of the image is related to the number of x-rays which are not transmitted through the brain because of interactions with the tissue in the form of Compton scattering. Thus, an x-ray CT essentially is a map of tissue density.

The x-ray tube, which rotates around the patient, is collimated so that at any one time the detector, opposite to the x-ray source, is imaging a single slice. Because the x-ray tube rotates, multiple "views" of the brain are taken. These views can then be back-projected to form a tomographic slice. Current CT scanners are capable of resolution on the order of 1 mm, and most common neurological lesions such as hemorrhage, infarction, and tumors are easily identified. Lesions may also be identified through the use of a CT contrast agent, an iodine-based substance which "absorbs" x-rays and demonstrates areas of blood brain barrier permeability. In addition to localizing lesions and measuring their size, CT can also be used to quantitate the size of normal brain structures (such as subarachnoid space and ventricles) and measure the density of brain tissue by direct quantitation. Since the reconstruction of the image requires assigning each volume element (voxel) a density relative to water (a Hounsfield unit), measurement of the Hounsfield number of a voxel can provide a quantitative estimate of the density of different brain regions.

MRI utilizes an entirely different principle in order to image the brain. The principle essentially makes use of the fact that atomic nuclei have a magnetic moment, and thus respond in predictable ways to externally applied magnetic fields. A variety of nuclei, such as ^{13}C, ^{23}Na, and ^{31}P are found in biological molecules and may be studied with MRI, yielding important physiological information. Because of the abundance of water in biological tissues, medical imaging has primarily been devoted to the study of ^{1}H, which reveals information of a largely structural nature.

The principles of magnetic resonance imaging are beyond the scope of this chapter and have been thoroughly reviewed in many recent monographs and papers (e.g., Budinger & Margulis, 1986; Brant-Zawadzki, 1987). Briefly, the procedure requires placing a patient in a strong magnetic field, which produces a net magnetization of the protons in the patient's tissues. A radio-frequency pulse is then applied, which re-orients the direction of the previously aligned protons. When the radio-frequency pulse is terminated, the protons emit energy, which can be used to create an image. The image reflects a number of parameters, including the abundance of protons and two separate relaxation parameters, T1 and T2, which are times required for the aligned protons to regain their original net magnetization vector and lose their new orientation, respectively. Because pathologic and normal tissues differ considerably in these three parameters, MR images show considerable contrast between grey matter, white matter, and cerebrospinal fluid, and show a variety of pathological processes such as infarction, edema, and tumor.

Because of the increased contrast sensitivity, MRI is capable of detecting small lesions, particularly when high proton-containing molecules, such as water, occur in the middle of hydrophobic structures such as myelin, as occurs in subcortical infarcts. In addition, many pathological processes are characterized by changes in brain water content at early stages. Thus infarcts, for example, may be imaged within hours of their occurrence. Differences in contrast between grey matter, white matter, and CSF allow the quantitation of the size of brain structures with more precision than is possible with CT.

Functional Imaging—PET and SPECT

Both PET and SPECT utilize emission tomography. The tomograph, an external detection system, maps the distribution of an injected radiotracer in three dimensions. The radiotracer consists of a radionuclide which is attached to a molecule of interest, and which may be a metabolic substrate, an inert molecule whose distribution parallels rCBF, or a neurotransmitter receptor ligand. The radionuclide emits a form of radioactivity which is detected by the tomograph, and the molecule permits the evaluation of a specific aspect of brain physiology. An integral part of emission tomographic imaging is the considerable preclinical research needed to clearly establish the metabolism of the tracer and document its *in vivo* biochemistry. Mathematical modeling of the behavior of the tracer is necessary in order to extract quantitative physiologic information from the PET or SPECT image.

The essential difference between PET and SPECT is in the type of radioactivity which is utilized. PET utilizes radionuclides which decay by positron emission. Common positron emitters include ^{11}C, ^{15}O, and ^{18}F. When a positron is emitted from such a nucleus, it travels a short distance in tissue and annihilates by interaction with an electron, producing two photons which travel at 180° opposite to each other. These photons can be detected by a pair of crystal detectors which are simultaneously excited by the annihilation photons. Thus, the tomograph can localize the positron emission to a line, and the reconstruction of an image is accomplished by the back projection of multiple such lines through each pair of opposing detectors. SPECT imaging makes use of radionuclides which decay by emitting single photons which are emitted in random directions. Typical SPECT isotopes are ^{99m}Tc and ^{123}I. Information about the location of the single photon emissions are obtained by collimation, a mechanical process which essentially limits the field of view of a detector to a line. SPECT images are obtained by the back projection of multiple such lines in a manner similar to PET.

The physical properties of positron emission and single photon emission have important consequences for the two imaging techniques. The mechanical collimation used in SPECT results in the loss of considerable data, representing the decay events which are not "viewed" by the collimated detectors. This diminishes the sensitivity of the tomograph, so that fewer counts are present in an image. As resolution increases, sensitivity decreases, so that effective increases in resolution are not practical beyond about 8–10 mm. The electronic collimation used with PET has no such limitations, as in-plane resolution can be increased by adding more detectors without affecting sensitivity, so that the theoretical limit of resolution is quite small. This also affects the temporal resolution of the techniques, as a greater number of counts can be obtained in a shorter time using PET compared to SPECT.

The radionuclides used in the two techniques are also different, as PET uses radioisotopes of atoms which are often common constituents of biological molecules of interest. Thus, the addition of an ^{11}C or a ^{15}O atom to such a molecule may not alter its biochemical behavior, while the addition of SPECT isotopes such as ^{99m}Tc or ^{123}I may have more profound consequences. Consequently, a large number of tracers have been used with PET to study glucose metabolism (^{18}F-labeled deoxyglucose, or FDG), blood flow (^{15}O-water), tissue pH, protein metabolism, and neurotransmitter receptor density and affinity. Clinical SPECT studies have been largely limited to studies of rCBF and some neurotransmitters, although considerable progress is now being made in the development of new tracers. Finally, the half-lives of positron emitters and single photon emitters are different, with many PET nuclides having extremely short half-lives, requiring an on-site cyclotron for their production and immediate use. SPECT radionuclides have half-lives which are longer and can be more easily synthesized and transported.

The differences in radionuclides used and their methods of detection also have bearing on the sorts of cognitive neuroimaging studies which can be done. The two most widely used PET nuclides, ^{15}O and ^{18}F, differ greatly in their half-lives (2 min and 110 min, respectively). Consequently, repeated studies using ^{15}O tracers can be performed in rapid sequence on the same subject, while ^{18}F tracers cannot be utilized in this manner. The most widely used ^{15}O tracer, ^{15}O-labeled water, enables the repeated measurement of rCBF by performing sequential studies of a subject in one session. Thus, one can study the effects on rCBF of several behavioral tasks which correspond to particular levels or modules of cognitive processing (see below). ^{15}O-labeled elemental oxygen (O_2) can also be used to study regional cerebral metabolic rates for O_2 (rCMRO_2), which is somewhat more cumbersome than rCBF studies. The nuclide ^{18}F has generally been utilized in ^{18}F-deoxyglucose (^{18}FDG) for the measurement of regional cerebral metabolic rates for glucose (rCMRglc). Because of the longer half-life of ^{18}FDG, stimulation studies either require each subject to participate in each of the stimulation and control conditions on different days, or require separate groups of subjects to participate in the various conditions. Recently, however, a technique for performing two PET-^{18}FDG studies in one sitting has been proposed (Chang, Duara, Barker, Apicella, & Finn, 1987). In addition, the shorter half-lived tracer ^{11}C has been used with deoxyglucose (^{11}CDG) to study cerebral metabolism. SPECT studies most commonly use the nuclides ^{123}I and ^{99m}Tc as ^{123}I-N-isopropyl-p-iodoamphetine (IMP) and ^{99m}Tc-hexamethyl propyl amine oxine (HMPAO), which have half-lives of 13 and 6 hrs, respectively. These half-lives necessitate the conduct of repeated SPECT studies for a given subject on separate occasions. While SPECT offers advantages over PET in its greater accessibility and less technical complexity, it is more limited in terms of resolution and quantitative precision.

STUDIES OF NEUROIMAGING AND COGNITION: LIMITATIONS

Overview of Structural Imaging Studies and Their Limitations

There is a vast literature relating lesions seen on CT scans to cognitive deficits. Also, there is a rapidly expanding literature relating the lesions revealed with MRI scans to one or another cognitive dysfunction. It would be impossible and, indeed, is not necessary for the purposes of this chapter to provide a thorough review of these structural imaging studies. The great majority of this literature deals with general cognitive functions or syndromes (for example, aphasic syndromes, constructional apraxia, anterograde amnesia, etc.) rather than correlating specific components (e.g., the word-finding component of language production, the semantic encoding component of a verbal learning and memory task, etc.) of a given cognitive function to anatomical lesion. The reader is referred to Kertesz (1983) and Heilman and Valenstein (1985) for summaries of the "classic" neuropsychology/localization-of-function literature. In the various sections of this chapter, we will include selected studies which relate specific cognitive deficits to structural lesions as seen on CT or MRI, with the caveats that follow.

It is important to keep in mind that the association of a particular brain lesion with a particular cognitive function is, in fact, only an association. One cannot infer from such an association that the brain area of interest is directly or solely responsible for the particular cognitive function which is disrupted. The interconnections among various brain regions are frequently complex and incompletely known: a lesion may have direct as well as indirect effects on the functions of brain areas distant from the lesion, areas which themselves may appear to be structurally intact on CT or MRI. Thus, we must limit our inferences from associations between brain lesions and cognitive dysfunction to those which posit some role (which is almost certainly not an exclusive role) for the brain region under study in the carrying out of the now disrupted cognitive function. We should also keep in mind the resolution limitations of structural imaging techniques. The brain areas which can be imaged are fairly gross, and if it were possible to image smaller brain regions (e.g., subregions of the hippocampus) one might see that lesions in these smaller regions would not have the same relationships to the cognitive dysfunction associated with damage to the medial temporal lobe, including the hippocampus (Squire, 1981). Nonetheless, lesion information, together with information derived from non-structural neuroimaging techniques can provide important information about the neurological bases of cognitive functions.

Overview of Correlational, Functional Imaging Studies and Their Limitations

Correlational, functional imaging studies are also "lesion studies," which rest on the same basic premise as do CT and anatomic MRI studies. In each case, the studies attempt to locate abnormal cerebral regions which are consistently associated with a specific cognitive abnormality. The potential advantage of resting state PET and SPECT studies is that they measure functional, as opposed to anatomic, boundaries of a cerebral lesion and may thus give a more complete view of the extent of the lesion, such as imaging functionally impaired brain regions which are remote from an anatomical lesion. Even this view of the lesion may be quite incomplete, however, for a PET or SPECT study measures a single physiologic parameter (e.g., oxygen utilization, blood flow, glucose metabolism), different physiologic processes are not always affected similarly, and other aspects of cerebral function (e.g., neurotransmitter levels) are not usually studied. Further, resting state physiology may not reflect functioning in response to stimulation.

Another weakness of lesion studies using functional imaging techniques is the relatively low spatial resolution of most PET and SPECT scanners. Information-processing models of cognitive function generally describe traditional cognitive domains such as reading or attention in terms of a set of highly specific subprocesses, each of which may itself be accomplished by narrowly localized and rather small structures. Consequently, functional imaging studies often have insufficient resolution to examine the postulated anatomic substrate of these models.

Overview of Investigative Approaches Used in Stimulation Studies and Their Limitations

Alternative Methods of Measurement of Cerebral Activity in Stimulation Studies

Most of the earlier stimulation studies (1970s, early 1980s) measured rCBF via two-dimensional techniques (spatial resolution of about 1 square cm) using the radioactive gas ^{133}Xe, which can either be injected or inhaled. SPECT procedures for three-dimensional (spatial resolution from 10 to 18 mm) rCBF determinations with ^{133}Xe, ^{123}IMP, and ^{99m}Tc isotopes have been developed more recently. The three-dimensionality of the SPECT procedure allows imaging of multiple brain slices. The majority of stimulation studies during the past decade have measured rCBF or rCMR (for glucose or oxygen) via PET, also a three-dimensional technique (spatial resolution from 2 to 18 mm), using short-lived positron-emitting isotopes (described above). Using a variety of activation techniques, changes in brain function can be imaged in regions which are considerably smaller than the resolution elements of the tomograph.

Temporal Resolution of the Various Neuroimaging Techniques

When studying cerebral activity as a function of the cognitive activity in which the subject is engaged, the period of time over which a reliable sampling of cerebral function can be obtained will directly limit the type of cognitive process that can be effectively manipulated in these studies. The measurement period required may vary from 30 min for ^{18}FDG used with PET to 40 sec for ^{15}O-water bolus injection used in a rCBF study. This difference affects both the duration of time the subject must perform a cognitive task, as well as the time needed between repeat studies on the same subject. Although the temporal specificity of cognitive-brain activity relationship which is now possible is tremendously improved compared to 10 years ago, we cannot yet measure localized brain metabolic responses to the discrete, very fast (taking place in milliseconds) mental events which cognitive psychologists can study via reaction time paradigms (e.g., serial search through memory, retrieval from memory, stepwise spread of activation in the semantic network, the scanning of a visual image, etc).

Approaches to Analysis of rCBF or rCMR Data Obtained in Stimulation Studies

There are at least three different approaches to the statistical analysis of the brain activity data obtained in stimulation studies. The first approach is to use the subtractive method, which involves testing the differences in, for example, rCBF between PET scans obtained during a resting state and a particular stimulation condition or during two different stimulation conditions. This method focuses on questions about whether one kind of cognitive activity leads to more or less regional activity than another kind of cognitive activity. A second method is the region-of-interest (ROI) correlation method. This method characterizes brain activity in terms of regional couplings, that is, in terms of pairs of ROIs that are significantly correlated during a particular type of stimulation. The focus is on questions concerning the extent to which different behavioral conditions are associated with different patterns of pairwise, regional correlation. A third approach to analyzing the data obtained in a stimulation study is the functional system approach. This approach derives from a conceptualization of higher cognitive functions being performed by large functional systems involving a number of ROIs; the regional make-up of the structural system can be evaluated for each of the stimulation conditions, using multivariate statistical analyses (e.g., Goldenberg, Podreka, Steiner, & Willmes, 1987).

LIMITATIONS IMPOSED BY CURRENT STATE OF COGNITIVE MODELING

In attempting to relate cognitive function (or dysfunction) to brain structure or function, one is, of course, limited by the current state of cognitive modeling and techniques available for measuring posited cognitive functions, as well as being limited by the neuroimaging techniques. A number of areas are under intensive study by cognitive scientists and the modeling in these areas is becoming much more sophisticated with regards to the specificity of cognitive functions included in these models. Examples include the visuospatial attention models of Posner and his colleagues (for a review see Posner, 1988), the language processing models of Morton (1969; 1979) and Fodor (1988), the connectionistic, parallel, distributed memory models being applied to visual word recognition (Rumelhart, McClelland, & PDP Research Group, 1986) and phonological processing (Dell, 1988), the sensory-semantic model of learning and memory (Nelson, 1981), Kosslyn's (1980) computational model of mental imagery, and the model of part/whole organization developed by Robertson and Lamb (1991; see also Robertson's discussion in Chapter 4). Nonetheless, there are many aspects of cognitive functioning that are not well understood by cognitive psychologists and for which models are either nonexistent or simplistic at this time. (In many of these cases, the behavioral techniques have yet to be discovered with which the specific cognitive functions of interest can be studied.) The examples we use in this chapter reflect an emphasis on studies which involve relatively specific cognitive dysfunctions (or functions, in the case of the stimulation studies with normal subjects) as well as an emphasis on studies which are motivated by a reasonably complete and well-tested cognitive model.

ATTENTION AND NEUROIMAGING

Structural Neuroimaging and Attention

Posner, Rafal, and colleagues have conducted a number of studies of selective attention with brain-lesioned patients, using the same types of reaction time tasks involving spatial cuing that have been used to study facilitation and inhibition of visual spatial attention in normal subjects (e.g., Posner, 1980). A model task of the type used in these studies is performed as follows: (1) the subject's vision is fixated at the center of the screen, where (2) an arrow (the "cue" for direction of attention) then points either to the right or to the left of center, and then (3) a target (described to the subject previously) is presented at varying intervals after the cue appearing either at the cued location or at the side opposite the cue. This type of task shows an advantage in reaction time for the validly- as compared to invalidly-cued location. In this paradigm, the cue (e.g., the arrow) increases overall alertness, and it also initiates a spatially selective movement of attention to the cued location. The cue also causes two forms of inhibition: "cost" (once attention is engaged at the cued location, all other locations will be inhibited), and "inhibition of return" (the efficiency of a previously cued location is decreased compared to other spatial locations for several seconds).

Posner and others (e.g., Posner, Walker, Friedrich, & Rafal, 1984; Morrow & Ratcliff, 1987) have studied patients with right parietal lesions on the spatial cuing tasks; these patients are those most frequently found to have hemispatial neglect and extinction (see DeRenzi, 1982; Heilman, Watson, & Valenstein, 1985; see also Robertson's discussion of neglect as part of a continuum of attentional disengagement deficit in Chapter 4). These patients, as one would expect, show an overall advantage for targets occurring ipsilateral as compared to contralateral to the lesion. However, little or no difference between ipsilateral and contralateral targets is seen for many of the parietal patients *if* the targets are validly cued. In contrast, when attention is cued to the side of the lesion and the target is presented to the side opposite the lesion (i.e., an invalid trial), the targets are either missed completely or the reaction time is significantly slowed. Thus, the main deficit in parietal patients occurs in the ability to disengage attention from a previously attended location to a new location.

A second patient group, with lesions of the midbrain (including the superior colliculus), progressive supranuclear palsy patients, has been studied by Rafal, Posner, Friedman, Inhoff, and Bernstein (1988). These patients have difficulty making voluntary eye movements, especially vertical ones, and often neglect the lower visual field. These patients show an overall slowing of reaction time, compared to the parietal patients, and show an effect of cue validity in the horizontal direction. However, they do not show a cue validity effect in the vertical direction at the 100 ms cue-target interval (as do the parietal patients); the validity effect does not occur until about 500 ms. Rafal et al. conclude that the deficit in the midbrain patients is in their ability to move covert attention in the vertical direction, which is the direction with the greatest eye movement difficulty.

A third group of patients, having thalamic lesions, has been shown to have

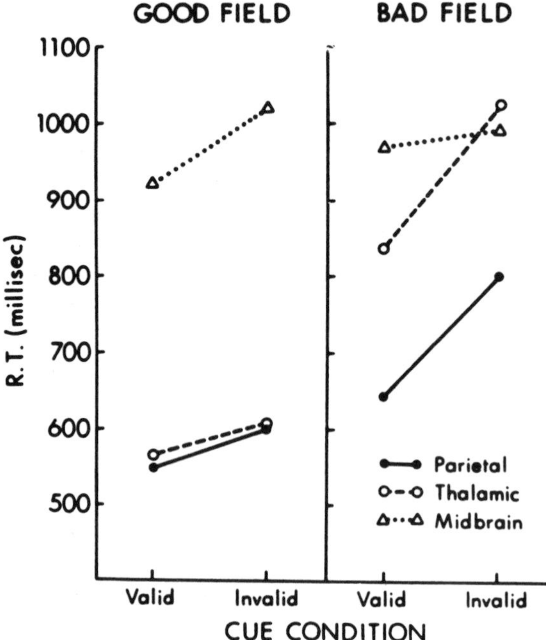

Figure 17-1 Three forms of neglect. The left panel shows performance when targets are in the nonneglected visual area, the right panel when they are in the neglected visual areas. Data are always from cue to target intervals of 100 ms or less. (This material has been reproduced from *Clinical neuropsychology and brain function: Research, measurement, and practice*, T. Boll & B. K. Bryant, Eds., 1988, p. 184. Copyright ©1988 by the American Psychological Association (APA). Reprinted by permission of the APA. Neither the original nor this reproduction can be republished, photocopied, reprinted, or distributed in any form, without the prior written permission of the APA.)

still another pattern of performance deficit on the cued attention task (Rafal & Posner, 1987). Although their performance in the "good" visual field is identical to that of the parietal patients, they show a very large increase in RT on both valid and invalid trials (still showing a significant validity effect) in their "bad" as compared to "good" field. It is important to note that these patients showed no evidence of ophthalmologic deficits. Rafal and Posner concluded that the thalamic patients had a deficit in the ability to engage attention on the contralesional side and that such a deficit was consistent with Crick's (1984) hypothesis that the thalamus has a role in controlling the "attentional spotlight."

These studies provide an excellent example of the application of a cognitive model to neuropsychological populations with known differences in lesion location (see Robertson's further discussion of this research in Chapter 4). In this example, Posner and his colleagues have shown differential impairments in a selective, cued attention task for the patients with parietal, midbrain, or thalamic lesions. The different patterns of cuing effects for the three patient groups are shown in Figure 17-1. The nature of each group's impairment seems to be explained by defective functioning of a particular module of selective attention.

Resting State Functional Imaging and Attention

At least one study has focussed on resting state functional imaging and attention; Bogousslavsky et al. (1988) used SPECT measures of rCBF to help explain the pathophysiology of two patients with hemispatial neglect. Both patients suffered infarctions of the right posterior limb of the internal capsule. While CT scans suggested (and autopsy confirmed, in one case) that the anatomic lesion was confined to that region, and did not involve the overlying cortex, both patients had left neglect syndromes with hemianopsia and hemiparesis. In each case, SPECT performed within 2 weeks post-ictus showed moderate hypoperfusion to the right parietal and frontal lobes, in addition to marked hypoperfusion of the right basal ganglia. Thus, the authors argue, the neglect syndrome may have resulted from disconnection of the right parietal lobe from the reticular activating formation.

Stimulation Studies of Neuroimaging and Attention

The effects of selective attention on rCBF (using the intracarotid ^{133}Xe injection method) have been studied in detail by Roland (1982). He presented subjects with simultaneous pairs of stimuli in each of three modalities (the same modality occurring within a pair), and subjects were required to make a two-choice discrimination in only one of the modalities while ignoring the other two modalities. Primary receptive cortex and immediate associative cortex for all three modalities were markedly activated in all three modes of selective attention (as they had been in the earlier single modality studies, on a modality specific basis), suggesting that ignored modalities were being processed at least preliminarily; this is especially relevant for early versus late filter models of selective attention (see Kahneman, 1973). Instructions to attend to the visual modality increased rCBF in the visual association cortex, the frontal eye fields, and also in the right posterior superior parietal cortex. Selection of the auditory modality increased rCBF in auditory association cortex, the midtemporal cortex, Broca's area, and the frontal eye fields. No modulation of rCBF was observed with the selection of somatosensory modality. In each selective attention condition, the superior mesial part of the prefrontal cortex was particularly strongly activated, compared to the earlier single modality studies, leading Roland to suggest that this area is involved in the control of "differential tuning" of attention, which results in modality specific modulation (at least for auditory and visual selection) across the selective attention conditions.

Posner (1988) and Posner, Sandson, Dhawan, and Shulman (1989) have utilized data from stimulation studies with normals as well as data on the association between structural lesion and attentional deficit in neglect patients (discussed above in the section on neuroimaging and attention) to derive a neuropsychological model of attention. They have proposed an attention system, separate from the data processing systems of the brain, comprised of a network of anatomical areas, with each area carrying out a different function that can be specified cognitively. This approach to studying the attention system is illustrated by Posner, Petersen, Fox, and Raichle (1988); this study compared the effects of word monitoring with target word detection on rCBF in the anterior cingulate versus the left lateral frontal area. In Posner et al.'s model, the anterior cingulate gyrus is identified as the part of the attention system which "selects for action," whereas the left lateral frontal area is associated with semantic network functions. (See the section on stimulation studies of language for a discussion of Posner, Petersen, and colleagues' work on semantic versus nonsemantic processing of words and rCBF.) As hypothesized, rCBF in the anterior cingulate increased when the number of target words (dangerous animals) was increased, whereas rCBF in the left lateral frontal region did not change. While the anterior cingulate may not be exactly the same brain region which Roland (1982) postulated to be involved in the tuning of attention, it is in the same area of prefrontal cortex to which Roland referred, and his "differential tuning" of attention seems very similar to Posner et al.'s "selection for action." (Posner, Petersen, and colleagues have also shown that the anterior cingulate gyrus is not specifically activated during performance of vigilance tasks with a low proportion of target items.)

Further support for the role of the anterior cingulate gyrus in "selection for action" has recently been reported by Pardo, Pardo, Janer, and Raichle (1990). These investigators measured rCBF via PET in young normals during performance of both the congruent and incongruent conditions of the well-known Stroop paradigm. In this paradigm, the subject is asked to name the color of printed words. The word can either be congruent or incongruent with the color of the print (e.g., the noun "red" displayed in a red color vs. the noun "red" displayed in a green color). The underlying assumption for the experiment was that differences in rCBF between the two conditions would reveal those brain regions that are involved in dealing with the attentional conflict set up by the Stroop task, that is, inhibiting the reading of the words while naming the color in which the words are printed. A number of brain regions showed significant differences in rCBF between the two Stroop conditions (the authors do not say how many regions were looked at altogether). The largest differences were found to be in the right anterior cingulate gyrus. The investigators cite other evidence from their laboratory, obtained with various word processing tasks, that the cingulate gyrus is particularly involved in selective attention (Petersen, Fox, Posner, Mintun, & Raichle, 1988; Posner et al., 1988; see subsection on stimulation studies of language). They also point out that, since many other brain areas showed significant differences between the congruent and incongruent Stroop conditions (including bilateral peristriate cortex, left premotor and left postcentral areas, left putamen, and left anterior inferior cingulate gyrus), the Stroop interference effect cannot be simply explained in terms of a single process such as encoding interference or response interference, as various behavioral researchers have suggested.

As discussed under the subsection "Structural Imaging and Attention," thalamic lesions seem to affect the orienting of attention. The pulvinar nucleus of the dorsal thalamus has been proposed by several investigators to play a critical role in selective attention (e.g., Petersen, Robinson, & Morris, 1987) as has the reticular nucleus (Crick, 1984). In fact, Crick has proposed that a network consisting of cells from both the reticular nucleus and a nucleus of the dorsal thalamus could support selective attention functions. LaBerge and Buchsbaum tested their hypothesis "that the pulvinar nucleus of the dorsal thalamus is the subcortical structure that interacts with cortical structures when a visual-identification task requires attentional filtering of a target object from other objects in its surround" (LaBerge & Buchsbaum, 1990; p. 613) in a stimulation study of rCMRglc. They used an attention task which required subjects to fixate on a central point while a filtering display (containing a to-be-detected target) was presented to one visual field, and a nonfiltering display (a single symbol which was sometimes equivalent to the to-be-detected target) was presented to the other visual field. Each subject participated in a session in which the filtering display was always on the right and in a session in which it was always on the left. The difference in rCMRglc between the two experimental conditions was assessed for the left and right pulvinar, mediodorsal nucleus of the thalamus, and two areas outside the thalamus (occipital area VI and an area of frontal white matter). The nonpulvinar regions served as controls for overall hemisphere differences caused by shifting the attention task between hemifields. For the pulvinar region, the rCMRglc data yielded a significant interaction of experimental session with hemisphere; this interaction was not significant for any of the other brain regions examined. Averaged across the two experimental sessions, the pulvinar showed greater glucose uptake when it was contralateral to the filtering display than when it was contralateral to the nonfiltering display. Although there was a sizeable hemisphere difference in rCMRglc in the predicted direction for the session in which the filtering display was presented to the right visual field (left hemisphere), there was a very small difference in the nonpredicted direction when the filtering display was presented to the left visual field (right hemisphere); no *t*-tests for these differences were reported. LaBerge and Buchsbaum suggested on the basis of their findings that the pulvinar may indeed act as a filtering mechanism between cortical areas involved in feature selection and cortical areas involved in object identification.

Yet another recent example of how PET-stimulation studies have yielded information about neurological underpinnings of selective attention is provided by Corbetta, Miezin, Dobmeyer, Shulman, and Petersen (1990). Corbetta et al. first developed a psychophysical task to study the effect of selective as compared to divided attention on discrimination of subtle changes in color, shape, or velocity of a visual stimulus. Four conditions were included: three conditions in which subjects were required to make a same-different judgment for two sequential stimuli on a single dimension, and a divided attention condition in which subjects responded "different" if any of the three dimensions differed. Then, a second group of subjects was tested under each of the four attention conditions while rCBF was measured via PET (with the ^{15}O-water, injection technique). The rCBF for the divided attention condition was subtracted from each of the selective attention conditions for a number of relatively small regions of extrastriate visual cortex. Although there were a couple of cortical foci that showed significant changes (i.e., z score > 1.96) with selective attention to either of two dimensions, there were about 15 foci that showed significant changes for only one of the three dimensions. Attention to shape resulted in bilateral increases in activation in several ventromedial occipital regions along the fusiform and parahippocampal gyri, a more distal focus in the occipitoparietal sulcus, and, on the lateral surface, an area midway along the superior temporal sulcus (between areas 21 and 22). Attention to color caused a bilateral increase in activation in a strip of cortical tissue on the lateral occipital gyri (area 19). Attention to velocity increased activation in a region within the inferior parietal lobule (area 19), but only on the left side. Corbetta et al. make a convincing case that these task-specific changes in neural activation are not due to sensory factors or to changes in general arousal (the divided attention task was, in fact, more difficult per the psychophysical measure of sensitivity in detecting a difference between the sequential stimuli). Rather, these researchers argue that the rCBF changes for each selective attention condition are based on a top-down attention-dependent modulation of activity in the visual cortex.

MEMORY AND NEUROIMAGING

Structural Neuroimaging and Memory

Clinico-neuropathological studies of Korsakoff's syndrome have shown two structures within the diencephalic midline, the mammillary bodies and the dorsomedial thalamic nucleus, to be linked to human amnesia (Victor, Adams, & Collins, 1971). The use of structural imaging with amnesic patients have supported the role of these diencephalic structures in the amnesic syndrome (Speedie & Heilman, 1982; Squire & Moore, 1979). The second general brain region which has been identified with human amnesia is the medial temporal area which includes the hippocampus. The well-known temporal lobe resection case, HM, established the significance of the medial temporal region (Scoville & Milner, 1957) and many other reports, using structural imaging as well as pathologic studies, have confirmed the importance of the hippocampus in normal memory functioning (see Squire & Butters, 1984; Squire, 1987). Common to the two general subgroupings of amnesic patients is a disruption of the ability to acquire new information, that is, an impairment in long-term, or secondary memory. In contrast, amnesics have normal short-term, or primary memory, in that they can hold a limited amount of information (not exceeding their immediate memory span) as long as it is consciously being rehearsed; once they are distracted, then the information is lost. Amnesics also have the ability to accurately recall remote memories, that is, information that was acquired prior to the brain injury (the time periods for which remote memory is intact varies a great deal across patients, but generally the memories for the time period closest to the brain injury are most disrupted). Based on these observations, Squire (1987, p. 180) concludes: "Amnesia appears to reflect neither direct injury to, nor loss of, those brain regions in which information is processed and stored. Instead, amnesia seems best explained by hypothesizing a neural system, which is damaged in amnesia, that ordinarily *participates* in memory storage without being itself a *site* of storage." Squire goes on to discuss the evidence that the hippocampus, the amygdala, the dorsomedial thalamic nucleus, the mammillary bodies, and perhaps also the prefrontal cortex are part of the neural system which, when intact, enables normal memory functioning.

Over the last 15 to 20 years, many studies of amnesic patients have been published in which the region of the brain lesion has been determined by structural neuroimaging (and in some cases by neuropathological examination as well) and in which the nature of the memory impairment has been described in terms of more specific memory functions than was the case in earlier studies. We now know that patients with damage to one or more areas within the neural memory system discussed above are impaired in the learning and memory of *declarative* information, which includes facts, lists, and the material of day-to-day remembering. In contrast, these same patients show a remarkable preservation of skill or *procedural* learning (e.g., mirror-reading, pursuit rotor tasks, puzzle completion) as well as preservation of *priming*, which, in this context, refers to the facilitation of performance by prior exposure to the "target" material (for a review see Cohen, 1984). In a study comparing explicitly to implicitly tested memory for studied words Squire, Shimamura, and Graf (1985) showed amnesics and controls common words and asked them to either recall the words, recall the words to cues consisting of the first three letters, or give the first word that came to mind which began with the same three letters. As expected, the amnesics were significantly impaired in the first two conditions, but performed normally in the third condition, which did not require explicit memory functions, and which could apparently benefit from the prior exposure to the words (i.e., they showed a priming effect). Based on this and other related findings, Squire has argued that "skills and priming are expressed through the operation of a memory system (or systems) that does not allow explicit access to the contents of the knowledge base. The memory can be expressed only in performance and it does not permit a patient's accumulating experience to be reflected either in verbal reports or in nonverbal tests asking for judgments of familiarity" (Squire, 1987; p. 158).

This same type of priming effect (i.e., a benefit from prior exposure to "targets") is reduced in Alzheimer's disease (which is associated with significant pathology of the hippocampus), but not in amnesic patients with comparable memory problems or in demented Huntington's disease patients (Shimamura, Salmon, Squire, & Butters, 1987); this may be indicative of the involvement of areas of cortex outside of the neural memory system in Alzheimer's disease that are normally involved in the storage of procedural information. Further support for differential storage of procedural and declarative knowledge comes from an animal lesion study by Zola-Morgan, Squire, and Mishkin (1982) in which a double dissociation was obtained for impairments in visual object memory versus visual pattern discrimination learning (a procedural task) and lesions in the hippocampus versus temporal stem, respectively. In a neuropsychological investigation of several types of procedural (or implicit) learning and memory across three different dementia groups, Heindel, Salmon, Shults, Walicke, and Butters (1989) have shown that Alzheimer patients are impaired on a verbal priming task, with normal performance on a motor learning task, whereas Huntington's disease patients showed the opposite pattern, and Parkinson's disease patients were impaired on both tasks. Based on these findings and knowledge about the brain regions affected in these three patient populations (knowledge based on both neuroimaging and neuropathological studies), Heindel et al. suggested that motor skill learning is mediated by a corticostriatal system, whereas verbal priming is mediated by the neocortical areas involved in storing semantic knowledge; Parkinson patients may in fact have damage to both neurologic systems.

Stimulation Studies of Neuroimaging and Memory

Mazziotta and colleagues (Mazziotta, Phelps, Carson, & Kuhl, 1982) compared PET-^{18}FDG images from a group of subjects listening to a story with instructions to remember its content to images from another group of subjects listening to the same stories without memory instructions. In both stimulation conditions, there were large areas of increased left as compared to right rCMRglc; however significant bilateral activations of the mesial temporal structures (containing hippocampus, parahippocampus) were seen only in the memory condition. This increased activity in the mesial temporal region is consistent with the large body of data showing correlations between anatomical lesions in the area of the hippocampus and memory deficits.

Changes (from resting state) in rCMRO$_2$ caused by the tactile learning of complex (nonmeaningful) geometric objects and by the tactile recognition of the previously studied objects (the right hand was used in each case) have been quantified by Roland, Eriksson, Widen, and Stone-Elander (1989). During tactile learning and during tactile recognition of old objects, significant ($p < .01$) increases in oxygen metabolism were seen in the same areas of prefrontal cortex, motor cortex, somatosensory cortex, insula, lingual gyrus, hippocampus, basal ganglia, thalamus, parasagittal anterior cerebellum, and neocerebellum. Based on these findings and related evidence (e.g., from lesion studies with monkeys), Roland et al. argue for the existence of a brain circuit which mediates tactile learning and recognition, the parts of which, however, are not themselves involved as storage sites for the tactile information.

When tactile learning was compared to tactile recognition, recognition resulted in increased oxygen use in the left premotor cortex, left somatosensory hand area, and the supplementary motor area, findings which are consistent with the higher recorded frequency of object manipulations during the recognition testing. Interestingly, however, the rCMRO$_2$ was significantly higher in the neocerebellar cortex during tactile learning than during tactile recognition, which Roland and colleagues take as an indication of the particular involvement of this area in the storage of tactile information.

The reader is referred to the section of "Mental Imagery and Neuroimaging" for discussion of the work by Goldenberg and colleagues on stimulation studies of memorization tasks with and without mental imagery.

LANGUAGE AND NEUROIMAGING

Resting State Functional Imaging and Language

It appears that studies have not been done which apply resting-state PET or SPECT to the study of information processing models of language. However, some of the potential for this type of work is demonstrated by studies looking at highly specific language disorders with functional imaging techniques. For example, Silver et al. (1988) used PET to study rCMRglc in a patient with pure alexia (alexia without agraphia). It has been argued that pure alexia is a disconnection syndrome created when a lesion blocks the transfer of information from the occipital cortices to the angular gyrus. This occurs most commonly when a cerebrovascular lesion in the periventricular white matter of the left occipital lobe extends to involve the splenum and thus isolates the angular gyrus from visual input from either hemisphere (Friedman & Albert, 1985). In Silver et al.'s patient, no such lesion was present, as was demonstrated by two CT scans and an MRI scan 7 months post onset. However, separate lesions of the splenum and of the left lateral geniculate were present, and PET scan demonstrated abnormally low glucose metabolism (over two standard deviations below control values) in the left occipital lobe (Brodmann areas 18–19). The authors hypothesized that this region was hypometabolic due to functional deafferentation resulting from these lesions, and conclude that the findings support the view that pure alexia is a disconnection syndrome.

Another example is the case report of Kushner et al. (1987) on rCMRglc in aphemia, an aphasia marked by dysfluency and literal paraphasias with preserved language in writing, and preserved comprehension. A CT scan failed to show any lesion of the left hemisphere, although it did demonstrate an old right parietal infarct. Successive PET scans demonstrated a persistent area of diminished glucose metabolism superior to the left lenticular nucleus, sparing Broca's area. The authors suggest that a circumscribed lesion at the base of the precentral gyrus affects the articulatory motor output, creating aphemia. In this case, as in that of Silver et al. (1988), the PET data did not result in a new anatomic account of the aphasic syndrome, but by demonstrating lesions not otherwise apparent, the data lent support to existing theories. They also demonstrate that narrowly defined aspects of language dysfunction can be correlated with resting state PET data.

Stimulation Studies of Neuroimaging and Language

The majority of stimulation studies using higher-level cognitive tasks with brain-intact individuals have employed language tasks. Ingvar, Larsen, Lassen, Roland & colleagues (see Ingvar, 1983) have conducted an extensive series of studies in which language tasks were given to patients without neurological disturbances and with normal speech, and in which rCBF was measured using the two-dimensional, ^{133}Xe technique. They found increased bilateral activation in the primary motor and sensory as well as parasensory areas expected to be involved in particular tasks (e.g., automatic speech engaging rolandic mouth-tongue-larynx areas and postcentral auditory regions, reading silently engaging visual areas and frontal eye fields, and reading aloud activating the mouth-tongue-larynx areas and postcentral auditory regions as well). However, the anterior and posterior speech areas on the left (Broca's and Wernicke's areas, respectively) were not unconditionally activated above their resting level during productive and receptive language tasks. Furthermore these rCBF studies showed that, in many cases, the right hemisphere homologs to Broca's and Wernicke's areas were activated above their resting state during language tasks (the regions of activation on the right were less well circumscribed than their counterparts on the left). Finally, this series of rCBF studies showed a significant involvement of the prefrontal cortex (Brodmann's areas, 6, 8, and 9), bilaterally, in a number of language production and reception tasks. These findings indicate that many brain areas are involved in normal language processing, in addition to those classically associated with language, and that claims about the left hemisphere being the "language hemisphere" are overly simplistic.

Wallesch, Henriksen, Kornhuber, and Paulson (1985) report a SPECT-rCBF (with ^{133}Xe) study in which normals were given each of several language and control tasks; the language tasks included syllable production, overt language production (retelling a story), and nonarticulatory language production (silently retelling a story). Unfortunately, no statistical tests of rCBF differences among the various stimulation conditions were done; we include the study here as an example of the use of multiple stimulation conditions which vary in terms of specified components of language behavior and because the patterns of rCBF across the different tasks suggest further investigations of this type would be fruitful. The authors reported that the overt language production task, compared to the syllable production task or resting, caused an increase in rCBF in Broca's area, the left anterior thalamic/pallidal region, bilaterally in the head of the caudate nucleus, and bilaterally in the retrorolandic areas. Additionally, rCBF was increased in the left temporal cortex for overt language production as compared to resting, but not as compared to syllable production. It is also interesting to note that during the nonarticulatory language production task there was still a bilateral rCBF increase in the caudate and thalamic regions, which the authors took as support for nonmotor cognitive functions of these nuclei.

The effects of phoneme monitoring (making a foot movement to target phonemes contained in a continuous list of single words) on regional cerebral couplings in rCMRglc were assessed by Bartlett, Brown, Wolf, and Brodie (1987; PET with ^{11}CDG was used). Sixteen ROIs were included in the pairwise, partial correlations, whereby the mean CMRglc across all slices was the control variable for the pairwise correlations. Using a significance level which was adjusted for the number of correlations, these investigators found: (1) more significant correlations in the stimulated as compared to unstimulated (resting) condition, (2) many significant correlations between left and right homologous areas in both conditions, (3) many significant within-hemisphere correlations in the stimulated condition which always occurred in the left hemisphere and which always involved the left inferior frontal area and, (4) no significant within-hemisphere correlations in the unstimulated condition. This study again suggests that many brain areas comprise the "neural language network" including areas of the right hemisphere, but also suggests that more inter-regional coupling of brain activity occurs in the left than the right hemisphere during linguistic processing.

In a recent series of studies designed to delineate the cortical areas involved in single-word processing, Petersen et al. (1988; see also Petersen, Fox, Posner, Mintun, & Raichle, 1989) and Posner et al. (1988) have used PET with ^{15}O-water to study rCBF as a function of single-word processing. For each of two modalities, visual and auditory, four behavioral conditions were used within subjects: fixation on a nonverbal stimulus, passive perception of single words, overt repetition of single words, and the generation of uses for a single-word referent. Each task added a small number of cognitive operations to its control (previous) state; subtracting the rCBF data of a "lower-level" condition from the rCBF data of the condition at the next level allowed the isolation of the cerebral regions involved in the particular cognitive operations of interest. For example, subtraction of the visual fixation point condition from the passive visual words condition would presumably show those brain regions automatically activated by visual word stimuli. The cortical foci of activation for each pair of subtraction conditions are shown in Figure 17-2.

For the visual modality, significant changes in rCBF were seen with passive perception of words (compared to the control state) in extrastriate occipital cortex; Petersen et al. (1988; see also Petersen et al., 1989; Posner et al., 1988) state that these areas are activated only by visually presented words and may represent a network which codes specifically for visual word forms (lesions near these regions can cause pure alexia). In the auditory modality, areas of activity for the auditorally presented words included the temporoparietal and anterior superior temporal regions, areas which are not activated by the presentation of nonverbal auditory stimuli. When words were repeated aloud, areas related to motor output and articulatory coding were activated bilaterally, with similar regions activated for the visual and auditory presentations. Regardless of the modality of word presentation, the semantic processing task—generating uses for items—activated a left inferior frontal area and the anterior cingulate gyrus. Petersen et al. (1988) argue that the first area is involved in processing of semantic association, and that the second area is part of an anterior attentional system involved in "selection for a response" (as discussed earlier in the section on attention). The findings of these word processing studies are also important in yielding evidence for parallel, as opposed to serial, processing of linguistic stimuli.

VISUOSPATIAL COGNITION AND NEUROIMAGING

Stimulation Studies of Object Discrimination vs. Spatial Location

Grady, Haxby, and colleagues (Haxby et al., 1988; Grady et al., 1989; Grady et al., 1990) have used PET and ^{15}O-water to measure rCBF changes in normal subjects which are the result of engaging in object discrimination versus spatial localization tasks. Both types of visual processing task required a two-choice, match-to-sample discrimination. In the case of object discrimination, subjects were asked to identify which of two lower squares contained a face that was of the same person shown in the single top square (under different lighting conditions or from a different angle). In the case of spatial location, subjects had to identify which of two lower squares contained a dot in the same location as the single upper square, with the lower squares rotated relative to the upper square. For each task, subjects responded by pressing either a left- or right-hand button. Ten young and ten old normal subjects participated in each of

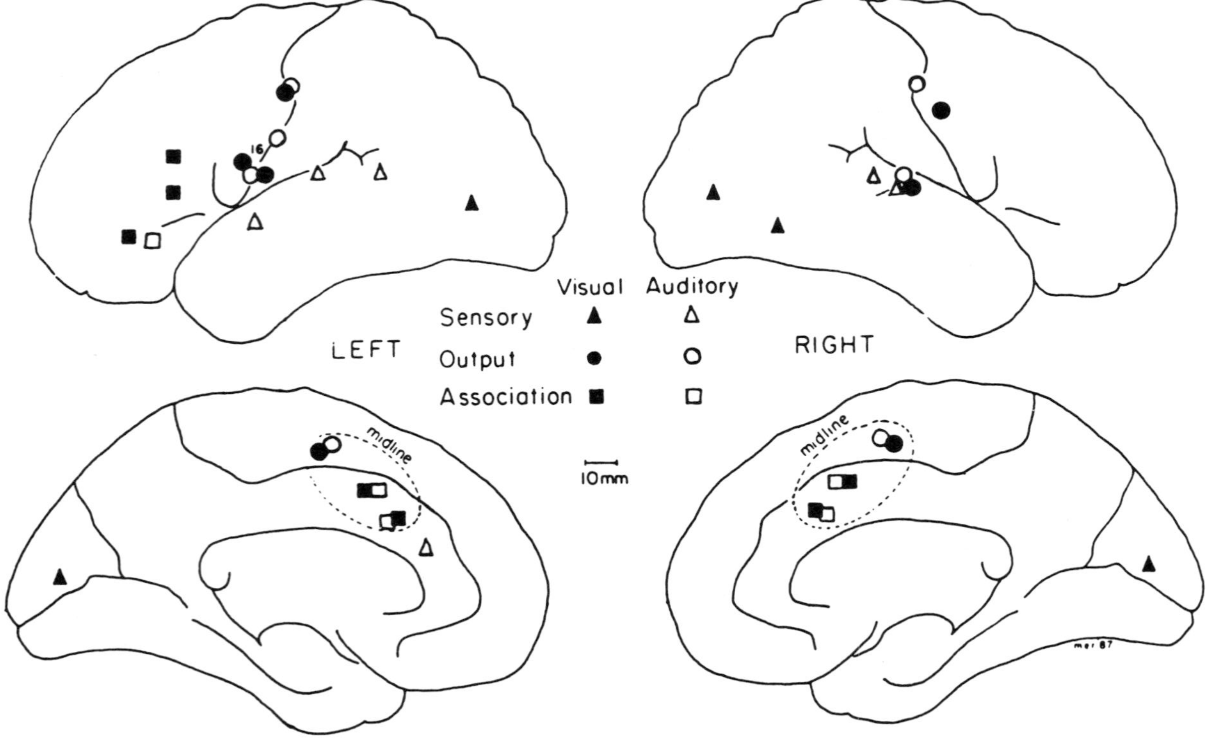

Figure 17-2 Results of an rCBF (PET with ^{15}O-water) stimulation study of single-word processing. Schematic lateral (upper) and medial (lower) surface views of the left and right hemispheres with superimposed cortical activation foci are shown. Each symbol represents a cortical focus for which the z-score of change in activation for the particular subtraction condition was significant at the .03 alpha level. Words were presented to subjects through either the visual or auditory modality. The subtraction conditions are: sensory (passive words–fixation point), output (repeat words–passive words) and association (generate uses for words–repeat words). Note that there is no overlap between the visual and auditory modalities for the sensory foci, in contrast to considerable overlap between the two modalities for the output and association foci. (Adapted from Petersen et al., 1988; reprinted with permission from *Nature*, Vol. 331, p. 586. Copyright ©1988 Macmillan Magazines Limited.)

these tasks as well as in a sensorimotor control task in which the squares were empty and subjects alternated left- and right-hand responses. The rCBF values were normalized by calculating ratios of regional to whole brain blood flow. For each subject and for each of the two experimental tasks, rCBF activation (within each 9 mm pixel) was calculated as a percentage difference between the experimental and the sensorimotor control task. Then, for each subject, areas were identified that had normalized rCBF increases greater than 30% in 12 contiguous pixels (48 mm^2).

Grady, Haxby, and colleagues (Haxby et al., 1988; Grady et al., 1990) found a double-dissociation (shown statistically with significant task by region interactions, bilaterally) for both young and old subjects, such that ventrolateral occipital association and occipito-temporal regions were activated more during the faces task, whereas superior parietal areas were activated only in the spatial task (see Figure 17-3). The researchers take these findings as evidence that two distinct pathways exist in man for object discrimination versus spatial location. In the Grady et al. (1990) study, there was no evidence for interactions between age and the pattern of rCBF changes seen with the two visual processing tasks, suggesting that normal aging has no effect on the location or magnitude of the rCBF changes.

Haxby et al. (1990) have also assessed the relations between rCBF increases during the object discrimination and spatial location tasks and performance for the young subjects who participated in the study just described. Neither reaction time nor accuracy on the two experimental tasks was correlated with the magnitude of rCBF increases in the two highly activated, anatomic regions described above, even though there was substantial inter-subject variation on the performance measures. Haxby and colleagues thus found no evidence that perceptual ability as measured by performance on object discrimination and spatial location is related to the capacity to activate relevant cortical regions in normal subjects.

Neuroimaging Studies of Mental Imagery

Mental imagery has been studied by numerous cognitive psychologists over the last 20–30 years. A major issue in the earlier years of this period was whether images were abstract/propositional or analog (directly containing visual and spatial information) representations. There is a general consensus that mental images do represent at least some of the visual and/or spatial properties of visual stimuli in an analog format (see Pinker, 1985, for a detailed discussion; but also see Pylyshyn, 1984, for arguments in favor of propositional representations of visual stimuli).

A recent case study by Farah, Levine, and Calvanio (1988) has provided evidence for the existence of imagery as a distinct functional system. The patient in this case study, RM, had suffered a left posterior cerebral artery infarction; structural neuroimaging (CT) showed a lesion in the left occipital and medial temporal region. On the (previously validated) imagery task, RM showed significantly worse performance on the true/false sentences which required imagery (68% correct, e.g., "a grapefruit is larger than an orange/a cantaloupe," for the

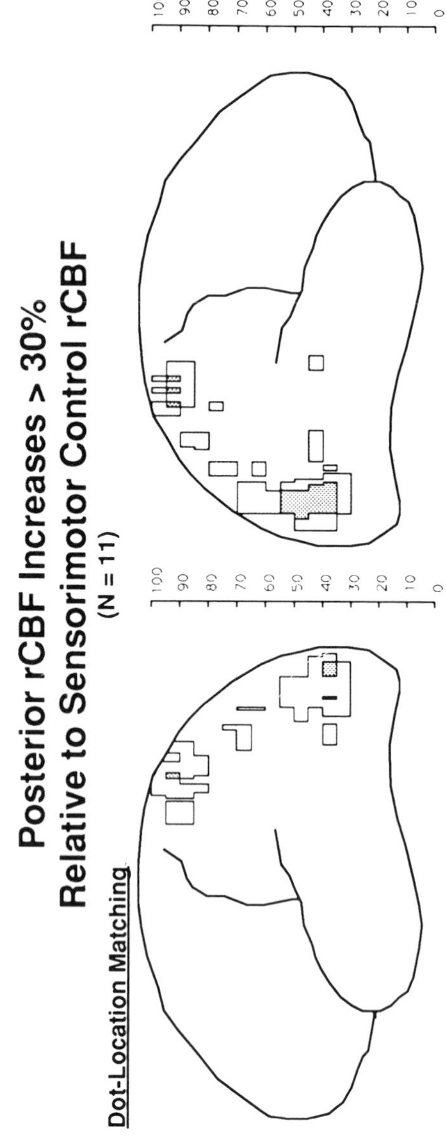
Posterior rCBF Increases > 30%
Relative to Sensorimotor Control rCBF
(N = 11)
Dot-Location Matching
100
90
80
70
60
50
40
30
20
10
0
100
90
80
70
60
50
40
30
20
10
0

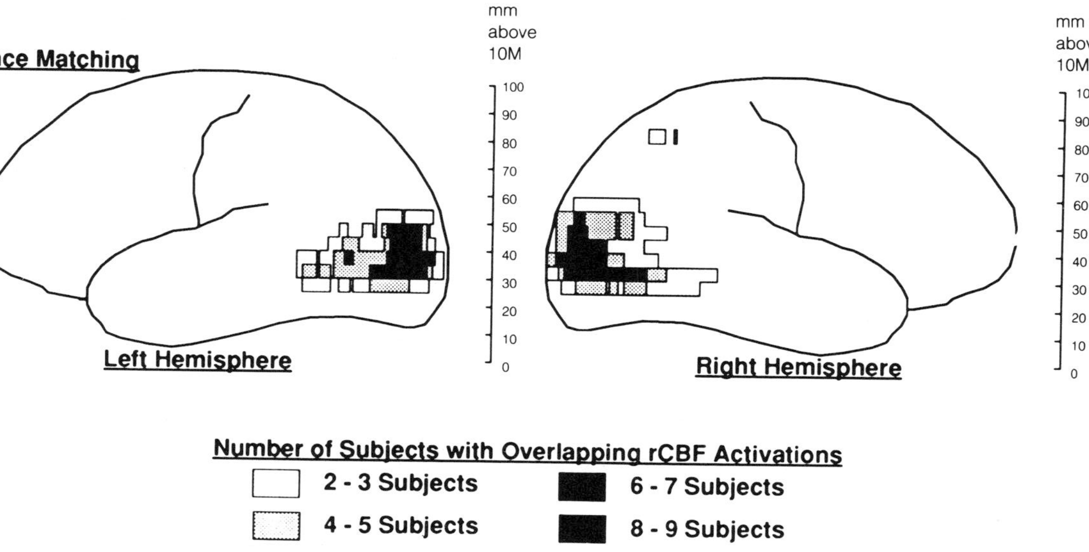

Figure 17-3 A mapping of rCBF in posterior brain regions, obtained via PET with ^{15}O-water. Only regions showing a 30% or greater increase in rCBF on each of two experimental perception tasks as compared to a sensorimotor control task are shown. (From Cheryl Grady and James Haxby; based on Grady, Haxby, et al., 1990.)

true and false versions, respectively) as compared to those which did not require imagery (97% correct, e.g., "the U.S. government functions under a two party/three party system," for the true and false versions, respectively). In contrast, a group of six right hemisphere-damaged patients performed equally (with an overall average of 77% correct on the two types of sentences). RM was also impaired on several imagery tasks that were not dependent on the processing of verbal information. Although RM had difficulties with tasks which required the use of mental imagery, he seemed to have no difficulties on visual recognition tasks. Kosslyn (1980) has suggested that the mental imagery system can be divided into four components: long-term visual memories, the visual buffer (a short-term representational medium for both images and percepts), the inspect process (this allows other cognitive systems to access the visual buffer), and image generation. Only image generation, which is the activation of representations from long-term memory into the visual buffer, is used exclusively by the mental imagery system. The other three components are used in both perception and imagery. Drawing upon Kosslyn's framework, Farah et al. concluded that the only component of imagery which is not also used in visual recognition—image generation—was the locus of RM's imagery deficit. These authors also refer to three additional, recently published cases with good lesion localization via CT, who also have intact recognition abilities in the face of impaired mental imagery, and who all have lesions in the left occipitotemporal region.

There have been three major directions in imagery research: (1) the delineation of the effects of imaginal as compared to nonimaginal encoding in learning and memory, (2) under the assumption that images are, indeed, analog representations, the determination of whether images are visual or spatial representations, and (3) the testing of the hypothesis that mental images function in the same manner as do perceptions of visual stimuli, engaging many of the same information processing mechanisms at multiple levels of the visual information processing system. Neuropsychological studies have been published recently which are concerned with each of these issues and which have related brain structure and/or function to some relatively specific imagery processes.

With regard to the effects of imagery on learning and memory, there is an often replicated finding that concrete (imageable) words are easier to remember than are abstract words, and that instructions to image the referents of a list of concrete words lead to better memory performance than when concrete words are learned without any special instruction. Paivio's (1979) dual-code model of memory postulated the existence of separate memory systems for visual versus verbal information, which were differentially involved in the encoding of abstract versus concrete words, as well as in the encoding of pictures versus words. This model stimulated a large number of experimental studies that used both episodic and semantic memory tasks in attempts to determine whether a single, amodal representational system or two separable (visual vs. verbal) representational systems existed.

A recent study by Goldenberg et al. (1987) looked at the effect on rCBF (measured via SPECT with IMP) of memorizing high- as compared to low-imagery words in an attempt to test the hypothesis that an anatomically distinct, right-hemisphere imagery system is activated by memorizing easily imaged, concrete nouns (Paivio, 1979; Ehrlichman & Barrett, 1983). All subjects underwent SPECT imaging while resting, and also while being given a word learning task, which involved nonsense words, abstract nouns, or concrete nouns. A subgroup of the subjects who were given concrete nouns were asked to use mental images to help them memorize the list. This study is particularly interesting in that both the region-by-region analysis of CBF differences among the stimulation conditions and a descriptive, multivariate, "functional cortical system" analysis for each stimulation condition was undertaken. The standard analysis of the rCBF data yielded no differences between any two stimulation conditions and no differences between the two hemispheres. The results of the "functional cortical system" analysis were also inconsistent with the assumption that the right hemisphere is specialized for visual imagery; rather, the results seemed to indicate that the memorization of concrete words, whether via an imagery or a verbal strategy, involves temporal and occipital regions within both hemispheres.

As mentioned above, the second major issue in imagery research (among cognitive psychologists who hold the analog view of imagery) is whether images are visual or spatial representations. "Visual representations are taken to be modality-specific representations that encode the literal appearance of objects. . . . Spatial representations are taken to be relatively abstract, amodal, or multimodal representations of the layout of objects in space with respect to the viewer and each other" (Farah, Hammond, Levine, & Calvanio, 1988, p. 442). Farah et al. review the evidence that visual and spatial information processing are subserved by anatomically separate and functionally distinct systems (in both monkeys and humans), and then argue that the same distinction between visual and spatial information processing applies to imagery as to perception, such that imagery involves *both* visual and spatial representations. These authors discuss a patient with a profound visual agnosia, i.e., with impaired visual object recognition who, nonetheless showed intact object localization, indicative of spared information processing. This patient, LH, suffered damage to both temporooccipital regions, the right temporal lobe, and the right inferior frontal lobe from a closed head injury and subsequent surgery. Farah et al. administered a number of imagery tasks to this patient, some of which required the processing of information concerning the visual appearance of imagined objects, and some of which required the processing of information concerning the spatial relationships among objects in the image. LH showed a dissociation between these two types of imagery tasks with the visual imagery tasks, but not the spatial imagery tasks, showing impaired performance (compared to 12 control subjects); this would seem to support the notion of two separable forms of imagery representations. Drawing again upon Kosslyn's model, Farah et al. conclude that LH has a deficit in the long-term visual memories required for both object recognition and the processing of visual appearance information in mental imagery.

An rCBF-SPECT (HMPAO as the tracer) stimulation study in which subjects were engaged in visual (colors, faces) or spatial (maps) imagery tasks has been reported recently by Goldenberg, Podreka, Uhl, et al. (1989). Only one of the 34 regions studied showed an overall significant difference ($p < .05$) in rCBF among the three imagery-"rest" differences and none of the *post-hoc* pairwise comparisons for this region, right inferior temporal cortex, were significant. This finding would seem to be inconsistent with the reports of Grady, Haxby, and colleagues, as discussed earlier, in which they describe differences in rCBF between spatial and visual *perception* conditions. This discrepancy is not surprising, however, given the differences in the types of tasks (other than the perceptual versus imaginal nature of the tasks) as well as differences in methods of measuring regional brain function between the two laboratories.

The third major direction in imagery research involves attempts to demonstrate that imagery and perception function in the same manner, i.e., sharing representations and utilizing the same visual information processing systems (for reviews see Farah, 1988; Finke, 1985). A recent study with normal subjects that supports the sharing of mental representations by imaginal and perceptual processes can be found in Farah (1989). Farah had subjects mentally project images of letters into the visual field and then detect point threshold stimuli that either fell on or off of the image. Stimuli falling on the image were detected significantly more often than those falling off of the image, showing that the array format representation was indeed shared by imaginal and perceptual processes.

Goldenberg, Podreka, Steiner, et al. (1989) have assessed the effects of processing sentences which vary in imageability on ongoing brain function. They conducted an rCBF-SPECT (HMPAO as the tracer) study, with 38 ROIs derived from four different levels or "slices." Goldenberg et al. had one group of subjects judge the correctness of a set of visual imagery sentences (e.g., "In a car the accelerator pedal is on the right side") and a set of motor imagery sentences (e.g., "To touch the floor with both hands, one has either to spread or to bend the legs") by flashing a hand-held light if they did not agree with the auditorally presented sentence. They had a separate group of subjects judge the correctness of a set of low imagery sentences (e.g., "Leap years have 366 days") and participate in a yes-no control condition, wherein they flashed the light only when they heard the word "no." They report several ROIs in which the visual imagery task led to greater rCBF than the low-imagery task or the yes-no control task; these ROIs were the left inferior temporal area and the left inferior occipital area. However, given the large number of comparisons made (each with a .05 alpha), the results are difficult to interpret. These authors also report nonsignificant, overall, left-right rCBF asymmetry for each of the four tasks. The results of a "functional cortical system" analysis also seemed to indicate the lack of any specificity in rCBF for imagery versus nonimagery tasks.

THE USE OF NEUROIMAGING WITH COGNITIVE DYSFUNCTION IN DEMENTIA

Dementia provides a good example of a disorder for which there is a major gap between neuroimaging and cognitive research. Most of the studies of cognition in dementia which have used information processing models have examined various aspects of episodic and semantic memory (for reviews, see Nebes, 1989; Jorm, 1986). Those studies which have looked at specific components of memory functioning in dementia do not include neuroimaging data; unfortunately, virtually all of the studies which have obtained neuroimaging data (usually correlational PET data) have obtained fairly general, neuropsychological measures of memory performance. However, several studies have compared diagnostically different dementia groups using memory tasks designed to focus on specific aspects of memory such as encoding or retrieval, or on specific types of memory such as declarative or procedural memory. An example of this kind of work is the series of studies produced by Butters and colleagues (Butters, Granholm, Salmon, Grant, & Wolfe, 1987; Granholm & Butters, 1988; Heindel et al., 1989). An important general finding is the existence of double dissociations of preserved and compromised memory functions between different patient groups. One example is provided by the Heindel et al. (1989) study discussed earlier (in the section on memory) in which Alzheimer's disease (AD) patients were shown to be impaired on word priming but not on motor learning, whereas Huntington's disease (HD) patients were shown to have normal word priming and impaired motor learning. Another double dissociation is evidenced in the recall versus recognition performance between AD and HD patients. Butters et al. (1987) and Granholm and Butters (1988) have demonstrated that even when the demented groups are equated for degree of impairment on free recall tasks they still display different patterns of errors in recall (AD but not HD patients making intrusion errors) and benefit differentially from cues (HD but not AD patients performing markedly better with cues).

Comparative studies of this type are of special interest because of increasing evidence that several major dementing illnesses are each associated with different patterns of anatomic and physiologic changes, and that these patterns of pathology have a degree of regional specificity which makes correlation with specific cognitive processes conceivable. Imaging techniques are able to measure certain features of the pathology of some dementing disorders *in vivo*. In HD, MRI and CT studies visualize the prominent atrophy of the caudate that is characteristic of this disorder. Focal metabolic (Kuhl et al., 1982) and blood flow (Reid, Besson, Best, Sharp, & Gemmell, 1988) abnormalities of this same region can also be demonstrated with PET and SPECT. In AD, the findings of structural imaging techniques are less specific; studies usually find cortical atrophy and ventricular enlargement which averages greater than that seen in normals, but which overlaps normal values substantially, and which lacks a characteristic regional pattern. Recent work suggests that more success may be attained in identifying MRI patterns specific to AD by using MRI study protocols that yield optimal views of those structures known to be heavily involved in AD, such as the hippocampus. Seab et al. (1988) found that morphometric measures of hippocampal atrophy clearly differentiated clinically diagnosed AD patients from age-matched controls (see Figure 17-4). PET and SPECT studies of AD have shown that diminished glucose metabolism and blood flow in temporal and parietal cortex are reasonably specific to AD (Jagust, Reed, Seab, Kramer, & Budinger, 1989; Jagust, Friedland, Budinger, Koss, & Ober, 1988; Sharp et al., 1986) (see Figure 17-5). These abnormalities seem to appear early in the disease (Duara et al., 1986; Reed, Jagust, Seab, & Ober, 1989), are generally bilateral but may be significantly asymmetric (Friedland et al., 1983; Grady, Haxby, Schlageter, Berg, & Rapoport, 1986), and worsen as symptoms progress (Jagust, Budinger, & Reed, 1987; Jagust et al., 1988). To date, however, there are few

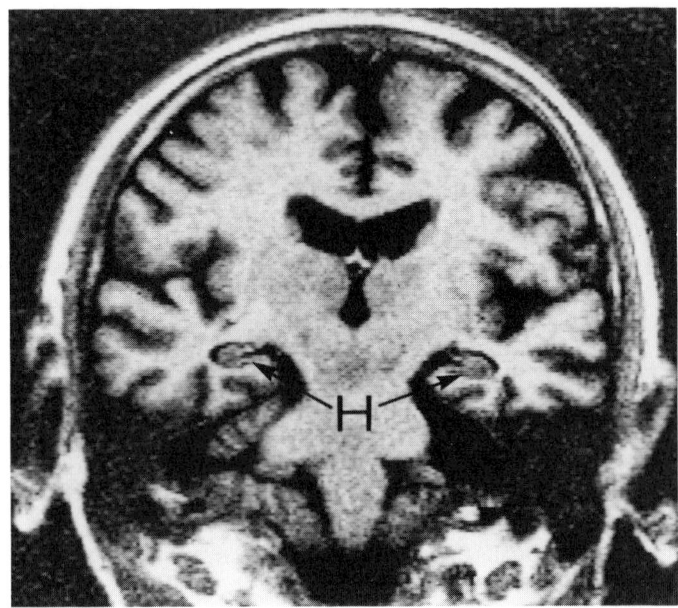

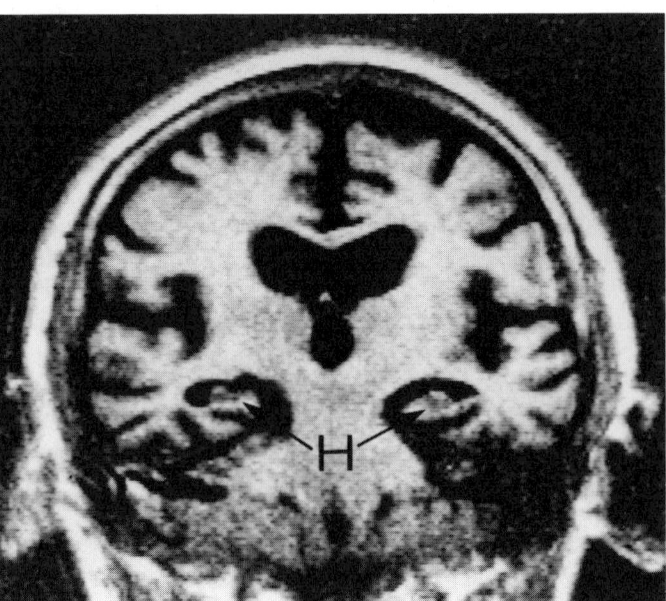

Figure 17-4 Coronal magnetic resonance images obtained from a control subject (top) and a patient with Alzheimer's disease (bottom). The hippocampus (H) is markedly atrophic in the Alzheimer patient, bilaterally. (Reprinted from Seab et al., 1988, with permission from *Magnetic resonance in medicine*, Vol. 8, p. 203. Copyright ©1988 Academic Press.)

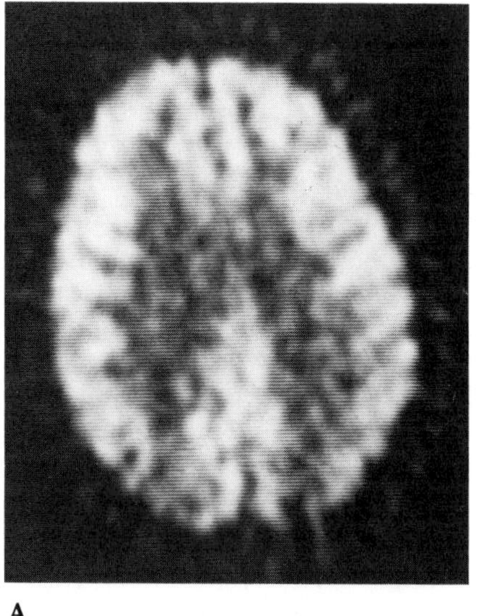
A

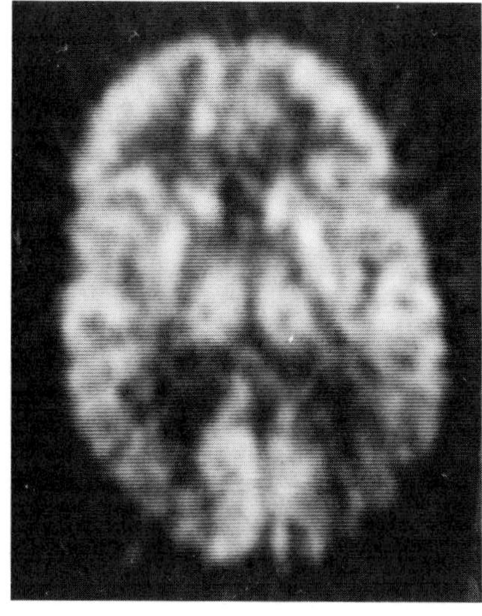
B

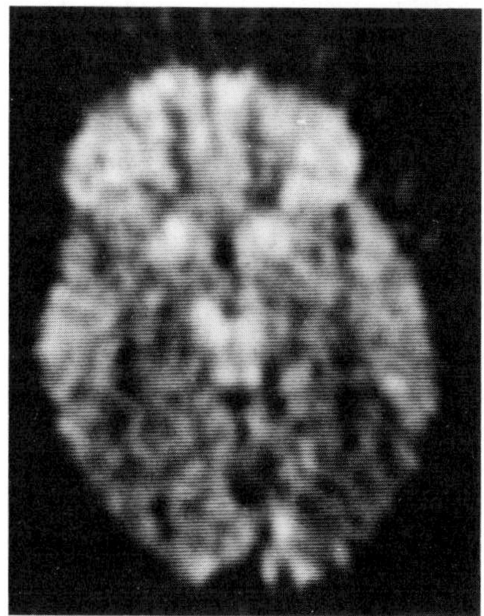
C

Figure 17-5 PET images using the tracer ^{18}F-fluorodeoxyglucose (FDG) in a patient with Alzheimer's disease. Images are obtained 7 (A), 5 (B), and 3 (C) cm above, and parallel to, the orbitomeatal line. These images demonstrate the characteristic hypometabolism seen in the temporal and parietal lobes.

studies that have examined information processing measures in dementia in relation to either structural or functional imaging. Studies which measure both cognition and structural imaging data have tended to use rather global cognitive measures in relation to large anatomic features. As an example, rate of cognitive deterioration has been shown to be significantly correlated with the rate of ventricular enlargement as measured by CT scan (Luxenberg, Haxby, Creasey, Sundaram, & Rapoport, 1987). Even when very specific anatomic measures have been used, the cognitive measures have remained general; for example, in Seab et al. (1988), the only cognitive measure reported was a mental status score which correlated significantly with cortical atrophy but not with hippocampal atrophy. The excellent spatial resolution of MRI appears to create the potential for many informative studies in this area. In working with humans, cognitive researchers have tended to use diagnostic status as a proxy variable for anatomic information; i.e., two groups with illnesses known to differ in their pathophysiology are compared and between-group cognitive differences are then inferred to be related to the group pathological differences. Valuable information might be gained by directly measuring pathology in regions of interest and correlating these measures with cognitive performance. Studies which attempt to examine the relation of information processing measures of cognition to the "metabolic landscape" of dementia appear to be lacking. A few studies, however, have related fairly broad cognitive functions (assessed by traditional neuropsychological tests) to functional neuroimaging data. Several investigations have shown that metabolic asymmetries are significantly correlated with discrepancies in lateralized cognitive functions (e.g., language vs. visuospatial performance, Haxby, Duara, Grady, Cutler, & Rapoport, 1985) and that when particular cognitive deficits are much more marked than the overall level of dementia severity, these deficits are related to markedly reduced physiologic function in the appropriate neocortical regions (e.g., Celsis, Agniel, Puel, Rascol, & Marc-Vergnes, 1987). Another example of a relatively general cognitive function being related to brain function is provided by Berent et al. (1988) who obtained a significant correlation of caudate metabolism with verbal memory performance in HD patients, but not in controls.

At least one study, Ober, Jagust, Koss, Delis, and Friedland (1991), has looked at the relationship of relatively specific components of a more general cognitive function and related performance on these components to rCMR in dementia patients. The general cognitive function involved visuoconstructive ability; patients' drawings (copied and drawn from memory) were scored on specific components such as attention to detail, attention to configuration, perseveration, etc., in addition to overall recognizability. Ober et al. found that several specific components of drawing performance, in addition to overall recognizability of the drawings (but not dementia severity), were significantly correlated with rCMRglc (assessed via PET with ^{18}FDG) in left and right temporal-parietal cortex and in left and right occipital cortex. This suggests that both left and right posterior cortices are involved in the visuoconstructive deficits seen in AD.

Attempts to examine the physiologic correlates of more specific cognitive processes are to some degree blocked by the limited spatial resolution of these techniques. For instance, it has generally not been possible to visualize adequately the hippocampus using either PET or SPECT. As the resolution of PET machines improves, studies examining specific aspects of memory in relation to metabolism in specific structures of interest will become possible (for example, studying rate of forgetting in relation to hippocampal glucose metabolism).

CONCLUSIONS

In this chapter we have provided a selective review of the literature which relates neuroimaging data to cognitive function. We limited our review to studies which were driven by a component process type of cognitive model and/or which looked at relatively specific cognitive functions. Based on this review, one comes to the obvious conclusion that stimulation studies in which high resolution PET or SPECT neuroimaging of regional cerebral function is obtained, while subjects are engaged in each of a series of component cognitive processes for a particular cognitive/behavioral task, is in many ways the "model" paradigm. When fairly well-developed models exist for the cognitive/behavioral task under study (such as word reading, selective attention, mental imagery, etc.) then the stimulation paradigm can be invaluable in enabling researchers to delineate within-subject differences in regional cerebral activation that occur as a result of engaging in a particular component process of the cognitive function under study.

We should keep in mind, however, that even these sorts of stimulation studies (e.g., using ^{15}O-water with PET to measure rCBF) can only tell us about the distribution of regional cerebral activity which results from the previous 2–3 minutes of cognitive function. Functional neuroimaging methods which utilize emission computed tomography do not permit the measurement of changes in brain function that occur within the time frame of individual word recognition trials or other discrete cognitive events taking place within milliseconds.

Correlative neuroimaging studies (both structural and functional imaging) which attempt to relate localized lesions to cognitive deficits also have advantages for understanding brain-cognition relationships. CT, MRI, and even SPECT studies are much less expensive and much less time consuming than the PET studies which have been employed in stimulation experiments. The correlational information about lesion location in patient groups or in neuropsychological case studies which can be obtained with CT, MRI, and SPECT, is quite useful when the component processes for the cognitive function of interest are unknown. Similarly, these correlational studies can be useful when the component processes have been modeled by cognitive psychologists, but the appropriate cognitive/behavioral tasks for assessing the intactness of these components (particularly in brain-damaged individuals) have not been devised and/or validated. In this light, the correlational imaging studies can be thought of as a fruitful means of delineating those brain areas which are likely to be involved in a particular cognitive function. For example, the correlational neuroimaging studies reviewed in the section on memory indicate a critical role for the hippocampus and for the diencephalic region in the transfer of information from short- to long-term memory. Future stimulation studies could look at the effects of engaging in particular long-term memory functions (e.g., retrieval of declarative vs. procedural knowledge) in both normals and in amnesic patients with hippocampal or diencephalic lesions.

In considering the clinical utility of neuroimaging techniques, it is important to remember that this chapter reviews only those studies in which the behavioral variables are being related to cognitive science models or at least to a specific cognitive process. This excludes a substantial portion of the neuroimaging literature, and happens to omit research on several applications of SPECT and PET that may soon affect clinical practice. While the use of PET is generally limited to tertiary care centers, its clinical utility has been demonstrated in the evaluation of patients with brain tumors (Valk et al., 1988), dementia, and stroke. SPECT is currently an accessible and affordable technique, with FDA-approved tracers for the measurement of rCBF. SPECT-rCBF studies may be useful in the differential diagnosis of dementia (Jagust et al., 1987; Reed et al., 1989) or in defining physiologic lesions in stroke (Nagata, Yunoki, Kabe, Suzuki, & Araki, 1986). Similar studies may prove to be useful in measuring changes in brain function, as in measuring deterioration in dementia (DeKosky, Shih, Schmitt, Coupal, & Kirkpatrick, 1990) or recovery from head injury or stroke.

The new information processing models mentioned in this chapter have already had a significant impact on clinical neuropsychology. Our understanding of memory failure, for example, has been changed tremendously by concepts such as implicit, explicit, episodic, and semantic memory. The application of these concepts to clinical phenomena has produced much progress in delineating patterns of amnesia that are differentially associated with different etiologies, and has provided intriguing hints about the treatment of memory loss. The impact of information processing models will expand as clinical neuropsychological tests are revised or created with them in mind.

Functional neuroimaging studies will hasten the day that information processing models become clinically useful by aiding our investigation of their physioanatomic substrate. The stimulation studies reviewed in this chapter show how PET can demonstrate a correspondence between a cognitive model's component processes and patterns of physiologic cerebral activity. Such studies can provide compelling support for a cognitive model and refine our understanding of the cognitive sequelae of cerebral lesions.

REFERENCES

Bartlett, E. J., Brown, J. W., Wolf, A. P., & Brodie, J. D. (1987) Correlations between glucose metabolic rates in brain regions of healthy male adults at rest and during language stimulation. *Brain and Language*, *32*, 1–18.

Berent, S., Giordani, B., Lehtinen, S., Markel, D., Penney, J. B., Buchtel, H. A., Starosta-Rubinstein, S., Hichwa, R., & Young, A. B. (1988). Positron emission tomographic scan investigations of Huntington's disease: Cerebral metabolic correlates of cognitive function. *Annals of Neurology*, *23*, 541–546.

Bogousslavsky, J., Miklossy, J., Regli, F., Deruaz, J. P., Assal, G., & Delaloye, B. (1988). Subcortical neglect: Neuropsychological, SPECT, and neuropathological correlations with anterior choroidal artery territory infarction. *Annals of Neurology*, *23*, 448–452.

Brant-Zawadzki, M. (1987). Magnetic resonance imaging principles: The bare necessities. In M. Brant-Zawadzki & D. Norman (Eds.), *Magnetic resonance imaging of the central nervous system* (pp. 1–13). New York: Raven Press.

Budinger, T. F., & Margulis, A. P. (Eds.). (1986). *Magnetic Resonance Imaging and Spectroscopy: A Primer*. Berkeley, CA: Society of Magnetic Resonance in Medicine.

Butters, N., Granholm, E., Salmon, D. P., Grant, I., & Wolfe, J. (1987). Episodic and semantic memory: A comparison of amnesic and demented patients. *Journal of Clinical and Experimental Neuropsychology*, *9*, 479–497.

Celsis, P., Agniel, A., Puel, M., Rascol, A., & Marc-Vergnes, J. P. (1987). Focal cerebral hypoperfusion and selective cognitive deficit in dementia of the Alzheimer type. *Journal of Neurology, Neurosurgery, and Psychiatry*, *50*, 1602–1612.

Chang, J. Y., Duara, R., Barker, W., Apicella, A., & Finn, R. (1987). Two behavioral states studied in a single PET/FDG procedure: Theory, method, and preliminary results. *Journal of Nuclear Medicine*, *28*, 852–860.

Cohen, N. J. (1984). Preserved learning in amnesia: Evidence for multiple memory systems. In L. R. Squire & N. Butters (Eds.), *Neuropsychology of memory*. New York: The Guilford Press.

Corbetta, M., Miezin, F. M., Dobmeyer, S., Shulman, G. L., & Petersen, S. E. (1990). Attentional modulation of neural processing of shape, color, and velocity in humans. *Science*, *248*, 1556–1559.

Crick, F. (1984). Function of the thalamic reticular complex: The searchlight hypothesis. *Proceedings of the National Academy of Science*, *81*, 4586–4590.

DeKosky, S. T., Shih, W. J., Schmitt, F. A., Coupal, J., & Kirkpatrick, C. (1990). Assessing utility of single photon emission computed tomography (SPECT) scan in Alzheimer's disease: Correlation with cognitive severity. *Alzheimer's Disease and Associated Disorders*, *4*, 14–23.

Dell, G. S. (1988). The retrieval of phonological forms in production: Tests of predictions from a connectionist model. *Journal of Memory and Language*, *27*, 124–142.

DeRenzi, E. (1982). *Disorders of space exploration and cognition*. New York: Wiley.

Duara, R., Grady, C., Haxby, J., Sundaram, M., Cutler, N. R., Heston, L., Moore, A., Schlageter, N., Larson, S., & Rapoport, S. I. (1986). Positron emission tomography in Alzheimer's disease, *Neurology*, *36*, 879–887.

Ehrlichman, H., & Barrett, J. (1983). Right hemispheric specialization for mental imagery: A review of the evidence. *Brain and Cognition*, *2*, 55–76.

Farah, M. J. (1988). Is visual imagery really visual? Overlooked evidence from neuropsychology. *Psychological Review*, *95*, 307–317.

Farah, M. J. (1989). Mechanisms of imagery-perception interaction. *Journal of Experimental Psychology: Human Perception and Performance*, *15*, 203–211.

Farah, M. J., Hammond, K. M., Levine, D. N., & Calvanio, R. (1988). Visual and spatial mental imagery: Dissociable systems of representation. *Cognitive Psychology*, *20*, 439–462.

Farah, M. J., Levine, D. N., & Calvanio, R. (1988). A case study of mental imagery deficit. *Brain and Cognition*, *8*, 147–164.

Finke, R. A. (1985). Theories relating mental imagery to perception. *Psychological Bulletin*, *98*, 236–259.

Fodor, J. (1988). On modularity in syntactic processing. *Journal of Psycholinguistic Research*, *17*, 125–168.

Friedland, R. P., Budinger, T. F., Ganz, E., Yano, Y., Mathic, C. A., Koss, B., Ober, B. A., Huesman, R. H., & Derenzo, S. E. (1983). Regional cerebral metabolic alterations in dementia of the Alzheimer type: Positron emission tomography with [18F]fluorodeoxyglucose. *Journal of Computer Assisted Tomography*, *7*, 590–598.

Friedman, R. B., & Albert, M. L. (1985). Alexia. In K. M. Heilman & F. Valenstein (Eds.), *Clinical neuropsychology* (pp. 75–96). New York: Oxford Press.

Goldenberg, G., Podreka, I., Steiner, M., & Willmes, K. (1987). Patterns of regional cerebral blood flow related to memorizing of high and low imagery words-an emission computer tomography study. *Neuropsychologia*, *25*, 473–485.

Goldenberg, G., Podreka, I., Steiner, M., Willmes, K., Suess, E., & Deecke, L. (1989). Regional cerebral blood flow patterns in visual imagery. *Neuropsychologia*, *27*, 641–664.

Goldenberg, G., Podreka, I., Uhl, F., Steiner, M., Willmes, K., & Deecke, L. (1989).

Cerebral correlates of imagining colours, faces and a map—I. SPECT of regional cerebral blood flow. *Neuropsychologia*, *27*, 1315–1328.

Grady, C. L., Haxby, J. V., Horwitz, B., Schapiro, M., Carson, R. E., Herscovitch, P., Ungerleider, L. G., Mishkin, M., Friedland, R. P., & Rapoport, S. I. (1989). Mapping human visual systems for object recognition and spatial localization by measurement of regional cerebral blood flow. *Journal of Cerebral Blood Flow and Metabolism*, *9*, S574 (Abstract).

Grady, C. L., Haxby, J. V., Horwitz, B., Schapiro, M., Ungerleider, L. G., Mishkin, M., Carson, R. E., Herscovitch, P., & Rapoport, S. I. (1990). Changes in regional cerebral blood flow (rCBF) demonstrate separate visual pathways for object discrimination and spatial location. *Journal of Clinical and Experimental Neuropsychology*, *12*, 93 (Abstract).

Grady, C. L., Haxby, J. V., Schlageter, N. L., Berg, G., & Rapoport, S. I. (1986). Stability of metabolic and neuropsychological asymmetries in dementia of the Alzheimer type. *Neurology*, *36*, 1390–1392.

Granholm, E., & Butters, N. (1988). Associative encoding and retrieval in Alzheimer's and Huntington's disease. *Brain and Cognition*, *7*, 335–347.

Haxby, J. V., Duara, R., Grady, C. L., Cutler, N. R., & Rapoport, S. I. (1985). Relations between neuropsychological and cerebral metabolic asymmetries in earlier Alzheimer's disease. *Journal of Cerebral Blood Flow and Metabolism*, *5*, 193–200.

Haxby, J. V., Grady, C. L., Horwitz, B., Schapiro, M. B., Carson, R. E., Ungerleider, L. G., Mishkin, M., Herscovitch, P., Friedland, R. P., & Rapoport, S. I. (1988). Mapping two visual pathways in man with regional cerebral blood flow (rCBF) as measured by positron emission tomography (PET) and $H_2{}^{15}O$. *Society for Neuroscience Abstracts*, *14*, 750.

Haxby, J. V., Grady, C. L., Horwitz, B., Ungerleider, L. G., Mishkin, M., Schapiro, M. B., & Rapoport, S. I. (1990). Relations between regional cerebral blood flow increases during visual processing and visuoperceptual performance. *Journal of Clinical and Experimental Neuropsychology*, *12*, 93–94 (Abstract).

Heilman, K. M., & Valenstein, E. (Eds.). (1985). *Clinical neuropsychology*. New York: Oxford University Press.

Heilman, K. M., Watson, R. T., & Valenstein, E. (1985). Neglect and related disorders. In K. M. Heilman & E. Valenstein (Eds.), *Clinical neuropsychology* (pp. 243–293). New York: Oxford.

Heindel, W. C., Salmon, D. P., Shults, C. W., Walicke, P. A., & Butters, N. (1989). Neuropsychological evidence for multiple implicit memory systems: A comparison of Alzheimer's, Huntington's, and Parkinson's disease patients. *Journal of Neuroscience*, *9*, 582–587.

Ingvar, D. H. (1983). Serial aspects of language and speech related to prefrontal cortical activity: A selective review. *Human Neurobiology*, *2*, 177–189.

Jagust, W. J., Budinger, T. F., & Reed, B. R. (1987). The diagnosis of dementia with single photon emission computed tomography. *Archives of Neurology*, *44*, 258–262.

Jagust, W. J., Friedland, R. P., Budinger, T. F., Koss, E., & Ober, B. A. (1988). Longitudinal studies of regional cerebral metabolism in Alzheimer's disease. *Neurology*, *38*, 909–912.

Jagust, W. J., Reed, B. R., Seab, J. P., Kramer, J. H., & Budinger, T. F. (1989). Clinical-physiologic correlates of Alzheimer's disease and frontal lobe dementia. *American Journal of Physiologic Imaging*, *4*, 89–96.

Jorm, A. F. (1986). Controlled and automatic information processing in senile dementia: A review. *Psychological Medicine*, *16*, 77–88.

Kahneman, D. (1973). *Attention and effort*. Englewood Cliffs, N.J.: Prentice-Hall.

Kertesz, A. (Ed.). (1983). *Localization in neuropsychology*. Orlando, FL: Academic Press.

Kosslyn, S. M. (1980). *Image and mind*. Cambridge, MA: Harvard University Press.

Kuhl, D. E., Phelps, M. E., Markham, C. H., Metter, E. J., Riege, W. H., & Winter, J. (1982). Cerebral metabolism and atrophy in Huntington's disease determined by ^{18}FDG and computed tomographic scan *Annals of Neurology*, *12*, 425–434.

Kushner, M., Reivich, M., Alavi, A., Greenberg, J., Stern, M., & Dann, R. (1987). Regional cerebral glucose metabolism in aphemia: A case report. *Brain and Language*, *31*, 201–214.

LaBerge, D., & Buchsbaum, M. S. (1990). Positron emission tomographic measurements of pulvinar activity during an attention task. *Journal of Neuroscience*, *10*, 613–619.

Luxenberg, J. S., Haxby, J. V., Creasey, H., Sundaram, M., & Rapoport, S. I. (1987). Rate of ventricular enlargement in dementia of the Alzheimer type correlates with rate of neuropsychological deterioration. *Neurology*, *37*, 1135–1140.

Mazziotta, J. C., Phelps, M. E., Carson, R. E., & Kuhl, D. E. (1982). Tomographic mapping of human cerebral metabolism: Auditory stimulation. *Neurology*, *32*, 921–937.

Morrow, L. A., & Ratcliff, G. (1987). Attentional mechanisms in clinical neglect. *Journal of Clinical and Experimental Neuropsychology*, *9*, 74–75 (Abstract).

Morton, J. (1969). The interaction of information in word recognition. *Psychological Review*, *76*, 165–178.

Morton, J. (1979). Facilitation in word recognition: Experiments causing change in the logogen model. In P. Kolers, M. Wrolstad, & H. Bouma (Eds.), *Processing of visible language* (Vol. 1, pp. 259–268.) New York: Plenum Press.

Nagata, K., Yunoki, K., Kabe, S., Suzuki, A., & Araki, G. (1986). Regional cerebral blood flow correlates of aphasia outcome in cerebral hemorrhage and cerebral infarction. *Stroke*, *17*, 417–423.

Nebes, R. D. (1989). Semantic memory in Alzheimer's disease. *Psychological Bulletin*, *106*, 377–394.

Nelson, D. L. (1981). Many are called but few are chosen: The influence of context on the effects of category size. *The Psychology of Learning and Motivation*, *15*, 129.

Ober, B. A., Jagust, W. J., Koss, E., Delis, D. C., & Friedland, R. P. (1991). Visuoconstructive performance and regional cerebral glucose metabolism in Alzheimer's disease. *Journal of Clinical and Experimental Neuropsychology*, *13*, 752–772.

Paivio, A. (1979). *Imagery and verbal processes*, 2nd Ed. Hillsdale, NJ: Lawrence Erlbaum.

Pardo, J. V., Pardo, P. J., Janer, K. W., & Raichle, M. E. (1990). The anterior cingulate cortex mediates processing selection in the Stroop attentional conflict paradigm. *Proceedings of the National Academy of Science*, *87*, 256–259.

Petersen, S. E. Fox, P. T., Posner, M. I., Mintun, M., & Raichle, M. E. (1988). Positron emission tomographic studies of the cortical anatomy of single-word processing. *Nature*, *331*, 585–589.

Petersen, S. E., Fox, P. T., Posner, M. I., Mintun, M., & Raichle, M. E. (1989). Positron emission tomographic studies of the processing of single words. *Journal of Cognitive Neuroscience*, *1*, 153–170.

Petersen, S. E., Robinson, D. L., & Morris, J. D. (1987). Contributions of the pulvinar to visual spatial attention. *Neuropsychologia*, *25*, 97–105.

Pinker, S. (1985). Visual cognition: An introduction. In S. Pinker (Ed.), *Visual cognition*. Cambridge, MA: MIT Press.

Posner, M. I. (1980). Orienting of attention. *Quarterly Journal of Experimental Psychology*, *32*, 3–25.

Posner, M. I. (1988). Structures and functions of selective attention. In T. Boll & B. K. Bryant (Eds.), *Clinical neuropsychology and brain function: Research, measurement, and practice* (pp. 169–202). Washington, DC: American Psychological Association.

Posner, M. I., Petersen, S. E., Fox, P. T., & Raichle, M. E. (1988). Localization of cognitive operations in the human brain. *Science*, *240*, 1627–1631.

Posner, M. I., Sandson, J., Dhawan, M., & Shulman, G. L. (1989). Is word recognition automatic? A cognitive-anatomical approach. *Journal of Cognitive Neuroscience*, *1*, 50–60.

Posner, M. I., Walker, J. A., Friedrich, F. J., & Rafal, R. D. (1984). Effects of parietal injury on covert orienting of visual attention. *Journal of Neuroscience 4*, 1863–1874.

Pylyshyn, Z. W. (1984). *Computation and cognition*. Cambridge, MA: MIT Press.

Rafal, R. D., & Posner, M. I. (1987). Deficits in human visual spatial attention following thalamic lesions. *Proceedings of the National Academy of Science*, *84*, 7349–7353.

Rafal, R. D., Posner, M. I., Friedman, J. H., Inhoff, A. W., & Bernstein, E. (1988). Orienting of visual attention in progressive supranuclear palsy. *Brain*, *111*, 267–280.

Reed, B. R., Jagust, W. J., Seab, J. P., & Ober, B. A. (1989). Memory and regional cerebral blood flow in mildly symptomatic Alzheimer's disease. *Neurology*, *39*, 1537–1539.

Reid, I. C., Besson, J. A. O., Best, P. V., Sharp, P. F., & Gemmell, H. G. (1988). Imaging of cerebral blood flow markers in Huntington's disease using single photon emission computed tomography. *Journal of Neurology, Neurosurgery, and Psychiatry*, *51*, 1264–1268.

Robertson, L. C., & Lamb, M. R. (1991). Neuropsychological contributions to theories of part/whole organization. *Cognitive Psychology*, *23*, 299–331.

Roland, P. E. (1982) Cortical regulation of selective attention in Man. A regional cerebral blood flow study. *Journal of Neurophysiology*, *48*, 1059–1078.

Roland, P. E., Eriksson, L., Widen, L., & Stone-Elander, S. (1989). Changes in regional cerebral oxidative metabolism induced by tactile learning and recognition in man. *European Journal of Neuroscience*, *1*, 3–18.

Rumelhart, D. E., McClelland, J. L., & PDP Research Group. (1986). *Parallel Distributed Processing: Explorations in the Microstructure of Cognition. Vol. 1: Foundations*. Cambridge, MA: MIT Press.

Scoville, W. B., &Milner, B. (1957). Loss of recent memory after bilateral hippocampal lesions. *Journal of Neurology, Neurosurgery, and Psychiatry*, *20*, 11–21.

Seab, J. P., Jagust, W. J., Wong, S. T. S., Roos, M. S., Reed, B. R., & Budinger, T. F. (1988). Quantitative NMR measurements of hippocampal atrophy in Alzheimer's disease. *Magnetic Resonance in Medicine*, *8*, 200–208.

Sharp, P., Gemmell, H., Cherryman, G., Besson, J., Crawford, J., & Smith, F. (1986). Application of iodine-123-labeled isopropylamphetamine imaging to the study of dementia. *Journal of Nuclear Medicine*, *27*, 761–768.

Shimamura, A. P., Salmon, D. P., Squire, L. R., & Butters, N. (1987). Memory dysfunction and word priming in dementia and amnesia. *Behavioral Neuroscience*, *101*, 347–351.

Silver, F. L., Chawluk, J. B., Bosley, T. M., Rosen, M., Dann, R., Sergott, R. C., Alavi, A., & Reivich, M. (1988). Resolving metabolic abnormalities in a case of pure alexia. *Neurology*, *38*, 730–735.

Speedie, L. J., & Heilman, K. M. (1982). Amnestic disturbance following infarction of the left dorsomedial nucleus of the thalamus. *Neuropsychologia*, *20*, 597–604.

Squire, L. R. (1981). Two forms of human amnesia: An analysis of forgetting. *Journal of Neuroscience*, *1*, 635–640.

Squire, L. R. (1987). *Memory and Brain*. New York: Oxford University Press.

Squire, L. R., & Butters, N. (Eds.) (1984). *Neuropsychology of memory*. New York: The Guilford Press.

Squire, L. R., & Moore, R. Y. (1979). Dorsal thalamic lesion in a noted case of human memory dysfunction. *Annals of Neurology*, *6*, 503–506.

Squire, L. R., Shimamura, A., & Graf, P. (1985). Independence of recognition memory and priming effects: A neuropsychological analysis. *Journal of Experimental Psychology: Learning, Memory, and Cognition*, *11*, 37–44.

Valk, P. E., Budinger, T. F., Levin, V. A., Silver, P., Gutin, P. H., & Doyle, W. K. (1988). PET of malignant cerebral tumors after interstitial brachytherapy. Demonstration of metabolic activity and correlation with clinical outcome. *Journal of Neurosurgery*, *69*, 830–838.

Victor, M., Adams, R. D., & Collins, G. H. (1971). *The Wernicke-Korsakoff syndrome*. Philadelphia: Davis.

Wallesch, C. W., Henriksen, L., Kornhuber, H. H., & Paulson, O. B. (1985). Observations on regional cerebral blood flow in cortical and subcortical structures during language production in normal man. *Brain and Language*, *25*, 224–233.

Zola-Morgan, S. Squire, L. R., & Mishkin, M. (1982). The neuroanatomy of amnesia: Amygdala-hippocampus vs. temporal stem. *Science*, *218*, 1337–1339.

Author Index

Subject Index